D1540626

Sex and Gender:
A Spectrum of Views

PHILIP E. DEVINE
Providence College

CELIA WOLF-DEVINE
Stonehill College

WADSWORTH
™
THOMSON LEARNING

Australia • Canada • Mexico • Singapore • Spain • United Kingdom • United States

WADSWORTH
THOMSON LEARNING

Publisher: *Holly J. Allen*
Philosophy Editor: *Steve Wainwright*
Assistant Editor: *Kara Kindstrom*
Editorial Assistant: *Anna Lustig*
Marketing Manager: *Worth Hawes*
Marketing Assistant: *Justine Ferguson*
Advertising Project Manager: *Bryan Vann*
Print/Media Buyer: *Robert King*

Composition Buyer: *Ben Schroeter*
Permissions Editor: *Bob Kauser*
Production Service: *Buuji, Inc.*
Copy Editor: *Linda Ireland*
Cover Designer: *Gopa & Ted 2*
Cover Image: *PhotoDisc*
Compositor: *Buuji, Inc.*
Cover and Text Printer: *Webcom, Limited*

Printed in Canada
1 2 3 4 5 6 7 06 05 04 03 02
For more information about our products, contact us at:
Thomson Learning Academic Resource Center
1-800-423-0563

For permission to use material from this text,
contact us by:
Phone: 1-800-730-2214   **Fax:** 1-800-730-2215
Web: http://www.thomsonrights.com

Library of Congress Cataloging-in-Publication Data
Sex and Gender : a spectrum of views / [edited by] Philip E. Devine, Celia Wolf-Devine.
     p. cm.
   Includes bibliographical references and index.
   ISBN 0-534-52338-2 (alk. paper)
   1. Sex. 2. Sex—Philosophy. 3. Sex role. 4. Sex differences (Psychology). 5. Man–Woman relationships—Philosophy I. Devine, Philip E., 1944– II. Wolf-Devine, Celia, 1942–

HQ21 .S4714 2003
306.7—dc21

2001056833

Wadsworth/Thomson Learning
10 Davis Drive
Belmont, CA 94002-3098
USA

Asia
Thomson Learning
60 Albert Street, #15-01
Albert Complex
Singapore 189969

Australia
Nelson Thomson Learning
102 Dodds Street
South Melbourne, Victoria 3205
Australia

Canada
Nelson Thomson Learning
1120 Birchmount Road
Toronto, Ontario M1K 5G4
Canada

Europe/Middle East/Africa
Thomson Learning
Berkshire House
168-173 High Holborn
London WC1 V7AA
United Kingdom

Latin America
Thomson Learning
Seneca, 53
Colonia Polanco
11560 Mexico D.F.
Mexico

Spain
Paraninfo Thomson Learning
Calle/Magallanes, 25
28015 Madrid, Spain

Contents

Preface for Instructors

Sex and Gender: A Spectrum of Views is, in our judgment, unique among textbooks devoted to the problems of human sexuality and male-female relationships. Its value consists, we think, in the fact that it presents a far wider range of viewpoints than other anthologies, but without sacrifice of quality or coherence. Our goal is to facilitate dialogue among the warring factions in our current cultural conflicts over sex and gender issues, and we have tried not to exclude any of the major participants. The editors are both philosophers, but our selections are chosen from a number of different disciplines, written in a variety of intellectual styles ranging from impassioned rhetoric to careful analytical reasoning, and for the most part are accessible to students without much philosophical background. Where some particular philosophical background is presupposed, we have tried to provide it in the introductory sections to each unit.

Presenting students with a wide spectrum of views has several pedagogical advantages. Students, in our experience, respond best when they are presented with both sides of issues. Since they may lack the sophistication to intelligently criticize views they disagree with, they often clam up or else try to give the teacher what they think that he or she wants (especially when the views presented in class seem strange and remote from their everyday lives). If students discover that views like their own have been defended, and their feelings taken seriously, by intelligent and articulate people, then they are likely to get more actively engaged with the material.

A further advantage of providing such a wide range of views is that it avoids the simplistic "taking sides" approach so common in anthologies. All too often students are given only two extreme positions and told they must choose one of them, rather than being encouraged to think in a nuanced way and consider the possibility of finding an acceptable compromise position.

The basic structure of the book has been described as Confucian. We begin with the smallest units, individual men and women, and gradually widen the circle in such a way that later units develop out of and build on earlier ones. From consideration of the nature of sexuality we move to reproduction which involves not just the two people, but their possible or actual offspring. The network of relationships thus generated leads to questions about how families should be structured, and this leads to broader policy questions about the political structure of society. And finally, we look at the way people's understanding of the meaning of sexuality and male-female differences is embedded in their broader worldview, including the way they conceive of Ultimate Reality. The material thus has a logical structure that is easy for students to follow, and that tracks the sorts of decisions the average student will face in his or her life.

Although heterosexuality is at the core of this unfolding structure, since only heterosexual intercourse can be reproductive, the perspectives of gay, lesbian, and transgendered people are also important for understanding sex, gender, and the relationship between them. Unit I, thus, begins with an account of the experience of a transsexual, and we have included material by gay and lesbian writers in a number of other sections, especially those on sexuality and politics. Our goal is to challenge students to critically examine their attitudes toward sexuality rather than just operating from their gut feelings.

Pedagogical Aids

We have included a variety of pedagogical aids to make the readings more accessible to students, to engage them critically with the material, and to provide resources for further research.

- Each unit begins with a fairly substantial introduction that provides a background framework to help students make sense of the readings and previews the main points made by each reading.
- Each unit introduction concludes with some broad reflection questions for students to keep in mind as they read through the selections in the unit.
- Following the reflection questions in each unit, there is a short glossary defining terms that are likely to be unfamiliar to students.
- Each reading selection is followed by more detailed questions geared to that particular reading. The questions highlight the most important points in the reading (often connecting it with other readings), and raise questions designed to touch off class discussion.
- Each unit ends with an extensive For Further Reading section.
- At the end of the For Further Reading section, we provide a list of Web sites that might be helpful to students doing research on the Internet, as well as search terms for use on InfoTrac® College Edition.

No one book can do everything. Since we believe that underlying differences in social philosophy are especially important for understanding disputes about sex and gender issues, we have touched on the debate between liberals and communitarians at several points in the introductory sections, and included short selections by John Rawls and Michael Sandel. But we have not attempted to provide students with any sort of systematic introduction to ethical theory. Instructors desiring to do this might wish to supplement this text with Louis Pojman's *Discovering Right and Wrong* or Robert Holmes's *Basic Moral Philosophy*.

Unfortunately, space limitations made it impossible to include cross-cultural material, much though we would have liked to. Doing so in enough depth to give more than an unrepresentative smattering of material from other cultures would have either destroyed the coherence of the book's structure or made the book prohibitively expensive. We have, however, given some suggestions in the For Further Reading sections for students interested in exploring cross-cultural material, as well as some Web sites that will be helpful. We also have not included much in the way of postmodernist or poststructuralist material. In order to make the selections intelligible, we would have had to provide more theoretical background material than we had room for. Literary theory lies largely outside the concerns of this book, and there are already a number of anthologies that do a good job of covering this material and could easily be used to supplement this text.

Finally, although we have attempted to be fair in presenting various positions, our own views may sometimes show through. This is inevitable; there is no such thing as a value neutral approach to any issue of human importance, particularly in such an emotionally charged area as sex and gender. We believe, however, that the material is presented in such a way that instructors with widely differing views will have room to put their own spin on it, and adapt it to different types of courses. This text would be appropriate for a wide range of classes in Philosophy or Feminist Thought, Applied Ethics, Gender Studies, Contemporary Political and Social Issues, as well as for interdisciplinary classes on gender issues or general education classes that touch on personal, professional, and public ethics. It could also fit well into Sociology or Psychology courses that focus on gender issues.

We would like to thank a number of people for their help: Sandra Keating for help with bibliography and Web site information on women in various world religions; Gary Culpepper for reading and giving helpful comments on an earlier draft of the introduction to the unit on religion; Josef Velasquez for thoughtful comments; and the library staff at Stonehill College for help tracking down obscure books and locating publishers for permissions. Peter Adams and Kara Kindstrom have been extremely helpful throughout this project, and the corrections and suggestions of a number of the following readers helped us to make this a better book:

> Raymond A. Belliotti, SUNY–Freedonia
> Joan Callahan, University of Kentucky
> Terri Elliott, California State University, Chico
> Michael Goodman, Humboldt State University
> Chris Horvath, Illinois State University
> John Mandle, SUNY–Albany
> Robert J. Rafalko, University of New Haven
> Jerome Shaffer, University of Connecticut
> James Sterba, University of Notre Dame
> Gail Sutherland, Louisiana State University
> Ronald K. Tacelli, Boston College
> Rosemarie Tong, University of North Carolina at Charlotte
> Michael Wreen, Marquette University

One of the editors has taught the material in this anthology to students at Stonehill College and found that it works very well as a catalyst for dialogue. Thus we offer it to you, both as a contribution to thought about some difficult issues, and as a teaching tool.

Philip E. Devine
Celia Wolf-Devine

Introduction for Students

A fact about the contemporary world, acknowledged both by those who celebrate it and those who lament it, is that we are surrounded by moral, intellectual, and cultural conflict. The essays reprinted here speak to one important area of conflict: sex. By "sex," we mean both sexual behavior and the difference between the two sexes. We further distinguish between *sex* (as a biological fact) and *gender* (the psychological and social meanings attached to biological differences).

The task of this book is to make sense of these two subjects, and of the relationship between them. This task is philosophical, insofar as the concepts *male* and *female* are central to the way most people think, act, and imagine. They enter deeply into our understanding of ourselves and our relationships with others; our social institutions both respond to and define gender differences. Even when we try to grasp a reality that surpasses the merely human, the concepts of male and female are often employed—for example, the *yang* and *yin* of Eastern philosophy, or the terms *Mother* and *Father* as applied to God. In this book, we include literary, legal, psychological, sociological, and theological writings, as well as philosophy in the narrow sense, for philosophical questions arise in many contexts, and are not encountered only in the writings of professional philosophers.

We do not approach these issues in a debate format in which the pros and cons are laid out and you are then told that you have to take one side or the other. People writing about sex and gender issues all too often take the lunatic fringe among their opponents to be representative, and then criticize them. Philosophers call this the "straw man fallacy." It involves first presenting your opponent's view in an unsympathetic and distorted way and then knocking it down. This is cheating. It makes your job too easy. We want to challenge you to get out of the "us versus them" mentality and try to understand the reasons people have for holding the beliefs they do. While it is not always the case that the correct position is to be arrived at by "splitting the difference," the issues are often sufficiently complicated that neither extreme position is quite adequate to them, and we want to encourage you to think in a nuanced way about the issues and to consider possible compromise positions.

We speak of a "spectrum" of views on sex and gender issues, but finding labels for the views we would place at the ends of the spectrum has proved difficult. After all, no one wants to have his or her views characterized as "extreme," and most people resist the label "radical" also, since this conjures up images of bomb-throwing fanatics or at least people who are strident and obsessive about their views. We had at one point proposed putting the teachings of the Roman Catholic Church at one end, but it was pointed out that Catholics might object to having their views characterized as "extreme." There are many people with far more extreme ideas—for example, those Hindus who believe that sexual intercourse is morally permissible only when performed with the deliberate intention of procreation (e.g., Gandhi), and many conservative Bible Christians who have far more authoritarian ideas about family structure than Catholics. The label "cultural radical" that we proposed for the other end of the spectrum gave rise to similar problems, since some proponents of the views we applied the label to were concerned that the word *radical* had pejorative connotations.

Leaving aside the problem of labels for the moment, the basic idea of the spectrum is that it ranges from those who want to retain or restore inherited ideas about sex and gender, to those who want to institute sweeping changes in inherited ways of thinking about sex and gender, replacing them with something entirely different. Liberals and communitarians fall in between the two extremes, believing that traditional institutions and ways of thinking need to be corrected and revised at some points, but not completely discarded. (The insistence of most liberals on tolerance of nonconforming ways of life guarantees that their reforms will be gradual and piecemeal.) The intent of the "cultural radical" label, then, was to distinguish people who want to make a clean sweep of traditional ideas from those who favor piecemeal reforms. The word *radical* comes from the Latin *radix* meaning "root," and thus a radical critique is one that goes to the root of something. For example, to suggest that our cultural concept of masculinity needs to be revised so that it is not thought unmasculine to openly express one's feelings would be proposing a reform in our way of thinking, but to propose that we eliminate *all* concepts of "masculine" and "feminine" and think of ourselves and others only as "persons" would be radical.

While understanding, then, that there are extremists at both ends of the spectrum, we have retained the label "cultural radical" for want of anything better. For the other end of the spectrum we use the term *traditionalists* (the term *tradition* is derived from the Latin *traditio*, meaning that which has been handed on), but it will be helpful here to clarify what sorts of views we mean to include under that label. Core beliefs shared by traditionalists are that monogamous, lifelong, heterosexual marriage is an institution that must be preserved and supported, and that sex and procreation should occur only within marriage. Orthodox Jews, Moslems, as well as many Christian Evangelicals and fundamentalists also emphasize the rightful authority of fathers within the family, and of parents over children. Roman Catholics have developed arguments to the effect that sex ought to always be open to procreation and that procreation should always take place within the context of a marital sexual union. These arguments, if sound, have implications for both contraception and reproductive technology. Catholics generally emphasize paternal authority less than some other traditionalists, but some people regard the Church's refusal to ordain women as manifesting a patriarchal attitude (i.e., one that advocates male dominance). Traditionalists generally regard heterosexuality as normative, and homosexuality as aberrant and socially undesirable, if not sinful. Finally, traditionalists are not all religiously inspired. There are many people, properly describable as "secular cultural conservatives," who think that traditional sexual mores (customs) are in the best interests of society as a whole and that tampering with them in any very substantive way is likely to be dangerous.

At the cultural radical end of the spectrum, there are also many groups with somewhat different concerns and interests. They all want to break decisively with inherited conceptions of marriage, family, and gender difference, but they differ among themselves over why they think such radical change is necessary, over just how radical the envisioned change should be, what we should put in the place of the traditional institutions, and how change is to be accomplished.

One central underlying concern of cultural radicals is that they believe traditional institutions have imposed certain sex role expectations on both women and men that limit their freedom to define themselves and find fulfillment as individuals. Male dominance has, they believe, been so deeply embedded in the traditional framework that dismantling the whole framework is necessary if women are to obtain true equality. The early feminist movement focused especially on the way in which traditional sex role expectations limit women's opportunities to live humanly fulfilling lives, but more recent feminists have tended to place more emphasis on the need to empower women. (The ideals of personal fulfillment and empowerment are related, but different; a person could have power but fail to lead a humanly fulfilling life, or live a humanly fulfilling life without having much power.) Another criticism that has been made of traditional institutions is that they wrongly privilege heterosexuality, thereby making it difficult for people with other sexual orientations to define themselves differently, achieve personal fulfillment, and attain full equality of power and esteem with heterosexuals.

Cultural radicals are not in complete agreement, however, over what should be put in place of the traditional gender system. One alternative is the ideal of androgyny. In this view, each of us has both masculine and feminine traits within us and we should strive to get these in balance so that we can become more whole as persons. Another view is that we should aim to transcend gender concepts altogether. In this view, no traits would be thought of as masculine or feminine, and each autonomous individual would simply choose those that he or she personally found attractive. According to some of the more extreme cultural radicals, we ought to transcend gender concepts to such an extent that biological sex differences are of no more importance in society than eye color. Just as a nonracist society would regard skin color as being of no importance, so a nonsexist one would regard sexual difference in the same way, perhaps even in sexual contexts (so that one would view one's sexual partners as persons and regard their sexual organs as irrelevant).

In seeking to root out all vestiges of patriarchy, the strongest forms of cultural radicalism reject not only the traditional male-female distinction, but also the adult-child distinction. They are especially opposed to the power of fathers over children, but go further and reject *all* social hierarchies, viewing them as oppressive and violative of people's autonomy. Some have welcomed new reproductive technologies, hoping that they will help set women free from the way in which their role in reproduction limits their freedom and autonomy. Others, however, worry about the dangers such innovations pose to women's psychological and physical health.

Finally, there is also disagreement among those who advocate a root-and-branch rejection of inherited ideas about sex and gender about how best to go about deconstructing the present sex-gender system. A few expect the changes to occur spontaneously, although more expect that intensive efforts to reeducate people will be necessary. Many propose to use legal and economic pressures mediated by the power of the state in order to reshape social institutions, and a few might sanction violence.

Large numbers of people, including most of the contributors to this anthology, fall somewhere in the middle of the spectrum. A wide range of views—they may usefully be called "liberal"—seek fairness and mutual toleration without attempting to redefine the meaning of sex and gender. Liberals define their positions by reference to the traditionalist and radical positions just outlined. Liberalism about sexual matters arose out of resentment of attempts to enforce traditional sexual morality, especially through the criminal law, and more broadly out of opposition to the use of state power to preserve "traditional family values." But in the present world, liberalism also opposes attempts to use state power to reshape family and sexual life in the novel directions proposed by the cultural radicals. Whatever their own choices in sexual matters, liberals support other people's freedom to follow their own preferences.

Some, however, have argued that the state cannot be neutral on such issues as family policy, and if this is so, then the line between liberals and cultural radicals becomes harder to draw. A group called "communitarians" is intermediate between liberals and those cultural conservatives who attempt to use state power to impose their moral codes. They are critical of the individualism underlying liberal political and economic theory and worried about the current breakdown of families and other communal structures that hold society together (neighborhoods, churches, voluntary associations, etc.). They acknowledge a public interest in stable families, and combat both public policies and market forces that subtly or blatantly disfavor them. The role of religion in sustaining families and other communities is controversial among communitarians, and they are cautious about pursuing family-friendly policies too far, because they want to avoid trying to enforce traditional morality.

The basic structure of this book is a simple one. We begin with a methodological prologue examining the relative roles of reason and emotion in understanding sex and gender issues. We then look at the issue of male-female difference, and expand our focus in ever–widening circles to include the nature of sexuality, reproduction, marriage and family, politics, and religion.

Judgments about sex and gender involve deep emotions on all sides, emotions which pose a methodological problem. Shall we regard such emotions as, while appropriate in nonintellectual contexts, mere obstacles to clarity in the study of sex and gender? Or should we treat our emotions as disclosing deep facts about ourselves, and "thinking with our blood" as the appropriate way to a proper understanding about sex and gender? Many people, including many feminists, have connected maleness with reason and femaleness with emotion. Is this connection defensible? The methodological prologue is concerned with such issues.

Unit I deals with the difference between male and female. Is the difference merely one of "plumbing," as one feminist has said? Are the observed differences in behavior between the sexes wholly the result of social conditioning, or are they connected with biological differences, and if so, how are they linked? The readings in this unit explore the relationship between sex and gender from a variety of different angles.

The issue has frequently been framed in terms of an opposition between the view that "biology is destiny" and the view that gender is wholly a social construction. (Extreme cultural radicals hold that even biological sex is a social construction.) "Biology is destiny" is taken to have the conservative implication that traditional sex roles are somehow grounded in our nature and hence unchangeable, while the view that gender is socially constructed is seen as liberating because it implies virtually unlimited possibilities of change. The issues, however, are considerably more complicated, and the essays reprinted here challenge any simplistic opposition between biology and culture.

Unit II has to do with the nature of sexuality. Some people hold that procreative sexual intercourse is a near-sacrament; others that it and other forms of sexual behavior are the pleasurable release of emotional tension. People who see things in such radically different ways frequently find each other's views shocking or incomprehensible. This is not surprising, since the way we understand sexuality is connected with our most basic beliefs about the world. This is why discussion of sexual issues is often so inflammatory. People feel that their most deeply held beliefs are under attack—the ones they rely on to make sense of the world and guide them in making moral decisions. Even those who regard sex as "no big deal" frequently react with blank incomprehension or hostility to those who feel passionately that it *is* a big deal—not surprisingly, since the view that it is no big deal is just as much bound up with their deepest worldview as their opponents' views are bound up with theirs.

To bring order into the welter of different understandings of sexuality, we introduce four frameworks (defined in more detail in the introductory text and glossary in Unit II). The first is paganism, which views sexuality as sacred; it manifests the operation of powerful deities. Thus, for example, the behavior of Helen of Troy (whose adultery was the cause of the Trojan War) was explained by saying that she had been taken over by the goddess Aphrodite (goddess of sex). Being regarded as sacred, then, the power of sexuality is regarded with awe and surrounded with taboos and rituals. Naturalism, on the other hand, strips the world of spiritual or supernatural powers of any kind, and sees sex as a normal, healthy human function like the need to eat. Manichaeanism holds that the physical world (including the body) is bad while the spirit is good. Consequently, sexuality is either spiritualized or regarded as degrading (in which case one may respond either by flight or wallowing). The final framework is that found in the Jewish and Christian view of nature. The created world is good and our embodiment is good. Sexuality is not itself divine (as in the pagan view) but participates in sacredness because sexual intercourse was ordained by God, and because through it we can cooperate with God in the generation of new human beings.

You are invited to reflect about the view of nature and our place in it underlying the selections in this unit, as well as about two controversial issues—the differences between male and female sexuality and between homosexual and heterosexual sex. (The difference between homosexual and heterosexual sex is also discussed in a political context in Unit V.)

In Unit III we consider two kinds of problems concerning reproduction: (1) the problems of those desiring to enjoy sexual activity while avoiding offspring, and (2) the problems of those who desire offspring but cannot get them in traditional ways. In the first group of problems are abortion, contraception, and sterilization; in the second group are adoption, artificial insemination, cloning, *in vitro* fertilization, and surrogate mothering. Among these issues, that of abortion has a special place, since it is not merely a sex-and-gender issue, but also involves the taking of life. The focus of this book, however, is not on fetal rights, but on gender differences and the way abortion bears on these.

Unit IV is concerned with issues of marriage and family. The way families are structured has enormous impact on the way in which the next generation is socialized; children learn largely by imitation. Boys learn how males should behave by imitating their fathers or older brothers, and likewise girls look to their mothers and older sisters for role models. Those critical of traditional sex roles, then, have been especially interested in finding ways to bring about changes in the division of labor, the distribution of power, and the emotional dynamics that obtain between the parents. Some also hope to break the hold of traditional sex roles by advocating alternative forms of family structure, such as same-sex marriages, communal child rearing, or various forms of loose groupings of several adults who cooperate in raising children. The readings in this unit center around the debate between those who believe traditional sex roles are a bad thing, and those who think that there is nothing wrong with them, or that they are actually a good thing. The interests of children must also be taken into account in evaluating various types of family structures, and their interests may sometimes be in tension with those of the adults who care for them.

Unit V, on sexual politics, takes as its focus the question of how men and women are to live together in society. This question is especially urgent in those arenas of male-female interaction that seem in danger of turning into war zones—consider, for example, the recent wave of sexual harassment charges in the work-place and the academic. (As a general rule, when social institutions are in flux and the rules of social life are unclear and contested, tensions among the members of society increase.) The two most important political movements concerned with gender issues in the second half of the twentieth century were feminism and the gay rights movement. Feminism has been concerned with male-female relation-ships, while the gay rights movement has called into question the idea that het-erosexuality should be considered the normal or standard form of sexuality.

We begin with two readings that explain some of the different sorts of fem-inism, followed by readings on both sides of controversial concrete issues that have grown out of concerns raised by the feminist movement: affirmative action for women and sexual harassment. We then turn to the gay rights movement. The first two readings explore the traditional assumption that heterosexuality should be normative; one defends this idea on the grounds that male-female comple-mentarity enriches both individuals and society as a whole, and one argues there are no significant differences between homosex and heterosex. The way in which we answer the broader theoretical question of whether or not homosexuality is entitled to parity of esteem with heterosexuality will have important implications for how we choose to design our social institutions. The unit ends, therefore, with readings on the concrete issue of whether or not the state should recognize same-sex marriages.

Unit VI deals with the significance of sex and gender in the structure of real-ity—in other words, with their religious significance. Many people think of sex and religion as representing the competing claims of individual pleasure and social duty, but there are deeper issues. When we think about a reality transcending the merely human, gender concepts continue to come into play. Taoists regard the interplay of *yang* and *yin* (the former being the masculine principle and the latter the feminine one) as fundamental to the structure of reality. Many religions have worshipped goddesses associated with the Earth and fertility. Jews and Moslems employ strongly masculine language when speaking of God, and Jesus taught his disciples to call God "Father." Feminist critics have argued that thinking of God in this way has served to support patriarchal social structures, and have called for changes in the way we think about God. How, then, does the way we think about God affect male-female relationships?

An anthology such as this will inevitably raise issues larger than it is able to answer. Our hope is that it will get you thinking about sex and gender issues, help you understand how those who disagree with you think, and ultimately enable you to articulate and defend your own positions on these sorts of issues intelligently.

About the Editors

Philip E. Devine is Professor of Philosophy at Providence College. He received his B.A. from Yale University and his Ph.D. from the University of California at Berkeley. During the academic year 1980–1981, he was Fellow in Law and Philosophy at the Harvard Law School. He is the author of *The Ethics of Homicide; Relativism, Nihilism, and God; Human Diversity and the Culture Wars;* and *Natural Law Ethics.* He is currently working on a book entitled *First Person Plural.*

Celia Wolf-Devine is Associate Professor of Philosophy at Stonehill College. She received her B.A. from Smith College and her Ph.D. from the University of Wisconsin at Madison. She is the author of *Descartes on Seeing: Epistemology and Visual Perception* and *Diversity and Community in the Academy: Affirmative Action in Faculty Appointments.*

About the Contributors

Sandra Lee Bartky teaches philosophy at the University of Illinois at Chicago. She completed the book from which this selection is taken at the Bunting Institute, Radcliffe College.

Edith Black is a freelance Roman Catholic theologian living in the San Francisco Bay area. She holds a B.A. from Smith College, an M. Div. from Union Theological Seminary, and an M.A. in Ancient Near Eastern Languages and Culture from the University of California at Berkeley. She is currently employed by Lindsay Wildlife Museum to teach natural history in the field to elementary school children.

Monsignor **Cormac Burke** was ordained a priest in 1955, and is also a Doctor of Canon Law and member of the Irish bar. He was appointed a Judge of the Roman Rota, the highest court of the Roman Catholic Church, by Pope John Paul II, a position from which he retired in 1999. He has taught at Trinity College, Dublin; the Catholic University of America; the Studium Rotale; and the Pontifical College of the Holy Cross. He now teaches anthropology at Strathmore University College, Nairobi, Kenya. He received the 1995 Lineacre Award of the National Federation of Catholic Physicians of the United States for his writings on marriage and sexuality. His book on marriage, *Covenanted Happiness*, has run into several editions, with translations into Italian, Spanish, and Portuguese.

Carol P. Christ, Ph.D. Yale, is author of the first Goddess theology, *Rebirth of the Goddess, Diving Deep and Surfacing*, and coeditor of the widely used anthologies *Womanspirit Rising* and *Weaving the Visions*. She now lives in Molivos, Lesbos, Greece, and conducts tours for the Adriadne Network.

Stephen B. Clark holds a B.A. from Yale University and an M.A. from the University of Notre Dame; he also studied Philosophy at Freiburg University. He served for many years as the Director of Research for the National Secretariat of the Cursillo Movement. At the time of writing, he was a coordinator of the Word of God, an interdenominational Christian community in Ann Arbor, Michigan. In addition to *Man and Woman in Christ*, his books include *Building Christian Communities* and *Unordained Elders and Renewal Communities.*

Richard J. Connell is a Professor Emeritus of Philosophy at the University of St. Thomas, St. Paul, Minnesota. He is the author of *The Empirical Intelligence—The Human Empirical Mode: Philosophy as Originating in Experience, From Observables to Unobservables in Science & Philosophy* and *Nature's Causes.*

David Orgon Coolidge is Director of the Marriage Law Project at the Columbus School of Law, Catholic University of America, and author of *Revitalizing the Institution of Marriage for the Twenty-First Century.*

Gary Culpepper is Associate Professor of Theology and Editor of *Providence: Studies in Western Civilization* at Providence College. He has published in *The Thomist, Communio,* and the *Josephinum Journal of Theology.*

Richard Davis is a gay Christian man living in Las Vegas. His fiction has appeared in the *The James White Review* and *Waves: An Anthology of New Gay Fiction,* edited by Ethan Mordden. He and his partner, Milton, are members of the Metropolitan Community Church of Las Vegas.

Andrea Dworkin is a noted radical feminist and collaborator, with Catharine MacKinnon, in the attempt to ban pornography as a form of sex-based discrimination. Her books include *Letters from a War Zone, Intercourse, Right Wing Women, Pornography: Men Possessing Women, Our Blood,* and *Woman Hating.*

Mircea Eliade is one of the founding figures in the study of comparative religion, and the author of numerous books, including *Images and Symbols; Myths, Dreams and Mysteries;* and *Patterns in Comparative Religions.* His best-known work is *The Sacred and the Profane.*

Jean Bethke Elshtain is Laura Spelman Rockefeller Professor of Ethics at the University of Chicago. Her works include *Women and War; Public Man, Private Woman; Power Trips and Other Journeys;* and *Who Are We?*

Paula Ettelbrick is the Family Policy Director for the Policy Institute of the National Gay and Lesbian Task Force, New York City. She is an adjunct professor of Law at the University of Michigan, Columbia University, and New York University.

Tamar Frankiel has taught history of religion at Stanford, Princeton, and the University of California at Berkeley. Her books include *Minding the Temple of the Soul, Entering the Temple of Dreams,* and *The Voice of Sarah.*

Robert P. George is McCormick Professor of Jurisprudence, Princeton University, and Director of the James Madison Program in American Ideals and Institutions, as well as a former member of the United States Commission on Civil Rights. He is the author of *Making Men Moral, In Defense of Natural Law,* and *The Clash of Orthodoxies.*

Sandra Gilbert is Professor of English at the University of California at Davis, and coauthor, with Susan Gubar, of *The Madwoman in the Attic* and *No Man's Land.* She has also published six collections of her own verse, most recently, *Kissing the Bread;* a book-length study of the poetry of D. H. Lawrence, *Acts of Attention;* a memoir, *Wrongful Death;* and a new anthology, *Inventions of Farewell.*

E. J. Graff is a Visiting Researcher at Brandeis Women's Studies Center and the author of *What Is Marriage For?*

Susan Gubar is Distinguished Professor of English at Indiana University and coauthor, with Sandra Gilbert, of *The Madwoman in the Attic* and *No Man's Land.*

Donald Hatcher is Professor of Philosophy; Director of the Science, Technology, and Human Values Program at Baker University; and author of *Science, Ethics and Technology* and *Reasoning and Writing: An Introduction to Critical Thinking.*

Susanne Heine is professor at the Protestant Faculty of Theology of Vienna and author of *Women and Early Christianity* and *Christianity and the Goddesses.*

Sylvia Ann Hewlett chairs the National Parenting Association and is the author of *A Lesser Life: The Myth of Women's Liberation in America, The War Against Parents: What We Can Do for America's Beleagured Moms and Dads,* and *Baby Hunger: Why Some Women Who Have It All Don't Have What They Want Most.*

Judith Hughes, when she wrote *Women's Choices* with Mary Midgley, taught at the University of Newcastle on Tyne, England.

Alison Jaggar is Professor of Philosophy at the University of Colorado at Boulder. She is the author of *Feminist Politics and Human Nature, Gender/Body/Knowledge,* and *Living with Contradictions;* and she is the editor of *A Companion to Feminist Philosophy.* She is working on a book tentatively titled *Sex, Truth, and Power.*

She was a founding member of the Society for Women in Philosophy.

Sr. Elizabeth Johnson, C.S.J., is Distinguished Professor of Theology, Fordham University, and the author of *Consider Jesus: Waves of Renewal in Christology; Friends of God and Prophets: A Feminist Theological Reading of the Communion of Saints;* and *She Who Is: The Mystery of God in Feminist Theological Discourse.*

Louis Katzner is Trustee Professor of Philosophy, Bowling Green State University, and author of *Man in Conflict: Traditions in Social and Political Thought.*

Suzanne Kessler teaches at State University of New York, College at Purchase, and is the author of *Lessons from the Intersexed.*

D. H. Lawrence (1885–1930) was an English novelist. His best-known work, *Lady Chatterley's Lover*, was long banned for its use of "four-letter words."

Susan Lydon graduated from Vassar in 1965. She is the author of *Take the Long Way Home: Memories of a Survivor* and *The Knitting Sutra: Craft as a Spiritual Practice*, both published by HarperSanFrancisco, as well as numerous reviews and magazine articles. She currently works as a columnist for the *Oakland Tribune.* "The Politics of Orgasm" was written in 1969, when she was a freelance writer active in Berkeley (California) Women's Liberation. She wishes to acknowledge Ann Koedt's essay "The Myth of the Vaginal Orgasm."

Catharine MacKinnon is a Professor of Law at the University of Michigan Law School. She is the author of *Feminism Unmodified* and *Only Words.* With Andrea Dworkin, she has sponsored attempts to outlaw pornography as a form of discrimination against women.

Father **Anthony Mastroeni** holds a J.D. from Rutgers University and an S.T.D. from the Pontifical University of St. Thomas Aquinas, Rome. He is professor of Moral Theology at the Franciscan University of Steubenville, and the author of *Fatima and the Church's Moral Teaching* and *A Moral Evaluation of Surgical Sex Reassignment.* He is also the editor of *Catholicity and the New Evangelization.*

Wendy McKenna teaches at Sarah Lawrence College.

Mary Midgley retired early from the University of Newcastle in 1980, in order to devote herself to writing. Her books include *Beast and Man, Heart and Mind, Animals and Why They Matter, Women's Choices* (with Judith Hughes), *Evolution as a Religion,* and *Wickedness.*

Richard Mohr teaches philosophy at the University of Illinois at Urbana-Champaign. He is the author of *Gays/Justice, Gay Ideas,* and many other writings on homosexual issues.

Jan Morris, formerly James Morris, is the author of many books including *Hong Kong: Return to the Heart of the Dragon, Over Europe, Coronation Everest, Venetian Bestiary,* and *Wales: Epic Views of a Small Country,* as well as *Conundrum.* Before the sexual transformation described in our selection, Morris had scaled Mount Everest, spent four years in the army, married, and fathered five children. Morris now lives in Wales.

Timothy F. Murphy teaches in the Department of Medical Education, College of Medicine, University of Illinois at Chicago. He is the author of *Ethics in an Epidemic: AIDS, Morality and Culture* and *Gay Science: The Ethics of Sexual Orientation Research.*

Thomas Nagel teaches at the New York University School of Law. He is the author of *The Last Word, Mortal Questions,* and *The View from Nowhere.*

Hilde Lindemann Nelson is an Associate Professor of Philosophy at Michigan State University. She is the author of *Damaged Identities* and, with James Lindemann Nelson, of *Alzheimer's: Answers to Hard Questions.*

James Lindemann Nelson is a Professor of Philosophy at Michigan State University and the author of *The Patient in the Family: An Ethics of Medicine and Families,* and coauthor with Hilde Lindemann Nelson of *Alzheimer's: Answers to Hard Questions.*

The late **Niles Newton** received her B.A. from Bryn Mawr and her Masters and Ph.D. from Columbia University, doing additional study with Margaret Mead in the 1960s. At the time of writing, Newton was a Research Associate in Obstetrics, School of Medicine, University of

Pennsylvania. In 1993 she retired as Professor Emeritus at Northwestern University School of Medicine, after 27 years in the Department of Psychiatry and Behavior Sciences. Newton was a behavioral scientist whose career focused on the broader aspects of reproduction. She was the author of *Maternal Emotions* and of more than 80 professional articles in such journals as *Obstetrics and Gynecology, Pediatrics, Birth,* and *The Journal of Human Lactation.* She also wrote for a popular audience, starting with her *Family Book of Childcare* (1957) and including regular columns for "Baby Talk" at the *Chicago Tribune.*

Michael Novak recently received the Templeton Prize for Religion. He works at the American Enterprise Institute, and his best-known book is *The Spirit of Democratic Capitalism.*

Susan Moller Okin is Martha Sara Weeks Professor of Ethics in Society, Stanford University. She is the author of *Justice, Gender and the Family; Women in Western Political Thought;* and *Is Multiculturalism Bad for Women?*

Plato (ca. 428-347 BC) is the first philosopher in the Western tradition whose works have survived largely intact. Besides the *Symposium,* his most important works are the *Republic* and a sequence of dialogues describing the trial and death of his teacher Socrates.

Laura Purdy is a Bioethicist for the University Health Network, University of Toronto, and author of *In Their Best Interest? The Case Against Equal Rights for Children* and *Reproducing Persons: Issues in Feminist Bioethics.*

John Rawls is Professor Emeritus of Philosophy, Harvard University. He is the author of *A Theory of Justice* and *Political Liberalism.*

Janet Radcliffe Richards is Reader in Bioethics at University College, London. She is the author of *The Sceptical Feminist* and *Human Nature After Darwin.*

John Robertson is Thomas West Gregory Professor in the School of Law at the University of Texas at Austin, as well as a fellow of the Hastings Center and a member of the American Fertility Society. He is the author of *The Rights of the Critically Ill* and *Children of Choice.*

Richard Rodriguez is the author of *Hunger of Memory* and *Days of Obligation.* He works as an editor for Pacific News Service in San Francisco, and is a contributing editor to *Harper's* and the Sunday "Opinion" section of the *Los Angeles Times.* He also frequently appears on television as an essayist.

Katie Roiphe holds a Ph.D. in English from Princeton University. Her work has appeared in *Harper's, Esquire,* and the *New York Times.* She is the author of *Still She Haunts Me* and *Last Night in Paradise: Sex and Morals at the Century's End.*

Rosemary Radford Ruether is Georgia Harkness Professor of Theology at Garrett Evangelical Seminary, Evanston, Illinois, and author of *Christianity and the Making of the Modern Family; Gaia and God: An Ecofeminist Theology of Earth Healing;* and *Sexism and God-Talk: Toward a Feminist Theology.*

Bertrand Russell (1872–1970) became third Earl Russell in 1931. His most important philosophical work, including *Principia Mathematica* with Alfred North Whitehead, was done between 1900 and 1914, after which he devoted himself primarily to popular writing and lecturing, educational experimentation, and political activism. He was twice jailed for his political activities, and was dismissed from Cambridge University and City College of New York for political reasons. He also received the Order of Merit and the Nobel Prize for Literature.

Michael Sandel is Associate Professor of Government at Harvard University, author of *Liberalism and the Limits of Justice* and *Democracy and its Discontents,* and editor of *Liberalism and Its Critics.*

Phyllis Schafly was educated at Washington University at St. Louis, and Harvard University. She has been a leader of the pro-family movement since 1972, when she founded the organization now called Eagle Forum. Besides *The Power of the Positive Woman,* her books on family issues include *Child Abuse in the Classroom, Who Will Rock the Cradle?,* and *First Reader.* She has also written and spoken on constitutional and national defense issues, and was a member of the Commission on the Bicentennial of the U.S. Constitution (1985–1991). She is best known for her successful campaign against the Equal Rights Amendment.

Roger Scruton recently retired as University Professor at Boston University. His works include *Sexual Desire, The Meaning of Conservatism,* and *The Philosopher at Dover Beach.*

Arlene Stein is Assistant Professor of Sociology at the University of Oregon. She is the editor of *Sisters, Sexpots, Queers* and the author of *Sex and Sensibility.*

Andrew Sullivan is a senior editor at the *New Republic,* and the author of *Virtually Normal* and *Love Undetectable.*

Judith Jarvis Thomson is Professor of Philosophy at Massachusetts Institute of Technology. Her works include *Rights, Restitution, and Risk: Essays in Moral Theory* and *The Realm of Rights.*

Sallie Tisdale worked as a registered nurse from 1983 to 1990. She is the author of *Talk Dirty to Me* and *Harvest Moon.* She received a James P. Phelan Award in 1986 and an NEA Fellowship in 1989.

Richard Wasserstom teaches at the University of California at Santa Cruz, where he held a Presidential Chair from 1988–1991. He is the author of *Philosophy and Social Issues,* and the editor of *War and Morality.*

Juli Loesch Wiley describes herself as a "worshiper of one God, wife of one husband, mother of two fine sons, living in East Tennessee." She has been active both in the peace movement (with Pax Christi) and the pro-life movement.

Methodological Prologue:
How Should We Think
About Sex and Gender?

ISSUES THAT INVOLVE SEX notoriously arouse strong emotions. This is true not just when discussing concrete issues like pornography or abortion, but even on the conceptual level. Defining a "family," for example, involves emotion-laden evaluations of various forms of human sexual, reproductive, and child-rearing association. Even factual questions such as the existence and nature of biological differences between men and women beyond their differing sexual organs, or what actually happened in some case of alleged sexual harassment, often become questions of emotional allegiance. These strong and pervasive emotions pose a challenge to us when we try to enter into dialogue with people who disagree with us about such issues.

What attitude should we adopt toward our strong, gut feelings about sexual issues? Should we try to disregard them as much as possible, to construct rational arguments, and to follow where those arguments lead us, even when they go against our feelings? Or should we regard our gut feelings as revelatory of certain truths about ourselves and our sexuality, and say so much the worse for rational arguments that seem to go against our deepest intuitive feelings?

The divide between those who strongly believe in reasoning about such matters and those who trust more in their feelings does not coincide with the divide between radicals and traditionalists. Some traditionalists believe that inherited sexual mores can be shown to be correct by rational argument. Others think that social institutions must respect and build upon our deepest gut feelings rather than challenge and confront them, believing that such strong feelings either have a genetic basis or are too deeply ingrained to change. And some, like D. H. Lawrence, believe that sexuality is so deeply connected with our emotions and our bodily nature, that reason is incapable of giving us any real understanding of sex. Cultural radicals, for their part, have often tried to override, in the name of reason, the emotions associated with inherited morality. In this spirit, they have written defenses of a strictly sex-blind society, of infanticide, and of the abolition of all inherited distinctions between human beings and other animals. On the other hand, some cultural radicals in repudiating tradition, have not spared those parts of our tradition that affirm devotion to truth and rational argument. This is especially true of those cultural radicals most strongly influenced by postmodernism. ("Farewell to Reason" has become a common slogan among postmodernists.)

There are several reasons for the current tendency to be skeptical about the claims of reason, some of which affect both traditionalists and radicals, and some of which do not. All parties to the discussion have been affected to some degree by recent developments in the field of moral philosophy. In the eighteenth century, Enlightenment thinkers aspired to free humanity from the darkness of superstition and inherited customs (especially religious morals), and to devise a purely rational morality that would be acceptable to all people. They were for the most part quite optimistic about reason's capacity to enable us to transform society in desirable ways, although skepticism about the power of reason in ethics was already articulated in the eighteenth century by David Hume, who thought morality had its basis in sentiments and said that "Reason is and ought to be the slave of the passions." Nineteenth century thinkers, for the most part, continued to believe that history was moving in the direction of greater human freedom, autonomy, scientific progress, and more rational social institutions.

But in the twentieth century, the horrors of two bloody world wars and the collapse of Marxism (the last of the optimistic Enlightenment ideologies) led to widespread discouragement about the power of reason and science to do much to improve the human condition. The worldwide resurgence of militant fundamentalist religious movements has thrown into serious question the idea that history is moving in the direction of increasingly rational and secular ways of thinking, and many societies seem to be breaking down into warring tribal groups (à la Yugoslavia) who are increasingly unable or unwilling to talk to each other.

But on the cultural radical side, there has also been an attack on reason that has grown out of the stereotypical conception of reason as masculine and emotion as feminine. Some feminists have argued that the concept of rationality within the Western tradition has been distorted by a masculine bias, but that this is not necessarily true of every possible conception of reason (see the book by Genevieve Lloyd listed in the For Further Reading section for an excellent example of this approach). Some feminists, however, have wholeheartedly accepted the association of women with emotion, and have chosen to celebrate the female perspective over and against the male one. Such women tend to frown upon other women who attempt to offer arguments for their views, accusing them of having "masculine minds." It is this sort of feminist that Janet Radcliffe Richards takes as her target in the selection here.

Most thinkers (rightly we believe) want to avoid being forced to choose reason *or* emotion and acknowledge the importance of both reason and emotion when dealing with moral issues generally and with sex and gender issues in particular. This is only the beginning, however. For people inevitably experience some tensions between reason and emotion, and a great deal of thought and work has to go into figuring out how to balance and integrate the two. The purpose of this first section is merely to present the reader with clear defenses of the claims of both emotion and reason.

Questions for Reflection

1. Do you think there is anything at all to the old association of emotion with women and reason with men?
2. To what extent can we resolve our differences about sex and gender issues rationally, or must we simply fall back on our gut responses?
3. Can emotions be sharply separated from reason? Don't emotions often have a cognitive element, as, for example, fear is associated with certain beliefs that may be rational or irrational?
4. Can reason be kept all that separate from the emotions? Some people passionately believe in reason, and Plato, for example, believed that human beings have a certain passionate (he would even use the term *erotic*) longing for wisdom and truth.
5. Can emotions sometimes be revelatory of reality or truth? If so, wouldn't it be irrational to ignore them?

Glossary

conditioning the nonrational ways in which a society transmits its values, especially to young children.

cultural radicals see Introduction for Students at beginning of book.

Enlightenment early modern movement that subjected all traditional ideas, especially religious doctrines, to severe rational examination, and tended to be optimistic about the possibility of progress.

feminism a highly contested concept. It is generally acknowledged that there are a number of different "feminisms." The general idea, however, is that feminists are people who evaluate institutions in terms of the interests and outlook of women. One important variety—call it *F*eminism—sees gender relations predominantly or exclusively in terms of power. See Unit V for more extended discussion.

four-letter words short, blunt, words for sexual and excretory functions, for example, *fuck*.

Lady Chatterley's Lover novel by D. H. Lawrence describing an affair between an aristocratic woman and a gamekeeper, notorious in its day for its use of four-letter words.

postmodernism a contemporary philosophical movement, predominantly secular and antitraditionalist in character, that criticizes Enlightenment understandings of reason and truth. Characteristically, postmodern thinkers *deconstruct* the philosophical tradition; that is, they try to show that it is incurably at war with itself.

rhetoric the use of language for persuasion, often opposed to sound argument.

traditionalists see Introduction for Students at beginning of book.

A Propos of *Lady Chatterley's Lover*

D. H. LAWRENCE

> D. H. Lawrence here defends the way he treats sexual issues in his controversial novel, *Lady Chatterley's Lover.* He protests the overcerebral way in which both "liberals" and "conservative" people discuss sex, and calls for a new conception of marriage based on a "correspondence of blood." Along the way, he expresses considerable (and, to many of his readers, surprising) sympathy for Roman Catholic ideas about sex and gender.

[I]N SPITE OF ALL ANTAGONISM, I put forth this novel as an honest, healthy book, necessary for us today. The words that shock so much at first don't shock at all after a while. Is this because the mind is depraved by habit? Not a bit. It is that the words merely shocked the eye, they never shocked the mind at all. People without minds may go on being shocked, but they don't matter. People with minds realize that they aren't shocked and never really were: and they experience a sense of relief. . . .

And this is the real point of this book. I want men and women to be able to think sex, fully, completely, honestly and cleanly.

Even if we can't act sexually to our complete satisfaction, let us at least think sexually, complete and clear. All this talk of young girls and virginity, like a blank white sheet on which nothing is written, is pure nonsense. A young girl and a young boy is a tormented tangle, a seething confusion of sexual feelings and sexual thoughts which only the years will disentangle. Years of honest thoughts of sex, and years of struggling action in sex will bring us at last where we want to get, to our real and accomplished chastity, our completeness, when our sexual act and our sexual thought are in harmony, and the one does not interfere with the other.

Far be it from me to suggest that all women should go running after gamekeepers for lovers. Far be it from me to suggest that they should be running after anybody. A great many men and women today are happiest when they abstain and stay sexually apart, quite clean: and at the same time, when they understand and realize sex more fully. Ours is the day of realization rather than action. There has been so much action in the past, especially sexual action, a wearying repetition over and over, without a corresponding thought, a corresponding realization. Now our business is to realize sex. Today the full conscious realization of sex is even more important than the act itself. After centuries of obfuscation, the mind demands to know and know fully. The body is a good deal in abeyance, really. When people act in sex, nowadays, they are half the time acting up. They do it because they think it is expected of them. Whereas as a matter of fact it is the mind which is interested, and the body has to be provoked. The reason being that our ancestors have so assiduously acted sex without ever thinking it or realizing it, that now the act tends to be mechanical, dull and disappointing, and only fresh mental realization will freshen up the experience.

The mind has to catch up, in sex: indeed, in all the physical acts. Mentally, we lag behind in our sexual thought, in a dimness, a lurking, grovelling fear which belongs to our raw, somewhat bestial ancestors. In this one respect, sexual and physical, we have left the mind unevolved. Now we have to catch up, and make a balance between the consciousness of the body's sensations and experiences, and these sensations and experiences themselves. Balance up the consciousness of the act, and the act itself. Get the two in harmony. It means having a proper reverence for sex, and a proper awe of the body's strange experience. It means being able to use the so-called obscene words, because these are a natural part of the mind's consciousness of the body. Obscenity only comes in when the mind despises and fears the body, and the body hates and resists the mind. . . .

Reprinted by permission of Haskell House Publishers.

But so it is. The mind has an old grovelling fear of the body and the body's potencies. It is the mind we have to liberate, to civilize on these points. The mind's terror of the body has probably driven more men mad than ever could be counted. The insanity of a great mind like Swift's is at least partly traceable to this cause. In the poem to his mistress Celia, which has the maddened refrain "But—Celia, Celia, Celia s***s," (the word rhymes with spits), we see what can happen to a great mind when it falls into panic. A great wit like Swift could not see how ridiculous he made himself. Of course Celia s***s! Who doesn't? And how much worse if she didn't. It is hopeless. And then think of poor Celia, made to feel iniquitous about her proper natural function, by her "lover." It is monstrous. And it comes from having taboo words, and from not keeping the mind sufficiently developed in physical and sexual consciousness.

In contrast to the puritan hush! hush!, which produces the sexual moron, we have the modern young jazzy and high-brow person who has gone one better, and won't be hushed in any respect, and just "does as she likes." From fearing the body, and denying its existence, the advanced young go to the other extreme and treat it as a sort of toy to be played with, a slightly nasty toy, but still you can get some fun out of it, before it lets you down. These young people scoff at the importance of sex, take it like a cocktail, and flout their elders with it. These young ones are advanced and superior. They despise a book like *Lady Chatterley's Lover.* It is much too simple and ordinary for them. . . .

So, between the stale grey puritan who is likely to fall into sexual indecency in advanced age, and the smart jazzy person of the young world, who says: "We can do anything. If we can think a thing we can do it," and then the low uncultured person with a dirty mind, who looks for dirt—this book has hardly a space to turn in. But to them all I say the same: Keep your perversions if you like them—your perversion of puritanism, your perversion of smart licentiousness, your perversion of a dirty mind. But I stick to my book and my position: Life is only bearable when the mind and the body are in harmony, and there is a natural balance between them, and each has a natural respect for the other.

And it is obvious, there is no balance and no harmony now. The body is at the best the tool of the mind, at the worst, the toy. The business man keeps himself "fit," that is, keeps his body in good working order, for the sake of his business, and the usual young person who spends much time on keeping fit does so as a rule out of self-conscious self-absorption, narcissism. The mind has a stereotyped set of ideas and "feelings," and the body is made to act up, like a trained dog: to beg for sugar, whether it wants sugar or whether it doesn't, to shake hands when it would dearly like to snap the hand it has to shake. The body of men and women today is just a trained dog. And of no one is this more true than of the free and emancipated young. Above all, their bodies are the bodies of trained dogs. And because the dog is trained to do things the old-fashioned dog never did, they call themselves free, full of real life, the real thing. . . .

What life could it have, of itself? The body's life is the life of sensations and emotions. The body feels real hunger, real thirst, real joy in the sun or the snow, real pleasure in the smell of roses or the look of a lilac bush; real anger, real sorrow, real love, real tenderness, real warmth, real passion, real hate, real grief. All the emotions belong to the body, and are only recognised by the mind. We may hear the most sorrowful piece of news, and only feel a mental excitement. Then, hours after, perhaps in sleep, the awareness may reach the bodily centres, and true grief wrings the heart.

How different they are, mental feelings and real feelings. Today, many people live and die without having had any real feelings—though they have had a "rich emotional life" apparently, having showed strong mental feeling. But it is all counterfeit. In magic, one of the so-called "occult" pictures represents a man standing, apparently, before a flat table mirror, which reflects him from the waist to the head, so that you have the man from head to waist, then his reflection downwards from waist to head again. And whatever it may mean in magic, it means what we are today, creatures whose active emotional self has no real existence, but is all reflected downwards from the mind. Our education from the start has *taught* us a certain range of emotions, what to feel and what not to feel, and how to feel the feelings we allow ourselves to feel. All the rest is just non-existent. The vulgar criticism of any new good book is: Of course nobody ever felt like that!—People allow themselves to feel a certain number of finished feelings. So it was in the last century. This feeling only what you allow yourselves to feel at last kills all capacity for feeling, and in the higher emotional range you feel nothing at all. This has come to pass in our present century. The higher emotions are strictly dead. They have to be faked.

And by the higher emotions we mean love in all its manifestations, from genuine desire to tender love, love of our fellow-men, and love of God: we mean love, joy, delight, hope, true indignant anger, passionate sense of justice and injustice, truth and untruth, honour and dishonour, and real belief in *anything:* for belief is a profound emotion that has the mind's connivance. All these things, today, are more or less dead. We have in their place the loud and sentimental counterfeit of all such emotion.

Never was an age more sentimental, more devoid of real feeling, more exaggerated in false feeling, than our own. Sentimentality and counterfeit feeling have become a sort of game, everybody trying to outdo his neighbour The radio and the film are mere counterfeit emotion all the time, the current press and literature the same. People wallow in emotion: counterfeit emotion. They lap it up: they live in it and on it. They ooze with it.

And at times, they seem to get on very well with it all. And then, more and more, they break down. They go to pieces. You can fool yourself for a long time about your own feelings. But not forever. The body itself hits back at you, and hits back remorselessly in the end. . . .

Sex lashes out against counterfeit emotion, and is ruthless, devastating against false love. The peculiar hatred of people who have not loved one another, but who have pretended to, even perhaps have imagined they really did love, is one of the phenomena of our time. The phenomenon, of course, belongs to all time. But today it is almost universal. People who thought they loved one another dearly, dearly, and went on for years, ideal: lo! suddenly the most profound and vivid hatred appears. If it doesn't come out fairly young, it saves itself till the happy couple are nearing fifty, the time of the great sexual change—and then—cataclysm!

Nothing is more startling. Nothing is more staggering, in our age, than the intensity of the hatred people, men and women, feel for one another when they have once "loved" one another. It breaks out in the most extraordinary ways. And when you know people intimately, it is almost universal. It is the char-woman as much as the mistress, and the duchess as much as the policeman's wife.

And it would be too horrible, if one did not remember that in all of them, men and women alike, it is the organic reaction against counterfeit love. All love today is counterfeit. It is a stereotyped thing. All the young know just how they ought to feel and how they ought to behave, in love. And they feel and they behave like that. And it is counterfeit love. So that revenge will come back at them, ten-fold. The sex, the very sexual organism in man and woman alike accumulates a deadly and desperate rage, after a certain amount of counterfeit love has been palmed off on it, even if itself has given nothing but counterfeit love. The element of counterfeit in love at last maddens, or else kills, sex, the deepest sex in the individual. . . .

Now the real tragedy is here: that we are none of us all of a piece, none of us *all* counterfeit, or *all* true love. And in many a marriage, in among the counterfeit there flickers a little flame of the true thing, on both sides. The tragedy is, that in an age peculiarly conscious of counterfeit, peculiarly suspicious of substitute and swindle in emotion, particularly sexual emotion, the rage and mistrust against the counterfeit element is likely to overwhelm and extinguish the small, true flame of real loving communion, which might have made two lives happy. Herein lies the danger of harping only on the counterfeit and the swindle of emotion, as most "advanced" writers do. Though they do it, of course, to counterbalance the hugely greater swindle of the sentimental "sweet" writers. . . .

When a woman's sex is in itself dynamic and alive, then it is a power in itself, beyond her reason. And of itself it emits its peculiar spell, drawing men in the first delight of desire. And the woman has to protect herself, hide herself as much as possible. She veils herself in timidity and modesty, because her sex is a power in itself, exposing her to the desire of men. If a woman in whom sex was alive and positive were to expose her naked flesh as women do today, then men would go mad for her. As David was mad for Bathsheba.

But when a woman's sex has lost its dynamic call, and is in a sense dead or static, then the woman *wants* to attract men, for the simple reason that she finds she no longer does attract them. So all the activity that used to be unconscious and delightful becomes conscious and repellent. The woman exposes her flesh more and more, and the more she exposes, the more men are sexually repelled by her. But let us not forget that the men are *socially* thrilled, while sexually repelled. The two things are opposites, today. Socially, men like the gesture of the half-naked woman, half-naked in the street. It is *chic,* it is a declaration of defiance and independence, it is modern, it is free, it is popular because it is strictly a-sexual, or anti-sexual. Neither men nor women *want* to feel real desire, today. They want the counterfeit, mental substitute.

But we are very mixed, all of us, and creatures of many diverse and often opposing desires. The very men who encourage women to be most daring and sexless complain most bitterly of the sexlessness of women. The same with women. The women who adore men so tremendously for their social smartness and sexlessness as males, hate them most bitterly for not being "men." In public, *en masse,* and socially, everybody today wants counterfeit sex. But at certain hours in their lives, all individuals hate counterfeit sex with deadly and maddened hate, and those who have dealt it out most perhaps have the wildest hate of it, in the other person—or persons. . . .

While sex is a power in itself, women try all kinds of fascinating disguise, and men flaunt. When the Pope insists that women shall cover their naked flesh in church, it is not sex he is opposing, but the sexless tricks of female immodesty. The Pope, and the priests, conclude that the flaunting of naked women's flesh in street and church produces a bad, "unholy" state of mind both in men and women. And they are right. But not because the exposure arouses sexual desire: it doesn't, or very rarely: even Mr. Shaw knows that. But when women's flesh arouses no sort of desire, something is specially wrong! Something is sadly wrong. For the naked arms of women today arouse a feeling of flippancy, cynicism and vulgarity which is indeed the very last feeling to go to church with, if you have any respect for the Church. The bare arms of women in an Italian church are really a mark of disrespect, given the tradition.

The Catholic Church, especially in the south, is neither anti-sexual, like the northern Churches, nor a-sexual, like Mr. Shaw and such social thinkers. The Catholic Church recognises sex, and makes of marriage a sacrament based on the sexual communion, for the purpose of procreation. But procreation in the south, is not the bare and scientific fact, and act, that it is in the north. The act of procreation is still charged with all the sensual mystery and importance of the old past. The man is potential creator, and in this has his splendour. All of which has been stripped away by the northern Churches and the Shavian logical triviality. . . .

. . . We are just in the throes of a great revolt against marriage, a passionate revolt against its ties and restrictions. In fact, at least three-quarters of the unhappiness of modern life could be laid at the door of marriage. There are few married people today, and few unmarried, who have not felt an intense and vivid hatred against marriage itself, marriage as an institution and an imposition upon human life. Far greater than the revolt against governments is this revolt against marriage.

And everybody, pretty well, takes it for granted that as soon as we can find a possible way out of it, marriage will be abolished. The Soviet abolishes marriage: or did. If new "modern" states spring up, they will almost certainly follow suit. They will try to find some social substitute for marriage, and abolish the hated yoke of conjugality. State support of motherhood, state support of children, and independence of women. It is on the programme of every great scheme of reform. And it means, of course, the abolition of marriage.

The only question to ask ourselves is, do we really want it? Do we want the absolute independence of women, State support of motherhood and of children, and consequent doing away with the necessity of marriage? Do we want it? Because all that matters is that men and women shall do what they *really* want to do. Though here, as everywhere, we must remember that man has a double set of desires, the shallow and the profound, the personal, superficial, temporary desires, and the inner, impersonal, great desires that are fulfilled in long periods of time. The desires of the moment are easy to recognise, but the others, the deeper ones, are difficult. It is the business of our Chief Thinkers to tell us of our deeper desires, not to keep shrilling our little desires in our ears.

Now the Church is established upon a recognition of some, at least, of the greatest and deepest desires in man, desires that take years, or a life-time, or even centuries to fulfil. And the Church, celibate as its priesthood may be, built as it may be upon the lonely rock of Peter, or of Paul, really rests upon the indissolubility of marriage. Make marriage in any serious degree unstable, dissoluble, destroy the permanency of marriage, and the Church falls. Witness the enormous decline of the Church of England.

The reason being that the Church is established upon the element of *union* in mankind. And the first element of union in the Christian world is the marriage-tie. The marriage-tie, the marriage bond, take it which way you like, is the fundamental connecting link in Christian society. Break it, and you will have to go back to the overwhelming dominance of the State, which existed before the Christian era. . . .

And the Church created marriage by making it a sacrament, a sacrament of man and woman united in the sex communion, and never to be separated, except by death. And even when separated by death, still not freed from the marriage. Marriage, as far as the individual went, eternal. Marriage, making one complete body out of two incomplete ones, and providing for the complex development of the man's soul and the woman's soul in unison, throughout a life-time. Marriage sacred and inviolable, the great way of earthly fulfilment for man and woman, in unison, under the spiritual rule of the Church. . . .

Augustine said that God created the universe new every day: and to the living, emotional soul, this is true. Every dawn dawns upon an entirely new universe, every Easter lights up an entirely new glory of a new world opening in utterly new flower. And the soul of man and the soul of woman is new in the same way, with the infinite delight of life and the ever-newness of life. So a man and a woman are new to one another throughout a lifetime, in the rhythm of marriage that matches the rhythm of the year.

Sex is the balance of male and female in the universe, the attraction, the repulsion, the transit of neutrality, the new attraction, the new repulsion, always different, always new. The long neuter spell of Lent, when the blood is low, and the delight of the Easter kiss, the sexual revel of spring, the passion of midsummer, the slow recoil, revolt, and grief of autumn, greyness again, then the sharp stimulus of winter of the long nights. Sex goes through the rhythm of the year, in man and woman, ceaselessly changing: the rhythm of

the sun in his relation to the earth. Oh, what a catastrophe for man when he cut himself off from the rhythm of the year, from his unison with the sun and the earth. Oh, what a catastrophe, what a maiming of love when it was made a personal, merely personal feeling, taken away from the rising and the setting of the sun, and cut off from the magic connection of the solstice and the equinox! This is what is the matter with us. We are bleeding at the roots, because we are cut off from the earth and sun and stars, and love is a grinning mockery, because, poor blossom, we plucked it from its stem on the tree of Life, and expected it to keep on blooming in our civilised vase on the table.

Marriage is the clue to human life, but there is no marriage apart from the wheeling sun and the nodding earth, from the straying of the planets and the magnificence of the fixed stars. Is not a man different, utterly different, at dawn from what he is at sunset? and a woman too? And does not the changing harmony and discord of their variation make the secret music of life? . . .

But—and this *but* crashes through our heart like a bullet—marriage is no marriage that is not basically and permanently phallic, and that is not linked up with the sun and the earth, the moon and the fixed stars and the planets, in the rhythm of days, in the rhythm of months, in the rhythm of quarters, of years, of decades and of centuries. Marriage is no marriage that is not a correspondence of blood. For the blood is the substance of the soul, and of the deepest consciousness. It is by blood that we are: and it is by the heart and the liver that we live and move and have our being. In the blood, knowing and being, or feeling, are one and undivided: no serpent and no apple has caused a split. So that only when the conjunction is of the blood, is marriage truly marriage. The blood of man and the blood of woman are two eternally different streams, that can never be mingled. Even scientifically we know it. But therefore they are the two rivers that encircle the whole of life, and in marriage the circle is complete, and in sex the two rivers touch and renew one another, without ever commingling or confusing. We know it. The phallus is a column of blood that fills the valley of blood of a woman. The great river of male blood touches to its depths the great river of female blood—yet neither breaks its bounds. It is the deepest of all communions, as all the religions, in practice, know.

Study Questions on D. H. Lawrence

1. Why does Lawrence think that the use of four-letter words contributes to a healthier attitude toward sex? Do you agree?
2. What does Lawrence mean by "realizing sex"? (Does this mean unrestrained indulgence?) How does he distinguish real from counterfeit sexual feelings?
3. Lawrence is, of course, writing with English culture in mind. Do you think he would say the same thing about contemporary American culture? Explain.
4. On what grounds might someone believe that Lawrence's attitudes toward sex would have bad personal or political consequences? What would be the results of extending his ways of thinking outside the sexual domain to politics, for example?

The Fruits of Unreason

JANET RADCLIFFE RICHARDS

Janet Radcliffe Richards here criticizes some feminists for attacking rationality as masculine, and for "taking the women's side in everything," whatever the merits of the issue. Doing so, she argues, undermines the feminist critique of patriarchal ideology, which necessarily includes the claim that this ideology is wrong because it is irrational.

1 The Undermined Foundations

SOME TIME AGO, as the recent wave of feminism was rising to its full intensity, a group called the New York Radical Women put out a statement of principles, beginning like this:

We take the woman's side in everything. We ask not if something is "reformist," "radical," "revolutionary," or "moral." We ask: is it good for women or bad for women?

At about the same time, and apparently not a thousand miles away, was produced another document, the *Redstockings Manifesto*, which contains a similar statement:

In fighting for our liberation we will always take the side of women against their oppressors. We will not ask what is "revolutionary" or "reformist," only what is good for women.

. . . [T]aken as they stand, these statements imply that in their determination to advance the cause of women, the feminists who formulated them are prepared to throw all constraints of morality to the winds; that right or wrong, fair or unfair, they will pursue anything whatever which is to the benefit of women. . . .

This conclusion cannot be avoided by arguing that since women have been badly treated throughout history there is now a balance to be

From *Janet Radcliffe Richards*, The Sceptical Feminist. *Reprinted by permission of David Highan Associates.*

restored, and women will have to be given far more than equal shares with men if justice is to be done. That is no doubt true, but it does not affect the point. If women need more than men in order to achieve sexual justice, the principles of justice will themselves determine how much more they need. There is no point at which it is reasonable to forget about the principles and concentrate only on the advantage of the oppressed group. However badly it has been treated, it is always possible that if it thought of nothing but its own interests it might eventually get too much, and begin to treat its former oppressor unjustly.

Nevertheless, someone might reply, even though that may well be true as a matter of theory, it is quite irrelevant to practice. In day to day activities, where we have to make decisions in far too great a hurry to allow for elaborate computations of justice, we have to be guided by rules of thumb. And since it is most unlikely in practice that women could ever achieve more than was their due, we are justified in taking the advantage of women as our general guide to action.

That is a stronger argument, but it still does not work. Even if sexual oppression is the worst type of oppression (a question to be left open for the time being), and even if the most oppressed people in the world are women (which is probably true), sexual oppression is still not the only form of oppression, and women are not the only oppressed people. Many men are far more oppressed than many women, and any feminist who was determined to support women in all situations would certainly encounter some where her support of women against men would increase the level of injustice in the world. Even though we may often have to make very rough guesses about the fairest thing to do, and even though in doing so we may often justifiably favour women against men, we cannot make a general rule that we should always do so. Or at least, if such a rule is justified, it needs far more elaborate defence than it has ever been given, and the onus is on any feminist who thinks it ought to be defended to provide reasons.

No feminist whose concern for women stems from a concern for justice in general can ever legitimately allow her only interest to be the advantage of women. Does this mean, then, that the New York Radical Women, the Redstockings and others like them have to be regarded as pursuing a different sort of feminism, one whose motivation is not moral? That is certainly what the evidence so far seems to suggest, but the trouble with that conclusion is that it seems completely at odds with the tone of the rest of the two statements from which the quotations are taken; the parts not quoted here. They are full of anger about suffering and abuse, disregarded feelings and unfair privileges, and convey the fiercest possible moral indignation. Even in the passages quoted above, chosen for their explicit non-moral stance, there is some indication of this where the Redstockings write of the oppressors of women. "Oppression" is not a morally neutral word. To claim that women are oppressed by men is not simply to say that men are in a position of advantage or power over women, but to imply that that power is unjustly held. But if all this is true, it looks as though it is after all a wish to see justice which motivates these feminists.

In other words, there is a contradiction. On the one hand there is the description of what is wrong with the position of women, written in terms of moral censure; on the other there is the statement of intended action, which seems to admit of no moral constraint at all. . . .

. . . The point about these groups is that they have apparently *not* abandoned their original concern for justice. What they seem to have done is allow their perception of the extent of women's oppression to extend itself until the elimination of women's suffering has become the criterion for justice. But this cannot be done. No matter how great the suffering of an oppressed group, and no matter how much it will have to be given before justice is done, its advantage can never be *the same thing* as justice. To identify the two is to allow for the possibility of the oppressed group's being given too much, and to set out on a path which leads to injustice, *injustice according to the very principles by which it was established that women were oppressed in the first place*. The heavenly city is being built with stones stolen from its own foundations.

. . . No group whose concern is for justice can reasonably be complacent about carelessly formulated principles which might lead away from fairness while appearing to support it.

2 The Extent of the Mistake

If we take it that the proper aim of feminism should be to establish a society in which there is sexual justice, it is obviously important that feminists should take care not to fall into moral confusion, and accidentally start on a course which could itself lead to injustice. However, important as that is, pointing it out was not the real purpose of the argument of the previous section. Its real importance was to illustrate a certain sort of mistake, which is just as serious for any feminist with no particular interest in morality as it is in the context of justice. Whatever your aims, it must go against your interests to act according to a hastily formulated maxim which is actually in conflict with those aims, and may lead by a different route to the position which you were trying to escape.

Here is another example of the same mistake, this time having nothing at all to do with morality. A feminist of my acquaintance said that the members of her group would not be interested in going to an evening class working on a non-polemical analysis of feminist issues. She said that they would have no interest in hearing evidence which might try to show that traditional ideas about women were right after all. People had for ages been producing spurious arguments to prove all kinds of absurdity about women, and there was no point whatever in listening to any more such nonsense.

. . . If feminists now have a better idea of what women are like than people used to have, that is only because some people eventually got round to looking at evidence about the nature of women, instead of being blinkered by prejudice and seeing only what happened to support what they wanted to believe. But now, it seems, some feminists may be falling into precisely the same mistake. Having used new evidence to revise the old ideas about women, and to put forward theories of their own which they find more attractive, they elevate them to too great a height, and presume them true. Having done that, they use their new theories to dismiss any further incoming evidence which conflicts with them.

But this way of going about things once again cuts the ground from under feminist feet. The whole point of challenging the traditional view of women was to prevent their being forced into uncongenial positions in society by people's wrong ideas about them. If feminists at any point start to presume their current theories in sociology, psychology or anything else can be taken as certainly true, when in fact there is always an overwhelming probability that the truth has not yet been reached, they are only heading for the same unhappy state of things by a different route. If we really want to make society as well suited to people's natures as possible, we cannot afford to ignore any evidence; not even when it is produced by the opposition.

The mistake is of just the same structure as the one described in the previous section. There, feminists were in search of justice; here, they want to understand the nature of women, to make an attack on the superstitions which are used to justify forcing them into uncongenial social situations. There, the perception that women were unjustly treated slipped into the idea that the well-being of women was the criterion for justice; here, the recognition that the original theories were wrong has slipped into the conviction that the new ones are right. In both cases the hastily reached conclusion has outgrown its roots and taken on an independent existence, *and has become a tool for undermining the very principles which were used to support the conclusion in the first place*. An attack on injustice has turned unnoticed into a device for perpetrating injustice; a determination to find out the truth about women has become an obstacle in the way of the truth's being found. . . .

Another example of the mistake is often connected with the idea of conditioning. Feminists quite rightly want women free, choosing for themselves what happens to them, but realize that as a result of the thoroughness of men's control over women, some women are not in a position to be able to choose effectively even when they seem entirely unconstrained. This may account for women's resistance to some feminist ideas. From there, however, it is all too easy to slide into the convenient idea that *whenever* women make choices which feminists think they ought not to make they must be conditioned, so giving feminists an excuse to discount those opinions. But if that happens there is obviously a risk of forcing women again, even though in a different direction from before, because the *nature* of someone's choice is not enough to show that it comes from conditioning. The attempt to free women turns into a different way of coercing them.

The examples go on and on. Feminists object legitimately to the tyranny of sexual roles, and complain if men and women are expected by virtue of their sex alone to do different sorts of work. But if, like some feminists, we go to the extent of presuming that we have not got rid of the tyranny until men and women are doing the same sorts of work, we risk a different problem: that of forcing them to do the same things even though they may possibly have inclinations (on average) to do different things. Or we complain about sexism, meaning that people count sex as relevant in contexts where it is not, and then slip into accusations of sexism whenever anyone has the temerity to suggest that there are *any* differences between the sexes. To do that is to say that sex should not count under circumstances where it *is* relevant, and that is a kind of sexism (making a special case of sex) in itself. Sometimes this self-defeating elevation of feminist insights into the standards by which everything else is to be tested even becomes quite formal. Irene Peslikis (one of the Redstockings) has a list of "Resistances to Consciousness," ideas which might beguile feminists into questioning prevailing ideology and are therefore to be rejected outright, apparently even when it looks as though there may be good evidence for believing them. Current doctrine is presented as the standard by which to assess the truth or acceptability of everything else, and is itself thereby made unquestionable.

When feminist theory is presented in that sort of way there is a special danger, because it conveys the impression that anyone who is against the dogma is against feminism. But to question these mistakes, even from outside the movement, is not to be against feminism. *Whatever* feminists want, whether it is justice, equality, freedom, happiness, female supremacy or the total elimination of men, they will not reach it by leaping to hasty conclusions and accepting as articles of faith principles which will undermine their real intentions. The fact that something is born of feminist effort, and comes out of the movement, is not enough to show that it is good for feminism.

3 *The Pursuit of Unreason*

No doubt it could be argued that the last thing any feminist ought to be doing is drawing public attention to widespread carelessness about reasoning in the feminist movement, as has just been done. It plays straight into the hands of the enemy. Of course feminists are incapable of reasoning, men are likely to say; women have never been able to reason. They are always full of emotion and apt to be carried away by strength of feeling, which is why all this pursuit of equality is nonsense in the first place. Whenever feminists try to deny their inferiority to men, they confirm it with every word they say.

We are actually forced to no such view of inherent feminine inadequacy in reasoning, in spite of the serious mistakes undoubtedly made by feminists. Apart from the fact that most men are none too marvellous when it comes to reasoning either, there is on the feminist side the very powerful argument that even if women are less good at reasoning than men that is hardly surprising, since men have always taken very good care that women should never have the opportunity to learn. That does not prove that when given the chance they will be competent, of course, but it certainly shows that men are not entitled to make many presumptions about women's potential on the basis of their present performance. A feminist should be quite happy to accept that women at present are likely (on average) to be less adept at argument than men, and one of the reasons for working through mistakes in reasoning is to get women better at it, and make their position less open to masculine attack.

. . . The trouble is that the traditional feminist who thinks that women are bound to have been held back by educational deprivation meets her most serious opponent not in men, but in *a new breed of anti-rational feminist, which unexpectedly embraces the enemy position.* Of course (this new feminist apparently thinks) women are less rational and more dependent on feeling than men. This has nothing to do with education. Women really are so by nature, and much the better for it. Rationality, like other things male, is something we are better without.

It is actually very difficult to prove that feminists hold these views. *Arguments* against *reason* do not start off on the firmest of ground, and they could hardly deceive even their proponents unless they were kept in a permanently slippery state, shifting from one meaning of "rational" or "logical" to another as the occasion demanded. They hardly ever get written down, therefore: to the extent that they can be seen directly they tend to live a precarious oral existence in the form of multiple ambiguous slogans such as "logic isn't everything," "people are more important than logic" and the like. More often their existence can only be inferred from other things which are said. But there is undoubtedly evidence that feminism has some tendency to get stuck in the quagmire of unreason from time to time, or at least to get dangerously close to its brink. Because of that the whole issue of rationality is an important matter in feminism. However, in case anyone should regard the whole accusation as totally implausible, and the attack as directed against nothing but straw women, some evidence for the claim must be produced.

There is, for example, Germaine Greer, one of the most attractive of recent feminist writers, and anything but straw. She writes with the utmost cheerfulness that her own arguments "have all the faults of an insufficient regard for logic and none of its strengths" (already implying that there are strengths in a disregard for logic) and goes on to say that in argument between women and their menfolk

> The rules of logical discourse are no more relevant than the Marquess of Queensberry's are to a pub brawl. Female hardheadedness rejects the misguided masculine notion that men are rational animals. Male logic can only deal with simple issues: women . . . are more aware of complexity. . . .

4 What Rationality Is

It cannot be denied that adopting an anti-rational stance has its uses; it can be turned into an all-purpose escape route from tricky corners. Whenever a feminist's conclusions are challenged by a man (or by an unliberated woman who has been conditioned into thinking the same way) she can say that the challenge is based on male reasoning, and refuse to argue any further. Nevertheless, in spite of these advantages of unreason, feminists should be cautious. Before so cheerfully consigning rationality to men it is necessary to be clear about precisely what it is, and make sure that it really is something women do not want for themselves. . . .

Logic covers a much smaller area than many people think. At root it is about *consistency*. It is not just an arbitrary set of rules which might have been otherwise and which could be done without, like the Marquess of Queensberry's, or like the various rules and conventions which keep women in their traditionally subservient place. It is a set of rules presupposed by the existence of language; not just some particular language, but any language. The most fundamental rule is that of non-contradiction. Essentially, whatever is meant when something is said, whether the words are used with their usual meanings or not, if the statement is to mean anything at all it must *exclude* some possibilities. In other words, to say for instance that something is red all over, in the standard use of those words, is to imply at the same time that it is *not* all kinds of other things, such as green or blue or spotted or striped. If, therefore, you say that something is red and blue all over at the same time, really meaning that and not something silly like constantly changing colour or being of a red and blue pattern, you have *failed to say anything at all* since to be red is, among other things, to be not-blue.

Similarly, to say "if it's red all over, it can't be blue," making an inference from redness to non-blueness, is to rely on the same rule; to assert both would be to say nothing because if one can truly be asserted, the other cannot. And that is what is wrong with being illogical. Being illogical is not having strong feelings, or mixed feelings, or changing your mind, or being unable to express things and prove things, or anything of the sort. It is maintaining that incompatible propositions are both true, and in doing so maintaining *nothing*, since to make an illogical statement is to make no statement at all. But since this is so, and since the purpose of language is to convey information, to use language at all is to rely on logic.

Feminists therefore cannot disregard logic. It is also quite clear (looking at the matter less fundamentally) that they do not even try to, since they are always accusing men of inconsistency of one sort or another. A feminist who thinks there is nothing wrong with inconsistency is in no position to complain if men expect women to carry heavy loads when those loads consist of children or shopping or washing, but say that they can't lift (the same) heavy loads when it is convenient to have rules excluding women from well-paid work. What is happening is that these men have committed themselves to *nothing at all* about what women can do, since they have implied that they both can and cannot lift loads of a certain weight. They invent the conflicting facts as they go along, to suit their convenience. Of course feminists complain, and they complain on grounds of logic.

That is why feminists must be logical. But logic is only part of rationality, though people sometimes use "logical" very loosely to mean generally rational, and often when women are accused of being illogical what is really intended is that they are irrational in relying too much on intuition. Instead of looking carefully at the available evidence before settling on a belief, which is supposed to be the rational thing to do, they are said to leap to unfounded conclusions. Men, conversely, are supposed to be much more careful about looking at the evidence for what they believe. And at this point the feminist who is sceptical about the value of reason may feel she is on much stronger ground. After all, she may say, for centuries men have been assembling facts and presenting what passed for proofs of this or that, and because we were brainwashed into thinking that male reason must be everything men said it was, we believed the lot. Now we are beginning to see that most of what they claimed was false.

So much for male rationality, the feminist may well say. We should have done a good deal better to rely on female intuition all along. . . .

The point is that rationality does not dictate how ideas should be arrived at, but only that they should not be stuck to obstinately in the face of strong conflicting evidence. Irrational people are not the ones who reach ideas without much explicit evidence, but those who refuse to look for and consider evidence which would count against those ideas. That is *prejudice,* a thing to which feminists must certainly be opposed. Men's prejudices about women are not the ideas they have which women do not like, nor the ones which happen to be false; they are the ones which are kept to irrationally, in spite of the evidence. If feminists defend irrationality they are in no position to complain if men resist all evidence and go on believing until the end of time that women are inherently weak, unreasonable and given to fits of the vapours. For that matter, they could not even complain if men took it into their heads to believe that women had black and yellow stripes and laid eggs. It is only through insisting that the evidence should be looked at carefully that women are able to attack the prejudices of men. Feminists cannot possibly support irrationality in any form.

Study Questions on Janet Radcliffe Richards

1. Have you encountered any of what Richards calls the "new breed of antirational feminists?" Do you agree with her that they embrace the enemy position?
2. Might the use of emotionalistic rhetoric rather than rational argument serve a positive political function by helping maintain group solidarity among feminists? If so, does this justify its use?
3. What do you think Richards would say about affirmative action for women and why? Do you agree? (See readings and For Further Reading in Unit V.)
4. What do you think D. H. Lawrence would say about Richards's way of addressing sexual issues?

For Further Reading

Ayer, (Sir) Alfred Jules. *Language, Truth, and Logic.* New York: Dover Publications, n.d. Chap. 6. A classic formulation of the emotive theory of ethics.

Brooke, John L. "Reason and Passion in the Public Sphere." *Journal of Interdisciplinary History,* 29, no. 1 (Summer 1998), 43ff. Available on InfoTrac® College Edition.

Clarke, Stanley G., and Evan Simpson, eds. *Anti-Theory in Ethics and Moral Conservatism.* Albany, N.Y.: SUNY, 1989. Includes Stuart Hampshire's defense of a key role for emotion in morals.

Devlin, Patrick (Lord). *The Enforcement of Morals.* Oxford: Oxford University Press, 1965. "Intolerance, indignation, and disgust" as elements of moral judgment.

Dodds, E. R. *The Greeks and the Irrational.* Berkeley: University of California Press, 1966.

Gilligan, Carol. *In a Different Voice.* Cambridge, Mass.: Harvard University Press, 1982.

Harding, S., and M. Hintikka, eds. *Discovering Reality: Feminist Perspectives on Epistemology, Metaphysics, and the Philosophy of Language.* Dodrecht: Reidel, 1983. Includes an important essay by Janice Moulton, "A Paradigm of Philosophy: The Adversary Method."

Hume, David. *A Treatise of Human Nature.* L. A. Selby-Bigge, ed. Oxford: Clarendon Press, 1888. Pts. II and III. Reason as the slave of the passions.

Jaggar, Alison. "Love and Knowledge in Feminist Epistemology." *Inquiry,* 32 (July 1989).

Kant, Immanuel. *Grounding for the Metaphysics of Morals.* James W. Ellington, trans. Indianapolis, Ind.: Hackett, 1981. Morality as centrally rational.

Kittay, Eva Feder, and Diana T. Meyers, eds. *Women and Moral Theory.* Totowa, N.J.: Rowman & Littlefield, 1987.

Lee-Hampshire, Wendy. "The Sound of Little Hummingbird Wings." *Feminist Studies,* 25, no. 2 (Summer 1999), 409ff. Available on InfoTrac® College Edition.

Lloyd, Genevieve. *The Man of Reason.* Minneapolis, Minn.: University of Minnesota Press, 1984.

MacIntyre, Alasdair. *After Virtue.* 2nd ed. Notre Dame, Ind.: University of Notre Dame Press, 1984. Esp. chaps. 1–3. Emotivism true of morality as actually practiced in the modern world.

Noddings, Nell. *Caring: A Feminine Approach to Ethics.* Berkeley: University of California Press, 1984.

Nussbaum, Martha. *Love's Knowledge.* Cambridge: Cambridge University Press, 1982.

Selby-Bigge, L. A. *British Moralists.* Indianapolis, Ind.: Bobbs-Merrill, 1964. Sentiment vs. reason as the ground of morality.

Solomon, Robert C. *The Passions.* Notre Dame, Ind.: Notre Dame University Press, 1983.

Storkenbloom, Dorothee. "Historicizing the Gender of Emotions." *Journal of Social History,* 34, no. 1 (Fall 2000), 55ff. Available on InfoTrac® College Edition.

Stout, Jeffrey. *Ethics After Babel.* Boston: Beacon Press, 1988.

Williams, Simon J. "Modernity and the Emotions." *Sociology,* 32, no. 4 (November 1998), 747ff. Available on InfoTrac® College Edition.

INFOTRAC COLLEGE EDITION To learn more about the topics from this chapter, you can use the following words to conduct an electronic search on InfoTrac College Edition, an online library of journals. Here you will find a multitude of articles from various sources and perspectives: *www.infotrac-college.com/wadsworth/access.html*

caring

enlightenment

feminist epistemology

masculine and feminine

mind and body

nature and culture

reason and passion

Web Sites

Americans for Better Care of the Dying
http://www.abcd.caring.org/mainpage.htm

Bly, Robert, "The Reunion of Masculine and Feminine" (Interview)
http://themenscenter.com/page47.html

Feminist Epistemology and Philosophy of Science (Stanford Encyclopedia of Philosophy)
http://plato.stanford.edu/entries/feminism-epistemology/

Internet Modern History Sourcebook: The Enlightenment
http://www.fordham.edu.halsall.modsbook.10html

Nature, Culture, and Spirit (Bioneers)
http://www.bioneers.org/track_pages101/nature_cs.html

Reason and Passion in Balance
web.bentley.edu/emplib/wbachhdz/articles/truthandtaste/idi4.html

Wozniak, Robert H., "Mind and Body: René Descartes to William James"
http://serendip./brynmayr.edu/Mind/Table.html

Male and Female:
Is the Distinction Natural
or Conventional?

FEW QUESTIONS HAVE RECEIVED MORE ATTENTION of late than the question of whether or not there are significant differences between males and females. At first blush, it might seem that this question should be easy to answer, and that all we need to do is to set psychologists to work using the most up-to-date research methods to investigate sex differences. A great deal of research has in fact already been done on this subject (see the book by Sarah Stein, listed in the For Further Reading section in this unit, for a summary of the results arrived at by Maccoby and Jacklin in their extensive cross-cultural research on male-female differences). But there are important reasons why empirical research alone cannot resolve the dispute over which observed differences are in some sense *real,* and which are simply the result of the way children have been socialized.

For one thing, given the fact that many researchers approach their research with strong ideological commitments, it is easy for them to select their samples and word their questions in such a way as to obtain the desired results. Research that relies on self-reporting by the subjects can be misleading, since people are often dishonest, self-deceiving, or just not very self-aware. And if we attempt to do experimental testing that relies on direct observation of the behavior of boys and girls, we quickly discover that standard sexual stereotypes—such as that males are more aggressive or more active than females—are very hard to define in a way that renders them amenable to experimental testing. To complicate matters further, there are certain clearly innate human dispositions (such as the smiling reflex) that require appropriate environmental stimulation to develop normally, so that genetics and environmental influences become virtually impossible to disentangle.

How, then, are we to make sense of the central theme of this unit—namely, the connection between *sex* and *gender.* According, at least, to the most common definitions of these terms, people's sex is a matter of their biology and, except for anomalous cases, is usually relatively uncontroversial. But gender has to do with how sexual differences are reflected on the social level, and is thus limited to humans, or at least to the higher animals. People present themselves as masculine or feminine in an enormous variety of ways—by how they walk, talk, dress, and laugh; by how they arrange their living quarters; by the hobbies they pursue; and so on. It is by means of these sorts of things that we perceive each other as gendered beings. Depending on the sort of relationship we have with a person, his or her gender may or may not be of central importance, but it is always there as a background. Consider, for example, how disquieting it can be to encounter someone whose sex or gender we cannot identify. Perhaps this is why sexually ambiguous persons (such as Tireseus in *Oedipus Rex* or the berdache in American Indian tribes) were often thought to possess spooky powers; they are transgressing one of the fundamental conceptual boundaries around which most people organize their lives.

In order to help clarify the way in which sex and gender are connected, we begin with the story of Jan Morris (born James Morris) who underwent a sex change operation. The reason for taking transsexualism as a focal point is not because it is an especially common phenomenon, but because it poses the problem of how sex and gender are related in a particularly sharp way. Prior to the sex change operation, Morris was undeniably biologically male (having married and fathered several children), but felt a deep contradiction between physical sex (male) and real gender (female)—a conviction of being a woman trapped in a man's body. In the course of hormonal and surgical treatments, Morris at last came to be endowed with the experiences and social role of a woman. Such phenomena are difficult to interpret philosophically. What sense can be made of the claim that one is really a woman trapped in a man's body (or vice versa)?

Two of the selections below argue that sex and gender cannot be separated in the way that Morris thinks they can. Mastroeni argues that transsexuals like Morris are simply suffering from psychological pathology, that arguments designed to justify transsexual surgery are based on an untenable form of mind-body dualism, and that after surgery someone like Morris has not become a woman, but merely a mutilated male. Clark brings in the social dimension by citing extensive cross-cultural similarities in the roles of men and women and pointing out that attempts to radically change these roles (e.g., in the Israeli kibbutzim) have failed. These facts would, he believes, indicate that at least some of the more general features of traditional sex roles flow naturally from the biological differences between men and women. This does not rule out cultural influence on behavioral differences between males and females, but cultures themselves develop as they do because women and men are as they are. While we can exert some control over cultural patterns, Clark argues that just as ecologists have shown us that small changes in the fragile and delicately balanced ecosystem can produce unforeseen and disastrous consequences, so also attempts to radically alter patterns of male and female roles that have been present throughout human history in favor of untried alternatives (as cultural radicals propose to do) could have equally disastrous consequences.

The next two readings develop an increasingly radical critique of the idea that gender is or needs to be closely tied to biological sex. Suzanne Kessler and Wendy McKenna argue that gender is a social construction, and emphasize the element of social construction even in the division of the world into two biological groups—males and females. Those American Indian cultures that have berdaches have, they would say, constructed social reality in such a way that there are three and not two genders. (A berdache is a biological male who is treated as female for social, including sexual, purposes.) Alternatively, they might say, they construct some biological males as female in gender. Which of these is the more accurate description is a matter for anthropological investigation. In any case, there is no reason why we could not construct gender in any number of different ways; there is no objective fact of the matter.

Richard Wasserstrom also emphasizes the idea that sex roles are social creations (and therefore changeable), but draws somewhat different conclusions from Kessler and McKenna. Wasserstrom concludes not just that there are a variety of different ways in which we could draw gender distinctions, but that we ought to cease constructing gender as a meaningful category at all. He rejects appeals to nature, and any other way of grounding sex-based limitations on legitimate forms of human life, in the name of an ideal of human autonomy. Just as a nonracist society (one which is assimilationist with respect to race) treats skin color as no more important than, say, eye color, so also a nonsexist society (one which is assimilationist with regard to sex) would be one in which anatomical sex differences have no importance at all for the way we treat persons or the behavior we expect from them, and thus bisexuality would be the typical form of intimate sexual association in the ideal society.

The last two readings articulate and defend a more moderate traditionalism. Mary Midgley argues that given the continuity between humans and other animals, and given the extensive morphological and hormonal differences between men and women, it is unreasonable to suppose that there are no biologically conditioned behavioral differences between the sexes. She also argues that we can admit such differences without succumbing to biological determinism, and that those feminists who attempt to completely deny the existence of biologically based differences between the sexes lapse into inconsistencies.

Roger Scruton, finally, articulates a moderate traditional view that takes account of the facts of cultural variation and concedes a great deal to Kessler and McKenna's view that gender is a social construction (although without accepting the idea that sex in the biological sense is a social construction). He compares sexuality to the soil out of which the leaves and fruit of gender grow. Gender differences are in a sense artifacts "whereby we embellish, exaggerate or conceal our sexual nature," but gender distinctions nonetheless lie very close to the heart of who we are as persons. He argues particularly against what he calls "Kantian feminism" (Wasserstrom's view) which holds that the only important thing about us is that we are persons who are free and rational. Scruton points out that in the sense in which gender is a social construction, so also is the concept of being a person. Gender, according to him, is a cultural creation, but one rooted in and expressive of biological difference. Gender distinctions are central to our understanding of ourselves, and make it possible for human sexuality to be something more than the purely physical reproductive acts of animals. It is important, thus, to preserve such distinctions, and Scruton would therefore oppose Wasserstrom's assimilationist idea.

The debate over the relationship between sex and gender, then, is interwoven with the broader philosophical debate over whether we can talk about human nature or objective reality at all, or whether all our institutions and concepts are essentially arbitrary social constructs. Generally speaking, cultural radicals tend to be social constructionists and look at our present gender system as a construct that we can and ought to change. Traditional thinkers like Mastroeni and Clark, by contrast, tend to believe in a close tie between our biological nature and our gender roles. But the issue is complicated, and there is no reason to suppose that those who believe gender to be a social construct must be cultural radicals or that those who believe in biologically based sexual differences must be traditionalists.

Those who believe in an objective human nature, including a biologically founded distinction between male and female, might be severely critical of present conventions on any number of grounds. They could argue that existing institutions fail to properly understand or respond to the *real* differences between men and women, and that they therefore ought to be changed in radical ways to bring them more in harmony with the way women and men really are. Similarly, it is quite possible to believe both that gender is wholly or partly a social construct, and that we either cannot or should not change our present gender system. Because something is socially constructed does not mean it can be changed; it may be too deeply ingrained to change. Nor does it mean that we *ought* to change it, for it is possible that attempts to change such deep features of our conceptual framework would produce such severe social and psychological disruptions that the negative consequences would outweigh the gains obtained by the change.

Questions for Reflection

1. Do you think that you could be the same person you now are, only the opposite sex from the one you now are?
2. Could you be a man in a woman's body or a woman in a man's body?
3. Do you feel that your autonomy (your freedom to become the person you want to be) is presently limited by your biological sex? Is it limited by gender role expectations?
4. In a world in which gender differences had been eliminated, being male or female would no longer be important to the ways in which people relate to each other, and no traits, behaviors, or ways of dressing would be thought of as masculine or feminine. Try to imagine in detail what such a world would be like.
5. What are some of the most important differences that would hold between such a world and the one you now find yourself in? How would your everyday life be different?
6. Would you like to live in such a world? Think about how it might be preferable to the social world you now inhabit, and ways in which it might be worse.

Glossary

alimony money traditionally paid to a wife after a divorce.

assimilationism the attempt to render some socially important distinction, for example, between men and women, unimportant.

autonomy self-rule.

berdache in American Indian practice, a biological male defined socially as a woman (some-times also a biological female defined socially as a man).

biodeterminism the belief that our biology determines our social practices.

conception variety of beliefs associated with a concept.

conventional created by human agreement rather than being a fact of nature.

cultural radicalism see Introduction for Students at beginning of book.

dichotomous divided into two classes, such as male and female.

dualism view of the human person that draws a sharp distinction between body and soul.

ecology the study of ecosystems; also a political movement founded on such study.

ecosystem system defined by the interaction of a variety of organisms or, in an extended sense, a variety of institutions and practices.

embodiment our character or experience as bodily beings.

enracinement rooting.

ethnomethodology the study of social practices from a perspective emphasizing social construction.

existentialism philosophy emphasizing the human capacity for free choice.

fatalism belief that our lives, and especially our social practices, are outside our control.

form and matter central metaphysical distinction in Aristotle's thought. The genotype is the form of the human body; the flesh its matter.

gender masculinity or femininity as a social or psychological category.

gender assignment gender attribution at birth.

gender attribution our "decision" to designate some person as a woman or man.

gender construction the fashioning of a gender identity.

gender identity defining oneself as male or female, or as masculine or feminine.

gender reassignment (or reconstruction) change in gender attribution.

gender roles social expectations associated with gender; also called *sex roles.*

hallucinogenic productive of altered states of consciousness (especially of a drug).

hyperspiritualism emphasis on the spiritual side of human beings, to the neglect of our bodily life.

ideal belief about what a man or woman (say) ought to be like.

incorrigible not open to being revised or abandoned.

individualism emphasizing the rights and needs of the isolated individual. Opposed to *corporate.*

innate present in an infant at birth, at least as a potentiality.

instinct innate tendency or drive (e.g., the sexual instinct or the maternal instinct).

intentional having to do with how sex (for example) is imagined or conceived, as opposed to its physiological character.

Kantian feminism the view that human beings should be regarded as persons, whose sex or gender is no more important than their eye or skin color.

kibbutzim Israeli utopian communities, founded on religious or socialist principles.

Lebenswelt world of ordinary human experience.

matriarchy social system in which social power is in the hands of women. Opposed to *patriarchy.*

matrilineal social system in which descent is traced in the female line. Opposed to *patrilineal.*

matrilocal social system in which a married couple lives with the wife's family. Opposed to *patrilocal.*

moral kind sort of action differing from others in morally relevant respects.

naturalistic confined to physical nature as understood by the natural sciences such as biology and physics. Opposed to *supernatural.*

nature-nurture controversy controversy about the relative roles of biology and social environment in determining human character and personality.

normative standard, normal.

passing acting so as to be taken as a man or woman, especially when this identity might be questioned.

pederasty homosexual intercourse, especially with a boy; often used to describe such activity between a man or older boy and a young boy.

person the distinctively human as a moral or metaphysical concept.

polyandry a social system in which a woman has more than one husband.

polygamy a social system in which a man has more than one wife. Opposed to *monogamy.*

principle of totality moral principle permitting the mutilation of one part of the human body for the good of the whole.

sex maleness or femaleness as defined by anatomy, for example, by the possession of a penis or vagina.

sexism irrational social distinctions between the sexes. In the view of some writers, any such distinctions, for example, the requirement that the parties to a marriage be of opposite sexes, are sexist.

shaman religious functionary known for trance states and the like.

social construction the fashioning of institutions and practices by human activity, not necessarily planned by anyone.

socialize bring up children to be members of a particular society.

subjectivity the mind or soul as understood by Descartes to exemplify a first-person perspective.

surrogate mother woman who carries in her womb a child not biologically her own, or who becomes pregnant having undertaken to give up the child at birth.

transsexual a person who believes that his or her gender differs from his or her sex.

transudate secretions.

transvestite a person who prefers to dress as a person of the opposite sex, sometimes as a means of sexual gratification.

Virgin Birth according to traditional Christian doctrine, the birth of Jesus from Mary without a human father. By reason of this belief, she is usually called *the Virgin Mary*.

yin and yang male and female principles in Chinese thought.

My Conundrum

JAN MORRIS

> In this autobiographical narrative, Jan Morris describes an early conviction of being born into the wrong body (being a girl in a boy's body), and tells how this conviction was sustained and reinforced by subsequent experiences. After marring and begetting several children, Morris at last decided to have hormonal and surgical treatments to remove this felt disharmony between bodily structure and true identity. The subtle changes wrought by hormone therapy are described in this selection, as well as the way in which the sex change operation affected Morris's personality and relationships with other people.

I WAS THREE OR PERHAPS FOUR years old when I realized that I had been born into the wrong body, and should really be a girl. I remember the moment well, and it is the earliest memory of my life. . . . [B]y every standard of logic I was patently a boy. I was James Humphry Morris, male child. I had a boy's body. I wore a boy's clothes. It is true that my mother had wished me to be a daughter, but I was never treated as one. It is true that gushing visitors sometimes assembled me into their fox furs and lavender sachets to murmur that, with curly hair like mine, I should have been born a girl.

As the youngest of three brothers, in a family very soon to be fatherless, I was doubtless indulged. I was not, however, generally thought effeminate. At kindergarten I was not derided. In the street I was not stared at. If I had announced my self-discovery beneath the piano, my family might not have been shocked (Virginia Woolf's androgynous *Orlando* was already in the house) but would certainly have been astonished.

Not that I dreamed of revealing it. I cherished it as a secret, shared for twenty years with not a single soul. At first I did not regard it as an especially significant secret. I was as vague as the next child about the meaning of sex, and I assumed it to be simply another aspect of differentness. For different in some way I recognized myself to be. . . .

My emotions, though, were far less distinct or definable. My conviction of mistaken sex was still no more than a blur, tucked away at the back of my mind, but if I was not unhappy, I was habitually puzzled. . . . Everything seemed more determinate for [other people]. *Their* lives looked preordained, as though like the old de Havilland they simply stuck dogged and content to their daily routes, comfortably throbbing. Mine was more like a glider's movements, airy and delightful perhaps, but lacking direction.

This was a bewilderment that would never leave me, and I see it now as the developing core of my life's dilemma. . . . Perhaps one day, when I grew up, I would be as solid as other people appeared to be; but perhaps I was meant always to be a creature of wisp or spindrift, loitering in this inconsequential way almost as though I were intangible. . . .

[T]here are thousands of people, perhaps hundreds of thousands, suffering from the condition today. It has recently been given the name "transsexualism," and in its classic form is as distinct from transvestism as it is from homosexuality. Both transvestites and homosexuals sometimes suppose they would be happier if they could change their sex, but they are generally mistaken. The transvestite gains his gratification specifically from wearing the clothes of the opposite sex, and would sacrifice his pleasures by *joining* that sex; the homosexual, by definition, prefers to make love with others of his own sort, and would only alienate himself and them by changing. Transsexualism is something different in kind. It is not a sexual mode or preference. It is not an act of sex at all. It is a passionate, lifelong, ineradicable conviction, and no true transsexual has ever been disabused of it. . . .

In any case, I myself see the conundrum in another perspective, for I believe it to have some higher origin or meaning. I equate it with the idea of soul, or self, and I think of it not just as a sexual enigma, but as a quest for unity. For me every aspect of my life is relevant to that quest—not only the sexual impulses, but all the sights, sounds, and smells of memory, the influences of buildings, landscapes, comradeships, the power of love and of sorrow, the satisfactions of the senses as of the body. In my mind it is a subject far wider than sex: I recognize no pruriency to it, and I see it above all as a dilemma neither of the body nor of the brain, but of the spirit. . . .

As I grew older my conflict became more explicit to me, and I began to feel that I was living a falsehood. I was in masquerade, my female reality, which I had no words to define, clothed in a male pretense. Psychiatrists have often asked me if this gave me a sense of guilt, but the opposite was true. I felt that in wishing so fervently, and so ceaselessly, to be translated into a girl's body, I was aiming only at a more divine condition, an inner reconciliation; and I attribute this impression not to the influences of home or family, but to an early experience of Oxford.

Oxford made me. I was an undergraduate there, and for much of my life I have owned a house there—doubly fulfilling my own criteria of possession by writing a book about the city too. But far more important, my first boarding school was there: the signs, values, and traditions of Oxford dominated my early boyhood, and were my first intimations of a world away from home, beyond my telescope's range. I have, I hope, no sentimental view of the place—I know its faults too well. It remains for me nevertheless, in its frayed and battered integrity, an image of what I admire most in the world: a presence so old and true that it absorbs time and change like light into a prism, only enriching itself by the process, and finding nothing alien except intolerance.

Of course when I speak of Oxford, I do not mean simply the city, or the university, or even the atmosphere of the place, but a whole manner of thought, an outlook, almost a civilization. I came to it an anomaly, a contradiction in myself, and were it not for the flexibility and self-amusement I absorbed from the Oxford culture—which is to say, the culture of traditional England—I think I would long ago have ended in that last haven of anomaly, the madhouse. For near the heart of the Oxford ethos lies the grand and comforting truth that there is no norm. We are all different; none of us is *entirely* wrong; to understand is to forgive.

I became a member of the University of Oxford in 1936, when I was nine years old, and my name will be found in the university calendars for that year. This is not because I was any kind of prodigy; but because I was first educated there at the choir school of Christ Church, a college so grand that its chapel is actually the cathedral of the Oxford diocese, and maintains its own professional choir. No education could leave a more lasting effect than this experience did on me, and I doubt if any other kind of school could have satisfied so curiously my inner cravings. A virginal ideal was fostered in me by my years at Christ Church, a sense of sacrament and fragility, and this I came slowly to identify as femaleness—"eternal womanhood," which, as Goethe says in the last lines of *Faust,* "leads us above." . . .

It has often been suggested to me that, in those post-Victorian years of the 1930s, conventions of the day might have distorted my sexual notions. Man was for hard things, making money, fighting wars, keeping stiff upper lips, beating errant schoolboys, wearing boots and helmets, drinking beer; woman was for gentler, softer purposes, healing, soothing, painting pictures, wearing silks, singing, looking at colors, giving presents, accepting admiration. . . .

The headiest influence of all, though, was the influence of life within the cathedral. I have never been a true Christian, and even now wish the great churches of Europe were devoted to some less preposterous exercise than worship. I except, though, from my iconoclasm your true-blue English cathedrals, if there are any left, where the Book of Common Prayer survives untampered, where the Bible is still King James's version, where fiery brides keep their fingers crossed as they promise to obey, where the smell is of must and candles, where the hassocks have been embroidered by the Diocesan Mothers' Guild, where the clergymen's vowels are as pure as their musical intonation is shaky, where gold plate gleams beneath rose windows, where organists lean genially from their organ-lofts during the sermon, where Stanford in C, *The Wilderness* or *Zadoc the Priest* thunder through the arches on feast days, and where at the end of evensong the words of the Benediction come frail, half inaudible but wonderfully moving from the distant coped figure raising his hand in blessing before the high altar. All these conditions were satisfied to perfection during my childhood attendance at the cathedral of Christ Church, Oxford, and beneath the orison of their mysteries I brooded and wondered, day after day, about the mystery of myself. . . .

[D]uring our daily hours at the cathedral, I could be myself. There I achieved some childish nirvana. Pink, white, and scarlet in my vestments, genuinely inspired by the music, the words, and the setting, I was not exactly a boy anyway, but had undergone some apotheosis of innocence to which I aspire even now—an enchantment less direct than my abandonment beneath the chestnuts, but more complete in its liberation. Perhaps it is how nuns feel. Certainly I felt sure that the spirits of the place approved of it, and perfectly understood my desires. How could they do otherwise? The noblest aspects of the liturgy aspired to what I conceived as the female principle. Our very vestments seemed intended to deny our manhood, and the most beautiful of all the characters of the Christian story, I thought, far more perfect and mysterious than Christ himself, was the Virgin Mary, whose presence drifted so strangely and elegantly through the Gospels, an enigma herself. . . .

Sex and My Conundrum • In the Hayloft • Gender and Bolsover

That my conundrum actually emanated from my sexual organs did not cross my mind then, and seems unlikely to me even now. Almost as soon as I reached my public school, Lancing, I learned very accurately the facts of human reproduction, and they seemed to me essentially prosaic. They still do. I was not in the least surprised that Mary had been invested with the beauty of virgin birth, for nothing could seem to me more matter-of-fact than the mechanics of copulation, which every living creature manages without difficulty, and which can easily be reproduced artificially too. That my inchoate yearnings, born from wind and sunshine, music and imagination—that my conundrum might simply be a matter of penis or vagina, testicle or womb, seems to me still a contradiction in terms, for it concerned not my apparatus, but my *self.* . . .

I hope I will not be thought narcissist if I claim that I was rather an attractive boy, not beautiful perhaps, but healthy and slim. Inevitably, the English school system being what it is, I was the object of advances, and thus my inner convictions were thrown into an altogether new relief. It seemed perfectly natural to me to play the girl's role in these transient and generally light-hearted romances, and in their platonic aspects I greatly enjoyed them. It was fun to be pursued, gratifying to be admired, and useful to have protectors in the sixth form. I enjoyed being kissed on the back stairs, and was distinctly flattered when the best-looking senior boy in the house made elaborate arrangements to meet me in the holidays.

When it came, nevertheless, to more elemental pursuits of pederasty, then I found myself not exactly repelled, but embarrassed. Aesthetically it seemed wrong to me. Nothing fitted. Our bodies did not cleave, and moreover I felt that, though promiscuity in flirtation was harmlessly entertaining, this intimacy of the body with mere acquaintances was inelegant. It was not what the fan vaulting expected of me. It was not what my girl friends had in mind, when they spoke in breathless undertones of their wedding night. It was a very far cry from Virgin Birth. It was also worrying for me, for though my body often yearned to give, to yield, to open itself, the machine was wrong. It was made for another function, and I felt myself to be wrongly equipped.

I fear my suitors thought me frigid, even the ones I liked best, but I did not mean to be ungrateful. I was not in the least shocked by their intentions, but I simply could not respond in kind. We indulged our illicit pleasures generally in the haylofts of farms, or the loose field-ricks they still built in those days, and I think it a telling fact that of those first sexual experiences I remember most vividly, and most voluptuously, not the clumsy embraces of Bolsover Major, not the heavy breathing of his passion or his sinuous techniques of trouser-removal, but the warm slightly rotted sensation of the hay beneath my body, and the smell of fermenting apples from the barns below. . . .

To me gender is not physical at all, but is altogether insubstantial. It is soul, perhaps, it is talent, it is taste, it is environment, it is how one feels, it is light and shade, it is inner music, it is a spring in one's step or an exchange of glances, it is more truly life and love than any combination of genitals, ovaries, and hormones. It is the essentialness of oneself, the psyche, the fragment of unity. Male and female are sex, masculine and feminine are gender, and though the conceptions obviously overlap, they are far from synonymous. As C. S. Lewis once wrote, gender is not a mere imaginative extension of sex. "Gender is a reality, and a more fundamental reality than sex. Sex is, in

fact, merely the adaptation to organic life of a fundamental polarity which divides all created beings. Female sex is simply one of the things that have feminine gender; there are many others, and Masculine and Feminine meet us on planes of reality where male and female would be simply meaningless." . . .

Yet I was not indifferent to magnetisms of the body. Some of the nameless craving that haunted me still was a desire for an earthier involvement in life. I felt that the grand constants of the human cycle, birth to death, were somehow shut off from me, so that I had no part in them, and could look at them only from a distance, or through glass. The lives of other people seemed more real because they were closer to those great fundamentals, and formed a homely entity with them. In short, I see now, I wished very much that I could one day be a mother, and perhaps my preoccupation with virgin birth was only a recognition that I could never be one. I have loved babies always, with the sort of involuntary covetousness, I suppose, that drives unhappy spinsters of a certain age to kidnap; and when later in life I reached the putative age of maternity, finding myself still incapable of the role, I did the next best thing and became a father instead. . . .

"Zero!"

One of the genuine and recurrent surprises of my life concerns the importance to men of physical sex. I was baffled by it when I left my poor friend distraught and apprehensive at the door of the Trieste brothel, when he would have had a far happier time, I felt sure, going to the pictures. I was astonished by it when the Bolsovers so suddenly transformed our agreeable trysts into frenzy. And even now, so many years older and more experienced, I am taken aback by the intensity with which mature, kind, and cultured men, reading early drafts of this book, looked in it for revelations about the sexual act. Even the most sensitive of my friends, I have come belatedly to realize, in following the course of my life with such kindly concern, have generally been much more interested in my sex than my psyche. . . .

But for me the actual performance of the sexual act seemed of secondary importance and interest. . . . My more immediate physical delights were far more superficial, and much easier to achieve. They were tactile, olfactory, visual, proximate delights—pleasures which, as it happened, I could handily transfer to inanimate objects too. . . .

I myself did not quite know what I wanted, or what I might allow myself to want, beyond the touch of the hand or lip, the warmth of the body, the long shared confidences at midnight, the smell of scent or tweed, the laughter and the company. . . . I felt more than ever isolated, neither one thing nor the other, neither seducing nor seducible—only, I flattered myself to think, reasonably seductive.

This was a paradox, and people often sensed it. It was as though I deliberately held myself back from fruition, in work as in pleasure. If sexually I found myself isolated, professionally, as I watched the world go by, I found myself more than ever outside mankind's commitments. More than ever [other people] seemed to be pursuing rounds of their own to which I was denied access—not minding their shops now, or sauntering with their holiday amours, but plotting revolutions, fighting elections, conspiring, warring, starving. I was there, by destiny it seemed as by vocation, only and always as an onlooker. An American colleague once described me as "so unobtrusive that one hardly knows he is there at all," while an English critic remarked upon "an odd tendency to disappear as the person behind the style." But it was not modesty that camouflaged me so, nor even professional technique: it was a detachment so involuntary that I often felt that I *really* wasn't there, but was viewing it all from some silent chamber of my own. If I could not be myself, my subconscious seemed to be saying, then I would not be. . . .

Meanwhile I watched our family grow. Believer as I could only be in omnisexuality, in the right and ability of humans of every kind to love one another carnally and spiritually, I always respected the emotions of homosexuals; but the truth and pathos of their condition seemed to me exemplified by their childlessness. Years ago I lived briefly in the same house as a devoted homosexual couple, one an eminent pianist, the other a businessman. Their life together was civilized without being in the least chi-chi. Their flat was full of handsome things, their conversation was kind and clever, and when the one was playing I would see the other listening with an expression of truest pride, pleasure, and

affection. So real was their bond that when the pianist died the businessman killed himself—and they left behind them, apart from the musician's records, only a void. A marriage as loyal as marriage could be had ended sterile and uncreative; and if the two of them had lived into old age their lives, I think, would have proved progressively more sterile still, the emptiness creeping in, the fullness retreating.

I could not have survived such a life, for my instinct to have children was profound. If I were not a writer, or an artist, I would certainly like to have been a plain mother, for I cannot think of a more fascinating profession than the raising of children, maddening though the little beasts can so often be. Indeed my children and my books, which I was now beginning to write, seemed to me oddly of a kind. With a sad pang I used to watch the aircraft flying overhead, when I had recently delivered a manuscript to my agents, for I imagined that in one of them my book was leaving for America—so long a friend, so quickly mashed into print and book reviews. Conversely my children I regarded rather as works of art. I am ashamed to think I might have loved them less if they *had* been plain or stupid, and perhaps the truth is that if they had been, I would not have known it; they seemed beautiful to me, anyway, slim in physique, nimble in mind, and I watched them developing with the pleasure I might derive from a very well-plotted novel. . . .

Changing Sex • Hormonal Effects • A Precarious Condition • Self-Protection • Rules

. . . Nobody in the history of humankind has changed from a true man to a true woman, if we class a man or a woman purely by physical concepts. Hermaphrodites may have shifted the balance of their ambiguity, but nobody has been born with one complete body and died with the other. When I say, then, that I now began a change of sex, I speak in shorthand. What was about to happen was that my body would be made as female as science could contemplate or nature permit, to reset (as I saw it) the pointer of my sex more sensibly and accurately along the scale of my gender. Doctors, whose conception of these matters is often simplistic to the degree of obscurantism, have devised many tests for the determination of sex, and divided the concept into several categories. There is anatomical sex, the most obvious: breasts, vagina, womb, and ovaries for the female, penis and testicles for the male. There is chromosomal sex, the most fundamental: the nuclear composition of the body, which need not necessarily conform to the anatomy, but which is accepted as a convenient rule of thumb for such purposes as international sport. There is hormonal sex, the chemical balance of male and female. There is psychological sex, the way people respond to the world, and feel themselves to be.

I was not much interested in these criteria, for I regarded sex merely as the tool of gender, and I believed that for me as for most people the interplay between the two lay very close to personality, not to be measured by blood tests or Freudian formulae. All I wanted was liberation, or reconciliation—to live as myself, to clothe myself in a more proper body, and achieve Identity at last. I would not hurry. First I would discover if it were feasible. Slowly, carefully, with infinite precaution against betrayal, I began the chemical experiments by which I would lose many of my male characteristics, and acquire some of the female; then, if all went well, several years later I would take the last step, and have the change completed by surgery.

To myself I had been woman all along, and I was not going to change the truth of me, only discard the falsity. But I *was* about to change my form and apparency—my status too, perhaps my place among my peers, my attitudes no doubt, the reactions I would evoke, my reputation, my manner of life, my prospects, my emotions, possibly my abilities. I was about to adapt my body from a male conformation to a female, and I would shift my public role altogether, from the role of a man to the role of a woman. It is one of the most drastic of all human changes, unknown until our own times, and even now experienced by very few; but it seemed only natural to me, and I embarked upon it only with a sense of thankfulness, like a lost traveler finding the right road at last. . . .

The change was infinitely gradual. I felt like a slow-motion Jekyll and Hyde, tinkering with testtubes and retorts in my dark laboratory; but the effects were so subtle that they seemed not to be induced at all, were not noticed for years by every-day acquaintances, and seemed to be part of the natural process of aging. Except that, fortunately, they worked backwards, and rejuvenated me. The first result was not exactly a feminization of my body, but a stripping away of the rough hide in which the male person is clad. I do not mean merely the body hair, nor even the leatheriness of the skin, nor all the hard protrusion of muscle; all these indeed vanished over the next few years, but there went with them something less tangible too, which I know now to be specifically masculine—a kind of unseen layer of accumulated resilience, which provides a shield for the male of the species, but at the same time deadens the sensations of the body. It is as though some protective substance has been sprayed onto a man from a divine aerosol, so that he is less immediately in contact with the air and the sun, more powerfully compacted within his own resources.

This suggestion, for it is really hardly more, was now stripped from me, and I felt at the same time physically freer and more vulnerable. I had no armor. I seemed to feel not only the heat and the cold more, but also the stimulants of the world about me. I relished the goodness of the sun in a more directly physical way, and for the first time in my life saw the point of lazing about on beaches. The keenness of the wind cut me more spitefully. It was as though I could feel the very weight of the air pressing on my person, or eddying past, and I thought that if I closed my eyes now the presence of the moonlight would cool my cheek. I was far lighter in weight, but I was lighter in motion too, not so brilliantly precipitate as I had been on Everest, but airier, springier. It was rather as though my sense of gravity had shifted, making me more delicate or subtle of balance. I dreamt frequently of levitation, and found it curiously more easy to slip around a corner when I observed some dour acquaintance approaching me up the street, as though for a moment or two I could levitate in real life.

All this helped to make me younger. It was not merely a matter of *seeming* younger; except in the matter of plain chronology, it was actually true. I was enjoying that dream of the ages, a second youth. My skin was clearer, my cheeks were rosier, my tread was lighter, my figure was slimmer. More important, I was actually starting again. It was as though I had slipped the gears of life, returning to an earlier cycle for a second time round; or had reached one of those repeats in a sonata which start identically, but end in piquant difference. Life and the world looked new to me. Even my relationship with Elizabeth, which soon lost its last elements of physical contact, assumed a new lucidity. My body seemed to be growing more complex, more quivering in its responses, but my spirit felt simpler. I had loved animals all my life, but I felt closer to them now, and sometimes I even found myself talking to the garden flowers, wishing them a Happy Easter, or thanking them for the fine show they made. . . .

. . . We are told that the social gap between the sexes is narrowing, but I can only report that having, in the second half of the twentieth century, experienced life in both roles, there seems to me no aspect of existence, no moment of the day, no contact, no arrangement, no response, which is not different for men and for women. The very tone of voice in which I was now addressed, the very posture of the person next in the queue, the very feel in the air when I entered a room or sat at a restaurant table, constantly emphasized my change of status.

And if others' responses shifted, so did my own. The more I was treated as a woman, the more woman I became. I adapted willy-nilly. If I was assumed to be incompetent at reversing cars, or opening bottles, oddly incompetent I found myself becoming. If a case was thought too heavy for me, inexplicably I found it so myself. Thrust as I now found myself far more into the company of women than of men, I began to find women's conversation in general more congenial. Women treated me with a frankness which, while it was one of the happiest discoveries of my metamorphosis, did imply membership of a camp, a faction, or at least a school of thought; and so I found myself gravitating always towards the female, whether in sharing a railway compartment or supporting a political cause. Men treated me more and more as a junior, as the Chevalier d'Éon had been obliged to accept a guardian in his womanhood—my lawyer, in an unguarded moment one morning, even called me "my child"; and so, addressed every day of my life as an inferior, involuntarily, month by month I accepted the condition. I discovered that even now men prefer women to be less informed, less able, less talkative,

and certainly less self-centered than they are themselves; so I generally obliged them.

It is hard for me now to remember what everyday life was like as a man—unequivocally as a man, I mean, before my change began at all. Sometimes, though, by a conscious effort I try to recapture the sensation, and realize the contrast in my condition now. It amuses me to consider, for instance when I am taken out to lunch by one of my more urbane men friends, that not so many years ago that fulsome waiter would have treated *me* as he is now treating *him*. Then he would have greeted me with respectful seriousness. Now he unfolds my napkin with a playful flourish, as if to humor me. Then he would have taken my order with grave concern, now he expects me to say something frivolous (and I do). Then he would have pretended, at least, to respect my knowledge of wines, now I am not even consulted. Then he would have addressed me as a superior, now he seems to think of me (for he is a cheerful man) as an accomplice. I am treated of course with the conventional deference that a woman expects, the moving of tables, the wrapping of coats, the opening of doors; but I know that it is really deference of a lesser kind, and that the man behind me is the guest that counts.

But it soon all came to feel only natural, so powerful are the effects of custom and environment. Late as I came in life to womanhood—"a late developer," as somebody said of me—the subtle subjection of women was catching up on me, and I was adjusting to it in just the way women have adjusted down the generations. It was, of course, by no means all unpleasant. If the condescension of men could be infuriating, the courtesies were very welcome. If it was annoying to be thought incapable of buying a second-class return to Liverpool, it was quite nice to have it done for one anyway. I did not particularly want to be good at reversing cars, and did not in the least mind being patronized by illiterate garagemen, if it meant they were going to give me some extra trading stamps. . . .

Physically I was no longer ambiguous of appearance. My body was no longer producing its male androgens, and the leanness left my face, indefinably changing the character of it. I filled out rather, in the cheeks, in the hips, in the bosom, and when I thought about it I found that

I now walked, sat, gesticulated altogether in a woman's way. . . .

Psychologically I was distinctly less forceful. . . . It is not merely the loss of androgens that has made me more retiring, more ready to be led, more passive: the removal of the organs themselves has contributed, for there was to the presence of the penis something positive, thrusting, and muscular. My body then was made to push and initiate, it is made now to yield and accept, and the outside change has had its inner consequences. . . .

My view of life shifted too. I was even more emotional now. I cried very easily, and was ludicrously susceptible to sadness or flattery. Finding myself rather less interested in great affairs (which are placed in a new perspective, I do assure you, by a change of sex), I acquired a new concern for small ones. My scale of vision seemed to contract, and I looked less for the grand sweep than for the telling detail. The emphasis changed in my writing, from places to people. The specious topographical essay which had been my *forte,* and my income, became less easy for me to write, and I found myself concentrating more on individuals or situations. Throughout the years of my change I was deeply engaged, though you might not guess it from this highly selective memoir, upon my most ambitious work, a trilogy about the Victorian Empire. The first volume I wrote while I was still a man, and it was above all an evocation of an era, and a world; the second I wrote during the last years of my metamorphosis, and it is far richer in personalities and episodes; the third I have not started yet, and I await its character with interest. Just as I feel emancipated as a person, so I do as a writer; perhaps I shall be a novelist yet. . . .

You are wondering how I now saw men and women. Clearly, I would say, for the first time. I had no inhibitions, no half-conscious restraints. Nor was I atrophied now, for I felt the sexual urges cheerfully revived. Looking back at my old persona, I sadly recognized my own frustrated desires, plain at last, but irretrievably wasted. I saw how deeply I had pined for the arms and the love of a man. I saw how proud and brave a wife I would like to have been, how passionate a mother, how forlornly my poor self had yearned to be released into its full sexuality—that flowering which, *faute de mieux,* I had so often redi-

rected into words, or patriotism, or love of place. The shutters were removed at last, no longer clamped down, like those clanking steel blinds of the Cairo shopkeepers, to keep the unwanted at bay during the long siesta. I was walking along Jermyn Street one day when I saw, for the first time in twenty years, a member of the Everest team of 1953. My goodness, I said to myself, what an extraordinarily handsome man. I knew he had been handsome all along, but I had allowed myself to like him only for his gentle manners, and it was only now that I permitted myself the indulgence of thinking him desirable.

I had found my own level, and looking frankly around me at the human species, admitted at last without embarrassment how attractive men could be, and what a pleasure it was to be cherished by them. At last I look at them with my sexuality unbound, and my attitude unpretending. I am asked sometimes if I plan to marry one, but no, the men I have loved are married already, or dead, or far away, or indifferent. Too late! Besides, though Elizabeth and I are divorced, we are locked in our friendship more absolutely than ever, and unless some blinding passion intervenes with one or the other of us, propose to share our lives happily ever after. She has a farmhouse in the Black Mountains of South Wales; I have a flat in Bath; we share the old buildings at Trefan; and linking us always wherever we are, and connecting us too with our children near and far, is a dear bond we cannot break. . . .

I have collated [gender] with the medieval idea of soul; but I am prepared to concede that one's sense of gender may be partly acquired, as the psychologists say, or at least powerfully influenced by the state of society. Would my conflict have been so bitter if I had been born now, when the gender line is so much less rigid? If society had allowed me to live in the gender I preferred, would I have bothered to change sex? Is mine only a transient phenomenon, between the dogmatism of the last century, when men were men and women were ladies, and the eclecticism of the next, when citizens will be free to live in the gender role they prefer? Will people read of our pilgrimage to Casablanca, a hundred years hence, as we might read of the search for the philosopher's stone, or Simeon Stylites on his pillar?

Study Questions on Jan Morris

1. What is the difference between sex and gender, according to Morris?
2. What sort of picture of femininity does Morris have? Do you find it acceptable?
3. Morris says that the desire to be a woman did not concern the sexual organs, but the self. If so, why did Morris find it necessary to get a sex change operation?
4. Was Morris a woman or a man before the operation? Is Morris a woman or a man now?

The Principle of Totality—A Possible Justification for Transsexual Surgery?

ANTHONY MASTROENI

Father Anthony Mastroeni, a Catholic moralist, here examines the moral acceptability of transsexual surgery of the sort Morris chose to undergo. He considers and rejects the attempt to justify such surgery by invoking the principle of totality, which permits mutilation of one part of the body for the sake of the health of the whole. His discussion includes a critique of the philosophical dualism that arguments for transsexual surgery characteristically invoke.

[O]NE OF THE PRINCIPLE moral justifications proposed for sex-reassignment surgery among some ethicians is the so-called extended notion of the principle of totality. Such a position attempts to view totality or total well-being in a context which includes not only somatic, but also psychic health. The ethical implications of this position in regard to transsexual surgery have already been noted in the recent work *Human Sexuality.* They are also clearly outlined in a work by Fr. John F. Dedek, wherein he offers the following rationale for transsexual surgery:

Behind the older moralists' absolute prohibition against transsexual surgery was the same premise that led them to absolutely forbid direct sterilization. Transsexual surgery, after

all, is a sterilizing operation, and direct sterilization was always considered by these authors as intrinsically evil. It could never be justified by the principle of totality because the sexual faculty has a wider finality than the good of the individual: it is also for the good of the species.

As we have seen, contemporary moral analysis questions this reasoning. Many Catholic theologians today argue that sterilization is justified by the principle of totality: direct sterilization is permissible when it is done for the welfare of the whole person.

There has been little contemporary ethical discussion of transsexual surgery, but it seems to me that is subject to the same kind of analysis as sterilization. In itself transsexual surgery is

Reprinted by permission of the author.

a disvalue. So is every form of surgery or physical mutilation. But in certain circumstances it is permissible in order to achieve a greater good.

This means that if transsexual surgery is medically indicated, it is morally licit. If in certain circumstances it is necessary for the total wellbeing of an individual, it is morally permissible according to the principle of totality.

For Dedek and others of similar persuasion, the parts of the body are seen as existing for the "total well-being of the individual," understood not only somatically, but also personally and even perhaps socially. The serious mutilation of direct sterilization, which comprises the major part of the surgery involved in sex-conversion, is accordingly justified by the claim that such a procedure is done for a greater good, presumably for the psychological and emotional welfare of the patient. . . .

Since man is obliged to exercise a wise stewardship over his whole bodily life, it sometimes happens that he must sacrifice a part of his bodily health for the greater good of the whole. Stewardship, then, is intimately related to totality. The former can be seen as an inhibiting principle, limiting man's power over his body to usufructuary rights, while the latter can be seen as an enabling principle, empowering man to sacrifice a part of the body for the greater good of the whole body over which he exercises a wise stewardship. Both principles, however, must be preserved in any well formed ethical doctrine of the disposition of the human body. . . .

The Extended Notion of Totality— A Neo-Dualism?

The efforts to extend the notion of totality to justify a vast array of surgical procedures, including the current phenomenon of sex-reassignment surgery, form part of an over-all blueprint for much of the Post-Kantian secular ethics that is largely deontological in character and latently dualistic in its understanding of human nature. Whether the claim is made that the bodily organism with its parts is subordinate to and expendible for either the "total vocation of the human person" or man's social nature, "his relationships to his family, community and the larger society"; or quite specifically, that the

destruction of healthy generative organs can be justified not only for the good of the body, but allegedly for more personal or social goods—for sociological, psychological or economic reasons, there is implicit in such reasoning—despite all its efforts to speak of "wholeness" and "unity"—a subtle dualism which seeks to disassociate man's bodily reality from his person, and ultimately to subordinate the former to the latter. As such, it stands in sharp contrast to the Biblical and Christian understanding of Creation, of man and his nature, and the significance of his moral acts.

As we shall see in the next section, the Biblical-Christian understanding of the human person is integrative in its character. As such, there is no dichotomy of body and soul. Essentially man is the "body of his soul" and the "soul of his body." This unitive view of man that permeates biblical anthropology is supported and further explicated by Aristotelian and Thomist Metaphysics. Proceeding from an analysis of the metaphysical structure of reality, it considers the human person as a unity of a rational soul united to the body as its form. As the intrinsic principle, the soul makes the person be the body he or she is; and, as the formal part of the body present throughout, it likewise makes the body be the person he or she is. The entire thrust here is one of substantial unity.

In contrast with this understanding is the ever-present tendency to substitute a radical dualism in the place of this unity, for it is the basic characteristic of dualism—whether Platonic, Neo-Platonic or Cartesian—to conceive of two distinct things where there is really only one. For Plato, who showed contempt for the sensible, the union of the soul with the body is a reproach. "The body is a tomb" and "as long as we have our soul kneaded into this evil thing we shall never possess in sufficiency the object of our desire." The soul, therefore, must isolate itself within, severing itself from the body, and "as far as possible breaking all contact with it, fleeing from it." For, according to Plato, "if ever we are to know something purely, we must stand aside from it and let the soul in itself look upon things in themselves."

Many of the Eastern mystery religions also have their roots within a dualistic matrix. Manichaeism, for instance, is the loyal heir of Mazdean Dualism. Basically, it scorns what it perceives to be the dark and seamy side of existence which it identifies with matter. Man, then, is seen as a fallen creature in so far as he is corporeal. Salvation, therefore, consists in the constant struggle of man to disengage himself from the bonds of his body—a sort of disincarnationalism. To achieve this end, the spirit must learn in the course of its earthly life to detach itself from all its fetters, its carnal appetites, and pursue instead only spiritual ones, for which death is seen as the perfect fulfillment. There is no question here of any sanctification of the body. "Not only will marriage be condemned, but also the stability of the marriage union, and its fruitfulness will be regarded with more horror than debauchery, considered merely a weakness, or than unnatural vice, which is necessarily unfruitful. . . ."

This dualistic perception of the human person was resurrected in classical modern philosophy through the aegis of René Descartes (1596–1650). It is perhaps more accurate in this respect to speak of the "Cartesian Spirit" whose ideas were fermenting long before Descartes, but through the internal logic of his thought, together with subsequent historical contingencies, coalesced into a system that has ruptured the human compound that is man.

The Cartesian understanding of the human person proceeds logically from its philosophical method. Personally dissatisfied with the philosophical and scientific doctrines he had been taught, and positively attracted by the mathematical sciences, Descartes attempted to establish a philosophical method of inquiry based on the certitude of a mathematical demonstration utilizing two functions of the intellect: intuition or the power of apprehending self-evident data, and deduction or the power of moving by uninterrupted sequence of self-evident steps from that data to their consequents.

Beginning with the methodical doubt as his starting point, Descartes agreed to set aside anything about which doubt was possible. The first were sensible things or the things of which man is aware by sensation. According to Descartes, it is possible to be deceived by shape, color, sound, etc., and even one's own body. What man cannot doubt, however, is the existence of himself as a thinking something—"Cogito, ergo sum." Accordingly, it is the nature of the soul to think, to

be conscious, and as such, it becomes identified with the conscious self. Conversely, the idea of body or matter does not include consciousness, but rather excludes it. The essential nature of the body or matter is not consciousness, but spatial extension with the roots of the secondary qualities of color, weight, hardness, shape, etc. The only true knowledge of the body, then, becomes a matter of mechanics.

Such reasoning left Descartes with an unbridgeable gap between the material world (*res extensa*) and the mind (*res cogitans*), all of which amounts to a striking substantial dualism when he attempts to establish the relationship between soul and body.

For Descartes, the body is identified with matter which he considers to be a distinct substance, a something in its own right, rather than an element or component of substance. He says, "First I considered myself having a face, hands, arms, and this whole machine of bone and flesh such as we see it in a corpse. To these I gave the name body." The assertion here is that man is two distinct substances: body or matter, and soul or unifying form that has been added to the body. Fundamentally, such a view renders unsolvable the problem of their union and reciprocal action. Unsuccessful attempts were made by Descartes to show that the soul resides in the pineal gland where it is supposedly in contact with the "animal spirits." However, in the final analysis such a view of the human person simply revived the radical dualism of the past. Soul becomes mind or consciousness, and body simply a matter of geometric extension. In effect, man becomes an angel inhabiting a machine and directing it by means of the pineal gland. . . .

The effects of all this are manifold. If, as Descartes maintains, "The body of man is nothing but a statue or a machine made of earth," then that same body ceases to be regarded as human by essence, and simply becomes an instrument, a matter of mechanics, a subject of technique. Maritain points out, "It is the Cartesian hyperspiritualism which has caused the mass-production of innumerable materialistic physicians rampant in science up to the close of the last century." Ruptured from the person, the body becomes part of the Cartesian world of nature over which the rational and conscious agent has complete dominion.

Furthermore, the rupture of thought from sense perception will occasion a complete disregard for the affective life, as Maritain observes:

Feeling is no longer anything more than a confused idea. The existence of love and of will as forming a distinct world, having its own life and its own laws in the heaven of the soul, is radically misunderstood.

Attempts to rediscover the unity of man have been made by some post-Hegelian philosophies. In an effort to insure the unity of the human person, some phenomenologists speak of man as an "incarnate spirit." However, upon closer examination, even this smacks of a residual Cartesian dualism, for it implies that man really has two natures rather than one, and that his spiritual subjectivity must work through an alien objectivity. In other words, the use of such a descriptive term implies that man is already complete as spirit, that he assumes a body which is other than the conscious subject. The real person, then, becomes identified with the conscious self to which a body is attached.

It is precisely this dualistic understanding of the human person that pervades many of the contemporary attempts that place themselves under the rubric of the so-called "new morality." For one thing, "if the person really is not his body, then the destruction of the life of the body is not directly and in itself an attack on a value intrinsic to the human person." If personhood is defined purely in terms of intentionality, rationality, consciousness, or the capacity for "meaningful activity" or "interpersonal relationships," then the destruction of fetal bodies need not necessarily be an attack on real persons. Or, to use another version of the same argument, if my body belongs to me as a possession over which I exercise dominion, then for a woman to do with "her own body" what she wishes becomes ample justification for the destruction of innocent human life in the womb. Furthermore, if the human person is not to be considered as a special type of body, with its bodily life and the biological processes which transmit it as constituting of themselves personal values, then there would be little to prevent the proposal that human beings be manufactured or fabricated in a petri dish. If human sexuality is simply a matter of technique for making body complexes, then there is little to prevent the transformation of the conjugal bed into a laboratory.

This rupture of the body from the personal self can also be seen in the current phenomenon of surrogate parenting. At a press conference Elizabeth Kane, the first American surrogate mother, urged women to "share their bodies for nine months." Her language (like the pro-abortion slogan about "women controlling their own bodies") reduces to a purely physical matter something as personal and intimate as mothering.

And as for the problematic that concerns us in this study, if the real self is to be located in consciousness, and the body is simply the material instrument of subjectivity (the Cartesian "*res extensa*"), then to mutilate the body—including the generative organs—that it might more easily fit the consciousness or self-image of the person, present in transsexualism, would appear to be morally justifiable. . . .

. . . [T]he mind or psyche exerts its supremacy and becomes the final arbiter in the question of conformity. . . . [T]he mind, instead of testing reality, begins to dictate the nature of it. The body, on the other hand, becomes an object of the mind or psyche and is reduced to the role of an instrument, to be altered, reshaped, deformed at will.

Continuing a bit further, on a matter that is tangential to the problem at hand but has, nonetheless, considerable importance in current discussions in moral theology—if we are not our bodies, then the use of sex in a manner inconsistent with its biological teleology (e.g., masturbation, contraception, or even bestiality) is not in itself a perversion of a good of the human person. It can be justified because it relieves tension, gives pleasure, and thus contributes to the good of the human person, all of which is located in the consciousness of the subject. "Sexuality can be liberated from regulation by mere biological laws—as advocates of the new morality regard them—so that it can be employed for 'interpersonal communication' or for the 'fostering of conjugal love.'" Such a view of human sexuality is predicated upon an understanding of the human person which distinguishes the self from the body. The latter is regarded as an object or an instrument of the self, something to be used or abused as the self chooses for the amusement and gratification of the self. Sex, then, becomes a matter of mechanics or technique, something to be learned from a manual. And when the maximum of pleasure has been reached, then pain is tried, which may explain the current phenomenon of sado-masochism especially among the chic set.

The dialogue for the entire scenario is clearly put forth by Joseph Fletcher:

> Physical nature—the body and its members, our organs and their functions—all of these things are a part of "what is over against us," and if we live by the rules and conditions set in physiology or any other *it* we are not men, we are not *thou*. When we discussed the problem of giving life to new creatures, and the authority of natural processes as over against the human values of responsibility and self-preservation (when nature and they are at cross-purposes), we remarked that spiritual reality and moral integrity belong to man alone, in whatever degree we may possess them as made *imago Dei* [sic]. Freedom, knowledge, choice, responsibility—all these things of personal or moral stature are in us, not *out there*. Physical nature is what is over against us, out there. It represents the world of *its*. Only man and God are *thou;* they only are persons.

In another work. Fletcher spells out his conclusions to such premises:

> The right of spiritual beings to use intelligent control over physical nature, rather than submit beastlike to its blind workings, is the heart of many crucial questions. Birth control, artificial insemination, sterilization, and abortion are medically discovered ways of fulfilling and protecting human values and hopes in spite of nature's failures or foolishnesses. Death control, like birth control, is a matter of human dignity.

It is evident from all of the above that a certain moral outlook, which presently seeks to gain ascendency, sees the body, its members, organs and functions as belonging to physical nature; and physical nature, in turn, is not to be identified with the person. Everything of moral significance is located within the person. The body, then, becomes a pure means. In no way is it an end in itself. No personal good or value inheres in the body, its functions or their inherent biological teleology.

Quite simply, if we are not our bodies, then there is no limit to what we can justify in the name of "personal or interpersonal values." Such a morality purports to liberate the person from biological laws, from nature for the benefit of more personal or interpersonal values. In effect, however, the so-called "new morality" succeeds in alienating the human person from his or her own bodily reality. A truly Christian morality, on the other hand, is fundamentally founded upon an integral understanding of the human person. It is grounded on a sound anthropology which maintains that the body of a human person is not something other than the person, but is rather constitutive of the very being of the person. Accordingly, it views the biological powers associated with sexuality—namely, generation—not simply as subhuman realities to be used by the conscious subject, not simply as possible goods for the person, but rather as goods of or intrinsic to the person. . . .

Ethical Implications

How does all of this affect the ethics of sex-reassignment? Gender Dysphoria has been described as a severely disordered mental state in which the patient claims that his mind (psyche, ego, soul) is said to have a sexual identity opposite to that which is somatically-given at birth. The proposed solution is to conform the body to the mental state by means of a series of hormonal and surgical procedures that destroy the unwanted bodily parts, most especially the generative organs, and then to surgically reconstruct facsimiles of organic parts belonging to the opposite sex.

As we have seen from an integrist perspective, man is essentially a psycho-somatic unity. Both body and soul determine man's ontological subjectivity and share in his dignity as a person. Within this unity the note of sexual identity is constitutive of the person himself, and therefore, shared by the whole person—both soma and psyche. Corporeal sexual differences, namely the generative organs, are outward signs of deeper ontological differences between the sexes. And since the person is substantially one, there being no antinomy between soma and psyche, it is therefore impossible for the soul (psyche or ego) to have in any objective sense a sexual identity different from that which is clearly evident in the body. The apparent conflict that exists in transsexuals cannot be attributed to any real, objective ontological disjunction between the self and the body, but rather is, as the weight of professional opinion shows, the result of gross psychological distortions in the area of self-perception. Indeed people can feel, act and make themselves look like members of the other sex, but they can only *be* a member of one sex. To speak, then, of sex-reassignment is really inaccurate. What occurs is not in any real, objective sense a change of sex, but rather a wholesale mutilation of healthy bodily organs, most especially the generative system, and the refashioning of artificial organs resembling those of the opposite sex. After surgery a male transsexual, for example, may feel and behave like, and even strongly resemble a woman, but in no real, objective sense can he be said to be a woman.

Moreover, such a procedure represents a massive assault on the integrity of the body and betrays an attitude of absolute dominion reserved only to the Creator. As such, transsexual surgery constitutes a seriously disordered action and is gravely immoral. . . .

Study Questions on Anthony Mastroeni

1. What is dualism? Why does Mastroeni believe that a dualistic understanding of human nature underlies justifications some ethicians offer for transsexual surgery? What alternative view of human nature does he advocate?
2. How would Mastroeni respond to the claim that prior to surgery, Morris had a male body and a female soul? How might Morris respond to Mastroeni?
3. What if anything is wrong with dualism? Is Mastroeni's rejection of dualism consistent with the Christian doctrine of personal immortality?
4. Why does Mastroeni believe that transsexual surgery is morally wrong?

The Universality of Sex Roles

STEPHEN B. CLARK

Stephen B. Clark here reports several significant patterns of sex role difference, discovered in all human societies. These are sexual division of labor, complementary roles in the communal and domestic spheres, some form of female subordination to the male, and expressions of gender difference in custom and tradition. He attempts to show that these patterns of men's and women's roles exhibit remarkable tenacity even in the face of an opposing ideology. Human behavior is malleable to some degree, and people may be able to condition themselves away from

Reprinted by permission of the author.

these natural patterns, but so far attempts to do so have either failed totally or had socially destructive results. Absent any evidence that the results will be good, then, feminist suggestions that we should radically change traditional sex roles ought to be rejected.

Consistent Cross-Cultural Patterns

KNOWLEDGE OF OTHER CULTURES has increased dramatically in the past hundred years. Anthropologists have studied the cultures of primitive peoples extensively, while the discipline of archaeology has developed methods of studying the earliest human societies. The new knowledge has often conveyed an impression of the stunning diversity of human life. What Western society has regarded as normative and universal often proves to be a unique practice or custom of Western culture. One example of this is the supernatural and corporate mentalities of primitive peoples. Primitive peoples tend to view the world without clear-cut distinctions between the natural and supernatural and between the individual and the community. The modern Western mind finds it difficult to grasp this way of looking at the world, but the obstacle is largely the individualistic, naturalistic Western cultural mentality—a point of view which is not shared by other peoples. Similarly, studies have demonstrated a wide variety of expressions of family life from culture to culture, many of them drastically different from the independent nuclear family system of technological society. Some family systems are polygamous, some monogamous, and a few polyandrous. Some societies trace descent through the father, some through the mother, while others trace it bilaterally. In some cultures a newly married couple lives with the man's family (patrilocal residence); in others they live with the woman's family (matrilocal residence); in still others they immediately establish their own residence (neolocal residence). Significant variations can also be observed in the expression of men's and women's roles. An activity (for example, painting) reserved for one sex in one society may be forbidden to that sex in another, and practiced by both sexes in still another. Cultures also differ in the degree of female involvement they permit in political and economic affairs and the degree of male involvement in domestic duties such as child-rearing. It is

no wonder that anthropological evidence can create an impression of unlimited cultural diversity.

Nevertheless, some human practices remain the same. Though cultures develop men's and women's roles differently, a careful examination of the anthropological evidence reveals that several significant underlying patterns can be discovered in all human societies. Four patterns appear to be especially significant:

1. *Sexual division of labor.* In every known society, past or present, the primary tasks of men and women are different. In his review of the anthropological literature related to men's and women's roles, Roy D'Andrade describes the pattern clearly: "One well-documented finding about behavioral sex differences is that men and women not only tend to perform different activities in every culture, but that men tend to perform particular types of activities and women to perform others. This division of labor is especially sharp for subsistence and other economic activities." Though the specific tasks assigned to men and women are not completely consistent from culture to culture (much consistency does exist), the fact that men and women perform different functions is a cross-cultural universal.

2. *Complementary roles in the communal and domestic spheres.* Men bear primary responsibility for the larger community. Women bear primary responsibility for domestic management and rearing of young children. Every known society, past or present, assigns to the men a primary responsibility for the government of the larger groupings within the society, and assigns to the women a primary responsibility for the daily maintenance of the household unit and the care of the younger children. As stated by Michelle Rosaldo, "an opposition between 'domestic' and 'public' provides the basis of a structural framework necessary to identify and explore the place of male and female in psychological, cultural, social, and economic aspects of human life. 'Domestic,' as used here, refers to those

minimal institutions and modes of activity that are organized immediately around one or more mothers and their children; 'public' refers to activities, institutions, and forms of association that link, rank, organize, or subsume particular mother-child groups. Though this opposition will be more or less salient in different social and ideological systems, it does provide a universal framework for conceptualizing the activities of the sexes." The degree of differentiation of male and female responsibility among communal/household lines varies from culture to culture. In almost all cultures, the father of a family or a father-surrogate exercises an overall responsibility for the family, and involves himself personally in the household life. In some cultures, women are allowed to participate actively in economic and political affairs. However, the general underlying pattern emerges universally regardless of the variations in expression.

3. *Some form of female subordination to the male.* In every known society, past or present, the female is in some sense subordinate to the male. As stated by Sherry Ortner, "I would flatly assert that we find women subordinate to men in every known society. The search for a genuinely egalitarian, let alone matriarchal, culture has proved fruitless." This subordination is found on two levels. First, the females are subordinate to the male governing of the communal structures. The "public" sphere, which includes the exercise of overall governmental authority, is the domain of males in every known society. Secondly, females are also customarily subordinate to males on a more personal level within the family. In all known societies, women are personally subordinate to a husband, father, uncle, or other male figure. This second type of subordination is usually minimal in societies in which adult males play only a peripheral role in family life, but it usually has at least some symbolic expression even in these societies. Personal subordination in the home appears to be related to communal subordination in the larger society. If the men are to effectively govern the society as a whole, they must also have some authority over the women who are managing the household units which make up the society. Once again, cultures express female subordination dif-

ferently. However, the underlying pattern of female subordination is the same.

4. *Cultural expression of gender differences between men and women.* Every known culture, past or present, includes some expressions of gender differences between men and women in its customs and traditions. Men and women dress differently, develop different character traits, and express respect with different customs. As stated by van den Berge, "It seems that virtually all societies, not content with the moderate amount of sexual dimorphism with which we are born, further stress sex role differentiation through highly visible social means. Clothing styles stand out most obviously, but even in societies in which nudity or near nudity is the rule, gender differences are visibly expressed through body adornment such as tattooing, scarification, jewelry, tooth mutilation, and the like. . . . Beyond differences in dress and body adornment, sex roles are also symbolically differentiated in most societies through a combination of rituals, taboos (for example, menstrual or post partum), spatial segregation (separate sleeping quarters, men's clubs), and rules of etiquette (for instance, "chivalry" and "gallantry" in the Western tradition). Some modern societies which have an ideological commitment to reduce male-female differentiation try to keep these cultural expressions to a minimum. For example, in China men and women dress in nearly identical ways. However, even these modern societies include some ways of expressing gender differences between men and women.

Some people respond skeptically to these assertions because they have a vague notion that some societies have been "matriarchal"—that is, the governing authorities have been women. However, anthropologists unanimously dismiss matriarchy as a characteristic of any known society, present or past. As stated by Rosaldo, "The issues involved here are complex, but the evidence of contemporary anthropology gives scant support to an argument for matriarchy." There are two main reasons for the persistent confusion about matriarchy. First, some primitive tribes have myths which tell of a time in their ancient past when women ruled. Anthropologists now generally regard these myths as justifications for some current aspect of the tribal life, such as male authority, and not as historically reliable tradition. Myths about Amazonian warrior women are also considered unhistorical by anthropologists. Secondly, anthropologists once used the term "matriarchy" to describe societies which are today called matrilineal or matrifocal. Matrilineal societies are those which trace lineage through the mother and not the father. Matrifocal societies are those in which the female role receives special attention and honor. Modern anthropologists no longer use the term "matriarchal" to describe these societies precisely because it implies that the women of the society actually govern the overall life of the group. In fact, men are the overall governing authorities in both matrilineal and matrifocal societies. Thus, the idea that matriarchal societies did or do exist is a popular misunderstanding, and a notion that modern anthropologists reject. . . .

The Strength of the Cross-Cultural Patterns

The tenacity of these four patterns of men's and women's roles in the midst of a hostile environment is especially visible in the light of opposing ideology. The Soviet Union, the People's Republic of China, and the Israeli Kibbutzim have all embraced radical programs intended to bring social equality among men and women. In these societies, socialist or communist ideology have at one time or another directly attacked each of the four universal patterns—division of labor by sex, complementary roles in the communal and domestic spheres, female subordination, and the cultural expression of men's and women's roles. Indeed, in important respects, men's and women's roles in these societies have been changed. Men and women in these societies live much differently today than they did in pre-communist China or Russia or in traditional Jewish society. The changes have been particularly marked in China, for women and their social role had little respect in traditional Chinese society in comparison to other traditional societies. While Chinese communist propaganda about the "bitter past" cannot be accepted on face value, it is certain that Chinese women no longer occupy such a role today. Significant, though not quite so strik-ing, changes in the roles of men and women have also occurred in the Soviet Union and the Kibbutzim. However, despite these changes, the four universal patterns are preserved intact in all three societies. Neither Russia, China, or the Kibbutzim have eliminated a sexual differentiation of labor. Women have greater job opportunities, but a division of labor still exists. Men still dominate the higher echelons of government, education, and the professions; women still dominate the care of children, though sometimes within a child-care institution rather than the family. There is still some sense of female subordination, though the ideological stand continues to assail it. There are still cultural expressions of men's and women's roles. It might be added that modern revolutionary societies such as Russia, China, and the Kibbutzim are better equipped than any previous societies to succeed in efforts to eradicate traditional social patterns. They possess new tools of propaganda such as mass state-controlled education, a new ideology which seeks to replace traditional social controls such as religion, and economic development plans which disrupt patterns of traditional life. Nevertheless, the universal patterns of men's and women's roles reassert themselves. They appear even in the midst of those societies which are earnestly seeking to undermine them.

The Kibbutzim present an especially important subject for study. Their potential to successfully reshape the roles of men and women is greater than either Communist China or the Soviet Union. The Kibbutz groupings are small, and thus are simpler and more manageable than a nation-state. Membership in the Kibbutzim is voluntary; and those who dislike the lifestyle can (and do) leave at any time. This ensures that the Kibbutz members will have a consistent and firm commitment to the ideals of the Kibbutz. Coercion is almost never necessary. Serious social problems rarely occur. The Kibbutzim need not deal with political subversion, criminality or insanity. Most men and women joining a Kibbutz have broken previous ties and are explicitly seeking to create a new society. Thus the Kibbutzim are in an excellent position to immediately establish a radical social policy regarding the family. The early founders of the Kibbutzim theoretically and practically dismantled the family unit. Children were reared corporately in common child-care facilities. Men and women shared an equal proportion of the labor of the Kibbutz and everyone had equal opportunity to share in the overall government of the group.

The Kibbutzim are also important because social scientists have studied them adequately. Western social scientists do not have accurate and thorough data on the social life of communist countries, especially Communist China. Governments of these countries generally forbid first-hand sociological study by Westerners, and official statistics and information are notoriously unreliable. Indeed, even if sociologists could freely study Russian and Chinese family life, the sheer size of the samples would complicate the researcher's task. In contrast, the Kibbutzim present miniature societies suitable for study and open to objective research. They are the best laboratories for assessing the success of a powerful and determined attempt to alter the universal patterns of men's and women's roles.

In their book *Women in the Kibbutz,* Lionel Tiger and Joseph Shepher report on their research into the current social structure of the Kibbutzim. Their research has been extensive, employing computer analysis and other sociological techniques. Their results are extremely significant. Tiger and Shepher show that the universal patterns have once again appeared despite the Kibbutzim's commitment to eliminate them. A division of labor exists in most occupations. Certain tasks are viewed as male, others as female. Men hold most high political positions. Women prefer to care for children, especially their own children. The women have begun to pressure the Kibbutzim authorities—mostly men—to allow greater parental involvement in child-rearing. The men appear to resist this trend and to reassert the Kibbutz ideal of eliminating family life and the distinctive roles of men and women. But the Kibbutz women persist. As Tiger and Shepher state it, "They (the women) have acted against the principles of their socialization and ideology, against the wishes of the men of their communities, against the economic interest of the Kibbutzim, in order to be able to devote more time and energy to private maternal activities rather than to economic and political public ones. Obviously these women have minds of their own;

despite obstacles, they are trying to accomplish what women elsewhere have been periodically urged to reject by critics of traditional female roles."

It can therefore be confidently asserted that several important patterns of men's and women's roles have been consistently observed in every culture yet studied. The qualification "yet studied" is added for scientific precision, but in fact the evidence implies that these patterns have existed in every human society. One should not overlook the implications of these universal patterns. . . . [T]he universality and tenacity of these patterns implies that some powerful underlying force is behind them. As Sherry Ortner, a feminist scholar with no "biodeterminist" sympathies, states it, "The universality of female subordination, the fact that it exists within every type of social and economic arrangement and in societies of every degree of complexity, indicates to me that we are up against something very profound, very stubborn, something we cannot root out simply by rearranging a few tasks and roles in the social system, or even by reordering the whole economic structure." In short, the unanimity and strength of the data concerning universal social structural patterns makes it one of the most significant areas in the study of the differences between men and women. . . .

The Argument Against Biodeterminism

An important question still remains: What is the proper attitude toward these differences between men and women? A strong movement today would pay as little attention as possible to these facts. This movement advances what could be described as "the argument against biodeterminism." In its strongest form, the argument against biodeterminism denies that there are real or significant differences between men and women. . . . [T]he evidence solidly refutes this strong form of the argument. A modified form of the argument against biodeterminism is more widely held. This is the view that some differences between men and women exist, but that we can and should recondition people so that they do not express these differences in any way other than in the physical necessities of sex and reproduction. This view holds that the human race is very malleable, that socialization and cultural conditioning are much more powerful in forming the human race than most biological factors, and hence that the human race should simply mold itself into whatever it wants to become.

This form of the argument against biodeterminism possesses some plausibility. To a great extent, the human race does possess the ability to condition itself away from what could be described as its "natural state." Humanity *is* malleable. Socialization is powerful. Humans can determine their own destiny in a way that animals cannot. However, human malleability has definite limits. There are physical limitations. There also appears to be a tendency to cling to a "natural" order. For example, women in the Kibbutzim have returned to a more traditional pattern of men's and women's roles despite an ideology which points in the opposite direction. Nonetheless, it does seem possible that the human race, through diligent and ingenious effort, could condition itself away from the pattern of men's and women's roles that has appeared in every human society.

However, the human race would attempt this change only at great risk. Developments in ecological studies in recent decades have demonstrated the fragility and complexity of the "natural" environment. Seemingly small changes in our physical environment can produce unexpected—even disastrous—consequences. The human race is not always adept at foreseeing the consequences of such changes because its understanding of the interrelationships of overall ecology lags well behind its technological ability to produce change.

The radical feminist movement has by its success shown its ability to produce vast social change. However, this could be one of the most destructive changes in the history of human society. The roles of men and women have proven useful in previous societies; in fact, past societies functioned well only when these roles were operating properly. Today a strong movement would destroy these roles without a firmly established understanding of the ecological consequences. The rationale is simply that human nature is "unbelievably malleable." In essence, the human race is told that it should make such changes sim-

ply because it is capable of doing so. In the face of such a claim, human beings would do well to acquire a humble sense of the limitations of human knowledge, and to recall recent lessons about some of the painful consequences of technological change.

For many years now our society has been experiencing a gradual weakening of men's and women's roles. Recent ideological and social movements have begun to hasten this process in many countries and this trend will probably continue. One should attempt to analyze the effects of this change. This is a complex and difficult task, but one can already observe in countries where the process is most advanced several destructive social trends that can probably be traced in part to the breakdown of men's and women's roles.

1. *Family life is weakened.* The breakdown of men's and women's roles weakens family life in two main ways. First, it undermines the subordination of the wife and turns her attention to her own life and career apart from her husband's career and apart from the life of the family. This takes away from the unity of the family, and is associated with the family's general loss of order and authority. Secondly, the breakdown of men's and women's roles leads men to take less responsibility for family groupings. As family life becomes an undifferentiated responsibility of husband and wife together with no defined male role of leadership, men often lose the motivation and commitment needed to care for their families. They tend to relate to women predominantly for sexual gratification. The man no longer focuses his desire for accomplishment on the family, but instead directs his interest elsewhere. As a consequence of these two trends—the increasing independence of the wife and irresponsibility of the husband—the family becomes less of a stable, ordered, and cohesive group, and more of a collection of individuals living together. These weaker families then produce weaker children with significant personal problems.

2. *Sexual relationships become troubled.* Confusion about roles may be a factor in the apparent increase of sexual disorders in Western culture. Evidence indicates that impotence in men is tied to the way their partners relate to them. When wives relate to their husbands in a challenging,

aggressive, or dominating way, men often lose interest in sexual relationships and sometimes become impotent. Some social scientists also believe that a breakdown in men's and women's roles is associated with homosexuality and confusion in sexual identity.

3. *Women often lose a sense of value.* The modern feminist movement—ostensibly a movement "for" women—normally devalues the very things that women feel the greatest desire to do: to be a wife and mother and have a home. Moreover, it often devalues precisely those elements of her personality that are most naturally feminine. Ironically, the effect of the feminist movement is largely to make women feel the "disadvantage" of being female more acutely. It puts them under greater pressure to compete with men.

4. *Womanly roles are neglected.* Our society neglects or institutionalizes roles involving care for personal needs—the roles traditionally filled by women. Thus home and family life becomes less supportive and charitable service is more impersonal and less charitable.

5. *Manly roles are neglected.* Our society provides less order, discipline, and personal protection in daily life than previous eras. Men are taught to avoid these traditionally male responsibilities; in fact, many men have become incapable of bearing these responsibilities because they have lost what was once the characteristically male approach to emotions and personal relationships.

6. *Men and women develop psychological instabilities.* There is some evidence that those groups in modern society most directly affected by the feminist movement have been specially plagued by psychological problems. The lack of social roles appears to make life more difficult for both men and women.

It probably cannot be proven that all these trends are caused by the erosion of men's and women's roles in our society. However, a reasonable case can be made for this position, and this case should be taken seriously until it is disproved. These trends amount to a picture of increasing social weakness. The fabric of our society could be seriously weakened by the continued breakdown of men's and women's roles.

Of the several social trends just described, the weakening of the family is of the greatest concern. Those who oppose the feminist program for restructuring society have long held that this program would undermine the most fundamental elements of family life. Radical adherents of the program agree with this analysis, and hail the undermining of the family as an essential step in social progress; more moderate adherents deny that the weakening of men's and women's roles must weaken the family. However, it is clear that the family in modern society is growing more fragile, and this fragility must stem at least in part from new approaches to men's and women's roles. This connection between weakened roles and a weakened family is illustrated in the following paragraph from Barbara Seaman, a feminist journalist who is writing from her own experience about families whose wives were actively involved in the feminist movement:

> I was in an early consciousness-raising group, which proved effective. We all went on to publish books, get PhDs, or rise up some way in the world. Years later, those of us who were mothers tried to reassemble in order to measure the price our families might have paid. The sessions were so painful that after five or six of them we quit. Too many husbands had deserted (one for a Playboy bunny), too many children had dropped out of school, turned gay, attempted suicide. To a man the divorced husbands, however affluent, were copping out on child support, college tuitions and psychiatrist bills. These were women, mind you, who never requested alimony for themselves.

Seaman's chronicle of family dissolution, children's problems, and male irresponsibility is a vivid testimony to some of the possible consequences of a feminist restructuring of society.

The argument against biodeterminism and similar forms of argumentation are seriously flawed in their very structure. Built into these theories and ideologies is a faulty view of where the burden of proof lies. They begin with the undeniable malfunctioning of many aspects of men's and women's roles today, and proceed to argue that distinctive roles for men and women should be abolished or substantially reduced. To be sure, they produce much evidence for the malfunctioning of the current remains of traditional men's and women's roles. However, this evidence alone cannot lead them to the conclusion they assert. If they are advocating a radical restructuring of society, then it is not enough to merely substantiate the problems and disadvantages of the present structure. Those arguing for change should also be required to show that their proposed new pattern can more successfully accommodate the natural differences between men and women and can provide a better basis for the structuring of society. They should be asked to show that a new approach would work *better than* the current system or the alternatives. If the present pattern of men's and women's roles is inadequate, but more promising than the alternatives, it would be a grave error to discard it in favor of a change that is even more inadequate. Nonetheless, those advocating the radical feminist positions today seldom try to show that their option is better. They are simply dismantling the remains of a traditional system of men's and women's roles without replacing this system with anything superior.

The feminist line of argumentation has another weakness. The argument advocates the abolition or reduction of role differences by documenting the problems in the current system of men's and women's roles. However, it can also be argued that the weaknesses in the current system point instead to the need for a restoration of fuller role differences. The current system of men's and women's roles is merely a remnant of the traditional patterns of men's and women's roles. These traditional patterns have been under ideological and cultural assault for over a hundred years. Therefore, the system of men's and women's roles in technological society today is largely the product of the very forces which would now take change even further, removing even the remnants of a traditional pattern. If the current system is any indication of the desirability of further change, the radical feminist program must appear highly undesirable.

Finally, the feminists are proposing sweeping, and untried, alternatives to a pattern of human life that has endured throughout all history. Surely the radicalness of their proposals puts the burden of proof upon them to justify the safety as well as the desirability of a program of eliminating all sexual role differences.

Study Questions on Stephen B. Clark

1. What features of male-female relationships does Clark claim can be found in all known societies? If he is right about the existence of the cross-cultural patterns, what, if anything, does this prove? What does he think it proves?
2. What results does Clark believe would follow from our attempting to condition people away from the sex role patterns that have prevailed throughout history? Do you agree with Clark that these consequences are bad? Are there also any good consequences?
3. Clark points out that the system we now have is a very weakened form of the traditional sex role system, and suggests that this is one reason for the problems we are experiencing. Do you think family systems worked better in the past than they do now? If so, when and for what reasons?
4. Explain his analogy between cultural systems and ecosystems. Do you find this analogy a persuasive one?

The Primacy of Gender Attribution

SUZANNE KESSLER AND WENDY McKENNA

Suzanne Kessler and Wendy McKenna here question the everyday assumption that every human being is naturally either a male or a female. A form of social construction called "gender attribution," they argue, is prior to other aspects of gender, including anatomical and physiological differences. No amount of information about a person, short of gender attribution itself, suffices to determine sexual identity.

As we go about our daily lives, we assume that every human being is either a male or a female. We make this assumption for everyone who ever lived and for every future human being. Most people would admit that the cultural trappings of males and females have varied over place and time, but that nevertheless, there is something essentially male and something essentially female. It is a fact that someone is a man or a woman, just as it is a fact that the result of a coin toss is either heads or tails, and we can easily decide the case by looking. Of course, the coin may be worn and we may have to inspect it very closely. Analogously, a person may not clearly be one gender or the other. But just as we assume that we can determine "heads" or "tails" by detailed inspection (rather than concluding that the coin has no heads or tails), we assume that we can do the same with a person's gender. Not even with biologically "mixed" individuals do we conclude that they are neither female nor male. Biologists may assert that a hermaphrodite's gender is not clear, but in everyday life ultimately some criteria can (and will) be found by which each one is placed in one of two mutually exclusive gender categories along with everyone else. Even the biologist would say that hermaphrodites are a combination of the two existing categories, rather than a third gender category.

If we ask by what criteria a person might classify someone as being either male or female, the answers appear to be so self-evident as to make the question trivial. But consider a list of items that differentiate females from males. There are none that *always and without exception* are true of only one gender. No behavioral characteristic (e.g., crying or physical aggression) is always present or never present for one gender. Neither can physical characteristics—either visible (e.g., beards), unexposed (e.g., genitals), or normally unexamined (e.g., gonads)—always differentiate the genders. According to Webster's dictionary (1973), males are those who beget young by performing the fertilization function in generation, and females are those who bear the young. Although this distinction may be useful for strictly biological considerations it is of little value in everyday encounters. The item "sperm-producer" may only appear on lists that describe men, but men are not always sperm-producers, and, in fact, not all sperm-producers are men. A male-to-female transsexual, prior to surgery, can be socially a woman, though still potentially (or actually) capable of spermatogenesis.

Substitute any item for "sperm-producer," and the statement will still be true. Penises, vaginas, beards, breasts, and so on in any combination are not *conclusive* evidence for categorizing someone as either a man or a woman in everyday life. Preoperative transsexuals can be men with vaginas or women with penises, and, of course, the bearded lady is still a lady.

We could make probability statements like most people with beards are men, or most people with breasts, high voices, vaginas, and long fingernails are women, but when we meet someone, the "decision"[1] that we make as to whether that person is a man or a woman is not stated in terms of probabilities. They are either one or the other, zero or 100 percent. We may modify our decision ("He is an effeminate man"), but we do not usually qualify it ("Maybe he is a man"). If we should have to qualify it, then we seek further information until the qualification is no longer necessary.

For example, we might look closely at the person's cheeks for signs of beard stubble, or we might even ask someone if they know the gender of the person in question. We make a *gender attribution*,[2] that is we decide whether someone is male or female, every time we see a new person. . . .

. . . [N]ot only is gender attribution far from a simple inspection process, but *gender attribution forms the foundation for understanding other components of gender,* such as gender role (behaving like a female or male) and gender identity (feeling like a female or male).

This perspective forms the core of our book. . . . [W]e lay the groundwork for this perspective by detailing the existence, importance, and primacy of the gender attribution process to both science and everyday life, and by raising questions about the inevitability of the gender *dichotomy.* Our final goal is not only to demonstrate that gender attribution is primary, but to delineate, as much as possible, both the necessary conditions for presenting oneself as female or male and the necessary rules for making sense out of such a presentation. Both of these are crucial in deciding a person's gender, We argue that the question of what it means to be a male or a female is merely another way of asking how one *decides* whether another is male or female.

Gender very clearly pervades everyday life. Not only can gender be attributed to most things, but there are certain objects (i.e., people) to which gender apparently *must* be attributed. The immediate concern with doing this when we meet an ambiguous person illustrates the pervasive, taken-for-granted character of the gender attribution process. Over and over again, transsexuals who were in the process of changing from one gender to the other, emphasized how uneasy people seemed to be interacting with them, until some sort of decision had been made about whether they were male or female—a decision that was often reached by asking them, "What are you?" Contrary to our expectations when we began researching gender, there does not seem to be a prohibition against asking certain people what gender they are, especially if it is done in a joking manner. However, those who were asked reported feeling embarrassed and uncomfortable, indicating that something had gone wrong with the interaction, that a "violation" of unstated rules had occurred. . . .

Ambiguous cases make the dichotomous nature of the gender attribution process extremely salient. In our culture, a person is *either* male *or* female. The gender dichotomy raises many questions. If Leslie is not male, is Leslie then necessarily female? Do we decide what someone is, or what they are not? This suggests that an analysis of "conditions of failure". . . might be appropriate in describing the gender attribution process. In other words, it may be that a "female" attribution is made when it is impossible to see the other person as a male, and vice versa. Whether attributions are made on the basis of the presence or the absence of cues is something we pursue.

The essential question we are asking is: How is a social reality where there are two, and only two, genders constructed?[3] Is the process the same for everyone, regardless of the person's reason for making the attribution? That is, does the biologist (for example) in making a gender attribution do

---

[1]The use of the term "decision" does not necessarily imply that people consciously deliberate or choose, nor that they could verbalize the "decision"-making process. The term is used in the ethnomethodological sense . . . to refer to the rule-guided, socially shared activity of gender attribution. . . . In no way do we mean to suggest that people have any trouble making these decisions, nor are we suggesting that unless they became aware of how they are deciding they might be making mistakes.

[2]We have chosen to use the word "attribution" because it implies an active process, based on information received, and involving implicit rules for assigning characteristics.

[3]Our use of the terms "construction" and "social construction" reflects our theoretical position that the sense of an objective world is accomplished by persons engaged in concrete day-to-day activities. (See the discussion which follows in the text.) This accomplishment or construction is social because those engaged in the activity are members; that is, they share a common method for producing the sense of objective facts like gender.

the same thing when in the laboratory as at a party? While it is important to understand scientific criteria for telling males from females, for the most part we will analyze gender attribution from the point of view of the "naive" person, that is, all of us when we are using our common sense understandings of everyday life. Even scientists must ultimately rely on their own common sense knowledge. In fact, "any scientific understanding of human action . . . must begin with and be built upon an understanding of the everyday life of the members performing those actions."

Our warrant for asking the question: How is a reality constructed where there are two genders? comes from the theoretical assumptions underlying the ethnomethodological approach. We can only present the briefest summary of these assumptions here, and in doing so we emphasize those that are most relevant to our particular interests. . . .

In our everyday lives and, for most of us, in our professional lives, we proceed on the basis of certain "unquestionable axioms" about the world which Mehan and Wood . . . call "incorrigible propositions" and others . . . call the "natural attitude." The most basic incorrigible proposition is the belief that the world exists independently of our presence, and that objects have an independent reality and a constant identity. For example, suppose you look out your window and see a rose in the garden, but when you go out to pick it, you cannot find it. You do not assume that there was a rose but now it has disappeared, nor do you assume that the rose turned into something else. You keep looking until you either find the rose or figure out what conditions existed to make you think there was a rose. Perhaps it was the configuration of shadows, or you might notice a butterfly which you mistook for a rose. By interpreting the results of your search in this way, you thereby verify the reality and constancy of objects like roses and butterflies, and validate that they exist independently of your interaction with them.

Not only the rose itself, but all its characteristics (color, fragrance, etc.) have this factual status. And what is true of roses is also true of people. In the natural attitude, there is reality and constancy to qualities like race, age, social class, and, of course, gender, which exist independently of any particular example of the quality. It is a fact that

there are two genders; each person is a mere example of one of them; and the task of the scientist is to describe, as accurately as possible, the constant characteristics that define male and female, for all people and for all time. This is reality in Western society.

By holding these beliefs as incorrigible propositions, we view other ways of seeing the world, other sets of beliefs about what reality is, as "incorrect," "primitive," or "misinformed." We know, for a fact, that people do not turn into birds, and if a Yaqui shaman thinks that they do . . ., he is wrong. His belief probably stems from "distorted" perceptions which occur under the influence of drugs. The shaman thinks that some plants carry the power to make him into a bird. According to Western reality, the *real* truth is that the plants are hallucenogenic and cause a physiological reaction which results in a distorted perception of the world.

Ethnomethodologists challenge this interpretation of the shaman's behavior, not by asserting that we are wrong in seeing his actions in this way, but rather by contending that the shaman's interpretation is as real for him as ours is for us. Indeed, both realities are created in the same way—through methodical (i.e., orderly, systematic, and thus recoverable), interactional work which creates and sustains whatever reality one is living, be it that of the shaman, the "man in the street," the biologist, or any other reality one could name.

In order to see the world as the ethnomethodologist does, it is necessary to ask the following questions: Suppose that we treat our belief in constancy and independent existences as just that, beliefs. Then suppose that, for the purpose of discovering what happens, we temporarily suspend our belief in these propositions. How does the world look then? This technique, known as "bracketing," is a method suggested by phenomenologists. . . . If we bracket the natural attitude, the constancy and independent existence of objects disappears, and we are left only with particular, concrete situations.

From this perspective we can then assert that, somehow, in each situation, a sense of "objective facts" which transcend the situation is produced. Thus we have grounds for asking the ethnomethodological question: What are the methodological ways by which members of a group produce, in each particular situation, this sense of external, constant, objective facts which have their own independent existences, not contingent on any concrete interaction? Applied to our interests in this book, the question becomes: How, in any interaction, is a sense of the reality of a world of two, and only two, genders constructed? How do we "do" gender attributions? That is, what kinds of rules do we apply to what kinds of displays, such that in every concrete instance we produce a sense that there are *only* men and women, and that this is an objective fact, not dependent on the particular instance.

Gender attribution is a complex, interactive process involving the person making the attribution and the person she/he is making the attribution about. (This distinction between attributor and other should not obscure the fact that in most interactions participants are simultaneously being both.) The process results in the "obvious" fact of the other being either male or female. On the one hand, the other person presents her or himself in such a way as to convey the proper cues to the person making the attribution. The presentation, however, cannot be reduced to concrete items that one might list as differentiating women from men. Most of the cues people assume play a role in the attribution process are really *post hoc* constructions. One transsexual we talked with put it well when he[4] said, "Gender is an anchor, and once people decide what you are they interpret everything you do in light of that."

The second factor in the interaction are the rules (methods) that the person doing the attributing uses for assessing these cues. These rules are not as simple as learned probabilities, such as people with beards are usually men. They are rules that construct for us a world of two genders, such that to say, "I knew he was a man because he had a beard" makes sense in the first place. In other words, "because he had a beard" is understood as a reason because of our methods for constructing "male" and "female." In another reality, "I knew he was a man because he carried a bow and arrow"

might be more sensible. . . . Part of being a socialized member of a group is knowing the rules for giving acceptable evidence for categorizing. In our culture, physical evidence is the most acceptable reason. Giving a reason is not the same, though, as making the categorization in the first place. We will argue that the fact of seeing two physical genders is as much of a socially constructed dichotomy as everything else.

Much of our work in this book consists of examining the treatment of gender in the social and biological sciences, in light of our perspective that the reality of gender is a social construction. Because of the confusion in terminology which pervades the literature on gender and gender differences, we must define certain terms, which, while overlapping in many ways with previous definitions, are not necessarily identical to them. Where appropriate we indicate how our meanings differ from those of others. One of the major differences is that our definitions are mutually exclusive and consequently narrower than those in current usage.

The term "gender" has traditionally been used to designate psychological, social, and cultural aspects of maleness and femaleness. . . . "Sex" generally designates the biological components of maleness and femaleness. Given this perspective, there are two sexes, male and female, and, correspondingly, two genders, masculine and feminine.

We will use gender, rather than sex, even when referring to those aspects of being a woman (girl) or man (boy) that have traditionally been viewed as biological. This will serve to emphasize our position that the element of social construction is primary in all aspects of being female or male, particularly when the term we use seems awkward (e.g., gender chromosomes). The word "sex" will be used only for references to reproductive and love-making activities and, at times, in reference to purely physical characteristics when explicating the position of someone else who uses this word.

The cultural/biological distinction traditionally associated with the usage of gender versus sex is a technical one, applicable to scientists in the laboratory and some textbooks, but little else. Gender is a word which, until very recently, was rarely used by people in everyday life, and even in technical

---

[4]Throughout this book, the gender pronoun we use for an informant (whether the informant is a professional, an "everyday" person, a transsexual, or anything else) refers to the attribution that we made in interacting with the person.

writings the two terms are often used interchangeably and confusingly. . . .

This brief discussion of terminology is important for what it reveals about the underlying ways of constructing our ideas of gender/sex. Although some social scientists are questioning the concepts of masculinity and femininity as mutually exclusive . . ., gender, as the cultural expression of all that is feminine or masculine in a person, is still treated as dichotomous. It may be easier today to see that particular individuals have both masculine and feminine features, but we still generally treat gender as dichotomous and most certainly treat sex that way. Even those who study biologically "mixed" persons (e.g., someone born with XY chromosomes and a vagina) prefer to treat those persons as special cases of dichotomous sex. "There are, with few exceptions, two sexes, male and female," states Stoller . . ., and although his and others' work is to a large extent based on these "few exceptions," he does not consider sex to be overlapping in the way gender may be.

GENDER ASSIGNMENT

Gender assignment is a special case of gender attribution which occurs only once—at birth. The cues for this special case are quite clear. The person making the assignment (doctor, midwife, etc.) inspects the genitals, categorizes them as vagina or penis, and announces the gender on the basis of that inspection. Vagina means the neonate is assigned the gender label "girl," and penis means the neonate is assigned the gender label "boy." Others have a right to check the assignment if they wish, but, again, genitals are all that is looked at. In cases where the genitals are ambiguous, assignment is withheld until other criteria are inspected. . . .

. . . If there has been a "mistake," a reassignment can be, and often is, made. However, since reassignment involves so much more than mere genital inspection, and, in fact, the "proper" physical genitals may not be there, "reassignment" is a misleading term. Reassignment could imply that the child had been one gender and is now the other, when actually the child is seen by everyone as having been the "new" gender all along. "Gender reconstruction" would be a better term,

since the child's history, as short as it may have been, must now be reinterpreted. For example, what was originally seen as an empty scrotum might later be seen as always having been misformed labia. This suggests that "gender assignment" and "gender construction" may be synonomous.

GENDER IDENTITY

Gender identity refers to an individual's own feeling of whether she or he is a woman or a man, or a girl or a boy. In essence gender identity is self-attribution of gender. Rules for self-attribution are not necessarily the same as rules for attributing gender to others, although it is as necessary to make a definite self-attribution as it is to make unqualified gender attributions about others. One young man who lived as a female for three years did not have a female gender identity. Even though successful at passing, he finally could not tolerate the conflict between his male gender identity and the female gender attributions which were consistently made to him. It was necessary to make a choice, and he decided to be a male. To him this meant not only living as a male in the eyes of others, but thinking of himself as a male without any doubts. This example not only points out the difficulty of trying to maintain a self-image without a clear gender identity, but it also shows how one's gender identity can be relatively independent of the gender attributions made by others.

The only way to ascertain someone's gender identity is to ask her/him. Clinicians may believe they can "get at" someone's gender identity by the use of projective tests, but they are probably measuring gender-role identity (see below). Of course, the person might lie and not reveal her/his true gender identity, but there is no other method of getting the answer besides asking. Another problem with asking is that the question, "Are you a boy/man or a girl/woman?" determines the nature of the answer. The question implicitly assumes that the respondent is either one or the other and there is no other category. Even if a less leading way of asking the question could be formulated (and all questions, to some extent, structure the desired answer) . . ., we still may not get accurate answers, either because the respondent knows that "I don't know" or "Neither" or "Both" are not acceptable answers or because she/he knows that the answer must be congruent with the evidence (e.g., physical characteristics) presented to the person who is asking. In any event, gender identity is what the person feels she/he is, regardless of the gender attribution other people would make about her/him, and regardless of the validity of our techniques for determining gender identity. To claim that your *gender* is what you feel yourself to be ignores the fact that people almost always attribute gender without asking one another. The equating of gender and gender identity is understandable, however, since the question, "Are you male or female?" can either be interpreted as, "What do you feel yourself to be?" or "How are you categorized by others?" The reason why most people do not have difficulty interpreting the question is that in the common-sense world there is no reason to distinguish gender identity from gender attribution. There is just gender.

The development of a gender identity appears to occur during a critical period. That is, there is a period of time in the young child's life before which she or he is too young to have a gender identity, and after which whatever gender identity has developed cannot be changed. There is only one reported case of a nonpsychotic person not developing either a male or female gender identity during childhood . . ., and even this case is not a clear one. Most of the evidence for the development of a gender identity during a critical period comes from cases where the initial assignment was deemed in error and an attempt was made to "correct" it by reassigning the child and making the necessary physical changes. Almost all attempts of this sort made after the age of about three are unsuccessful, in the sense that the individual either retains her/his original gender identity or becomes extremely confused and ambivalent. When the child *is* able to develop a new gender identity to go along with the reassignment, professionals conclude that the earlier gender identity had not been firmly entrenched. This circularity is a rather obvious example of the operation of incorrigible propositions. Given a belief in the permanence of gender identity after a critical period, the inability to reassign a child in some cases *and* the ability to

do so in others serves as proof of the "truth" of the invariance of gender identity. Even though emphasis on a critical period makes the acquisition of a gender identity seem like an all-or-nothing event there is a developmental process involved in learning that you are either a girl or a boy, what it means to be one or the other, and that this is a permanent aspect of your life.

Instead of thinking in terms of "critical periods," a term that suggests innate biological mechanisms, it is possible to discuss gender identity from a different perspective. It may be that gender can be successfully reassigned up to the point when the child incorporates the rules which construct gender, specifically, the "fact" that gender is unchangeable. . . .

Gender identity should not be confused with the similar-sounding concept of gender-role identity. . . . Gender-role identity refers to how much a person approves of and participates in feelings and behaviors, which are seen as "appropriate" for his/her gender. . . . Failing to separate the two concepts leads many scientists . . . to conclude that someone with atypical feelings about how their maleness or femaleness should be expressed in behavior has a gender identity problem. This could lead one to assert that the lessening rigidity in gender behaviors will result in a large number of persons who do not know whether they are male or female. There is no evidence to support that assertion, although gender identity and gender-role identity might influence one another in various ways. For example, given rigid expectations, a boy could think that because he does not like "boy things" and does like "girl things" he might be a girl. . . . As expectations become more flexible, such gender identity conflicts may be less likely to occur.

GENDER ROLE

A role, as the concept is used in sociology, is a set of prescriptions and proscriptions for behavior—expectations about what behaviors are appropriate for a person holding a particular position within a particular social context. A gender role, then, is a set of expectations about what behaviors are appropriate for people of one gender. People can be categorized as role occupants either through their own efforts ("achieved" roles, such as doctor, mother, student) or on the basis of attributes over which they are seen to have no control ("ascribed" roles, such as Black, infant, Italian). Obviously, gender roles in our society are treated as ascribed roles.

According to the traditional perspective, someone is "born into" the category "male" or "female," and by virtue of her or his birth becomes obligated to perform the male or female role. In other words, one is expected to behave in accordance with the prescriptions and proscriptions for one's gender. . . .

The obligatory nature of gender roles is so firm that when dictionaries attempt to define woman and man, they often do so by listing gender role behaviors. ("Man: one possessing a high degree of . . . courage, strength, and vigor" *Webster's,* 1973, p. 889). Even Stoller, who is so aware of the ambiguities surrounding gender, cites, as proof that an XO chromosome individual is as natural a woman as any XX woman, the fact that she likes to cook and sew.

Gender roles have many components, including interests, activities, dress, skills, and sexual partner choice. For each of these components, there are clear, and different, expectations for those who occupy the male role and the female role. . . . Because these role expectations are so pervasive, it is not necessary to list exactly what they are.

As with other roles, sanctions against violating various pre- and proscriptions vary. In fact, the sanctions, rather than the expectations, may be what is changing in contemporary society. Women are still expected, in general, to want a home and family, but deviance from that expectation is now more permissible. On the other hand, men still cannot wear skirts, if they want to be taken seriously.

A *stereotype* is a set of beliefs about the characteristics of the occupants of a role, not necessarily based on fact or personal experience, but applied to each role occupant regardless of particular circumstances. In addition, stereotypes are conceived of as having an evaluative component. That is, they are not merely descriptive of expected behaviors, but these expected behaviors are evaluated as good, bad, desirable, and so on. For example, the stereotyped female role in our society consists of such low-valued behaviors and traits as passivity

and helplessness and such high-valued ones as "very tactful." . . . [W]e are not particularly concerned with stereotypes, *per se*, because, by definition, stereotypes are not assumed to be "objective" in the way gender role, in which stereotypes are grounded, is seen to be.

Because gender is an ascribed role, certain gender role expectations are seen as being an expression of the biological (i.e., unchangeable) foundations of gender. . . .

. . . Theories of gender role development (i.e., how children learn the proper behavior associated with their gender) vary in the emphasis which they place on biological and environmental factors. All the major theories, however, make the assumption that dichotomous roles are a natural (and hence proper) expression of the dichotomous nature of gender. This assumption is being increasingly reexamined, but the grounds for questioning existing dichotomous gender roles do not question the existence of two genders. It is only by questioning dichotomous criteria for gender attributions that the dichotomous nature of gender, itself, becomes problematic.

The Primacy of Gender Attribution

Having provided definitions of gender assignment, gender identity, and gender role, we now explore how these components form the foundation for some gender-based categories which our society has for describing people: transsexual/nontranssexual; transvestite/nontransvestite; homosexual/heterosexual. What we demonstrate through this discussion is that knowing someone's gender assignment, identity, or role, or knowing that they belong in one of the gender-based categories, or even knowing *all* of this will give a great deal of information about a person but will not inform the person's gender because there will never be sufficient information for a definite gender attribution to be made. However, once a gender attribution has been made, the meaning of gender-related information for any particular individual can be interpreted.

TRANSSEXUAL

"Transsexualism is the conviction in a biologically normal person of being a member of the opposite sex. This belief is these days accompanied by requests for surgical and endocrinological procedures that change anatomical appearance to that of the opposite sex." . . . By opposite sex, Stoller means opposite from that which one was assigned. (Note how the use of the word "opposite" serves to underscore the dichotomous sense of gender.)

If you know that an individual's gender identity and gender assignment conflict then you know that the person is a transsexual. This certainly gives you important information about someone, but it does not tell you whether he/she is female or male. We are not asking about biological criteria for being male or female, nor are we concerned with value judgments about "real" men and "real" women. Our interest is in the everyday process of gender attribution, a process that even members of the medical team engage in when evaluating transsexuals according to medical criteria. . . . Even when transsexuals are in transitional stages, they still receive definite gender attributions. For example, genetic males at the initial stages of estrogen treatment may look like "feminine" *men*, and at some later stage may look like "masculine" *women*. No matter what stage of "transformation" transsexuals we have met were in, in each and every case it has been possible, necessary, and relatively easy for us to make a gender attribution.

Once a gender attribution has been made the "transsexual" label becomes clarified. For example, if you attribute "man" to a person who is a male (assignment) to female (identity) transsexual, you know that he has not begun to "pass"[5] or is not "passing" well. On the other hand, if you make the gender attribution "female" to this person, you know that she is credible as a woman in every way. Gender attribution gives meaning to the gender-based category.

[5]The term "passing" commonly refers to being taken for something one is really not. For example, a Black person who is light-skinned might attempt to be taken for a white person. In this sense she/he is passing as white. Our usage, on the other hand, carries no implication that a person is *really* not what she/he appears to be. . . . In the sense that we mean passing, everyone is passing, i.e., doing something in order to be taken as she/he intends.

TRANSVESTITE

Clinically, a transvestite is someone whose gender identity corresponds to her/his assignment, but who obtains erotic pleasure by dressing ("dress" includes hairstyle and accessories) as the other gender. Only when the gender of the individual's dress is in conflict with *both* assignment and identity is that individual labeled "transvestite." (We recognize that the female/male dichotomization of dress is forced because it ignores the fact that some individuals dress androgynously and that most transvestites cross-dress only on occasion.)

There is some question as to whether "transvestite," in the preceding sense, is an appropriate category for an individual with a female assignment and a female identity who dresses as a male, since there is no evidence that dressing in male clothing (e.g., jockey shorts) is erotic for someone with a female identity. Nevertheless, there are women who dress as the male gender role dictates. Therefore, we will talk about "cross-dressing," a more neutral term which does not imply eroticism.

Knowing that someone is a cross-dresser does not tell you if they are a woman or a man. Knowing that they are a woman or a man, on the other hand, allows you to make an interpretation of their cross-dressing. The clinical usage of "transvestite" contrasts with the everyday usage of the term. A transvestite, for most people, is someone who is *known* to be one gender but who dresses as the other, for example, a man who wears female clothes. Some transvestites are called "drag queens." Such individuals are often assumed to be mimicking the members of the other gender or trying to be like them rather than responding to a fetish. . . . This may be especially true in regard to females who cross-dress. The term "butch" implies imitation rather than eroticism. People categorize a person as a transvestite based on the gender attribution they have made about that person and their conclusion that this gender attribution conflicts with the way the person is dressed. In everyday life we rarely if ever, have any knowledge of another's gender identity or gender assignment. The fact that the attribution comes first, suggests that neither knowing how people dress, nor their gender identity, nor their gender assignment is necessary in order to make a gender attribution.

HETEROSEXUAL/HOMOSEXUAL

People are classified as heterosexual or homosexual on the basis of their gender and the gender of their sexual partner(s). When the partner's gender is the same as the individual's, then the person is categorized as homosexual. When the partner's gender is other than the individual's, then the label "heterosexual" is applied. (The label "lesbian" is dependent on a definite prior gender attribution, i.e., that both partners are female.) This homosexual/heterosexual distinction is as forced as the others, since clearly there are degrees of preference in sexual partner choice.

This gender-based categorization makes the primacy of gender attribution particularly salient. Knowing that someone is homosexual or heterosexual tells you something about the person, but it does not tell you if they are male or female. In fact, attaching one of these gender-based labels to someone first of all depends on the gender attributions made about *both* partners (e.g., that one is male and the other is female). The gender attribution determines the label "homosexual" or "heterosexual" but the label itself does not lead to a gender attribution.

FEMININE/MASCULINE

We have discussed how the way one dresses and the inferences made regarding the motivation to dress in a particular way, whom one chooses as a sexual partner, and whether one's identity is in accord with one's gender assignment, determine whether one is placed in a particular gender-based category with its own name, etiology, and prognosis. One's interests, activities, and personality traits, on the other hand, do not have this status. Although people rarely exhibit only male or only female interests, and so on, an individual who has predominantly male interests, as defined by the particular culture, is "masculine," and an individual with predominantly female interests is "feminine." ("Effeminate" describes men who caricature stereotypical femi-

nine behavior. Obviously, in order to use this adjective, a gender attribution must already have been made.) Interests, activities, and personality traits give no information about the type of gender attribution that would be made, but knowing the person's gender would give meaning to their "masculinity" or "femininity."

There are no separate nouns in the English language to refer to people with stereotypical male or female interests. The slang terms "pansy" or "bulldyke" refer more to expressive style, in conjunction with choosing a sexual partner of the same gender, than they do to interests, activities, and personality traits. The fact that we have nouns for style but only adjectives for interests is important, because style may be a cue for gender attribution, whereas interests may not.

Conclusion

Knowing the relationship among the gender components is, as we have shown, not sufficient for making a gender attribution. What is the gender of a masculine, homosexual, transsexual who cross-dresses? Not even having concrete information about these components is sufficient. Consider the following: (1) Lee was assigned the gender "male" at birth. (2) Ronnie has a female gender identity. (3) Chris wears female clothing and hair styles. (4) Sandy chooses men as sexual partners. (5) Leslie has feminine interests and engages in feminine activities. Do any of these pieces of information tell you whether Lee, Ronnie, Chris, Sandy, or Leslie are men or women? For example, Lee might be a man, or, on the other hand, Lee could . . . have been born with an enlarged clitoris that was mistaken for a penis. If this were discovered early enough, a "reassignment" could have been made and Lee might be a woman. Or, Lee might be a postoperative transsexual, and therefore a woman in just about any sense of the word.

This same type of exercise could be done for the rest of the examples. It becomes clear that no *one* piece of information about a component of gender is sufficient for making a gender attribution.

Not only are we not able to make gender attributions from only one piece of information, but the knowledge itself is relatively meaningless without a prior gender attribution. For example, if you already know Sandy is a man, the fact that Sandy chooses men as sexual partners conveys very different information than it does if you know that Sandy is a woman.

Even information about *all* the components is insufficient. Is a person with a male gender assignment, a female gender identity, male interests, male sexual partners, and female clothing, a male or a female?

There is no way to answer this question in the absence of concrete interaction with the individual described. No amount of descriptive information we could give you about the person would allow you to attribute gender with absolute certainty, short of our making the attribution for you. Information about secondary gender characteristics might enable you to make a more educated guess than knowledge about gender components or gender-based categories alone. You might be right most of the time in guessing that a feminine heterosexual with facial hair, a deep voice, and broad shoulders was someone to whom you would make a "male" gender attribution were you to interact with the person. However, the person could turn out to be a woman, and your tentative gender attribution would just be a guess. Gender attributions are not guesses. In our everyday world people are either male or female, not probably one or the other.

Even knowledge about what many consider the ultimate criteria for telling women from men, namely genitals, is not the answer. Attributions are almost always made in the absence of information about genitals, and most people do not change their gender attributions even if they discover that someone does not have the "appropriate" genitals. On occasion, friends of ours have interacted with persons whom they later accidentally discovered were preoperative transsexuals. In other words, they found out that someone about whom they had made a gender attribution did not have the "right" genitals. In no case did they change their gender attribution in light of this knowledge, although there may have been changes in other attributions made about the person. Secondary gender characteristics and genitals are important cues, but they are never sufficient for making a gender attribution. Whether someone is a man or a woman is determined in the course of interacting. . . .

The primacy of gender attribution becomes obvious when we recognize that assignment and identity can be seen as special cases of attribution, and, even more importantly, that in order to meaningfully interpret someone's assignment, identity, and role, and the relationship among them, *one must first attribute gender.* Identity, role, and assignment are not the same as attribution, but they can only be interpreted when placed in context by the gender attribution process.

The gender attribution process is the method by which we construct our world of two genders. As we mentioned earlier, a defining feature of reality construction is to see our world as being the only possible one. . . .

Study Questions on Suzanne Kessler and Wendy McKenna

1. What do Kessler and McKenna mean by *gender attribution, gender assignment, gender identity,* and *gender role?* Apply each of these terms to Jan Morris. In what sense do Kessler and McKenna believe that gender attribution is primary?
2. We normally think of gender attribution as something that can be done by simple inspection. Why do the authors disagree?
3. Do you agree that asking what it means to be a male or a female is the same as asking how one decides whether another is male or female? What philosophical assumptions underlie this claim?
4. In what cases, if any, would you stick with the attribution of gender to someone if you discovered that the person had the genitals of the sex opposite to the one you thought he or she was?

Sex Roles and the Ideal Society

RICHARD WASSERSTROM

Richard Wasserstrom here defends one conception of a nonsexist society—one in which an individual's sex is of no more importance than his or her eye color in our own. In such a society, bisexuality, not homosexuality or heterosexuality, would be the normative sexual orientation. Wasserstrom appeals to the restrictive character of all role-differentiated living in support of this proposal.

. . . [O]NE CONCEPTION OF A NONRACIST SOCIETY is that which is captured by what I shall call the assimilationist ideal: a nonracist society would be one in which the race of an individual would be the functional equivalent of the eye color of individuals in our society today. In our society no basic political rights and obligations are determined on the basis of eye color. No important institutional benefits and burdens are connected with eye color. Indeed, except for the mildest sort of aesthetic preferences, a person would be thought odd who even made private, social decisions by taking eye color into account. It would, of course, be unintelligible, and nor just odd, were a person to say today that while he or she looked blue-eyed, he or she regarded himself or herself as really a brown-eyed person. Because eye color functions differently in our culture than does race, there is no analogue to passing for eye color. Were the assimilationist ideal to become a reality, the same would be true of one's race. In short, according to the assimilationist ideal, a nonracist society would be one in which an individual's race was of no more significance in any of these three areas than is eye color today.

What is a good deal less familiar is an analogous conception of the good society in respect to sexual differentiation—one in which an individual's sex were to become a comparably unimportant: characteristic. An assimilationist society in respect to sex would be one in which an individual's sex was of no more significance in any of the three areas than is eye color today. There would be no analogue to transsexuality, and, while physiological or anatomical sex differences would remain, they would possess only the kind and degree of significance that today attaches to the physiologically distinct eye colors persons possess.

It is apparent that the assimilationist ideal in respect to sex does not seem to be as readily plausible and obviously attractive here as it is in the case of race. In fact, many persons invoke the possible realization of the assimilationist ideal as a reason for rejecting the Equal Rights Amendment and indeed the idea of women's liberation itself. The assimilationist ideal may be just as good and just as important an ideal in respect to sex as it is in respect to race, but it is important to realize at the outset that this appears to be a more far-reaching proposal when applied to sex rather than race and that many more persons think there are good reasons why an assimilationist society in respect to sex would not be desirable than is true for the comparable racial ideal. Before such a conception is assessed, however, it will be useful to provide a somewhat fuller characterization of its features. . . .

To begin with, it must be acknowledged that to make the assimilationist ideal a reality in respect to sex would involve more profound and fundamental revisions of our institutions and our attitudes than would be the case in respect to race. On the institutional level we would, far instance, have to alter significantly our practices concerning marriage. If a nonsexist society is a society in which one's sex is no more significant than eye color in our society today, then laws which require the persons who are getting married to be of different sexes would clearly be sexist laws.

More importantly, given the significance of role differentiation and ideas about the psychological differences in temperament that are tied to sexual identity, the assimilationist ideal would be incompatible with all psychological and sex-role differentiation. That is to say, in such a society the ideology of the society would contain no proposition asserting the inevitable or essential attributes of masculinity or feminity; it would never encourage or discourage the ideas of sisterhood or brotherhood; and it would be unintelligible to talk about the virtues or the disabilities of being a woman or a man. In addition, such a society would not have any norms concerning the appropriateness of different social behavior depending upon whether one were male or female. There would be no conception of the existence of a set of social tasks that were more appropriately undertaken or performed by males or by females. And there would be no expectation that the family was composed of one adult male and one adult female, rather than, say, just two adults—if two adults seemed the appropriate number. To put it simply, in the assimilationist society in respect to sex, persons would not be socialized so as to see or understand themselves or others as essentially or significantly who they were or what their lives would be like because they were either male or female. And no political rights or social institutions, practices, and norms would mark the physiological differences between males and females as important.

Were sex like eye color, these kinds of distinctions would make no sense. Just as the normal, typical adult is virtually oblivious to the eye color of other persons for all significant interpersonal relationships, so, too, the normal, typical adult in this kind of nonsexist society would be equally as indifferent to the sexual, physiological differences of other persons for all significant interpersonal relationships. Bisexuality, not heterosexuality or homosexuality, would be the typical intimate, sexual relationship in the ideal society that was assimilationist in respect to sex. . . .

. . . [T]here appear to be very few, if any, respects in which the ineradicable, naturally occurring differences between males and females *must* be taken into account. The industrial revolution has certainly made any of the general differences in strength between the sexes capable of being ignored by the good society for virtually all significant human activities. And even if it were true that women are naturally better suited than men to care for and nurture children, it is also surely the case that men can be taught to care for and nurture children well. Indeed, the one natural or biological fact that seems *required* to be taken into account is the fact that reproduction of the human species requires that the fetus develop *in utero* for a period of months. Sexual intercourse is not necessary, for artificial insemination is available. Neither marriage nor the nuclear family is necessary either for conception or child rearing. Given the present state of medical knowledge and what might be termed the natural realities of female pregnancy, it is difficult to see why any important institutional or interpersonal arrangements are constrained to take the existing biological differences as to the phenomenon of *in utero* pregnancy into account.

But to say all this is still to leave it a wholly open question to what degree the good society *ought* to build upon any ineradicable biological differences, or to create ones in order to construct institutions and sex roles which would thereby maintain a substantial degree of sexual differentiation. . . .

The point that is involved here is a very general one that has application in contexts having nothing to do with the desirability or undesirability of maintaining substantial sexual differentiation. It has to do with the fact that humans possess the ability to alter their natural and social environment in distinctive, dramatic, and unique ways. An example from the nonsexual area can help bring out this too seldom recognized central feature. It is a fact that some persons born in human society are born with congenital features such that they cannot walk or walk well on their legs. They are born naturally crippled or lame. However, humans in our society certainly possess the capability to devise and construct mechanical devices and institutional arrangements which render this natural fact about some persons relatively unimportant in respect to the way they and others will live together. We can bring it about, and in fact are in the process of bringing it about, that persons who are confined to wheelchairs can move down sidewalks and across streets because the curb stones at corners of intersections have been shaped so as to accommodate the passage of wheelchairs. And we can construct and arrange buildings and events so that persons in wheelchairs can ride elevators, park cars, and be seated at movies, lectures, meetings, and the like. Much of the environment in which humans live is the result of their intentional choices and actions concerning what that environment shall be like. They can elect to construct an environment in which the natural incapacity of some persons to walk or walk well is a major difference or a difference that will be effectively nullified vis-à-vis the lives that they, too, will live.

Nonhuman animals cannot do this in anything like the way humans can. A fox or an ape born lame is stuck with the fact of lameness and the degree to which that will affect the life it will lead. The other foxes or apes cannot change things. This capacity of humans to act intentionally and thereby continuously create and construct the world in which they and others will live is at the heart of what makes studies of nonhuman behavior essentially irrelevant to and for most if not all of the normative questions of social, political, and moral theory. Humans can become aware of the nature of their natural and social environment and then act intentionally to alter the environment so as to change its impact upon or consequences for the individuals living within it. Nonhuman animals cannot do so. This difference is, therefore, one of fundamental theoretical importance. At the risk of belaboring the obvious, what it is important to see is that the case against any picture of the good society of an assimilationist sort—if it is to be a defensible critique—ought to rest on arguments concerned to show why some other ideal would be preferable; it cannot plausibly rest in any significant respect upon the claim that the sorts of biological differences typically alluded to in contexts such as these require that the society not be assimilationist in character.

There are, though, several other arguments based upon nature, or the idea of the "natural" that also must be considered and assessed. First, it might be argued that if a way of doing something is natural, then it ought to be done that way. Here, what may be meant by "natural" is that this way of doing the thing is the way it would be done if culture did nor direct or teach us to do it differently. It is not clear, however, that this sense of "natural"

is wholly intelligible; it supposes that we can meaningfully talk about how humans would behave in the absence of culture. And few if any humans have ever lived in such a state. Moreover, even if this is an intelligible notion, the proposal that the natural way to behave is somehow the appropriate or desirable way to behave is strikingly implausible. It is, for example, almost surely natural, in this sense of "natural," that humans would eat their food with their hands, except for the fact that they are, almost always, socialized to eat food differently. Yet, the fact that humans would naturally eat this way, does not seem in any respect to be a reason for believing that that is thereby the desirable or appropriate way to eat food. And the same is equally true of any number of other distinctively human ways of behaving.

Second, someone might argue that substantial sexual differentiation is natural not in the sense that it is biologically determined nor in the sense that it would occur but for the effects of culture, but rather in the sense that substantial sexual differentiation is a virtually universal phenomenon in human culture. By itself, this claim of virtual universality, even if accurate, does not directly establish anything about the desirability or undesirability of any particular ideal. But it can be made into an argument by the addition of the proposition that where there is a widespread, virtually universal social practice or institution, there is probably some good or important purpose served by the practice or institution. Hence, given the fact of substantial sex-role differentiation in all, or almost all, cultures, there is on this view some reason to think that substantial sex-role differentiation serves some important purpose for and in human society.

This is an argument, but it is hard to see what is attractive about it. The premise which turns the fact of sex-role differentiation into any kind of a strong reason for sex-role differentiation is the premise of conservatism. And it is no more or less convincing here than elsewhere. There are any number of practices or institutions that are typical and yet upon reflection seem without significant social purpose. Slavery was once such an institution; war perhaps still is. . . .

To put it another way, the question that seems fundamentally to be at issue is whether it is desirable to have a society in which sex-role differences are to be retained in the way and to the degree they are today—or even at all. The straightforward way to think about the question is to ask what would be good and what would be bad about a society in which sex functioned like eye color does in our society; or alternatively, what would be good and what would be bad about a society in which sex functioned in the way in which religious identity does today; or alternatively, what would be good and what would be bad about a society in which sex functioned in the way in which it does today. We can imagine what such societies would look like and how they might work. It is hard to see how thinking about answers to this question is substantially advanced by reference to what has typically or always been the case. If it is true, for instance, that the sex-role-differentiated societies that have existed have tended to concentrate power and authority in the hands of males, have developed institutions and ideologies that have perpetuated that concentration, and have restricted and prevented women from living the kinds of lives that persons ought to be able to live for themselves, then this, it seems to me, says far more about what may be wrong with any strongly nonassimilationist ideal than does the conservative premise say what may be right about any strongly nonassimilationist ideal. . . .

One strong, affirmative moral argument on behalf of the assimilationist ideal is that it does provide for a kind of individual autonomy that a substantially nonassimilationist society cannot provide. The reason is because any substantially nonassimilationist society will have sex roles, and sex roles interfere in basic ways with autonomy. The argument for these two propositions proceeds as follows.

Any nonassimilationist society must have some institutions and some ideology that distinguishes between individuals in virtue of their sexual physiology, and any such society will necessarily be committed to teaching the desirability of doing so. That is what is implied by saying it is nonassimilationist rather than assimilationist. And any substantially nonassimilationist society will make one's sexual identity an important characteristic so that there will be substantial psychological, role, and status differences between persons who are

male and those who are female. That is what is implied by saying that it is substantially nonassimilationist. Any such society will necessarily have sex roles, a conception of the places, characteristics, behaviors, etc., that are appropriate to one sex or the other but not both. That is what makes it a *sex* role.

Now, sex roles are, I think, morally objectionable on two or three quite distinct grounds. One such ground is absolutely generic and applies to all sex roles. The other grounds are less generic and apply only to the kinds of sex roles with which we are familiar and which are a feature of patriarchal societies, such as our own. I begin with the more contingent, less generic objections.

We can certainly imagine, if we are not already familiar with, societies in which the sex roles will be such that the general place of women in that society can be described as that of the servers of men. In such a society individuals will be socialized in such a way that women will learn how properly to minister to the needs, desires, and interests of men; women and men will both be taught that it is right and proper that the concerns and affairs of men are more important than and take precedence over those of women; and the norms and supporting set of beliefs and attitudes will be such that this role will be deemed the basic and appropriate role for women to play and men to expect. Here, I submit, what is objectionable about the connected set of institutions, practices, and ideology—the structure of the prevailing sex role—is the role itself. It is analogous to a kind of human slavery. The fundamental moral defect— just as is the case with slavery—is not that women are being arbitrarily or capriciously assigned to the social role of server, but that such a role itself has no legitimate place in the decent or just society. As a result, just as in the case with slavery the assignment on *any* basis of individuals to such a role is morally objectionable. A society arranged so that such a role is a prominent part of the structure of the social institutions can be properly characterized as an *oppressive* one. It consigns some individuals to lives which have no place in the good society, which restrict unduly the opportunities of these individuals, and which do so in order improperly to enhance the lives and opportunities of others.

But it may be thought possible to have sex roles and all that goes with them without having persons of either sex placed within a position of general, systemic dominance or subordination. Here, it would be claimed, the society would not be an oppressive one in this sense. Consider, for example, the kinds of sex roles with which we are familiar and which assign to women the primary responsibilities for child rearing and household maintenance. It might be argued first that the roles of child rearer and household maintainer are not in themselves roles that could readily or satisfactorily be eliminated from human society without the society itself being deficient in serious, unacceptable ways. It might be asserted, that is, that these are roles or tasks that simply must be filled if children are to be raised in a satisfactory way. Suppose this is correct, suppose it is granted that society would necessarily have it that these tasks would have to be done. Still, if it is also correct that, relatively speaking. these are unsatisfying and unfulfilling ways for humans to concentrate the bulk of their energies and talents, then, to the degree to which this is so, what is morally objectionable is that if this is to be a *sex* role, then women are unduly and unfairly allocated a disproportionate share of what is unpleasant, unsatisfying, unrewarding work. Here the objection is the degree to which the burden women are required to assume is excessive and unjustified vis-à-vis the rest of society i.e., the men. Unsatisfactory roles and tasks, when they are substantial and pervasive, should surely be allocated and filled in the good society in a way which seeks to distribute the burdens involved in a roughly equal fashion.

Suppose, though, that even this feature were eliminated from sex roles, so that, for instance, men and women shared more equally in the dreary, unrewarding aspects of housework and child care, and that a society which maintained sex roles did not in any way have as a feature of that society the systemic dominance or superiority of one sex over the other, there would still be a generic moral defect that would remain. The defect would be that any set of sex roles would necessarily impair and retard an individual's ability to develop his or her own characteristics, talents, capacities, and potential life-plans to the extent to which he or she might desire and from which he or she might derive genuine satisfaction. Sex roles, by definition, constitute empirical and normative limits of varying degrees of strength—restrictions on what it is that one can expect to do, be, or become. As such, they are, I think, at least prima facie objectionable.

To some degree, all role-differentiated living is restrictive in this sense. Perhaps, therefore, all role differentiation in society is to some degree troublesome, and perhaps all strongly role-differentiated societies are objectionable. But the case against sex roles and the concomitant sexual differentiation they create and require need not rest upon this more controversial point. For one thing that distinguishes sex roles from many other roles is that they are wholly involuntarily assumed. One has no choice about whether one shall be born a male or female. And if it is a consequence of one's being born a male or a female that one's subsequent emotional, intellectual, and material development will be substantially controlled by this fact, then it is necessarily the case that substantial, permanent, and involuntarily assumed restraints have been imposed on some of the most central factors concerning the way one will shape and live one's life. The point to be emphasized is that this would necessarily be the case, even in the unlikely event that substantial sexual differentiation could be maintained without one sex or the other becoming dominant and developing oppressive institutions and an ideology to support that dominance and oppression. Absent some far stronger showing than seems either reasonable or possible that potential talents, abilities, interests, and the like are inevitably and irretrievably distributed between the sexes in such a way that the sex roles of the society are genuinely congruent with and facilitative of the development of those talents, abilities, interests, and the like that individuals can and do possess, sex roles are to this degree incompatible with the kind of respect which the good or the just society would accord to each of the individual persons living within it. It seems to me, therefore, that there are persuasive reasons to believe that no society which maintained what I have been describing as *substantial* sexual differentiation could plausibly be viewed as a good or just society.

Study Questions on Richard Wasserstrom

1. Explain what Wasserstrom means by a society that is assimilationist with respect to sexual differentiation. How is it parallel with a society that is assimilationist with respect to race? Why does the assimilationist model lead him to think of bisexuality as normative?

2. How does he answer the arguments of those who claim that sexual differentiation is natural? Of those who argue that because it is found in all societies it ought to be retained? In particular how would he respond to the arguments offered by Clark, and how might Clark respond? Which do you agree with more and why?

3. Does Wasserstrom give any reason for his belief that personal autonomy is of such a high value that anything which interferes with it in any way must be eliminated? Can he give a reason without falling back on some sort of conception of human nature?

4. Is Wasserstrom's ideal society possible? if so, could it be implemented without coercion, and if not, what implications does this have for personal autonomy?

5. Wasserstrom begins with a characteristically liberal emphasis on personal autonomy, but pushes it so far that he arrives at a position that can only be characterized as radical. Does this seem odd to you?

Biology, Mere and Otherwise

MARY MIDGLEY AND JUDITH HUGHES

Mary Midgley and Judith Hughes write in defense of an open-minded approach to the nature-nurture controversy, as applied to the differences between men and women. For such an approach, male-female differences may arise partly from the genetic constitution of the species, and partly from culture and history, and the task of working out the relative importance of the two is one for empirical investigation rather than ideological contention. They point to feminists' use of the term *sisterhood* (though not *motherhood*) to evoke a solidarity grounded in forms of oppression that are, in part at least, biologically based. They argue that biological influences on our behavior need be no more destructive of human freedom than cultural forces.

From Women's Choices: Philosophical Problems Facing Feminism. © *Mary Midgley and Judith Hughes. Reprinted by permission of St. Martin's Press, LLC.*

"She's a rum 'un, is Natur . . . Natur," said Mr. Squeers solemnly, *"is more easier conceived than described."*

Charles Dickens, *Nicholas Nickleby*

What Sort of Difference?

IS THE DIFFERENCE BETWEEN men and women natural, or is it produced by culture? Here is another false antithesis. In other fields today this one is usually nailed as false quite quickly, being unkindly referred to as "the old nature-nurture controversy." In most contexts, people now see that any aspect of human affairs can in principle have some biological sources in the genetic constitution of the species, and also some in recent culture and history. The two sets do not compete. The job of working out their details and relative importance is done by empirical enquiry, not by dying on the barricades.

Many feminists, however, still tend to resist this open-minded approach strongly. In the early stages of the movement they often dismissed any suggestion of natural sex differences as not only mistaken but wicked. Thus Kate Millett, complaining of "the threadbare tactic of justifying social and temperamental differences by biological ones," writes: "The sexes are inherently in everything alike, save reproductive systems, secondary sexual characteristics, orgasmic capacity, and genetic and morphological structure. Perhaps the only things they can uniquely exchange are semen and transudate." The extraordinary assumption that everything physical (the whole "genetic and morphological structure") could be different and yet everything mental could remain the same was rather widespread at that time among social scientists. Although every cell in our bodies is sexed, and although there are marked sex differences in the structure of the brain and working of the nervous system, the human spirit was treated as a separate entity, somehow immune to such gross influences. This attitude, which is luckily less common now, will be our business shortly. We must notice first, however, that Kate Millett's position cannot stand in any case because it is inconsistent with some ideas central to feminism itself.

In itself, it is understandable as a reaction to confused male theorists, who have repeatedly justified local customs in this area which were just crude devices to protect masculine interests, or which were plain foolish, as laws fixed by unalterable dictates of nature. If what we want is merely to find food for satire and indignation, shooting them down can keep us occupied for a long time. But we do not only want that. Moreover, feminists need to be careful about shooting in this direction, since they may hit their own windows.

The assumption of natural causes is such a deep-rooted one that even those who officially disown it often find that they are using it. There are two prominent feminist concepts which seem to depend on that assumption. One is the idea of the natural superiority of women, either in general or in certain special respects. (It will be remembered that the strict, exclusive definition of feminism, to which Janet Radcliffe Richards referred, included belief in "the inherent equality of the sexes *or the superiority of the female.*" (Italics ours.) These two alternatives may look alike to the casual eye, but they call for opposite views on innateness.) The other is *sisterhood*, considered—as it usually seems to be—not just as an external community in misfortune, but as a natural bond of sympathy, resting on intrinsic likeness.

Neither of these ideas makes sense without the assumption of distinct, innate dispositions in the two sexes. We shall see that there is in fact nothing alarming in this suggestion. Innate difference does not have to be inferiority; it is just difference. And as we have already seen, people do not need to be standard, indistinguishable units like frozen peas, "in everything alike," in order to be political equals. They need just enough minimal likeness to make them members of the community. We shall lose nothing by jettisoning the dogma that the two sexes have to be inherently indistinguishable. And if we want to retain the use of these two feminist concepts, we must jettison it. The use and standing of these concepts remains to be discussed. They are mentioned here just to point out that the question of natural difference is not a simple one, settled at once by reference to what is politically edifying. There are, too, some influential feminists, such as

Elaine Morgan, for whom biological considerations are central.

The issue is in any case a bit too serious for dogmatic bickering. We need the truth. In examining current attitudes to the sex difference and working to humanize them, we need the fullest understanding we can get of its real sources. To rule out the possibility of genetic ones in advance, simply because that area has been put to bad use in the past, is arbitrary. If there are such sources, even minor ones, we need to know about them. There is no substitute for this open-minded temper. Questions of fact cannot be settled in the lump on political grounds. If certain facts are dangerous, the remedy is, as usual, not suppression but more facts.

The Fear of Fatalism

All this may in general be admitted. But there is a special difficulty which apparently stops people from even considering propositions about human nature as candidates for belief. This is the suspicion of fatalism, usually described now as "biological determinism" or "genetic determinism." People feel that, if our conduct had any genetically determined causes, we would be condemned to the status of automata, doomed to stick helplessly in our grooves. Must we not therefore believe instead only in social causes, so as to give ourselves the option of initiating change?

It is a very mysterious point about this way of thinking that it treats social causes as so much less compelling than genetic ones. As is often remarked, we are all "conditioned by our culture."

This belief, however, is not thought to turn us into automata. Yet the account of social conditioning can be built up, quite as easily as that of physical causes, in such a way as to make us seem like robots. And it has the extra disadvantage that it makes social change seem impossible. Since, however, we know that social change continually takes place, there must be something wrong with this notion of conditioning—which is, indeed, a very crude one. Human beings are not lumps of putty, passively accepting a mould, but active creatures with their own individual natures, able to select among the suggestions which they get, and to transform customs, gradually and cumulatively, by their distinctive responses. It is our individual

natures, and the use we make of them, which save us from the tyranny of culture.

There is no fatalism here. Fatalism is the belief that there are, not just causes, but overwhelming and unmanageable causes, opposing and dooming the enterprises that we value. In fact, originally fatalism is the belief in unbeatable hostile beings who are bound to get us whatever we do, as in the story of Oedipus. This is something quite different from determinism, which is just the modest assumption that events in the world may be expected to be regular. This assumption is needed for everyday science, though apparently not for the study of quantum mechanics. It need not rest on private information from heaven that events actually *are* regular. It is simply a convenient assumption, made for the sake of getting on with enquiry. Deterministic calculations can indeed sometimes be depressing, because they point out awkward facts about the world which we would have wished otherwise—such as that we are probably not going to be able to invent anti-gravity, so that weights will go on being heavy to lift. But we need to know these things. And just as often they point out welcome facts, such as the reliable good qualities of the plants and animals on which we depend. And in our observations of human conduct we depend on this calculation for our general expectations of good and evil alike. Human conduct is not random and unpredictable.

No doubt there are problems about explaining the relation of these predictions to free will. But they are problems about description, not about the facts. Human choice is a matter of common experience, not a hazardous theoretical speculation. Both in ourselves and others, we are all familiar with the difference between normal, relatively free decision and decision driven by such things as threats and illicit influence from without, or by obsessions and diseases and neurotic compulsions from within. It is the latter which approximate us to automata. People do not, for instance, feel driven, automaton-like, by the talents and natural emotions which make up their inheritance. We do not think of a genius as a helpless automaton driven by a specially powerful motor. Yet genius certainly is thought of as a gift, as a piece of rather sublime luck for which the owner should be thankful, not as a pure achievement of the will. The same is true, on a more modest scale, of the gifts belonging to the rest of us. This idea of inherited gifts is not, and ought not to be, frightening. And it does not become so merely because scientists can discover a good deal about the working of our brains.

Biology is an enquiry, not a sinister force. All academic disciplines are tools, not empires. It is strangely common now for people to speak of being "threatened by their biology" and the like. Thus Shulamith Firestone writes that "women throughout history before birth control were at the continual mercy of their biology," and that the substitution of *in vitro* pregnancy for current methods would "free women from their biology." What this complaint really seems to express is a horror of the body—especially, of course, of childbirth—as a threat to the free mind and soul. We will discuss this idea shortly. But it clearly cannot be properly expressed in this way.

The impression that biology, and physical science in general, constitutes a threat seems to be a response to a certain kind of illicit scientific reductionism which brings out with an air of triumph, as if exposing a fraudulent medium, the claim that we are "nothing but" certain scientific entities. About the physical basis of thought and feeling, this is usually done by claiming that the physical phenomena—secretions and the like—which accompany our experiences are their only real causes, and concluding that people are therefore really only the pawns or playthings of their secretions. The reducer's point is to exclude souls, vital force and other extras from the scientific scene, and this he is quite entitled to do. But to suggest that this shows ordinary experience to be unreal is sheer meaningless melodrama. Certainly we think and feel by means of our brains and nervous systems. If they fail us, our thought falters. But that is true of our hearts and livers as well, and is part of our general dependence on the physical world.

As whole beings, we think with our brains just as we jump with our legs. But to understand what we are doing requires much more than the physical sciences; it calls for a grasp of our purposes and the facts in the world to which they relate, all of which are perfectly real—indeed, their reality is far less problematical than that of, say, the basic entities of physics. The neurological explanation cannot therefore be the only one—or in some sense

the only "real" one—and the reduction fails. So, and more resoundingly, does the still odder and more recent sociobiological one, which says that all we are really doing is maximizing the spread of our genes ("the organism is only DNA's way of making more DNA"). This is not biology, it is rhetoric.

What is needed in order to prevent causes from looking like fates is a full recognition of their complexity. This will show the presence of genetic causes to be inoffensive in both the areas where it impinges on left-wing thought generally and feminism in particular. The first of these areas concerns capacity, the second, motivation.

Capacity and Competition

Of these, capacity is the one which has been better ventilated and is now probably the easier to handle. That we do have inherited capacities—different from those of other species, and different again for each individual—is something which it makes little sense to deny, and which has no sinister consequences. What has made it seem dangerous is the insistence of theorists on forcing these capacities into a ranking order by means of concepts like IQ. The trouble with this is not really anything to do with inheritance. Ranking people would be just as objectionable if their capacities really were, by some miracle, formed during their childhood. It is still too late for them to do anything about it. The trouble lies in our age's obsession with the racecourse model. . . .

. . . The Greeks were obsessed enough with their Games, but we are far worse. The worship of IQs is only one aspect of this strange obsession, and the insistence that IQs are not hereditary does very little to make it less sinister. It needs to be plainly said that people's general capacities cannot be measured in this way. Measurement, by its nature, always measures a special, limited capacity relative to something already taken as a goal. But to consider people's capacities in general is to wonder, much more widely, what kinds of things each of them can or cannot do. This can call on us to recognize things as achievements, as strengths, even as aims, which we had not thought of as such before. It can alter our whole idea of what an achievement is. It is in this sort of spirit that we need to ask, with an open mind, whether there are in fact, as has often been supposed, differences in capacity between men and women.

Yin, Yang and Others

Are there then any systematic differences, any specializations here? Let us look first at the tradition. It has been very widely believed that there are, and that they are profoundly, perhaps metaphysically, important. Many peoples believe that creation arises from a mystical marriage between male and female elements, often between heaven and earth, and still expresses a combination of these two natures. The Chinese notion of "yin" and "yang," and the Aristotelian one of form and matter, are just two of many more sophisticated versions of this thinking. It has deep roots, and would not be easy to get rid of. These ideas have practical consequences, which are reflected back onto everyday life. They have also been drawn from that life in the first place. We need to look at their possible meanings.

They posit a sexual specialization which can look more or less alarming according to how you treat it. It can be formulated in a sweeping way which draws a firm line between the whole faculty of thought (male) and the faculty of feeling (female); or it can appear in a less drastic version which deals only with specialization within thought itself, and holds that men reason logically and articulately, while women use intuition—that is, they reach the same cognitive goals by different and more mysterious means. These are very different ideas, and need to be looked at separately.

We had better look first at the more sweeping yin/yang or reason/emotion kind of formula. Its symbolic and religious uses do not concern us now. At a very abstract level, it may have a real point. But we want to know what it says about actual men and women, and what consequences for them flow from accepting it. And here there is an obvious danger. Unless the interdependence of these elements is strongly stressed we will be landed with a sharp division of labour, in which women are not expected to think, nor men to feel. And though this sort of specialization cannot possibly be kept up in actual life, it does seem to have operated as a background ideal in our culture, and caused a mass of confusions.

Its clearest expression in modern times may have been that of Otto Weininger, the brilliant young Austrian follower of Schopenhauer, whose psychology influenced Freud. Weininger's MW theory posited two basic elements in every human being, never found in isolation but existing everywhere as polar extremes. Of these, the M factor was responsible for everything positive, active and intellectual, while the W stood simply for emotion. Absolute W, if she existed, would be wholly unconscious. She has no cognitive element at all. (Weininger unfortunately shot himself when he found that his reasoning proved him to be homosexual, so he never explained his ideas further.)

The trouble about this kind of thing is that it rules out, *a priori,* any possibility of noticing the distinctive forms of female life and character. This is what made it so easy for Freud to give his account of women as a kind of shadowy, defective non-man, forever haunted by penis envy. Emotion on its own figures here as a kind of elemental force, a head of steam or water-power, which needs specifically male thinking before it can be translated into any kind of action. The formulation differs from the old Aristotelian one where emotion, equally with women, is treated as passive. Weininger seems to see both rather as the energy-source of all activity. He thus expresses, more directly than the older formulas, the terror of woman as a strange, uncontrollable force. But he calms this anxiety by keeping the idea that she is essentially formless and indeterminate. Until programmed by some male instructions, the whirlwind will not, it seems, know what to do. . . .

Sisterhood and Motherhood

. . . The degree to which male dominance is a general feature of [human cultures] has been questioned. But there is no doubt about something else, which has to be happening before that question can even arise—namely the universal division of men and women into separate groups, with distinct social roles. Why would this happen if they did not differ in character? It is no use accounting for this as a case of the strong oppressing the weak, because that can be done without any division of roles at all. Some women, too, are stronger than some men, and in any case many of the differences do not seem to have anything to do with oppression. They are just differences, not tyrannies.

This notion of a natural, irremovable likeness binding women and distinguishing them from men is taken for granted as underlying the notion of sisterhood, which has been so important to the women's movement. It is scarcely possible to think of that bond as just a link connecting fellow-sufferers from a particular kind of deceptive or distorting treatment—a conditioning which has persuaded women that they were different. If that were the idea, women's groups would surely want to *cure* them of the illusion, and send them out into the world as individuals who would no longer specially need each other's company. Far from this, women cultivate their own distinctness, and find great relief in discovering not just that other women share their misfortunes, but that they respond to them similarly. This cannot possibly just mean that, as behaviourism requires, they have been stamped in the same mill.

The thinking of the women's movement, then, already agrees with the anthropological evidence which indicates that women and men are not a single standard item. . . . Characteristic sex differences in the average levels of hormones have long been known, and more recently considerable differences in the arrangements of the two brain hemispheres are also emerging. Of course misuse of this evidence must be resisted, but that is a different thing from dismissing it all wholesale as irrelevant to psychology. That dismissal shows not just a disregard for the unity of science, but also a more than Christian desire to detach the soul from the physical world, which we must presently consider.

Against all these considerations, what horrific objection still stands? Undoubtedly, the obstacle is still the peculiarly crude and unreal idea, still current, of what an innate disposition is. This is well seen in Elisabeth Badinter's book, *The Myth of Motherhood*. This book is devoted to proving that women have "no natural maternal instinct." The word "instinct" is freely used in it, but the author refuses to define that word, saying that everybody knows perfectly well what it means. But unluckily they do not, as she herself shows. She cites evidence from history to show many cases where women have neglected and ignored their children. This shows indeed that there is no automatic, sim-

ple, unfailing mechanism which secures that women will care for children. But then instincts never are mechanisms of this simple unfailing kind. Even weaver birds, whose nest-building is indeed instinctive, can fail to build nests at the proper time, or can build them badly: something can go wrong. In any case the parental instincts of animals are not, properly speaking, detailed, "closed" instincts of this kind at all. They are what Tinbergen has called "major instincts"—general tendencies to a *kind* of behaviour.

Other examples, comparable to parental interest, are curiosity, hunting, cleanliness or fear. Each of these general groupings typically contains a number of more specific behaviour patterns which are appropriate to it. A bird with strong parental motivation is likely to brood its chicks, and also to bring them food if they are hungry. But this same motivation can also lead to a wide variety of other, miscellaneous, activity which is not in itself instinctive at all, such as protecting them from new dangers and helping them out of new difficulties. Thus a mother elephant, swept away with her calf by a flooded river, was seen to perform the unparalleled feat of lifting the calf with her trunk and placing it on a ledge in safety from the water. The action resulted from general maternal instinct, but was not regular "instinctive behaviour" in the simple sense of a fixed action pattern like nest-building. In a dangerous and changing world, this range of behaviour is highly variable and complex, especially with intelligent creatures. . . .

Primate mothers are in general particularly devoted parents. Because of their high intelligence baby primates cannot mature quickly. They need a long period of dependence, during which they learn flexible behaviour, instead of relying on a few basic instinctive patterns and a little experience to make them independent. Mothers must therefore not just keep their babies alive, but take a real interest in them, play with them, show them what they need to know and generally draw them into the community. They are not left alone to do this. Males, other females and particularly other young play a very important part in the process. A liking for children thus becomes a strong general emotional tendency in primates, as in other very social creatures. In some species, too, fathers or other males play a special part in this bonding. And it seems clear that our own species owes its success to an important degree to becoming one of these. All the same, even in these species the mother remains the irreplaceable centre of her infant's life. Although bouts of exploration soon interrupt the period of total dependence and grow longer and longer as growth proceeds, they are still for a very long time alternated with returns to the mother for comfort and reassurance, particularly if anything goes wrong. This rhythm of adventure and return to base is fundamental to the development of the young. Primate mothers have to show, and commonly do show, just those qualities of devotion, patience and intelligent affection for which human mothers are justly celebrated.

The Existentialist Protest

Are we, however, forbidden by respect for human dignity to draw any conclusions from this about maternity in human beings? Was there a total change—a miraculous Rise of Man, in which our species levitated away from the physical world altogether—when this whole instinctive mechanism vanished and was replaced by the radically different workings of social conditioning? Or did advanced intellect and culture emerge rather as a further development, enriching and organizing these simpler motivations into a new and splendid whole, not needing to destroy them first?

The first idea, which treats nature and culture as sharply exclusive alternatives, is one of the false antitheses which are the main business of this book.

This awkward cleavage is still popular among some social scientists; but no adequate reason for it, or plausible story about how it could occur, has ever been given. And in any detailed application it produces endless difficulties, of which the batch concerning motherhood are typical. How is it really supposed to work? Are the hormonal arrangements (which in human beings are very similar to those in the higher apes) supposed to have lost their function, become idle and ceased to be connected with the emotions? Or do they stay connected but only one way round—are they now passive, accepting social conditioning from outside but contributing nothing of their own? Is there now one-way causation? If this strange state of

affairs were really working, nobody surely ought to be able to have emotions which their society did not demand of them. But they do, and it happens notoriously in this very case of motherhood.

On the one hand, some mothers cannot feel the love for their children which their society unanimously demands of them. Their instinctive responses fail, as do those of some apes. On the other, mothers often persist tenaciously in loving and clinging to babies whom their societies require them to forget. This has often happened in the case of illegitimate babies. To retain them was often certain to wreck the mother's life. Some indeed were lightly abandoned:

> Sink ye or swim ye, my bonny babe,
> For ye'll get no more of me.

But many were kept in the face of appalling difficulties and continued to supply the central motivation of their mothers' lives, compensating for the general rejection of society. There have been recent cases, too, of girls arranging to have their babies adopted, and finding to their intense surprise after the birth that they could not do so because of the unexpected bond which had developed. (It is a common experience of mothers to be surprised by the nature and strength of this bond, even when they expected, in a general way, that something of the sort would appear.) If we are tempted to say that what happens here is still some expression of local Christian ideas on what ought to happen, it is worth noticing how things go in societies where ideas are different. In classical Greece, a poor country where infanticide was socially accepted as a proper and necessary way of controlling population, mothers (it is said) still voiced their indignant protests in the teeth of respectable opinion.

Those who are determined to admit only social causes usually deal with this kind of evidence by saying that the conditioning must have been more complex than it looked—that there has been counter-conditioning at a deeper level, producing the conflicting motives. At this point, however, the notion of conditioning stops being an empirical one at all. If unnoticed conditioning can always be invoked as a hidden cause, anything goes.

It is very interesting that feminists should treat motherhood so differently from sisterhood. Obviously, one reason for this is the way in which the idealization of motherhood has been misused to justify narrowing women's lives. . . . Simone de Beauvoir, among many others, declares that there is something not just frightening, but metaphysically degrading, about pregnancy and childbirth. A pregnant woman is, she says, "alienated"; in her, the species is taking over the individual; she is "in the iron grip of the species." Both the father and the child are violating her sacred individuality.

Moreover, she will not be recompensed for this outrage by achieving anything of value. She is merely being used as a passive, uninvolved vehicle:

> The [primitive] woman who gave birth, therefore, did not know the pride of creation; she felt herself the plaything of obscure forces, and the painful ordeal of childbirth seemed a useless and even troublesome accident. But in any case, giving birth and suckling are not *activities*, they are natural functions; no project is involved; and that is why woman found in them no reason for a lofty affirmation of her existence—she submitted passively to her biologic fate.

The premiss needed to make sense of this amazing piece of nonsense is the existentialist one that no act has value unless it is an entirely solitary choice and achievement. Since most human enterprises are in fact communal, it is hard, by these rules, to find anything at all which is worth doing. Everybody (including, of course, the artist) relies deeply on tradition. Everybody wants their achievements to be received and valued by others. The romantic idea of a dignity which could be sustained in solitude is grotesque. The examples which Simone de Beauvoir gives of genuine, male, forms of creation are the invention of "the stick and the club with which he armed himself." These, it seems, are new, whereas going on having the same old babies and decorating the same old houses, century after century, "imprisons her in repetition and immanence." But if creativity means

only doing a thing for the first time, it seems rather a minor value, and men are going to spend as much of their time without it as women.

What matters, most of the time, is doing the expected thing in the right way, which will sometimes (but not always) be a new and better way. This plainly can just as well be done when practising the difficult arts of childbirth and suckling and house-decorating as when hunting. The idea that there is something specially passive about these demanding occupations is a piece of ignorant traditional foolishness. Occasionally Simone de Beauvoir does see this, at least over sexual intercourse:

> As a matter of fact, man, like woman, is flesh, therefore passive, the plaything of his hormones and of the species, the restless prey of his desires. And she, like him, in the midst of the carnal fever, is a consenting, a voluntary gift, an activity; they live out in their several fashions the strange ambiguity of existence made body.

That goes for childbirth too. There is plenty of scope for initiative in both activities. Nietzsche and Sartre, moreover, were not just making a mistake. They were making a special kind of directed mistake. Their peculiar idea of human dignity and independence is specifically a male one and is designed as such. One point of it is to elevate the male condition and represent the female one as degraded. It is just as easy, if one is interested in this sort of game, to exalt the female as being the only one who can break through the bounds of solitude, who can have the mystical experience of being both one and two, and who therefore is not afraid of otherness and constitutes our species's link with the glories of the physical universe. Either sex can, if it likes, claim superiority. You can take your choice. But it is best to take it while remembering that both parties are here for keeps.

Study Questions on Mary Midgley and Judith Hughes

1. What was Kate Millet's understanding of sex differences, and what is Midgley and Hughes's criticism of her view?

2. Many people believe that if sexual differences are biologically based then this takes away our freedom, but if they are the result of social conditioning then our freedom is not constrained. How do Midgley and Hughes argue against this view?
3. Why do feminists treat sisterhood and motherhood so differently? Do you agree with Midgley and Hughes that they are being inconsistent?
4. Are Midgley and Hughes committed to the view that "biology is destiny"? What do you think they would say about transsexualism?

Sex and Gender

ROGER SCRUTON

> Roger Scruton argues that, though there is a biological basis for our sexual conduct, it does not provide the core of sexual experience. Sexual difference is nonetheless a prominent and immovable part of sexual life. Even if there is no such thing as a "natural" distinction of gender, the "Kantian feminist" view—that, fundamentally, I am a person to whom bodily difference of sex is irrelevant—is untenable. For gender is as much as personhood an inescapable feature of our world, no less real through being our own construction.

MEN REPRODUCE SEXUALLY, and, biologically speaking, reproduction is the function of the sexual act. That platitude has enormous consequences for our subject and two will be of particular concern to us. First, it is sometimes argued that the reproductive function of the sexual act is part of its nature *as an act.* Hence sexual performance severed from its reproductive consequences—as in homosexual or contracepted intercourse—is a different act, intentionally and perhaps also morally, from the sexual act allied to its biological function. According to that view, reproduction is not only a biological but also a spiritual feature of the sexual act.

In the present chapter I shall consider another, related thought, suggested by the biological destiny of human desire. It is evident that there are things which are not persons, with neither self-knowledge nor responsibility, which also reproduce sexually, and which are therefore compelled by whatever urge induces them to engage in the act of copulation, and rewarded by whatever pleasure accompanies its performance. We must surely be subject to the same urges, and the same pleasures, as govern the reproductive activities of other sexual beings. Why is that not the basic fact of sexual experience? There may indeed be interpersonal attitudes of the kind that I have described—attitudes of love and desire, attached by whatever cultural process to the basic urge to copulate. Nevertheless it is the urge which is fundamental, and which reveals the truth of our condition.

. . . The objection raises in its widest form the general subject of the relation between our erotic lives as persons and our sexual lives as animals. It therefore bears once again on the vexed question of embodiment: the question, how can one and the same thing be both a person and an animal?

From Sexual Desire: A Moral Philosophy of the Erotic *by Roger Scruton.* © 1986 by *Roger Scruton. Reprinted with permission from The Free Press, a division of Simon & Schuster, Inc.*

I shall argue that there is indeed a biological basis to our sexual conduct; but I shall reject the implication that it provides the core of sexual experience. The best way to understand the position for which I shall argue is in terms of an analogy. A tree grows in the soil, from which it takes its nourishment, and without which it would be nothing. And it would be almost nothing *to us* if it did not also spread itself in foliage, flower and fruit. In a similar way, human sexuality grows from the soil of the reproductive urge, from which it takes its life, and without which it would be nothing. Furthermore, it would be nothing *for us,* if it did not flourish in personal form, clothing itself in the flower and foliage of desire. When we understand each other as sexual beings, we see, not the soil which lies hidden beneath the leaves, but the leaves themselves, in which the matter of animality is intelligible, only because it has acquired a personal form. Animal and person are, in the end, inextricable, and just as the fact of sexual existence crucially qualifies our understanding of each other as persons, so does our personal existence make it impossible to understand sexuality in "purely animal" terms.

Sex and Gender

I have conducted the entire discussion until this point without explicitly mentioning sex—the fact, that is, of sexual differentiation. The reader might reasonably wonder what *sex* has to do with the interpersonal attitude that I have been describing. Of course, sexual desire does not occur only between people of different sex: an account of sexual desire that could not be extended to homosexuality would be ludicrous in itself and also totally ineffective as a basis for coherent moral judgement. It is surely one of the vital questions of sexual morality, whether homosexual is morally distinguishable from heterosexual intercourse. If the first is not an expression of desire, it would be difficult to see in what terms this question could be posed, let alone answered.

Even in homosexuality, however, the fact of sexual differentiation is a prominent, and indeed immovable, part of the experience. The male homosexual desires the other (in the first instance) *as a man;* the female homosexual desires the other (in the first instance) *as a woman.* Of course there

are complexities here: I may, for example, desire you as a man, but only on condition that you also play at being a woman. Nevertheless, the complexities are no different from those which attend the sex-lives of heterosexuals. It is integral to both heterosexual and homosexual experience that the object is a sexual being, and a representative of the particular sex that is his. It is only on this assumption, I shall argue, that the phenomena of homosexual love become intelligible.

Such thoughts already alert us to a vital distinction—that between the material and the intentional concepts of sexuality. The material concept of sexuality is the concept of a division between natural kinds—the division, in most cases, between male and female. In the material sense, it is for science to determine what it is to be male or female, and to describe the biological and functional characteristics of sexual union. In this sense, it is clear that we have discovered much about sexuality; indeed, it could be said that no one knew very much about it until a century ago.

In the intentional sense, however, people knew as much before the Darwinian revolution as after it. (Indeed, they probably knew more.) The intentional concept of sexuality is of a perceivable division within the world of phenomena, which incorporates not only the distinct observable forms of man and woman, but also the differences in life and behaviour which cause us selectively to respond to them. I shall refer to this intentional distinction as that between masculine and feminine *gender*—thereby giving a respectable use to a term that has a disreputable history.

In addition to the concept of gender, it is also important to acknowledge the varying *conceptions* and the varying ideals which have been associated with it. To the extent that you and I both distinguish the masculine and the feminine in the immediate objects of experience, and identify the same central examples of each, then we share a concept of gender. But you may associate with that concept a variety of beliefs about men and women which I reject; in which case we have separate conceptions of the distinction. Likewise, I may have an ideal of masculine conduct, or of feminine conduct, which is repugnant to you. And both of us may disagree in our conceptions and ideals, while agreeing not only in our possession of the concept of gender, but also in our possession of the concept of sex. We may even have identical *conceptions* of sex—accepting the same body of scientific reports and theories about the real distinction between woman and man. The separation of concept, conception and ideal is familiar to philosophers. But it is important to refer to it at the outset, before entering a terrain that is fraught with moral and intellectual dangers.

Failure to distinguish sex and gender—to distinguish the material base from the intentional superstructure—is responsible for many interesting confusions, and in particular for the once popular attempt to identify a masculine and a feminine character, and to associate these characters with the separate physiological conditions of man and woman. . . .

. . . I propose, in what follows, to explore the concept of gender, and to show its place in focussing the experience of sexual union. It has been argued that distinctions of gender are entirely arbitrary, and may be either abolished or constructed in any way, depending upon the social conventions, prejudices and ideological purpose of the person who makes them. Such, at any rate, is a frequent claim of feminists, as well as of certain exponents of "gay liberation." For such thinkers, there is no such thing as a "natural" distinction of gender, even though there is a natural distinction between the sexes. . . .

Gender Construction

Gender denotes, in my usage, an intentional classification: an order elicited in reality by our way of seeing and responding to it. But in this case we are also the object of our classification, and have a consuming interest in the facts which it records. Hence the existence of the classification changes the thing described: we match reality to our perception, and so justify the intentional understanding that is expressed in it. The phenomenon perceived through the concept of gender is also to some extent the product of that concept.

The term "gender" therefore verges on ambiguity—or, at least, it has two semantic levels. It expresses the concept which informs our intentional understanding of sex; it also denotes the artefact which we construct in response to that understanding, and whereby we embellish, exag-

gerate or conceal our sexual nature. In such a case, to parody Frege, sense does not merely *determine* reference; it also changes it. In what follows, therefore, I shall use the term "gender" to denote both a way of perceiving things and a particular artificial feature of the thing perceived (its "gender construction").

There are other concepts belonging to our intentional understanding which have this effect of changing the reality to which they are applied. One such is the concept of the person. By seeing ourselves as persons, we also motivate ourselves to *become* persons—to reconstruct ourselves according to the requirements of a fundamental perception. I shall suggest that we cannot engage in this "personal construction" without engaging in gender construction too.

Kantian Feminism

In so arguing, I shall be expressly opposing the philosophical picture behind the claims considered above. I shall describe this picture in its clearest form, as the "Kantian feminist" theory of gender. According to this theory, what I really and fundamentally am, for myself and for another, is a person. My nature as a person establishes completely and exclusively all my claims to be treated with consideration, and is the true basis of every interpersonal reaction to me. Although I am incarnate, my being so is, so to speak, the instrument of my "realisation," in the public world of personal emotion. My personality is distinct from its bodily form, and is the true locus of my rights, my privileges, my values, my choices and—to use the Kantian term—my "freedom." Features of my body, which distinguish my body from yours, cannot give reasonable ground for any judgement as to my nature as a person. If am crippled, or black, or handsome, I am as much a person as you, who are whole, white and ugly. The category "person" is a unity: there is only *one* kind of thing that falls under it, and distinctions between persons are simply distinctions among accidental personal properties—distinctions expressed and revealed in free choices. There is no real distinction between the masculine and the feminine, except in so far as human freedom has been bent in certain directions, by whatever social pressures, so as to take on two contrasting forms. Distinctions of gender cannot lie in the *nature of things*. For, while there may be two kinds of human body—the male and the female—there cannot be two corresponding kinds of human *person*. For that would mean attributing these bodily distinctions to the "freedom" of the persons which they divide, in the way that the racist attributes the race or skin colour of another to his responsibility. Although the enslaved black wears the character induced by his slavery, he is, in himself, something independent of the social conditions which produced him. To say that he wears his personality *by nature*—as in the Aristotelian defence of slavery—is to say that his physiological distinction from his white master is the outward sign of a distinct moral identity. The Kantian feminist argues that it is as absurd and wicked to suppose that persons are fundamentally masculine or feminine as that they are fundamentally enslaved or free. Such *natural* differences as there are, are *merely* bodily—the difference between the male and the female, the difference between the Caucasian and the Negro. All differences of personality are the outcome of social conditions which, because they are the product of choice, might also be freely altered.

That argument—which has been given eloquent expression in recent years by Simone de Beauvoir—is undeniably appealing. I have given it in what is perhaps its most popular form, as a corollary of the categorical imperative, expressed in terms of the Kantian notion of freedom. However, it can be re-expressed in the language of my previous argument, as follows: the distinction between the sexes lies in the nature of things, and, although there may be odd cases of sex change, the basic division between male and female is one between two separate natural kinds. The kind "person" is not, however, a natural kind, and divisions within the natural kind "human animal" do not imply divisions in the "social" kind "person." On the contrary. The kind "person" owes its existence to our sense that human beings are alike in respect of their rationality, and that the possession of this attribute is sufficient to found a distinct pattern of response towards them. The kind "person" ranges indifferently across all beings with a capacity for rational response, and the "deep" characteristics of the person—the possession of a first-person perspective, and of the attitude towards agency that I have called responsibility—are exemplified by every specimen, or at least are possessed alike by men and women. Hence, there is no inference from the sexual distinction within the natural kind "human being," to the gender distinction within the social kind "person." The latter is artificial, changeable and in any case not of the essence, while the former is natural, unchangeable and essential to the nature of the things which display it.

There are other kinds of feminism, and if I choose to discuss the Kantian variety, it is only on account of its intellectual purity, and its consequent ability to display what is really at stake, and not because it is intrinsically plausible. The Kantian feminist position, I contend, must be criticised on three counts. First, it assigns an implausible role to the concept of gender. Secondly, it fails to take seriously the fact of embodiment: it is at war with the truth that we *are* our bodies, and, in separating personal freedom entirely from biological destiny, it is misled by a transcendental illusion. Finally, Kantian feminism fails to recognise that, in the sense that distinctions of gender are "artificial," so too is the human person.

The Role of Gender

The feminist claims that concepts of gender have no validity outside the attitudes which they serve to convey. There is no *fact of the matter* about gender, only distinctions of attitude that can be redrawn at any time. To put it another way: the idea of gender is purely intentional; it neither engages with the material distinction between the sexes, nor does it have any explanatory purpose that would lead us to assign an independent reality to the division that it records.

That would be plausible only if the deep division between man and woman (the division of natural kind) were such that it did not intrude into our intentional understanding. To *assume* that it does not intrude is, however, to beg the question. The anti-feminist claims that the distinction between man and woman *determines* distinct responses towards the two natural kinds, and that we employ concepts of gender so as to focus those responses upon the relevant features of their objects. For the feminist, the distinction of sex is hidden, in the way that the distinction between onyx and porphyry is hidden. The two stones can be made to look very different; they can also be made to look very similar. We are interested in their similarity, and therefore we classify them together, despite the vast distinction of natural kind. Likewise, the feminist argues, men and women, considered as *persons,* can be made to seem very similar, or they can be made to seem very different. It depends upon our interests. If we choose, we can reconstruct the social world, so that the two sexes appear equally as persons. And in such a world we should have no use for the concept of gender.

The anti-feminist will argue, however, that sex is more *apparent* than that suggests, and hence that our conceptions of gender embody an attempt, not merely to project our attitudes, but to understand the inward constitution of reality. They are responsive to the *deep* facts about man and woman, in the way that the concept "ornamental marble" is not responsive to the deep facts about stones. Even if we have no knowledge of the science of sex, we may yet be responsive to the facts of sex. And one of our responses to these facts is our formation of a concept of gender. To some extent, therefore, our conceptions of gender may record the underlying facts of sexual differentiation. Indeed, if they did not, it would be difficult to see how we could describe them as conceptions of gender. They can be such only if they aim to distinguish man from woman, and the masculine from the feminine, in terms which convey the intentional content of responses that would be meaningless but for the underlying distinction of sex.

It is difficult to determine *a priori* which of those views is correct. The best we can do is to study, first, what *might* be true concerning the capacity of sex to intrude into our sexual experience, and secondly, what *is* true of the experience itself—and, in particular, how the distinction between man and woman is *seen.*

Man and Woman

It is widely recognised that the biological distinction between the sexes is not as absolute in reality

as it tends to be in our thoughts. While sexuality is not exactly a matter of degree, there is a scale upon which male and female characteristics may be placed. There are also cases which cannot be placed on this scale: cases such as hermaphroditism, in which characteristics of both sexes are exhibited, and neuterism, in which neither sex seems properly to have emerged, and the creature is endowed either with no reproductive organs at all, or with only atrophied organs, incapable of carrying out any serious sexual task. The existence of these cases leads us to an idea of sexual normality— of the man or woman, in whom everything relevant to the reproductive function is also optimally suited to it. This way of seeing sex is so natural, and relies on facts that are so vivid and so interesting to us, that it would not be surprising to find that it has permeated our conceptions of gender. In gender too, we recognise masculine and feminine characteristics, and ambiguous or puzzling cases which seem to defy classification. We also recognise a scale of masculine and feminine— although, as I shall argue below, it is a scale that is unlike other polarities. Finally our ideas of gender are saturated with a conception of normality which, while it only partly corresponds to the idea of sexual normality, contains an essential reference, if not to the function of the sexual act, at least to the nature of desire.

Far more important than the sexual scale, however, is the sexual distinction itself. Men and women differ in their bodily appearance and in their bodily capacities. They develop according to a different rhythm, and seem to possess different intellectual aptitudes. There are lessons to be drawn about the genetic constitution of men and women from the observation that they are *socially* so distinct. Men and women differ in their powers, in their energies and in their approach to practical problems. But in nothing do they differ so much as in their sexual dispositions and experiences. For women may become pregnant; and their bodies have a rhythm, and a destiny, that are conditioned by the fact of childbirth.

From the genetic point of view, the distinction between the sexes is a deep characteristic, determined from the earliest stages of foetal development by a chromosome mechanism. In a thousand ways, the development of the male is minutely different from the development of the female, and we can expect these differences to survive in enduring dispositions and biologically determined habits. But what are the implications for our idea of gender? Here it is instructive to engage in a piece of *a priori* sociobiology. The relentless struggle of the gene to perpetuate itself, which—according to the sociobiologist—is the root cause of sexual union, is furthered by distinct behaviour in the male and the female. The male helps his genes to the extent that he impregnates females, and ensures that his own offspring have a better chance of survival than their competitors. The female perpetuates her genes to the extent that she is impregnated, and is able to nourish her offspring. The genes of the male are benefited, therefore, by his determination to assert exclusive sexual use of the females whom he has impregnated, while the genes of the woman are benefited by her determination to secure the enduring cooperation of a strong, reliable male, in the maintenance of her life and the support of her offspring. These two functions are not incompatible—indeed, they form, for the sociobiologist, the true material reality that underpins the marriage contract. But they indicate that the genetic ambitions of male and female would be furthered by distinct psychological dispositions. Suppose we were to allow ourselves a little imaginative licence, and attempt to describe, from sociobiological premises, the psychological dispositions of man and woman that would be most favourable to the perpetuation of their genes. We might paint the following picture:

The man is active in the pursuit of women; he does not confine his attentions to one woman only, but moves on restlessly after new conquests, and attempts to exclude other men from enjoying their favours. Moreover, his jealousy has a peculiar focus. He is pained, not so much by the attempt by other men to help and support his woman, as by their attempt to unite with her sexually. Indeed, it is the thought of her copulating with another which causes him the greatest outrage. (Our imaginary sociobiologist would not be surprised by the tribe (described by Buffon) who close the maiden vagina with a ring, and who on marriage replace that ring with another that may be opened, although with a key guarded by the husband.) At the same time, he has a disposition to provide for

her, and to seek food and shelter that will facilitate the nourishment of his children.

The woman is not active in the pursuit of men, but modest and retiring. She thereby guarantees that she can be obtained only at the cost of effort and determination, and so ensures that her genes will unite with the strongest available strain, thus furthering their chances of survival. Once possessed, she does her utmost to secure the services of the man, and to bind him to her, so as to enjoy the fruits of his protection during the times ahead. She is jealous of other women, but her jealousy focusses not so much on the sexual act—provided it is performed in a spirit of indifference—as on the enduring relationships which threaten her own protection. She is frightened more by the thought that her man's love may be enticed away from her than by the thought of his copulating with another. To prevent what she fears, she provides comforts for him that will bind him to their common home.

The disparity between the genetic requirements of man and woman is reflected also—according to the imaginary portrait that I am offering—in the structure of male and female desire. The man will be attracted to those features in the woman which promise healthy offspring and easy childbirth. He will be moved by her youth, vitality and regular features; by her readiness for domestic life, and by her modesty. He will value chastity, and even virginity: the harbingers of his own genetic triumph. And he will try to win her by a display of strength and competence.

She, however, will respond to the man who promises the greatest protection to her offspring. She is impressed less by his youth than by his power. Everything that promises security is capable of arousing her affections, and even a far older man may excite her, provided there is, in his look, his smell, his conversation or his social manner, the necessary virtues of a father. The authoritative glance, the resolute action, the confident enjoyment of social pre-eminence: all such qualities will be as important in the woman's eyes as her youth, freshness and vitality are important in the eyes of a man. At the same time, she will not be indifferent to a man's physical character, and—like him—will be turned away by evident deformities, and by the signs of intellectual or emotional decay.

Of course, it is stretching the imagination beyond the bounds of probability to suppose that real human beings would behave like that. If sociobiology implies that they do, so much the worse for sociobiology. As a matter of fact, however, sociobiology can hardly fail to have some such implication. For it is committed to the view that reproductive behaviour is to be explained functionally, in terms of its capacity to further the propagation of the genes of those who engage in it. Moreover, it is not only sociobiology that is guilty of this horrendous description of the difference between man and woman. It seems to be a received idea of the literature of love, from Theocritus to D. H. Lawrence. Almost all agree in distinguishing male desire from female desire, male jealousy from female jealousy and male love from female love, in ways that are already suggested in my piece of *a priori* sociobiology. *Tantum imaginatio potuit suadere malorum!*

Suppose, however, that such a picture—which I have presented in the broadest outline—were true to our biological condition, and to the psychological dispositions that are rooted in it. Would this not have the greatest imaginable implications for our ideas of gender? In particular, would it not suggest that the traditional conception of gender, according to which men and women have different characters, different emotions, and different social and domestic roles, is neither a biological accident nor a social superfluity? May it not even refute the view that gender distinctions have been manufactured "for the convenience of the male," and "at the expense of the female," by a society in which men have been peculiarly dominant? (If we do not think that it refutes that view, we must explain *why* men have been so dominant. We will then be forced to suppose just the kind of biological differentiation that is being questioned.) . . .

Embodiment

At this point the reader might reasonably object that I am failing to acknowledge one of my own persistently reaffirmed premises: that the intentional and the material are conceptually distinct, and that the first is determined at best only by our *conception* of the second. Why cannot our conception of gender take whatever form is required by

our moral understanding, without regard for the scientific truth concerning sexual differentiation? For, after all, this "truth" is a comparatively recent "discovery"—perhaps even a recent invention—and more like a scientistic apology for an old ideology than a scientific basis for a new one.

While there is some force in that objection, I have already suggested that it fails to be wholly persuasive. Our conceptions of gender are permeable to our conceptions of sex, and the facts of sex are sufficiently important, and sufficiently vivid, to make an indelible impact upon our experience. We recognise the biological division between man and woman, and it is resurgent in our perceptions. But we also recognise other distinctions, not so obviously biological, which we perceive in conjunction with the biological reality. It is an integral part of the experience of sexual desire that we regard the subject as overwhelmed, in that moment, by his *sex*. It is this bodily condition which comes to the surface, and which takes command of him. And in this moment all that is associated with his existence as a sexual being—everything from his tone of voice to his social role—is gathered into his sexuality and made part of it. Gender is an elaborate social prelude; when the curtain rises, what is disclosed is not gender, but sex.

There is no doubt that we are never so revealed as animals as in the sexual act. The physical reality of the body is exposed in this act, and becomes the object of exploration and curiosity. Precisely those parts which distinguish the sexes take on the most overwhelming significance. Our perception of the animal basis of our existence is therefore shot through with our knowledge of sexual differentiation. All our attempts to elaborate or diminish the distinction, to give it social and moral identity, to redeem it from the stigma of the "merely animal," end by confirming the ultimate fact—that our nature as incarnate animals is revealed precisely in the physiology which divides us. In the final surrender to desire, we experience our incarnate nature; we know, then, the "truth" of gender: which is that, as embodied creatures, we are inseparable from our sex.

The experience of embodiment in sexual desire is, then, one of the root responses that are focussed by our concept of gender. What happens in the sexual act enforces upon us a sense of our "gender identity," while compelling us to experience the embodiment of gender in sex. At the same time, very little of the observed distinction of gender could be explained by "reference back" to the sexual act. Our perception of gender is responsive to our experience of intercourse, but far from determined by it. If the roles adopted by man and woman in the sexual act seem to explain the social distinction of gender, this is partly because the sexual act is performed under the influence of a conception of gender. In sexual intercourse I experience, not only the embodiment of my *self,* but also the incarnation of a "moral kind."

What, then, is the origin of that "moral kind"? Clearly, people attempt to signal their sex in their social behaviour, and to signal their fitness for desire. The basic differences between the sexes— hair, skin, voice, form and movement—are redeemed from their arbitrariness by being represented as integral to a moral condition. In this way, both the creation of gender and its rooting in sex become parts of a common social enterprise.

That exercise is, indeed, "culturally determined." Even if gender distinctions are in some sense natural—perhaps even inevitable—consequences of our experience of sexual embodiment, it does not follow that there is some *one* distinction of gender which every society must attempt to construct or obey. The universality of gender is, however, confirmed by the evidence of anthropologists, whose findings are summarised in the following terms by Margaret Mead:

> In every known society, mankind has elaborated the biological division of labour into forms often very remotely related to the original biological differences that provided the original clues. Upon the contrast in bodily form and function men have built analogies between sun and moon, night and day, goodness and evil, strength and tenderness, steadfastness and fickleness, endurance and vulnerability. . . .

> . . . we know of no culture that has said, articulately, that there is no difference between men and women except in the way they contribute to the next generation.

Nor is the social construction of gender confined to heterosexuals. Although the homosexual's con-

ception, both of his sex and of his gender, must inevitably reflect his predilections, he is as active in the affirmation of his gender as any heterosexual. Indeed, we may agree with Hocquenghem that if it were not for gender homosexuality would be unintelligible. The thesis of the "effeminacy" of the homosexual, once so popular, and especially among those who wished . . . to give a biological theory of homosexual behaviour, is now rightly repudiated. Although there are homosexuals who cultivate the habits and manners of the opposite sex, they are the exception rather than the rule, and in any case seldom advance beyond a state of transparent theatricality, designed to draw attention, at one and the same time, and often in a single gesture, both to their posture as a representative of one sex, and to their reality as a member of the other. We should not be surprised, therefore, at the enhanced effort of gender construction exhibited by the homosexual, whose consciousness of his own sex is magnified by his own attraction towards it. (Consider, for example, the "sun and steel" ethos of Mishima.) But the process which the homosexual exhibits at its most developed is displayed also by the rest of humanity.

The artefact of gender is not merely one of display. Men and women develop separate characters, separate virtues, separate vices and separate social roles. The modern consciousness is less disposed to admit those facts than was Aristotle, say, or Hume. Nevertheless, it cannot be denied that, whatever men and women *ought* to do, they have persistently conspired to create an effective "division of moral labour," with the virtues and aptitudes attributed to the one sex being complemented, but by no means always imitated, by the other. Hence it has often been held that a single disposition might be a virtue in one sex and a vice, or a neutral attribute, in the other. The case of chastity—mentioned in this connection by Hume—is perhaps too emotive to bear consideration. A more bearable instance is that of gossiping. This is regarded by many people as a harmless and indeed justifiable extension of woman's desire to break down the barriers of privacy and create a common social world, so blocking the secret paths to violence and immorality. The same disposition, however, is frequently regarded as the most scandalous vice in a man—indeed as a paradigm of "unmanliness," on a par with the disposition to flee from enemies or to abandon one's wife and child.

As I earlier remarked, however, this practice of "gender construction" may well be "culturally determined." If Margaret Mead is to be trusted, there are societies in which gossiping is regarded as a male prerogative, and in which women are assigned the arduous duties of organised labour, in order that men should be free to lie in the shade, discussing the great concerns of human destiny and also the trivial tidbits of the hearth. The important point is not whether a particular *conception* of gender is a human universal, but whether the *concept* of gender is such: whether human beings must experience the world according to this artificial fracture. The argument that I have given suggests at least that something integral to the experience of sex is missing without it. Without gender, sex ceases to play a part in human embodiment, and the sexual act, far from being liberated from its "mere animality," is in fact detached from its most natural moral interpretation.

Embodiment and Gender Construction

Our embodiment is no more "natural" than the phenomena that are expressed in it. It is a result of the social process which transfigures us from animal to person. Hence embodiment expresses both the compulsions and the choices which that process involves. Just as we attach our interpersonal attitudes to our bodily reality, so do we remake the body, in order that it should be a more effective vehicle for the meanings which it is instructed to reveal. The most striking example of this is provided by clothing, which dramatises the sexuality of the body in the act of concealing it. Sex is hidden, so that it might be revealed as gender. Men and women are able to perceive each other sexually in the veils which hide their sex. Thus the most daring thought of another's sexual nature may take up peaceful residence in a perception of his clothes, as when Herrick transforms his desirous perception of Julia:

When as in silks my Julia goes,
Then, then (me thinks) how sweetly flows
The liquefaction of her clothes.

The representation of the body in the clothes that cover it is matched, in Western art, by a reciprocal representation of the clothes in the body. Anne Hollander has persuasively argued that the tradition of Western erotic painting, in which the naked form provides the object of a sustained and contemplative interest, represents the body as "unclothed"— i.e. as *lacking* the clothes which "belong" to it. It is a tradition, in Kenneth Clark's terms, of the naked rather than the nude. Painters have frequently accomplished this, Hollander adds, by representing the body in terms of the shapes and movements of the garments which have been peeled from it. Hence is captured, in a single visual image, both the desirable body and the process of unveiling which disclosed it. The body unclothed (*desnuda*) is the visible record of a sexual transaction.

Clothes have to some extent lost that representational function. But the function has not been lost. Instead it has been transferred to the body itself. Through weight-lifting, sun-bathing, massage and dieting, the modern person attempts to express his gender in his body, to achieve a *direct* embodiment, without the mediation of clothes— to establish before our eyes the living identity of sex and gender, in a manner that hides nothing of sex. The result admits of much moral commentary. Let us only note the enormous loss of freedom that is entailed when sexual embodiment must be achieved by such painful means. How much more lightly could one wear one's gender when one wore it in one's clothes!

I have argued that gender distinctions are artificial, but only in the way that persons are artificial. At the same time, I have conceded that they are more variable, and more easily changed, than many other features in which our ideas of personality are rooted. Hence there inevitably arises the question of justification. How ought the gender distinction to be constructed? . . . To understand it, . . . it is necessary to have some idea of the *process* of gender construction. We must identify the precise occasions for change; for these will be the places where justification *counts.* . . .

The result of gender construction is that we perceive the *Lebenswelt* as subject to a great ontological divide. Not only is there an intentional distinction between person and thing, there is another between the masculine and the feminine, which is initially a distinction among persons. But this second onto-logical divide, while it takes its sense from our understanding of persons, is not confined to the personal realm. On the contrary, it reaches through all nature, presenting us with a masculine and a feminine in everything. A willow, a Corinthian column, a Chopin nocturne, a Gothic spire—in all these one may receive the embodied intimation of femininity, and someone who could not understand the possibility of this is someone with impoverished perceptions. Thus the intentional world reflects back to us the ontological division which we exemplify. We absorb and reabsorb the ideas of the masculine and the feminine, as intentional contents, already impressed with the mark of human sexuality and human desire. Gender thereby becomes an inescapable feature of our world, none the less real through being our own creation.

Although gender is an artefact, it is also, in another sense, as natural a feature of the *Lebenswelt* as the human person himself. No person can easily refrain from thinking of himself as "of" a certain sex, and of rationalising that thought in a conception of gender. The experience of sexual embodiment, which so compromises and diverts our projects, forces us to be aware of our sex as a channel through which will and consciousness flow. Gender is the concept whereby sex *enters* our lives, giving a persistent and reasoned form to otherwise inchoate projects. It is hard to avoid this way of identifying myself, since it is hard to avoid the impulse which prompts me to see myself in sexual terms. My sexual desire stems, not from some accidental part of me, but from my *self*. Hence, I think, not of my body, but of *myself*, as being of a certain sexual kind. However I may divest my "inner" self of attributes, I find it hard to divest it of this one. Even those pure "first-person perspectives"—the gods who move in transcendental spheres—are identified in terms of their gender. The most abstract religion will attribute a gender to its god: not to do so is to cast in doubt the whole *style* of God's agency. (Thus the God of Islam has a gender, despite his wholly discarnate nature; and this gender is made explicit, even when the Koran is translated into a gender-free language, such as Turkish.)

If Kantian feminism were correct, it would be impossible to think of myself as a man, rather than as a person with a man's body. Yet it is precisely to the self that we attribute the feature which bears most overwhelming witness to our incarnate condition. Confirmation is to be found in a case which at first might seem to refute the claim—the case of the "sex change." So persuasive is the idea that gender is an artefact, and so immovable is the human prejudice that sex is nothing but gender, that the theory has arisen of sex, too, as an artefact. It suffices to make a few adjustments to the physical constitution of the body, and any child could be brought up indifferently as a boy or as a girl: the social relativity of his gender is tantamount to the social relativity of his sex. Such ideas are biological nonsense. But this has not prevented them from being extremely influential, or from nurturing the fantasy that each person may have a "real sex," which is belied by his bodily form, but which is revealed in his own conception of his gender. The sex-change patient undertakes this hazardous operation, not in order to change his "real sex," but in order to change his *body*, to the sex that is really *his*. In other words, he identifies his sex through his gender, and his gender not through his body but through his conception of himself. His body, he feels, belongs to a kind to which he himself does not belong. It is on this ground that sex-change operations are both desired by those who undergo them and justified by those who perform them. No more vivid example exists of the human determination to triumph over biological destiny, in the interests of a moral idea. . . .

It is tempting to conclude, therefore, that there is a *real distinction* of gender: that "man" and "woman" denote two kinds of person, whose biological distinction is gathered up within a division of kinds. This is intimated, at least, by our habits of self-identification, and in particular by our identification of ourselves in and through our gender. At the same time, it might be held that, since distinctions of gender are distinctions, not among natural, but among "phenomenological" kinds, there can be no sense to the idea of a *real* distinction. Since these kinds are in some sense created by us, how can we speak of a "real essence" which unites whatever is included by them? In which case, what is the content of our belief that men and women are two kinds of person? . . .

I have no argument for the conclusion that gender *is* an essential property of whatever possesses it:

such arguments are always hard to produce, and always inconclusive. But even without that strong conclusion, we can surely accept that gender is a morally *significant* property of whatever possesses it, and hence that the Kantian feminist position, which banishes gender to the periphery of human freedom, is mistaken. For it is precisely the existence of gender that serves to unite our sexual nature to the moral life that grows from it. Gender—in my analogy—is the trunk through which the flower and foliage of desire are nurtured.

The Root of Desire

Given the existence of gender, we can no longer assume that the sexual act between humans is the *same* act as that performed by animals. Every feature of the sexual act, down to its very physiology, is transformed by our conception of gender. When making love I am consciously being a man, and this enterprise involves my whole nature, and strives to realise itself in the motions of the act itself. Although the man who enters a woman, or the woman who encloses a man, are satisfying a primitive urge, and experiencing whatever sensations and palpitations may accompany the fulfilment of that urge, this is not a description of "what they are doing" in the act of love. Even if they are acutely conscious of the process—and it is to be supposed that their thoughts abound in fantasies which direct them constantly to the source of their physical pleasure—it is not the physical process, described as such, which constitutes the object of their intention. They are intending to "make love," that is, to unite as sexual beings, in an experience guided by the concept of gender. It is "man uniting with woman" rather than "penis entering vagina" which focuses their attention. The latter episode is perceived simply as a "moment" in the former, which provides its indispensable context.

Hence the physical performance, in becoming a human action, is lifted out of its biological circumstance. It is adapted to the morphological requirements of sexual desire, by being reconstituted in terms of gender. The pleasurable exercise of copulation is moralised by the concept of gender, and made into something distinctively human, just as the pleasurable exercise of skipping and jumping is

moralised by the idea of the dance. Animals can skip and jump and feel the corresponding pleasure. But they cannot dance, for they cannot perceive their movements in the way required by dancing— as things significant in themselves. Hence, though they can experience the pleasure of skipping, they cannot experience the pleasure of dancing. Nor, for similar reasons, can they experience the pleasure of sex, in which the movements of copulation embody a moral idea of sex-membership, and are engaged in, not simply by impulse, but because of what they mean.

However, in the words of James Thurber—is sex necessary? I mean, is it necessary for sexual desire, with its peculiar interpersonal intentionality, to lead us into precisely *this* predicament? Of course, we should not call it *sexual* desire if it habitually and normally expressed itself in some other way. But that is merely a verbal matter. What is it about the intentionality of desire that requires its attachment to the sexual act?

The introduction of sex into desire is not without the most far-reaching consequences. In particular, it introduces an element of universality into the object of desire. He or she is desired *as* a man or *as* a woman, and it is from this thought that much of the phenomenology of desire arises—a point that I have already tried to illustrate in discussing shame and jealousy. The universality in question is, however, not that of sex, but that of gender. The other appears to me, even in the sexual act, not as the naked animal, but as a person, clothed in the moral attributes of his gender. In desiring him I see him as essentially embodied, and his body as essentially ensouled; the gap between soul and body is closed for me by my desire. It is hard to imagine this utter unity in the intentional object arising from a non-sexual motive. Interpersonal union which culminates in swimming together, walking together, talking together, does not focus upon the reality of the other's body in quite the way of the sexual act. It is only when kisses and caresses become part of the aim of interpersonal union, and the true source of pleasure, that we are forced to see the other's body as truly him, and contact with his body as contact with him. Sexual desire must therefore involve such activities as kissing and caressing if it is to fulfil its fundamental aim. It is surely obvious, therefore, that the natural culmination of these activities—the sexual act—should become incorporated into the intentional content of desire. Desire both exploits and confirms our concept of gender, by refusing to countenance the separation between a person and his body. The sexual act is, both biologically and intentionally, the culmination of a process of physical intimacy, in which a person is joined to another through his body. None of our bodily functions is so well fitted to this union as is the sexual function, provided that sex is perceived under the aspect of gender—perceived, in other words, as a personal attribute, rather than as a merely biological fact.

Hence we find enormous difficulty in envisaging true sexual desire between fishes and other creatures which reproduce sexually but without sexual contact. The female mackerel may deposit an egg which is later fertilised and guarded by a male. But what, in this solitary action, bears the aspect of desire? Not only physical contact, but every conceivable mutuality, has been extruded from the sexual process, which in consequence cannot be seen, by any stretch of the imagination, as a form of desire. How much easier is it to see desire in the copulation of dogs, or even that of insects. (Thus, whatever else it is, artificial insemination is never adultery.)

It seems, therefore, that, so long as sex is perceived as gender, there is an intrinsic fittingness which unites the sexual act to the interpersonal attitude of desire. Hence, just as the intentionality of desire takes root in the pleasures of sexual congress, so does an idea of gender enter into the intentional content of desire, determining the "kind of thing" which is its proper object. The individual is always pursued under the aspect of his gender, as one instance of a sexual kind. . . .

Homosexuality and Gender

All the features of our sexual perception that I have referred to in this chapter, from the bare distinction of biological kinds to the high point of aesthetic contemplation, serve to emphasise not only the distinction between the sexes, but also the otherness of the other sex, and the familiarity of one's own. Kantian feminism has tended to assume—with Simone de Beauvoir—that it is only

one sex that has perceived the other in terms of its "otherness." In that very observation, however, is revealed the covert recognition that man is as much the "other" for woman as woman is the "other" for man. Man is the "other" whose otherness resides in his "creation" of woman's otherness. If Kantian feminism were true, it would be impossible to think of men, as a class, engaged in this supposedly false representation and in its associated oppressive action. Only individual persons—who happen to be male—could be responsible for such a crime. But, *ex hypothesi*, their maleness, not being a feature of their personality, would have no part to play in their responsibility. In which case it could never be said that the division of the world into genders, and the erection of a myth of the "other" sex, was the doing of men, or in any other way an upshot of masculine dominion. To put it shortly, if the claims made by Kantian feminists were true, Kantian feminism would be false.

For the Kantian feminist, the *enracinement* of the person in the soil of animal activity is a single phenomenon, exemplified alike by man and woman. One and the same person might have taken root in either soil. If this were so, there can be no moral difference between homosexual and heterosexual desire. The body's sex would be irrelevant to the interpersonal emotions that are displayed in it; just *this* person might have had just *this* desire, whatever his sex. Otherwise we must say that desire is not, after all, an interpersonal attitude, but simply a residue of bodily experience, indicating not the person but his biological destiny, in the manner of sensory pleasure and sensory pain. In other words, Kantian feminism has radical moral consequences. Either it denies the moral distinction between heterosexual and homosexual desire—and, along with it, the idea of a sexual "normality" answerable to our nature as sexually reproducing beings. Or else it forces us to accept the Platonic view of desire as "merely animal." Neither view is acceptable. . . .

The plain fact is that, because we live in a world structured by gender, the other sex is forever to some extent a mystery to us, with a dimension of experience that we can imagine but never inwardly know. In desiring to unite with it, we are desiring to mingle with something that is deeply—perhaps essentially—not ourselves, and which brings us to experience a character and inwardness that challenge us with their strangeness. . . .

This might imply that there is a distinction between homosexual and heterosexual desire. The heterosexual ventures towards an individual whose gender confines him within another world. The homosexual unites with an individual who does not lie beyond the divide which separates the world of men from the world of women. Hence the homosexual has a peculiar inward familiarity with what his partner feels. His discovery of his partner's sexual nature is the discovery of what he knows. . . .

Study Questions on Roger Scruton

1. What is "Kantian feminism" and what are Scruton's three main arguments against it?
2. What does Scruton mean in saying that "in the sense that gender is an artefact, so too is the human person" and that we cannot engage in personal construction without also engaging in gender construction?
3. Scruton sees gender both as culturally conditioned and as a deep and inescapable fact about human beings. Do you see these as consistent?
4. Could you be the same person you are now but the opposite sex? What does Scruton believe and why? What do you think and why?

For Further Reading

Allen, Prudence, R. S. M. *The Concept of Woman: The Aristotelian Revolution, 750 BC–AD 1250.* Grand Rapids, Mich.: Eerdmans, 1997.

Anthony, Louise. "Natures and Norms." *Ethics,* 111, no. 1 (October 2000), 8ff. Available on InfoTrac® College Edition.

Bly, Robert. *Iron John.* Reading, Mass.: Addison-Wesley, 1990.

Butler, Judith. *Bodies That Matter.* New York: Routledge, 1993.

Daly, Mary. *Gyn/Ecology.* Boston: Beacon Press, 1990.

de Beauvoir, Simone. *The Second Sex.* H. M. Parshley, trans. New York: Vintage, 1974.

Durden-Smith, Jo, and Diane deSimone. *Sex and the Brain.* New York: Arbor House, 1985.

Estés, Clarissa Pinkola. *Women Who Run with the Wolves.* New York: Ballantine, 1992.

Evans, Debra. *The Mystery of Womanhood.* Westchester, Ill.: Crossway, 1987.

Gilligan, Carol. *In a Different Voice.* Cambridge, Mass.: Harvard University Press, 1982.

Gilmore, David D. *Manhood in the Making: Cultural Concepts of Masculinity.* New Haven, Conn.: Yale University Press, 1990.

Gray, John. *Men Are from Mars, Women Are from Venus.* New York: HarperCollins, 1992.

Griffin, Susan. *Woman and Nature: The Roaring Inside Her.* New York: Harper & Row, 1980.

Griffiths, Morwena, and Margaret Whitford, eds. *Feminist Perspectives in Philosophy.* Bloomington: Indiana University Press, 1988.

Joyce, Mary Rosera. *Women and Choice: A New Beginning.* St. Cloud, Minn.: LifeCom, 1986.

LeGuin, Ursula. *The Left Hand of Darkness.* New York: Ace, 1983. Fantasy about an androgynous society.

Macoby, Eleanor E., and Carol N. Jacklin. *The Psychology of Sex Differences.* Stanford, Calif.: Stanford University Press, 1974.

May, Larry, and Robert A. Strikwerda, eds. *Rethinking Masculinity.* 2nd ed. Lanham, Md.: Rowman & Littlefield, 1996.

Mead, Margaret. *Sex and Temperament in Three Primitive Societies.* New York: William Morrow, 1935.

_____. *Male and Female.* New York: William Morrow, 1949.

Noddings, Nell. *Caring: A Feminine Approach to Ethics.* Berkeley: University of California Press, 1964.

Purdy, Laura. "Nature and Nurture: A False Dichotomy." *Hypatia,* 1, no. 1 (1986), 167–174.

Rothenberg, Paula S. *Racism and Sexism.* New York: St. Martin's, 1988. The reputed Bible of political correctness.

Scheman, Naomi. "Feminist Epistemology." Response by Louise Anthony. American Philosophical Association (Eastern Division), December 29, 1994.

Stein, Sarah. *Girls and Boys: The Limits of Nonsexist Childrearing.* New York: Scribner's, 1983.

Travis, Carol. *The Mismeasure of Woman.* New York: Simon & Schuster, 1992.

Tuana, Nancy. *The Less Noble Sex.* Bloomington: Indiana University Press, 1993.

_____. "Re-fusing Nature/Nurture." *Hypatia,* 3 (1983), 621–632.

Vatterling-Braggin, Mary, ed. *"Femininity," "Masculinity," and "Androgyny": A Modern Philosophical Discussion.* Totowa, N.J.: Allanheld, 1982.

Wilson, Edward O. *Sociobiology: The New Synthesis.* Cambridge, Mass.: Harvard University Press, 1975.

_____. *Of Human Nature.* Cambridge, Mass.: Harvard University Press, 1978.

INFOTRAC COLLEGE EDITION To learn more about the topics from this chapter, you can use the following words to conduct an electronic search on InfoTrac College Edition, an online library of journals. Here you will find a multitude of articles from various sources and perspectives: *www.infotrac-college.com/wadsworth/access.html*

Androgyny	Masculine and Feminine
Feminism	Nature and Nurture
Gender	Sexism
Human Nature	Sociobiology
Man and Woman	

Web Sites

Androgyny RAQ (Rarely Asked Questions)
http://www.chaparrltree.com/raq

Feminist Activist Resources on the Net
http://igc.org/women.feminist.html

Gender and Sexuality
http://www.eserver.org/gender

Human Nature.Com
http://www.human-nature.com

National Organization of Men Against Sexism
http://www.nomas.org/

Nature, Nurture, and Psychology
http://www.apa.org/431824.html

Sociobiology (C.G. Boeree)
http://www.ship.edu/~cgboeree/sociobiology.html

Unit II

Sexuality: The Flesh and the Spirit

SEXUALITY IN THE SENSE OF SEXUAL ACTIVITY brings into play many aspects of the human person: physical, instinctual, emotional, and spiritual. It grows out of our experience of ourselves as embodied and gendered beings and has the potential to bring new human beings into being, as well as to generate and strengthen intense emotional ties between individuals. It also plays a very important role in the formation of the complex webs of familial and broader kinship relationships that have played such an important role in all human societies (a topic we will turn to in Unit IV).

As we explore the ways in which people understand sex, it is important not to neglect the deep feelings people have about it. This does not mean that it is impossible to reason about sex, but only that to accurately understand the phenomenon of sexuality, it is necessary to be aware of the deep emotions it arouses. The selections from Andrea Dworkin and Richard Mohr, especially, challenge modern rationalism by emphasizing the dark side of sexuality and the primal fears and passions connected with it; in fact, Mohr celebrates these features of the sexual life. The book by Camile Paglia listed in the For Further Reading section of this unit is perhaps the most forceful presentation of this dimension of sexuality.

In American society, the debate about the nature of sexuality has tended to be between those who propose to understand it purely naturalistically as an activity that is pleasurable, relaxing, and productive of intimacy between individuals, and those whose religious beliefs lead them to understand sex as having an important spiritual dimension as well. The deeply different worldviews of the parties to this debate make it difficult for them to understand each other. Sex makes us very aware of ourselves as embodied beings who are male or female, and especially of those parts of our bodies that are characteristic of our sex and that of the other. It also puts us in touch with instinctual drives that have deep roots in our animal nature. Human beings are very often ambivalent about their animality, and cling to the deeply held intuition that they are more than just animals; the major religions teach that this intuition is correct, and even people who are not religious frequently hold something like this view.

Four Worldviews

Since understanding sexuality involves locating it within a broader understanding of the nature of human beings and our place in nature, we propose to broaden the debate somewhat beyond merely naturalism versus the Jewish and Christian traditions, and include two other worldviews that have deep roots in the human psyche—namely, paganism and Manichaeanism. Both of these have been historically important, are present in varying degrees in non-Western religions, and are influential upon many of those involved in the current controversy about sexuality in spite of the fact that there are few self-professed Manichaeans in the contemporary world, and most people who think of themselves as neo-pagans are highly selective about which aspects of paganism they want to revive (frequently being guided largely by therapeutic or political aims). It has not been possible, therefore, to arrange the selections neatly under these four headings, but nonetheless we believe that these frameworks underlie contemporary disputes, and bringing them into the open will help us to understand why people so often find each other's sexual views not just wrong, but incomprehensible.

The pagan view of nature sees nature as being full of spiritual powers of various sorts that must be respected or placated. Sexuality and reproduction are the domain of powerful forces that have been personified in various ways as Ishtar, Astarte, Aphrodite, Venus, and so on. Sexuality can be a great power either for good or for evil. Because of this, pagans have regarded sexuality with awe and surrounded it with rituals and taboos. D. H. Lawrence (in the Prologue) presents a kind of neo-pagan view of sex, praising the mysterious power of sex to unite lovers in a "correspondence of blood" and to bring them into contact and harmony with the primal forces of nature—with the rhythms of the stars and the seasons.

The positive side of paganism has been celebrated by various kinds of fertility cults that have flourished throughout history in an enormous variety of cultures. These hold in awe the mysterious life-giving power of sexuality, particularly female sexuality, since it is, after all, women who give birth. But the dark side of paganism cannot be ignored; not all the spiritual forces that pervade nature are benevolent. Near the shrine of Astarte were found the skeletons of infants sacrificed to her. Neither celibacy nor self-indulgence is entirely safe. Our best hope, according to paganism, lies in moderation and continued attempts to placate the goddess, though nothing guarantees that we can avoid being caught between two gods (say the goddesses of sex and family life) and having to take drastic measures to remedy a bad situation.

A worldview that has come more lately on the scene, but which has become enormously influential if not entirely dominant in our culture, is naturalism. Naturalism denudes the world of all spiritual forces, positive or negative. It would not be fair to say that naturalism, by eliminating the transcendent dimension, reduces sexuality to mere animality; we are after all rational and social animals. Naturalists, however, characteristically lack either the sense of awe that pagans feel toward sexuality or the poignant sense of tension between the spirit and the flesh characteristic of Manichaeans or of those in the Jewish and Christian traditions. Sex is demythologized and regarded as merely a normal and natural human need.

Since sex is a powerful desire, of course, it is important to regulate it by reason in order to avoid social chaos and other disastrous consequences. Sex should be enjoyed in such a way as to avoid disease ("safe sex") and with careful rational consideration of whether reproduction would be desirable in light of our needs and circumstances. But the normal, healthy expression of one's sexuality is a legitimate source of pleasure, relaxation, and, sometimes at least, growth in intimacy between people. It is also bound up with many valuable things in our culture—the production of art and poetry, our appreciation of beauty, romance, and our pursuit of happiness.

Sex and reproduction are thus good only to the degree that they are conducive to our happiness, as they are when properly regulated by reason. Attempts to suppress sexuality only lead to psychological disorders, obsessions, and unhappiness. Among the selections presented here, Bertrand Russell most clearly articulates the naturalistic approach to sexuality. A popular form of it also underlies the "Playboy philosophy," which regards sexual activity as an enjoyable form of recreation.

Manichaeanism also has a very ancient pedigree, and has been a constantly recurring theme in both Western and Oriental cultures. It regards the physical world as essentially bad and the spirit as good, and sees our goal in life as attempting to transcend and free ourselves from the body. As a result, sexuality must be either spiritualized (as it could be argued that Nagel does) or else regarded as degrading—or perhaps both. Manichaeans, not surprisingly, tend to be rather tormented over sex. Certainly its reproductive dimension would be regarded with horror by a Manichaean, since each new birth traps another soul in the mire and muck of the physical world. This sort of thinking reemerges constantly in various vaguely gnostic religious groups, and has often pervaded Christianity also. (Augustine, for example, was strongly influenced by it in his youth and arguably also in later life.) Dworkin manifests a strongly Manichaean attitude toward sexuality; she regards the created order as evil because it degrades women—"God, who does not exist, you hate women, otherwise you'd have made them different."

A Manichaean attitude can certainly produce a horrified flight from sexuality. But traces of it linger also among those who pursue sex avidly while consciously or unconsciously regarding it as low, nasty, and dirty. Since all that really matters is the spirit, perhaps we can wallow in bodily pleasures while retaining purity. This attitude is aptly expressed by a contemporary poet, C. P. Cafavy, who says:

> Fortified by theory and by study,
> I shall not fear my passions like a coward.
> I shall yield my body to sensual delights,
> to enjoyments that one dreams about,
> to the most audacious amorous desires,
> to the wanton impulses of my blood, without
> a single fear, for whenever I wish—
> and I shall have the will, fortified
> as I shall be by theory and by study—
> at moments of crisis, I shall find again
> my spirit, as before, ascetic.[1]

Another form of Manichaeanism (rather more pragmatic and less poetic and mystical) concludes that sexuality is too powerful to resist. Therefore we must allow the

From "Perilous Things" in The Complete Poems of Cavafy, *copyright © 1961 and renewed 1989 by Rae Dalven, reprinted by permission of Harcourt, Inc.*

body its pleasures so that it will cease clamoring for satisfaction and leave us free to pursue higher things. After all, the spirit itself remains unsullied by the flesh.

Manichaeans standardly have a very elevated view of the spirit, and regard it as something akin to the divine. It can happen, however, that someone with a basically Manichaean view of reality loses belief in any sort of higher reality—there is no God, no eternal forms as in Plato, or anything else of that sort. In this case what results is a kind of inverted Manichaeanism. The mind and the body are still regarded as in deep opposition to each other, but the values are reversed. It is the body that is regarded as good, while the mind is nothing but the empty, needless chatter of thoughts and concepts that must be somehow dissolved back into the body and silenced, until at last we are merely the body sensing. This sort of view is articulated in the selection by Mohr.

The last view to be considered is that of the Jewish and Christian traditions. Both regard the world as the creation of a good and all-powerful God. Since human beings were created as embodied beings, it must be good that we have bodies. This is in sharp contrast to the standard Manichaean view that being trapped in a body is a misfortune and that there exists an ineradicable hostility between flesh and spirit. Sexuality itself, however, is not divine, as it is in the pagan view. It partakes in sacredness both because it has its origins in God's creative act, and because humans can, in the sexual act, share in His creative power by cooperating with Him in the generation of new human beings. (*He* is traditional for Christians and Jews; we do not beg the question of God's gender.) Thus the sort of awe of sexuality characteristic of paganism lingers also in the Jewish and Christian attitude. Our sexuality must be submitted to God's will, and rules governing its use have been revealed by God. Due to original sin, we sometimes have to struggle to submit our sexuality to God, and if we do not do this we risk unleashing the horrors envisioned by the dark side of paganism.

The Jewish and Christian traditions are not in complete opposition to naturalism, however. Jews and Christians both believe that, since nature was created by God, one can get a certain amount of guidance about sexuality and its proper use by rationally reflecting upon our human nature as we find it. This is the underlying assumption of the Catholic natural law tradition that has its roots in Aquinas. And naturalists, for their part, may find themselves moving toward the natural law tradition. If values cannot be derived from facts, then the natural order as we find it cannot give us any practical guidance. Naturalists, however, often refer to nature with a capital *N* and try to discern Her purposes.

The most popular form of natural law sexual ethics has been the attempt to ground sexual morality in the natural teleology of the sexual organs and the sexual act, and our obligation to respect this natural teleology. While this approach does not limit itself to biology, since consideration of the needs and interests of the children who may result from sexual acts does enter into reasoning about the morality of certain sexual acts, not violating the natural teleology of the sexual organs remains at least a necessary condition for a sexual act to count as morally good. The reading by Richard Connell is an example of this tradition. So also is the reading by Cormac Burke in Unit III, although Burke arrives at his conclusion by a very different route than Connell does.

A different form of natural law theory has been developed recently and applied to sexuality by John Finnis in collaboration with Germain Grisez and Joseph Boyle; see the selections by Finnis, Ford, and Lawler in the For Further Reading section in this unit. (Robert George, whose discussion of same-sex marriage is reprinted in Unit IV, is also of this school.) These writers focus more on the teleology of human acts understood in terms of the basic goods they aim at, and claim to have discovered a small number of basic human goods that exhaust the goods at which people aim. The basic goods are incommensurable and we therefore cannot weigh and balance one against another, or in any way act directly against a basic good. Since life is one of the basic goods, we ought not to act directly against this good, and they take this to imply a ban on artificial contraception as well as abortion, suicide, murder, and so on.

The four worldviews presented here are not intended to be exhaustive; no doubt there are both alternatives to these outlooks and mixtures of them. The authors selected here are not, for the most part, engaged primarily in articulating or defending their worldviews, but in trying to answer specific questions about the nature of sexuality such as, for example, whether sex is inherently private and if so why, whether there is such a thing as sexual perversion and if so what it is, whether a morally good sex act must be open to procreation and if so why, and so on.

Male and Female

Since the burdens and joys of reproduction fall unequally on women and men, the question arises of how or whether this impacts the way in which women and men experience their sexuality. The selection from Susan Lydon argues that female sexuality has been systematically misunderstood (particularly by those in the Freudian tradition) in ways that emphasize female inferiority and dependence on men. Niles Newton argues that an overemphasis on orgasm wrongly overlooks what is distinctively female in sexuality in favor of the one thing they share with men. Similar views are defended by Sidney Callahan; see the article listed in the For Further Reading section of Unit III. Newton holds that pregnancy, childbirth, and breastfeeding are also sexually charged experiences for women and that the way women experience intercourse is connected in deep and complex ways with their feelings about these phenomena.

Homosexuality

Homosexual sex necessarily lacks the reproductive dimension that is present in heterosexual sex, but carries with it equally intense physical sensations and emotions as well as various complex social and psychological meanings. The reading by Mohr presents a vision of homosexual sexual activity focusing on its intimacy, emotional intensity, and privacy, while the reading by Richard Rodriguez explores in a sensitive and nuanced way the emotional and social dimensions of homosexual culture as it has developed in San Francisco. Adrienne Rich has argued that lesbian sex is as least as natural for women as the heterosexual variety (and that all women fall on a "lesbian continuum"). Arlene Stein, in the account of the new lesbianism of the 1970s reprinted here, develops this idea in a more pointedly political direction: "*all* women were born 'that way,' all had the capacity to be lesbians but were hampered by the system of male domination. . . . [Lesbians] were different only in terms of their political commitment to affirm women's autonomy." The reader is also referred to the selections by Michael Novak and Timothy

Murphy in Unit V for further reflections on whether homosexuality is fundamentally different from heterosexuality.

Among the writers in the Western tradition, Plato is unusual in that he combines two features usually thought incompatible with one another. Sex for him meant primarily the homosexual sort, especially that between a man and a younger man or a boy. Yet he also held that virtue required that the sexual impulse be disciplined and directed to higher ends (ultimately toward a vision of the Good)—hence our expression "Platonic love," and a recurrent belief within our tradition that the deepest aims of sexuality are spiritual rather than fleshy.

The next two units will explore the implications of the reproductive dimension of sexuality and consider ethical issues surrounding: (1) the genesis of new human life, and (2) the institutions of marriage and family that have developed in large part to provide for the care and nurture of the next generation of human beings.

Questions for Reflection

1. For each reading: What is the author's vision of the nature of human sexuality? What understanding of human beings and our place in nature is implicit in that vision?
2. Which of the four worldviews considered here, if any, most closely represents the way you think about sex?
3. Is there a fifth, omitted here, that better represents your views?
4. Does everyone have a worldview, even if he or she has never bothered to articulate it? Are people's views on sexuality always closely connected with their worldviews?
5. How does female sexuality differ from male sexuality, and how (if at all) is that difference important?
6. Is there an essential difference between homosexual sex—whether that of gay men or that of lesbians—and heterosexual sex, apart from the question of reproduction?

Glossary

clitorectomy surgical removal of the clitoris, practiced in some African and Arab societies.

coprophilia sexual interest in excrement.

Eros passionate love, the son of Resource and Need.

Good, the the highest reality in Platonic philosophy, roughly similar to the Christian conception of God.

incommensurable incapable of being measured on a common scale.

lesbian continuum a range of forms of female-female intimacy, from a girl infant sucking at her mother's breast to overt lesbian sexuality.

Manicheanism a religion founded by the Persian prophet Mani (216–77 BC), which taught a radical dualism grounded in coeternal and independent powers of Light and Darkness. More broadly, any view that sharply opposes flesh and spirit, usually treating the flesh as bad and the spirit as good.

naturalism the belief that the natural order is all that exists (specifically excluding a Creator God).

natural law ethics attempt to derive moral requirements from the requirements of human nature.

paganism belief in a multitude of gods and goddesses. In sophisticated versions, these are natural, social, and psychological forces that determine human destiny (e.g., Venus or Aphrodite stands for the social and psychological power of sex).

patriarchy strictly, a political system in which husbands and fathers have the power of life and death over their wives and children; loosely, any system of male dominance.

Platonic love passionate love without physical sex, in its original form between a man and a boy.

teleology purpose, especially that held to be inherent in biological processes.

white slave traffic prostitution as an international business.

worldview an overall perspective on life that sums up what we know or believe about the world, how we evaluate it, and how we respond to it in practice.

The Inherent Privacy of Sex

RICHARD MOHR

Richard Mohr here argues for a right to sexual privacy from a phenomenology of sexual experience. Sexual acts are "world excluding" in the following ways. Sexually aroused people experience the world in an altered way. Social relations alter importantly during the shift into erotic reality, so that appeal to one's sexual tastes overrides every other feature of a potential partner. All parties become increasingly identified with their bodies, submerged in the flesh. The everyday world of will and deeds fades away with sexual arousal. In conclusion, he suggests that nothing about the privacy of sexual acts requires that the number of sexual actors be limited, so that, for example, gay cruising zones in parks at night are private in the requisite sense.

EVEN IF THERE WERE NO SOCIAL CUSTOMS that generate a right to privacy from the obligation to privacy, sex acts would still be covered by any general, substantive right to privacy. For the privacy of sex acts is not only culturally based but is inherent to them. Sex acts are what I shall call "world excluding." Custom and taboo aside, sexual arousal and activity, like the activities of reading a book or praying alone, are such as to propel away the ordinary world, the everyday world of social function and public observation.

There are several ways in which sex acts are world-excluding. First, sexually aroused people experience the world in an altered way. Sexual arousal alters the perception of reality in some of the same ways powerful drugs do. It withdraws one from everyday reality, from the workaday world, from ordinary activities and day-to-day

From American Philosophical Quarterly, 2 *(1987): 57–69. Reprinted by permission of the University of Pittsburgh.*

encounters with largely functionary others, from public spaces, from the world of waking and talking, from reason, persuasion, and thought.

Space recedes. Arousal is an immersion into a different medium, as into sleep fraught with scarey possibilities, or as into a liquid, where one either is contiguous with another or has no contact at all. One could not have a public, shared space in syrup. In continued arousal, perception becomes more and more focused and narrow. One's gaze no longer roams or scans at large, but increasingly becomes a form of attention. The focusing process calls for and is enhanced by nightfall. Only what is near, if anything at all, is seen. Gradually perception is channelled away from vision—the supreme sense of the everyday public world, a sense that requires a gulf of open space. Perception shifts from vision to touch, the sense which requires the absence of open space.

At peak arousal, as in a liquid or in a blizzard, the horizon is but the extent of one's flesh. One is hermetic save for the continuation of one's flesh with and in the flesh of another. And so too, sex is essentially a world of silence; words, such as they are, are not reports, descriptions or arguments but murmurs and invocations which emphasize silence and its awe.

One attends only what is near. Even the comfort and irritation of immediate environments pale with increased arousal. A chief difficulty in producing convincing visual pornography is how to address the omnipresence of a background, which is necessarily in the visual field but necessarily not part of what is to be presented. In sex one becomes segregated from one's environment.

Time, like space, recedes with arousal. Suspended is the time by which one gauges the regularity and phases of the workaday world. Time is interrupted and becomes inconsequential, as in the spontaneity and attention-absorbing fascination of games.

Second, social relations alter importantly during the shift into erotic reality; people who were important in everyday reality recede from importance. People with whom one has functional, public roles fade away entirely or at least as having those roles. Colleagues and service personnel fade

from consciousness. One becomes focused only upon those who potentially jibe with one's tastes, the particularities of one's erotic choices or desires. Anyone could have sold you a train ticket through a wicket, even a computer could, but only someone particular in appearance, mien, pose and act could arouse you. Even the most "impersonal" or "anonymous" sexual encounters are intimate in this way—rarely does a name arouse—and communist ideology aside, such encounters are not marked by mere functioning in accord with social or economic roles. Even in sexual environments where there are ample numbers of ready, willing, able and intentionally sexual bodies, as in bathhouses, parks, and backroom bars, still virtually everyone is picky about their partners, even to the point of completely frustrated desire.

Third, in the process of sexual arousal, one becomes increasingly incarnate, submerged in the flesh, a process which, when mutual and paired with the shift in perception to touch, achieves an unparalleled intimacy, which leaves the everyday social world far behind. Social and psychological characteristics, one's own and those of the object of erotic desire, pale in this focusing on and submerging into flesh. In sexual disengagement from spatial, social and psychological circumstances, the body ceases to be merely a coathanger for personality, but assumes for the first time a life of its own.

One perceives the other as flesh and desires the other to be flesh. Usually one becomes, in turn, flesh for the other, in part because one's own submersion into the flesh sparks or enhances desire in the other. The recognition of this effect on the other, in turn again, prompts one's own further submersion. This process of mutual reciprocal incarnations may be iterated at many levels, though eventually the body submerges even the mind's ability to carry out the requisite recognitions and one becomes just the body sensing.

This sexually aroused body, in turn, works as an alembic on sensations typical of the everyday world. A touch, say, a light brushing of the flesh, that would go largely unnoticed in the everyday world, save possibly for its social significance, here becomes an intense yet diffuse pleasure, and, as the non-timid masochist knows, what was pain in the ordinary world, say, one's tits being tweaked, here transmutes into a coursing yet careening pleasure.

The recognitions constitutive of mutual incarnations and especially the very slide into the purely sensing body produce a transparency in the flow of information and sensation between partners. This transparency is further clarified by a number of concurrent and mutually reinforcing enhanced states: a heightened awareness of touch, the heightened significance of touch, the heightened profile of the body in sex and the immediacy and simultaneity of touching and being touched. The vagueness and ambiguity typical of everyday interactions and the obscurity of connections between intent and response are here distilled into a clarity of cause and effect unmatched in human experience. One is as intimate as one could be.

Fourth, the everyday world of will and deeds fades away with sexual arousal. For will is not a chief causal factor in the fulfillment of sexual desire and indeed impedes sexual arousal. One can effectively use one's will to raise one's arm but one can not use one's will to raise, well, to effect the transition from sexual desire—horniness—to sexual arousal—the engorging and sexual sensitizing of the genitals. Indeed, quite the opposite is true: willing sexual arousal guarantees it will not occur. Sexual arousal must come over one; it is a passion, not an action, project, or deed. And so too, it can only occur in situations in which one is not observing one's progress and judging how one is doing. As Masters and Johnson have shown, the willing of arousal, self-observation, and self-judging, all guarantee and are the chief causes of impotence. One has to be lost in sex for it to work upon one.

For all these reasons, the sexual realm is inherently private. The sex act creates its own sanctuary which in turn is necessary for its success. The whole process and nature of sex is interrupted and destroyed if penetrated by the glance of an intruder—unless that glance itself becomes incorporated in the processes just described. The gazes of non-participating others in sex are not the harmless matrix of intersecting looks of the marketplace or townmeeting, which, for their very complexity, cancel each other out like randomly

intersecting waves. Rather, being viewed by an uninvited other is as intrusive in sex as the telephone ringing. For, like the telephone ringing, it brings crashing in its train the everyday world of duration and distance, function and duty, will and action. Further, the gaze of others injects into sex the waking world of vision not flesh: and, most importantly, it judges—even if sympathetically—causing self-reflection, even if only in the form of felt uncertainty, but virtually always causing a great deal more. For in social circumstances where an act is blanketed by an obligation to privacy which mounts to the level of taboo (as is the case with sex and excretion in America), then *any* observation, even a seemingly disinterested one, is bound to be construed by the observed as a harsh intrusive judgment. There is no such thing as casual observation of people fucking.

Each component, then, of the world-excluding nature of sexual encounters is destroyed by an intruding observer. To observe sex but not participate in it is to violate the sexual act. Sex is only possible in the realm of *presumed* privacy, and so is violated even by an unobserved observer. Sex is inherently private. Any moral theory that protects privacy as sanctuary and as repose from the world must presumptively protect sexual activity.

. . . Nothing about the nature of sexual encounters requires that members of private sexual acts be limited numerically. The traditional and sometimes legally enforced belief that two participants at most constitute a sexual encounter as private—that three or more people automatically make a sex act public—is a displaced vestige of the view that sex is only for procreation, which, since humans have litters of but one, only two can effect.

. . . [M]any perhaps find orgy rooms at bathhouses and backrooms in bars not private. This is wrong, for if the participants are all consenting to be there with each other for the possibility of sex polymorphic, then they fulfill the proper criterion of the private in the realm of the sexual. If, as is the case, gay cruising zones of parks at night have as their habitues only gay cruisers, police cruisers, and queerbashers, then they too are private in the requisite sense; and, in the absence of complaints against specific individuals, arrests should not occur there for public lewdness. . . .

Study Questions on Richard Mohr

1. In what ways is privacy somehow natural to sexual acts (as opposed to required by custom) according to Mohr?
2. Mohr speaks of the intimacy of impersonal or anonymous sex. What does intimacy mean in this context? Does whether one knows one's partner deeply make a difference to the sexual act itself? Would knowing the person make it harder or easier to immerse one's mind in one's body in the way Mohr regards as desirable?
3. Can sexual acts performed in "private" (in Mohr's sense) have important social consequences? If so, can claims to privacy ever be absolute in your opinion? (Consider, e.g., public regulation of homosexual bath houses.)
4. Do you think Mohr's characterization of the nature of sex is equally applicable to all sorts of sexual activity? Is there anything distinctively male about his view? He identifies himself as a homosexual. Do you think that affects his understanding of sexuality, or could this selection equally well have been written by a heterosexual?

Intercourse

ANDREA DWORKIN

Complaining to the "God who does not exist" for the way he has made women, Andrea Dworkin argues that the female body is designed to have less privacy, less integrity of body, and less sense of self than the male. Intercourse, she argues, occurs in a context of a pervasive and indisputable power relation, and expresses dominance, hostility, or anger rather than affection. What women want is not conventional intercourse, but a diffuse sensuality that involves the whole body and polymorphous tenderness.

Oh, God, who does not exist, you hate women, otherwise you'd have made them different.

Edna O'Brien,
Girls in Their Married Bliss

A HUMAN BEING has a body that is inviolate; and when it is violated, it is abused. A woman has a body that is penetrated in intercourse: permeable, its corporeal solidness a lie. The discourse of male truth—literature, science, philosophy, pornography—calls that penetration *violation*. This it does with some consistency and some confidence. *Violation* is a synonym for intercourse. At the same time, the penetration is taken to be a use, not an abuse; a normal use; it is appropriate to enter her, to push into ("violate") the boundaries of her body. She is human, of course, but by a standard that does not include physical privacy. She is, in fact, human by a standard that precludes physical privacy, since to keep a man out altogether and for a lifetime is deviant in the extreme, a psychopathology, a repudiation of the way in which she is expected to manifest her humanity.

. . . By definition, as the God who does not exist made her, she is intended to have a lesser privacy, a lesser integrity of the body, a lesser sense of self, since her body can be physically occupied and in the occupation taken over. By definition, as the God who does not exist made her, this lesser privacy, this lesser integrity, this lesser self, establishes her lesser significance: not just in the world of social policy but in the world of bare, true, real existence. She is defined by how she is made, that hole, which is synonymous with entry; and intercourse, the act fundamental to existence, has consequences to her being that may be intrinsic, not socially imposed.

There is no analogue anywhere among subordinated groups of people to this experience of being made for intercourse: for penetration, entry, occupation. There is no analogue in occupied countries or in dominated races or in imprisoned dissidents or in colonialized cultures or in the submission of children to adults or in the atrocities that have marked the twentieth century ranging from Auschwitz to the Gulag. There is nothing exactly the same, and this is not because the political invasion and significance of intercourse is banal up against these other hierarchies and brutalities. Intercourse is a particular reality for women as an inferior class; and it has in it, as part of it, violation of boundaries, taking over, occupation, destruction of privacy, all of which are construed to be normal and also fundamental to continuing human existence. There is nothing that happens to any other civilly inferior people that is the same in its meaning and in its effect even when those people are forced into sexual availability, heterosexual or homosexual; while subject people, for instance, may be forced to have intercourse with those who dominate them, the God who does not exist did not make human existence, broadly speaking, dependent on their compliance. The political

meaning of intercourse for women is the fundamental question of feminism and freedom: can an occupied people—physically occupied inside, internally invaded—be free; can those with a metaphysically compromised privacy have self-determination; can those without a biologically based physical integrity have self-respect?

There are many explanations, of course, that try to be kind. Women are different but equal. Social policy is different from private sexual behavior. The staggering civil inequalities between men and women are simple, clear injustices unrelated to the natural, healthy act of intercourse. There is nothing implicit in intercourse that mandates male dominance in society. Each individual must be free to choose—and so we expand tolerance for those women who do not want to be fucked by men. Sex is between individuals, and social relations are between classes, and so we preserve the privacy of the former while insisting on the equality of the latter. Women flourish as distinct, brilliant individuals of worth in the feminine condition, including in intercourse, and have distinct, valuable qualities. For men and women, fucking is freedom; and for men and women, fucking is the same, especially if the woman chooses both the man and the act. Intercourse is a private act engaged in by individuals and has no implicit social significance. Repression, as opposed to having intercourse, leads to authoritarian social policies, including those of male dominance. Intercourse does not have a metaphysical impact on women, although, of course, particular experiences with individual men might well have a psychological impact. Intercourse is not a political condition or event or circumstance because it is natural. Intercourse is not occupation or invasion or loss of privacy because it is natural. Intercourse does not violate the integrity of the body because it is natural. Intercourse is fun, not oppression. Intercourse is pleasure, not an expression or confirmation of a state of being that is either ontological or social. Intercourse is because the God who does not exist made it; he did it right, not wrong; and he does not hate women even if women hate him. Liberals refuse categorically to inquire into even a possibility that there is a relationship between intercourse per se and the low status of women. Conservatives use what appears to be God's work to justify a social and moral hierarchy in which women are lesser than men. Radicalism on the meaning of intercourse—its political meaning to women, its impact on our very being itself—is tragedy or suicide. "The revolutionary," writes Octavio Paz paraphrasing Ortega y Gasset, "is always a radical, that is, he [*sic*] is trying to correct the uses themselves rather than the mere abuses. . . ." With intercourse, the use is already imbued with the excitement, the derangement, of the abuse; and abuse is only recognized as such socially if the intercourse is performed so recklessly or so violently or so stupidly that the man himself has actually signed a confession through the manner in which he has committed the act. What intercourse *is* for women and what it *does* to women's identity, privacy, self-respect, self-determination, and integrity are forbidden questions; and yet how can a radical or any woman who wants freedom not ask precisely these questions? The quality of the sensation or the need for a man or the desire for love: these are not answers to questions of freedom; they are diversions into complicity and ignorance. . . .

Intercourse occurs in a context of a power relation that is pervasive and incontrovertible. The context in which the act takes place, whatever the meaning of the act in and of itself, is one in which men have social, economic, political, and physical power over women. Some men do not have all those kinds of power over all women; but all men have some kinds of power over all women; and most men have controlling power over what they call *their* women—the women they fuck. The power is predetermined by gender, by being male. . . .

Despite all efforts to socialize women to want intercourse—e.g., women's magazines to pornography to *Dynasty;* incredible rewards and punishments to get women to conform and put out—women still want a more diffuse and tender sensuality that involves the whole body and a polymorphous tenderness. . . .

. . . Women have a vision of love that includes men as human too; and women want the human in men, including in the act of intercourse. Even without the dignity of equal power, women have believed in the redeeming potential of love. There has been—despite the cruelty of exploitation and forced sex—a consistent vision for women of a sexuality based on a harmony that is both sensual and possible. In the words of sex reformer Ellen Key:

She will no longer be captured like a fortress or hunted like a quarry; nor will she like a placid lake await the stream that seeks its way to her embrace. A stream herself, she will go her own way to meet the other stream.

A stream herself, she would move over the earth, sensual and equal; especially, she will go her own way. . . .

These visions of a humane sensuality based in equality are in the aspirations of women; and even the nightmare of sexual inferiority does not seem to kill them. They are not searching analyses into the nature of intercourse; instead they are deep, humane dreams that repudiate the rapist as the final arbiter of reality. They are an underground resistance to both inferiority and brutality, visions that sustain life and further endurance.

They also do not amount to much in real life with real men. There is, instead, the cold fucking, duty-bound or promiscuous; the romantic obsession in which eventual abandonment turns the vagina into the wound Freud claimed it was; intimacy with men who dread women, coital dread—as Kafka wrote in his diary, "coitus as punishment for the happiness of being together." . . .

Physically, the woman in intercourse is a space inhabited, a literal territory occupied literally: occupied even if there has been no resistance, no force; even if the occupied person said yes please, yes hurry, yes more. Having a line at the point of entry into your body that cannot be crossed is different from not having any such line; and being occupied in your body is different from not being occupied in your body. It is human to experience these differences whether or not one cares to bring the consequence of them into consciousness. . . .

. . . Male sexual discourse on the meaning of intercourse becomes our language. It is not a second language even though it is not our native language; it is the only language we speak, however, with perfect fluency even though it does not say what we mean or what we think we might know if only we could find the right word and enough privacy in which to articulate it even just in our own minds. We know only this one language of these folks who enter and occupy us: they keep telling us that we are different from them; yet we speak only their language and have none, or none that we remember, of our own; and we do not dare, it seems, invent one, even in signs and gestures. Our bodies speak their language. Our minds think in it. The men are inside us through and through. We hear something, a dim whisper, barely audible, somewhere at the back of the brain; there is some other word, and we think, some of us, sometimes, that once it belonged to us.

There are female-supremacist models for intercourse that try to make us the masters of this language that we speak that is not ours. They evade some fundamental questions about the act itself and acknowledge others. They have in common a glorious ambition to see women self-determining, vigorous and free lovers who are never demeaned or diminished by force or subordination, not in society, not in sex. The great advocate of the female-first model of intercourse in the nineteenth century was Victoria Woodhull. She understood that rape was slavery; not less than slavery in its insult to human integrity and human dignity. She acknowledged some of the fundamental questions of female freedom presented by intercourse in her imperious insistence that women had a *natural* right—a right that inhered in the nature of intercourse itself—to be entirely self-determining, the controlling and dominating partner, the one whose desire determined the event, the one who both initiates and is the final authority on what the sex is and will be. Her thinking was not mean-spirited, some silly role reversal to make a moral point; nor was it a taste for tyranny hidden in what pretended to be a sexual ethic. She simply understood that women are unspeakably vulnerable in intercourse because of the nature of the act—entry, penetration, occupation; and she understood that in a society of male power, women were unspeakably exploited in intercourse. Society—men—had to agree to let the woman be the mind, the heart, the lover, the free spirit, the physical vitality behind the act. The commonplace abuses of forced entry, the devastating consequences of being powerless and occupied, suggested that the only condition under which women could experience sexual freedom in intercourse—real choice, real freedom, real happiness, real pleasure—was in having real and absolute control in each and every act of intercourse, which would be, each and every time, chosen by the woman. She would have the incontrovertible authority that would make intercourse possible:

To woman, by nature, belongs the right of sexual determination. When the instinct is aroused in her, then and then only should commerce follow. When woman rises from sexual slavery to sexual freedom, into the ownership and control of her sexual organs, and man is obliged to respect this freedom, then will this instinct become pure and holy; then will woman be raised from the iniquity and morbidness in which she now wallows for existence, and the intensity and glory of her creative functions be increased a hundred-fold. . . .

The consent standard is revealed as pallid, weak, stupid, second-class, by contrast with Woodhull's standard: that the woman should have authority and control over the act. . . .

Male-dominant gender hierarchy, however, seems immune to reform by reasoned or visionary argument or by changes in sexual styles, either personal or social. This may be because intercourse itself is immune to reform. In it, female is bottom, stigmatized. Intercourse remains a means or the means of physiologically making a woman inferior: communicating to her cell by cell her own inferior status, impressing it on her, burning it into her by shoving it into her, over and over, pushing and thrusting until she gives up and gives in—which is called *surrender* in the male lexicon. In the experience of intercourse, she loses the capacity for integrity because her body—the basis of privacy and freedom in the material world for all human beings—is entered and occupied; the boundaries of her physical body are—neutrally speaking—violated. What is taken from her in that act is not recoverable, and she spends her life—wanting, after all, to have something—pretending that pleasure is in being reduced through intercourse to insignificance. She will not have an orgasm—maybe because she has human pride and she resents captivity; but also she will not or cannot rebel—not enough for it to matter, to end male dominance over her. She learns to eroticize powerlessness and self-annihilation. The very boundaries of her own body become meaningless to her, and even worse, useless to her. The transgression of those boundaries comes to signify a sexually charged degradation into which she throws herself, having been told, convinced, that identity, for a female, is there—somewhere beyond privacy and self-respect.

It is not that there is no way out if, for instance, one were to establish or believe that intercourse itself determines women's lower status. New reproductive technologies have changed and will continue to change the nature of the world. Intercourse is not necessary to existence anymore. Existence does not depend on female compliance, nor on the violation of female boundaries, nor on lesser female privacy, nor on the physical occupation of the female body. But the hatred of women is a source of sexual pleasure for men in its own right. Intercourse appears to be the expression of that contempt in pure form, in the form of a sexed hierarchy; it requires no passion or heart because it is power without invention articulating the arrogance of those who do the fucking. Intercourse is the pure, sterile, formal expression of men's contempt for women; but that contempt can turn gothic and express itself in many sexual and sadistic practices that eschew intercourse per se. Any violation of a woman's body can become sex for men; this is the essential truth of pornography. So freedom from intercourse, or a social structure that reflects the low value of intercourse in women's sexual pleasure, or intercourse becoming one sex act among many entered into by (hypothetical) equals as part of other, deeper, longer, perhaps more sensual lovemaking, or an end to women's inferior status because we need not be forced to reproduce (forced fucking frequently justified by some implicit biological necessity to reproduce): none of these are likely social developments because there is a hatred of women, unexplained, undiagnosed, mostly unacknowledged, that pervades sexual practice and sexual passion. Reproductive technologies are strengthening male dominance, invigorating it by providing new ways of policing women's reproductive capacities, bringing them under stricter male scrutiny and control; and the experimental development of these technologies has been sadistic, using human women as if they were sexual laboratory animals— rats, mice, rabbits, cats, with kinky uteri. For increasing numbers of men, bondage and torture of the female genitals (that were entered into and occupied in the good old days) may supplant intercourse as a sexual practice. The passion for hurting women is a sexual passion; and sexual hatred of women can be expressed without intercourse.

There has always been a peculiar irrationality to all the biological arguments that supposedly predetermine the inferior social status of women. Bulls mount cows and baboons do whatever; but human females do not have estrus or go into heat. The logical inference is not that we are *always* available for mounting but rather that we are never, strictly speaking, "available." Nor do animals have cultures; nor do they determine in so many things what they will do and how they will do them and what the meaning of their own behavior is. They do not decide what their lives will be. Only humans face the often complicated reality of having potential and having to make choices based on having potential. We are not driven by instinct, at least not much. We have possibilities, and we make up meanings as we go along. The meanings we create or learn do not exist only in our heads, in ineffable ideas. Our meanings also exist in our bodies—what we are, what we do, what we physically feel, what we physically know; and there is no personal psychology that is separate from what the body has learned about life. Yet when we look at the human condition, including the condition of women, we act as if we are driven by biology or some metaphysically absolute dogma. We refuse to recognize our possibilities because we refuse to honor the potential humans have, including human women, to make choices. Men too make choices. When will they choose not to despise us? . . .

Study Questions on Andrea Dworkin

1. What does Dworkin mean by "the God who does not exist"?
2. What does intercourse express according to Dworkin? Why, in Dworkin's view, is the fact that the female body is penetrated in intercourse a source of grievance?

3. Men too can be sexually penetrated. A double standard according to which the passive partner is degraded by sex but the active partner is not, is something that has been around since ancient Greece, and has been applied both to heterosexual intercourse and homosexual intercourse. How is men's situation different from that of women, according to Dworkin?

4. Dworkin looks at the physiology of sexual intercourse and reads from it the meaning of intercourse. Interestingly, so does Cormac Burke (see Unit III), and to a slightly lesser degree, Richard Connell (in this unit), but they find radically different meanings in the act. What does each of them see when he or she looks at sexual intercourse? How can they be talking about the same thing? *Are* they talking about the same thing? Could they all be right?

The Place of Sex Among Human Values

BERTRAND RUSSELL

Bertrand Russell argues that moralists should regard sex as they regard food: as the object of a natural human need, to be regulated only for reasons such as the protection of health. Yet he also maintains that a comprehensive sexual ethic cannot regard sexual desire merely as natural hunger and as a possible source of danger, since it is connected with some of the greatest goods of human life, such as lyric love, happiness in marriage, and art.

THE WRITER WHO DEALS with a sexual theme is always in danger of being accused, by those who think that such themes should not be mentioned, of an undue obsession with his subject. It is thought that he would not risk the censure of prudish and prurient persons unless his interest in the subject were out of all proportion to its importance. This view, however, is only taken in the case of those who advocate changes in the conventional ethic. Those who stimulate the appeals to harry prostitutes and those who secure legislation, nominally against the White Slave Traffic, but really against voluntary and decent extra-marital relations; those who denounce women for short skirts and lipsticks; and those who spy upon sea beaches in the hope of discovering inadequate bathing costumes, are none of them supposed to be the victims of a sexual obsession. Yet in fact they probably suffer much more in this way than do writers who advocate greater sexual freedom. Fierce morality is generally a reaction against lustful emotions, and the man who gives expression to it is generally filled with indecent thoughts—thoughts which are rendered indecent, not by the mere fact that they have a sexual content, but that morality has incapacitated the thinker from thinking cleanly and wholesomely on this topic. I am quite in agreement with the Church in thinking that obsession with sexual topics is an evil, but I am not in agreement with the Church as to the best methods of avoiding this evil. It is notorious that St. Anthony was more obsessed by sex than the most extreme voluptuary who ever lived. . . .

. . . [I]f sex is not to be an obsession, it should be regarded by the moralists as food has come to be regarded, and not as food was regarded by the hermits of the Thebaid. Sex is a natural human need like food and drink. It is true that men can survive without it, whereas they cannot survive without food and drink, but from a psychological standpoint the desire for sex is precisely analogous to the desire for food and drink. It is enormously enhanced by abstinence, and temporarily allayed by satisfaction. While it is urgent, it shuts out the rest of the world from the mental purview. All other interests fade for the moment, and actions may be performed which will subsequently appear insane to the man who has been guilty of them. Moreover, as in the case of food and drink, the desire is enormously stimulated by prohibition. I have known children refuse apples at breakfast and go straight out into the orchard and steal them, although the breakfast apples were ripe and the stolen apples unripe. . . .

. . . In like manner, Christian teaching and Christian authority have immensely stimulated interest in sex. The generation which first ceases to believe in the conventional teaching is bound, therefore, to indulge in sexual freedom to a degree far beyond what is to be expected of those whose views on sex are unaffected by superstitious teaching, whether positively or negatively. Nothing but freedom will prevent undue obsession with sex, but even freedom will not have this effect unless it has become habitual and has been associated with a wise education as regards sexual matters. I wish to repeat, however, as emphatically as I can, that I regard an undue preoccupation with this topic as an evil, and that I think this evil widespread at the present day, especially in America, where I find it particularly pronounced among the sterner moralists, who display it markedly by their readiness to believe falsehoods concerning those whom they regard as their opponents. The glutton, the voluptuary, and the ascetic are all self-absorbed persons whose horizon is limited by their own desires, either by way of satisfaction or by way of renunciation. A man who is healthy in mind and body will not have his interests thus concentrated upon himself. He will look out upon the world and find in it objects that seem to him worthy of his attention. Absorption in self is not, as some have supposed, the natural condition of unregenerate man. It is a disease brought on, almost always, by some thwarting of natural impulses. The voluptuary who gloats over thoughts of sexual gratification is in general the result of some kind of deprivation, just as the man who hoards food is usually a man who has lived through a famine or a period of destitution. Healthy, outward-looking men and women are not to be produced by the thwarting of natural impulse, but by the equal and balanced development of all the impulses essential to a happy life.

I am not suggesting that there should be no morality and no self-restraint in regard to sex, any more than in regard to food. In regard to food we have restraints of three kinds, those of law, those of manners, and those of health. We regard it as wrong to steal food, to take more than our share at a common meal, and to eat in ways that are likely to make us ill. Restraints of a similar kind are essential where sex is concerned, but in this case they are much more complex and involve much more self-control. Moreover, since one human being ought not to have property in another, the analogy of stealing is not adultery but rape, which obviously must be forbidden by law. The questions that arise in regard to health are concerned almost entirely with venereal disease, a subject which we have already touched upon in connection with prostitution. Clearly, the diminution of professional prostitution is the best way, apart from medicine, of dealing with this evil, and diminution of professional prostitution can be best effected by that greater freedom among young people which has been growing up in recent years.

A comprehensive sexual ethic cannot regard sex merely as a natural hunger and a possible source of danger. Both these points of view are important, but it is even more important to remember that sex is connected with some of the greatest goods in human life. The three that seem paramount are lyric love, happiness in marriage, and art. Of lyric love and marriage we have already spoken. Art is thought by some to be independent of sex, but this view has fewer adherents now than it had in former times. It is fairly clear that the impulse to every kind of aesthetic creation is psychologically connected with courtship, not necessarily in any direct or obvious way, but none the less profoundly. In order that the sexual impulse may lead to artistic expression, a number of conditions are necessary. There must be artistic capacity; but artistic capacity, even within a given race, appears as though it were common at one time and uncommon at another, from which it is safe to conclude that environment, as opposed to native capacity, has an important part to play in the development of the artistic impulse. There must be a certain kind of freedom, not the sort that consists in rewarding the artist, but the sort that consists in not compelling him or inducing him to form habits which turn him into a philistine. When Julius II imprisoned Michelangelo, he did not in any way interfere with that kind of freedom which the artist needs. He imprisoned him because he considered him an important man, and would not tolerate the slightest offence to him from anybody whose rank was less than papal. When, however, an artist is compelled to kow-tow to rich patrons or town councillors, and to adapt his work to their aesthetic canons, his artistic freedom is lost. And when he is compelled by fear of social and economic persecution to go on living in a marriage which has become intolerable, he is deprived of the energy which artistic creation requires. Societies that have been conventionally virtuous have not produced great art. Those which have, have been composed of men such as Idaho would sterilize. America at present imports most of its artistic talent from Europe, where, as yet, freedom lingers, but already the Americanization of Europe is making it necessary to turn to the negroes. The last home of art, it seems, is to be somewhere on the Upper Congo, if not in the uplands of Tibet. But its final extinction cannot be long delayed, since the rewards which America is prepared to lavish upon foreign artists are such as must inevitably bring about their artistic death. Art in the past has had a popular basis, and this has depended upon joy of life. Joy of life, in its turn, depends upon a certain spontaneity in regard to sex. Where sex is repressed, only work remains, and a gospel of work for work's sake never produced any work worth doing. Let me not be told that some one has collected statistics of the number of sexual acts *per diem* (or shall we say *per noctem*?) performed in the United States, and that it is at least as great per head as in any other country. I do not know whether this is the case or not, and I am not in any way concerned

to deny it. One of the most dangerous fallacies of the conventional moralists is the reduction of sex to the sexual act, in order to be the better able to belabour it. No civilized man, and no savage that I have ever heard of, is satisfied in his instinct by the bare sexual act. If the impulse which leads to the act is to be satisfied, there must be courtship, there must be love, there must be companionship. Without these, while the physical hunger may be appeased for the moment, the mental hunger remains unabated, and no profound satisfaction can be obtained. The sexual freedom that the artist needs is freedom to love, not the gross freedom to relieve the bodily need with some unknown woman; and freedom to love is what, above all, the conventional moralists will not concede. If art is to revive after the world has been Americanized, it will be necessary that America should change, that its moralists should become less moral and its immoralists less immoral, that both, in a word, should recognize the higher values involved in sex, and the possibility that joy may be of more value than a bank-account. Nothing in America is so painful to the traveller as the lack of joy. Pleasure is frantic and bacchanalian, a matter of momentary oblivion, not of delighted self-expression. Men whose grandfathers danced to the music of the pipe in Balkan or Polish villages sit throughout the day glued to their desks, amid typewriters and telephones, serious, important and worthless. Escaping in the evening to drink and a new kind of noise, they imagine that they are finding happiness, whereas they are finding only a frenzied and incomplete oblivion of the hopeless routine of money that breeds money, using for the purpose the bodies of human beings whose souls have been sold into slavery.

It is not my intention to suggest, what I by no means believe, that all that is best in human life is connected with sex. I do not myself regard science, either practical or theoretical, as connected with it, nor yet certain kinds of important social and political activities. The impulses that lead to the complex desires of adult life can be arranged under a few simple heads. Power, sex, and parenthood appear to me to be the source of most of the things that human beings do, apart from what is necessary for self-preservation. Of these three, power begins first and ends last. The child, since he has very little power, is dominated by the desire to have more. Indeed, a large proportion of his activities spring from this desire. His other dominant desire is vanity—the wish to be praised and the fear of being blamed or left out. It is vanity that makes him a social being and gives him the virtues necessary for life in a community. Vanity is a motive closely intertwined with sex, though in theory separable from it. But power has, so far as I can see, very little connection with sex, and it is love of power, at least as much as vanity, that makes a child work at his lessons and develop his muscles. Curiosity and the pursuit of knowledge should, I think, be regarded as a branch of the love of power. If knowledge is power, then the love of knowledge is the love of power. Science, therefore, except for certain branches of biology and physiology, must be regarded as lying outside the province of sexual emotions. As the Emperor Frederick II is no longer alive, this opinion must remain more or less hypothetical. If he were still alive, he would no doubt decide it by castrating an eminent mathematician and an eminent composer and observing the effects upon their respective labours. I should expect the former to be nil and the latter to be considerable. Seeing that the pursuit of knowledge is one of the most valuable elements in human nature, a very important sphere of activity is, if we are right, exempted from the domination of sex.

Study Questions on Bertrand Russell

1. How close do you think the parallel is between our need for food and drink and our need for sex? How are the needs similar and different?
2. Is Russell's statement that "no civilized man, and no savage that I have ever heard of," is content with merely physical sex consistent with his earlier description of sex as a natural need like hunger and thirst? How is the mental hunger connected with the physical one?
3. Do you agree with Russell that sex has very little connection to power?
4. In your experience, does sexual self-restraint lead to obsession with sex? Does sexual self-indulgence?

Sexual Perversion

THOMAS NAGEL

Thomas Nagel here investigates the question of exactly what about human sexuality qualifies it to admit of perversions. In his view, the connection between sex and reproduction has no bearing on sexual perversion; what is crucial, instead, is the fact that sexual desire is a feeling about other persons. Drawing on the

From Thomas Nagel, "Sexual Perversion," Journal of Philosophy, LXVI, *1 (January 16, 1969):*
5–17 (edited version). Reprinted by permission of The Journal of Philosophy.

philosophies of Sartre and H. P. Grice, he argues that sex involves a desire that one's partner be aroused by the recognition of one's desire that he or she be aroused. On these premises, he attempts to distinguish between those deviations from standard intercourse that are perversions and those that are not.

THERE IS SOMETHING to be learned about sex from the fact that we possess a concept of sexual perversion. I wish to examine the concept, defending it against the charge of unintelligibility and trying to say exactly what about human sexuality qualifies it to admit of perversions. . . .

Some people do not believe that the notion of sexual perversion makes sense, and even those who do disagree over its application. Nevertheless I think it will be widely conceded that, if the concept is viable at all, it must meet certain general conditions. First, if there are any sexual perversions, they will have to be sexual desires or practices that can be plausibly described as in some sense unnatural, though the explanation of this natural/unnatural distinction is of course the main problem. Second, certain practices will be perversions if anything is, such as shoe fetishism, bestiality, and sadism; other practices, such as unadorned sexual intercourse, will not be; about still others there is controversy. Third, if there are perversions, they will be unnatural sexual *inclinations* rather than merely unnatural practices adopted not from inclination but for other reasons.

I wish to declare at the outset my belief that the connection between sex and reproduction has no bearing on sexual perversion. The latter is a concept of psychological, not physiological interest, and it is a concept that we do not apply to the lower animals, let alone to plants, all of which have reproductive functions that can go astray in various ways. (Think of seedless oranges.) Insofar as we are prepared to regard higher animals as perverted, it is because of their psychological, not their anatomical similarity to humans. Furthermore, we do not regard as a perversion every deviation from the reproductive function of sex in humans: sterility, miscarriage, contraception, abortion.

Another matter that I believe has no bearing on the concept of sexual perversion is social disapprobation or custom. Anyone inclined to think that in each society the perversions are those sexual practices of which the community disapproves, should consider all the societies that have frowned upon adultery and fornication. These have not been regarded as unnatural practices, but have been thought objectionable in other ways. What is regarded as unnatural admittedly varies from culture to culture, but the classification is not a pure expression of disapproval or distaste. In fact it is often regarded as a *ground* for disapproval, and that suggests that the classification has an independent content.

. . . The skeptical argument runs as follows:
"Sexual desire is simply one of the appetites, like hunger and thirst. As such it may have various objects, some more common than others perhaps, but none in any sense 'natural.' An appetite is identified as sexual by means of the organs and erogenous zones in which its satisfaction can be to some extent localized, and the special sensory pleasures which form the core of that satisfaction. This enables us to recognize widely divergent goals, activities, and desires as sexual since it is conceivable in principle that anything should produce sexual pleasure and that a nondeliberate, sexually charged desire for it should arise (as a result of conditioning, if nothing else). We may fail to empathize with some of these desires, and some of them, like sadism, may be objectionable on extraneous grounds, but once we have observed that they meet the criteria for being sexual, there is nothing more to be said on *that* score. Either they are sexual or they are not: sexuality does not admit of imperfection, or perversion, or any other such qualification—it is not that sort of affection."

This is probably the received radical position. It suggests that the cost of defending a psychological account may be to deny that sexual desire is an appetite.

Let us approach the matter by asking whether we can imagine anything that would qualify as a gastronomical perversion. Hunger and eating are importantly like sex in that they serve a biological function and also play a significant role in our inner lives. It is noteworthy that there is little temptation to describe as perverted an appetite for substances that are not nourishing. We should probably not consider someone's appetites as *perverted* if he liked to eat paper, sand, wood, or cotton. Those are merely rather odd and very unhealthy tastes: they lack the psychological complexity that we expect of perversions. (Coprophilia, being already a sexual perversion, may be disregarded.) If on the other hand someone liked to eat cookbooks, or magazines with pictures of food in them, and preferred these to ordinary food—or if when hungry he sought satisfaction by fondling a napkin or ashtray from his favorite restaurant—then the concept of perversion might seem appropriate (in fact it would be natural to describe this as a case of gastronomical fetishism). It would be natural to describe as gastronomically perverted someone who could eat only by having food forced down his throat through a funnel, or only if the meal were a living animal. What helps in such cases is the peculiarity of the desire itself, rather than the inappropriateness of its object to the biological function that the desire serves. Even an appetite, it would seem, can have perversions if in addition to its biological function it has a significant psychological structure.

If we can imagine perversions of an appetite like hunger, it should be possible to make sense of the concept of sexual perversion. I do not wish to imply that sexual desire is an appetite—only that being an appetite is no bar to admitting of perversions. Like hunger, sexual desire has as its characteristic object a certain relation with something in the external world; only in this case it is usually a person rather than an omelet, and the relation is considerably more complicated. This added complication allows scope for correspondingly complicated perversions.

The fact that sexual desire is a feeling about other persons may tempt us to take a pious view of its psychological content. There are those who believe that sexual desire is properly the expression of some other attitude, like love, and that when it occurs by itself it is incomplete and unhealthy—or at any rate subhuman. (The extreme Platonic version of such a view is that sexual practices are all vain attempts to express something they cannot in principle achieve: this makes them all perversions, in a sense.) I do not believe that any such view is

correct. Sexual desire is complicated enough without having to be linked to anything else as a condition for phenomenological analysis. It cannot be denied that sex may serve various functions—economic, social, altruistic—but it also has its own content as a relation between persons, and it is only by analyzing that relation that we can understand the conditions of sexual perversion.

I believe it is very important that the object of sexual attraction is a particular individual, who transcends the properties that make him attractive. When different persons are attracted to a single person for different reasons: eyes, hair, figure, laugh, intelligence—we feel that the object of their desire is nevertheless the same, namely that person. There is even an inclination to feel that this is so if the lovers have different sexual aims, if they include both men and women, for example. Different specific attractive characteristics seem to provide enabling conditions for the operation of a single basic feeling, and the different aims all provide expressions of it. We approach the sexual attitude toward the person through the features that we find attractive, but these features are not the objects of that attitude.

The importance of this point will emerge when we see how complex a psychological interchange constitutes the natural development of sexual attraction. This would be incomprehensible if its object were not a particular person, but rather a person of a certain *kind*. Attraction is only the beginning, and fulfillment does not consist merely of behavior and contact expressing this attraction, but involves much more.

In particular, narcissistic practices and intercourse with animals, infants, and inanimate objects seem to be stuck at some primitive version of the first stage. If the object is not alive, the experience is reduced entirely to an awareness of one's own sexual embodiment. Small children and animals permit awareness of the embodiment of the other, but present obstacles to reciprocity, to the recognition by the sexual object of the subject's desire as the source of his (the object's) sexual self-awareness.

Sadism concentrates on the evocation of passive self-awareness in others, but the sadist's engagement is itself active and requires a retention of deliberate control which impedes awareness of himself as a bodily subject of passion in the required sense. The victim must recognize him as the source of his own sexual passivity, but only as the active source. De Sade claimed that the object of sexual desire was to evoke involuntary responses from one's partner, especially audible ones. The infliction of pain is no doubt the most efficient way to accomplish this, but it requires a certain abrogation of one's own exposed spontaneity. All this, incidentally, helps to explain why it is tempting to regard as sadistic an excessive preoccupation with sexual technique, which does not permit one to abandon the role of agent at any stage of the sexual act. Ideally one should be able to surmount one's technique at some point.

A masochist on the other hand imposes the same disability on his partner as the sadist imposes on himself. The masochist cannot find a satisfactory embodiment as the object of another's sexual desire, but only as the object of his control. He is passive not in relation to his partner's passion but in relation to his nonpassive agency. In addition, the subjection to one's body characteristic of pain and physical restraint is of a very different kind from that of sexual excitement: pain causes people to contract rather than dissolve.

Both of these disorders have to do with the second stage, which involves the awareness of oneself as an object of desire. In straightforward sadism and masochism other attentions are substituted for desire as a source of the object's self-awareness. But it is also possible for nothing of that sort to be substituted, as in the case of a masochist who is satisfied with self-inflicted pain or of a sadist who does not insist on playing a role in the suffering that arouses him. Greater difficulties of classification are presented by three other categories of sexual activity: elaborations of the sexual act; intercourse of more than two persons; and homosexuality.

If we apply our model to the various forms that may be taken by two-party heterosexual intercourse, none of them seem clearly to qualify as perversions. Hardly anyone can be found these days to inveigh against oral-genital contact, and the merits of buggery are urged by such respectable figures as D. H. Lawrence and Norman Mailer. There may be something vaguely sadistic about the latter technique (in Mailer's writings it seems to be a method of introducing an element of rape), but it is not obvious that this has to be so. In general, it

would appear that any bodily contact between a man and a woman that gives them sexual pleasure, is a possible vehicle for the system of multi-level interpersonal awareness that I have claimed is the basic psychological content of sexual interaction. Thus a liberal platitude about sex is upheld.

About multiple combinations, the least that can be said is that they are bound to be complicated. If one considers how difficult it is to carry on two conversations simultaneously, one may appreciate the problems of multiple simultaneous interpersonal perception that can arise in even a small-scale orgy. It may be inevitable that some of the component relations should degenerate into mutual epidermal stimulation by participants otherwise isolated from each other. There may also be a tendency toward voyeurism and exhibitionism, both of which are incomplete relations. The exhibitionist wishes to display his desire without needing to be desired in return; he may even fear the sexual attentions of others. A voyeur, on the other hand, need not require any recognition by his object at all: certainly not a recognition of the voyeur's arousal.

It is not clear whether homosexuality is a perversion if that is measured by the standard of the described configuration, but it seems unlikely. For such a classification would have to depend on the possibility of extracting from the system a distinction between male and female sexuality; and much that has been said so far applies equally to men and women. Moreover, it would have to be maintained that there was a natural tie between the type of sexuality and the sex of the body, and also that two sexualities of the same type could not interact properly.

Certainly there is much support for an aggressive-passive distinction between male and female sexuality. In our culture the male's arousal tends to initiate the perceptual exchange, he usually makes the sexual approach, largely controls the course of the act, and of course penetrates whereas the woman receives. When two men or two women engage in intercourse they cannot both adhere to these sexual roles. The question is how essential the roles are to an adequate sexual relation. One relevant observation is that a good deal of deviation from these roles occurs in heterosexual intercourse.

The best discussion of these matters that I have seen appears in part III of Sartre's *Being and*

Nothingness. Since it has influenced my own views, I shall say a few things about it now. Sartre's treatment of sexual desire and of love, hate, sadism, masochism, and further attitudes toward others, depends on a general theory of consciousness and the body which we can neither expound nor assume here. He does not discuss perversion, and this is partly because he regards sexual desire as one form of the perpetual attempt of an embodied consciousness to come to terms with the existence of others, an attempt that is as doomed to fail in this form as it is in any of the others, which include sadism and masochism (if not certain of the more impersonal deviations) as well as several nonsexual attitudes. According to Sartre, all attempts to incorporate the other into my world as another subject, i.e., to apprehend him at once as an object for me and as a subject for whom I am an object, are unstable and doomed to collapse into one or other of the two aspects. Either I reduce him entirely to an object, in which case his subjectivity escapes the possession or appropriation I can extend to that object; or I become merely an object for him, in which case I am no longer in a position to appropriate his subjectivity. Moreover, neither of these aspects is stable; each is continually in danger of giving way to the other. This has the consequence that there can be no such thing as a *successful* sexual relation, since the deep aim of sexual desire cannot in principle be accomplished. It seems likely, therefore, that the view will not permit a basic distinction between successful or complete and unsuccessful or incomplete sex, and therefore cannot admit the concept of perversion.

I do not adopt this aspect of the theory, nor many of its metaphysical underpinnings. What interests me is Sartre's picture of the attempt. He says that the type of possession that is the object of sexual desire is carried out by "a double reciprocal incarnation" and that this is accomplished, typically in the form of a caress, in the following way: "I make myself flesh in order to impel the Other to realize *for herself* and *for me* her own flesh, and my caresses cause my flesh to be born for me in so far as it is for the Other *flesh causing her to be born as flesh.*" . . . The incarnation in question is described variously as a clogging or troubling of consciousness, which is inundated by the flesh in which it is embodied.

The view I am going to suggest, I hope in less obscure language, is related to this one, but it differs from Sartre's in allowing sexuality to achieve its goal on occasion and thus in providing the concept of perversion with a foothold.

Sexual desire involves a kind of perception, but not merely a single perception of its object, for in the paradigm case of mutual desire there is a complex system of superimposed mutual perceptions—not only perceptions of the sexual object, but perceptions of oneself. Moreover, sexual awareness of another involves considerable self-awareness to begin with—more than is involved in ordinary sensory perception. The experience is felt as an assault on oneself by the view (or touch, or whatever) of the sexual object.

Let us consider a case in which the elements can be separated. For clarity we will restrict ourselves initially to the somewhat artificial case of desire at a distance. Suppose a man and a woman, whom we may call Romeo and Juliet, are at opposite ends of a cocktail lounges with many mirrors on the walls which permit unobserved observation, and even mutual unobserved observation. Each of them is sipping a martini and studying other people in the mirrors. At some point Romeo notices Juliet. He is moved, somehow, by the softness of her hair and the diffidence with which she sips her martini, and this arouses him sexually. Let us say that X *senses* Y whenever X regards Y with sexual desire. (Y need not be a person, and X's apprehension of Y can be visual, tactile, olfactory, etc., or purely imaginary; in the present example we shall concentrate on vision.) So Romeo senses Juliet, rather than merely noticing her. At this stage he is aroused by an unaroused object, so he is more in the sexual grip of his body than she of hers.

Let us suppose, however, that Juliet now senses Romeo in another mirror on the opposite wall, though neither of them yet knows that he is seen by the other (the mirror angles provide three-quarter views). Romeo then begins to notice in Juliet the subtle signs of sexual arousal: heavy-lidded stare, dilating pupils, faint flush, et cetera. This of course renders her much more bodily, and he not only notices but senses this as well. His arousal is nevertheless still solitary. But now, cleverly calculating the line of her stare without actually looking her in the eyes, he realizes that it is directed at him through the mirror on the opposite wall. That is, he notices, and moreover senses, Juliet sensing him. This is definitely a new development, for it gives him a sense of embodiment not only through his own reactions but through the eyes and reactions of another. Moreover, it is separable from the initial sensing of Juliet; for sexual arousal might begin with a person's sensing that he is sensed and being assailed by the perception of the other person's desire rather than merely by the perception of the person.

But there is a further step. Let us suppose that Juliet, who is a little slower than Romeo, now senses that he senses her. This puts Romeo in a position to notice, and be aroused by, her arousal at being sensed by him. He senses that she senses that he senses her. This is still another level of arousal, for he becomes conscious of his sexuality through his awareness of its effect on her and of her awareness that this effect is due to him. Once she takes the same step and senses that he senses her sensing him, it becomes difficult to state, let alone imagine, further iterations, though they may be logically distinct. If both are alone, they will presumably turn to look at each other directly, and the proceedings will continue on another plane. Physical contact and intercourse are perfectly natural extensions of this complicated visual exchange, and mutual touch can involve all the complexities of awareness present in the visual case, but with a far greater range of subtlety and acuteness.

Ordinarily, of course, things happen in a less orderly fashion—sometimes in a great rush—but I believe that some version of this overlapping system of distinct sexual perceptions and interactions is the basic framework of any full-fledged sexual relation and that relations involving only part of the complex are significantly incomplete. The account is only schematic, as it must be to achieve generality. Every real sexual act will be psychologically far more specific and detailed, in ways that depend not only on the physical techniques employed and on anatomical details, but also on countless features of the participants' conceptions of themselves and of each other, which become embodied in the act. (It is a familiar enough fact, for example, that people often take their social roles and the social roles of their partners to bed with them.)

The general schema is important, however, and the proliferation of levels of mutual awareness it involves is an example of a type of complexity that typifies human interactions.

Another example of such reflexive mutual recognition is to be found in the phenomenon of meaning, which appears to involve an intention to produce a belief or other effect in another by bringing about his recognition of one's intention to produce that effect. (That result is due to H. P. Grice, whose position I shall not attempt to reproduce in detail.) Sex has a related structure: it involves a desire that one's partner be aroused by the recognition of one's desire that he or she be aroused.

It is not easy to define the basic types of awareness and arousal of which these complexes are composed, and that remains a lacuna in this discussion. I believe that the object of awareness is the same in one's own case as it is in one's sexual awareness of another, although the two awarenesses will not be the same, the difference being as great as that between feeling angry and experiencing the anger of another. All stages of sexual perception are varieties of identification of a person with his body. What is perceived is one's own or another's *subjection* to or *immersion* in his body, a phenomenon which has been recognized with loathing by St. Paul and St. Augustine, both of whom regarded "the law of sin which is in my members" as a grave threat to the dominion of the holy will. In sexual desire and its expression the blending of involuntary response with deliberate control is extremely important. For Augustine, the revolution launched against him by his body is symbolized by erection and the other involuntary physical components of arousal. Sartre too stresses the fact that the penis is not a prehensile organ. But mere involuntariness characterizes other bodily processes as well. In sexual desire the involuntary responses are combined with submission to spontaneous impulses: not only one's pulse and secretions but one's actions are taken over by the body; ideally, deliberate control is needed only to guide the expression of those impulses. This is to some extent also true of an appetite like hunger, but the takeover there is more localized, less pervasive, less extreme. One's whole body does not become saturated with hunger as it can with desire. But the most characteristic feature of a specifically sexual immersion in the body is its ability to fit into the complex of mutual perceptions that we have described. Hunger leads to spontaneous interactions with food; sexual desire leads to spontaneous interactions with other persons, whose bodies are asserting their sovereignty in the same way, producing involuntary reactions and spontaneous impulses in *them*. These reactions are perceived, and the perception of them is perceived, and that perception is in turn perceived; at each step the domination of the person by his body is reinforced, and the sexual partner becomes more possessible by physical contact, penetration, and envelopment.

Desire is therefore not merely the perception of a preexisting embodiment of the other, but ideally a contribution to his further embodiment which in turn enhances the original subject's sense of himself. This explains why it is important that the partner be aroused, and not merely aroused, but aroused by the awareness of one's desire. It also explains the sense in which desire has unity and possession as its object: physical possession must eventuate in creation of the sexual object in the image of one's desire, and not merely in the object's recognition of that desire, or in his or her own private arousal. (This may reveal a male bias: I shall say something about that later.)

To return, finally, to the topic of perversion: I believe that various familiar deviations constitute truncated or incomplete versions of the complete configuration, and may therefore be regarded as perversions of the central impulse.

Women can be sexually aggressive and men passive, and temporary reversals of role are not uncommon in heterosexual exchanges of reasonable length. If such conditions are set aside, it may be urged that there is something irreducibly perverted in attraction to a body anatomically like one's own. But alarming as some people in our culture may find such attraction, it remains psychologically unilluminating to class it as perverted. Certainly if homosexuality is a perversion, it is so in a very different sense from that in which shoe-fetishism is a perversion, for some version of the full range of interpersonal perceptions seems perfectly possible between two persons of the same sex.

In any case, even if the proposed model is correct, it remains implausible to describe as perverted every deviation from it. For example, if the partners in heterosexual intercourse indulge in private heterosexual fantasies, that obscures the recognition of the real partner and so, on the theory, constitutes a defective sexual relation. It is not, however, generally regarded as a perversion. Such examples suggest that a simple dichotomy between perverted and unperverted sex is too crude to organize the phenomena adequately.

Study Questions on Thomas Nagel

1. Nagel's account of sexual perversion relies, he says, on a psychological theory about sexual desire. Explain that theory with reference to his story about Romeo and Juliet.

2. In terms of the worldviews discussed in the Introduction for Students in this book, how would you classify Nagel? Do you think that Nagel overspiritualizes sex?

3. Both Nagel and Mohr (in this unit) talk about the experience of embodiment in sex. Do they seem to mean the same thing by this?

4. Do you think there is such a thing as sexual perversion? If so, what sorts of things are perversions and why? How serious a matter is sexual perversion? Does the concept of perversion make sense without a background conception of nature?

Reproduction as the Goal of Sexuality

RICHARD CONNELL

Richard Connell argues that reproduction is the natural goal of sexual activity. In nature generally, and in the human animal as well, reproduction is for the benefit of the species, for the coming-into-existence of new individuals ensures its continuation. Reproduction also includes the processes of development that produce both physical and nonphysical maturation. Human sexuality is under voluntary control; we ought to engage only in those forms of sexual activity that are in accord with these purposes.

Two Kinds of Activity

IF WE USE THE TERM "activity" in its broadest sense—to signify any movement, behavior, or operation whatsoever of living and non-living things alike—then we have a class, a category of thing that can be divided into two main subcategories, one of which is called "goal-directed," the other "random." An action belonging to the first of these two categories is characterized by the end-state or entity (thing) toward which it is oriented and which is, as we say, determinative of the action itself; whereas members of the second category are characterized by the absence of any such orientation toward a determinate end-state or entity. This difference is important, and therefore, our aim here is to elaborate upon the distinction between these two sorts of activity.

Egg-laying is a part of the reproductive process of birds, and it is ordinary for a particular species of bird to have a fairly well defined clutch number, which is important to the species in that it represents the number of offspring for which the parent(s) is able to care at one time. One is not surprised, then, to learn that clutch size plays a role in determining how long the laying continues. Normally, the female will produce until the appropriate number is attained, at which time the egg-laying ceases. Farmers have made use of this phenomenon for years, for they know that by gathering their eggs—thereby preventing the normal clutch number from being reached—they can keep the laying process going. In short, our point is this: actions of this type persist until the goal is reached; the end, therefore, is determinative of the action; the action exists for its goal.

A similar relationship exists between other activities and their goals, and the production of red blood cells within the mammalian body is an example. If bleeding occurs, diminishing the number of red cells, the body immediately begins to produce them, continuing the production until the normal limits are reached. On the other hand, if a transfusion is made very quickly after the hemorrhage starts, little or no production of cells takes place; and, if more red cells are introduced than are needed, a destructive process, known as phagocytosis, brings the number within the established limits. . . .

Natural actions are not the only ones to be goal-directed. Conscious human activities are also oriented toward a definite entity or end-state. When we act consciously we think about an object we wish to produce or some state or condition we wish to achieve, and then we do something in order to obtain what we thought about. To illustrate: Mental skills and the activities which they enable us to perform are the goal of education; health is the end of exercise; refreshment as the looked-for result of recreation; clothing is the goal of sewing, etc. . . .

Purely random activity, on the other hand, is characterized by the absence of directedness altogether, and consequently it is defined as a lack of

Reprinted by permission of Laval Théologique et Philosophique.

orientation to a determinate end-state or entity, a lack which is accompanied by an absence of a corresponding preexisting pattern or "program" through which the orientation is realized. . . .

Physical and Voluntary Actions

We have already talked about activities from the point of view of their being random or goal-directed; now we wish to discuss certain human operations from the point of view of how they are initiated. Although what follows is evident to all, we think it wise to include it here.

Two kinds of goal-directed, bodily activity occur within the human being: 1) those which are controlled voluntarily, and 2) those which are not subject to such control but issue from purely physical causes. The movement of one's legs is an example of the first; the flow of digestive enzymes in the stomach is an instance of the second. Obviously a large part of the human organism functions on the basis of physical causes, which are not *directly* subject to voluntary direction, and certainly we are fortunate that this is so. Were we encumbered with the need to regulate voluntarily all of our physiological activities, it is certain we could not survive. . . .

. . . In man's capacity to choose from among many, in his ability to direct and to control in much broader measure his mode of living, lies his superior status. On this is founded his human dignity; this is what we call his freedom. In short, the dignity of the human person is based principally upon two things: 1) the voluntary, free, self-regulating, self-directing mode of behavior; 2) the goals toward which these actions can be oriented. . . .

It is important to note, however, the obvious fact that only the *use* of certain human powers is under voluntary direction. The natural operative capacities that we possess are determined in their character before we exercise them. (We do not cause them to be what they are, and for that reason we speak of them as given to us.) For example, we may apply the power of sight to this or that object, but we do not say whether we shall see with the eye or do something else with it. We can introduce meat or vegetables into the stomach, but once they are there we have nothing fur-

ther to say about the digestive process. Again, human voluntary control extends only to the *use* of human powers. We can decide to apply them or not, but we are unable to determine what their functions shall be. . . .

The God of Reproduction

In nature generally reproduction is for the benefit of the species, for the coming-into-existence of new individuals ensures its continuation. Similarly in the human animal. But the reproductive process is inadequately considered if one views its goal to be simply the birth of a new individual. The adults of other species do not abandon their young until they are ready to function by themselves; so, too, human parents are obliged to care for their children until they are reared, until such time as the children are equipped to direct their own lives. One could put the matter another way by saying that reproduction has two stages: 1) the process of biological generation (one part of which is coitus) that brings about the physical separation of the offspring from its parents; 2) the processes of development, from which ensue both a physical and a non-physical maturation. In short, the young adult is the goal of procreation. . . .

The use of the human procreative powers is subject to voluntary control, for coitus is an activity in which men consciously and willfully engage. In addition, the use of such operational capacities ought to be in accord with the goals which they are given by nature; yet as long as one recognizes these conditions, to regulate births by voluntary means in view of a family size commensurate with the goal of reproduction lies within a man's moral province.

However, the use of medications which alter the physiological processes of the ovulatory cycle in a healthy organ or which inhibit the production of sperm by healthy parts is not morally licit. As in all other cases, medications may be used morally only to stimulate processes that are insufficient, or to inhibit those that are excessive. They could, for example, be used to stimulate an inadequate production of sperm or inhibit—if such occurs—an overly active mechanism. Similarly, medicines can be used to correct defective parts of an oestrous cycle. But one may not morally introduce a medication to stimulate or inhibit—to disrupt—what is already healthy; such a use of medicines is immoral.

The employment of mechanical or chemical contraceptive devices (their use is not a medical question, but it is related to the same principles) also introduces a disorder into the human mode of operation. People who employ them are attempting to exercise the activity but at the same time to prevent the realization of the goal toward which the activity is naturally—by its constitution—directed. Because the organ exists for its function, the use of these means is morally equivalent to temporarily damaging the part for the sake of inhibiting its operation. Clearly, damage to a part is bad because of the ensuing interference with the function. Consequently, to interpose a mechanical device for the sake of interferring with the normal deposit of sperm is, as we said, morally equivalent to doing temporary damage to the part at the same time that its operation is sought; the act is, therefore, immoral. One must constantly keep in mind that human art may treat what is defective, but it may not disrupt what is biologically normal as this is determined by nature. . . .

Study Questions on Richard Connell

1. Do you think that there can be goal-directed activity without conscious purpose? Does Connell's argument depend on belief in a God, Who creates human beings and their sexuality for His purposes? Does Darwin's theory of evolution invalidate Connell's way of speaking about biological purposes?
2. Do you find Connell's picture of sexuality adequate? Incomplete? Hopelessly mistaken?
3. Do you find Connell's understanding of sexuality too animalistic (or, as it is often put, "biologistic")? Are the purposes of sexuality adequately served by an adolescent male who impregnates large numbers of females, then dies in a street fight?
4. Do you think Connell has articulated a serious moral objection to artificial contraception?

Sexual Intercourse: Its Relation to the Rest of Women's Sexual Role

NILES NEWTON

Niles Newton protests the cultural tendency to limit investigation of female sexuality to coitus and orgasm. Menstruation, pregnancy, childbirth, and breastfeeding, she argues, are equally important aspects of women's sexual experience. We can understand women's response in intercourse only in this larger context.

From Maternal Emotions *by Niles Newton, Paul Hoeber, Inc., Harper & Bros., 1955, pp. 85–94. Reprinted by permission of Elizabeth Reid.*

SEXUAL INTERCOURSE IS, of course, just as important a phase of women's reproductive role as menstruation, pregnancy, childbirth, and lactation. However, it has often been singled out as if it were the *only* important part of women's sexuality and unrelated to any other phase of women's sexual role. An excellent example of this cultural tendency is to be seen in Kinsey, *et al.*'s book on women. A huge volume purporting to cover *Sexual Behavior of the Human Female* deals in fact only with the orgastic and coital aspects of female sexuality. Menstruation, pregnancy, childbirth, and breast feeding are simply excluded from serious consideration as if they were not part of women's sexual behavior. The Kinsey study concentrates on only those portions of women's sexual behavior that are similar to what men experience. The fact that this discrepancy was seldom, if at all, noticed by reviewers shows that Kinsey *et al.*'s habits of thought are in keeping with those of most of the culture.

Actually, there is considerable research evidence that feeling about intercourse may be closely related to every other phase of women's sexuality. The evidence is as follows:

Menstruation and Intercourse

Sexual feeling and sexual activity vary with the menstrual cycle. McCance, Luff, and Widdowson studied the cyclic behavior through detailed and extensive daily records made by 167 normal women—each over a period of several months. They analyzed 780 complete menstrual cycles. Inaccuracies due to memory were kept to a minimum since records were made daily through each cycle. They found that single women reached a peak of sexual feeling at about the eighth day after the onset of menstruation, with the period of lowest incidence of sexual feeling during the early part of the menstrual flow. Married women similarly experienced a low of sexual feeling during the first days of the menstrual flow, and then their incidence of desire rose rapidly to reach its peak on the eighth day. Intercourse in married women also reached its peak incidence on the eighth day and its low point during the first three days after the onset of menstruation.

Questionnaire methods have also found that women report variations in desire, according to the phase of the menstrual cycle, but they suggested a later peak for the period of greatest sexual desire.[5] This latter finding, however, might well be discounted since more accurate methods indicate earlier peaks of desire, and since these early peaks are more in accord with new research suggesting that ovulation usually takes place well before the middle of the menstrual cycle.[2]

Additional evidence about the relation of menstruation and intercourse comes from a study of menstrual pain. A report on married women with dysmenorrhea showed that 77 percent were maladjusted sexually. whereas only 27 percent of the control group were sexually maladjusted.

An exploratory study, done in connection with this research, found that women who had positive feelings about menstruation desired intercourse more frequently than those who had negative feelings about menstruation. There was a 34 percent difference between the two groups; but since the numbers were small, this is not a statistically significant difference.

Pregnancy and Intercourse

There is some evidence that sexual feelings also vary with pregnancy. Landis studied the rise and ebb of sexual desire during pregnancy in more than 200 couples by the questionnaire method. Although a few women reported increased desire during the beginning months of pregnancy, most tended to have less sexual desire as pregnancy progressed. Twenty-seven percent of the women noticed a decrease in desire by the first three months of pregnancy, 43 percent by the second three months of pregnancy, and 79 percent by the last three months.

Absence of orgasm coupled with frequent undesired intercourse is reported to be related to nausea and vomiting in pregnancy. Robertson, who did the study, was in an unusually good position to obtain the information because he studied his own private obstetrical cases. He found that all of the pregnant women with severe nausea had disturbed sexual function, whereas only one in ten of the pregnant women without nausea had similar sexual problems.

An exploratory study, done in connection with this research, found that women who had positive feelings about pregnancy desired intercourse more frequently than those who had negative feelings about pregnancy. There was a 37 percent differ- ence between the two groups, but since the num-

bers were small this is not a statistically significant difference.

Childbirth and Intercourse

There are some interesting similarities between the physiology of uninhibited, undrugged childbirth and the physiology of sexual excitement. The most strikingly similar points are as follows:

UNINHIBITED, UNDRUGGED CHILDBIRTH

SEXUAL EXCITEMENT

Breathing

In the first stage of labor breathing becomes deeper during contractions.

During early stages breathing becomes faster an deeper.

Second stage brings on very deep breaths with breath holding.

As orgasm approaches breathing becomes inter- rupted.

Tendency to make noises, grunts, etc.

Tendency to make gasping, sucking noises.

Facial Expression

As delivery approaches face gets intense, strained look which makes observers often assume woman is suffering great pain.

As orgasm approaches face gets what Kinsey, *et al.* call a "tortured expression." Mouth open, glassy eyes, tense muscles.

Face looks like that of an athlete undergoing great physical strain.

Face looks like that of an athlete under great phys- ical strain.

Uterus

The upper segment of the uterus contracts rhyth- mically.

The upper segment of the uterus contracts rhyth- mically.

Loosening of mucus plug from os of cervix is one of the standard signs of labor.

Cervical secretion may loosen mucus plug which ordinarily lies at os of cervix thus opening it for spermatozoa.

Abdominal Muscles

Contract periodically. A strong, instinctive urge to bear down by using abdominal muscles as delivery approaches.

Abdominal muscles contract periodically with con- siderable force. Movement builds up as orgasm approaches.

Legs wide apart and bent.

This position is used by women in intercourse.

Central Nervous System

Woman becomes uninhibited particularly during second stage of labor. All veneer of "refinement" disappears.

Inhibitions and psychic blockages are relieved and often eliminated.

Delivery of the baby through the narrow passage calls for unusual strength and body expansion.

Unusual muscular strength. Many persons become capable of bending and distorting body in ways they could not otherwise do.

Sensory Perception

The vulva becomes anesthetic with full dilatation, so that woman often must be told of birth of baby's head.

Amnesia, tendency to become insensitive to surroundings as delivery approaches.

Suddenly, delivery completed, woman becomes wide awake.

Whole body of person who becomes sexually aroused becomes increasingly insensitive even to sharp blows and severe injury.

As orgasm approaches loss of sensory perception is nearly complete—sometimes leading to moments of unconsciousness.

After orgasm, sudden return of sensory acuity.

Emotional Response

After the birth of the baby there is a flood of joyful emotion. Read describes it as "complete and careless ecstasy."

There is a strong feeling of well being in most persons. Many psychologists believe that this relief from tension is the chief source of satisfaction gained from intercourse.

The sexual data for this comparison came almost entirely from Kinsey, *et al.* They base their statements not only on interviews with thousands of persons, but also on reports of scientifically trained persons observing human sexual activities, physiological experiments on human beings, and on evidence from other mammals.

The data on birth were gained chiefly from Grantly Dick Read, who has analyzed 516 consecutive labors. Read made every effort to keep women free from fear or disturbance, and thus uninhibited. Some of the birth data are corroborated by some movies and photographs of women in labor. Since in this country it is the custom to move, strap down, and otherwise disturb even undrugged women as they approach the birth climax, the behavior noted by Read may be not so frequent nor so pronounced here.

Feelings about childbirth may influence sexual adjustment. Landis, in his study of couples after the birth of their first child, found that those who did *not* fear childbirth had a higher proportion of very good sexual adjustment. Fewer of those who feared childbirth had very good sexual adjustments. The difference was statistically significant.

Landis's study done on 212 couples should be weighed much more heavily than the small exploratory study done in connection with this research which found no indication that feelings toward childbirth and feelings toward intercourse were related.

Breast Feeding and Intercourse

The function of the breast is closely related to the function of the other female organs. The breast develops about the time of the onset of menstruation and develops still further during pregnancy. Sexual excitement causes uterine contractions[3] and so does breast feeding.[6]

Uterine contractions during breast feeding are very sensitive to psychological stimuli. Experimental evidence indicates that this let-down reflex (which involves uterine contractions) does not occur when the mother is frightened or disturbed.[7, 18]

The absence of uterine contractions may be a sign of breast feeding failure. Uterine contractions are easily noted in the early puerperium since they frequently cause pain to women in our society. Newton and Newton[8] asked mothers about these painful uterine contractions that occur *during* breast feeding. Mothers who went on to breast feed abundantly reported significantly more of such painful contractions than women who went on to have an inadequate milk supply. On the second day postpartum, 64 percent of the successful breast feeders as opposed to 38 percent of the unsuccessful breast feeders had painful uterine contractions during breast feeding.

The same hormone extract (Pitocin) that starts the let-down of milk is widely used to start the uterine contractions of labor. Oxytocin works both on breast and uterus. Although the let-down of milk is usually set off by the sucking of the baby, cows have been induced to let down their milk by stimulating their vulva or vagina.[9]

The breast and particularly the nipple are very sensitive organs. The nipple becomes erect on stimulation. Kinsey, *et al.* believe that about one out of every two women derives distinct satisfaction when the breast is involved in sexual play. They have records of some men and some women even reaching orgasm through breast stimulation.

Extensive breast stimulation occurs during breast feeding. The baby's mouth strokes the nipple for many minutes at a time. Often the little arm waves in an instinctive rhythmic motion, stroking the breast. When mother and baby are undressed they press firmly together, skin against skin. This kind of firm, continuous pressure is described by Kinsey, *et al.* as leading to sexual excitement.

Our culture makes every effort to minimize the possibilities of sensuous enjoyment of breast feeding. Usually the mother and baby are clothed and sucking time is limited. There is even an ingenious device called the nipple shield, whose purpose is to protect the nipple from the direct sucking of the baby. It can be found in almost every hospital. The popularity of manual expression of milk rather than letting the baby suck as much as it desires may also in part stem from this aversion to direct contact between mother and baby.

There is some evidence that breast feeding is somewhat of an antithesis of the menstruation-intercourse portion of woman's sexual cycle. Lactation delays ovulation and menstruation, and decreases the probability of conception. Lactation of long duration causes the uterus to atrophy. The muscle fibers shrink from their enormous enlargement at the time of delivery to become smaller than their pre-pregnant state.[17]

Virtually all of the women included in this research study were lactating, and therefore might be expected to show evidence that their sexual energies were flowing into lactation. The exploratory study found that women who wanted to continue breast feeding said they desired less intercourse than women who planned to bottle feed. There was a 40 percent difference between the two groups. Women who liked breast feeding also expressed less enjoyment in intercourse. There was a 27 percent difference between the two groups. These differences, however, are not statistically significant since the numbers involved in the exploratory study were small.

Motherliness and Intercourse

Although religious institutions frequently emphasize that the enjoyment of sexual intercourse is for the purpose of procreation, this is frequently regarded as just a "moral" law. There is, however, some evidence that it may be also a psychological and physiological law for women, at least to some extent. Certainly intercourse behavior is related to many aspects of parenthood.

Sterility is related to sexual responsiveness in some instances. Wittkower and Wilson compared 30 sterile women with 30 women pregnant with their first babies. The sterile women had fertile husbands and no obvious abnormality of the genital tract. Eighty-seven percent of the sterile women reported such difficulties as failure to have orgasm, no sexual feeling, pain during intercourse, painful vaginal spasm. Only 27 percent of the control group reported similar troubles.

Parenthood may lead to lessened sexual desire. Landis in his study of 212 couples found that there was a significantly lower level of sex desire in both wives and husbands after the birth of their first child as compared with before the pregnancy. The relation between devaluation of motherhood and poor sexual adjustment is suggested in a study of 50 college women who expressed futility. Fifty-four percent of these women did *not* have "being a good and successful mother" as *even one* of their major life goals, and 80 percent expressed futility about sexual adjustment.[20]

The desire for children does not necessarily increase the orgasm rate of women. The Terman study on 556 selected women found no relation between orgasm and the conscious desire for children. Nor were number of children related to orgasm. However, fear of having children may be related to poor sexual adjustment. Landis found that wives who distrust their contraceptive methods reported a significantly lower rate of sexual adjustments than wives who did not distrust their contraceptive methods. . . .

Practical Application

One of the most fundamental and well-demonstrated psychological laws states that the whole is *not* equal to the sum of its parts. For instance, a pencil drawing of an apple is not just a lot of pencil lines—it has a meaning over, above, and beyond those pencil lines. Similarly, women's sexuality can be viewed with more understanding if it is viewed as a whole rather than as disconnected parts.

One of the chief difficulties in viewing women's sexuality as a whole is that the taboos against some aspects of it are much greater than others. The intercourse aspect of women's sexuality is quite freely discussed in the popular press. The experiences of childbirth and pregnancy are just beginning to be freely discussed and even photographed. Equally frank talk about menstruation is still taboo, and the idea that successful breast feeding gives sensuous pleasure is generally considered utterly unprintable!

Another difficulty is that those women who use all the potentialities of their female bodies are the least likely to write, to speak, and to do research because they are absorbed in the task of growing children. Thus verbalization about women's sexuality tends to be left to men or to women who have rejected part of their female biological role.

The study of women's total sexuality is a great and fruitful area for future study. Women's wider sexual role forms the primitive basis of family life. Father and siblings have no bodily relationship between themselves. However, they share one common bond. All members of the family have had or do have a direct psychosomatic relationship with the mother. The problems of family life, the interactions of family life, and the satisfactions of family life cannot be fully understood without considering *all* aspects of these psychosomatic relationships.

Summary

1. An exploratory study done in connection with this research yielded the suggestive finding that women who had the least desire for intercourse were more likely to have negative feelings toward menstruation and pregnancy, and to have positive feelings toward lactation.

2. Women's feelings toward intercourse may be closely related to every phase of her sexual role. Extensive controlled studies have found the following tendencies in certain groups of women:

    A. Sexual desire and sexual activity waxes and wanes with the course of the menstrual cycle. Married women with severe menstrual pain are likely to be sexually maladjusted.

    B. Pregnancy materially alters the sexual desires. Nausea and vomiting in pregnancy frequently are related to experiences of undesired intercourse.

    C. Women who fear childbirth are less likely to have very good sexual adjustment. Uninhibited, undrugged childbirth is very similar to sexual excitement and orgasm in regard to the following points: Manner of breathing, facial expression, contractions of the uterus, contractions of the abdominal muscles, position of the body, reactions of the central nervous system, sensory perception, and emotional response.

  D. Both breast feeding and sexual excitement cause uterine contractions. Women who fail to have uterine contractions during nursing are likely to have an insufficient milk supply. The breast is a very sensitive erotic area that gets extensive stimulation during breast feeding. The lactation portion of women's sexual cycle is physically somewhat the antithesis of the menstruation-intercourse portion of women's sexual cycle.

  E. Marriages are happiest when the wife becomes a mother. Marriage failure is extremely frequent when the woman remains childless. Even if a childless woman remains undivorced till middle age, her marriage is likely to be unhappier than that of a similar woman who has become a mother.

3. In view of these findings, it seems reasonable to assume that women's response in intercourse can probably only be understood if the rest of her sexual role is fully considered as well.

References

1. Douglas, J. W. B. The extent of breast feeding in Great Britain in 1946, with special reference to the health and survival of children. *J. Obst. & Gynaec. The Brit. Emp.* 57:335, 1950.

2. Farris, E. J. *Human Fertility and Problems of the Male.* White Plains, N.Y., Author's Press, 1950.

3. Kinsey, A. C., *et al. Sexual Behavior in the Human Female.* Philadelphia, Saunders, 1953.

4. Landis, J. T. The effects of first pregnancy upon the sexual adjustment of 212 couples. *Am. Soc. Rev.* 15:767, 1950.

5. McCance, R. A., *et al.* Physical and emotional periodicity in women. *J. Hyg.* 37:571, 1937.

6. Moir, Chassar. Recording the contractions of the human pregnant and non-pregnant uterus. *Tr. Edinburgh Obst. Soc.* 54:93, 1934.

7. Newton, M., and Newton, Niles. The letdown reflex in human lactation. *J. Pediat.* 33:698, 1948.

8. Newton, Niles, and Newton, M. Relation of the let-down reflex to ability to breast feed. *Pediatrics* 5:726, 1950.

9. Nüesch, A. Uber das sogenannte Aufziehen der Milch bei der Kuh. Inaug. Diss. Zürich, 1904. As cited by Hammond, J. *Veterinary Rec.* 16:519, 1936.

10. Popenoe, P. Infertility and the stability of marriage. *Western J. Surg.* 56:309, 1948.

11. Read, G. D. *Childbirth Without Fear.* New York, Harper & Brothers, 1944.

12. Read, G. D. The discomforts of childbirth. *Brit. M. J.* 1:651, 1949.

13. Read, G. D. Observations on a series of labors with special reference to physiological delivery. *Lancet* 1:721, 1949.

14. Read, G. D. *The Birth of a Child.* New York, Vanguard, 1950.

15. Read, G. D. *Introduction to Motherhood. New York, Harper & Brothers, 1950.*

16. *Robertson, G. G. Nausea and vomiting in pregnancy.* Lancet 2:336, 1946.

17. Sanger, M. Die Ruckbildung der Muscularis des Puerperalen Uterus. *Beitr. Z. path., Anat. U. Klin. Med. Von Wagner's Schülen,* 1887, p. 134. quoted by Beck, A. C. *Obstetrical Practice* (2 Ed.). Baltimore, Williams and Wilkins, 1939.

18. Steere. Discussion of paper by Moir, C.[6]

19. Terman, L. M. Correlates of orgasm adequacy in a group of 556 wives. *J. Psychol.* 32:115, 1951.

20. Wilson, Pauline. *College Women Who Express Futility.* New York, Bureau of Publications, Teacher's College, Columbia University, 1950.

21. Wittkower, E., and Wilson, A. T. M. Dysmenorrhea and sterility. *Brit. M. J.* 2:586, 1940.

Study Questions on Niles Newton

1. Do you normally think of things like pregnancy, lactation, menstruation, and childbirth as important aspects of female sexuality? If not, does this mean you have adopted a masculine way of thinking about sexuality?
2. Do you think that Newton's understanding of female sexuality leads to a view of women as dependent on or inferior to men? What do you think Lydon (see the next article) would say? What do you think?
3. Does the idea that women experience a sort of sexual pleasure while breast-feeding shock you? Should it?
4. What implications might Newton's view of female sexuality have for the question of what sort of social institutions are most conducive to the sexual and psychological flourishing of women?

The Politics of Orgasm

SUSAN LYDON

Women's sexuality, Susan Lydon argues, defined by men to benefit men, has been downgraded and perverted, repressed and channeled, denied and abused so that women no longer, as they did in pagan times, get more pleasure from lovemaking than do men. The principal villain is Freud's doctrine that, in psychosexually mature women, the vagina replaces the clitoris as the leading erogenous zone. The doctrine of the vaginal orgasm helps keep women down—making them sexually as well as economically, socially, and politically subservient. But the doctrine of the clitoral orgasm liberates women by making their sexual pleasure independent of the man's erect penis.

TIRESIAS, WHO HAD BEEN both man and woman, was asked, as Ovid's legend goes, to mediate in a dispute between Jove and Juno as to which sex got more pleasure from lovemaking. Tiresias unhesitatingly answered that women did. Yet in the intervening 2,000 years between Ovid's time and our own, a mythology has been built up which not only holds the opposite to be true, but has made this belief an unswerving ideology dictating the quality of relations between the sexes. Woman's sexuality, defined by men to benefit men, has been downgraded and perverted, repressed and channeled, denied and abused until women themselves, thoroughly convinced of their sexual inferiority to men, would probably be dumfounded to learn that there is scientific proof that Tiresias was indeed right.

The myth was codified by Freud, as much as by anyone else. In *Three Essays on the Theory of Sexuality*, Freud formulated his basic ideas concerning feminine sexuality: for little girls, the leading erogenous zone in their bodies is the clitoris; in order for the transition to womanhood to be successful, the clitoris must abandon its sexual primacy to the vagina; women in whom this transition has not been complete remain clitorally-oriented, or "sexually anaesthetic" and "psychosexually immature."

> The fact that women change their leading erotogenic zone in this way, [Freud wrote] together with the wave of repression at puberty, which, as it were, puts aside their childish masculinity, are the chief determinants of the greater proneness of women to neurosis and especially to hysteria. These determinants, therefore, are intimately related to the essence of feminity.

In the context of Freud's total psychoanalytic view of women—that they are not whole human beings but mutilated males who long all their lives for a penis and must struggle to reconcile themselves to its lack—the requirement of a transfer of erotic sensation from clitoris to vagina became a *prima facie* case for their inevitable sexual (and moral) inferiority. In Freud's logic, those who struggle to become what they are not must be inferior to that to which they aspire.

Freud wrote that he could not "escape the notion (though I hesitate to give it expression) that for women the level of what is ethically normal is different from what it is in men. . . . We must not allow ourselves to be deflected from such conclusions by the denials of the feminists, who are anxious to force us to regard the two sexes as completely equal in position and worth."

Freud himself admitted near the end of his life that his knowledge of women was inadequate. "If you want to know more about femininity, you must interrogate your own experience, or turn to the poets, or wait until science can give you more information," he said; he also expressed the hope that the female psychoanalysts who followed him would be able to find out more. But the post-Freudians adhered rigidly to the doctrine of the master, and, as in most of his work, what Freud hoped would be taken as a thesis for future study became instead a kind of canon law.

. . . The superiority of the vaginal over the clitoral organism was particularly useful as a theory, since it provided a convenient basis for categorization: clitoral women were deemed immature, neurotic, bitchy, and masculine; women who had vaginal orgasms were maternal, feminine, mature, and normal. Though frigidity should technically be defined as total inability to achieve orgasm, the orthodox Freudians (and pseudo-Freudians) preferred to define it as inability to achieve vaginal orgasm, by which definition, in 1944, Edmond Bergler adjudged between 70 and 80 percent of all women frigid. The clitoral *vs.* vaginal debate raged hot and heavy among the sexologists—although Kinsey's writings stressed the importance of the clitoris to female orgasm and contradicted Bergler's statistics—but it became clear that there was something indispensable to the society in the Freudian view which allowed it to remain unchallenged in the public consciousness.

In 1966, Dr. William H. Masters and Mrs. Virginia E. Johnson published *Human Sexual Response,* a massive clinical study of the physiology of sex. Briefly and simply, the Masters and Johnson conclusions about the female orgasm, based on observation of and interviews with 487 women, were these:

1) That the dichotomy of vaginal and clitoral orgasms is entirely false. Anatomically, all orgasms are centered in the clitoris, whether they result from direct manual pressure applied to the clitoris, indirect pressure resulting from the thrusting of penis during intercourse, or generalized sexual stimulation of other erogenous zones like the breasts.

2) That women are naturally multi-orgasmic; that is, if a woman is immediately stimulated following orgasm, she is likely to experience several orgasms in rapid succession. This is not an exceptional occurrence, but one of which most women are capable.

3) That while women's orgasms do not vary in kind, they vary in intensity. The most intense orgasms experienced by the research subjects were by masturbatory manual stimulation, followed in intensity by manual stimulation by the partner; the least intense orgasms were experienced by women during intercourse.

4) That the female orgasm is as real and identifiable a physiological entity as the male's; it follows the same pattern of erection and detumescence of the clitoris, which may be seen as female equivalent of the penis.

5) That there is an "infinite variety of female sexual response" as regards intensity and duration of orgasms.

. . . Before Masters and Johnson, female sexuality had been objectively defined and described by men; the subjective experience of women had had no part in defining their own sexuality. And men defined feminine sexuality in a way as favorable to themselves as possible. If woman's pleasure was obtained through the vagina, then she was totally dependent on the man's erect penis to achieve orgasm; she would receive her satisfaction only as a concomitant of man's seeking his. With the clitoral orgasm, woman's sexual pleasure was independent of the male's, and she could seek her satisfaction as aggressively as the man sought his, a prospect which didn't appeal to too many men. The definition of normal feminine sexuality as vaginal, in other words, was a part of keeping women down, of making them sexually, as well as economically, socially, and politically subservient.

In retrospect, particularly with the additional perspective of our own time, Freud's theory of feminine sexuality appears an historical rationalization for the realities of Victorian society. Culture-bound in the Victorian ethos, Freud had to play the role of *pater familias*. Serving the ethos, he developed a psychology that robbed Victorian women of possible politics. In Freud's theory of penis envy, the penis functioned as the unalterable determinant of maleness which women could symbolically envy instead of the power and prestige given men by the society. It was a refusal to grant women acknowledgment that they had been wronged by their culture and their times; according to Freud, woman's lower status had not been conferred upon her by men, but by God, who had created her without a penis.

Freud's insistence on the superiority of the vaginal orgasm seems almost a demonic determination on his part to finalize the Victorians' repression of feminine eroticism, to stigmatize the remaining vestiges of pleasure felt by women, and thus make them unacceptable to the women themselves. For there were still women whose sexuality hadn't been completely destroyed, as evidenced by one Dr. Isaac Brown Baker, a surgeon who performed numerous clitoridectomies on women to prevent the sexual excitement which, he was convinced, caused "insanities," "catalepsy," "hysteria," "epilepsy," and other diseases. The Victorians had needed to repress sexuality for the success of Western industrialized society; in particular, the total repression of woman's sexuality was crucial to ensure her subjugation. So the Victorians honored only the male ejaculation, that aspect of sexuality which was necessary to the survival of the species; the male ejaculation made women submissive to sex by creating a mystique of the sanctity of motherhood; and, supported by Freud, passed on to us the heritage of the double standard.

When Kinsey laid to rest the part of the double standard that maintained women got no pleasure at all from sex, everyone cried out that there was a sexual revolution afoot. But such talk, as usual, was deceptive. Morality, outside the marriage bed, remained the same, and children were socialized as though Kinsey had never described what they would be like when they grew up. Boys were taught that they should get their sex where they could find it, "go as far" as they could. On the old assumption that women were asexual creatures, girls were taught that since they needed sex less than boys did, it was up to them to impose sexual restraints. In whatever sex education adolescents did manage to receive, they were told that men had penises and women vaginas; the existence of the clitoris was not mentioned, and *pleasure* in sex was never discussed at all.

Adolescent boys growing up begging for sexual crumbs from girls frightened for their "reputations"—a situation that remains unchanged to this day—hardly constitutes the vanguard of a sexual revolution. However, the marriage-manual craze that followed Kinsey assumed that a lifetime of psychological destruction could, with the aid of a little booklet, be abandoned after marriage, and that husband and wife should be able to make sure that the wife was not robbed of her sexual birthright to orgasm, just so long as it was *vaginal* (though the marriage manuals did rather reluctantly admit that since the clitoris was the most sexually sensitive organ in the female body, a little clitoral stimulation in foreplay was in order), and so long as their orgasms were *simultaneous*.

The effect of the marriage manuals of course ran counter to their ostensible purpose. Under the guise of frankness and sexual liberation, they dictated prudery and restraint. Sex was made so mechanized, detached, and intellectual that it was robbed of its sensuality. Man became a spectator of his own sexual experience. And the marriage manuals put new pressure on women. The swing was from repression to preoccupation with the orgasm. Men took the marriage manuals to mean that their sexuality would be enhanced by bringing women to orgasm and, again co-opting feminine sexuality for their own ends, they put pressure on women to perform. The endorsement by the marriage manuals of the desirability of vaginal orgasm ensured that women would be asked not only, "Did you come?," but also, "Did you conform to Freud's conception of a psychosexually mature woman, and thereby validate my masculinity?"

Rather than being revolutionary, the present sexual situation is tragic. Appearances notwithstanding, the age-old taboos against conversation about personal sexual experience still haven't broken down. This reticence has allowed the mind-manipulators of the media to create myths of sexual supermen and superwomen. So the bed becomes a competitive arena, where men and women measure themselves against these mythical rivals, while simultaneously trying to live up to the ecstasies promised them by the marriage manuals and the fantasies of the media ("If the earth doesn't move for me, I must be missing something," the reasoning goes.) Our society treats sex as a sport, with its record-breakers, its judges, its rules, and its spectators.

As anthropologists have shown, women's sexual response is culturally conditioned; historically, women defer to whatever model of their sexuality is offered them by men. So the sad thing for women is that they have participated in the destruction of their own eroticism. Women have helped make the vaginal orgasm into a status symbol in a male-dictated system of values. A woman would now perceive her preference for clitoral orgasm as a "secret shame," ignominious in the eyes of other women as well as those of men. This internalization can be seen in the literature: Mary McCarthy's and Doris Lessing's writings on

orgasm do not differ substantially from D. H. Lawrence's and Ernest Hemingway's, and even Simone de Beauvoir, in *The Second Sex,* refers to vaginal orgasm as the only "normal satisfaction."

Rather than working to alleviate the pressure on them, women have increased it. Feeling themselves insecure in a competitive situation, they are afraid to admit their own imagined inadequacies, and lie to other women about their sexual experiences. With their men, they often fake orgasm to appear "good in bed" and thus place an intolerable physical burden on themselves and a psychological burden on the men unlucky enough to see through the ruse.

One factor that has made this unfortunate situation possible is ignorance: the more subtle and delicate aspects of human sexuality are still not fully understood. For example, a woman's ability to attain orgasm seem to be conditioned as much by her emotions as by physiology and sociology. Masters and Johnson proved that the orgasm experienced during intercourse, the mis-named vaginal orgasm, did not differ *anatomically* from the clitoral orgasm. But this should not be seen as their most significant contribution to the sexual emancipation of women. A difference remains in the *subjective* experience of orgasm during intercourse and orgasm apart from intercourse. In the complex of emotional factors affecting feminine sexuality, there is a whole panoply of pleasures: the pleasure of being penetrated and filled by a man, the pleasure of sexual communication, the pleasure of affording a man his orgasm, the erotic pleasure that exists even when sex is not terminated by orgasmic release. Masters and Johnson's real contribution was to stress an "infinite variety of female sexual response." One should be able to appreciate the differences, rather than impose value judgments on them.

. . . Women don't aspire to imitate the mistakes of men in sexual matters, to view sexual experiences as conquest and ego-enhancement, to use other people to serve their own ends. But if the Masters and Johnson material is allowed to filter into the public consciousness, hopefully to replace the enshrined Freudian myths, then woman at long last will be allowed to take the first step toward her emancipation, to define and enjoy the forms of her own sexuality.

Study Questions on Susan Lydon

1. According to Lydon, how did Freud's understanding of female sexuality lead him to see women as sexually and morally inferior to men? Why does she think Freud's views represent "almost a demonic determination on his part to finalize the Victorians' repression of feminine eroticism"? Are you persuaded that she is right about Freud?

2. What seems to be at issue in the debate over whether the "vaginal orgasm" is superior to the "clitoral orgasm"? Why does it matter which we choose? What social implications does Lydon think follow from the view that the "vaginal orgasm" is superior? Are you persuaded?

3. Is there some reason why sensations from both the clitoris and the vagina cannot be involved in bringing about orgasm in women?

4. Many radical feminists argue that women are socialized into "compulsory hetero-sexuality." if Lydon is right, does her view have implications for whether hetero-sexuality is natural or normative for women as opposed to being just something socially imposed upon them?

Late Victorians

RICHARD RODRIGUEZ

Richard Rodriguez describes the gay culture of San Francisco at the outset of the AIDS epidemic. He discusses the gentrification of San Francisco brought about by gays and yuppies, unpacking the symbolism inherent in the transformation of the old Victorian mansions in the Castro area from homes designed for the multigenerational family to studio apartments occupied largely by gay men. Homosexuals, he argues, made a covenant against nature in the name of freedom; the AIDS epidemic required them to consent to nature and necessity.

ST. AUGUSTINE WRITES from his cope of dust that we are restless hearts, for earth is not our true home. Human unhappiness is evidence of our immortality. Intuition tells us we are meant for some other city.

Elizabeth Taylor, quoted in a magazine article of twenty years ago, spoke of cerulean Richard Burton days on her yacht, days that were nevertheless undermined by the elemental private reflection: This must end.

On a Sunday in summer, ten years ago, I was walking home from the Latin Mass at St. Patrick's,

From Days of Obligation *by Richard Rodriguez.* © *1992 by Richard Rodriguez. Used by permission of Viking Penguin, a division of Penguin Putnam, Inc.*

the old Irish parish downtown, when I saw thousands of people on market Street. It was the Gay Freedom Day parade—not the first, but the first I ever saw. Private lives were becoming public. There were marching bands. There were floats. Banners blocked single lives thematically into a processional mass, not unlike the consortiums of the blessed in Renaissance paintings, each saint cherishing the apparatus of his martyrdom: GAY DENTISTS. BLACK AND WHITE LOVERS. GAYS FROM BAKERSFIELD. LATINA LESBIANS. From the foot of Market Street they marched, east to west, following the mythic American path toward optimism.

I followed the parade to Civic Center Plaza, where flags of routine nations yielded sovereignty to a multitude. Pastel billows flowed over all.

Five years later, another parade. Politicians waved from white convertibles. "Dykes on Bikes" revved up, thumbs-upped. But now banners bore the acronyms of death. AIDS. ARC. Drums were muffled as passing, plum-spotted young men slid by on motorized cable cars.

Though I am alive now, I do not believe an old man's pessimism is necessarily truer than a young man's optimism simply because it comes after. There are things a young man knows that are true and are not yet in the old man's power to recollect. Spring has its sappy wisdom. Lonely teenagers still arrive in San Francisco aboard Greyhound buses. The city can still seem, by comparison with where they came from, paradise.

Four years ago on a Sunday in winter—a brilliant spring afternoon—I was jogging near Fort Point while overhead a young woman was, with difficulty, climbing over the railing of the Golden Gate Bridge. Holding down her skirt with one hand, with the other she waved to a startled spectator (the newspaper next day quoted a workman who was painting the bridge) before she stepped onto the sky.

To land like a spilled purse at my feet.

Serendipity has an eschatological tang here. Always has. Few American cities have had the experience, as we have had, of watching the civic body burn even as we stood, out of body, on a hillside, in a movie theater. Jeanette MacDonald's loony scatting of "San Francisco" has become our go-to-hell anthem. San Francisco has taken some heightened

pleasure from the circus of final things. To Atlantis, to Pompeii, to the Pillar of Salt, we add the Golden Gate Bridge, not golden at all, but rust red. San Francisco toys with the tragic conclusion.

For most of its brief life, San Francisco has entertained an idea of itself as heaven on earth, whether as Gold Town or City Beautiful or the Haight-Ashbury.

San Francisco can support both comic and tragic conclusions because the city is geographically *in extremis,* a metaphor for the farthest-flung possibility, a metaphor for the end of the line. Land's end.

To speak of San Francisco as land's end is to read the map from one direction only—as Europeans would read it or as the East Coast has always read it. In my lifetime San Francisco has become an Asian city. To speak, therefore, of San Francisco as land's end is to betray parochialism. My parents came here from Mexico. They saw San Francisco as the North. The West was not west for them. They did not share the Eastern traveler's sense of running before the past—the darkening time zone, the lowering curtain.

I cannot claim for myself the memory of a skyline such as the one César saw. César came to San Francisco in middle age; César came here as to some final place. He was born in South America; he had grown up in Paris; he had been everywhere, done everything; he assumed the world. Yet César was not condescending toward San Francisco, not at all. Here César saw revolution, and he embraced it.

Whereas I live here because I was born here. I grew up ninety miles away, in Sacramento. San Francisco was the nearest, the easiest, the inevitable city, since I needed a city. And yet I live here surrounded by people for whom San Francisco is the end of quest.

I have never looked for utopia on a map. Of course I believe in human advancement. I believe in medicine, in astrophysics, in washing machines. But my compass takes its cardinal point from tragedy. If I respond to the metaphor of spring, I nevertheless learned, years ago, from my Mexican father, from my Irish nuns, to count on winter. The point of Eden for me, for us, is not approach but expulsion.

After I met César in 1984, our friendly debate concerning the halcyon properties of San Francisco ranged from restaurant to restaurant. I spoke of limits. César boasted of freedoms.

It was César's conceit to add to the gates of Jerusalem, to add to the soccer fields of Tijuana, one other dreamscape hoped for the world over. It was the view from a hill, through a mesh of tram wires, of an urban neighborhood in a valley. The vision took its name from the protruding wedge of a theater marquee. Here César raised his glass without discretion: To the Castro.

There were times, dear César, when you tried to switch sides, if only to scorn American optimism, which, I remind you, had already become your own. At the high school where César taught, teachers and parents had organized a campaign to keep kids from driving themselves to the junior prom, in an attempt to forestall liquor and death. Such a scheme momentarily reawakened César's Latin skepticism.

Didn't the Americans know? (His tone exaggerated incredulity.) Teenagers will crash into lampposts on their way home from proms, and there is nothing to be done about it. You cannot forbid tragedy.

By California standards I live in an old house. But not haunted. There are too many tall windows, there is too much salty light, especially in winter, though the windows rattle, rattle in summer when the fog flies overhead, and the house creaks and prowls at night. I feel myself immune to any confidence it seeks to tell.

To grow up homosexual is to live with secrets and within secrets. In no other place are those secrets more closely guarded than within the family home. The grammar of the gay city borrows methaphors from the nineteenth-century house. "Coming out of the closet" is predicated upon family laundry, dirty linen, skeletons.

I live in a tall Victorian house that has been converted to four apartments; four single men.

Neighborhood streets are named to honor nineteenth-century men of action, men of distant fame. Clay. Jackson. Scott. Pierce. Many Victorians in the neighborhood date from before the 1906 earthquake and fire.

Architectural historians credit the gay movement of the 1970s with the urban restoration of San Francisco. Twenty years ago this was a bor-derline neighborhood. This room, like all the rooms of the house, was painted headache green, apple green, boardinghouse green. In the 1970s, homosexuals moved into black and working-class parts of the city, where they were perceived as pioneers or as block-busters, depending.

Two decades ago, some of the least expensive sections of San Francisco were wooden Victorian sections. It was thus a coincidence of the market that gay men found themselves living within the architectural metaphor for family. No other architecture in the American imagination is more evocative of family than the Victorian house. In those same years—the 1970s—and within those same Victorian houses, homosexuals were living rebellious lives to challenge the foundations of domesticity.

Was "queer-bashing" as much a manifestation of homophobia as a reaction against gentrification? One heard the complaint, often enough, that gay men were as promiscuous with their capital as otherwise, buying, fixing up, then selling and moving on. Two incomes, no children, described an unfair advantage. No sooner would flower boxes begin to appear than an anonymous reply was smeared on the sidewalk out front: KILL FAGGOTS.

The three- or four-story Victorian house, like the Victorian novel, was built to contain several generations and several classes under one roof, behind a single oaken door. What strikes me at odd moments is the confidence of Victorian architecture. Stairs, connecting one story with another, describe the confidence that bound generations together through time—confidence that the family would inherit the earth. The other day I noticed for the first time the vestige of a hinge on the topmost newel of the staircase. This must have been the hinge of a gate that kept infants upstairs so many years ago.

If Victorian houses assert a sturdy optimism by day, they are also associated in our imaginations with the Gothic—with shadows and cobwebby gimcrack, long corridors. The nineteenth century was remarkable for escalating optimism even as it excavated the backstairs, the descending architecture of nightmare—Freud's labor and Engels's.

I live on the second story, in rooms that have been rendered as empty as Yorick's skull—gutted, unrattled, in various ways unlocked—added skylights and new windows, new doors. The hallway remains the darkest part of the house.

This winter the hallway and lobby are being repainted to resemble an eighteenth-century French foyer. Of late we had walls and carpet of Sienese red; a baroque mirror hung in an alcove by the stairwell. Now we are to have enlightened austerity—black-and-white marble floors and faux masonry. A man comes in the afternoons to texture the walls with a sponge and a rag and to paint white mortar lines that create an illusion of permanence, of stone.

The renovation of Victorian San Francisco into dollhouses for libertines may have seemed, in the 1970s, an evasion of what the city was actually becoming. San Francisco's rows of storied houses proclaimed a multigenerational orthodoxy, all the while masking the city's unconventional soul. Elsewhere, meanwhile, domestic America was coming undone.

Suburban Los Angeles, the prototype for a new America, was characterized by a more apparently radical residential architecture. There was, for example, the work of Frank Gehry. In the 1970s, Gehry exploded the nuclear-family house, turning it inside out intellectually and in fact. Though, in a way, Gehry merely completed the logic of the postwar suburban tract house—with its one story, its sliding glass doors, Formica kitchen, two-car garage. The tract house exchanged privacy for mobility. Heterosexuals opted for the one-lifetime house, the freeway, the birth-control pill, minimalist fiction.

The age-old description of homosexuality is of a sin against nature. Moralistic society has always judged emotion literally. The homosexual was sinful because he had no kosher place to stick it. In attempting to drape the architecture of sodomy with art, homosexuals have lived for thousands of years against the expectations of nature. Barren as Shakers and, interestingly as concerned with the small effect, homosexuals have made a covenant against nature. Homosexual survival lay in artifice, in plumage, in lampshades, sonnets, musical comedy, couture, syntax, religious ceremony, opera, lacquer, irony.

I once asked Byron, an interior decorator, if he had many homosexual clients. *"Mais non,"* said he, flexing his eyelids. "Queers don't need decorators. They were born knowing how. All this ASID [American Society of Interior Decorators] stuff—tests and regulations—as if you can confer a homosexual diploma on a suburban housewife by granting her a discount card."

A knack? The genius, we are beginning to fear in an age of AIDS, is irreplaceable—but does it exist? The question is whether the darling affinities are innate to homosexuality or whether they are compensatory. Why have so many homosexuals retired into the small effect, the ineffectual career, the stereotype, the card shop, the florist? *Be gentle with me?* Or do homosexuals know things others do not?

This way power lay. Once upon a time, the homosexual appropriated to himself a mystical province, that of taste. Taste, which is, after all, the insecurity of the middle class, became the homosexual's licentiate to challenge the rule of nature. (The fairy in his blood, he intimated.)

Deciding how best to stick it may be only an architectural problem or a question of physics or of engineering or of cabinetry. Nevertheless, society's condemnation forced the homosexual to find his redemption outside nature. *We'll put a little skirt here.* The impulse is not to create but to re-create, to sham, to convert, to sauce, to rouge, to fragrance, to prettify. No effect is too small or too ephemeral to be snatched away from nature, to be ushered toward the perfection of artificiality. *We'll bring out the highlights there.* The homosexual has marshaled the architecture of the straight world to the very gates of Versailles—that great Vatican of fairyland—beyond which power is tyrannized by leisure.

In San Francisco in the 1980s, the highest form of art became interior decoration. The glory hole was thus converted to an eighteenth-century foyer.

I live away from the street, in a back apartment, in two rooms. I use my bedroom as a visitor's room—the sleigh bed tricked up with shams into a sofa—whereas I rarely invite anyone into my library, the public room, where I write, the public gesture.

I read in my bedroom in the afternoon because the light is good there, especially now, in winter, when the sun recedes from the earth.

There is a door in the south wall that leads to a balcony. The door was once a window. Inside the door, inside my bedroom, are twin green shutters. They are false shutters, of no function beyond wit. The shutters open into the room; they have the effect of turning my apartment inside out.

A few months ago I hired a man to paint the shutters green. I wanted the green shutters of Manet—you know the ones I mean—I wanted a weathered look, as of verdigris. For several days the painter labored, rubbing his paints into the wood and then wiping them off again. In this way he rehearsed for me decades of the ravages of weather. Yellow enough? Black?

The painter left one afternoon, saying he would return the next, leaving behind his tubes, his brushes, his sponges and rags. He never returned. Someone told me he has AIDS.

A black woman haunts California Street between the donut shop and the cheese store. She talks to herself—a debate, wandering, never advancing. Pedestrians who do not know her give her a wide berth. Somebody told me her story; I don't know whether it's true. Neighborhood merchants tolerate her presence as a vestige of dispirited humanity clinging to an otherwise dispiriting progress of "better" shops and restaurants.

Repainted façades extend now from Jackson Street south into what was once the heart of the "Mo"—black Fillmore Street. Today there are watercress sandwiches at three o'clock where recently there had been loudmouthed kids, hole-in-the-wall bars, pimps. Now there are tweeds and perambulators, matrons and nannies. Yuppies. And gays.

The gay-male revolution had greater influence on San Francisco in the 1970s than did the feminist revolution. Feminists, with whom I include lesbians—such was the inclusiveness of the feminist movement—were preoccupied with career, with escape from the house in order to create a sexually democratic city. Homosexual men sought to reclaim the house, the house that traditionally had been the reward for heterosexuality, with all its selfless tasks and burdens.

Leisure defined the gay-male revolution. The gay political movement began, by most accounts, in 1969 with the Stonewall riots in New York City,

whereby gay men fought to defend the nonconformity of their leisure.

It was no coincidence that homosexuals migrated to San Francisco in the 1970s, for the city was famed as a playful place, more Catholic than Protestant in its eschatological intuition. In 1975, the state of California legalized consensual homosexuality, and about that same time Castro Street, southwest of downtown, began to eclipse Polk Street as the homosexual address in San Francisco. Polk Street was a string of bars. The Castro was an entire district. The Castro had Victorian houses and churches, bookstores and restaurants, gyms, dry cleaners, supermarkets, and an elected member of the Board of Supervisors. The Castro supported baths and bars, but there was nothing furtive about them. On Castro Street the light of day penetrated gay life through clear plate-glass windows. The light of day discovered a new confidence, a new politics. Also a new look—a noncosmopolitan, Burt Reynolds, butch-kid style: beer, ball games, Levi's, short hair, muscles.

Gay men who lived elsewhere in the city, in Pacific Heights or in the Richmond, often spoke with derision of "Castro Street clones," describing the look, or scorned what they called the ghettoization of homosexuality. To an older generation of homosexuals, the blatancy of Castro Street threatened the discreet compromise they had negotiated with a tolerant city.

As the Castro district thrived, Folsom Street, south of Market, also began to thrive, as if in contradistinction to the utopian Castro. Folsom Street was a warehouse district of puddled alleys and deserted corners. Folsom Street offered an assortment of leather bars—an evening's regress to the outlaw sexuality of the fifties, the forties, the nineteenth century, and so on—an eroticism of the dark, of the Reeperbahn, or of the guardsman's barracks.

The Castro district implied that sexuality was more crucial, that homosexuality was the central fact of identity. The Castro district, with its ice-cream parlors and hardware stores, was the revolutionary place.

Into which carloads of vacant-eyed teenagers from other districts or from middle-class suburbs would drive after dark, cruising the neighborhood for solitary victims.

The ultimate gay-basher was a city supervisor named Dan White, ex-cop, ex-boxer, ex-fireman, ex–altar boy. Dan White had grown up in the Castro district; he recognized the Castro revolution for what it was. Gays had achieved power over him. He murdered the mayor and he murdered the homosexual member of the Board of Supervisors.

Katherine, a sophisticate if ever there was one, nevertheless dismisses two men descending the aisle at the Opera House: "All so sleek and smooth-jowled and silver-haired—they don't seem real, poor darlings. It must be because they don't have children."

Lodged within Katherine's complaint is the perennial heterosexual annoyance with the homosexual's freedom from childrearing, which does not so much place the homosexual beyond the pale as it relegates the homosexual outside "responsible" life.

It was the glamour of gay life, after all, as much as it was the feminist call to career, that encouraged heterosexuals in the 1970s to excuse themselves from nature, to swallow the birth-control pill. Who needs children? The gay bar became the paradigm for the singles bar. The gay couple became the paradigm for the selfish couple—all dressed up and everywhere to go. And there was the example of the gay house in illustrated life-style magazines. At the same time that suburban housewives were looking outside the home for fulfillment, gay men were reintroducing a new generation in the city—heterosexual men and women—to the complaisancies of the barren house.

Puritanical America dismissed gay camp followers as yuppies; the term means to suggest infantility. Yuppies were obsessive and awkward in their materialism. Whereas gays arranged a decorative life against a barren state, yuppies sought early returns—lives that were not to be all toil and spin. Yuppies, trained to careerism from the cradle, wavered in their pursuit of the Northern European ethic—indeed, we might now call it the pan-Pacific ethic—in favor of the Mediterranean, the Latin, the Catholic, the Castro, the Gay.

The international architectural idioms of Skidmore, Owings & Merrill, which defined the skyline of the 1970s, betrayed no awareness of any street-level debate concerning the primacy of play in San Francisco or of any human dramas resulting from urban redevelopment. The repellent office tower was a fortress raised against the sky, against the street, against the idea of a city. Offices were hives where money was made, and damn all.

In the 1970s, San Francisco divided between the interests of downtown and the pleasures of the neighborhoods. Neighborhoods asserted idiosyncrasy, human scale, light. San Francisco neighborhoods perceived downtown as working against their influence in determining what the city should be. Thus neighborhoods seceded from the idea of a city.

The gay movement rejected downtown as representing "straight" conformity. But was it possible that heterosexual Union Street was related to Castro Street? Was it possible that either was related to the Latino Mission district? Or to the Sino-Russian Richmond? San Francisco, though complimented worldwide for holding its center, was in fact without a vision of itself entire.

In the 1980s, in deference to the neighborhoods, City Hall would attempt a counterreformation of downtown, forbidding "Manhattanization." Shadows were legislated away from parks and playgrounds. Height restrictions were lowered beneath an existing skyline. Design, too, fell under the retrojurisdiction of the city planner's office. The Victorian house was presented to architects as a model of what the city wanted to uphold and to become. In heterosexual neighborhoods, one saw newly built Victorians. Downtown, postmodernist prescriptions for playfulness advised skyscrapers to wear a party hats, buttons, comic mustaches. Philip Johnson yielded to the dollhouse impulse to perch angels atop one of his skyscrapers.

I can see downtown from my bedroom window. But days pass and I do not leave the foreground for the city. Most days my public impression of San Francisco is taken from Fillmore Street, from the anchorhold of the Lady of the Donut Shop.

She now often parades with her arms crossed over her breasts in an "X," the posture emblematic of prophecy. And yet gather her madness where she sits on the curb, chain-smoking, hugging her knees, while I disappear down Fillmore Street to make Xerox copies, to mail letters, to rent a video, to shop for dinner. I am soon pleased by the faint breeze from the city, the slight agitation of the homing crowds of singles, so intent upon the path of least resistance. I admire the prosperity of the corridor, the shop windows that beckon inward toward the perfected life-style, the little way of the City of St. Francis.

Turning down Pine Street, I am recalled by the prickly silhouette of St. Dominic's Church against the scrim of the western sky. I turn, instead, into the Pacific Heights Health Club.

In the 1970s, like a lot of men and women in this city, I joined a gym. My club, I've even caught myself calling it.

In the gay city of the 1970s, bodybuilding became an architectural preoccupation of the upper middle class. Bodybuilding is a parody of labor, a useless accumulation of the laborer's bulk and strength. No useful task is accomplished. And yet there is something businesslike about habitués, and the gym is filled with the punch-clock logic of the workplace. Machines clank and hum. Needles on gauges toll spent calories.

The gym is at once a closet of privacy and an exhibition gallery. All four walls are mirrored.

I study my body in the mirror. Physical revelation—nakedness—is no longer possible, cannot be desired, for the body is shrouded in meat and wears itself.

The intent is some merciless press of body against a standard, perfect mold. Bodies are "cut" or "pumped" or "buffed" as on an assembly line in Turin. A body becomes so many extrovert parts. Delts, pecs, lats, traps.

I harness myself in a Nautilus cage.

Lats become wings. For the gym is nothing if not the occasion for transcendence. From homosexual to autosexual. . . .

I lift weights over my head, baring my teeth like an animal with the strain.

. . . to nonsexual. The effect of the overdeveloped body is the miniaturization of the sexual organs—of no function beyond wit. Behold the ape become Blakean angel, revolving in an empyrean of mirrors.

The nineteenth-century mirror over the fireplace in my bedroom was purchased by a decorator from the estate of a man who died last year of AIDS. It is a top-heavy piece, confusing styles. Two-ebony-painted columns support a frieze of painted glass above the mirror. The frieze depicts three bourgeois graces and a couple of free-range cherubs. The lake of the mirror has formed a cataract, and at its edges it is beginning to corrode.

Thus the mirror that now draws upon my room owns some bright curse, maybe—some memory not mine.

As I regard this mirror, I imagine St. Augustine's meditation slowly hardening into syllogism, passing down through centuries to confound us: evil is the absence of good.

We have become accustomed to figures disappearing from our landscape. Does this not lead us to interrogate the landscape?

With reason do we invest mirrors with the superstition of memory, for they, though glass, though liquid captured in a bay, are so often less fragile than we are. They—bright ovals, or rectangles, or rounds—bump down unscathed, unspilled through centuries, whereas we. . . .

The man in the red baseball cap used to jog so religiously on Marina Green. By the time it occurs to me that I have not seen him for months, I realize he may be dead—not lapsed, not moved away. People come and go in the city, it's true. But in San Francisco death has become as routine an explanation for disappearance as Mayflower Van Lines.

AIDS, it has been discovered, is a plague of absence. Absence opened in the blood. Absence condensed into the fluid of passing emotion. Absence shot through opalescent tugs of semen to deflower the city.

And then AIDS, it was discovered, is a non-metaphorical disease, a disease like any other. Absence sprang from substance—a virus, a hairy bubble perched upon a needle, a platter of no intention served round: fever, blisters, a death sentence.

At first I heard only a few names—names connected, perhaps, with the right faces, perhaps not. People vaguely remembered, as through the cataract of this mirror, from dinner parties or from intermissions. A few articles in the press. The rumored celebrities. But within months the slow beating of the blood had found its bay.

One of San Francisco's gay newspapers, the *Bay Area Reporter,* began to accept advertisements from funeral parlors and casket makers, inserting them between the randy ads for leather bars and tanning salons. The *Reporter* invited homemade obituaries—lovers writing of lovers, friends remembering friends and the blessings of unexceptional life.

Peter. Carlos. Gary. Asel. Perry. Nikos.

Healthy snapshots accompany each annal. At the Russian River. By the Christmas tree. Lifting a beer. In uniform. A dinner jacket. A satin gown.

He was born in Puerto La Libertad, El Salvador.

He attended Apple Valley High School where he was their first male cheerleader.

From El Paso. From Medford. From Germany. From Long Island.

I moved back to San Francisco in 1979. Oh, I had had some salad days elsewhere, but by 1979 I was a wintry man. I came here in order not to be distracted by the ambitions or, for that matter, the pleasures of others but to pursue my own ambition. Once here, though, I found the company of men who pursued an earthly paradise charming. Skepticism became my demeanor toward them—I was the dinner-party skeptic, a firm believer in Original Sin and in the limits of possibility.

Which charmed them.

He was a dancer.

He settled into the interior-design department of Gump's, where he worked until his illness.

He was a teacher.

César, for example.

César had an excellent mind. César could shave the rind from any assertion to expose its pulp and jelly. But César was otherwise ruled by pulp. César loved everything that ripened in time. Freshmen. Bordeaux. César could fashion liturgy from an artichoke. Yesterday it was not ready (cocking his head, rotating the artichoke in his hand over a pot of cold water). Tomorrow will be too late (Yorick's skull). Today it is perfect (as he lit the fire beneath the pot). We will eat it now.

If he's lucky, he's got a year, a doctor told me. If not, he's got two.

The phone rang. AIDS had tagged a friend. And then the phone rang again. And then the phone rang again. Michael had tested positive. Adrian, well, what he had assumed were shingles. . . Paul was back in the hospital. And César, dammit, César, even César, especially César.

That winter before his death, César traveled back to South America. On his return to San Francisco, he described to me how he had walked with his mother in her garden—his mother chafing her hands as if she were cold. But it was not cold, he said. They moved slowly. Her summer garden was prolonging itself this year, she said. The cicadas will not stop singing.

When he lay on his deathbed, César said everyone else he knew might get AIDS and die. He said I would be the only one spared—"spared" was supposed to have been chased with irony, I knew, but his voice was too weak to do the job. "You are too circumspect," he said then, wagging his finger upon the coverlet.

So I was going to live to see that the garden of earthly delights was, after all, only wallpaper—was that it, César? Hadn't I always said so? It was then I saw that the greater sin against heaven was my unwillingness to embrace life.

César said he found Paradise at the baths. He said I didn't understand. He said if I had to ask about it, I might as well ask if a wife will spend eternity with Husband #1 or Husband #2.

The baths were places of good humor, that was Number One; there was nothing demeaning about them. From within cubicles men would nod at one another or not, but there was no sting of rejection, because one had at last entered a region of complete acceptance. César spoke of floating from body to body, open arms yielding to open arms in an angelic round.

The best night. That's easy, he said, the best night was spent in the pool with an antiques dealer—up to their necks in warm water—their two heads bobbing on an ocean of chlorine green, bawling Noël Coward songs.

But each went home alone?

Each satisfied, dear, César corrected. And all the way home San Francisco seemed to him balmed and merciful, he said. He felt weightlessness of being, the pavement under his step as light as air.

It was not as in some Victorian novel—the curtains drawn, the pillows plumped, the streets strewn with sawdust. It was not to be a matter of custards in covered dishes, steaming possets, *Try a little of this, my dear.* Or gathering up the issues of

Architectural Digest strewn about the bed. Closing the biography of Diana Cooper and marking its place. Or the unfolding of discretionary screens, morphine, parrots, pavilions.

César experienced agony.

Four of his high-school students sawed through a Vivaldi quartet in the corridor outside his hospital room, prolonging the hideous garden.

In the presence of his lover Gregory and friends, Scott passed his life. . . .

He died peacefully at home in his lover Ron's arms.

Immediately after a friend led a prayer for him to be taken home and while his dear mother was reciting the 23rd Psalm, Bill peaceful took his last breath.

I stood aloof at César's memorial, the kind of party he would enjoy, everyone said. And so for a time César lay improperly buried, unconvincingly resurrected in the conditional: would enjoy. What else could they say? César had no religion beyond aesthetic bravery.

Sunlight remains. Traffic remains. Nocturnal chic attaches to some discovered restaurant. A new novel is reviewed in *The New York Times*. And the mirror rasps on its hook. The mirror is lifted down.

A priest friend, a good friend, who out of naïveté plays the cynic, tells me—this is on a bright, billowy day; we are standing outside—"It's not as sad as you may think. There is at least spectacle in the death of the young. Come to the funeral of an old lady sometime if you want to feel an empty church."

I will grant my priest friend this much: that it is easier, easier on me, to sit with gay men in hospitals than with the staring old. Young men talk as much as they are able.

But those who gather around the young man's bed do not see Chatterton. This doll is Death. I have seen people caressing it, staring Death down. I have seen people wipe its tears, wipe its ass; I have seen people kiss Death on his lips, where once there were lips.

Chris was inspired after his own diagnosis in July 1987 with the truth and reality of how such a terrible disease could bring out the love, of so many friends and family.

Sometimes no family came. If there was family, it was usually Mother. Mom. With her suitcase and with the torn flap of an envelope in her hand.

Brenda. Pat. Connie. Toni. Soledad.

Or parents came but then left without reconciliation, some preferring to say "cancer."

But others came. They walked Death's dog. They washed his dishes. They bought his groceries. They massaged his poor back. They changed his bandages. They emptied his bedpen.

Men who sought the aesthetic ordering of existence were recalled to nature. Men who aspired to the mock-angelic settled for the shirt of hair. The gay community of San Francisco, having found freedom, consented to necessity—to all that the proud world had for so long held up to them, withheld from them, as "real humanity."

And if gays took care of their own, they were not alone. AIDS was a disease of the entire city. Nor were Charity and Mercy only male, only gay. Others came. There were nurses and nuns and the couple from next door, co-workers, strangers, teenagers, corporations, pensioners. A community was forming over the city.

Cary and Rick's friends and family wish to thank the many people who provided both small and great kindnesses.

He was attended to and lovingly cared for by the staff at Coming Home Hospice.

And the saints of this city have names listed in the phone book, names I heard called through a microphone one cold Sunday in Advent as I sat in Most Holy Redeemer Church. It might have been any of the churches or community centers in the Castro district, but it happened at Most Holy Redeemer at a time in the history of the world when the Roman Catholic Church pronounced the homosexual a sinner.

A woman at the microphone called upon volunteers from the AIDS Support Group to come forward. Throughout the church, people stood up, young men and women, and middle-aged and old, straight, gay, and all of them shy at being called. Yet they came forward and assembled in the sanctuary, facing the congregation, grinning self-consciously at one another, their hands hidden behind them.

I am preoccupied by the fussing of a man sitting in the pew directly in front of me—in his seventies, frail, his iodine-colored hair combed forward and pasted upon his forehead. Fingers of porcelain clutch the pearly beads of what must have been his mother's rosary. He is not the sort of man any gay man would have chosen to become in the 1970s. He is probably not what he himself expected to become. Something of the old dear about him, wizened butterfly, powdered old pouf. Certainly he is what I fear becoming. And then he rises, this old monkey, with the most beatific dignity, in answer to the microphone, and he strides into the sanctuary to take his place in the company of the Blessed.

So this is it—this, what looks like a Christmas party in an insurance office, and not as in Renaissance paintings, and not as we had always thought, not some flower-strewn, some sequined curtain call of greasepainted heroes gesturing to the stalls. A lady with a plastic candy cane pinned to her lapel. A Castro clone with a red bandana exploding from his hip pocket. A perfume-counter lady with an Hermès scarf mantled upon her shoulder. A black man in a checkered sports coat. The pink-haired punkess with a jewel in her nose. Here, too, is the gay couple in middle age; interchangeable plaid shirts and corduroy pants. Blood and shit and Mr. Happy Face. These know the weight of bodies.

Bill died.

. . . Passed on to heaven.

. . . Turning over in his bed one night and then gone.

These learned to love what is corruptible, while I, barren skeptic, reader of St. Augustine, curator of the earthly paradise, inheritor of the empty mirror, I shift my tailbone upon the cold hard pew.

Study Questions on Richard Rodriquez

1. The restoration and transformation of the old Victorian mansions in San Francisco in the 1970s is taken by Rodriguez as a kind of metaphor for broader cultural changes connected with the influx of gay men and ambitious young yuppies into what had formerly been black and working-class neighborhoods. Spell out the symbolism of the house, and explain how he understands the connection between the architectural changes and the cultural changes.

2. How does Rodriguez understand "queer-bashing"? (For example, how does he explain Dan White's murder of the mayor and the gay member of the Board of Supervisors?)

3. How does he understand gay culture? What does he mean in saying that "homosexuals have made a covenant against nature"? What impact did AIDS have on gay culture?

4. Is the childlessness of gay male couples essentially different from the childlessness (voluntary or involuntary) of some heterosexual couples? What does Rodriguez think? What do you think?

5. Many people regard the gay bath houses as instantiating a particularly degrading form of sex. What was it that César found in the bathhouses? What do you think about the sort of sexual encounters that occurred in them? Compare, also, Mohr's view of sex in Unit II.

6. Rodriguez begins by citing St. Augustine, and subsequently contrasts an old man's pessimism with a young man's optimism. Explain the point of these remarks for his understanding of San Francisco culture. In particular, explain how they are related to the significance César has for Rodriguez.

From Old Gay to New

ARLENE STEIN

> Arlene Stein here provides a short history of recent lesbian culture. She distinguishes older forms of lesbianism, founded on desires strong enough to overcome social pressures, from the "new lesbianism," which presents itself as a choice open to all women.

CONTRARY TO THE HISTORIES WRITTEN in the afterglow of lesbian feminism and gay liberation, lesbian life in this country did not begin in 1970. In the 1930s and 1940s, and even earlier in many places, were lively, albeit secretive and stigmatized, lesbian subcultures in American towns and cities. World War II had led to the flowering of homosexual life in the United States, mainly in port cities like San Francisco and New York, but also in many smaller cities and towns, where active communities sprang up; they were frequently working class and mixed race in character, centering mainly on bars. By the postwar period, there were many subcultural niches in which women who loved other women congregated: informal networks of young lesbians of color in Harlem and other urban areas; professional networks comprising middle-class women, some of whom were involved in the first lesbian organization, the Daughters of Bilitis; homosexual resort communities; and untold other groupings. Even as homosexuals were being vilified, gender roles were being shored up, and the definition of "proper femininity" was narrowing, there were unprecedented opportunities to construct a different kind of life in the relative safety of the lesbian subculture.

Outside the homosexual subculture, women who engaged in same-sex behavior learned to "manage" their stigma; being a lesbian shaped one's life choices in practically every respect—particularly with regard to one's job. Middle-class women who were upwardly mobile were forced at work to conform to feminine norms, carefully managing their identities to avoid being found out. But in the bars, women met friends and lovers, were initiated into the rules and rituals of lesbian life, escaped from the constraints of heterosexual society, and developed a sense of their common difference. Audre Lorde recalled her early gay life in New York in the 1950s: "All of us who survived those common years had to be a little strange . . . a little proud. Keeping ourselves together and on our own tracks, however wobbly, was like trying to play the Dinizulu War Chant or a Beethoven sonata on a tin dog-whistle. . . . You had to have a place. Whether or not it did justice to whatever you felt you were about, there had to be some place to refuel and check your flaps." Gay subcultures allowed women, in Lorde's words, to "refuel and check their flaps." They promoted and protected the expression of same-sex desire and shielded "gender outlaws"—women who, by choice or necessity, failed to conform. What participants in these various subcultures held in common was a sense of marginality, of difference, of exclusion from gender and sexual norms and from the codes of behavior they implied. "The culture of gayness that I came out in," as one woman described the 1950s, "very much emphasized and was aware of our difference from the people who were not queer. We were constantly reminded of our difference, and built an identity that was based on it."

Membership in lesbian subcultures was regulated through codes, signals, and complex in-group rules, such as those governing butch-femme roles. Joan Nestle has characterized butch-femme during this period as "a conspicuous flag of rebellion" in a highly stigmatized, secretive world, a means of survival in an age when gender rules were

Reprinted by permission of the author.

leaden weights. She describes butch-femme as a "style of self-presentation that made erotic competence a political statement in the 1950's." Roles eroticized differences between partners. The butch, or active partner, orchestrated the sexual interaction, but her pleasure was dependent upon pleasing her partner. "We labeled ourselves," Nestle writes, "as part of our cultural ritual, and the language reflected our time in history, but the words stood for complex sexual and emotional exchanges."

Butch-femme roles linked sexuality, appearance, and frequently economic position in a highly ritualized way. Dress was a reflection of sexual style, a signal to potential sexual and nonsexual partners, and a pretty good indicator of whether you were a secretary or a manual worker. The writer Ann Bannon fashioned a series of paperback novels around the character Beebo Brinker, a strapping tomboy who worked as an elevator operator so that she could wear a man's uniform. The system of roles, as practiced in the 1950s, implied a great deal of permanence and consistency. Identity as butch or femme was an essential, integral part of one's being. Once a femme, always a femme—and likewise for butches. By imposing rules and placing limits on self-expression, roles eroticized difference, providing security and regularity in a tenuous, secretive world. While they were often proud statements of lesbian resistance, they were also the expression of an oppressed minority faced with a paucity of alternatives.

Butch-femme roles were not universally adopted within the subculture, however. Many women objected to roles on the grounds that they confined individuals to certain modes of conduct and limited individual self-expression. In addition, butch-femme couples may have embarrassed some because they made lesbians culturally visible, which was, Nestle writes, "a terrifying act for the 1950's." Working-class butches, who wore men's suits and kept their hair short and slicked back, presented a strong visual message. Historical accounts describe in harrowing detail the brutality meted out to lesbians, particularly strongly butch women in the 1950s and 1960s. Many bars monitored their clients' clothing, requiring that no more than one piece of men's apparel be worn, and frequent police raids enforced these rules. While

the medical profession "policed" the boundaries that delineated the normal from the abnormal, those boundaries were quite literally policed as officers kept the subculture in line.

The effect of this is easy to imagine: those who identify as homosexual cannot escape an either/or situation. Either one is "in the closet," passing for straight and experiencing the loss of self that that entails, or one is "out" and facing the harassment, threat of violence, economic deprivation, and loss of family support that so often follow. To become a part of the lesbian world was to give up many of one's privileges. In the face of these dangers, only those who felt that they had relatively little to lose in terms of social status—or who, despite extreme social disapproval, could incorporate "deviant" sexuality into a favorable sense of themselves—came to self-identify as lesbian.

It was principally sexual desire that shaped lesbian communities before the convergence of Stonewall and the second wave of feminism. As one woman who lived through this period put it, "If you weren't particularly sexually driven, if you didn't care one way or another, why put up with all the social opprobrium? If you could just as easily sleep with a man as with a woman, why go through hell to go to bed with a woman? Or if you were just as happy celibate, why not just be a spinster? The hell we went through was just not worth it unless the rewards were pretty intense." One might speculate that "old gay" women, who claimed lesbian identities in the 1950s and early 1960s, were more likely to be of working-class or upper-class origin: working class, because they had little to lose; upper class, because they had access to greater resources and the freedom to maneuver outside the structures of "straight" society. These women were also less likely to have had significant sexual and emotional relationships with men, or to have developed stable identities as heterosexuals. In the 1950s and 1960s, this "core" group probably constituted the bulk of the population of lesbian-identified women. . . .

"Smash the Categories"

Now! Enter the young; the new morality; the belief that the individual has the RIGHT to be different. Basic to this attitude is the assertion that the larger society cannot legitimately dictate the life patterns or social habits of its individual members. . . . Fortified wi th this idea, increasing numbers of younghomosexuals and Lesbians perceive their sexuality in the same manner as other socialdifferences; placing sex practices (not just homosexuality) on the same level as variations in dress or life-style habits.

> Fen Gregory, "Before the Gap
> Becomes a Chasm," *The Ladder,*
> April–May 1970

Women who reached adolescence and young adulthood during the 1950s and 1960s lived their formative years in a period of relative conservatism and conformity, only to have their assumptions about the world radically challenged by protests against the Vietnam War and by the civil rights movement. These movements dramatized the glaring contradiction between American values of liberal individualism and the conventional social practices that denied rights to many.

Gay people, some suggested, should take their place alongside other "legitimate" minority groups vying for power in American society. "The revolution must be fought for us, too, not only for blacks, Indians, welfare mothers, [and] grape pickers," proclaimed lesbian activist Martha Shelley in 1969. That same year, a crowd of drag queens, dykes, street people, and bar boys battled police as they attempted to shut down a bar in Greenwich Village in New York, in what became known as the Stonewall rebellion. Stonewall represented what sociologist George Herbert Mead might call a "problematic occurrence," a moment at which people become conscious of themselves and their circumstances, of what they have previously taken for granted, and of the need to seek alternative ways of acting.

But early gay liberationists never thought of themselves solely as building a civil rights movement for a particular minority, in the style of "ethnic" politics. They believed they were waging a revolutionary struggle to free the homosexual in everyone. "New gay" activists redefined the frontiers of lesbian/gay existences. They popularized a new vocabulary, tied to a new set of concepts: "sexual identity," "gay lifestyle," "gay pride," "coming out." They equated the adoption of a

homosexual identity with the development of "gay consciousness," thus making gay identity, and even desire, a much more reflexive matter than ever before. They proclaimed that homosexuals were a radical vanguard that posed a challenge to the dominant heterosexist and masculinist sex/gender system.

In "Notes of an 'Old Gay,'" an important gay liberation tract, a woman who had experienced lesbian desires before Stonewall, a self-described tomboy from an early age, related her encounter with psychiatry, crediting the movement with her eventual challenge of the hegemony of medical knowledges in defining homosexuality: "I read the usual psychiatric shit and found deviance writ large in my personal history: inadequate identification with same-sex parent; infantile narcissism; penis envy; penis-fear; body-shame; 'urethral' personality; fear of adult intimacy; degradation fantasies; equation of sex with dirt, etc. In short, I had 'introjected' our culture beautifully; now I had to be cured of it." She and others had been viewed as "not women," "the third sex," "inverts," and "dwellers in the half-world," but they had, finally, a theory that defined them as "normal women" or even an avant-garde. "I see now that I, in line with the society around me, my psychotherapist, and all my friends (gay and straight), was firmly resisting an interpretation of lesbianism that would bring into question the essential rightness of the male sexist ethic, or suggest the kind of drastic overhaul our society really needs."

Gay liberationists emphasized the innate "polymorphous perversity" of individuals and the artificiality of the roles imposed upon them by society. In 1970, activist Carl Wittman suggested the radical potential of homosexuality:

> Nature leaves undefined the object of sexual desire. The gender of that object has been imposed socially. . . . As kids, we refused to capitulate to demands that we smother our feelings toward each other. Somewhere we found the strength to resist being indoctrinated, and we should count that among our assets. . . . Homosexuality is NOT . . . a makeshift in the absence of the opposite sex; it is not hatred or rejection of the opposite sex; it is not genetic; it is not the result of broken homes (except inasmuch as we could see the sham of American marriage).

Wittman turned conventional explanations of homosexuality—as genetic, as the problem of a "failure" of the family—on their heads, portraying homosexuals as rebels against a failed system. But rather than substitute homosexuality for heterosexuality, he and others hoped that in a liberated society, homosexuality and heterosexuality would flourish side by side, as sexual and gender roles of all sorts became meaningless. As a popular wall poster at the time proclaimed, it was time to "smash the categories." What if every person or even a small percentage of those who had had feelings for a member of his or her own sex let that be known? If left to their own polymorphously perverse devices, individuals would reject the constraints of both homosexuality and heterosexuality and be bisexual.

Sexual behavior was changing. A study by the Institute of Sex Research showed that the number of women engaging in premarital sexual intercourse had doubled in the 1960s. As Lillian Faderman observed, "heterosexuality began to look somewhat like homosexuality, as nonreproductive sex and cohabitation without marriage came to be commonplace." In mixed-sex communal households, as the boundaries between friends and lovers blurred, "free love" and the practices of group sex and nonmonogamy occasionally allowed women to find one another beneath the sheets. But in a society in which men held the upper hand, could love ever really be "free"? Some women came to suggest that sexual liberation was a "male plot." "Sexual freedom has meant more opportunity for men, not a new kind of experience for women," declared one. Perhaps gender was the real locus of women's oppression. And so women began to form feminist organizations and their own movement for liberation.

Lesbians were not particularly welcome in this movement. In 1970, an important anthology of writings from the women's liberation movement, Robin Morgan's *Sisterhood Is Powerful*, collected the writings of fifty-four women. Only two of the articles and one poem mentioned lesbianism. Martha Shelley, in her piece "Notes of a Radical Lesbian," provided a scathing critique of femininity in American culture:

For women, as for other groups, there are several American norms. All of them have their rewards, and their penalties. The nice girl next door, virginal until her marriage—the Miss America type—is rewarded with community respect and respectability. She loses her individuality and her freedom, to become a toothpaste smile and a chastity belt. The career woman gains independence and a large margin of independence and a large margin of freedom—if she is willing to work twice as hard as a man for less pay. . . . The starlet, call girl, or bunny, whose source of income is directly related to her image as a sex object, gains some financial independence and freedom from housework . . . but she pays through psychological degradation as a sex object, and through the insecurity of knowing that her career, based on her youthful good looks, is short-lived.

Others within the movement had leveled similar charges. . . . But where Shelley's critique differed from other versions of radical feminism was in posing lesbianism as the solution to women's oppression: "The Lesbian, through her ability to obtain love and sexual satisfaction from other women, is freed of dependence on men for love, sex, and money. She does not have to do menial chores for them (at least at home), nor cater to their egos, nor submit to hasty and inept sexual encounters. She is freed from fear of unwanted pregnancy and the pains of childbirth, and from the drudgery of child raising." Lesbians, because they stood outside the norms of the sex/gender system, because they were financially and emotionally independent of men, childbirth, and child raising, were the only women who were truly free. The boldness of this statement was a telling indication of the growing self-consciousness of lesbians within the heterosexual-dominated women's movement. In the same year that *Sisterhood Is Powerful* was published, lesbians fled what they perceived as virulent homophobia among heterosexual feminists, forming an autonomous lesbian feminist movement.

"It is the primacy of women relating to women, of women creating a new consciousness of and with each other which is at the heart of women's liberation." So declared "The Woman Identified Woman," the 1970 essay that is generally considered to be the first statement of an autonomous lesbian feminist politic. This essay circulated widely among young radical feminists and achieved enormous influence. It reconceptualized the meaning of *lesbian,* equating it with female independence and suggesting that the label had been used to divide women: "When a woman hears this word tossed her way, she knows she is stepping out of line . . . for a woman to be independent means she *can't be* a woman—she must be a dyke. . . . As long as the label 'dyke' can be used to frighten women into a less militant stand, keep her separate from her sisters, keep her from giving primacy to anything other than men and family—then to that extent she is controlled by the male culture." In this view, the category *lesbian* was predicated on the existence of gender inequality; the practice of labeling independent women as lesbians was intended to force their conformity to conventional gender roles. . . . By logical extension, in order to create a freer, more egalitarian society, these limiting categories must be destroyed.

In order to do this, however, they first must be embraced, in a "reverse affirmation" of the characteristics assigned by the dominant culture. Lesbians were not failed women, but actually rebels against gender inequality. If the "exchange of women," compulsory heterosexuality, was the bedrock of the sex/gender system, then women who made lives with other women were actually subverting the dominant order. Lesbians . . . were the only truly independent women.

> Women's Liberation and Homosexual Liberation are both struggling toward a common goal: a society free from defining and categorizing people by virtue of gender and/or sexual preference. . . .

Once lesbians were redefined as "autonomous women," it was but a short step to argue that women's "authentic" nature, repressed by the dominant culture, was to love other women. Lesbians were born "that way," lesbian feminists asserted; indeed, *all* women were born "that way," all had the capacity to be lesbians but were hampered by the system of male domination. In this universalizing conception, lesbians were not "essentially" different from heterosexual women. They were different only in terms of their political commitment to affirm women's autonomy. . . .

There was little room in this politics for gay men, who, like heterosexual men, were considered to be part of the problem. Young women who "came out through feminism" believed that female homosexuality had a different source and a different meaning than male homosexuality. While gay liberationists had earlier criticized the limitations of binary identity categories, embracing the belief that everyone was naturally bisexual, feminists claimed that lesbianism was the only viable alternative to compulsory heterosexuality. Gay men, said feminists, separated sex from emotional involvement and were preoccupied with superficial issues, such as the right to have sex in public places. Lacking a radical analysis of sex and sex roles, they advocated solutions that made no basic changes in the system that oppressed lesbians as women.

In contrast, "woman identification," feminists believed, was an act of self-affirmation and love, an act of identification rather than desire. Ultimately, it was much more than simply a matter of sex, poet Judy Grahn declared: "Men who are obsessed with sex are convinced that lesbians are obsessed with sex. Actually, like other women, lesbians are obsessed with love and fidelity." Reconceptualizing the nature of sexuality, some feminists perceived desire itself as a social construct; there is no essential, undifferentiated sexual impulse, sex drive or lust, that resides in the body. The part that sexual behavior played in lesbianism was only small, and not always necessary.

Adrienne Rich suggested that primary identification with women, "a range . . . of woman-identified experience," and practices designed to make women central to one's life—and accordingly to minimize the influence of men—could or should be placed along a "lesbian continuum." The operation of compulsory, or normative, heterosexuality has meant that sexual preference is never a "free choice." "For women heterosexuality may not be a 'preference' at all but something that has to be imposed, managed, organized, propagandized, and maintained by force." Rich blurred the boundaries between homosexual and heterosexual women, universalizing the possibility of lesbianism. While providing a critique of the limiting definitions of lesbianism that derived from sexology, she maintained a commitment to the political utility of organizing around the category. . . . [S]ame-sex *desire* became secondary to same-sex *identification.* Radical feminists consciously downplayed the sexual aspects of lesbianism, at least in their public rhetoric. The process of desexualizing lesbianism may have begun when early lesbian feminists, such as the Furies, attempted to make lesbianism acceptable to heterosexual feminists who were uncomfortable with overt lesbian sexuality. Lesbianism was imagined as a kind of "female bonding," a more inclusive category with which a larger number of women could identify, and for which there was a historical precedent: the "passionate friendships" of eighteenth- and nineteenth-century women.

These and other social constructionist ideas had an enormous impact on the emergent lesbian feminist culture. Lesbianism was no longer assigned at birth or in early childhood. It was no longer the product of biological imprinting—the inheritance of genes or hormones—or a psychological aberration, such as a rejecting mother, unresolved oedipal crisis, or traumatic early sexual experience. Neither explanation had been very popular, because feminists were wary of both biological determinism and the psychotherapeutic system. Instead, lesbianism was a choice open to any woman.

Writing in *The Ladder*, the newsletter of the Daughters of Bilitis, one woman described her transformation from "old dyke" to "new lesbian" in terms of her rejection of essentialist concepts of lesbian identity.

> I clung to the conviction that most women quite naturally were attracted to men as I was attracted to women. I found it impossible to understand, in any way meaningful to me, how a woman could love a man with the total involvement of her sexuality but nothing would shake loose my belief that somehow she did. My rationalization was that, being a lesbian, I could not expect to understand. . . . But at the same time I insisted on trying to understand them. And I experienced and observed things that did not quite fit my comfortable assumption that some women are born lesbians and most are not. I cannot pinpoint just when I took the plunge and threw out the silly assumption (as it now appears to me) that most women are naturally drawn to men, but it happened as a direct result of the women's liberation movement.

That "silly assumption"—that women are naturally drawn to men—would go unchallenged no longer.

Identities in Motion

The most popular novel of the lesbian feminist period, *Rubyfruit Jungle* by Rita Mae Brown, told the story of Molly Bolt, an unapologetic, fiery young lesbian who captivated cheerleaders, heiresses, and other seemingly straight women at every turn. She briefly dates a married woman named Polina.

> The wine went directly to Polina's tongue and she told me how freaked out she was and how secretly she thought lesbianism attracted and frightened every woman, because every woman could be a lesbian, but it was all hidden and unknown. Did I get into it because of the allure of the forbidden? She then went on to say what a wonderful relationship she had with her husband . . . and wasn't heterosexuality just grand?
> "It bores me, Polina."
> "Bores you—what do you mean?"
> "I mean men bore me. If one of them behaves like an adult it's cause for celebration, and even when they do act human, they still aren't as good in bed as women."
> "Maybe you haven't met the right man?"
> "Maybe you haven't met the right woman. And I bet I've slept with more men than you have, and they all work the same show. Some are better at it than others but it's boring once you know what women are like."

Women around the nation took to heart Molly's assertion that every woman could be a lesbian, that lesbianism was the exciting, alluring alternative to garden-variety heterosexuality. A woman who had been married for twenty-two years, interviewed in the early 1970s, described the origins of her lesbian identification: "I began . . . to become involved with women's consciousness-raising groups, and I began to hear . . . of the idea of women being turned on to each other. It was the first time I heard about it in terms of people that I knew. . . . I was receptive but had no previous, immediate history. Like there was a part of me that had been thinking about it, and thinking, 'Gee, that sounds like intellectually that's a good idea.'" This was a very different narrative of lesbian development than the dominant essentialist one. Fading was the image of the tomboy, the girl who had never fit into heterosexual femininity, who had been castigated by her family and shunned by schoolmates, and who became a woman forced to live her life on the margins of society.

Feminists contested popular conceptions of lesbianism, renegotiating the boundaries of permissible sexuality and creating more ways of "being" a lesbian. They constructed far more voluntaristic conceptions of desire, which many women believed could be resocialized and reshaped at will. Thus women coming of age in the early 1970s, though they had little contact with the mainly underground tradition of working-class lesbian bars, had access to a wider variety of different accounts of lesbianism than those in the 1950s, when medical discourses controlled the terms of sexual knowledge. It was more common for women, particularly middle-class women, to be faced with a *choice* about which sexual identity—heterosexual or homosexual—to adopt.

Some have suggested that for the most fervent proponents of radical feminism in the 1970s, lesbianism was often less a choice than an imperative. How could one possibly support the liberation of women and sleep with the enemy? Lesbianism became the privileged option of the vanguard of the women's movement, the only viable position for those who considered themselves truly committed politically to the liberation of their sex. This does not mean that radical feminists universally developed sexual relationships with women. But many previously heterosexual women did withdraw from their relationships with men. Armed with the homosocial concepts of the "woman-identified woman" and the "lesbian continuum," which emphasized identifica-

tions over desires, many declared themselves to be lesbians.

Certainly, the new discourse of lesbian feminism enabled many women who had never considered the possibility of claiming a lesbian lifestyle to leave their husbands and boyfriends—some for political motives, others in expression of deeply rooted desires, many for both reasons. It allowed many of those living primarily closeted lives to come out and declare their lesbianism openly. Prefeminist lesbian subcultures located in the bars had been composed mainly of working-class women. Upper-class women had their own social networks and secretive institutions. By redefining lesbianism as a political challenge to male domination, feminists made lesbianism more public and opened up the possibility of homosexuality to greater numbers of middle-class women than ever before. Lesbianism became a more public, visible, and self-conscious basis for identity. As Lillian Faderman notes, "There were probably more lesbians in America during the 1970s than any other time in history, because radical feminism had helped redefine lesbianism to make it almost a categorical imperative for all women truly interested in the welfare and progress of other women."

Feminist-style lesbianism resonated with many women who had long experienced their sexuality in relational rather than simply erotic terms, who had never thought of themselves as "exclusive" homosexuals, or indeed as homosexuals at all. Lesbianism had become, through the influence of feminist ideas, a highly self-conscious and reflexive identity—"on a head level and not just a 'gut' level." . . .

Study Questions on Arlene Stein

1. Distinguish between the old lesbianism and the new. What role did feminism play in the emergence of the new lesbianism according to Stein? Explain the connection the new lesbians saw between their strong political commitment to feminism and their choice to become lesbians. Do you agree that there is a natural connection between feminism and lesbianism? Could a strongly heterosexual woman be as committed to feminism as a lesbian one?
2. Stein says that the new lesbians believe that female homosexuality has a different source and meaning than male homosexuality. Explain. Do you agree?

3. How is lesbian culture as described by Stein similar to male homosexual culture as described by Rodriguez (see previous article)? How is it different? Is there any male analogue to Stein's new lesbianism?

4. Do you agree that all women are potentially lesbians? What assumptions motivate the claim that they are? If this is true of women, are all men potentially gay in the same sense that women are, or do you think that female sexuality is more malleable than male sexuality? It might help you think about this if you know people who have changed from being practicing heterosexuals to being practicing homosexuals or vice versa. Do women, in your experience, tend to change their sexual orientation more often than men?

5. Members of the gay and lesbian movement often describe their opponents as *homophobes*, suggesting that they are the victims of irrational fears. In the light of the selection from Stein, is there anything for them to be afraid of?

The Ladder of Eros

Plato

Plato describes Love (*Eros*) as a spirit, or envoy that mediates between heaven and earth. He is the son of Resource and Need, at once desirous and full of wisdom, a lifelong seeker after truth, an adept in sorcery, enchantment, and seduction. All of us long for procreation: those men whose procreative power is of the body turn to a woman, and raise a family, in the hope that they will keep their memory alive forever; but those whose procreative power is of the spirit attempt to beget the goods of the spirit on beautiful boys. They then go from the love of the beauty of individuals to the love of beautiful institutions and the love of learning, and at last to the heavenly Beauty itself. Such men attain immortality if anyone does.

. . . [SPIRITS] ARE THE ENVOYS and interpreters that ply between heaven and earth, flying upward with our worship and our prayers, and descending with the heavenly answers and commandments, and since they are between the two estates they weld both sides together and merge them into one great whole. They form the medium of the prophetic arts, of the priestly rites of sacrifice, initiation, and incantation, of divination and of sorcery, for the divine will not mingle directly with the human, and it is only through the mediation of the spirit world that man can have any intercourse, whether waking or sleeping, with the gods. And the man who is versed in such matters is said to have spiritual powers, as opposed to the mechanical powers of the man who is expert in the more mundane arts. There are many spirits, and many kinds of spirits, too, and Love is one of them.

Then who were his parents? I asked.

I'll tell you, she said, though it's rather a long story. On the day of Aphrodite's birth the gods were making merry, and among them was

From E. Hamilton, *The Collected Dialogues of Plato.* © 1961, renewed 1989 by Princeton University Press. Reprinted by permission of the publisher.

Resource, the son of Craft. And when they had supped, Need came begging at the door because there was good cheer inside. Now, it happened that Resource, having drunk deeply of the heavenly nectar—for this was before the days of wine—wandered out into the garden of Zeus and sank into a heavy sleep, and Need, thinking that to get a child by Resource would mitigate her penury, lay down beside him and in time was brought to bed of Love. So Love became the follower and servant of Aphrodite because he was begotten on the same day that she was born, and further, he was born to love the beautiful since Aphrodite is beautiful herself.

Then again, as the son of Resource and Need, it has been his fate to be always needy; nor is he delicate and lovely as most of us believe, but harsh and arid, barefoot and homeless, sleeping on the naked earth, in doorways, or in the very streets beneath the stars of heaven, and always partaking of his mother's poverty. But, secondly, he brings his father's resourcefulness to his designs upon the beautiful and the good, for he is gallant, impetuous, and energetic, a mighty hunter, and a master of device and artifice—at once desirous and full of wisdom, a lifelong seeker after truth, an adept in sorcery, enchantment, and seduction.

He is neither mortal nor immortal, for in the space of a day he will be now, when all goes well with him, alive and blooming, and now dying, to be born again by virtue of his father's nature, while what he gains will always ebb away as fast. So Love is never altogether in or out of need, and stands, moreover, midway between ignorance and wisdom. You must understand that none of the gods are seekers after truth. They do not long for wisdom, because they are wise—and why should the wise be seeking the wisdom that is already theirs? Nor, for that matter, do the ignorant seek the truth or crave to be made wise. And indeed, what makes their case so hopeless is that, having neither beauty, nor goodness, nor intelligence, they are satisfied with what they are, and do not long for the virtues they have never missed. . . .

. . . We are all of us prolific, Socrates, in body and in soul, and when we reach a certain age our nature urges us to procreation. Nor can we be quickened by ugliness, but only by the beautiful. Conception, we know, takes place when man and woman come together, but there's a divinity in human propagation, an immortal something in the midst of man's mortality which is incompatible with any kind of discord. And ugliness is at odds with the divine, while beauty is in perfect harmony. In propagation, then, Beauty is the goddess of both fate and travail, and so when procreancy draws near the beautiful it grows genial and blithe, and birth follows swiftly on conception. But when it meets with ugliness it is overcome with heaviness and gloom, and turning away it shrinks into itself and is not brought to bed, but still labors under its painful burden. And so, when the procreant is big with child, he is strangely stirred by the beautiful, because he knows that beauty's tenant will bring his travail to an end. So you see, Socrates, that Love is not exactly a longing for the beautiful, as you suggested.

Well, what is it, then?

A longing not for the beautiful itself, but for the conception and generation that the beautiful effects. . . .

Well then, she went on, those whose procreancy is of the body turn to woman as the object of their love, and raise a family, in the blessed hope that by doing so they will keep their memory green, "through time and through eternity." But those whose procreancy is of the spirit rather than of the flesh—and they are not unknown, Socrates—conceive and bear the things of the spirit. And what are they? you ask. Wisdom and all her sister virtues; it is the office of every poet to beget them, and of every artist whom we may call creative. . . .

Well now, my dear Socrates, I have no doubt that even you might be initiated into these, the more elementary mysteries of Love. But I don't know whether you could apprehend the final revelation, for so far, you know, we are only at the bottom of the true scale of perfection.

Never mind, she went on, I will do all I can to help you understand, and you must strain every nerve to follow what I'm saying.

Well then, she began, the candidate for this initiation cannot, if his efforts are to be rewarded, begin too early to devote himself to the beauties of the body. First of all, if his preceptor instructs him as he should, he will fall in love with the beauty of one individual body, so that his passion may give life to noble discourse. Next he must consider how nearly related the beauty of any one body is to the beauty of any other, when he will see that if he is to devote himself to loveliness of form it will be absurd to deny that the beauty of each and every body is the same. Having reached this point, he must set himself to be the lover of every lovely body, and bring his passion for the one into due proportion by deeming it of little or of no importance.

Next he must grasp that the beauties of the body are as nothing to the beauties of the soul, so that wherever he meets with spiritual loveliness, even in the husk of an unlovely body, he will find it beautiful enough to fall in love with and to cherish—and beautiful enough to quicken in his heart a longing for such discourse as tends toward the building of a noble nature. And from this he will be led to contemplate the beauty of laws and institutions. And when he discovers how nearly every kind of beauty is akin to every other he will conclude that the beauty of the body is not, after all, of so great moment.

And next, his attention should be diverted from institutions to the sciences, so that he may know the beauty of every kind of knowledge. And thus, by scanning beauty's wide horizon, he will be saved from a slavish and illiberal devotion to the individual loveliness of a single boy, a single man, or a single institution. And, turning his eyes toward the open sea of beauty, he will find in such contemplation the seed of the most fruitful discourse and the loftiest thought, and reap a golden harvest of philosophy, until, confirmed and strengthened, he will come upon one single form of knowledge, the knowledge of the beauty I am about to speak of.

And here, she said, you must follow me as closely as you can.

Whoever has been initiated so far in the mysteries of Love and has viewed all these aspects of the beautiful in due succession, is at last drawing near the final revelation. And now, Socrates, there bursts upon him that wondrous vision which is the very soul of the beauty he has toiled so long for. It is an everlasting loveliness which neither comes nor goes, which neither flowers nor fades, for such beauty is the same on every hand, the same then as now, here as there, this way as that way, the same to every worshiper as it is to every other.

Nor will his vision of the beautiful take the form of a face, or of hands, or of anything that is of the flesh. It will be neither words, nor knowledge, nor a something that exists in something else, such as a living creature, or the earth, or the heavens, or anything that is—but subsisting of itself and by

itself in an eternal oneness, while every lovely thing partakes of it in such sort that, however much the parts may wax and wane, it will be neither more nor less, but still the same inviolable whole.

And so, when his prescribed devotion to boyish beauties has carried our candidate so far that the universal beauty dawns upon his inward sight, he is almost within reach of the final revelation. And this is the way, the only way, he must approach, or be led toward, the sanctuary of Love. Starting from individual beauties, the quest for the universal beauty must find him ever mounting the heavenly ladder, stepping from rung to rung—that is, from one to two, and from two to *every* lovely body, from bodily beauty to the beauty of institutions, from institutions to learning, and from learning in general to the special lore that pertains to nothing but the beautiful itself—until at last he comes to know what beauty is.

And if, my dear Socrates, Diotima went on, man's life is ever worth the living, it is when he has attained this vision of the very soul of beauty. And once you have seen it, you will never be seduced again by the charm of gold, of dress, of comely boys, or lads just ripening to manhood; you will care nothing for the beauties that used to take your breath away and kindle such a longing in you, and many others like you, Socrates, to be always at the side of the beloved and feasting your eyes upon him, so that you would be content, if it were possible, to deny yourself the grosser necessities of meat and drink, so long as you were with him.

But if it were given to man to gaze on beauty's very self—unsullied, unalloyed, and freed from the mortal taint that haunts the frailer loveliness of flesh and blood—if, I say, it were given to man to see the heavenly beauty face to face, would you call *his,* she asked me, an unenviable life, whose eyes had been opened to the vision, and who had gazed upon it in true contemplation until it had become his own forever?

And remember, she said, that it is only when he discerns beauty itself through what makes it visible that a man will be quickened with the true, and not the seeming, virtue—for it is virtue's self that quickens him, not virtue's semblance. And when he has brought forth and reared this perfect virtue, he shall be called the friend of god, and if ever it is given to man to put on immortality, it shall be given to him. . . .

Study Questions on Plato

1. How does Diotima rank the forms of Love, from lowest to highest? Do you accept her ranking? Does it strip lower forms of love and friendship of all value?
2. Do what seem to be uncomplicated physical urges in fact involve a desire for Eternity?
3. Plato wrote in a society in which respectable women had little or no life outside the home, and in which sexual passion for young boys on the part of men was an established institution. How do these facts affect our ability to accept and apply his philosophy today? (For example, is Platonic love between men and women now possible?)
4. Investigate Plato's larger philosophy, and examine the role of the doctrine of Love (Eros) within it. Can Plato's views on Love be separated from his distinctive metaphysics?

For Further Reading

Aquinas, Thomas. *Summa Theologiae.* Dominican Fathers, trans. New York: Benziger Brothers, 1948. IIa IIae, QQ. 51–54.

Augustine. *Confessions.* Many translations. Books II–III.

Baker, Robert, and Frederick Elliston, eds. *Philosophy and Sex.* New rev, ed. Buffalo, N.Y.: Prometheus, 1984.

Barth, Karl. *Church Dogmatics: A Selection.* Helmut Gollwizer, ed. G. W. Bromiley, trans. New York: Harper Torchbooks, 1962. Chaps. 6 and 7. A statement of the Christian view of sex by a conservative Protestant theologian.

Berns, Walter. "Pornography versus Democracy. *Society,* 36, no. 6 (September 1999), 16ff. Available on InfoTrac® College Edition.

Brownmiller, Susan. *Against Our Will.* New York: Simon & Schuster, 1975.

Cameron, Paul. "A Case Against Homosexuality." *Human Life Review,* 4 (Summer 1978), 17–49.

Derrick, Christopher. *Sex and Sacredness.* San Francisco: Ignatius, 1982. A defense of a conservative Catholic view of sex in the light of an interpretation of paganism.

Devine, Philip E. "Birth, Copulation, and Death." *New Scholasticism,* (Summer 1985).

Euripides. "Hipplolytus." Many translations. A pagan view of the dangers of sex.

Ferguson, Ann. "Patriarchy, Sexual Identity, and the Sexual Revolution." *Signs,* 7, no. 1 (1981), 158-172. Available: www.infoexchange.net/au/wise/HEALTH/Les4.htm

Finnis, John. "Law, Morality, and 'Sexual Orientation.'" *Notre Dame Journal of Law, Ethics. and Public Policy,* 9 (1995).

Ford, John, S. J. et al. *The Teaching of "Humanae Vitae."* San Francisco: Ignatius, 1988. Includes important contributions by Germain Grisez.

Gibbs, Liz, ed. "Daring to Dissent: Lesbian Culture from Margin to Mainstream." In Roy Hopkins, Liz Gibbs, and Christina Ruse, eds., *Women on Women.* London: Cassell, 1994.

Great Britain. Committee on Obscenity and Film Censorship. *Obscenity and Film Censorship: An Abridgment of the Williams Report.* Cambridge: Cambridge University Press, 1981.

Greer, Germaine. *Sex and Destiny.* New York: Harper and Row, 1984.

Heron, Alastair, ed. *Towards a Quaker View of Sex.* London: Friends Service Committee, 1964.

Horney, Karen. *Feminine Psychology.* New York: W. W. Norton, 1973.

Johnston, Jill. *Lesbian Nation: The Feminist Solution.* New York: Simon & Schuster, 1973.

Lawler, Ronald, O.F.M. Cap., Joseph Boyle, and William E. May. *Catholic Sexual Ethics.* Huntington, Ind.: Our Sunday Visitor, 1985.

Mann, Thomas. *Death in Venice.* Eric Heller, ed. Kenneth Burke, trans. New York: Modern Library, 1970. A classic portrayal of death wish sexuality, in the form of desire for a young boy.

Mill, John Stuart. *On Liberty.* Many editions.

Mitchell, Juliet. *Psychoanalysis and Feminism.* New York: Vintage, 1975.

Munt, Sally, ed. "New Lesbian Criticism: Literary and Cultural Readings." In Lillian Freeman and Larry Gross, eds., *Between Men–Between Women: Lesbian and Gay Studies.* New York: Columbia University Press, 1972.

Paglia, Camile. *Sexual Personae.* New York: Yale University Press, 1990.

Plato. *Phaedrus.* Many translations.

Purtill, Richard L. *Moral Dilemmas.* Belmont, Calif.: Wadsworth, 1965. Contains an exceptionally good section on issues in sexual morality.

Ramsey, Paul. "On Taking Sexual Responsibility Seriously Enough." *Christianity and Crisis,* 23 (1964).

Raymond, Janice. "Putting the Politics Back into Lesbianism." *Women's Studies International Forum,* 12, no. 2 (1989), 149–156. Available: www.infoexchange.net.au/wise/Les3.htm.

Rich, Adrienne. "Compulsory Heterosexuality and Lesbian Existence." *Signs,* 5, no. 4 (1989), 631–660.

Rieff, Philip. *Freud: The Mind of the Moralist.* Garden City, N.Y.: Doubleday, 1961.

Ruse, Michael. *Homosexuality.* Oxford: Basil Blackwell, 1988. Comprehensive.

Sacred Congregation for the Doctrine of the Faith. "Declaration on Sexual Ethics." (December 29, 1975). In James E. White, ed., *Contemporary Moral Issues.* St. Paul, Minn.: West, 1985. Pp. 175–80.

Sartre, Jean-Paul. *Being and Nothingness.* Hazel Barnes, trans. New York: Gramercy Books; Avanerel, N.J.: Random House, 1994. Pt. III, Chap. 3.

Schopenhauer, Arthur. *The World as Will and Representation.* E. J. Payne, trans. New York: Dover, 1969. Vol. I, § 60; Vol. II, Chap. 44. Classical expression of sexual pessimism.

Scruton, Roger. *Sexual Desire.* London: Weidenfeld & Nicholson, 1986.

Soble, Alan. *Pornography.* New Haven, Conn.: Yale University Press, 1986.

Stein, Arlene. "Sisters and Queers: The Decentering of Lesbian Feminism." *Socialist Review,* 22, no. 1 (January–March 1992), 33–55.

Stewart, Robert M. *Philosophical Perspectives on Sex and Love.* New York: Oxford University Press, 1995.

Vincent, Norah. "A Normal Lesbian." *New Republic,* 214, nos. 2–3 (January 8, 1996), 15ff.

Wasserstrom, Richard. "Is Adultery Immoral?" In Wasserstrom, ed., *Today's Moral Problems.* New York: Macmillan, 1979. Pp. 288–299.

Weissberg, Robert, "The Abduction of Tolerance." *Society,* 36, no. 1 (November–December, 1998), 8ff. Available on InfoTrac® College Edition.

INFOTRAC COLLEGE EDITION To learn more about the topics from this chapter, you can use the following words to conduct an electronic search on InfoTrac College Edition, an online library of journals. Here you will find a multitude of articles from various sources and perspectives: *www.infotrac-college.com/wadsworth/access.html*

Adultery

Homosexuality

Obscenity

Platonic Love

Perversion

Pornography

Psychoanalysis

Rape

Sex, Love, and Friendship

Sexual Desire

Sexual Morality

Web Sites:

Freedom from Pornography
http://www.go.to/freefromporn

Homosexuality and Bisexuality (Religioustolerance.org)
http://www.religioustolerance.org/hom.htm

Kelb, Jim, "Sexual Morality FAQ"
http: //www/freespeech.org.antitechnocrat/sex. html

Men Can Stop Rape
http://www.mencanstoprape.org/

Morality in Media
http://www.moralityinmedia.org/

Perversion. Sexual (Encyclopedia.com)
http://www.encylopedia.com/articles.10068.html

Platonic Love
http: //www.uh.edu/~cfreelan/courses/platoniclove.html

Psychoanalysis
http://www.ipjia.org/

Stokes, David. "Marriage a la Mode: What's Adultery amid Decadence?"
http://www.nd.edu/~afreddos/papers/stokes.htm

Sullivan. Andrew, "Love Undetectable"
http://www.tbook.com/alternative_medicine/Men'sHealth/Love_Undetectable_Notes_on_
Friendship_Sex_and_Survival_0679451.htm

Tatchell, Peter, "Liberate Sexual Desire"
http://www.tatchellgayarchive.freeserve.co.uk/queer%20theory/liberating.htm

Unit III

Reproduction: How Far Should We Try to Control It?

As WE MOVE FROM DISCUSSING the meaning of sexual acts themselves to considering the ethical issues that arise from the reproductive dimension of sex, our focus expands to include not only the sexual partners, but also their possible and actual offspring. Having children is something people have strong feelings about. Infertile couples often spend huge amounts of money and go through annoying, uncomfortable, and sometimes even dangerous medical procedures in the hope of being able to have a baby. And unwanted pregnancies generate all sorts of powerful and conflicted emotions. Furthermore, whether or not a woman becomes pregnant is not entirely under her control. No method of contraception is 100 percent effective (even sterilization has been known to fail occasionally), and fertility problems are quite common these days for a variety of reasons.

We take it as a biological given that babies must be gestated in the wombs of women. Perhaps someday science will develop methods of implanting babies in men's intestines (this has been done with some animals) or growing them wholly in artificial wombs, but for the moment these can be ruled out as practical alternatives. Normally the womb the child grows in is that of the woman whose egg was fertilized by the father's sperm, but in some forms of surrogate mothering this is not the case. The ethical issues surrounding reproduction cannot be resolved by technology, whose only function is the instrumental one of keeping the customer satisfied. We therefore have to fall back on some sort of ethical principles to help us determine where we should draw the line in hard cases.

In Unit I, we found that in order to think about the relationship between sex and gender, it is necessary to give some thought to our background assumptions about the nature of the mind and its relation to the body—for example, can one be a woman in a man's body? In Unit II, we found that looking at people's broader worldviews is helpful in making sense of why they think about sex in the way they do. Likewise, in this unit and the next two units, it will be easier to understand what is going on if we keep in mind not only the kinds of background assumptions already discussed in the first two units, but also the vision of society held by the authors—in a word, their social philosophy.

Differing Social Philosophies

The dominant paradigm in social philosophy in the latter part of the twentieth century (especially in the United States) was liberal individualism, which has its root in Enlightenment thinkers like Thomas Hobbes, but whose most recent influential spokesman is John Rawls (see selection in Unit IV). Liberals characteristically think of human social life in terms of bargaining, on terms of at least rough equality, among persons whose identity is already given; the result is called the social contract. Our obligation to obey the laws, then, is founded on implied or real consent to this social contract; we are bound only by obligations that we have ourselves assumed (or at least could reasonably be expected to accept). For Hobbes, our fear of one another leads to the acceptance of an absolute sovereign. Unlike Hobbes, most liberals place a high value on autonomy and attempt to secure tolerance for diversity and to place limits on the power of the state even when its policies have the support of the majority. Thus Rawls, in his *Theory of Justice,* set out to derive basic principles of justice that could be used to design social institutions appropriate to a pluralistic society. His idea was that we should think of justice as fairness or impartiality, and that fair rules are ones that everyone would agree to *if* we could somehow screen out our tendency to choose those principles that we think will favor people like us. In order to derive the principles of justice, then, he devised the idea of a "veil of ignorance"—extending to our moral and religious convictions as well as to our talents, race, and sex—and supposed that under this veil the contractors would come to unanimous agreement about the principles of justice. Bargaining would not occur, since the contractors would be ignorant of their own identities—which makes Rawls a limiting case for the social contract tradition.

Just principles, then, are the ones that those setting up the social contract *would* come up with if they were ignorant of their own particular individual talents, social class, and beliefs about religion and about what constitutes the good life. In other words, if you do not know whether, after you emerge from the "veil of ignorance," you will turn out to be smart or stupid, male or female, gay or straight, a believer or an atheist, and so on, then, Rawls thought, you will choose principles or rules that will not seriously disfavor any group, but rather ensure that the competition among individuals is a fair one. The principles of justice, according to Rawls, are that everyone is entitled to the maximum personal liberty consistent with equal liberty for others, and that inequalities of wealth, income, opportunity, power, and the social bases of self-respect are permissible only when they are to the advantage of the worst off. The principles thus arrived at will guide those designing society's most basic institutions. In this unit, the two selections that represent the liberal individualist perspective most clearly are those by Judith Jarvis Thomson and John Robertson, though neither author follows Rawls exactly (see John Rawls and also Susan Moller Okin in Unit IV).

Questions having to do with reproduction and the rearing of children, however, are difficult to deal with within the liberal individualist framework. When discussing reproductive issues, we might try to imagine ourselves reasoning in ignorance about whether we have been born, but decisions now made about the uses of reproductive technologies will have an impact on the existence and genetic structure of future generations and on the character of the society they will find themselves in. Attempts have been made to conceptualize these issues in terms of existing individuals existing "downstream" from us in time, or in terms of the potential human beings latent in presently existing ones, but the whole problem is a very messy one. Issues of family structure and education of the young (to be discussed in Unit IV) are particularly difficult. Such issues are bound up with the question of what sort of people we want the next generation to become, and it is impossible to reason about this under a veil of ignorance about our own conceptions of what the good life for human beings is like; liberals at least need to assume that autonomy is valuable.

Communitarianism is a social philosophy that has arisen largely as a reaction against liberal individualism, and the areas communitarians are most interested in are precisely those areas where liberal theory seems most inadequate—namely, those involving families and the education of the young. Communitarians are deeply troubled by the dissolution of the social bonds that hold families and neighborhoods together and by the fact that increasing numbers of children seem to be growing up to be materialistic, greedy, and self-indulgent. In part these problems can be traced to the corrosive effects of a highly competitive capitalistic economy. But communitarians also criticize liberal political theory on the grounds that its structure favors possessive individualism, even though most liberals have no intention of defending greed or self-indulgence. Rawls, for example, focuses on goods that can be distributed and possessed by individuals (omitting friendship from his list of basic goods) and screens out shared ideals of the good life from deliberations about the requirements of social justice.

Liberal democracy, communitarians argue, cannot continue to function well unless we begin to give more thought to inculcating civic virtues in the young—things like honesty, a willingness to work hard, and fidelity to one's commitments. Many important moral obligations, they point out, are not voluntarily assumed, with familial obligations being an especially important case in point. Virtues emphasized by liberals, such as a sense of justice and autonomy, must be supplemented by such virtues as a sense of responsibility to help the less fortunate, and a willingness to subordinate one's own personal interests to the common good. Since the family is the place where children receive their earliest and most important character formation, communitarians have been especially interested in families and concerned about their ability to adequately perform the necessary socialization of the next generation. They tend to favor something like the traditional family and support family-friendly policies. The selections by Celia Wolf-Devine and Jean Bethke Elshtain in this unit represent the communitarian tendency (see also Michael Sandel and Juli Loesch Wiley).

The readings in this unit center around two sorts of problems: (1) the problems facing those who want to avoid pregnancy, and (2) the problems facing those who want children but cannot get them by the usual means.

Preview of Readings

Abortion

Abortion is by far the most conspicuous issue in the ethics of reproduction now under discussion; the literature is endless. Much of the discussion of this issue has centered on the status of the fetus—whether its destruction is murder, elective surgery, or something in between. But here we concentrate on an issue whose presence off the page has often decisively influenced answers to the fetus question. What is the significance of pregnancy and abortion for the women who undergo them? Thus, in reading the selections by women, you should ask yourselves how, if at all, the authors' experiences as women have affected their understanding of the issues. Judith Jarvis Thomson attempts to cross gender lines by offering analogies to an unwanted pregnancy that apply to men as well as to women (such as waking with a violinist attached to one's kidneys), but we can still ask how her choice of analogies is colored by her experience as a woman, and how this contributes to their effectiveness.

Although all of the selections on abortion are by women, we do not mean to suggest that men as men have no distinctive experience of abortion. A man may have pressured a woman into an abortion, paid for one, or had his offspring aborted against his will, and these experiences can have lasting effects. But, for complicated cultural reasons, the many men who have written on the abortion issue have done so almost exclusively from abstract philosophical, medical, or political perspectives, rather than reflecting in an incisive way on the impact abortion has on the men involved. (Interestingly, this is exactly what those who distinguish the masculine from the feminine voice in ethics would lead us to expect.)

We begin with a description of life in an abortion clinic. The author (a nurse in an abortion clinic) believes abortion to be, in her own words, a form of "necessary violence," and is prepared to take part in abortions on that ground. Next comes Judith Jarvis Thomson's defense of abortion, one that rests on the invasive character of the fetus or embryo's presence regardless of its human status. Thomson compares the woman pregnant against her will with someone who has been kidnapped and attached to a comatose violinist whose life can only be sustained by use of her kidneys. Just as it would be permissible for the victim to disconnect herself from the violinist even though doing so would result in his death, so also the involuntarily pregnant woman may disconnect herself from the fetus, even though doing so will cause its death. Celia Wolf-Devine examines abortion in the context of the distinction between the "feminine voice" and the "masculine voice" in ethics (concepts developed by Carol Gilligan). She suggests that abortion should be understood as itself an invasive procedure springing from a "masculine voice" approach to an unwanted pregnancy. It manifests a drive to control nature through technological manipulation, a willingness to use violence to maintain control, and an abdication of the values associated with an ethics of care (the "feminine voice") such as preserving relationships, taking responsibility to care for others, and nonviolence.

Contraception

Behind the abortion issue there lurks that of contraception, which is sometimes linked with abortion and sometimes proposed as a means of avoiding it. This is not as "hot" a topic as abortion, obviously. Opposition to it is mostly confined these days to Catholics (and many Catholics dissent from this particular Church teaching), but some evangelicals worry about it because they think there may be a slippery slope argument leading from contraception to abortion, and there are some flutters of interest in natural family planning among those troubled by the fact that many other forms of birth control turn out to have harmful effects on women. The reason for including contraception is not because it is in the headlines, but because it is conceptually connected in interesting ways with abortion, and thinking about it sheds light on some of the broader issues involved.

First, the line between contraception and abortion is not a sharp one (see the works by Andre Hellegers and Norman Ford listed in the For Further Reading section in this unit). Some forms of contraception—for example, the IUD—result in the destruction of an already fertilized ovum, and thus can be understood as early forms of abortion. Morning-after pills do the same thing (preventing implantation of the fertilized ovum). Should they be classified as abortifacients?

Second, there is some dispute over whether readily available contraception actually leads to fewer abortions or more abortions. Obviously, successful use of contraception obviates the need for abortion, so it would seem that contraception is the answer to the problem of unwanted pregnancies. But on the other side, it has been argued that widespread use of contraception has resulted in more extra-marital sex, so that given the fallibility of contraception and the fact that many people are careless in their use of it, we may wind up with more abortions overall, particularly since people may feel abortion is more legitimate in cases of contraceptive failure (after all, they *tried* to avoid pregnancy).

Third, contraception engages the dispute between a conception of medicine that regards the human body as a machine to be modified to suit the purposes of its "owner," and a holistic-organic approach that tries to be guided by the body's immanent norms. The same issues are raised by cosmetic surgery, transsexual surgery, sterilization, and genetic engineering, as well as cloning and various forms of assisted reproduction. Worries about what, if any, limits should be placed on such practices and why are quite widespread, and not confined to those with religiously grounded qualms about "playing God."

And finally, looking at the arguments for and against contraception brings into clear focus the connection between sexual intercourse and reproduction. The Catholic position is that sexual intercourse should be open to the possibility of reproduction—that people should not deliberately intervene in the natural processes of the human body in order to render intercourse sterile. Three types of arguments have been offered to defend this position. One, typified by Richard Connell in Unit II, focuses on the natural teleology of the sexual organs themselves; reproduction just is, he argues, what the reproductive organs are *for*. A second, articulated by Finnis and Grisez (cited in the For Further Reading sections of Units II and III), relies instead on a general type of argument that we must never act directly against one of the basic goods (in this case the good of life). And the third argument, illustrated by the selections in this unit, is a more personalistic one, focusing on the way in which contraception impacts the marital relationship. Rosemary Ruether argues that, in the world in which we find ourselves, the use of contraception is consistent with married love, and in fact is likely to contribute to the health and stability of the marriage. Cormac Burke argues that if one deliberately destroys the power of the conjugal act to give life, one necessarily destroys its power to signify the love and union proper to marriage.

Assisted Reproduction

The issue of reproductive technology is the flip side of the issue of contraception. We must ask to what extent it is legitimate to separate reproduction from sex, just as we have asked whether it is legitimate to separate sex from reproduction. Those who condemn all forms of artificial birth control also condemn all (or virtually all) forms of reproductive technology. But opposition to assisted reproduction is also widespread among feminists worried about its impact on women. It is also common among those who are becoming worried about the sort of high-tech manipulation of the human body that is becoming common, and generally favor a more holistic and organic approach.

The first reading on this topic is a libertarian defense of "collaborative reproduction" by the legal theorist John Robertson. The next reading is a critique of the new reproductive technologies by Jean Bethke Elshtain who expresses concern about the impact of new reproductive technologies on women and about their implications for the dignity and equality of all people. Finally, James and Hilde Lindemann Nelson argue that biological parenthood, especially when freely chosen, carries with it obligations to one's child that are violated by "surrogate mothering."

Liberal individualism encourages us to frame the issue of surrogate mothering in terms of informed consent, since women are frequently not properly informed about the dangers and probabilities of success of the procedures they are undergoing (see Corea and Evans in For Further Reading in this unit). But taking informed consent to be the central issue runs into a serious problem, for only those who are party to a surrogacy contract can consent to it, and one party crucially affected by such arrangements—namely, the resulting child—cannot have consented either to conventional or to innovative methods of reproduction.

Questions for Reflection

1. Explain the difference between abortion and contraception. How important do you think this distinction is?

2. Do you think there is an emotional or psychological difference between sexual intercourse in which contraception is employed, and sexual intercourse where it is not? Has this any moral significance?

3. Aside from objections to the particular means employed, are there any moral problems with intervening in human reproduction?

4. Do you think our present abortion laws that place very few restrictions on the procedure are good for women or not?

5. Do you think that fathers should have any say over whether or not their offspring is aborted? What if the man is willing to take full responsibility for the child at birth? Does it make a difference whether the couple is married?

6. Should a woman who would never have an abortion herself drive a friend to an abortion clinic?

7. Is there anyone in your circle of acquaintances who has had an abortion? What effect did it have on her? Has this had any impact on your opinion about the rightness or wrongness of abortion?

8. If you do not wholly reject reproductive technologies, how would you distinguish between those that inherently lend themselves to an unconscionable level of manipulation of women and those that can, if properly regulated, be acceptable? Or do you think that the dangers of reproductive technology are sufficient to require a veto on all such procedures?

9. Think about the effects of reproductive technologies on the children so conceived. Would it make a difference to you if you discovered that your biological father had sold his sperm to a sperm bank, or that your biological mother had signed a surrogacy contract and handed you over at birth to the woman who you thought was your mother?

Glossary

abortifacient producing an abortion (usually a pill or medicine).

amniocentesis testing the cells of the placenta to determine whether the fetus is "defective."

anencephalic lacking a brain.

artificial insemination fertilizing a woman with a man's sperm by methods other than sexual intercourse; where the man is not expected to have a role in the child's life, this is called *artificial insemination by donor.*

Baby M. case famous New Jersey case concerning surrogate motherhood.

basic good a good taken as fundamental in moral reasoning, such as friendship or procreation.

biologism understanding of sex as mainly or solely a biological phenomenon.

biophilic favorable to life.

biopolitics political manipulation of human reproduction.

birth-parent genetic parent (in contrast with adoptive parents); woman who gives birth to a child (in contexts of surrogacy).

care perspective viewing society as a web of relationships sustained by a process of communication, in which the demands of the particular other are paramount.

collaborative reproduction practices in which an infertile couple employs an outsider in order to get children (for example, artificial insemination by donor).

colonized minds the outlook of those members of an oppressed group who adopt the perspective of their oppressors.

conjugal act see *marital act* in this Glossary.

dualism view of the human person that draws a sharp distinction between body and soul.

ecofemininst a group that attempts to blend the concerns of feminists with the ecology movement. See *ecology* in the Glossary in Unit I.

embryo flushing removal of a live embryo from the womb.

Enlightenment early modern movement that subjected all traditional ideas, especially religious doctrines, to severe rational examination, and tended to be optimistic about the possibility of progress.

eugenics attempt to improve the quality of the human stock by encouraging the reproduction of superior people and discouraging the reproduction of inferior people.

feminine voice vs. masculine voice two approaches to moral reasoning identified by Carol Gilligan; the first emphasizes concern for the particular other, care, and relationships, while the second emphasizes rights, rules, and principles.

gametes reproductive cells (sperm and ova).

gestation pregnancy.

gestational hostess woman carrying another woman's child in her womb.

grim options the view that it is sometimes necessary to do morally unpleasant things.

Heinz dilemma situation in which a man can only get medicine for his sick wife by stealing.

individualism emphasizing the rights and needs of the isolated individual. Opposed to *corporate.*

information speck a bit of embodied genetic information, such as a fertilized ovum.

IUD (intrauterine device) a possibly abortifacient form of contraception.

IVF (in vitro fertilization) fertilization outside a woman's body, say in a test tube.

liberalism political tradition that conceptualizes social life in terms of a contract among independent individuals.

licitness moral acceptability.

marital act sexual intercourse in marriage.

natural family planning controlling reproduction by timing intercourse to coincide with infertile times, determined by basal body temperature, vaginal secretions, as well as the number of days since the last menstrual period. More reliable than the rhythm method.

objectification treating persons as objects.

oral-steroid the Pill, which prevents reproduction by changing a woman's hormones.

parturition childbirth.

periodic continence rhythm method or natural family planning.

personalism approach to philosophical and theological issues that takes the person as central.

Playboy Philosophy column in the men's magazine *Playboy*, expressing the editor's views on sexual issues.

procreativeness sex as capable of producing children.

relational aspect of sexuality sex as an element in a (usually long-term) relationship between two persons.

reproductive rights right to control reproduction, especially by abortion; also *reproductive choice.*

rhythm method avoiding reproduction by timing sexual intercourse according to the number of days since the last menstrual period.

Roe v. Wade United States Supreme Court decision (1973) legalizing abortion.

spermicidal destroying semen.

surrogate embryo transfer taking an embryo from one woman's womb and putting it in another.

surrogate mother woman who carries in her womb a child not biologically her own, or who becomes pregnant having undertaken to give up the child at birth.

womb rental employment of another woman's womb to bear one's child.

We Do Abortions Here

SALLIE TISDALE

> Sallie Tisdale describes life in an abortion clinic, including its grim, weary moments, and her problems in dealing with clients who persist in using the word *baby* and inquiring about the baby's sex. Despite everything she has experienced, she remains pro-choice.

WE DO ABORTIONS HERE; that is all we do. There are weary, grim moments when I think I cannot bear another basin of bloody remains, utter another kind phrase of reassurance. So I leave the procedure room in the back and reach for a new chart. Soon I am talking to an eighteen-year-old woman pregnant for the fourth time. I push up her sleeve to check her blood pressure and find row upon row of needle marks, neat and parallel and discolored. She has been so hungry for her drug for so long that she has taken to using the loose skin of her upper arms; her elbows are already a permanent ruin of bruises. She is surprised to find herself four months pregnant. I suspect she is often surprised, in a mild way, by the blows she is dealt. I prepare myself for another basin, another brief and chafing loss.

"How can you stand it?" Even the clients ask. They see the machine, the strange instruments, the blood, the final stroke that wipes away the promise of pregnancy. Sometimes I see that too: I watch a woman's swollen abdomen sink to softness in a few stuttering moments and my own belly flip-flops with sorrow. But all it takes for me to catch my breath is another interview, one more story that sounds so much like the last one. There is a numbing sameness lurking in this job: the same questions, the same answers, even the same trembling tone in the voices. The worst is the sameness of human failure, of inadequacy in the face of each day's dull demands.

In describing this work, I find it difficult to explain how much I enjoy it most of the time. We laugh a lot here, as friends and as professional peers. It's nice to be with women all day. I like the sudden, transient bonds I forge with some clients: moments when I am in my strength, remembering weakness, and a woman in weakness reaches out for my strength. What I offer is not power, but solidness, offered almost eagerly. Certain clients waken in me every tender urge I have—others make me wince and bite my tongue. Both challenge me to find a balance. It is a sweet brutality we practice here, a stark and loving dispassion.

I look at abortion as if I am standing on a cliff with a telescope, gazing at some great vista. I can sweep the horizon with both eyes, survey the scene in all its distance and size. Or I can put my eye to the lens and focus on the small details, suddenly so close. In abortion the absolute must always be tempered by the contextual, because both are real, both valid, both hard. How can we do this? How can we refuse? Each abortion is a measure of our failure to protect, to nourish our own. Each basin I empty is a promise—but a promise broken a long time ago.

I grew up on the great promise of birth control. Like many women my age, I took the pill as soon as I was sexually active. To risk pregnancy when it was so easy to avoid seemed stupid, and my contraceptive success, as it were, was part of the promise of social enlightenment. But birth control fails, far more frequently than laboratory trials predict. Many of our clients take the pill; its failure to protect them is a shocking realization. We have clients who have been sterilized, whose husbands have had vasectomies; each one is a statistical misfit, fine print come to life. The anger and shame of these women I hold in one hand, and the basin in the other. The distance between the two, the length I pace and try to measure, is the size of an abortion.

The procedure is disarmingly simple. Women are surprised, as though the mystery of conception, a dark and hidden genesis, requires an elaborate finale. In the first trimester of pregnancy, it's a mere few minutes of vacuuming, a neat tidying up. I give a woman a small yellow Valium, and when it has begun to relax her, I lead her into the back, into bareness, the stirrups. The doctor reaches in her, opening the narrow tunnel to the uterus with a succession of slim, smooth bars of steel. He inserts a plastic tube and hooks it to a hose on the machine. The woman is framed against white paper that crackles as she moves, the light bright in her eyes. Then the machine rumbles low and loud in the small windowless room; the doctor moves the tube back and forth with an efficient rhythm, and the long tail of it fills with blood that spurts and stumbles along into a jar. He is usually finished in a few minutes. They are long minutes for the woman; her uterus frequently reacts to its abrupt emptying with a powerful, unceasing cramp, which cuts off the blood vessels and enfolds the irritated, bleeding tissue.

I am learning to recognize the shadows that cross the faces of the women I hold. While the doctor works between her spread legs, the paper drape hiding his intent expression, I stand beside the table. I hold the woman's hands in mine, resting them just below her ribs. I watch her eyes, finger her necklace, stroke her hair. I ask about her job, her family; in a haze she answers me; we chatter, faces close, eyes meeting and sliding apart.

I watch the shadows that creep up unnoticed and suddenly darken her face as she screws up her features and pushes a tear out each side to slide down her cheeks. I have learned to anticipate the quiver of chin, the rapid intake of breath and the surprising sobs that rise soon after the machine starts to drum. I know this is when the cramp deepens, and the tears are partly the tears that follow pain—the sharp, childish crying when one bumps one's head on a cabinet door. But a well of woe seems to open beneath many women when they hear that thumping sound. The anticipation of the moment has finally come to fruit; the moment has arrived when the loss is no longer an imagined one. It has come true.

I am struck by the sameness and I am struck every day by the variety here—how this commonplace dilemma can so display the differences of women. A twenty-one-year-old woman, unemployed, uneducated, without family, in the fifth month of her fifth pregnancy. A forty-two-year-old mother of teenagers, shocked by her condition, refusing to tell her husband. A twenty-three-year-old mother of two having her seventh abortion, and many women in their thirties having their first. Some are stoic, some hysterical, a few giggle uncontrollably, many cry.

I talk to a sixteen-year-old uneducated girl who was raped. She has gonorrhea. She describes blinding headaches, attacks of breathlessness, nausea. "Sometimes I feel like two different people," she tells me with a calm smile, "and I talk to myself."

I pull out my plastic models. She listens patiently for a time, and then holds her hands wide in front of her stomach.

"When's the baby going to go up into my stomach?" she asks.

I blink. "What do you mean?"

"Well," she says, still smiling, "when women get so big, isn't the baby in your stomach? Doesn't it hatch out of an egg there?"

My first question in an interview is always the same. As I walk down the hall with the woman, as we get settled in chairs and I glance through her files, I am trying to gauge her, to get a sense of the words, and the tone, I should use. With some I joke, with others I chat, sometimes I fall into a brisk, business-like patter. But I ask every woman, "Are you sure you want to have an abortion!" Most nod with grim knowing smiles. "Oh, yes," they sigh. Some seek forgiveness, offer excuses. Occasionally a woman will flinch and say, "Please don't use that word."

Later I describe the procedure to come, using care with my language. I don't say "pain" any more than I would say "baby." So many are afraid to ask how much it will hurt. "My sister told me—" I hear. "A friend of mine said—" and the dire expectations unravel. I prick the index finger of a woman for a drop of blood to test, and as the tiny lancet approaches the skin she averts her eyes, holding her trembling hand out to me and jumping at my touch.

It is when I am holding a plastic uterus in one hand, a suction tube in the other, moving them together in imitation of the scrubbing to come, that women ask the most secret question. I am speaking in a matter-of-fact voice about "the tissue" and "the contents" when the woman suddenly catches my eye and asks, "How big is the baby now?" These words suggest a quiet need for a definition of the boundaries being drawn. It isn't so odd, after all, that she feels relief when I describe the growing bud's bulbous shape, its miniature nature. Again I gauge, and sometimes lie a little, weaseling around its infantile features until its clinging power slackens.

But when I look in the basin, among the curd-like blood clots, I see an elfin thorax, attenuated, its pencilline ribs all in parallel rows with tiny knobs of spine rounding upwards. A translucent arm and hand swine beside.

A sleepy-eyed girl, just fourteen, watched me with a slight and goofy smile all through her abortion. "Does it have little feet and little fingers and all?" she'd asked earlier. When the suction was over she sat up woozily at the end of the table and murmured, "Can I see it?" I shook my head firmly.

"It's not allowed," I told her sternly, because I knew she didn't really want to see what was left. She accepted this statement of authority, and a shadow of confused relief crossed her plain, pale face.

Privately, even grudgingly, my colleagues might admit the power of abortion to provoke emotion. But they seem to prefer the broad view and disdain the telescope. Abortion is a matter of choice, privacy, control. Its uncertainty lies in specific cases: retarded women and girls too young to give consent for surgery, women who are ill or hostile or psychotic. Such common dilemmas are met with both compassion and impatience: they slow things down. We are too busy to chew over ethics. One person might discuss certain concerns, behind closed doors, or describe a particularly disturbing dream. But generally there is to be no ambivalence.

Every day I take calls from women who are annoyed that we cannot see them, cannot do their abortion today, this morning, now. They argue the price, demand that we stay after hours to accommodate their job or class schedule. Abortion is so routine that one expects it to be like a manicure: quick, cheap, and painless.

Still, I've cultivated a certain disregard. It isn't negligence, but I don't always pay attention. I couldn't be here if I tried to judge each case on its merits; after all, we do over a hundred abortions a week. At some point each individual in this line of work draws a boundary and adheres to it. For one physician the boundary is a particular week of gestation; for another, it is a certain number of repeated abortions. But these boundaries can be fluid too: one physician overruled his own limit to abort a mature but severely malformed fetus. For me, the limit is allowing my clients to carry their own burden, shoulder the responsibility themselves. I shoulder the burden of trying not to judge them.

This city has several "crisis pregnancy centers" advertised in the Yellow Pages. They are small offices staffed by volunteers, and they offer free pregnancy testing, glossy photos of dead fetuses, and movies. I had a client recently whose mother is active in the anti-abortion movement. The young woman went to the local crisis center and was told that the doctor would make her touch her dismembered baby, that the pain would be the most horrible she could imagine, and that she might, after an abortion, never be able to have children. All lies. They called her at home and at work, over and over and over, but she had been wise enough to give a false name. She came to us a fugitive. We who do abortions are marked, by some, as impure. It's dirty work.

When a deliveryman comes to the sliding glass window by the reception desk and tilts a box toward me, I hesitate. I read the packing slip, assess the shape and weight of the box in light of its supposed contents. We request familiar faces. The doors are carefully locked; I have learned to half glance around at bags and boxes, looking for a telltale sign. I register with security when I arrive, and I am careful not to bang a door. We are all a little on edge here.

Concern about size and shape seem to be natural, and so is the relief that follows. We make the powerful assumption that the fetus is different from us, and even when we admit the similarities, it is too simplistic to be seduced by form alone. But the form is enormously potent—humanoid, powerless, palm-sized, and pure, it evokes an almost fierce tenderness when viewed simply as what it appears to be. But appearance, and even potential, aren't enough. The fetus, in becoming itself, can ruin others; its utter dependence has a sinister side.

When I am struck in the moment by the contents in the basin, I am careful to remember the context, to note the tearful teenager and the woman sighing with something more than relief. One kind of question, though, I find considerably trickier.

"Can you tell what it is!" I am asked, and this means gender. This question is asked by couples, not women alone. Always couples would abort a girl and keep a boy. I have been asked about twins, and even if I could tell what race the father was.

An eighteen-year-old woman with three daughters brought her husband to the interview. He glared first at me, then at his wife, as he sank lower and lower in the chair, picking his teeth with a toothpick. He interrupted a conversation with his wife to ask if I could tell whether the baby would be a boy or a girl. I told him I could not.

"Good," he replied in a slow and strangely malevolent voice, "'cause if it was a boy I'd wring her neck."

In a literal sense, abortion exists because we are able to ask such questions, able to assign a value to the fetus which can shift with changing circumstances. If the human bond to a child were as primitive and unflinchingly narrow as that of other animals, there would be no abortion. There would be no abortion because there would be nothing more important than caring for the young and perpetuating the species, no reason for sex but to make babies. I sense this sometimes, this wordless organic duty, when I do ultrasounds.

We do ultrasound, a sound-wave test that paints a faint, gray picture of the fetus, whenever we're uncertain of gestation. Age is measured by the width of the skull and confirmed by the length of the femur or thighbone; we speak of a pregnancy as being a certain "femur length" in weeks. The usual concern is whether a pregnancy is within the legal limit for an abortion. Women this far along have bellies which swell out round and tight like trim muscles. When they lie flat, the mound rises softly above the hips, pressing the umbilicus upward.

It takes practice to read an ultrasound picture, which is grainy and etched as though in strokes of charcoal. But suddenly a rapid rhythmic motion appears—the beating heart. Nearby is a soft oval, scratched with lines—the skull. The leg is harder to find, and then suddenly the fetus moves, bobbing in the surf. The skull turns away, an arm slides across the screen, the torso rolls. I know the weight of a baby's head on my shoulder, the whisper of lips on ears, the delicate curve of a fragile spine in my hand. I know how heavy and correct a newborn cradled feels. The creature I watch in secret requires nothing from me but to be left alone, and that is precisely what won't be done.

These inadvertently made beings are caught in a twisting web of motive and desire. They are at least inconvenient, sometimes quite literally dangerous in the womb, but most often they fall somewhere in between—consequences never quite believed in come to roost. Their virtue rises and falls outside their own nature: they become only what we make them. A fetus created by accident is the most absolute kind of surprise. Whether the blame lies in a failed IUD, a slipped condom, or a false impression of safety, that fetus is a thing whose creation has been actively worked against. Its existence is an error. I think this is why so few women, even late in a pregnancy, will consider giving a baby up for adoption. To do so means making the fetus real—imagining it as something whole and outside oneself. The decision to terminate a pregnancy is sometimes so difficult and confounding that it creates an enormous demand for immediate action. The decision is a rejection; the pregnancy has become something to be rid of, a condition to be ended. It is a burden, a weight, a thing separate.

Women have abortions because they are too old, and too young, too poor, and too rich, too stupid, and too smart. I see women who berate themselves with violent emotions for their first and only abortion, and others who return three times, five times, hauling two or three children, who cannot remember to take a pill or where they put the diaphragm. We talk glibly about choice. But the choice for what? I see all the broken promises in lives lived like a series of impromptu obstacles. There are the sweet, light promises of love and intimacy, the glittering promise of education and progress, the warm promise of safe families, long years of innocence and community. And there is the promise of freedom: freedom from failure, from faithlessness. Freedom from biology. The early feminist defense of abortion asked many questions, but the one I remember is this: Is biology destiny? And the answer is yes, sometimes it is. Women who have the fewest choices of all exercise their right to abortion the most.

Oh, the ignorance. I take a woman to the back room and ask her to undress; a few minutes later I return and find her positioned discreetly behind a drape, still wearing underpants. "Do I have to take these off too?" she asks, a little shocked. Some swear they have not had sex, many do not know what a uterus is, how sperm and egg meet, how sex makes babies. Some late seekers do not believe themselves pregnant; they believe themselves *impregnable*. I was chastised when I began this job for referring to some clients as girls: it is a feminist heresy. They come so young, snapping gum, sockless and sneakered, and their shakily applied eyeliner smears when they cry. I call them girls with maternal benignity. I cannot imagine them as mothers.

The doctor seats himself between the woman's thighs and reaches into the dilated opening of a five-month pregnant uterus. Quickly he grabs and crushes the fetus in several places, and the room is filled with a low clatter and snap of forceps, the click of the tanaculum, and a pulling, sucking sound. The paper crinkles as the drugged and sleepy woman shifts, the nurse's low, honey-brown voice explains each step in delicate words.

I have fetus dreams, we all do here: dreams of abortions one after the other; of buckets of blood splashed on the walls; trees full of crawling fetuses. I dreamed that two men grabbed me and began to drag me away. "Let's do an abortion," they said with a sickening leer, and I began to scream, plunged into a vision of sucking, scraping pain, of being spread and torn by impartial instruments that do only what they are bidden. I woke from this dream barely able to breathe and thought of kitchen tables and coat hangers, knitting needles striped with blood, and women all alone clutching a pillow in their teeth to keep the screams from piercing the apartment-house walls. Abortion is the narrowest edge between kindness and cruelty. Done as well as it can be, it is still violence—merciful violence, like putting a suffering animal to death.

Maggie, one of the nurses, received a call at midnight not long ago. It was a woman in her twentieth week of pregnancy; the necessarily gradual process of cervical dilation begun the day before had stimulated labor, as it sometimes does. Maggie and one of the doctors met the woman at the office in the night. Maggie helped her onto the table, and as she lay down the fetus was delivered into Maggie's hands. When Maggie told me about it the next day, she cupped her hands into a small bowl— "It was just like a little kitten," she said softly, wonderingly. "Everything was still attached."

At the end of the day I clean out the suction jars, pouring blood into the sink, splashing the sides with flecks of tissue. From the sink rises a rich and humid smell, hot, earthy, and moldering; it is the smell of something recently alive beginning to decay. I take care of the plastic tub on the floor, filled with pieces too big to be trusted to the trash. The law defines the contents of the bucket I hold protectively against my chest as "tissue." Some would say my complicity in filling that bucket gives me no right to call it anything else. I slip the tissue gently into a bag and place it in the freezer, to be burned at another time. Abortion requires of me an entirely new set of assumptions. It requires a willingness to live with conflict, fearlessness, and grief. As I close the freezer door, I imagine a world where this won't be necessary, and then return to the world where it is.

Study Questions on Sallie Tisdale

1. "Each abortion is a measure of our failure to protect, to nourish our own." What does Tisdale mean by this statement? Why is she still prepared to take part in abortions nonetheless?
2. Why is the failure of contraception or sterilization to protect women shocking?
3. "Abortion exists because we are . . . able to assign a value to the fetus which can shift with changing circumstances." Ought we to do so?
4. What do you think of Tisdale's attitude toward her patients? Does she respect them? Should a nurse tell the truth about fetal development to a patient coming in for abortion, or should she shade the truth to make the patient feel better?

A Defense of Abortion

JUDITH JARVIS THOMSON

Judith Jarvis Thomson defends abortion, though not unqualifiedly. (She does not defend a right to secure the death of the unborn child.) She compares an unwanted pregnancy to waking up suddenly back to back with a famous unconscious violinist, having been kidnapped by the Society of Music Lovers who has attached him to your kidneys. She then tries to extend her argument to cases besides those of conception due to rape which this analogy suggests. She compares a woman who chooses to continue an unwelcome pregnancy to the Good Samaritan, who made large personal sacrifices to rescue a stranger. It may be noble to be willing to make such sacrifices, but no one should be forced to do so.

From Philosophy and Public Affairs, 1, *1 (1971): 47–66.* © *The Johns Hopkins University Press.*
Reprinted by permission of the publisher.

MOST OPPOSITION TO ABORTION relies on the premise that the fetus is a human being, a person, from the moment of conception. The premise is argued for, but, as I think, not well. Take, for example, the most common argument. We are asked to notice that the development of a human being from conception through birth into childhood is continuous; then it is said that to draw a line, to choose a point in this development and say "before this point the thing is not a person, after this point it is a person" is to make an arbitrary choice, a choice for which in the nature of things no good reason can be given. It is concluded that the fetus is, or anyway that we had better say it is, a person from the moment of conception. But this conclusion does not follow. Similar things might be said about the development of an acorn into an oak tree, and it does not follow that acorns are oak trees, or that we had better say they are. Arguments of this form are sometimes called "slippery slope arguments"—the phrase is perhaps self-explanatory—and it is dismaying that opponents of abortion rely on them so heavily and uncritically.

I am inclined to agree, however, that the prospects for "drawing a line" in the development of the fetus look dim. I am inclined to think also that we shall probably have to agree that the fetus has already become a human person well before birth. . . .

I propose, then, that we grant that the fetus is a person from the moment of conception. How does the argument go from here? Something like this, I take it. Every person has a right to life. So the fetus has a right to life. No doubt the mother has a right to decide what shall happen in and to her body; everyone would grant that. But surely a person's right to life is stronger and more stringent than the mother's right to decide what happens in and to her body, and so outweighs it. So the fetus may not be killed; an abortion may not be performed.

It sounds plausible. But now let me ask you to imagine this. You wake up in the morning and find yourself back to back in bed with an unconscious violinist. A famous unconscious violinist. He has been found to have a fatal kidney ailment, and the Society of Music Lovers has canvassed all the available medical records and found that you alone have the right blood type to help. They have therefore kidnapped you, and last night the violinist's circulatory system was plugged into yours, so that

your kidneys can be used to extract poisons from his blood as well as your own. The director of the hospital now tells you, "Look, we're sorry the Society of Music Lovers did this to you—we would never have permitted it if we had known. But still, they did it, and the violinist now is plugged into you. To unplug you would be to kill him. But never mind, it's only for nine months. By then he will have recovered from his ailment, and can safely be unplugged from you." Is it morally incumbent on you to accede to this situation? No doubt it would be very nice of you if you did, a great kindness. But do you *have* to accede to it? What if it were not nine months, but nine years? Or longer still? What if the director of the hospital says, "Tough luck, I agree, but you've now got to stay in bed, with the violinist plugged into you, for the rest of your life. Because remember this. All persons have a right to life, and violinists are persons. Granted you have a right to decide what happens in and to your body, but a person's right to life outweighs your right to decide what happens in and to your body. So you cannot ever be unplugged from him." I imagine you would regard this as outrageous, which suggests that something really is wrong with that plausible-sounding argument I mentioned a moment ago.

In this case, of course, you were kidnapped; you didn't volunteer for the operation that plugged the violinist into your kidneys. Can those who oppose abortion on the ground I mentioned make an exception for a pregnancy due to rape? Certainly. They can say that persons have a right to life only if they didn't come into existence because of rape; or they can say that all persons have a right to life, but that some have less of a right to life than others, in particular, that those who came into existence because of rape have less. But these statements have a rather unpleasant sound. Surely the question of whether you have a right to life at all, or how much of it you have, shouldn't turn on the question of whether or not you are the product of a rape. And in fact the people who oppose abortion on the ground I mentioned do not make this distinction, and hence do not make an exception in case of rape.

Nor do they make an exception for a case in which the mother has to spend the nine months of her pregnancy in bed. They would agree that would be a great pity, and hard on the mother; but all the same, all persons have a right to life, the fetus is a person, and so on. I suspect, in fact, that they would not make an exception for a case in which, miraculously enough, the pregnancy went on for nine years, or even the rest of the mother's life.

Some won't even make an exception for a case in which continuation of the pregnancy is likely to shorten the mother's life; they regard abortion as impermissible even to save the mother's life. Such cases are nowadays very rare, and many opponents of abortion do not accept this extreme view. . . .

. . . Where the mother's life is not at stake, the argument I mentioned at the outset seems to have a much stronger pull. "Everyone has a right to life, so the unborn person has a right to life." And isn't the child's right to life weightier than anything other than the mother's own right to life, which she might put forward as ground for an abortion?

This argument treats the right to life as if it were unproblematic. It is not, and this seems to me to be precisely the source of the mistake.

For we should now, at long last, ask what it comes to, to have a right to life. In some views having a right to life includes having a right to be given at least the bare minimum one needs for continued life. But suppose that what in fact *is* the bare minimum a man needs for continued life is something he has no right at all to be given? If I am sick unto death, and the only thing that will save my life is the touch of Henry Fonda's cool hand on my fevered brow, then all the same, I have no right to be given the touch of Henry Fonda's cool hand on my fevered brow. It would be frightfully nice of him to fly in from the West Coast to provide it. It would be less nice, though no doubt well meant, if my friends flew out to the West Coast and carried Henry Fonda back with them. But I have no right at all against anybody that he should do this for me. Or again, to return to the story I told earlier, the fact that for continued life that violinist needs the continued use of your kidneys does not establish that he has a right to be given the continued use of your kidneys. He certainly has no right against you that *you* should give him continued use of your kidneys. For nobody has any right to use your kidneys unless you give him such a right; and nobody has the right against you that you shall give him this right—if you do allow him to go on using your kidneys, this is a kindness on your part, and not something he can

claim from you as his due. Nor has he any right against anybody else that *they* should give him continued use of your kidneys. Certainly he had no right against the Society of Music Lovers that they should plug him into you in the first place. And if you now start to unplug yourself, having learned that you will otherwise have to spend nine years in bed with him, there is nobody in the world who must try to prevent you, in order to see to it that he is given something he has a right to be given.

Some people are rather stricter about the right to life. In their view, it does not include the right to be given anything, but amounts to, and only to, the right not to be killed by anybody. But here a related difficulty arises. If everybody is to refrain from killing that violinist, then everybody must refrain from doing a great many different sorts of things. Everybody must refrain from slitting his throat, everybody must refrain from shooting him—and everybody must refrain from unplugging you from him. But does he have a right against everybody that they shall refrain from unplugging you from him? To refrain from doing this is to allow him to continue to use your kidneys. It could be argued that he has a right against us that *we* should allow him to continue to use your kidneys. That is, while he had no right against us that we should give him the use of your kidneys, it might be argued that he anyway has a right against us that we shall not now intervene and deprive him of the use of your kidneys. I shall come back to third-party interventions later. But certainly the violinist has no right against you that *you* shall allow him to continue to use your kidneys. As I said, if you do allow him to use them, it is a kindness on your part, and not something you owe him.

The difficulty I point to here is not peculiar to the right to life. It reappears in connection with all the other natural rights; and it is something which an adequate account of rights must deal with. For present purposes it is enough just to draw attention to it. But I would stress that I am not arguing that people do not have a right to life—quite to the contrary, it seems to me that the primary control we must place on the acceptability of an account of rights is that it should turn out in that account to be a truth that all persons have a right to life. I am arguing only that having a right to life does not guarantee having either a right to be given the use of or a right to be allowed continued use of another person's body—even if one needs it for life itself. So the right to life will not serve the opponents of abortion in the very simple and clear way in which they seem to have thought it would.

There is another way to bring out the difficulty. In the most ordinary sort of case, to deprive someone of what he has a right to is to treat him unjustly. Suppose a boy and his small brother are jointly given a box of chocolates for Christmas. If the older boy takes the box and refuses to give his brother any of the chocolates, he is unjust to him, for the brother has been given a right to half of them. But suppose that, having learned that otherwise it means nine years in bed with that violinist, you unplug yourself from him. You surely are not being unjust to him, for you gave him no right to use your kidneys, and no one else can have given him any such right. But we have to notice that in unplugging yourself, you are killing him; and violinists, like everybody else, have a right to life, and thus in the view we were considering just now, the right not to be killed. So here you do what he supposedly has a right you shall not do, but you do not act unjustly to him in doing it.

The emendation which may be made at this point is this: the right to life consists not in the right not to be killed, but rather in the right not to be killed unjustly. This runs a risk of circularity, but never mind: it would enable us to square the fact that the violinist has a right to life with the fact that you do not act unjustly toward him in unplugging yourself, thereby killing him. For if you do not kill him unjustly, you do not violate his right to life, and so it is no wonder you do him no injustice.

But if this emendation is accepted, the gap in the argument against abortion stares us plainly in the face: it is by no means enough to show that the fetus is a person, and to remind us that all persons have a right to life—we need to be shown also that killing the fetus violates its right to life, i.e., that abortion is unjust killing. And is it?

I suppose we may take it as a datum that in a case of pregnancy due to rape the mother has not given the unborn person a right to the use of her body for food and shelter. Indeed, in what pregnancy could it be supposed that the mother has given the unborn person such a right? It is not as if there were unborn persons drifting about the world, to whom a woman who wants a child says "I invite you in."

But it might be argued that there are other ways one can have acquired a right to the use of another person's body than by having been invited to use it by that person. Suppose a woman voluntarily indulges in intercourse, knowing of the chance it will issue in pregnancy, and then she does become pregnant; is she not in part responsible for the presence, in fact the very existence, of the unborn person inside her? No doubt she did not invite it in. But doesn't her partial responsibility for its being there itself give it a right to the use of her body? If so, then her aborting it would be more like the boy's taking away the chocolates, and less like your unplugging yourself from the violinist—doing so would be depriving it of what it does have a right to, and thus would be doing it an injustice.

And then, too, it might be asked whether or not she can kill it even to save her own life: If she voluntarily called it into existence, how can she now kill it, even in self-defense?

The first thing to be said about this is that it is something new. Opponents of abortion have been so concerned to make out the independence of the fetus, in order to establish that it has a right to life, just as its mother does, that they have tended to overlook the possible support they might gain from making out that the fetus is *dependent* on the mother, in order to establish that she has a special kind of responsibility for it, a responsibility that gives it rights against her which are not possessed by any independent person—such as an ailing violinist who is a stranger to her.

On the other hand, this argument would give the unborn person a right to its mother's body only if her pregnancy resulted from a voluntary act, undertaken in full knowledge of the chance a pregnancy might result from it. It would leave out entirely the unborn person whose existence is due to rape. Pending the availability of some further argument, then, we would be left with the conclusion that unborn persons whose existence is due to rape have no right to the use of their mothers' bodies, and thus that aborting them is not depriving them of anything they have a right to and hence is not unjust killing.

And we should also notice that it is not at all plain that this argument really does go even as far as it purports to. For there are cases and cases, and the details make a difference. If the room is stuffy, and I therefore open a window to air it, and a burglar climbs in, it would be absurd to say, "Ah, now he can stay, she's given him a right to the use of her house—for she is partially responsible for his presence there, having voluntarily done what enabled him to get in, in full knowledge that there are such things as burglars, and that burglars burgle." It would be still more absurd to say this if I had had bars installed outside my windows, precisely to prevent burglars from getting in, and a burglar got in only because of a defect in the bars. It remains equally absurd if we imagine it is not a burglar who climbs in, but an innocent person who blunders or falls in. Again, suppose it were like this: people-seeds drift about in the air like pollen, and if you open your windows, one may drift in and take root in your carpets or upholstery. You don't want children, so you fix up your windows with fine mesh screens, the very best you can buy. As can happen, however, and on very, very rare occasions does happen, one of the screens is defective; and a seed drifts in and takes root. Does the person-plant who now develops have a right to the use of your house? Surely not—despite the fact that you voluntarily opened your windows, you knowingly kept carpets and upholstered furniture, and you knew that screens were sometimes defective. Someone may argue that you are responsible for its rooting, that it does have a right to your house, because after all you *could* have lived out your life with bare floors and furniture, or with sealed windows and doors. But this won't do—for by the same token anyone can avoid a pregnancy due to rape by having a hysterectomy, or anyway by never leaving home without a (reliable!) army.

It seems to me that the argument we are looking at can establish at most that there are *some* cases in which the unborn person has a right to the use of its mother's body, and therefore *some* cases in which abortion is unjust killing. There is room for much discussion and argument as to precisely which, if any. But I think we should sidestep this issue and leave it open, for at any rate the argument certainly does not establish that all abortion is unjust killing.

There is room for yet another argument here, however. We surely must all grant that there may be cases in which it would be morally indecent to detach a person from your body at the cost of his life. Suppose you learn that what the violinist needs is not nine years of your life, but only one hour: all you need do to save his life is to spend one hour in that bed with him. Suppose also that letting him use your kidneys for that one hour would not affect your health in the slightest. Admittedly you were kidnapped. Admittedly you did not give anyone permission to plug him into you. Nevertheless it seems to me plain you *ought* to allow him to use your kidneys for that hour—it would be indecent to refuse.

Again, suppose pregnancy lasted only an hour, and constituted no threat to life or health. And suppose that a woman becomes pregnant as a result of rape. Admittedly she did not voluntarily do anything to bring about the existence of a child. Admittedly she did nothing at all which would give the unborn person a right to the use of her body. All the same it might well be said, as in the newly emended violinist story, that she *ought* to allow it to remain for that hour—that it would be indecent in her to refuse.

Now some people are inclined to use the term "right" in such a way that it follows from the fact that you ought to allow a person to use your body for the hour he needs, that he has a right to use your body for the hour he needs, even though he has not been given that right by any person or act. They may say that it follows also that if you refuse, you act unjustly toward him. This use of the term is perhaps so common that it cannot be called wrong; nevertheless it seems to me to be an unfortunate loosening of what we would do better to keep a tight rein on. Suppose that box of chocolates I mentioned earlier had not been given to both boys jointly, but was given only to the older boy. There he sits, stolidly eating his way through the box, his small brother watching enviously. Here we are likely to say "You ought not to be so mean. You ought to give your brother some of those chocolates." My own view is that it just does not follow from the truth of this that the brother has any right to any of the chocolates. If the boy refuses to give his brother any, he is greedy, stingy, callous—but not unjust. I suppose that the people I have in mind will say it does follow that the brother has a right to some of the chocolates, and thus that the boy does act unjustly if he refuses to give his brother any. But the effect of saying this is to obscure what we should keep distinct, namely the difference between the boy's refusal in this case and the boy's refusal in the earlier case, in which the box was given to both boys jointly, and in which the small brother thus had what was from any point of view clear title to half.

A further objection to so using the term "right" that from the fact that A ought to do a thing for B, it follows that B has a right against A that A do it for him, is that it is going to make the question of whether or not a man has a right to a thing turn on how easy it is to provide him with it; and this seems not merely unfortunate, but morally unacceptable. Take the case of Henry Fonda again. I said earlier that I had no right to the touch of his cool hand on my fevered brow, even though I needed it to save my life. I said it would be frightfully nice of him to fly in from the West Coast to provide me with it, but that I had no right against him that he should do so. But suppose he isn't on the West Coast. Suppose he has only to walk across the room, place a hand briefly on my brow—and lo, my life is saved. Then surely he ought to do it, it would be indecent to refuse. Is it to be said "Ah, well, it follows that in this case she has a right to the touch of his hand on her brow, and so it would be an injustice in him to refuse"? So that I have a right to it when it is easy for him to provide it, though no right when it's hard? It's rather a shocking idea that anyone's rights should fade away and disappear as it gets harder and harder to accord them to him.

So my own view is that even though you ought to let the violinist use your kidneys for the one hour he needs, we should not conclude that he has a right to do so—we should say that if you refuse, you are, like the boy who owns all the chocolates and will give none away, self-centered and callous, indecent in fact, but not unjust. And similarly, that even supposing a case in which a woman pregnant due to rape ought to allow the unborn person to use her body for the hour he needs, we should not conclude that he has a right to do so; we should conclude that she is self-centered, callous, indecent, but not unjust, if she refuses. The complaints are no less grave; they are just different. However, there is no need to insist on this point. If anyone does wish to deduce "he has a right" from "you ought," then all

the same he must surely grant that there are cases in which it is not morally required of you that you allow that violinist to use your kidneys, and in which he does not have a right to use them, and in which you do not do him an injustice if you refuse. And so also for mother and unborn child. Except in such cases as the unborn person has a right to demand it—and we were leaving open the possibility that there may be such cases—nobody is morally *required* to make large sacrifices, of health, of all other interests and concerns, of all other duties and commitments, for nine years, or even for nine months, in order to keep another person alive.

We have in fact to distinguish between two kinds of Samaritan: the Good Samaritan and what we might call the Minimally Decent Samaritan. The story of the Good Samaritan, you will remember, goes like this:

> A certain man went down from Jerusalem to Jericho, and fell among thieves, which stripped him of his raiment, and wounded him, and departed, leaving him half dead.
>
> And by chance there came down a certain priest that way; and when he saw him, he passed by on the other side.
>
> And likewise a Levite, when he was at the place, came and looked on him, and passed by on the other side.
>
> But a certain Samaritan, as he journeyed, came where he was; and when he saw him he had compassion on him.
>
> And went to him, and bound up his wounds, pouring in oil and wine, and set him on his own beast, and brought him to an inn, and took care of him.
>
> And on the morrow, when he departed, he took out two pence, and gave them to the host, and said unto him, "Take care of him; and whatsoever thou spendest more, when I come again, I will repay thee." (Luke 10:30–35)

The Good Samaritan went out of his way, at some cost to himself, to help one in need of it. We are not told what the options were, that is, whether or not the priest and the Levite could have helped by doing less than the Good Samaritan did, but assuming they could have, then the fact they did nothing at all shows they were not even Minimally Decent Samaritans, not because they were not Samaritans, but because they were not even minimally decent.

These things are a matter of degree, of course, but there is a difference, and it comes out perhaps most clearly in the story of Kitty Genovese, who, as you will remember, was murdered while thirty-eight people watched or listened, and did nothing at all to help her. A Good Samaritan would have rushed out to give direct assistance against the murderer. Or perhaps we had better allow that it would have been a Splendid Samaritan who did this, on the ground that it would have involved a risk of death for himself. But the thirty-eight not only did not do this, they did not even trouble to pick up a phone to call the police. Minimally Decent Samaritanism would call for doing at least that, and their not having done it was monstrous.

After telling the story of the Good Samaritan, Jesus said "Go, and do thou likewise." Perhaps he meant that we are morally required to act as the Good Samaritan did. Perhaps he was urging people to do more than is morally required of them. At all events it seems plain that it was not morally required of any of the thirty-eight that he rush out to give direct assistance at the risk of his own life, and that it is not morally required of anyone that he give long stretches of his life—nine years or nine months—to sustaining the life of a person who has no special right (we were leaving open the possibility of this) to demand it.

Indeed, with one rather striking class of exceptions, no one in any country in the world is *legally* required to do anywhere near as much an this for anyone else. The class of exceptions is obvious. My main concern here is not the state of the law in respect to abortion, but it is worth drawing attention to the fact that in no state in this country is any man compelled by law to be even a Minimally Decent Samaritan to any person; there is no law under which charges could be brought against the thirty-eight who stood by while Kitty Genovese died. By contrast, in most states in this country women are compelled by law to be not merely Minimally Decent Samaritans, but Good Samaritans to unborn persons inside them. This doesn't by itself settle anything one way or the other, because it may well be argued that there should be laws in this country—as there are in many European countries—compelling at least Minimally Decent Samaritanism. But it does show that there is a gross injustice in the existing state of the law. And it shows also that the groups currently working against liberalization of abortion laws, in fact working toward having it declared unconstitutional for a state to permit abortion, had better start working for the adoption of Good Samaritan laws generally, or earn the charge that they are acting in bad faith.

I should think, myself, that Minimally Decent Samaritan laws would be one thing, Good Samaritan laws quite another, and in fact highly improper. But we are not here concerned with the law. What we should ask is not whether anybody should be compelled by law to be a Good Samaritan, but whether we must accede to a situation in which somebody is being compelled—by nature, perhaps—to be a Good Samaritan. We have, in other words, to look now at third-party interventions. I have been arguing that no person is morally required to make large sacrifices to sustain the life of another who has no right to demand them, and this even where the sacrifices do not include life itself; we are not morally required to be Good Samaritans or anyway Very Good Samaritans to one another. But what if a man cannot extricate himself from such a situation? What if he appeals to us to extricate him? It seems to me plain that there are cases in which we can, cases in which a Good Samaritan would extricate him. There you are, you were kidnapped, and nine years in bed with that violinist lie ahead of you. You have your own life to lead. You are sorry, but you simply cannot see giving up so much of your life to the sustaining of his. You cannot extricate yourself, and ask us to do so. I should have thought that—in light of his having no right to the use of your body—it was obvious that we do not have to accede to your being forced to give up so much. We can do what you ask. There is no injustice to the violinist in our doing so.

Following the lead of the opponents of abortion, I have throughout been speaking of the fetus merely as a person, and what I have been asking is whether or not the argument we began with, which proceeds only from the fetus' being a person, really does establish its conclusion. I have argued that it does not.

But of course there are arguments and arguments, and it may be said that I have simply fastened on the wrong one. It may be said that what is important is not merely the fact that the fetus is a person, but that it is a person for whom the woman has a special kind of responsibility issuing from the fact that she is its mother. And it might be argued that all my analogies are therefore irrelevant—for you do not have that special kind of responsibility for that violinist, Henry Fonda does not have that special kind of responsibility for me. And our attention might be drawn to the fact that men and women both *are* compelled by law to provide support for their children.

I have in effect dealt (briefly) with this argument . . . above; but a (still briefer) recapitulation now may be in order. Surely we do not have any such "special responsibility" for a person unless we have assumed it, explicitly or implicitly. If a set of parents do not try to prevent pregnancy, do not obtain an abortion, and then at the time of birth of the child do not put it out for adoption, but rather take it home with them, then they have assumed responsibility for it, they have given it rights, and they cannot *now* withdraw support from it at the cost of its life because they now find it difficult to go on providing for it. But if they have taken all reasonable precautions against having a child, they do not simply by virtue of their biological relationship to the child who comes into existence have a special responsibility for it. They may wish to assume responsibility for it, or they may not wish to. And I am suggesting that if assuming responsibility for it would require large sacrifices, then they may refuse. A Good Samaritan would not refuse—or anyway, a Splendid Samaritan, if the sacrifices that had to be made were enormous. But then so would a Good Samaritan assume responsibility for that violinist; so would Henry Fonda, if he is a Good Samaritan, fly in from the West Coast and assume responsibility for me.

My argument will be found unsatisfactory on two counts by many of those who want to regard abortion as morally permissible. First, while I do argue that abortion is not impermissible, I do not argue that it is always permissible. There may well be cases in which carrying the child to term requires only Minimally Decent Samaritanism of the mother, and this is a standard we must not fall below. I am inclined to think it a merit of my account precisely that it does *not* give a general yes or a general no. It allows for and supports our sense that, for example, a sick and desperately frightened fourteen-year-old schoolgirl, pregnant due to rape, may *of course* choose abortion, and

that any law which rules this out is an insane law. And it also allows for and supports our sense that in other cases resort to abortion is even positively indecent. It would be indecent in the woman to request an abortion, and indecent in a doctor to perform it, if she is in her seventh month, and wants the abortion just to avoid the nuisance of postponing a trip abroad. The very fact that the arguments I have been drawing attention to treat all cases of abortion, or even all cases of abortion in which the mother's life is not at stake, as morally on a par ought to have made them suspect at the outset.

Secondly, while I am arguing for the permissibility of abortion in some cases, I am not arguing for the right to secure the death of the unborn child. It is easy to confuse these two things in that up to a certain point in the life of the fetus it is not able to survive outside the mother's body; hence removing it from her body guarantees its death. But they are importantly different. I have argued that you are not morally required to spend nine months in bed, sustaining the life of that violinist; but to say this is by no means to say that if, when you unplug yourself, there is a miracle and he survives, you then have a right to turn round and slit his throat. You may detach yourself even if this costs him his life; you have no right to be guaranteed his death, by some other means, if unplugging yourself does not kill him. There are some people who will feel dissatisfied by this feature of my argument. A woman may be utterly devastated by the thought of a child, a bit of herself, put out for adoption and never seen or heard of again. She may therefore want not merely that the child be detached from her, but more, that it die. Some opponents of abortion are inclined to regard this as beneath contempt—thereby showing insensitivity to what is surely a powerful source of despair. All the same, I agree that the desire for the child's death is not one which anybody may gratify, should it turn out to be possible to detach the child alive.

At this place, however, it should be remembered that we have only been pretending throughout that the fetus is a human being from the moment of conception. A very early abortion is surely not the killing of a person, and so is not dealt with by anything I have said here.

Study Questions on Judith Jarvis Thomson

1. Thomson's argument is essentially an argument from analogy. Just as it would be morally permissible to detach oneself from a violinist, it is also morally permissible for a pregnant woman to detach herself from the fetus, although this will cause its death (even if we concede that it is a person). How close is the analogy? List all the ways in which an unwanted pregnancy is like being kidnapped and hooked up to a violinist, and all the ways in which the two cases are different.

2. Is there a morally relevant difference between pregnancy arising from rape and pregnancy arising from voluntary intercourse? What effect does the use of contraceptives have on Thomson's argument? Do you find the "people seeds" analogy persuasive? Why or why not?

3. Thomson's argument has been criticized from the Left on the grounds that she places property rights over human lives by so strongly emphasizing the fact that the body (or womb) belongs to the woman, so that the fetus has no right to use it. Does this seem to you a fair criticism?

4. Does Thomson represent the feminine voice in moral reasoning, as described by Wolf-Devine (see next article) and the authors she cites? Why or why not?

5. Explain the limits Thomson places on legitimate abortions. (Consider, e.g., the current controversy over partial-birth abortion.)

Abortion and the "Feminine Voice"

CELIA WOLF-DEVINE

Celia Wolf-Devine describes the efforts of some feminists to articulate the feminine voice, and to articulate a distinctively feminine approach to moral reasoning, human nature, our relationship to nature, and human social life. All of these theories, she argues, imply that abortion manifests a masculine voice rather than a feminine voice approach to an unwanted pregnancy. She concludes with a critique of some attempts to defend abortion on feminine voice premises.

A GROWING NUMBER OF FEMINISTS now seek to articulate the "feminine voice," to draw attention to women's special strengths, and to correct the systematic devaluation of these by our male-dominated society. Carol Gilligan's book, *In a Different Voice*, was especially important to the emergence of this strain of feminist thought. It was her intention to help women identify more

Used by permission of the author.

positively with their own distinctive style of reasoning about ethics, instead of feeling that there
is something wrong with them because they do
not think like men (as Kohlberg's and Freud's
theories would imply). Inspired by her work,
feminists such as Nel Noddings, Annette Baier,
and the contributors to *Women and Moral
Theory,* have tried to articulate further the feminine voice in moral reasoning. Others such as
Carol McMillan, Adrienne Rich, Sara Ruddick,
and Nancy Harstock agree that women have distinct virtues, and argue that these need not be
self-victimizing. When properly transformed by a
feminist consciousness, women's different characteristics can, they suggest, be productive of new
social visions.

Similar work is also being done by feminists
who try to correct for masculine bias in other areas
such as our conception of human nature, the way
we view the relationship between people and
nature, and the kinds of paradigms we employ in
thinking about society.

Some of those engaged in this enterprise hold
that women *by nature* possess certain valuable
traits that men do not, but more frequently, they
espouse the weaker position that, on the whole,
the traits they label "feminine" are more common
among women (for reasons which are at least
partly cultural), but that they also can be found in
men, and that they should be encouraged as good
traits for a human being to have, regardless of sex.[1]

Virtually all of those feminists who are trying to
reassert the value of the feminine voice, also
express the sort of unqualified support for free
access to abortion which has come to be regarded
as a central tenet of feminist "orthodoxy." What I
wish to argue in this paper is that: (1) abortion is,
by their own accounts, clearly a masculine response
to the problems posed by an unwanted pregnancy,
and is thus highly problematic for those who seek
to articulate and defend the "feminine voice" as
the proper mode of moral response, and that
(2) on the contrary the "feminine voice" as it has
been articulated generates a strong presumption

against abortion as a way of responding to an
unwanted pregnancy.[2]

These conclusions, I believe, can be argued
without relying on a precise determination of the
moral status of the fetus. A case at least can be
made that the fetus is a person since it is biologically a member of the human species and will, in
time, develop normal human abilities. Whether
the burden of proof rests on those who defend
the personhood of the fetus, or on those who
deny it, is a matter of moral methodology, and for
that reason will depend in part on whether one
adopts a masculine or feminine approach to moral
issues.

I. *Masculine Voice/Feminine Voice*

A. MORAL REASONING

According to Gilligan, girls, being brought up by
mothers, identify with them, while males must
define themselves through separation from their
mothers. As a result, girls have "a basis for empathy built into their primary definition of self in a
way that boys do not." Thus while masculinity is
defined by separation and threatened by intimacy,
femininity is defined through attachment and
threatened by separation; girls come to understand
themselves as imbedded within a network of personal relationships.

A second difference concerns attitudes toward
general rules and principles. Boys tend to play in
larger groups than girls, and become "increasingly
fascinated with the legal elaboration of rules, and
the development of fair procedures for adjudicating conflicts." We thus find men conceiving of
morality largely in terms of adjudicating fairly
between the conflicting rights of self-assertive
individuals.

Girls play in smaller groups, and accord a
greater importance to relationships than to following rules. They are especially sensitive to the needs

[1]In this paper I shall use the terms "masculine" and "feminine" only in this weaker sense, which is agnostic about the
existence of biologically based differences.

[2]A strong presumption against abortion is not, of course, the
same thing as an absolute ban on all abortions. I do not
attempt here to resolve the really hard cases; it is not clear
that the feminine voice (at least as it has been articulated so
far) is sufficiently fine-grained to tell us exactly where to
draw the line in such cases.

of the particular other, instead of emphasizing impartiality, which is more characteristic of the masculine perspective. They think of morality more in terms of having responsibilities for taking care of others, and place a high priority upon preserving the network of relationships which makes this possible. While the masculine justice perspective requires detachment, the feminine care perspective sees detachment and separation as themselves the moral problem.

Inspired by Gilligan, many feminist philosophers have discovered a masculine bias in traditional ethical theories. Nel Noddings has written a book called *Caring: A Feminine Approach to Ethics.* Annette Baier has praised Hume for his emphasis on the role of the affections in ethics and proposed that trust be taken as the central notion for ethical theory. Christina Hoff Sommers has argued for giving a central role to special relationships in ethics. And Virginia Held has suggested that the mother-child relationship be seen as paradigmatic of human relationships, instead of the economic relationship of buyer/seller (which she sees to be the ruling paradigm now).

The feminine voice in ethics attends to the particular other, thinks in terms of responsibilities to care for others, is sensitive to our interconnectedness, and strives to preserve relationships. It contrasts with the masculine voice, which speaks in terms, of justice and rights, stresses consistency and principles, and emphasizes the autonomy of the individual and impartiality in one's dealings with others.

B. HUMAN NATURE: MIND AND BODY

Feminist writers have also discovered a masculine bias in the way we think of mind and body and the relationship between them. A large number of feminists, for example, regard radical mind/body dualism as a masculine way of understanding human nature. Alison Jaggar, for example, criticizes what she calls "normative dualism" for being "male biased," and defines "normative dualism" as "the belief that what is especially valuable about human beings is a particular 'mental' capacity, the capacity for rationality."

Another critic of dualism is Rosemary Radford Reuther, a theologian. Her book *New Woman, New Earth* is an extended attack upon what she calls transcendent hierarchical dualism, which she regards as a "male ideology." By "transcendent dualism" she means the view that consciousness is "transcendent to visible nature" and that there is a sharp split between spirit and nature. In the attempt to deny our own mortality, our essential humanity is then identified with a "transcendent divine sphere beyond the matrix of coming to be and passing away." In using the term "hierarchical," she means that the mental or spiritual component is taken to be superior to the physical. Thus "the relation of spirit and body is one of repression, subjugation and mastery." . . .

Feminists critical of traditional masculine ways of thinking about human nature also examine critically the conception of "reason" which has become engrained in our Western cultural heritage from the Greeks on. Genevieve Lloyd, for example, in *The Man of Reason: Male and Female in Western Philosophy,* suggests that the very notion of reason itself has been defined in part by the exclusion of the feminine. And if the thing which makes us distinctively human—namely our reason—is thought of as male, women and the things usually associated with them such as the body, emotion and nature, will be placed in an inferior position.

C. OUR RELATIONSHIP WITH NATURE

Many feminists hold that mind-body dualism which sees mind as transcendent to and superior to the body, leads to the devaluation of both women and nature. For the transcendent mind is conceived as masculine, and women, the body and nature assigned an inferior and subservient status. As Rosemary Radford Ruether puts it:

> The woman, the body and the world are the lower half of a dualism that must be declared posterior to, created by, subject to, and ultimately alien to the nature of (male) consciousness in whose image man made his God.

Women are to be subject to men, and nature may be used by man in any way he chooses. Thus the male ideology of transcendent dualism sanctions unlimited technological manipulation of nature; nature is an alien object to be conquered. . . .

Feminists who stress the deep affinities between feminism and the ecology movement are often called "ecofeminists." . . .

Interconnectedness, which we found to be an important theme in feminist ethics, thus reappears in the writings of the ecofeminists as one of the central aspects of the feminine attitude toward nature.

D. PARADIGMS OF SOCIAL LIFE

Feminists' descriptions of characteristically masculine and feminine paradigms of social life center around two different focusses. Those influenced by Gilligan tend to stress the contrast between individualism (which they take to be characteristic of the masculine "justice tradition") and the view of society as "a web of relationships sustained by a process of communication" (which they take to characterize the feminine "care perspective"). According to them, the masculine paradigm sees society as a collection of self-assertive individuals seeking rules which will allow them to pursue their own goals without interfering with each other. The whole contractarian tradition from Locke and Hobbes through Rawls is thus seen as a masculine paradigm of social life; we are only connected to others and responsible to them through our own choice to relinquish part of our autonomy in favor of the state. The feminine care perspective guides us to think about societal problems in a different way. We are already imbedded in a network of relationships, and must never exploit or hurt the other. We must strive to preserve those relationships as much as possible without sacrificing the integrity of the self.

The ecofeminists, pacifist feminists, and those whose starting point is a rejection of dualism, tend to focus more on the contrast between viewing social relationships in terms of hierarchy, power, and domination (the masculine paradigm) and viewing them in a more egalitarian and nonviolent manner (the feminine one). Feminists taking this position range from the moderate ones who believe that masculine social thought tends to be more hierarchical than feminine thought, to the extreme radicals who believe males are irre-

deemably aggressive and dominating, and prone to violence in order to preserve their domination.

The more moderate characterization of masculine social thought would claim that men tend to prefer a clear structure of authority; they want to know who is in control and have a clear set of procedures or rules for resolving difficult cases. The more extreme view, common among ecofeminists and a large number of radical feminists, is that males seek to establish and maintain patriarchy (systematic domination by males) and use violence to maintain their control. These feminists thus see an affinity between feminism (which combats male violence against women) and the pacifist movement (which does so on a more global scale). Mary Daly, for example, holds that "the rulers of patriarchy—males with power—wage an unceasing war against life itself. . . . [F]emale energy is essentially biophilic." Another radical feminist, Sally Miller Gearhart, says that men possess the qualities of objectification, violence, and competitiveness, while women possess empathy, nurturance, and cooperation. Thus the feminine virtues must prevail if we are to survive at all, and the entire hierarchical power structure must be replaced by "horizontal patterns of relationship."

Women are thus viewed by the pacifist feminists as attuned in some special way to the values and attitudes underlying a pacifist commitment. Sara Ruddick, for example, believes that maternal practice, because it involves "preservative love" and nurtures growth, involves the kinds of virtues which, when put to work in the public domain, lead us in the direction of pacifism.

II. Abortion

A person who had characteristically masculine traits, attitudes and values as defined above would very naturally choose abortion, and justify it ethically in the same way in which most feminists do. Conversely, a person manifesting feminine traits, attitudes and values would not make such a choice, or justify it in that way.

According to the ecofeminists, the masculine principle is insensitive to the interconnectedness of all life; it strives to discriminate, separate and control. It does not respect the natural cycles of nature, but objectifies it, and imposes its will upon it through unrestrained technological manipulation. Such a way of thinking would naturally lead to abortion. If the woman does not *want* to be pregnant, she has recourse to an operation involving highly sophisticated technology in order to defend her control of her body. This fits the characterization of the masculine principle perfectly.

Abortion is a separation—a severing of a life-preserving connection between the woman and the fetus. It thus fails to respect the interconnectedness of all life. Nor does it respect the natural cycles of nature. The mother and the developing child together form a delicately balanced ecosystem with the woman's entire hormonal system geared towards sustaining the pregnancy. The abortionist forces the cervical muscles (which have become thick and hard in order to hold in the developing fetus) open and disrupts her hormonal system by removing it.

Abortion has something further in common with the behavior ecofeminists and pacifist feminists take to be characteristically masculine; it shows a willingness to use violence in order to maintain control. The fetus is destroyed by being pulled apart by suction, cut in pieces, or poisoned. It is not merely killed inadvertently as fish might be by toxic wastes, but it is deliberately targeted for destruction. Clearly this is not the expression of a "biophilic" attitude. This point was recently brought home to me by a Quaker woman who had reached the conclusion that the abortion she had had was contrary to her pacifist principles. She said, "we must seek peaceableness both within and without."

In terms of social thought, again, it is the masculine models which are most frequently employed in thinking about abortion. If masculine thought is naturally hierarchical and oriented toward power and control, then the interests of the fetus (who has no power) would naturally be suppressed in favor of the interests of the mother. But to the extent that feminist social thought is egalitarian, the question must be raised of why the mother's interests should prevail over the child's.

Feminist thought about abortion has, in addition, been deeply pervaded by the individualism which they so ardently criticize. The woman is supposed to have the sole authority to decide the outcome of the pregnancy. But what of her interconnectedness with the child and with others? Both she and the unborn child already exist within a network of relationships ranging from the closest ones—the father, grandparents, siblings, uncles and aunts, and so on—to ones with the broader society—including the mother's friends, employer, employees, potential adoptive parents, taxpayers who may be asked to fund the abortion or subsidize the child, and all the numerous other people affected by her choice. To dismiss this already existing network of relationships as irrelevant to the mother's decision is to manifest the sort of social atomism which feminist thinkers condemn as characteristically masculine.

Those feminists who are seeking to articulate the feminine voice in ethics also face a *prima facie* inconsistency between an ethics of care and abortion. Quite simply, abortion is a failure to care for one living being who exists in a particularly intimate relationship to oneself. If empathy, nurturance, and taking responsibility for caring for others are characteristic of the feminine voice, then abortion does not appear to be a feminine response to an unwanted pregnancy. If, as Gilligan says, "an ethic of care rests on the premise of non-violence—that no one should be hurt," then surely the feminine response to an unwanted pregnancy would be to try to find a solution which does not involve injury to anyone, including the unborn.

"Rights" have been invoked in the abortion controversy in a bewildering variety of ways, ranging from the "right to life" to the "right to control one's body." But clearly those who defend unrestricted access to abortion in terms of such things as the woman's right to privacy or her right to control her body are speaking the language of an ethics of justice rather than an ethics of care. For example, Judith Jarvis Thompson's widely read article "A Defense of Abortion" treats the moral issue involved in abortion as a conflict between the rights of the fetus and the mother's rights over her own body. Mary Anne Warren also sees the issue in terms of a conflict of rights, but since the fetus does not meet her criteria for being a person, she weighs the woman's rights to "freedom, happiness and self-determination" against the rights of other people in the society who would like to see the fetus preserved for whatever reason. And, insofar as she appeals to consciousness, reasoning, self-motivated activity, the capacity to communicate, and the presence of self-concepts and self-awareness as criteria of personhood, she relies on the kind of opposition between mind and nature criticized by many feminists as masculine. In particular, she is committed to what Jaggar calls "normative dualism"—the view that what is especially valuable about humans is their mental capacity for rational thought.

It is rather striking that feminists defending abortion lapse so quickly into speaking in the masculine voice. Is it because they feel they must do so in order to be heard in our male dominated society, or is it because no persuasive defense of abortion can be constructed from within the ethics of care tradition? We now consider several possible "feminine voice" defenses of abortion.

III. Possible Responses and Replies

Among the feminists seeking to articulate and defend the value of the feminine voice, very few have made any serious attempt to grapple with abortion. The writings of the ecofeminists and the pacifist feminists abound with impassioned defenses of such values as non-violence, a democratic attitude towards the needs of all living things, letting others be and nurturing them, and so on, existing side by side with impassioned defenses of "reproductive rights." They see denying women access to abortion as just another aspect of male domination and violence against women.

. . . [But] it is not true that males are the chief opponents of abortion. Many women are strongly opposed to it. The pro-life movement at every level is largely composed of women. For example, as of May 1988, 38 of the state delegates to the National Right to Life Board of Directors were women, and only 13 were men. Indeed as Jean Bethke Elshtain has observed, the pro-life movement has mobilized into political action an enormous number of women who were never politically active before. And a Gallup poll in 1981 found that 51% of women surveyed believed a person is present at conception, compared with only 33% of the men. The pro-life movement, thus, cannot be dismissed as representing male concerns and desires only. Granted, a pro-choice feminist could argue that women involved in the pro-life

movement suffer from "colonized minds," but this sort of argument clearly can be made to cut both directions. After all, many of the strongest supporters of "reproductive rights" have been men—ranging from the Supreme Court in *Roe v. Wade* to the Playboy Philosopher. . . .

Secondly, terms like violence and domination are used far too loosely by those who condemn anti-abortion laws. If there are laws against wife abuse, does this mean that abusive husbands are being subjected to domination and violence? One does not exercise violence against someone merely by crossing his or her will, or even by crossing his or her will and backing this up by threats of legal retribution.

Finally, those who see violence and domination in laws against abortion, but not in abortion itself, generally fail to look at the nature of the act itself, and thus fail to judge that act in light of their professed values and principles. This is not surprising; abortion is a bloody and distressing thing to contemplate. But one cannot talk about it intelligently without being willing to look concretely at the act itself.

One line of thought is suggested by Gilligan, who holds that at the highest level of moral development, we must balance our responsibility to care for others against our need to care for ourselves. Perhaps we could, then, see the woman who has an abortion as still being caring and nurturing in that she is acting out of a legitimate care for herself. This is an implausible view of the actual feelings of women who undergo abortions. They may believe they are "doing something for themselves" in the sense of doing what they must do to safeguard their legitimate interests. But the operation is more naturally regarded as a violation of oneself than as a nurturing of oneself. This has been noted, even by feminists who support permissive abortion laws. For example, Carolyn Whitbeck speaks of "the unappealing prospect of having someone scraping away at one's core," and Adrienne Rich says that "Abortion is violence: a deep, desperate violence inflicted by a woman upon, first of all, herself."

We here come up against the problem that a directive to care, to nurture, to take responsibility for others, and so on, provides a moral orientation, but leaves unanswered many important questions and hence provides little guidance in problem situations. What do we do when caring for one person involves being uncaring toward another? How widely we must extend our circle of care? Are some kinds of not caring worse than others? Is it caring to give someone what they want even though it may be bad for them?

Thinking in terms of preserving relationships suggests another possible "feminine" defense of abortion—namely that the woman is striving to preserve her interconnectedness with her family, husband, or boyfriend. Or perhaps she is concerned to strengthen her relationship with her other children by having enough time and resources to devote to their care. To simply tell a woman to preserve *all* her existing relationships is not the answer. Besides the fact that it may not be possible (women *do* sometimes have to sever relationships), it is not clear that it would be desirable even if it were possible. Attempting to preserve our existing relationships has conservative tendencies in several unfortunate ways. It fails to invite us to reflect critically on whether those relationships are good, healthy or worthy of preservation. It also puts the unborn at a particular disadvantage, since the mother's relationship with him or her is just beginning, while her relationships with others have had time to develop. And not only the unborn, but any needy stranger who shows up at our door can be excluded on the grounds that caring for them would disrupt our existing pattern of relationships. Thus the care perspective could degenerate into a rationalization for a purely tribal morality; I take care of myself and my friends.

But how are decisions about severing relationships to be made? One possibility is suggested by Gilligan in a recent article. She looks at the network of connections within which the woman who is considering abortion finds herself entangled, and says "to ask what actions constitute care or are more caring directs attention to the parameters of connection and the *costs of detachment* . . . (emphasis added)" Thus, the woman considering abortion should reflect upon the comparative costs of severing various relationships. This method of decision, however, makes her vulnerable to emotional and psychological pressure from others, by encouraging her to sever whichever connection is easiest to break (the squeaky wheel principle).

But perhaps we can lay out some guidelines (or, at least, rules of thumb) for making these difficult decisions. One way we might reason, from the point of view of the feminine voice, is that since preserving interconnectedness is good, we should prefer a short term estrangement to an irremediable severing of relationship. And we should choose an action which *may* cause an irremediable break in relationship over one which is certain to cause such a break. By either of these criteria, abortion is clearly to be avoided.

Another consideration suggested by Gilligan's work is that since avoiding hurt to others (or nonviolence) is integral to an ethics of care, severing a relationship where the other person will be only slightly hurt would be preferable to severing one where deep or lasting injury will be inflicted by our action. But on this criterion, again, it would seem she should avoid abortion, since loss of life is clearly a graver harm than emotional distress.

Two other possible criteria which would also tell against abortion are: (1) that it is permissible to cut ties with someone who behaves unjustly and oppressively toward one, but not with someone who is innocent of any wrong against one, or (2) we have special obligations to our own offspring, and thus should not sever relationship with them.

Criteria can, perhaps, be found which would dictate severing relationship with the fetus rather than others, but it is hard to specify one which clearly reflects the feminine voice. Certainly the right to control one's body will not do. The claim that the unborn is not a person and therefore does not deserve moral consideration can be faulted on several grounds. First, if the feminine voice is one which accepts the interconnectedness of all life and strives to avoid harm to nature and to other species, then the non-personhood of the fetus (supposing it could be proved) would not imply that its needs can be discounted. And secondly, the entire debate over personhood has standardly been carried on very much in the masculine voice. One feminist, Janice Raymond, has suggested that the question of when life begins is a masculine one, and if this is a masculine question, it would seem that personhood, with its juridical connotations, would be also. It is not clear that the care perspective has the resources to resolve this issue. If it cannot, then, one cannot rely on the non-personhood of the fetus in constructing a "feminine voice" defense of abortion. A care prespective would at least seem to place the burden of proof on those who would restrict the scope of care, in this case to those that have been born.

It seems that the only way open to the person who seeks to defend abortion from the point of view of the feminine voice is to deny that a relationship (or at least any morally significant relationship) exists between the embryo/fetus and the mother. The question of how to tell when a relationship (or a morally significant relationship) exists is a deep and important one, which has, as yet, received insufficient attention from those who are trying to articulate the feminine voice in moral reasoning. The whole ecofeminist position relies on the assumption that our relationship with nature and with other species is a real and morally significant one. They, thus, have no basis at all for excluding the unborn from moral consideration.

There are those, however, who wish to define morally significant relationships more narrowly—thus effectively limiting our obligation to extend care. While many philosophers within the "justice tradition" (for example, Kant) have seen moral significance only where there is some impact upon rational beings, Nel Noddings, coming from the "care perspective" tries to limit our obligation to extend care in terms of the possibility of "completion" or "reciprocity" in a caring relationship. Since she takes the mother-child relationship to be paradigmatic of caring, it comes as something of a surprise that she regards abortion as a permissible response to an unwanted pregnancy.

There are, on Noddings's view, two different ways in which we may be bound, as caring persons, to extend our care to one for whom we do not already have the sort of feelings of love and affection which would lead us to do the caring action naturally. One is by virtue of being connected with our "inner circle" of caring (which is formed by natural relations of love and friendship) through "chains" of "personal or formal relations." As an example of a person appropriately linked to the inner circle, she cites her daughter's fiancé. It would certainly *seem* that the embryo in one's womb would belong to one's "inner circle" (via natural caring), or at least be connected to it by a "formal relation" (that is, that of parenthood). But Noddings does not concede this. Who is part of my inner circle, and who is connected to it in such a way that I am obligated to extend care to him or her seems to be, for Noddings, largely a matter of my feelings toward the person and/or my choice

to include him or her. Thus the mother *may* "confer sacredness" upon the "information speck" in her womb, but need not if, for example, her relationship with the father is not a stable and loving one. During pregnancy "many women recognize the relation as established when the fetus begins to move about. It is not a question of when life begins, but of when relation begins."

But making the existence of a relation between the unborn and the mother a matter of her choice or feelings, seems to run contrary to one of the most central insights of the feminine perspective in moral reasoning—namely that we already *are* interconnected with others, and thus have responsibilities to them. The view that we are connected with others only when we choose to be or when we *feel* we are, presupposes the kind of individualism and social atomism which Noddings and other feminists criticize as masculine.

Noddings also claims that we sometimes are obligated to care for "the proximate stranger." She says:

> We cannot refuse obligation in human affairs by merely refusing to enter relation; we are, by virtue of our mutual humanity, already and perpetually in potential relation.

Why, then, are we not obligated to extend care to the unborn? She gives two criteria for when we have an obligation to extend care: there must be "the existence of or potential for present relation" and the "dynamic potential for growth in relation, including the potential for increased reciprocity. . . ." Animals are, she believes, excluded by this second criterion since their response is nearly static (unlike a human infant).

She regards the embryo/fetus as not having the potential for present relationships of caring and reciprocity, and thus as having no claim upon our care. As the fetus matures, he or she develops increasing potential for caring relationships, and thus our obligation increases also. There are problems with her position, however.

First of all, the only relationships which can be relevant to *my* obligation to extend care, for Noddings, must be relationships with *me*. Whatever the criteria for having a relationship are, it must be that at a given time, an entity either has a relationship with me or it does not. If it does not, it may either have no potential for a morally significant relationship with me (for example, my word processor), or it may have such potential in several ways: (1) The relationship may become actual at the will of one or both parties (for example, the stranger sitting next to me on the bus). (2) The relationship may become actual only after a change in relative spatial locations which will take time, and thus can occur only in the future (for example, walking several blocks to meet a new neighbor, or traveling to Tibet to meet a specific Tibetan). Or (3) The relationship may become actual only after some internal change occurs within the other (for example, by waiting for a sleeping drug to wear off, for a deep but reversible coma to pass, or for the embryo to mature more fully) and thus can also happen only in the future.

In all three of these cases there is present now in the other the potential for relations of a caring and reciprocal sort. In cases (1) and (2) this is uncontroversial, but (3) requires some defense in the case of the unborn. The human embryo differs now from a rabbit embryo in that it possesses potential for these kinds of relationships although neither of them is presently able to enter into relationships of any sort. That potential becomes actualized only over time, but it can become actualized only because it is there to be actualized (as it is not in the rabbit embryo). Noddings fails to give any reason why the necessity for some internal change to occur in the other before relation can become actual has such moral importance that we are entitled to kill the other in case (3), but not in the others, especially since my refraining from killing it is a sufficient condition for the actualization of the embryo's potential for caring relationships. Her criterion as it stands would also seem to imply that we may kill persons in deep but predictably reversible comas.

Whichever strand of Noddings thought we choose, then, it is hard to see how the unborn can be excluded from being ones for whom we ought to care. If we focus on the narrow, tribal morality of "inner circles" and "chains," then an objective connection exists tying the unborn to the mother and other relatives. If we are to be open to the needy stranger because of the real potential for relationship and reciprocity, then we should be open to the unborn because he or she also has the real and present potential for a relationship of reciprocity and mutuality which comes with species membership.

Many feminists will object to my argument so far on the grounds that they do not, after all, consider abortion to be a *good* thing. They aren't pro-abortion in the sense that they encourage women to have abortions. They merely regard it as something which must be available as a kind of "grim option"—something a woman would choose only when the other alternatives are all immeasurably worse.

First of all, the grim options view sounds very much like the "masculine voice"—we must grit our teeth, and do the distasteful but necessary deed (the more so where the deed involves killing).[3] Furthermore, it is in danger of collapsing into total subjectivism unless one is willing to specify some criteria for when an option is a genuinely grim one, beyond the agent's feeling that it is. What if she chooses to abort in order not to have to postpone her trip to Europe, or because she prefers sons to daughters? Surely these are not grim options no matter what she may say. Granted, the complicated circumstances surrounding her decision are best known to the woman herself. But this does not imply that no one is *ever* in a position to make judgments about whether her option is sufficiently grim to justify abortion. We do not generally concede that only the agent is in a position to judge the morality of his or her action.

---

[3]Granted, this sort of judgment is, at least in part, an impressionistic one. It is supported, however, by Gilligan's findings about the difference between boys and girls in their response to the "Heinz dilemma" (where the man is faced with a choice between allowing his wife to die or stealing an expensive drug from the druggist to save her). Although the females she studies do not all respond to the dilemma in the same way (e.g., Betty at first sounds more like Hobbes than like what has been characterized as the feminine voice—pp. 75–76), some recurring patterns which she singles out as representative of the feminine voice are: resisting being forced to accept either horn of the dilemma, seeing all those involved as in relationship with each other, viewing the dilemma in terms of conflicting responsibilities rather than rights, and seeking to avoid or minimize harm to anyone (see, e.g., Sarah p. 95). Since the abortion decision involves killing and not merely letting die, it would seem that the impetus to find a way through the horns of the dilemma would be, if anything, greater than in the Heinz dilemma.

Feminists standardly hold that absolutely no restrictions may be placed on a woman's right to choose abortion.[4] This position cannot be supported by the grim options argument. One who believes something is a grim option will be inclined to try to avoid or prevent it, and thus be willing, at least in principle, to place some restrictions on what counts as a grim option. Granted, practical problems exist about how such decisions are to be made and by whom. But someone who refuses in principle to allow any restrictions on women's right to abort, cannot in good faith claim that they regard abortion only as a grim option.

Some feminists will say: yes, feminine virtues are a good thing for any person to have, and yes, abortion is a characteristically masculine way of dealing with an unwanted pregnancy, but in the current state of things we live in a male dominated society, and we must be willing to use now weapons which, ideally, in a good, matriarchal society, we would not use. But there are no indications that an ideal utopian society is just around the corner; thus we are condemned to a constant violation of our own deepest commitments. If the traits, values and attitudes characteristic of the "feminine voice" are asserted to be good ones, we ought to act according to them. And such values and attitudes simply do not lend support to either the choice of abortion as a way of dealing with an unwanted pregnancy in individual cases, or to the political demand for unrestricted[5] access to abortion which has become so entrenched in the feminist movement. Quite the contrary.

[4] For example, one feminist, Roberta Steinbach, argues that we must not restrict a woman's right to abort for reasons of sex selection *against females* because it might endanger our hard won "reproductive rights"! (See "Sex Selection: From Here to Fraternity" in Carol Gould (ed.), *Beyond Domination* (Totowa, NJ: Rowman & Allanheld, 1984), p. 280.)

[5] Restrictions can take many forms, including laws against abortion, mandatory counselling which includes information about the facts of fetal development and encourages the woman to choose other options, obligatory waiting periods, legal requirements to notify (and/or obtain the consent of) the father, or in the case of a minor the girl's parents, etc. To defend the appropriateness of any particular sort of restric-

Study Questions on Celia Wolf-Devine

1. Do you think that anyone—male or female—reasons exclusively in masculine voice terms or exclusively in feminine voice terms about moral issues? Should anyone attempt to do so?
2. Can you think of a way to defend abortion in feminine voice terms? Or a way of opposing abortion in masculine voice terms?
3. What would a feminine voice approach be to the issue of contraception? To the issue of reproductive technologies?
4. Can the feminine voice approach to moral issues be rendered fine-grained enough to resolve hard cases about abortion, given that it tends to shy away from hierarchical thinking and strict principles? What are we to do when women's moral intuitions clash?

Birth Control and the Ideals of Marital Sexuality

ROSEMARY RADFORD RUETHER

Written shortly before the promulgation of the papal enclyclical *Humanae Vitae* (1968), which reaffirmed traditional Catholic teachings about artificial contraception, this selection by Rosemary Radford Ruether attempts to defend "artificial" birth control in terms of Catholic ideals of marital sexuality. She argues from the fact that, in actual life, the achievement of the ideal nature of the sexual act is not always possible, to the conclusion that contraceptive sex may be a second best expression of the ideal in our present situation.

THE PRESENT CONTROVERSY in the Catholic Church over the licitness or illicitness of various methods of birth control is so heated and fraught with polemic that it seems increasingly difficult to think through the whole issue in a simple and sane fashion, and yet such simple and sane thinking is desperately needed on this issue, now more than ever. The Church can scarcely afford to perpetuate the present muddle much longer without the gravest danger to the consciences of thousands of sincere persons within the Church as well as the general disrespect and contempt which the situation is engendering among non-Catholics both Christian and non-Christian.

Much of the difficulty which impedes clear thinking on this issue is a frightful semantic muddle. Words used by one person to mean one thing are used by another school of thought to mean another. Thus the present author wrote in the *Saturday Evening Post* (April 10, 1964) that the Church should clearly recognize that the relational aspect of the marital act is a genuine value and purpose in itself, and cannot just be subsumed as a means to the end of procreation. The critics immediately replied that this meant promiscuity and extra-marital intercourse, since, for some strange reason, procreation in their minds necessarily implied marriage whereas the relational aspect of the marital act did not seem to imply any permanent bond between two human beings. Now obviously one can have babies outside of marriage just as well as one can have sexual relationships outside of marriage. If we are to have any intelligent discussion of this problem at all, we must be convinced that we are talking about *marriage* and not promiscuity. Within this context we must then make clear that the procreational and the relational aspects of the sexual act are two semi-independent and interrelated purposes which both are brought together in their meaning and value within the total marriage project, although it is not only unnecessary but even biologically impossible that both purposes be present in every act.

Another semantic muddle exists in regard to the term "procreation" or, more specifically "procreativeness." The present proponents of the rhythm method have redefined procreativeness until it simply means a kind of formal structure of the sexual act, irrespective of whether that act can procreate or not. Thus, since rhythm doesn't interfere with this formal procreative structure, it is licit, while mechanical contraceptives, which supposedly interfere with this procreative structure, are illicit. Now it is very strange that procreativeness should be defined only in terms of the operation of the sperm as it travels into the uterus, but the presence or absence of the ovum is deemed irrelevant to the definition of procreativeness. One almost suspects some hangover of the medieval notion that the sperm alone was the generative agent, the existence of the ovum being then unknown. In any case it is obvious that procreative means nothing less than the actual possibility of the act procreating, although this may not always occur, and this capacity to procreate entails the presence of ovum just as much as the viability of the sperm. Hence, sexual acts which are calculated to function only during times of sterility are sterilizing the act just as much as any other means of rendering the act infertile. It is difficult to see why there should be such an absolute moral difference between creating a spatial barrier to procreation and creating a temporal barrier to procreation.

First, let us think about marital morality in terms of the full expression of its ideal nature. The sexual act exists on several levels of meaning and purpose. First of all, it is a biological act whose purposive goal is the generation of a new human being. Secondly, it is an act of love in which the married couple express their union with each other. In this union they both express their union and make this union; that is, the sexual act does not merely express the union of their persons, but in this expression it also makes this union, and so it is the cement that holds together the relationship, and not only of the couple to each other, but also as the parents of their children. This union does not just exist on a physiological level, but it expresses the mutuality of their union on all levels of their being, their total I and Thou with each other.

The sexual act would be expressed ideally when all these purposes and meanings could be present in a total and harmonious whole. This would mean that the couple truly give themselves to each other in deep devotion and love; that from this act of love a child should actually spring, as its natural fruition, and that the act of love and the biological cause and effect that produce the child be no mere chance coincidence, but, in loving each other, the couple should also choose to create a child as an authentic act of will. For man is not just an animal, and should not just procreate as an animal does as the servant of biological chance, but he should choose his own existence, and the effects of his own acts in an authentically human way.

This, then, would be the nature of the sexual act under ideal circumstances. This is, perhaps, the way it might have been before the fall of Adam, when nature was as God intended it to be before it became disordered and its existence as a created image of God was blurred. However, in actual reality, under our present situation, this complete unification of all the goals of marriage in a single and harmonious act can only occasionally occur at best.

First of all, man never knows when his sexual acts will actually procreate, so that he cannot will a sexual act to be an act of procreation and know that he has actually effected this end. In the order of fallen nature, the sexual act is used many hundreds of times and only procreative occasionally. Secondly, the limitations of man's social life, particularly in the modern world, are such that man feels less and less free to procreate. The psychological demands of living within a sexual union impel a relatively frequent use of the sexual act, and yet man, particularly in our urban society, only feels really free to allow himself, perhaps, between two and five children. Many couples may have more than that, and society today will make these couples feel (and with some reason since we cannot ignore the realities of economic and social life) that they have produced more children than is in the common good. Thus we see that the actual use of the sexual act and the number of children that can be positively desired are radically out of tune with each other.

We have discussed the sexual act from the point of view of its ideal completion in procreation and shown how the limitations imposed upon man, both from biological nature and the social structure, create a radical and inevitable falling away from the ideal in practice. Let us now consider the marital act from the point of view of its expression of the person to person relationship of the couple. This purpose of the sexual act also has its inner laws of perfection. Above all an authentic act of love should be given freely, without external force. The couple should not feel forced to love when they are not genuinely drawn together, or forced not to love for reasons external to their personal well being. Above all it should be an act arising from the total communion of the couple, without calculation, so that, for example, a conversation in the evening which brings with it a deepened sense of person to person understanding might lead on into the expression of their relationship in physical union. All traces of lust should be expelled, so that one partner never approaches the other as a mere thing to be used for his own gratification, but the pleasure of the sexual act should arise as a by-product of their mutual self-giving to each other.

However, in actual practice, the limitations of a man's lack of charity, preoccupation with selfish concerns or mere day to day business create a falling away from this ideal. Most couples do not express the full mutuality of their persons in the sexual act for the simple reason that they have not achieved such mutuality, because their understanding of each other is distorted and fraught with petty tensions and dislikes. A thousand concerns press upon them and fragment the wholeness of their persons and thus impede their communion. The sexual act, in practice, may seldom be an expression of deeper commingling, but may be a casual thing, or even forced upon the one partner by the desires of the other. Seldom are the moments when the two turn equally to each other in full openness to the spirit of each other. The sexual natures themselves of man and woman make union difficult, for the two are not temperamentally compatible, but the man's sexual desires are more constant, while the woman's are more variable, and the two have different cycles of crescendo in the act itself. Thus many factors, both in the biological nature and in the social nature of the relationship, tend toward a falling away from the ideal of full mutuality.

Having accepted the fact that, in actual life, the achievement of the ideal nature of the sexual act at all times is impossible, because man can neither desire nor have a child with each sexual act, nor can he give himself to his partner as lovingly as he ought, what should be our guidelines in coming as close as possible to the various ideals and purposes of marital sexuality? When we spoke of the perfection of the procreative nature of the sexual act, it was clear that this purpose of the act is best expressed when man does choose to procreate as an authentic act of desire. But man, as we have seen, can only desire perhaps three, four or five children (and there is no point telling people they ought to have more children when the circumstances of their life mitigate against it). The second best expression of the ideal would then be that those children which are born are genuinely desired and authentically chosen; that is, at the time they are begotten, the couple is actually making use of the sexual act with a desire to procreate. Now we come to the ironic fact that in our present situation man is only able fully to say "yes" to procreation if he is also able to say "no." If, on the other hand, he has at his disposal only an ineffective method of birth control which does not give him the freedom to say "no," then he will not

really have the freedom to say "yes" either, because his efforts will be expended on trying to prevent the birth of more children than he feels he can provide for, and to space those children with an insecure method; and so the children. that he does have tend to be "accidents" rather than products of authentic human will. Only when he can be confident that the "accident" will not occur is he then able to feel free to stop holding his procreative powers in abeyance at appropriate intervals and to make love with the full intention of creating a child, although, of course, he can never be absolutely sure when or if a child will be conceived. Therefore, we arrive at the paradox that, in man's present situation, his ability to approach the ideal of marital sexuality, where all the purposes of the sexual act can be present harmoniously, is dependent on his ability to hold his procreative powers in abeyance at other times.

Having shown that man's ability to choose procreation authentically is dependent on his ability not to choose it at other times, let us look at the various methods for holding the procreative powers in abeyance, to see which are suited to the best ordering of the primary and auxiliary purposes of the marital act. Looking at the question from one point of view we might be inclined to feel that man should only make love when he can really desire a child, and when he does not so desire, he should dispense with the sexual act altogether. This might be the ideal situation from the standpoint of radical morality, but in actual practice it is both impossible and inadvisable for most couples. As we have seen, man's sexual desires and his desire for procreation are not actually in tune, and this is a fact of his nature which he cannot well overcome. The demands of living in the sexual union are real and meaningful demands which impose a far more frequent use of the sexual act for its relational function than could ever be brought into harmony with procreation itself. Man needs to express his mutuality with his partner, and in the sexual act this mutuality is both expressed and recreated; and in this sense the sexual act as a relational act is a genuinely purposeful act, and not mere play or unleashing of passion. Since this is the case, the couple cannot well dispense with the act and yet continue to live in a sexual relationship without doing extensive emotional damage to the basic stability of their marriage. Since the firmness of their relational cohesion with each other is the cement that holds the marriage together, and this, in turn, is the milieu in which the children which have been born are nurtured, the first ideal of marriage, the ideal of procreation itself mitigates against the use of a method of birth control which would undermine the stability of the sexual union of the couple. Thus the continued use of the sexual act for its relational purpose, even when its procreational purpose is impeded, may be said to be required by the procreational purpose itself, because the procreational purpose extends to the nurture of the child; and if the continued use of the sexual act is necessary in order to maintain the union of the couple and their ability to carry out their continued responsibility to the child, then the primary purpose of marriage itself points to the use of the sexual act for its purely relational function.

Thus in actual practice man has no real choice (except perhaps in the case of a couple both called to a life of virginity), but to find some method of birth control which allows him to continue to use the sexual act for its relational purpose and to do this under as ideal emotional circumstances as possible. Among these methods there are four main types: permanent sterilization, periodic continence, the mechanical or chemical contraceptive and the oral-steroid pill.

Permanent sterilization is undesirable chiefly because of its finality. It takes from man his ability to choose in favor of procreation and leaves him only with his previous choice against it. It thus dehumanizes him by depriving him of his freedom to make authentically human choices.

The rhythm method has several defects which cause a falling away from the ideals we have outlined. First, the method forces a mechanization of the affections of the couple who must artificially "schedule" their mutual affection at the time of the infertile period, and this takes from the couple their freedom to choose to love as an expression of true mutuality, and makes them subservient to an impersonal biological cycle which has no genuine relationship to their human expression of mutual love. Secondly, this method is very insecure and so forces a constant calculation and worry which is psychologically debilitating and tends to undermine the couple's stability and introduces fear and conflict into their relationship.

Thus the rhythm method is undesirable for the same reasons as total abstinence, that its demands upon the psychological cohesion of the couple often exceed what can be reconciled with the stability of their relationship, and thus not in the best interests of the family as a whole. Thirdly, this method does not give fully effective control over procreation, but the natural fluctuations of sterility are such that the most careful use of the method (and we must remember that the method is being practiced by human beings, and not laboratory rats, and that the psychological tensions created by the method also are a permanent contributing factor to its ineffectiveness) will produce many accidental babies, often exceeding the total number of children the couple feels they can accept, and so it does not give the couple the freedom to fully affirm their desire for children—rather, in practice, the couple has to spend so much energy in trying to make the method work, i.e. to get it to effectively impede procreation, that the freedom authentically to desire a child and plan for his conception is lost.

The third method is that of the traditional contraceptive: condom, diaphragm, spermicidal jelly and the like. All have the undesirable quality that they tend to intrude themselves into the psychological dynamics of the sexual act itself, because the couple must calculate the time of the sexual act in order to be armed in advance, and they are made psychologically aware of the means being used to impede procreation in a way esthetically distasteful to many people. However, one must make distinctions within this general group of mechanical and chemical means. Certain means, such as condom and *coitus interruptus,* definitely do not allow for the full completion of the sexual act as a relational act, and so they may be said to devalue the relational aspect of the act in a way which is morally intolerable. Other methods, such as the diaphragm, operate at the base of the cervix, or even within the womb. They do not prevent the full and natural sexual play between the couple and the depositing of the seed in the vagina. Thus they can be condemned only if one condemns any method which prevents the procreative fulfillment of the act, and this, as we have said, is equally true of all methods of birth control, including the rhythm method. Some of these mechanical means are still inesthetic, and this may cause some falling away from the ideal of marital mutuality, but it is questionable whether esthetic criteria alone can brand these methods as absolutely immoral. The esthetic criterion is a highly subjective one, and many persons do not feel such methods are inesthetic or that they prevent the full expression of mutual self-giving (in the relational rather than the procreational sense of the word). These people simply accept such means in the same way that one accepts a pair of reading spectacles, as an aid to nature which one uses but psychologically ignores.

Finally, there are the new oral-steroid pills, which, assuming that they are medically safe, would seem to hold the best possibility for a reasonable balance of goals and ideals in marriage. First, this method is fully effective, and gives to the couple the power to hold their procreative powers in abeyance when this is necessary, and, in turn, to release these powers to create a child, when they can and do desire to so choose (—and this choice may often require a great sacrificial effort. We do not intend to suggest that this voluntary choice of procreation by which man dares to live up to the highest ideal of the sexual act will existenially be an easy one to make). Furthermore, when the woman discontinues the use of the pills, she has a jump-back of heightened fertility and so receives a "bonus" of added assurance that the desire for a child may actually he brought to fruition. Thirdly, the method is totally divorced from the physical and psychological setting of the sexual act, and as such it is preferable from the esthetic point of view. Finally, it allows the couple full freedom to use or control the sexual act according to the true laws of their love and respect for each other, without being forced into subservience to its external considerations, such as the "safe period," or the need to calculate the relationship in order to have the contraceptive in place.

Study Questions on Rosemary Radford Ruether

1. What is Ruether's characterization of the ideal sexual act? She is working within the Catholic tradition, but some non-Christian religions agree with her characterization of the ideal sexual act. Does the belief that this is the ideal depend necessarily on some religious framework, or are there nonreligious reasons for taking it to be the ideal?

2. Why does she think this is not fully attainable "in actual reality, under our present situation"? When, if ever, *was* it attainable?

3 What are Ruether's objections to the rhythm method? To what extent do they rest on the unreliability of the method and to what extent do they rest on other considerations? Many proponents of natural family planning (a more sophisticated form of periodic abstinence as a way of spacing births) argue that using this method helps couples become attuned to their natural bodily rhythms, to respect each other, to develop self-discipline, and to find alternative ways of expressing love besides sex. How would Ruether respond to these arguments? What do you think?

4. Ruether limits herself to consideration of the use of contraceptives in marriage. What do you think she would say about the use of contraceptives outside of marriage?

5 Write an essay explaining how you think Ruether would respond to the arguments given by Cormac Burke (see next article) and how Burke would respond to Ruether's arguments (being sure to clearly state the arguments on both sides). Which do you find more persuasive?

Marriage and Contraception

CORMAC BURKE

Cormac Burke asks two questions: why must marital sex be open to procreation, and why must procreation be the consequence of marital sex (rather than of various forms of artificial reproduction)? He denies that the procreative and unitive aspects of marital sex are separable: If we deliberately destroy the power of the conjugal act to give life, we also necessarily destroy its power to signify the love and union proper to marriage. Contraceptive sex is disfigured body language; it expresses a rejection of the other. Artificial fertilization ignores the fact that the child is meant to be, not just the fruit of the union, however brought about, of two cells, but of the loving union of two persons (which means the union of two souls and two bodies).

THERE ARE TWO RELATED, QUestions before us asking for clear and, if possible, simple answers: why must the conjugal act be open to procreativity and why must procreation be the consequence of a true conjugal act?

Of these two questions, the first is bigger; it is of importance everywhere round the world and of moral significance to practically all married couples. It has been the subject of intense debate for some twenty-five years, and at this stage, I feel that well-matured answers are available.

The second question is of much more recent appearance. It also is intensely debated, although primarily in academic circles with echoes in the press. It is of practical interest to relatively few couples. Probably it will take some years before its finer points (as in certain forms of homologous artificial fertilization) can be fully seen in satisfactory light. I feel that a clear answer to this second question will largely come in consequence of having dearly answered the first, to which most of my remarks will be addressed. My main endeavor, therefore, will be to show why one cannot annul the procreative aspect or the procreative reference of the marital act without necessarily destroying its unitive function and significance.

There is a modern argument for contraception that claims to speak in personalist terms and that could be summarized as follows. The marital act expresses love; it unites. It has, indeed, a possible procreative side effect, which can result in children. But since this side effect depends on biological factors, which science today permits us to control, the procreative aspect of marital intercourse can be nullified, and its unitive function left intact.

Until quite recently, the traditional argument against birth control has been that the sexual act is naturally designed for procreation, and it is wrong to frustrate this design because it is wrong to interfere with man's natural functions. The defenders of contraception dismiss this traditional argument as mere "biologism," that is, as an understanding of the marital act that fails to go beyond its biological function or possible biological consequences and ignores its spiritual function of signifying and effecting the union of the spouses. They feel they are on strong and positive ground here. While the marital act is potentially a procreative act, it is actually and in itself an act of love, a unitive act. Although contraception frustrates the biological or procreative aspect of the act, it fully respects the spiritual and unitive aspect and even facilitates it by removing tensions or fears capable of impairing the expression of love in married intercourse.

This is the contraceptive argument couched in apparently personalist terms. If we are to offer an effective answer to it and show its radical defectiveness, I would suggest that we need to develop a personalist argument based on a true personalist understanding of sex and marriage.

Reprinted by permission of the author.

The contraceptive argument is built on an essential thesis: the procreative and the unitive aspects of the marital act are *separable,* that is, the procreative aspect can be nullified without in any way vitiating the conjugal act or making it less a unique expression of true marital love and union. This thesis is explicitly rejected by the Church. The main reason why contraception is unacceptable to a Christian conscience is, as Paul VI puts it in *Humanae Vitae,* the "inseparable connection, established by God . . . between the unitive significance and the procreative significance which are both inherent to the marriage act."

Paul VI affirms this inseparable connection, He does not, however, go on to explain why these two aspects of the marital act are so inseparably connected, or why this connection is such that it is the very ground of the moral evaluation of the act. Yet I think that serene reflection easily enough discovers the reasons why the connection between the two aspects of the act is such that the destruction of the act's procreative reference necessarily destroys its unitive and personalist significance; why, in other words, if one deliberately destroys the power of the conjugal act to give life, one necessarily destroys its power to signify the love and union proper to marriage.

The Marital Act as an Act of Union

Why is the act of intercourse regarded as the foremost act of self-giving, the most distinctive expression of marital love? Why is this act, which is but a passing and fleeting thing, particularly regarded as an act of *union?* After all, people in love express their love and desire to be united in many ways: they send letters, exchange looks or presents, hold hands. What makes the sexual act unique? Why does this act unite the spouses in a way that no other act does? What is it that makes it not just a physical experience but an experience of love?

Is it the special pleasure attached to it? Is the unitive meaning of the conjugal act contained just in the sensation, however intense, that it can produce? If intercourse unites two people simply because it gives special pleasure, then it would seem that one or both of the spouses could, at times, find a more meaningful union outside of marriage than within it. It would follow too that

sex without pleasure becomes meaningless, and that sex with pleasure—even homosexual sex—becomes meaningful. No. The conjugal act may or may not be accompanied by pleasure, but the meaning of the act does not consist in its pleasure. The pleasure provided by marital intercourse may be intense, but it is transient. The *significance* of marital intercourse is also intense, and it is not transient; it lasts.

Why should the marital act be more significant than any other expression of affection between the spouses? Why should it be a more intense expression of love and union? Surely because of what happens in that marital encounter, which is not just a touch, not a mere sensation, however intense, but a communication, an offer and acceptance, an exchange of something that uniquely represents the gift of oneself and the union of two selves.

It should not be forgotten that while two persons in love want to give themselves to one another, to be united to one another, this desire of theirs remains, humanly speaking, on a purely volitional level. They can bind themselves to one another, but they cannot actually give themselves. The greatest expression of a person's desire to give himself is to give the seed of himself. Giving one's seed is much more significant, and in particular is much more real, than giving one's heart. "I am yours, I give you my heart; here, take it" remains mere poetry, to which no physical gesture can give true body. But "I am yours; I give you my seed; here, take it" is no poetry; it is love. It is conjugal love embodied in a unique and privileged physical action whereby intimacy is expressed ("I give you what I give no one else") and union is achieved. "Take what I have to give. This will be a new me. United to you, to what you have to give, to your seed, this will be a new *you-and-me,* fruit of our mutual knowledge and love." In human terms, this is the closest one can get to giving oneself conjugally and to accepting the conjugal self-gift of another, and so achieving spousal union.

Therefore, what makes marital intercourse express a unique relationship and union is not the sharing of a sensation, but the sharing of a power: an extraordinary, life-related, creative, physical, sexual power. In a true conjugal relationship, each spouse says to the other, "I accept you as somebody like no one else in my life. You will be unique to me and I to you. You and you alone will be my husband; you alone will be my wife. And the proof of your uniqueness to me is the fact that with you, and with you alone, am I prepared to share this God-given life-oriented power." In this consists the singular quality of intercourse. Other physical expressions of affection do not go beyond the level of a mere gesture; they remain a symbol of the union desired. But the conjugal act is not a mere symbol. In true marital intercourse, something real has been exchanged; and there remains, as witness to their conjugal relationship and the intimacy of their conjugal union, the husband's seed in the wife's body.[1]

Now if one deliberately nullifies the orientation to life of the conjugal act, one destroys its essential power to signify union. Contraception turns the marital act into self-deception or into a lie. "I love you so much that with you, and with you alone, I am ready to share this most unique power"; but *what* unique power? In contraceptive sex, no unique power is being shared, except a power to produce pleasure. The uniqueness of the marital act is reduced to pleasure. Its significance is gone.

Contraceptive intercourse is an exercise in meaninglessness. It could perhaps be compared to going through the actions of singing without letting any sound of music pass one's lips. . . . Contraceptive spouses involve each other in bodily movements, but their body language is not truly human. They refuse to let their bodies communicate sexually and intelligibly with one another. They go through the motions of a song, but there is no song.

Contraception is not just an action without meaning; it is an action that contradicts the essential meaning that true conjugal intercourse should have as signifying total and unconditional self-giving. Instead of accepting each other totally, contraceptive spouses reject part of each other because fertility is part of each one of them. They reject the power of their mutual love to be fruitful. A couple may say, "We do not want our love to be fruitful." But if that is so, there is an inherent contradiction in their trying to express their love by means of an act that of its nature implies fruitful love; and there is even more of a contradiction if, when they engage in the act, they deliberately destroy the orientation to fertility from which precisely it derives its capacity to express the uniqueness of their love.

In true marital union, husband and wife are meant to experience the vibration of human vitality in its very source.[2] In the case of contraceptive union, the spouses experience sensation, but it is drained of real vitality. The anti-life effect of contraception does not stop at the "No" that it addresses to the possible fruit of love. It tends to take the very life out of love itself. Within the hard logic of contraception, anti-life becomes anti-love. Its devitalizing effect devastates love, threatening it with early aging and premature death.

At this point, let us anticipate the possible criticism that our argument so far is based upon an incomplete disjunction, inasmuch as it seems to affirm that the conjugal act is either procreative or else merely hedonistic. Can contraceptive spouses not counter this with the sincere affirmation that, in their intercourse, they are not merely seeking pleasure, but that they are also experiencing and expressing love for one another? Let us clarify our position on this particular point. We do not claim that contraceptive spouses may not love each other in their intercourse, nor, insofar as they are unwilling to have such intercourse with a third person, that it does not express a certain uniqueness in their relationship. Our thesis is that it does not express *conjugal* uniqueness. Love may somehow be present in their contraceptive relationship; conjugal love is not expressed by it. Conjugal love may, on the contrary, soon find itself threatened by it. Contraceptive spouses are constantly haunted by the suspicion that although the act in which they share could indeed be for each one of them a

---

[1]In this way, the uniqueness of the decision to marry a particular person is reaffirmed in each marital act. By every single act of true intercourse, each spouse is confirmed in the unique status of being husband or wife to the other.

[2]This still remains true even in cases where, for some reason or another, the spouses cannot have children. Their union in such cases, just as their union during the wife's pregnancy, draws its deepest meaning from the fact that both their conjugal act and the intention behind it are open to life, even though no life can actually result from the act. It is their openness to life that gives the act its meaning and dignity, but as the absence of this openness undermines the dignity and meaning of the act when the spouses, without serious reason, deliberately limit their marital intercourse to the infertile periods.

privileged giving of pleasure, it could also be a mere selfish taking of pleasure. It is logical that their sexual acts be troubled by a sense of falseness or hollowness, for they are attempting to found the uniqueness of the spousal relationship on an act of pleasure, which tends ultimately to close each one of them sterilely in on himself or herself. They are refusing to found that relationship on the truly unique conjugal dimension of loving co-creativity, capable in its vitality of opening each of them out, not merely to one another, but to the whole of life and creation.

Sexual Love and Sexual Knowledge

The mutual and exclusive self-giving of the marriage act consists in its being the gift and acceptance of something unique. Now this something unique is not just the seed (this indeed could be biologism), but the fullness of the sexuality of the other person.

That it is not good for man to be alone provided the context in which God made him sexual. He created man in a duality, male and female, with the potential to become a trinity. The differences between the sexes speak therefore of a divine plan of complementarity, of self-completion and self-fulfillment through self-perpetuation. It is not good for man to be alone because man on his own cannot fulfill himself. He needs others. He especially needs one other: a companion, a spouse. Union with a spouse, giving oneself to a spouse, sexual and marital union in self-giving, are normal conditions of human growth and fulfillment.

Marriage, then, is a means of fulfillment through union. Husband and wife are united in mutual knowledge and love. This love is not just spiritual but also bodily; and this knowledge underpinning their love is not just speculative or intellectual but also bodily. That marital love is meant to be based on this *carnal* knowledge is fully human and fully logical. How significant it is that the Bible, in the original Hebrew, refers to marital intercourse in terms of a man and a woman "knowing" each other. Adam, Genesis says, knew Eve, his wife (Gn 4:1). What comment can we make on this equivalence, which the Bible draws, between conjugal intercourse and mutual knowledge? What is the distinctive knowledge that husband and wife communicate to one another? It is the knowledge

of each other's integral human condition as spouse. Each discloses to the other the most intimate secret of his or her personal sexuality. Each one is revealed to the other truly as spouse and comes to know the other in the uniqueness of that spousal self-revelation and self-gift. Each one lets himself or herself be known by the other and surrenders to the other, precisely as husband or wife.

Nothing can undermine a marriage so much as the refusal fully to know and accept one's spouse or to let oneself be fully known by him or her. A marriage is endangered when one spouse holds something back from the other or keeps back some knowledge that he or she does not want the other to possess.[3] This can occur on all levels of interpersonal communication, physical as well as spiritual.

In many modern marriages, there is something in the spouses, and between the spouses, that each does not want to know or face up to, but rather, wants to avoid; this something is their sexuality. Since they will not allow each other full mutual carnal knowledge, they do not truly know each other sexually or humanly or spousally. This places their married love under a tremendous existential tension, which can tear it apart.

In true marital intercourse, each spouse renounces protective self-possession, so as fully to possess and be fully possessed by the other. This fullness of true sexual gift and possession is only achieved in marital intercourse open to life. Only in procreative intercourse do the spouses exchange true knowledge of one another, do they truly speak humanly and intelligibly to one another, do they truly reveal themselves to one another in their full human potential and actuality. Each offers and each accepts full spousal knowledge of the other.

In the body language of intercourse, each spouse utters a word of love that is both a self-expression, an image of each one's self, as well as an expression of his or her longing for the other. These two words of love meet and are fused into one. As this new unified word of love takes on flesh, God shapes it into a person, the child, who is the incarnation of

---

[3]We are not referring here to those occasions in which, out of justice to a third party, one of the spouses is under an obligation to observe some secret, for example, of a professional nature. Fulfillment of such an obligation is in no way a violation of the rights of married intimacy.

the husband's and the wife's sexual knowledge of one another and sexual love for one another.

In contraceptive intercourse, the spouses will not let the word, which their sexuality longs to utter, take flesh. They will not even truly speak the word to each other. They remain humanly impotent in the face of love, sexually dumb and carnally speechless before one another.

Sexual love is a love of the whole male or female person, body and spirit. Love is falsified if body and spirit do not say the same thing. This happens in contraceptive intercourse. The bodily act speaks of a presence of love or of a degree of love that is denied by the spirit. The body says, "I love you totally," whereas the spirit says, "I love you reservedly." The body says, "I seek you"; the spirit says, "I will not accept you, not all of you."

Contraceptive intercourse falls below mere pantomime. It is disfigured body language; it expresses a rejection of the other. In it, each says, "I do not want to know you as my husband or my wife; I am not prepared to recognize you as my spouse. I want something from you but not your sexuality, and if I have something to give to you, something I will let you take, it is not my sexuality."[4]

This enables us to develop a point we touched on a few pages back. The negation that a contraceptive couple are involved in is not directed just toward children or just toward life or just toward the world. They address a negation directly toward one another. "I prefer a sterile you" is equivalent to saying "I do not want all you offer me. I have calculated the measure of my love, and it is not big enough for that, it is not able to take all of you. I want a you cut down to the size of my love." The fact that both spouses may concur in accepting a cut-rate version of each other does not save their love or their lives or their possibilities of happiness from the effects of such radical human and sexual devaluation.

Normal conjugal intercourse fully asserts masculinity and femininity. The man asserts himself as man and husband, and the woman equally asserts herself as woman and wife. In contraceptive intercourse, only a maimed sexuality is asserted. Sexuality, in the truest sense, is not asserted at all. Contraception represents such a refusal to let oneself be known that it simply is not real carnal knowledge. A deep human truth underlies the theological and juridical principle that contraceptive sex does not consummate marriage.

Contraceptive intercourse, then, is not real sexual intercourse at all. That is why the disjunctives in this whole matter are insufficiently expressed by saying that if intercourse is contraceptive, then it is merely hedonistic. This may or may not be true. What is true, at a much deeper level, is that if intercourse is contraceptive, then it is not sexual. In contraceptive intercourse there is an intercourse of sensation but no real sexual knowledge or sexual love, no true sexual revelation of self or sexual communication of self or sexual gift of self. The choice of contraception is the rejection of sexuality. The warping of the sexual instinct from which modern society suffers reflects not so much an excess of sex as a lack of true human sexuality.

True conjugal intercourse unites. Contraception separates, and the separation works right along the line. It not only separates sex from procreation, it also separates sex from love. It separates pleasure from meaning and body from mind. Ultimately and surely, it separates wife from husband and husband from wife.

Contraceptive couples who stop to reflect realize that their marriage is troubled by some deep malady. The alienations they experience are a sign as well as a consequence of the grave violation of the moral order involved in contraception. Only a resolute effort to break with contraceptive practices can heal the sickness affecting their married life. . . .

Why Does Only Procreative Sex Fulfill?

Our argument so far is that contraceptive marital sex does not achieve any true personalist end. It does not bring about self-fulfillment in marriage but rather, prevents and frustrates it. One may still ask, however, whether it follows that procreative

---

[4]If it is not sexuality that each spouse in contraceptive intercourse gives to or takes from the other, what does each one take or give? In what might be termed the better cases, it is a form of love divorced from sexuality. In other cases, it is merely pleasure, also, be it noted, divorced from sexuality. In one case or the other, contraceptive spouses always deny their sexuality. Their marriage, deprived of a true sexual relationship, suffers in consequence.

marital sex alone leads to the self-fulfillment of the spouses? I think it does and that the reason lies in the very nature of love. Love is creative. God's love (if we may put it this way) drove him to create. Man's love, made in the image of God's, is also meant to create. If it deliberately does not do so, it frustrates itself. Love between two persons makes them want to do things together. While this is true of friendship in general, it has a singular application to the love between spouses. A couple truly in love want to do things together; if possible, they want to do something original together. Nothing is more original to a couple in love than their child, the image and fruit of their love and their union. That is why *"the* marital thing" is to have children, and other things, as substitutes, do not satisfy conjugal love.

Procreative intercourse fulfills also because only in such intercourse are the spouses open to all the possibilities of their mutual love, ready to be enriched and fulfilled not only by what it offers to them but also by what it demands of them.

Further, procreative intercourse fulfills because it expresses love and does not contradict it, as contraceptive intercourse does. Love can thrive only on life-wishes, not on death-wishes. When a married couple have a child, they joyfully pass their child to each other. If their child dies, there is no joy; there are tears as they pass the dead body to one another. Spouses should weep over a contraceptive act. This barren, desolate act rejects the life that is meant to keep love alive; it kills the life to which their love naturally seeks to give origin. There may be physical satisfaction, but there should be no joy in passing dead seed or in passing living seed only to kill it.

The vitality of sensation in sexual intercourse should correspond to a vitality of meaning (remembering, as we have said, that sensation is not meaning). The very explosiveness of sexual pleasure suggests the greatness of the creativity of sex. In each conjugal act, there should be something of the magnificence, scope, and power of Michelangelo's *Creation* in the Sistine Chapel. It is the dynamism, not just of a sensation, but of an event—of something that happens, of a communication of life. A lack of true sexual awareness characterizes the act if the intensity of the pleasure does not serve to stir a fully conscious understanding of the greatness of the conjugal experience: I am committing myself and my creative life-giving power, not just to another person, but to the whole of creation, to history, to mankind, to the purposes and design of God. In each act of conjugal union, teaches Pope John Paul II, "there is renewed, in a way, the mystery of creation in all its original depth and vital power."

A last point should be made. The whole question we are considering is tremendously complicated precisely by the strength of the sexual instinct. Nevertheless, the very strength of this instinct should itself point toward an adequate understanding of sexuality. Elementary common sense says that the power of the sexual urge must correspond to deep human aspirations or needs. It has been traditional to explain the sexual urge in cosmic or demographic terms: just as we have a food appetite to maintain the life of the individual, so we have a sexual appetite to maintain the life of the species. This explanation makes sense, as far as it goes; however, it clearly does not go far enough. The sexual appetite, in all its strength, surely corresponds not only to cosmic or collectivist needs but also to personalist needs. If a man and a woman feel a deep longing for sexual union, it is because each one personally has a deep longing for all that is involved in true sexuality: self-giving, self-complementarity, self-realization, self-perpetuation, in spousal union with another.

The experience of such complete spousal sexuality is filled with a many-faceted pleasure, in which the simple physical satisfaction of a mere sense instinct is accompanied and enriched by the personalist satisfaction of the much deeper and stronger longings involved in sex and not marred and soured by their frustration. Continuous and growing sexual frustration is a main consequence of contraception because the contraceptive mentality deprives the very power of the sexual urge of its real meaning and purpose and then tries to find full sexual experience and satisfaction in what is little more than physical release.

Why Does Procreation Have to Be the Fruit of a Conjugal Act?

Human life has its origin in sex; it cannot be passed on other than by sexual reproduction. The generation of each child, which marks the renewal and perpetuation of creation, is always and necessarily the result of the union of sexual differences. Modern science has made procreation possible by fusing these sexual differences without any actual union of the bodies of husband and wife. It is the teaching of the Catholic Church that this gravely violates the God-given rule and mode of procreation, as well as the use and purpose of sex within marriage. This teaching has been most recently set forth in the Instruction on Respect for Human Life. The few remarks that I set down here simply constitute some incidental thoughts on the topic of artificial fertilization, in line with the reasoning of the preceding pages on human sexuality.

The child is meant to be, not just the fruit of sexuality in a purely biological sense (that is, the fruit of the union, however brought about, of two cells), but the fruit of *human and spousal* sexuality. The child is and has the right to be the fruit of the living union of two *persons,* which means the union of two souls and two bodies, not just of two wills with no true bodily union. A union of wills without a union of bodies lacks the proper composition of parental love. It does not constitute a sufficient human basis for the creation of a new life, nor does the simple union of seed without the union of bodies. The union of bodies is conjugal and human; it is the mere union of seed that is biological.

A child is not meant to be the fruit of a bodiless union. In such a union, his origin is less than human; he is de-humanized in his origins. If the child is not the fruit of true marital intercourse between the parents, the fruit of that act by which they have human sexual knowledge of one another, he is not actually conceived. He remains, all his life, a *product* of the knowledge of technology, but not an *incarnate concept* of his parents' spousal and bodily knowledge of each other. Humanly, if not biologically, he will suffer the consequences. He may easily end up as a misfit in a life that has certainly started as a misconception.

Study Questions on Cormac Burke

1. Do you agree that contraceptive intercourse is unable to express the full self-giving of the spouses? Is it only a kind of "going through the motions"?
2. Suppose we agree with Burke that a true marriage must include acts that are both unitive and open to procreation. Is it necessary that each and every sexual act in marriage should have this character?
3. What if a couple are physically unable to have children, say because the wife has had a hysterectomy? Does Burke's argument imply that they are incapable of truly marital sexual acts? Does natural family planning—or timing intercourse to avoid fertile periods—escape Burke's criticisms?
4. Do spouses ever fully possess one another? What would it mean if they did (that neither of them keeps anything secret from the other, for example)?

Collaborative Reproduction: Donors and Surrogates

JOHN ROBERTSON

John Robertson argues that what he calls "collaborative reproduction" is an important part of the procreative liberty of both infertile couples and the donors and surrogates who assist them. Rather than discouraging such practices, public policy should ensure that it occurs in a safe, effective, and mutually satisfying way; and that appropriate provision is made for counseling, informed consent, record keeping, and rights and duties in child rearing.

ALL REPRODUCTION IS COLLABORATIVE, for no mortal person reproduces alone. The term "collaborative reproduction" is nonetheless useful for describing those situations in which someone other than one's partner provides the gametes or gestation necessary for reproduction, such as occurs with sperm, egg, or embryo donation, or surrogate motherhood. These technologies play an increasingly central role in infertility treatment and raise basic questions about the scope of procreative liberty.

The Dilemmas of Collaborative Reproduction

A basic commitment to procreative liberty—to the freedom to have and rear offspring—should presumptively protect most forms of collaborative reproduction. After all, collaborative reproduction occurs for the same reason as IVF—the couple is infertile and cannot produce offspring. They need donor or surrogate assistance if they are to have children. Even if both rearing partners are not reproducing in the strict genetic sense, at least one partner will have a genetic or gestational relationship with their child. The same techniques may also be sought by a single woman or a same-sex couple that wishes to have offspring. In a few cases, donor gametes are used to avoid genetic handicap in offspring.

Despite its clear link to procreative choice, collaborative reproduction often generates controversy and even calls for prohibition. Collaborative reproduction is problematic because it intrudes a

third party—a donor or surrogate—into the usual situation of two-party parenthood, and separates or deconstructs the traditional genetic, gestational, and social unity of reproduction. A child could in theory end up with three different biologic parents (a genetic mother, a gestational mother, a genetic father) and two separate rearing parents, with various combinations among them. Such collaboration risks confusing offspring about who their "true" parent is and creating conflict about parental rights and duties. At the same time, the isolation of the particular components of parenthood tends to depersonalize the contributions of gamete donors and surrogates.

Collaborative reproduction thus poses several challenges for a regime of procreative liberty. On the one hand, it greatly expands procreative options, both for infertile couples seeking to form a family with biologically related offspring, as well as for persons who find satisfaction or meaning in serving as donors or surrogates.

On the other hand, it involves a novel set of practices and relationships in which social and psychological meanings and legal rights and duties have not yet been clearly defined. Given the ample room presented for misunderstanding and conflict, the use of technology to alter fundamental or traditional family relationships seems risky, and should occur only under conditions that protect the welfare of offspring, couples, and collaborators.

Indeed, the decomposition of the usually unified aspects of reproduction into separate genetic, gestational, and social strands calls into question the very meaning of procreative liberty. Are couples who use these techniques "procreating" in a significant way, even though one of them may lack a genetic or biological connection to offspring? Is a collaborator meaningfully procreating if he or she is merely providing gametes or gestation without any rearing role? Do such limited procreative roles deserve the same respect and protection that traditional coital reproduction warrants? Answers to these questions will help determine the extent to which such arrangements are permitted, regulated, or prohibited. . . .

Harm to Offspring

Although no organized movement to ban collaborative reproduction exists, many persons—usually those who have not themselves faced infertility—find these practices to be ethically troubling and socially deviant. In their eyes the central problem is that intrusion of a gamete donor or surrogate into the marital relationship confuses family and lineage in a way that is ultimately harmful to offspring. To protect offspring from the problems of multiple parents, they would strictly limit, if not prohibit altogether, the use of donors and surrogates to treat infertility.

ARE OFFSPRING HARMED BY COLLABORATIVE REPRODUCTION?

The concern about the impact on offspring is an important one. Genetic and biological ties are so central to our notions of individual identity and family that the possibility of adverse effects from deliberate separation of these elements must be taken seriously. Indeed, participants in these endeavors are often nervously aware that they are engaged in an enterprise for which the psychological, social, and legal rules have not yet been written.

Yet the claim that these practices should be prohibited because they are so inimical to offspring welfare is not convincing. The chief danger is that children will be reared by a person who is not their genetic mother or father, and that they may not know who their "true" father or mother is. In addition to causing conflict between the rearing partners and collaborator, the nonbiologic rearing partner may subtly or explicitly reject the child, and the child may experience a sense of loss or abandonment by the absent biologic parent.

Such experiences, of course, are not unique to donor- and surrogate-assisted reproduction. More than 25 percent of children are now raised in a nonnuclear family, and 28 percent of children are now born out of wedlock. Many children are being raised by adoptive, step, or foster parents, by relatives or by other persons in situations in which they will have no or limited contact with their genetic or gestational parents and have close ties with non-biologic rearers.

If the phenomenon of split biologic and social rearing is so widespread, one may question why collaborative reproduction should be of special concern. Of course, most instances of adoption, stepparentage, and other forms of blended or mixed families are a postnatal response to death, divorce, economic travail, abuse, or abandonment. In contrast, collaborative families are intentionally created. The intention is to create a loving home for a child who has a biological connection to one or both rearing parents.

The intentional creation of families with an absent genetic or gestational parent is a problem only if being reared in a situation in which one biologic parent is missing is itself generally harmful. Even if not ideal, we must ask what the risks of serious psychosocial problems in such families are, and what steps are possible to minimize them. Even then, one must also ask whether the likely problems are so great that offspring of collaborative reproduction, who have no other way to be born, would be better off never existing. . . .

The data on sperm donation suggest that the impact of collaborative reproduction on offspring will depend largely on how well the infertile couple and their family accept and adjust to the situation. . . .

Yet even if couples or offspring have difficulties adjusting to the fact of donor or surrogate assistance, it does not follow that collaborative assistance should be discouraged in order to prevent harm to offspring. But for the technique in question, the child never would have been born. Whatever psychological or social problems arise, they hardly rise to the level of severe handicap or disability that would make the child's very existence a net burden, and hence a wrongful life. Measures to minimize such effects are needed, but their absence alone would not justify banning collaborative techniques.

PROTECTING OFFSPRING BY DISCLOSURE

Given that collaborative reproduction serves individual procreative interests, makes possible children who would not otherwise be born, and does not appear to generate undue psychological or social conflict, such practices should generally be permitted. Rather than try to stop such practices, public policy should focus on preventing the problems that can arise. Legal rules for allocating rearing rights and duties among the participants are discussed in the next section. Later sections also discuss the need to protect collaborators by assuring that they act freely and knowingly. Questions of secrecy and disclosure, which directly affect offspring, are discussed here. This concern raises two questions: (1) should children be told of their donor- or surrogate-assisted birth? (2) What information about donors and surrogates should be provided to offspring?

Secrecy Versus Disclosure of Collaborative Birth

. . . [T]he question of secrecy or disclosure to the child is best left to the couple to resolve. Although most psychologists see no good reason for secrecy and emphasize the energy that keeping the secret entails, they recognize that disclosure entails its own complications. At what age to tell the child? What information about the donor is needed? What if the child wants to meet the missing biologic parent? Such questions will recur many times, restimulating the parents' own unresolved conflicts about their infertility, and may take on special urgency during adolescence or times of conflict. . . .

Rearing Rights and Duties in Collaborative Reproduction

A major policy issue in collaborative reproduction is the allocation of rearing rights and duties in offspring. Given that there may be more than two biologic parents and multiple possible social parents, who will have the legal right or duty to rear the child? This issue is of central importance to infertile couples, to donors and surrogates, and to the children born of these arrangements.

While these issues have been largely resolved for sperm donation to a married couple, legal questions remain about the status of sperm donation to a married woman and situations where donor and recipient intend to share rearing. The legal status of rearing is even less clear with donor eggs, embryo donation, and surrogacy. A major issue concerns whether the preconception intentions of the parties for rearing shall be determinative, or whether lawmakers should adopt some other system for allocating rearing roles.

In my view there are compelling reasons for recognizing the preconception intentions of the parties as the presumptive arbiter of rearing rights and duties, as long as the welfare of the offspring will not be severely damaged by honoring those intentions. This standard, of course, assumes that the child's best interest does not automatically depend on being reared by a particular genetic or gestational parent.

A main reason for presumptively enforcing the preconception agreement for rearing is procreative liberty. . . . [T]he procreative liberty of infertile married couples (and arguably unmarried persons as well) should include the right to use noncoital means of conception to form families. If the couple lacks the gametes or gestational capacity to produce offspring, a commitment to procreative liberty should also permit them the freedom to enlist the assistance of willing donors and surrogates.

Reliance on preconception agreements are thus necessary to give the couple—as well as the donors and surrogates—the assurance they need to go forward with the collaborative enterprise. Without some contractual assurance, the parties may be unwilling to embark on the complicated enterprise of collaborative reproduction. The infertile couple needs assurance that their efforts to become parents, if medically successful, will be legally recognized. Donors and surrogates also need assurance that they will not acquire unwanted rearing duties, or, if they have bargained for a more active rearing role, that their intentions will be honored. Without some advance certainty about legal consequences, they or the couple might be unwilling to collaborate, thus depriving the couple of the ingredients needed to have and rear offspring.

In addition to giving parties advance certainty, honoring preconception intentions will minimize the frequency of disputes and the costs of resolving them if they occur. If preconception agreements concerning rearing are generally binding, there will be less chance that participants will violate them. If disputes do arise, presumptively recognizing those intentions will be the most efficient way to resolve the dispute. Holding the parties to the promises on which the other parties relied also seems to be a fair solution. If enforcement of those agreements does not hurt the child, the only question will be whether the agreement was knowingly and freely made.

The idea of allowing preconception intentions or contracts to control postbirth rearing, however, is objectionable to many people. They point to the rejection of a contractual approach to adoption, the disparities in bargaining position that may exist, and the disregard of the child's best interests. However, the position asserted here is not necessarily antithetical to those points. The parties' preconception agreement about postbirth rearing is not enforced if it was not freely made or if enforcing the rearing provisions will clearly harm the child. However, if the parties who have contracted to rear are adequate child rearers, their preconception agreement should trump the claims of donors or surrogates who later insist on a different rearing role than they had agreed upon. If all parties are equally good child rearers and the collaborative agreement was freely and knowingly entered, the preconception agreement for rearing should be enforced. . . .

Surrogacy

Collaborative reproduction is also practiced with the assistance of a woman who gestates the embryo of the infertile couple. The wife may have functioning ovaries but no uterus or is otherwise medically unable to carry a fetus to term. Through IVF, she and her husband produce an embryo which is then placed in the uterus of the gestational surrogate. The resulting child is the genetic offspring of the rearing parents, but has been gestated or carried to term by another.

Surrogacy may also occur with the surrogate providing the egg as well as gestation. The collaborator in this case is artificially inseminated with the husband's sperm, and relinquishes the child to the father and his wife at birth. At some point after

birth she terminates her parental rights, and the father's wife—the child's stepmother—adopts the child. In this case, the rearing husband will have a biologic connection with the child. The rearing mother will have none.

The question of enforcing preconception surrogacy agreements for rearing is the most controversial issue in collaborative reproduction. Although most surrogates relinquish the child as agreed, widely publicized cases of surrogates seeking custody or visitation in violation of their agreement have arisen. The few courts that have dealt with the matter have usually applied the long standing adoption law principle that preconceptual or prenatal agreements to relinquish for adoption will not be enforced. They reject the notion that the child's best interests can be determined prior to birth or conception by contract, or that women can know their true wishes about rearing offspring before birth occurs. Some persons oppose enforcing surrogate contracts because women may enter into these arrangements under financial pressure, because it is their labor that has produced the child, or because contract law reflects patriarchal notions of rights that use women's bodies for the sake of male reproduction.

In my view, the preconception intentions of the parties should be binding both for gestational and full surrogacy. In both cases the couple will have invested considerable time, energy, and emotion in finding the surrogate and initiating pregnancy in reliance on her promise. In the case of gestational surrogacy, they will also have entrusted their embryo to her. Given these competing interests, it is not obvious that the surrogate's disappointment or loss at having to relinquish the child as promised should be privileged over the loss which the couple will feel if she now insists on rearing. Assuming that both the couple and the surrogate are fit rearers, there is no reason to think that the child is always better off with the birth mother. In addition, overriding preconception intentions interferes with the couple's procreative interest in using this method of forming a family. . . .

While a mix of reasons contribute to the view that the gestational mother's wish to rear should be privileged, they are not sufficient to override the procreative interests at stake. Indeed, in the final analysis, rejection of preconception intentions to fix postbirth rearing rights and duties seems to be based on paternalistic attitudes toward women or on a symbolic view of maternal gestation. Privileging the surrogate's wishes over the reliance interests of the couple assumes that women cannot make rational decisions about reproduction and child rearing prior to conception. It also treats gestational motherhood as a near sacred endeavor, which preconception contracts that separate gestational and social parentage violate. However, paternalistic and symbolic attitudes over which reasonable persons differ do not justify trumping the fundamental right to use collaborative means of procreation.

No court, however, has yet held that enforcement of preconception rearing agreements is required by procreative liberty. The New Jersey Supreme Court rejected it in the Baby M. case by characterizing procreation as genetic only, ignoring the rearing relationship that William Stern and most genetic reproducers intend as a result. Most states that have legislated on surrogate motherhood since Baby M. also protect the surrogate's right to retain rearing rights, despite her preconception promise to the contrary. . . .

ASSURING INFORMED CONSENT AND AVOIDING DISAPPOINTMENT

An essential step to protect the collaborating parties is to make sure that they are fully informed of the particular risks that they run in participating in collaborative reproduction. In most instances, this will require actions by physicians and other intermediaries. In some cases, laws or professional guidelines will be necessary. . . .

Surrogates

Special attention must be paid to the needs of surrogates. They will be embarking on a major life event—pregnancy and childbirth—with the intention of then relinquishing the child they have gestated. Accurate information about medical difficulties in initiating and completing pregnancy is essential. Counseling is also essential to prepare surrogates for probable feelings of disappointment, depression, and guilt. Counseling should be pro-

vided both prior to conception and after birth to help them adjust to their situation.

A class bias in most surrogacy arrangements may also be inevitable. While most surrogates are high school graduates, and many will have gone to college, they are more likely to be less educated and less well off than the infertile couples who hire them. . . .

Until regulatory legislation is passed, surrogate brokers have special duties to make sure that the women they recruit are well informed and counseled about the risks they face. Although this has not always been the practice, surrogate brokers should inform prospective surrogates at the earliest possible time in the recruitment process, such as in the material that they send out to women responding to newspaper ads, that surrogacy is disappointing and difficult for some women. Brokers should also make clear to prospective surrogates that they represent the infertile couple, not the surrogate, and advise the surrogate to seek her own legal counsel. They should also screen prospective surrogates psychologically, so that women who appear likely to have problems are excluded or so infertile couples have full information on the psychological profile of the prospective surrogate. They may also have legal duties to make sure that medical tests that protect the surrogate are performed.

Whether privately or publicly imposed, measures to assure that surrogates are adequately counseled and screened will increase costs, and interfere to some extent with the wishes of individuals to engage or function as a surrogate. Such restrictions, however, do not violate procreative liberty, for they are not likely to prevent couples from use of this technique. Moreover, the additional burden they create is justified as a reasonable measure to enhance autonomy and protect the parties in surrogate reproduction.

PAYING MONEY AND THE REIFICATION OF REPRODUCTION

A major concern about collaborative reproduction arises from paying donors and surrogates for their services. Commercializing reproduction is said to exploit and depersonalize women, turning them into mere cogs in the machinery of reproduction. It also risks turning children into commodities that are purchased via the payments for donor and surrogate services that make them possible.

Objections to payment, however, vary with the procedure in question. Some countries, such as France, England, and Australia, have banned payments to gamete donors and depend solely on volunteers. The prevailing practice in the United States is for commercial sperm banks or physician intermediaries to pay sperm donors for their time and effort, thus proving the inaccuracy of the term "donor." Egg donors are also paid on a graduated schedule according to the procedures they undergo. A fee of $1,500 to $2,000 is now common. Some embryo donors have requested compensation to cover the costs incurred in producing the donated embryos. Federal and state laws outlaw the sale of solid organs and nonrenewable tissue, but usually do not apply to the sale of gametes.

Payment to surrogate mothers, however, is much more controversial and is illegal in many states and abroad. Several states have recently passed statutes that expressly forbid commercial surrogacy, banning payments both to surrogates and to the brokers who arrange for their services. Other states reach the same result by construing laws against baby selling, which prohibit payments other than medical expenses for adoption, as prohibiting payments to surrogates. Such laws do not usually distinguish between gestational and other forms of surrogacy. In most states the legal status of payment to surrogates remains uncertain. . . .

Paying surrogates (though perhaps not gamete donors) is probably necessary if infertile couples are to obtain surrogacy services. Although surrogates usually act out of a mix of motivations, few women not related to the couple are likely to undergo pregnancy and childbirth unless they are paid for their services. Also, it seems unfair not to pay surrogates for their very substantial efforts, while egg and sperm donors and the doctors and lawyers arranging surrogate services are well paid. If a ban on payment significantly reduced access to surrogacy, it would infringe the infertile couple's procreative liberty, for it would prevent them from obtaining the collaborative services they need to rear biologically related offspring. Such an infringement could be justified only if banning payment prevented a substantial

harm that clearly outweighed the burden on procreative choice.

Yet the arguments for banning payment do not appear to reach that level of justification. A main argument is that a ban on payment will prevent exploitation of surrogates, who in most cases will be poorer and of a different social class than the infertile couples hiring them. Exploitation should not be confused with coercion. Women volunteering to be paid surrogates are not being coerced, even if they need the money, because they are not deprived of anything that they are otherwise entitled to if they refuse the couple's offer.

Nor is it clear that they are being exploited to any greater degree than labor markets generally exploit financial need. In this regard, markets for the sale of gestational services are no more exploitive than the sale of other kinds of physical labor. If people are free to sell their labor as petrochemical workers, cleaning persons, or construction workers in the hot Texas sun, why should the sale of gestational services be treated any differently? Much paid labor is equally or even more risky to health.

Proponents of the exploitation claim point to the very different nature of maternal gestation, and argue that women should not be asked to trade their gestational capacity for their need for money. Their argument, in effect, rests on an objection to the perceived risks and demeaning effects of commercializing motherhood. Yet reasonable people have differing moral perceptions about paid surrogacy, with many not finding the symbolic demeaning of motherhood that others see as so glaringly wrong. With such splits in perception, such symbolic concerns alone should not override the couple's interest in having and rearing biologic offspring with the help of a freely consenting, paid collaborator.

A second argument against payment—that it commodifies children and surrogates—also reduces to a perception of the symbolic effects of treating gestation as a product to be sold for money. Professor Margaret Radin has developed this argument more fully than anyone else. But she has failed to show that payment will lead to monetizing or commodifying all children or women, or why certain attributes such as gestation and sexuality may not be sold, while other attributes, such as physical size, skill, attractiveness, and intellectual prowess may be. Her claim that her list of non-monetizable attributes are more essential "to our deepest understanding of what it is to be human" is not convincing, since one could just as reasonably argue that the physical and mental attributes that drive the market for models, professional athletes, and computer scientists are also essential to "our deepest understanding of what it is to be human." . . .

Collaborative Reproduction and the Future of Families

Discussion of these issues inevitably brings us to a recurring concern about collaborative reproduction—that it will accelerate the decline of the nuclear family at a time when that institution is under severe pressure from divorce, teenage pregnancy, single mothers, blended families, gay and lesbian life-styles, and other forces.

Yet such fears exaggerate the effect of collaborative reproduction and do not justify limiting the joint efforts of infertile couples, donors, and surrogates. In most cases, collaborative reproduction enables a married couple to have biologically related offspring, with the gamete donor or surrogate excluded from any significant rearing role. While contracts to include the donor or surrogate in rearing offspring are theoretically possible, they are likely to be rare except where a friend or family member provides the service. Even then, one would expect there to be at most two primary rearers, even if some contact with other biologic parents and their relatives occurs.

Given the great number of families in which nonbiologic parents are primary rearers due to death, divorce, abandonment, and the like, it is difficult to see how collaborative reproduction, with its small number of intentionally blended families, poses a threat to the nuclear family. Indeed, with its emphasis on enabling a married couple to have and rear biologic offspring, it supports that institution more than it diminishes it, despite the social, psychological, and legal complications that might ensue. . . .

Study Questions on John Robertson

1. What does Robertson mean by collaborative reproduction? How does it differ from the ordinary sort?
2. On what grounds does he reject the claim that such reproduction is harmful to offspring, or to the family as an institution? Are you persuaded?
3. How does he propose to handle the question of rearing rights and duties? Do you find his proposal satisfactory?
4. Explain the picture of social life, and the family as an institution, that underlies Robertson's arguments. How does it fall within the liberal-communitarian debate described in the introduction to this unit? What do you think of this picture?
5. Why does Robertson place such a high value on "procreative liberty" or "procreative choice?" Do sterile people or people who find reproductive sexuality repellant, have a right to have children? On what grounds might someone assert such a right?

Technology as Destiny

JEAN BETHKE ELSHTAIN

> Jean Bethke Elshtain urges feminists to attend to the newer technologies for controlling reproduction. What, she asks, are the implications when life becomes a commodity? How are we to avoid the biopolitics of the Nazis? She raises concerns about the nature of intimacy and the family, which are threatened by the revival of eugenics and the transformation of human procreation into a technical operation.

ALMOST EVERY DAY, strange newspaper headlines trumpet even stranger content:

MAN FILES TEST-TUBE EMBRYO SUIT. In this bizarre case, a Tennessean divorcing his wife went to court to stop her from becoming pregnant with fertilized eggs they had put in frozen storage as a couple. Decision pending.

YALE RESEARCHERS TO TEST TRANSPLANTS OF FETAL TISSUE. Shorthand for this technique might be, "Parkinson's is the disease; abortion is the cure." The procedure in question involves transplanting brain cells from aborted fetuses into patients with Parkinson's to stem the degenerative course of the disease. For some, this is a potentially marvelous medical advance; for others, a morally sordid situation that raises the specter of pregnancy-for-hire to "harvest" fetal tissue from aborted fetuses for a variety of purposes.

HOSPITAL PUTS INFANT IN ORGAN DONOR WARD. The hospital in question, Loma Linda in Los Angeles, seems to specialize in the macabre, having pioneered the unsuccessful transplant of a chimpanzee heart into a baby. The latest twist is to keep anencephalic newborns alive in order to "harvest" their organs.

Each of the articles detailing these late-breaking developments indicates that they raise "profound" and "troubling" ethical questions. This follows a course that has become almost routine: First, certain techniques are perfected or modeled; then, we consult professional ethicists to advise us on whether we ought to be doing what we are, in fact, already doing.

Ethics has a kind of desperate post-hoc character these days. Biomedical technology, on the other hand, is preemptive, aggressive, on-the-move—and searching for big profits. Reproduction is shaping up as a kind of industrial production: the manufacture of particular goods for a price. The names that genetic-engineering firms choose for themselves tell the tale: Select Embryos; Quality Embryo Transfer Company, Ltd.; Sunshine Genetics; Reproduction Enterprises, Inc.; Treasure Valley Transplants.

What are the implications when life becomes a commodity? Who become our candidates for what was tagged, in Nazi biopolitics, "life unworthy of life"? We don't call it eugenics anymore, because the biopolitics of the Nazi regime gave that word a bad name. But the new eugenics is here.

To be sure, we have a long way to go before we approach the ruthless rules of Nazi biopolitics, which required eliminating unworthies of all sorts—the physically and mentally handicapped, inferior races, and the useless elderly, among others. But we have gone farther down this road than most Americans realize or want to acknowledge.

It has all come to us in the guise of "quality of life," and "reproductive choice." And, of course, it has a lofty rationale: to "free" women of "unwanted" fetuses (unwanted because they are defective or, increasingly, because they are of the wrong sex), or to "free" women to have babies by means of highly touted, enormously expensive, rarely successful methods such as in-vitro fertilization or through the costly but physically painless route of surrogacy, where another woman's body labors.

In this brave new world, who speaks, or claims to speak, *for* women? This is an issue on which feminism surely ought to be heard, raising the alarm against a clear and present danger. But matters are by no means so clear-cut. Feminist discourse since the mid-1960s has been lodged securely, with few dissenting voices, in the notion of reproductive freedom.

Until recently, mainstream feminism paid little attention to newer technologies for controlling human reproduction, except when it came to issuing briefs in behalf of a 100 percent safe and effective contraceptive and in defense of abortion-on-demand. The voices within the feminist camp that questioned arguments for abortion couched *exclusively* in the language of absolute freedom of choice, or in terms of contractual rights to control one's own body, did not prevail in the debates. Those voices now seem to have astutely anticipated the past decade's runaway developments in reproductive technology and genetic engineering.

In-vitro fertilization, embryo flushing, surrogate embryo transfer, surrogate motherhood, sex pres-election, cloning—the entire panoply of real or potentially realizable techniques for manipulating, redirecting, controlling, and altering human reproduction are upon us *now*. Radical intrusion into human biology is an especially vexing issue for feminists because most of these techniques take place in, or are practiced upon, or require the use of the female body.

Feminist philosopher Anne Donchin contends that feminists have sorted themselves out into three major, conflicting positions on the matter of reproductive technology and its mind-boggling implications: pro-interventionists, who celebrate techniques that sever women from "biological determinism"; anti-interventionists, who oppose the new reproductive technologies as an intensification of patriarchal control over women and nature; and those who share bits and pieces of both the pro- and anti-interventionist positions.

For the radical pro-interventionists, the new eugenics presents no problem so long as it can be wrested from male control. They regard that as the only political dilemma, and assess all moral ques-

tions with reference to women's freedom. And that means freeing women from what has been tagged as "biological tyranny" in the interventionist credo.

Once women have been liberated from biological tyranny, the pro-interventionists assert, all systems of oppression—the economy, the state, religion, and the law—will erode and collapse. Deploying rhetoric dominated by market metaphors, strong pro-interventionists seek an end to the "barbarism" of biological reproduction and foresee a feminist utopia to come when every aspect of human life rests in the beneficent hands of a "new elite of engineers, cyberneticians"—the words of Shulamith Firestone, who set the tone for interventionist feminism.

Feminist interventionists share an overall world-view with the new eugenicists for they, too, believe that nature must be overcome and that human beings should aspire to godlike power. Those who see only our animal origins and patriarchal control in women's links to biology, birth, and nurture are bound to applaud anything that breaks those links. The feminist revolution, in this scheme of things, is a technological solution to women's "control deficit."

The pro-interventionists, whose voices once tended to dominate the movement, are now on the defensive. A powerful feminist anti-interventionist presence has taken center stage in current debates, conjuring up nightmarish worst-case scenarios of the eugenically engineered world to come. As they continue to demand the right to choose, noninterventionists ponder the many "coercive choices" the new reproductive technology seems to entail.

For example, is amniocentesis really a free choice or is it more and more a manipulated, subtly coercive procedure with only one *correct* outcome—to abort if the fetus is "defective"? As younger and younger women submit to amniocentesis, physicians speak of "maternal anxiety" as the motivation. In the words of one thirty-two-year-old woman, "Having a baby isn't like buying a car, but in a way, he [her husband] wanted to know what he was getting. . . ." So, it seems, did she as she embraced the ever more common "perfect-baby syndrome."

But how liberally are we to define "defect"? And what about the much proclaimed "right" to bear a child—is this not another imposition of a male-dominant society upon women who see themselves as "failures" if they cannot get pregnant and are thus driven to place themselves in the hands of "techno-docs" (Gena Corea's term) to try to rectify their failure?

According to anti-interventionists, all modern technology is designed to deepen and extend patriarchal control. They are deeply skeptical that *this* technology can be turned to good purpose. Radical anti-interventionists insist that just as males moved successfully to control female "sex parts" through various forms of prostitution (including marriage), so they now seek a new reality: the reproductive brothel.

Writes Andrea Dworkin, "Women can sell reproductive capacities the same way old-time prostitutes sold sexual ones. . . . While sexual prostitutes sell vagina, rectum, and mouth, reproductive prostitutes will sell other body parts: Wombs. Ovaries. Eggs."

Not all statements of anti-interventionists are so extreme. Many of the scenarios conjured up by Gena Corea in her book *The Mother Machine* are genuinely frightening, showing how methods first developed as part of animal husbandry—to control the reproduction of non-human animals—are making their way into human lives.

But the anti-interventionist position unravels philosophically—and politically—where one finds assertions of an absolute right to choose, but only so long as the choices are "true," not "false," according to ideologically correct doctrine.

Thus, some feminists claim that the lesbian who wants to assert her right to "independent motherhood" is entitled both to artificial insemination and to sex selection as a basis for abortion should the fetus turn out to be male when she wants a female. But the woman in a heterosexual relationship who, with her husband, opts for in-vitro fertilization is viewed as a hapless dupe of patriarchal wiles. And, should she choose sex selection as a basis for abortion because she and her husband want a male child, that suddenly becomes "feticide" rather than the "right to choose."

This won't do. To offer a genuinely compelling argument, the anti-interventionists would have to extend their opposition to eugenics to include gender preselection on the part of female as well as male-female couples going through artificial insemination by donor. Either one does or does not have moral permission to eliminate the unborn solely on the basis of gender. But for some anti-interventionists, a preferential option for the female fetus is part of the arsenal or weapons to fight patriarchal society.

By sanctioning sex selection of the "right sort" as the basis for abortion, radical feminists are playing with fire—and with social reality. Especially poignant for women is the fact that female fetuses are prime candidates for our version of what might be called "life less worthy of life." There is no doubt that the modern technology of sex preselection will result in a higher proportionate destruction of female fetuses—at least for the *first* birth.

A recent *New York Times* piece proclaimed, "In a major change in medical attitudes and practice, many doctors are providing prenatal diagnoses to pregnant women who want to abort a fetus on the basis of sex alone." We have reached the point of disrupting the "natural lottery"—the fact that no human being can control whether he or she is white or black, male or female, a Down's syndrome child or a musical prodigy. When we do that, we undermine the very basis of human equality. The *Times* piece goes on to note that it is only "in very rare instances" that "there is a valid medical reason for sex selection." The reasons are social and political.

The erosion of human equality—the fragile insistence that each of us has an ontological dignity that we did not create and over which society has no control—requires that we accept and welcome life in all its variety. Once we claim that we do, in fact, have such control—that we can ensure more males and fewer females, that we can prevent the appearance of the Down's syndrome child and, maybe, in the even braver new world to come, manipulate genes to get the musical prodigy—we pave the way for nightmarish biological totalitarianism.

At that sorry point, some among us—"perfect" white males—will have been given top priority by a three-to-two majority, if current studies are any indication. Others will be inferior, having been placed lower on the preference list. And still others will be disallowed life at all. Should any of this last sort sneak through, there will be no moral basis for insisting that they be given decent treatment as members of the human community since, if the controls had been working right, they wouldn't be here in the first place.

The radical interventionists are right to insist that technical progress is never neutral. But to counterpose good female values (feminism rightly understood) to bad male values gets us nowhere. There are women as well as men who support these technologies—some in the name of feminism.

To insist, as does anti-interventionist Maria Mies, that the "so-called new technology does not bring us and our children any kind of qualitative or quantitative improvement in our lives; it solves none of our basic problems; it will advance even more the exploitation and humiliation of women; therefore we do not need it," strikes a sympathetic chord with many, myself included, who do not share the full range of anti-interventionist assumptions. And warning flags are going up in unexpected places including *The Village Voice*, which featured a piece on "the selling of in-vitro fertilization" in which the author, Andrea Boroff Eagan, indicated that "tears of gratitude" sprang to her eyes when a Catholic priest on an ethics panel mentioned "conjugal intimacy"—the only person to do so in a week-long discussion of reproduction that was otherwise "desexed, disembodied, dehumanized."

Most feminists and I would guess, most people generally belong somewhere between the radical pro- and anti-interventionist positions, hoping that real help might come to infertile couples but in ways that seem human and humane; concerned to "do something" about human suffering but worried about eliminating human beings according to someone else's definition of suffering. (The decision to withhold treatment and nourishment from imperfect newborns is usually directly traceable to the premises of a eugenics politics that dictates that a handicap devalues life and undermines any right to it.)

Most people support contraception and do not want abortion made illegal—but neither are they "pro-abortion." Studies consistently find a shaky combination of "yes" and' "no" answers to the vast array of powers and projects currently, and dubiously, lumped under the heading of "reproductive freedom."

The Baby M. case crystallized this queasiness and prompted further elaboration of what might be called the moderate position. Here was a situation in which biological motherhood and social parenting were severed—as feminists had long claimed they should be. Here was a situation in which a biological father insisted he wanted to assume the responsibilities of fatherhood—as feminists had long claimed men ought to want to do. Here was a case in which everyone "freely" agreed to a contract. Yet as the case unraveled, more and more feminists expressed opposition to commercial surrogacy and outrage at the initial court decision, which got all woozy ever the man's desire for genetic offspring while dismissing Mary Beth Whitehead's frenzied struggle to keep the child to which she had given birth.

The case demonstrated, at times with almost unbearable pathos, the inadequacy of such terms as "procreative liberty," "gestational hostess," "womb rental," "risk pay for pregnancy services," and the host of other depersonalizing euphemisms which seek to transform childbearing into a morally and emotionally neutral activity. As Betty Friedan pointed out the initial decision denying Whitehead *any* claim—she was no mother of any kind in any way—had "frightening implications for women" because it was a "terrifying denial of what should be basic rights for women, an utter denial of the personhood of women, the complete dehumanization of women. It is an important human-rights case. To put it on the level of contract law is to dehumanize women and the human bond between mother and child."

Yet, the business of surrogacy had, in fact, taken off as a venture at the furthest frontiers of reproductive freedom—and, of course, of profit. To condemn the latter required a critical look at the former and at what was now being done under the banner of individualist versions of such freedom.

Some feminists did point to the fine print in the surrogacy contract: Whitehead was to abort on William Stern's demand should the fetus show any signs of "physiological abnormality" following amniocentesis. Many found this repugnant, even immoral, because the male got to order it, not because such abortion is dubious on principle.

Feminists aroused by this case circled around a vital point—that, in Friedan's words, "the claim of the woman who has carried the baby for nine months should take precedence over the claim of the man who has donated one of his fifty million sperm." When Lee Salk noted psychologist, called Whitehead a "rented uterus" in his testimony in behalf of the Sterns, he earned a permanent place in the rogue's gallery. The most eloquent statement of feminist outrage came from Katha Pollitt who wrote, in *The Nation,* "What William Stern wanted, however, was not just a perfect baby: the Sterns did not, in fact, seriously investigate adoption. He wanted a perfect baby with his genes and a medically vetted mother who would get out of his life forever immediately after giving birth."

Surrogacy and other new eugenics questions bring us back, inevitably, to concerns about the nature of human intimacy and the family. That is as it should be. The new eugenics cannot be separated from the wider cultural and social environment.

All approaches to eugenics with which I am familiar—from Plato's elegant *Republic* to Hitler's vulgar *Reich*—aimed to eliminate, undermine, or leap-frog over the family to achieve their aims. To modern eugenicists, too, the family and "traditional morality" are obstacles in the path of radical social and genetic engineering. As the surrogacy case demonstrated, women's attachment to their own children is a problem. It would be far easier if natural pregnancy could somehow be phased out. But, in the meantime, newer and better ways to convince people to participate in eugenics (under other names, of course) must be devised.

Paradoxically, the new eugenics, operating under the umbrella of reproductive freedom, may have opened women's lives to more invasive forms of control. The search for intervention in human reproduction comes, at least initially, from those able to command the resources of genetic engineers and medical experts. They are prepared to accept a remarkable degree of surveillance and manipulation of their lives to satisfy their demand that babies be made (or unmade) whenever they want and as soon as a "valid contract" can be drafted.

In this way, human procreation is transformed into a technical operation. Writes social critic Jeanne Schuler, "Reproductive liberty sounds as if it was written for women but it signals a new level of alienated sexuality. . . . Behind the effort to make all things equal in the realm of reproduction figures a new form of discrimination. The hazards of reproductive freedom are not easily visible to liberal politics. . . . However, liberalism nurtures freedom without cultivating a vision of family, let alone community. Thus it is easily drafted to the side of the status quo, once so-called negative liberties are intact."

Many feminists are troubled by the Frankenstein monster we seem to be unleashing. All women are affected by these developments. The political battles over definitions of motherhood—and, indeed, of human life itself—are only beginning. The new eugenics, in the meantime, has passed one green light after another and is rolling at breakneck speed, claiming "gender equality" and "freedom" on its side.

Erecting a stop sign at future intersections requires that we reject the view that freedom can be narrowed to contractual terms, that human bodies can be bartered, that we have a "right" to eliminate those human beings who don't look or act like our perfect image of ourselves. And it requires that we forge alliances however fragile, to preserve human dignity, which must be the basis for any genuine project of human equality and justice.

Study Questions on Jean Bethke Elshtain

1. How, in Elshtain's view, do the slogans "quality of life" and "reproductive choice" threaten us with the biopolitics of the Nazis?
2. Some feminists argue that new reproductive technologies are a form of renewed male dominance—for example, because these technologies are likely to be controlled by men. Does Elshtain's argument support this concern?

3. Is there a tenable middle ground between reproductive interventionism and reproductive anti-interventionism? If so, what is it? (In framing your answer, consider as many forms of reproductive technology as possible, including abortion and contraception.)

4. Would you describe Elshtain's argument as liberal, conservative, or what? (Her article was published in the Leftist magazine *The Progressive*.) How does the liberal-communitarian debate, described in the introduction to this unit, bear on this question?

5. Compare and contrast Elshtain's argument with Robertson's (see previous article). Which do you agree with more and why?

Cutting Motherhood in Two

HILDE AND JAMES LINDEMANN NELSON

Hilde and James Lindemann Nelson deal with moral problems that arise from the inability to have children. They examine the implications of separating gestation and parturition from nurturing, and of extending the free-market model to parent-child relations. They maintain a view of parental obligation based on the causal relationship between parents and offspring. By bringing a child into the world, parents have put the child at risk of harm, since he or she is extremely needy and vulnerable to a vast assortment of forms of physical and psychological damage. Those who have created the child's vulnerability cannot escape the obligation to provide for the child's care.

IF UNWANTED PREGNANCIES are a problem in our culture, so too is the inability to have children. With the widespread use of the Pill and other contraceptive devices, in conjunction with more relaxed social attitudes toward abortion, women have achieved a measure of control over their pregnancies that their great-grandmothers never dreamed of. Is it any wonder, then, that women and men who have experienced the agonizing frustration of remaining childless despite all their best efforts should turn to medical technology for control over their infertility?

Many infertile couples feel a strong desire to bring into being the children they rear; for them, adoption is distressingly inadequate. They may feel that the bond between them is deepened if they have a biological link to the next generation, or they may simply feel shame at the inability to do something as natural as producing a baby. Some people without partners are content to stay single, but want to have their own—not someone else's—children. The urge to reproduce oneself may relate to the desire to survive one's death; it is surely akin to the artist's urge to make something that will outlast its creator's lifetime.

Whatever the reason, it is clear that people will go to considerable lengths to have children of their own. When the time-honored method fails, the would-be parents may turn to artificial insemination by donor. This remedy will not meet the

From Hypatia, 4, *3 (Fall 1989): 85–94. Reprinted by permission of Indiana University Press.*

case, however, if the prospective mothe'rs reproductive equipment isn't functioning properly, or if her general state of health is so poor as to make childbearing an even more risky business than it is ordinarily. In such a situation, the parents may seek a surrogate mother.

By "surrogate mother" we mean a woman who is hired to bear a child whom she turns over at birth to her employer. Typically, she supplies the egg while the man who purchases her services provides the sperm, but the egg need not be hers. Our concern here is not so much with ménage-à-trois arrangements in which the surrogate participates, along with the contracting couple, in the rearing of the child; we focus instead on standard agreements that grant sole custody to the contracting couple—or, just as likely, the contracting father.

Now, on the face of it, "surrogate mother" is an odd designation for the woman hired to gestate the child.. The *O.E.D.* defines "surrogate" as "a person appointed by authority to act in the place of another;" "mother" as "a woman who has given birth to a child." it would seem, then, that the surrogate mother would actually be someone to whom the child is surrendered, and who will then act in place of the mother. The person who does the surrendering, it seems clear, is a *real* mother, not a surrogate anything.

Common usage indicates that we have a richer conception of motherhood than does the *O.E.D.;* it includes not only the process of gestation and parturition, but also of nurturing. These strands of the concept are generally tightly braided. Sometimes—as in the case of adoption—the strands come apart, and so we distinguish between a biological and a social sense of mothering.

The evaluation of social vs. biological mothering which is implicit in the "surrogate mother" tag may seem a piece of obfuscation, designed to hide some of the reality involved in this practice, or at least to mute a point that deserves the most careful kind of ethical scrutiny. But we think that there is a sense in which what appears to be an ad hoc conceptual move, designed to hide possibly troubling facts, is actually quite revealing. What our current practice with the label indicates is that we have evaluated the significance of those strands in cases where they come apart and regard the social sense of mothering as so significant that it overrides the biological sense when they conflict. That the social sense of mothering can be seen as an elective response to a pregnancy (whether one's own or another's) may explain what seems to be a widespread tendency to conclude that maternal duties as such rest wholly on our decisions; we shall argue that this is not so.

We maintain a view of parental obligation which is based on the *causal* relationships between parents and their offspring, rather than on any intensional ties; it is, we think, not the *decision* to have children but rather the *fact* of having done so, which primarily creates responsibilities. The leading idea of our view is that in bringing a child into the world, the parents have put it at risk of harm; it is extremely needy and highly vulnerable to a vast assortment of physical and psychological damage. Because they have exposed it to that risk, they have at least a prima facie obligation to defend it; further, they may not transfer their parental duties to another caretaker simply as a matter of choice, for it is the child who holds the claim against both mother and father, and it cannot release them.

In our final section we develop this view by defending it against objection and considering its implications for cases other than surrogacy where the strands of motherhood part. Before that, we show how a causal perspective on parental obligation coheres more comfortably with prominent themes in feminist ethics than more permissive accounts.

II

A causal perspective on parental obligation renders surrogate motherhood morally dubious—certainly a position consistent with much feminist analysis of the issue—but it may not be immediately clear that it does so on feminist grounds. The stress, after all, seems more on a putative right of a child to both her parents' care, than on considerations explicitly involving the interests of women. Christine Sistare has written that a "fundamental moral issue in the surrogacy debate is the nature and extent of women's freedom: their freedom to control their bodies, their lives, their reproductive powers, and to determine the social use of those reproductive capacities." . . . She goes on to claim that "the question which ought primarily to occupy us, therefore, is this: is there sufficient justification for society to deny to adult women the disposition of their reproductive capacities according to their own desires?"

The question Sistare raises is certainly important. But as we see it, her theoretical reliance on liberal presuppositions not only obscures the significance of the connection between parent and child, it also distorts the goal of women's autonomy by offering a crucially one-sided view of the way in which women's freedom is threatened by surrogacy.

Recent work by Christine Overall suggests two ways in which women's control over their lives is impaired by surrogacy. Overall examines models that are frequently used in thinking about surrogacy—the free market model and the prostitution model—and comes to the conclusion that neither is adequate, because both see surrogacy as a job when in fact it is nothing of the kind. In her view, a job implies the selling of a service or other commodity, and it also implies that the worker has control over the work.

The first half of the definition ought to seem suspicious to academics. Embittered joking aside, there is a certain vulgarity in the attempt to commodify learning: a liberal arts institution can't readily be reduced to an "information delivery system." But surrogacy doesn't seem much like college teaching. There is no special expertise involved, nor any interest in the spiritual or intellectual growth of the person paying the fee. If anything, surrogacy is more like the selling of a service. Yet this will not do either, because the surrogate mother has little if any control over the service she is supposedly selling. Pregnancy and birth are not volitional processes; they are simply natural bodily functions she cannot help. Overall quotes Mary O'Brien's application to motherhood of Marx's distinction between the architect and the bee. The mother cannot use her skills and her imaginative vision to create the baby; "like the bee, she cannot help what she is doing."

It is this lack of autonomy over the enterprise that pushes surrogacy off the far end of the scale of alienated labor and thus distinguishes it, in Overall's mind, from prostitution. We tend to agree with her that "surrogate motherhood is no

more a job than being occupied, for a fee, is a job," but then, "being occupied, for a fee," strikes us as such an apt description of prostitution that we wonder if there mightn't be closer parallels between the two than Overall allows. The prostitute, like the bee, is certainly exercising a natural bodily function, and like the bee she has little autonomy with regard to the act. While there can be an art to erotic activity, it is more often practiced by experienced lovers than by a hooker turning twenty tricks a night. The hooker is renting out her body much as another might rent out a room; she has only slightly more control than the room does over what goes on in there.

If prostitutes and surrogate mothers both resemble the bee more than the architect in the nonvolitional nature of the "jobs" themselves, they also lack control over another aspect of the proceedings, namely, the agreements they make with their clients. As the prostitutes have pimps to set the terms of employment, so the surrogate mothers have their clients' lawyers. Overall directs us to the work of Susan Ince, who has found that surrogate contracts are usually written to favor the contracting father. Acting from a postion of relative wealth, he hires a lawyer to assure the preeminence of his interests over not only the surrogate but also his infertile wife, whose consent is not typically required. It is the father to whom the baby must be delivered, and the primary concern of the contract is to "make certain the child has the sperm and name of the buyer."

But we don't suppose that any of this is going to impress Sistare—nor should it, given her assumptions. Supposing there were a well-regulated system of surrogate motherhood—one free of coercion, with legally enforced safeguards built in for the surrogate that set conditions of service that were highly to her advantage. Wouldn't such a system allow women new ways to profit from their abilities, while speaking to the deep needs of those who chose to employ them—including women who wish to be mothers, but who cannot themselves give birth? Aren't Overall's concerns about surrogacy's not being a job beside the point? Women's bodies are their property, and if surrogates are *rentiers* rather than workers, fine: our society allows one to execute contracts to rent property, as well as to render service. Wouldn't

Sistare be absolutely right in seeing argument against participation in such an arrangement—still more, argument for making it illegal—as condescending and disrespectful to mature adult women?

Embedded in questions of this sort are the classical liberal values of freedom, self-fulfillment, individual dignity, and the equality of opportunity to pursue one's own interests. These interests are to be defined by the individual, because traditional liberal theory is skeptical regarding the justifiability of establishing political institutions that promote any specific conception of human good.

Now, not all feminists look askance at such skepticism, but it is certainly a rich and powerful theme in much of their thinking. Alison Jaggar, for example, has pointed out a serious problem with liberalism's epistemic posture, which she sees as resulting, at least in part, from "normative dualism," her phrase for the view that "what is especially valuable about human beings is their 'mental' capacity for rationality." In concentrating on the rationality of our social interaction, in the focus on consensual models such as social contract theory, we have overlooked human biology. "No adequate philosophical theory of human need can ignore the facts of biology: our common need for air, water, food, warmth, etc. Far from being irrelevant to political philosophy, these facts must form its starting point."

Instead of starting with the facts of human biology, liberal theory has started with "abstract individualism"—a model of autonomous, self-interested entities interacting contractually in pursuit of their own goods. These individuals, untouched by any particular language, culture, or socialization, seem woefully inadequate to the facts of biological existence.

Feminists have perhaps all the more readily seen the shortcomings of abstract individualism in that the abstract individual looked so little like a woman or a child. There is something distinctly hairy-chested about Hobbes's state of nature, about the social contract, about revealed preference theory, about the conception of equality that accords to every rational individual equal rights regardless of gender, economic class, race or age. As Virginia Held remarks, "It stretches credulity even further than most philosophers can tolerate to imagine babies as little rational calculators contracting with their mothers for care."

Sistare does not deny that the kind of individual autonomy on which she centers has been associated with patriarchal structures of thought. She is, however, confident that the association can be dissolved, claiming that "the admittedly real connections of such phenomena and values are historically contingent." But, as Cheshire Calhoun has recently pointed out, patriarchal systems of thought such as liberal individualism, or that version of it that serves as Calhoun's example—the "justice perspective" in ethics—have causal as well as logical implications: women and children can perhaps be accommodated within such systems in principle, but in fact, they tend to inculcate a "moral ideology" that blinds us to morally important features of situations—especially to those involving women and children.

As Held considers the drawbacks to the contractual "economic man" model of classical liberal theory, she reaches a conclusion that is shared by many feminists:

> At some point contracts must be embedded in social relations that are noncontractual. . . . Although there may be some limited domains in which rational contracts are the appropriate form of social relations, as a foundation for the fundamental ties which ought to bind human beings together, they are clearly inadequate.

The contractual model, Jaggar argues, is incapable of providing a "substantive conception of the good life and a way of identifying genuine human needs."

In the context of surrogacy, contractual models are inappropriate because they tend to leave out the interests of infants, who are not contracting parties. They also distort an important feature of human agency: the freedom to do as we ought. This is not, of course, the kind of freedom that we usually associate with "rational contractors" in pursuit of their own good. It is not egoistic or acquisitive; it is not part of the ideology we naturally associate with the occupants of Hobbes's state of nature. But it is morally significant all the same, and surrogacy contracts are incompatible with it. The most meticulously worded contract Sistare could devise cannot protect the surrogate's freedom, not only because of current patterns of patriarchy, and not only because of the nonvolitional nature of the functioning of her body. These issues of control are serious enough, both for the surrogate and for the prostitute, but there is an even more fundamental control issue at stake for the surrogate, and the contract cannot safeguard it because its relinquishing is an essential element of the contract. This is the control over the rearing of the child. In the rest of this paper, we argue why the surrogate mother may not relinquish this control.

III

In her paper, "Begetting, Bearing, and Rearing," Onora O'Neill argues that parental obligations come from voluntary undertakings. In the case of biological parents, it is not always plain what kinds of actions or inactions count as voluntarily undertaking the parental role and its responsibilities, but for her purposes this is not crucially important, for O'Neill's central interest is in clearly elected procreation—which, of course, encompasses surrogacy. Bearers and begetters may, as she sees it, either care for the child themselves, or (leaving abortion, infanticide, and malign neglect to one side) arrange for the competent rearing of the child. Whether these alternatives are morally on a par for O'Neill is not clear.

The problem with this view is that causal responsibility—particularly when it does not result from coercion—is closely linked to moral responsibility. In choosing to give birth, parents bring about the presence of a new individual who is both extremely important and extremely needy. As they brought about these needs, parents are primarily responsible for seeing to their satisfaction. Looked at in this way, procreation is more like running someone over in one's car than like signing a contract. Where I create a vulnerability, I have at least a prima facie obligation to stand by the victim.

O'Neill sees a crucial difference between accident victims and children of unconsenting parents: however neglectful or abusive unconsenting parents are, they do not worsen their children's lives (and therefore they haven't harmed them), since, without the unintentional conception, their children wouldn't exist at all. "Worse" is a comparative judgment, and as comparisons between nonexistence and a given life are thoroughly obscure, we cannot say that the child is worse off.

Let's take this apart. In the first place, if I neglect my children, I make them worse off than they would have been had I not done so. But, as it stands, this does not seem to support a claim of special responsibility to satisfy needs; there are, presumably, any number of people who are the worse for my neglect. Yet in the case of my children, I am causally responsible for their needs, and this causal relationship is sufficient to undergird a special moral responsibility to satisfy them.

As an illustration, consider the following case: suppose a woman is infertile, and can conceive only if she takes a certain drug. Suppose, further, that one of the side-effects of the drug is that, some years after conception, the resulting child will contract a hideous disease unless it is provided with an antidote which the manufacturers are capable of supplying. Is there any doubt that they have a duty to make sure that the antidote is available? The drug didn't make the children any worse off than they would have been, but we would find it reprehensible if the manufacturers denied the child the antidote on those grounds.

Of course, unlike the hypothetical corporation, parents are sometimes incapable of supplying their children's needs. Consider the paradigm instance of "cutting motherhood in two": adoption. When a woman (or more often, a teen-aged child) decides she is unable to care for a baby and either chooses not to have an abortion, or because of her beliefs or social constraints, finds that abortion is not an option, she may bear the baby and then give it up. She is doing what she can to see to it that the baby's needs are met, and this is praiseworthy. Sara Ruddick tells the story of a woman of her acquaintance who gave her baby up for adoption, not because she was *unable* to care for it, but because she figured that the child would have a better life elsewhere than the one she could provide. Ruddick points out that this too is a gesture of care, and one which probably ought to be practiced more often. We regard it as more problematic than Ruddick, for reasons we will develop shortly. But whatever the precise motivation, adoption differs from surrogacy at least in that it is a response to an already-existing pregnancy that is somehow troublesome. Something has gone wrong; the situation has an element of the calamitous about it that calls for extraordinary measures. We don't, after all, casually remark to a friend or a neighbor, "Oh, a new baby. How nice! Are you going to keep this one or give it up for adoption?"

Another instance in which the birth-parent may not rear the child is in the aftermath of divorce. In this case the child cannot live with both its parents simultaneously (although, when feasible, joint custody allows the child participation in both parents' lives). Surrogate mothering (especially where the surrogate provides the egg) is very like a divorce in which the mother consents to give up custody of the child. But as with adoption, a salient difference is that in the aftermath of divorce, the child already exists, and the custody arrangement has come about because something has gone wrong between the parents.

A third case in which the procreative function splits off from childrearing is one we are apt to overlook because it is so familiar to us. This is the case in which one parent (almost always the father) says to the other: "All right, we'll have this baby if that's what you want, but my job is far too demanding to permit me to care for it, so you'll have to raise it." Further along the same spectrum is the case of the unwed father who disclaims any responsibility for the child he has sired, or the man whose sperm is used for Artificial Insemination by Donor.

In this last cluster of cases, the morally significant variable seems to be the consent of the other parent. The father is a scoundrel if he leaves the mother holding the baby; we certainly don't think being a parent is so contractual a matter that fathers can unilaterally absent themselves if they change their minds about whether they're "comfortable" with the commitment. On the other hand, if the mother *wants* to take full responsibility for rearing the child, why shouldn't she? Our answer should be apparent by now: it is because of the debt that the father owes *to the child*.

Setting abandonment to one side, the strands of parenthood typically come apart because the parent cannot undertake the burden of adequate care. In surrogacy cases, this is often not true. The parting does not take place because it is in the child's best interests; it is not on its behalf, but on behalf of others, that the placement is made. What the surrogate mother has done is to put herself in a position where it is extremely difficult—perhaps impossible—to ensure continued adequate care over a period of many years for her child. She has compromised her ability to discharge her obligation to the child, when there was no necessity to drive her to this extreme.

It's natural to reply that if a prospective surrogate mother takes care in the selection of her clients that she has answered this objection. But this is at least questionable. Serious disagreements on what constitutes appropriate treatment of children often break out between adults who have had a great deal of opportunity to get to know one another over a period of years. It is not uncommon, for instance, for divorced women who share the custody of children with ex-spouses to find that their conception of proper care progressively and seriously diverges from their former partners as time goes on—even if they have known their spouses intimately for years, and reared the children with them for long periods. It seems unlikely that a surrogate mother could get to know the prospective parents as intimately as she knows her ex-spouse.

Besides, the point isn't whether someone else would do as good a job; it's that it's *her* job—and his. A parent on the scene is in a position to continually monitor her own efforts with respect to the child's well-being. She cannot do this for anyone else, especially if she removes herself from daily involvement in the child's life. Her relationship to the agency of others is categorically different from her relationship to her own agency. She can at best *predict* that another person will meet the child's needs; she herself is the only person she can bring to *perform* the required services. To engineer a situation in which the biological father can discharge his responsibility daily, but the mother cannot, is to put her under an obligation to the child that she does not intend to meet. Apart from making deceitful promises to Nazis, there would seem to be few cases where we can legitimately act in such bad faith.

The job falls on those who created the vulnerability, and if this is a social decision that could have been made otherwise, it is not so much a decision about parents and children as it is about something more fundamental: the moral link between cause and culpability. If we are right, it follows that sperm donation too is ethically dubious, and that divorced parents may have a duty to do what they can to stay in close contact with their children. On the other hand, it might be quite all right for a surrogate mother to join the household of an infertile couple and participate, along with the couple, in the upbringing of the child she bears for them. But that would be surrogate motherhood of a different kind. In its typical form, surrogacy seems to us to threaten important ideals and duties that bind us together. The assumptions that underlie the practice seem to hold an impoverished view of the full significance of women's freedom, and an inadequate recognition of the child's moral stake in the matter.

Study Questions on Hilde and James Lindemann Nelson

1. Are you persuaded by the Nelsons' argument that serving as a surrogate mother is morally wrong? Why or why not? Does it make a difference whose egg it is?
2. In your view, how should custodial decisions be made after a divorce? Should children remain with their biological parents rather than their stepparents? How does your answer apply to the various forms of surrogacy?
3. A woman gives up a child for adoption, on the grounds that the child will receive better care from others. A man agrees to impregnate a woman who desires a child, on the condition that he have no responsibility for the child's upbringing. Explain the Nelsons' evaluation of these decisions. Do you agree with them, and why?
4. What is the implication of the Nelsons' argument for other issues in reproductive ethics—for example, abortion?

For Further Reading

Abrams, Natalie, and Michael D. Bruckner, eds. *Medical Ethics.* Cambridge, Mass.: MIT Press, 1983. Secs. 88–99. Abortion, Genetic Counselling, and Reproductive Technologies.

Adritti, Rita, Renata Duelli Klein, and Shirley Minden, eds. *Test-Tube Women.* London: Pandora Press, 1984.

Arras, John, and Robert Hunt, eds. *Ethical Issues in Modern Medicine.* 2nd ed. Palo Alto, Calif.: Mayfield, 1983. Pts. II and V. Abortion and Human Genetics.

"Baby, It's You, and You, and You . . . Renegade Scientists Say They Are Ready to Start Applying the Technology of Cloning to Human Beings." *Time,* 157, no. 7 (February 19, 2001), 46ff. Available on InfoTrac® College Edition.

Brody, Baruch. *Abortion and the Sanctity of Human Life.* (Cambridge, Mass.: MIT Press, 1975.

Brown, Harold O. J. et al. "Contraception: A Symposium." *First Things,* no. 88 (December 1998), 17–29.

Callahan, Daniel, ed. *The Catholic Case for Contraception.* London: Collier-Macmillan, 1969. Contains Paul VI, *Humanae Vitae* (1968), and the majority and minority commission reports that preceded it.

Callahan, Sidney. "Abortion and the Sexual Agenda." *Commonweal* (April 25, 1986).

Campbell, Courtney et al. "Abortion: Searching for Common Ground." *Hastings Center Report,* 19 (July/August, 1989), 22–37.

Cohen, Marshall, Thomas Nagel, and Thomas Scanlon, eds. *The Rights and Wrongs of Abortion.* Princeton, N.J.: Princeton University Press, 1974.

Congregation for the Doctrine of the Faith. "Instruction on Respect for Human Life in Its Origin" (1984). In Thomas A. Shannon, ed., *Bioethics,* 3rd ed. Mahauwak, N.J.: Paulist Press, 1987. Pp. 590–620.

Corea, Gina. *The Mother Machine.* New York: Harper & Row, 1985.

Curran, Charles, ed. *Contraception: Authority and Dissent.* New York: Herder & Herder, 1969.

Denes, Magda. "Performing Abortions." *Commentary* (October 1976).

Devine, Philip E. *The Ethics of Homicide.* Ithaca, N.Y.: Cornell University Press, 1978. Paperback edition; Notre Dame, Ind.: Notre Dame University Press, 1990.

D'Sousa, Dinesh. "Staying Human: The Danger of Techno-utopia." *National Review,* 53, no. 1 (January 22, 2001). Available on InfoTrac® College Edition.

Ely, John Hart. "The Wages of Crying Wolf." *Yale Law Journal,* 82 (1973), 923–1947. A critique of *Roe v. Wade.*

Evans, Debra. *Without Moral Limits.* Westchester, Ill.: Crossway, 1989. Similar to Corea, but from a Christian perspective.

Feinberg, Joel. *The Problem of Abortion.* 2nd edition. Belmont, Calif.: Wadsworth, 1984.

Ford, John C., S. J. et al. *The Teaching of "Humanae Vitae."* San Francisco: Ignatius, 1988.

Ford, Norman M., S.N.D. *When Did I Begin?* Cambridge: Cambridge University Press, 1988.

Glover, Jonathan et al. *Reproductive Technologies.* DeKalb, Ill.: Northern Illinois University Press, 1989.

Greer, Germain. *Sex and Destiny.* New York: Harper & Row, 1984.

Grisez, Germain. *Abortion.* New York: Corpus, 1970.

_____. *Contraception and the Natural Law.* Milwaukee, Wisc.: Bruce, 1964.

_____. "When Do People Begin?" In Seamus J. Heaney, ed., *Abortion: A New Generation of Catholic Responses.* Braintree, Mass.: Pope John Center, 1992.

Griswold v. Connecticut, 381 U.S. 479 (1965). Recognizing a constitutional right to practice contraception.

Hellegers, Andre. "Fetal Development." *Theological Studies,* 30 (1970), 3–9.

Luker, Kristin. *Abortion and the Politics of Motherhood.* Berkeley: University of California Press, 1984.

McGee, Glen. "Cloning, Sex, and New Kinds of Families." *The Journal of Sex Research,* 34, no. 3 (August 2000), 266ff. Available on InfoTrac® College Edition.

Noonan, John T. *Contraception.* Enlarged ed. Cambridge, Mass.: Harvard University Press, 1986.

_____, ed. *The Morality of Abortion.* Cambridge, Mass.: Harvard University Press, 1974.

O'Neill, Onora, and William Ruddick, eds. *Having Children: Philosophical and Legal Perspectives.* New York: Oxford University Press, 1979.

Pluhar, Werner. "Abortion and Simple Consciousness." *Journal of Philosophy,* 24 (1977), 159–172.

Pojman, Louis P., and Francis Beckwith, eds. *The Abortion Controversy 25 Years after Roe v. Wade.* Belmont, Calif.: Wadsworth, 1998.

Pollit, Katha. "The Strange Case of Baby M." In Alison M. Jaggar and Paula S. Rothenberg, eds., *Feminist Frameworks,* 3rd edition. New York: McGraw-Hill, 1993. Pp. 385–394.

Ramsey, Paul. *Fabricated Man.* New Haven, Conn.: Yale University Press, 1970.

Reardon, David C. *Aborted Women: Silent No More.* Chicago: Loyola University Press, 1987.

Riyali, Norbert. "Words and Contraception." *America,* 183, no. 8 (September 23, 2000), 8ff. Available on InfoTrac® College Edition.

Roe v. Wade, 410 U.S. 179 (1973). Recognizing a constitutional right to abortion. Other important cases include *Webster v. Reproductive Health Services* (1989), and *Planned Parenthood v. Casey* (1992).

Sartre, Jean-Paul. *The Age of Reason.* Eric Sutton, trans. New York: Vintage, 1992. Novel about an undesired pregnancy.

Schwartz, Stephen S., and Tacelli, R. D. "Abortion and Some Philosophers." *Public Affairs Quarterly,* 3 (1989), 81ff.

Shalit, Wendy. "Whose Choice?" *National Review,* 50, no. 9 (May 18, 1998), 3ff. Available on InfoTrac® College Edition.

Smith, Janet. *Why Humanae Vitae Is Right.* San Francisco: Ignatius, 1993.

Stith, Richard. "A Critique of Abortion Rights." *Democracy* (Fall 1983), 60–70.

_____. "Nominal Babies." *First Things,* no. 90 (February, 1999), 16–20.

Sumner, L. W. *Abortion and Moral Theory.* Princeton, N.J.: Princeton University Press, 1981.

Tiger, Lionel. "The Decline of Males." *Society,* 27, no. 2 (January 2000), 6ff. Available on InfoTrac® College Edition.

Tooley, Michael. *Abortion and Infanticide.* Oxford: Clarendon Press, 1983.

Warren, Mary Anne. "On the Moral and Legal Status of Abortion." *Monist,* 57 (1973), 43–61.

Wilcox, John T. "Nature as Demonic in Thomson's Defense of Abortion." *New Scholasticism,* 73 (Autumn 1989), 463–484.

Will, George F. "Life and Death at Princeton." *Newsweek,* 134, no. 11 (September 13, 1999), 80. Available on InfoTrac® College Edition.

INFOTRAC COLLEGE EDITION To learn more about the topics from this chapter, you can use the following words to conduct an electronic search on InfoTrac College Edition, an online library of journals. Here you will find a multitude of articles from various sources and perspectives: *www.infotrac-college.com/wadsworth/access.html*

Abortion and Fathers	*Humanae Vitae*
Assisted Reproduction	Pro-Choice
Cloning	Pro-Life
Contraception	Reproductive Rights
Genetic Counselling	Reproductive Technology

Web Sites

Assisted Reproduction Foundation
http://www.reproduction.org.

Contraception Information Center
http://www.amaassn. org/special/contra/contra/htm

Feminists for Life of America
http://www.feministsforlife.org

Humanae Vitae (On the Regulation of Birth). 1968
http://www.ncbusc.org/prolife/tdocs/humanaevitae.htm

Moreland. J. P., and Scott Rae. "Body and Soul"
http:/gospel.com.net/title/tool/1577.html

NARAL: Reproductive Freedom and Choice
http://www.naral.org

NYM Ministries: Abortion Affects Fathers, Too
http://www.nyinministries.org/tnflloc.html

Pro-choice Views
http://prochoice.about.com.newsissues/prochoice.mbody.htm

Pro-life: The Ultimate Resource Center
http://www.prolife.info.org/

Resta, Robert G. "Coping with the Human Impact of Genetic Diseases"
http://www.accessexcellence. com/AE/AEC/CC/counselling_background.html

Unit IV

Marriage and Family: Is the Traditional Family a Good Thing?

CONTROVERSIES OVER FAMILY POLICY generate strong feelings on all sides. This is not surprising. Such issues are deeply connected with the question of what sort of people we want the next generation to become (since it is within the family that children receive their earliest and most important socialization), and thus engage people's worldview on a deep level. Some regard the traditional family as an oppressive, patriarchal institution and wish to institute radical changes in it, while others cling to it as our main bulwark against social chaos. "Traditional family values" are invoked and attacked, often without a clear sense of what is meant. Thus it is necessary to begin by clarifying what is meant by the "traditional family." In its most central sense a family arises when a heterosexual couple produces a child. The concept has been extended to include childless married couples, and couples who have adopted children or obtained them through the use of a sperm donor or surrogate mother, and of course second marriages in which the children are genetically unrelated to one of the parents they live with. A variety of other morally important relationships develop out of this core, such as those between siblings, between aunts and uncles and their nieces and nephews, between grandparents and grandchildren, and between cousins of various degrees of closeness. Traditionalists wish to retain this core concept of family and reject suggestions that same-sex couples or group marriages, for example, be recognized as "families."

Furthermore, a great many of those who defend the "traditional family" would add the provision that a traditional family is one in which the mother has the primary, although not the sole, responsibility for homemaking and for care of the children, while the father is the primary breadwinner (although he is also expected to spend as much time with his children as his job allows). A smaller number of them would also include in their definition of the traditional family the idea that the husband is, in some sense, the "head of the family," and rightly exercises authority over his wife and children. In practice this can mean anything from titular leadership to extreme authoritarianism. The traditional family is also transgenerational. Grown children continue to have special obligations to their parents. And given that women have traditionally taken a larger share in caring for children and maintaining the home, they have also assumed a larger share of care for the elderly.

The goal in this unit is to explore what is at issue between supporters and critics of the "traditional family." Since this anthology centers on gender issues, the readings focus particularly on the traditional division of labor between the sexes in marriage and the effects this has on both women and men. Its effects on children cannot, however, be overlooked. For children are socialized into sex roles largely by modeling themselves on their parents. And children are also affected by the way their parents apportion tasks between them if this affects the amount of time each parent can spend with the children or the long-term stability of the family.

In posing the question of whether or not the traditional family should be preserved, we do not mean to imply that what we have now (the status quo) *is* the traditional family, and that the issue is whether or not to change it. Family structures are currently in flux, and patterns vary widely according to economic class, ethnic background, race, religion, and region of the country. Nor do we mean to imply that "we" (whoever that is) can just *decide* whether to eliminate it or keep it. Our power to change social institutions like marriage and family is real but limited. There are all sorts of factors that have an impact on family structure over which we have very little control—for example, changes in the global economy. And, since cultures evolve over the course of many generations, they cannot simply be imposed by those in political authority, especially in the area of marriage and family where the emotions involved are so powerful. Sexual possessiveness, women's fierce feelings of attachment to their children, and men's deep feelings about their masculinity are facts that must be acknowledged even if one would like to change them, and different emotions cannot simply be generated at will.

Nonetheless, your decisions will have an impact on what the family structure of the future will be like. You will choose whether or not to marry; and if you marry, you and your spouse must make decisions about how to apportion the duties of child care, housework, and work outside the home between you (these decisions must also be made by couples who raise children together but do not get married). Furthermore, as a voter, you will be called to make decisions about such things as the laws governing marriage and divorce, tax policies, child support allowances, publicly mandated maternity leaves, or provision of day care at state expense; and in the long run, the policies we adopt in these areas will have a significant influence on the structure and function of the family. Is the "traditional family," then, a good thing? If so, are its functions sufficiently important that it is deserving of public support (e.g., through giving tax breaks to families in which the mother stays home and cares for the children)?

Before introducing the readings, a few preliminaries are in order. These are of two sorts: (1) a cross-cultural perspective on the family; and (2) a discussion of the way in which the liberalism-communitarianism dispute described in the introduction to Unit III bears upon the current controversy over the traditional family.

Cross-Cultural Perspective. Those interested in gender issues have been tending increasingly to introduce global and cross-cultural perspectives, in part because this helps free us from unthinkingly taking the way we do things to be the natural or the only way of doing them, and opens us up to new possibilities. When one looks at family structures across cultures, one quickly discovers that assumptions taken for granted here do not hold everywhere. Differences between cultures exist on a number of levels. There are differences in the laws governing marriage, divorce, property ownership, and so on, as well as practices of a more informal sort that have profound effects on the relationship between the spouses and the status of children (e.g., conventions governing bride prices or dowries). On a more philosophical level, cultures differ in the way they think about familial bonds and about social structure generally.

One important way in which cultures differ is in how much authority or power the husband exercises over his wife and children. The range here is from egalitarian to highly patriarchal. In very patriarchal societies, married women have few legal rights (in Zimbabwe, e.g., women cannot own property in their own names), marriages are often arranged in ways that involve the man making a payment of some sort to the woman's parents for her, husbands make all the important decisions, and males are generally more highly prized, better fed, and better educated than females. The most extreme case here would be China where women and children are literally sold on the black market. European and North American cultures are clearly more toward the egalitarian end of the spectrum. Although patriarchal attitudes have not been wholly eliminated, the sorts of blatant inequalities so common in other countries would provoke virtually universal outrage here, and even extreme traditionalists in America would be regarded in many cultures as dangerous radicals whose ideas, if put into practice, would threaten the very bases of their social order. When viewed in historical and cross-cultural context, then, the parties in our current controversies over the "traditional family" have a lot more in common than is sometimes realized.

Cultures also range along a spectrum from those that are highly familial and communal to those that are more individualistic (emphasizing individual autonomy and rights over and against the claims of family and community). This is a matter of one's social philosophy—one's picture of society and the place of individuals in it. Most African societies, for example, are highly communal. People think of themselves more as members of a particular family or tribe than as independent individuals, polygamy is not uncommon, children are very highly prized, people want large families, and extended family and kinship groups are far more important than they are in North America, for example. Hindus strongly emphasize the religious and familial dimension of marriage, and arranged marriages are common. The idea that marriages should be freely contracted by the two people involved purely on the basis of their mutual feelings of love (independent of the preferences of their families) is one that would be rejected in a large number of societies. On this particular spectrum, then, customs in Europe and North America are closer to the individualistic end than to the communal/familial end. And this fact is not of merely theoretical interest. In the wake of large waves of immigration, decisions must be made about such things as whether or not to recognize the polygamous marriages of immigrants (there has been a lot of controversy over this in France lately), or how to handle cases like the one where a man from rural Iraq who had brought his family to the United States gave his 13- and 14-year-old daughters in marriage to two friends of his, aged 28 and 34, claiming that this was the practice in his culture.

Liberal and Communitarian Visions of Society. A more global perspective helps to put the debate between liberals and communitarians (see the introduction to Unit III) in perspective. Communitarians are reacting against the view of society as composed of competing individuals engaged in a race for various social goods—

a position they see as implied, if not necessarily intended, by people like Rawls. They argue that we should view it more organically as a web or network of relationships into which children are born and socialized. They believe that competitive individualism is taking a heavy toll on the most vulnerable members of our society (children and the elderly), and that we could fruitfully move more in the direction of strengthening familial and communal ties. If we keep in mind the broader spectrum that includes non-Western cultures, communitarians can be seen as trying to move us more toward the center of the spectrum.

There are, however, deep issues involved here—issues that will be explored by the selections in this unit. For familial bonds are a two-edged sword. Yes, they do hold society together, provide support for the vulnerable and a way to inculcate socially important virtues in the next generation, and they give people a sense of identity and belonging. But families can also severely limit people's freedom to define themselves, develop their own talents, and follow what they believe to be their own calling or vocation in life. The demands of being the breadwinner for a family or of being the primary caretaker for children and maintaining a home can make it difficult for the parents to develop their talents and pursue their own interests. Parents may pressure their children to adopt a particular type of career or to marry within their own ethnic group or religion, and duties to care for aging parents can constitute a very heavy burden, requiring considerable self-sacrifice. (For interesting philosophical discussions of the nature and source of grown children's obligations to their aging parents, see the essays by Jane English, Lin Yutang, and Christina Sommers in the For Further Reading section at the end of this unit.)

Preview of Selections

The selections reprinted here by Hatcher, Bartky, and Okin criticize the traditional family, focusing on its damaging effects on women, but they differ about the precise nature of the harm involved.

One of the earliest feminist criticisms of the traditional family was that developed by Simone de Beauvoir, one of the founding mothers of contemporary feminism (whose views are summarized in our selection by Donald Hatcher). She believed that traditional sex roles dehumanize women. To understand why this is so, we need to look at her underlying metaphysical assumptions about human nature—namely, her commitment to existentialism. According to the existentialists, our ability to transcend our merely biological nature and be autonomous, free, self-creating beings is the characteristic most central to our humanity. De Beauvoir believed that women are less able to develop and exercise their autonomy than men, and thus are condemned to be second-class citizens, unable to fully realize their humanity in the way men can. The problem according to her is both biological and social. Pregnancy is particularly degrading; the pregnant woman is "ensnared by nature" and feels "the immanence of her body." This stands in contrast with "the transcendence of the artisan, of the man of action." De Beauvoir hoped that new medical technologies would at last free women from the burden of pregnancy. Being a woman is more than biology, however, and de Beauvoir also argued that the bourgeois institutions of marriage and family restrict women's potential for being free, creative, and autonomous. Since her argument is at bottom a metaphysical one, the preferences of women themselves have no weight, and those who enjoy child rearing and homemaking are to be censured for having abdicated their full humanity. (For a philosophical response to de Beauvoir's criticism of traditional sex roles, see the essay by Midgley and Hughes in Unit I.)

Radical feminists offer rather different sorts of criticisms. Their central focus is on *power,* and they seek to expose the deep ways in which the traditional family maintains male dominance and female subordination. In doing so, they analyze not only economic or political institutions, but also the intimate emotional and sexual dimensions of male-female relationships in terms of how they distribute power. Sandra Lee Bartky explores the way in which women are disempowered through their emotional caregiving in marriage. Women, she argues, provide emotional sustenance to men in a way men do not provide it to women. And this pattern contributes in an important way to the construction of women as inferior in the gender hierarchy. Her basic categories are drawn from Marxist theory, and she argues that the mechanisms involved in the disempowerment of women resemble those involved in establishing the racial hierarchy that subordinates black people to white people.

Other radical feminists find the source of the subordination of women in the act of heterosexual intercourse itself, holding that it is inherently degrading to be sexually penetrated (see Dworkin in Unit II for this view). (More precisely, even homosexual penetration is degrading to the receptive partner, whereas heterosexual sex without penetration can be a worthwhile way of expressing affection.) Since heterosexual intercourse is at the heart of the traditional family, then, they naturally reject the traditional family.

Liberal feminists, finally, criticize the traditional family specifically on the grounds that it is unfair or unjust to women. The selection by Susan Moller Okin represents this strand in feminist thought. Since she develops her argument that the traditional (gender-structured) family is an unjust institution against the background of John Rawls's *Theory of Justice* and its communitarian critics, we have included short selections by Rawls and Sandel in order to set up the framework within which Okin addresses the issue.

Rawls argues here that just institutions are those that would be agreed upon by rational agents who had to decide what sort of institutions to adopt under what he calls a "veil of ignorance." Specifically, the contractors in the original position would be ignorant of their own place in society, their physical characteristics, and even their own moral and religious convictions (they would not know, e.g., whether they are atheists or religious believers). The family is a problematic institution for Rawls, since his principles of justice require that all citizens ought to enjoy equality of opportunity to become successful and attain the various social goods (like wealth, income, and power), and the existence of the family (of any sort) is in tension with this goal. Children whose families provide them with material advantages, good early moral training, and adequate emotional support will have a far better chance of success than those whose families cannot or do not provide these things.

Rawls, however, does not go so far as to recommend abolition of the family, and refrains from applying his theory of justice within the family itself (maintaining, as liberals do, a dichotomy between the public and private spheres, and regarding the contractors in the original position as "heads of households"). It is not surprising that Rawls does not submit the traditional family to scrutiny in terms of his political principles of justice. For the contractors are supposed to reason about social institutions under a veil of ignorance about their personal conception of "the good life." But since the family functions to educate and form the next generation, we cannot decide between competing sorts of family structures without a conception of what sort of people we want our children to become. Attempts have been made to defend something resembling the family along Rawlsian lines (see, e.g., Jeffrey Blustein, listed in the For Further Reading section of this unit), but they necessarily assume that certain character traits such as autonomy or the capacity to form intimate relationships are good.

Michael Sandel, the leading communitarian critic of Rawls, challenges the idea that justice is the highest virtue, and argues that the virtues obtainable by families (at their best) are higher or better than mere justice (and thus agrees with Rawls against Okin in allowing for a private space immune to the principles of liberal justice). Justice, he believes, is called for in situations of scarcity and conflict of interest, but given that the family is a "solidaristic" association (i.e., one in which each of the members has an interest in the interests of the other), emphasizing questions of justice can actually cause a decline in the moral character of family life.

Okin argues that Sandel's picture of the traditional family is unrealistic; conflicts of interest among family members can be real and deep. Against Rawls, she argues that it is necessary to scrutinize the traditional family and its internal structure to be sure that it is a just institution. Supposing that you did not know whether you were a man or a woman (i.e., under a "veil of ignorance" about your sex), would you choose the traditional family as an institution or not? Her answer, articulated in the selection from *Justice, Gender and the Family,* is "no." The traditional division of labor in which women assume a larger share of homemaking and child rearing is unjust, she argues, because: (1) given that in the traditional family the mother is primarily responsible for homemaking and child care, *and* that so many mothers now work outside the home also, women carry a double burden that exhausts them and disadvantages them in their careers; and (2) the economic dependence of the traditional wife (exacerbated by the loss of earning power resulting from her being out of the workforce or working part-time while her children are little) renders her vulnerable to domination and even abuse by her husband, and leaves her impoverished and unable to provide for herself and her children in the event of divorce. Okin therefore advocates important changes in tax policies, divorce law, and education in order to discourage the gender-structured family.

The remaining authors in this unit defend the traditional family against various criticisms and give reasons why they think we ought to support it.

Phyllis Schlafly represents a strong traditionalist view, arguing that older forms of family are in the best interests of women as well as of men. Women, she believes, have a natural need to care for others. Therefore they find raising children and maintaining a home fulfilling rather than alienating. The fact that they are not proportionally represented in positions of economic and political power is, she argues, a result of their preference for the domestic life and an unwillingness to make the sorts of sacrifices of one's familial life that attaining such positions requires. In any case, most of the jobs men do are no more fulfilling than housework and child care. A wife's cheerful disposition and her ability to make her husband feel appreciated and admired are the pillars of a happy marriage. Activities outside the home, including a healthy involvement in community service, will increase a woman's sense of worth, keep her from being dependent on her husband in an unhealthy way, and increase her husband's respect for her.

Jean Bethke Elshtain represents a communitarian response to those feminists who reject the traditional family (she herself can be regarded as representing one kind of feminism; we will examine the question of the meaning of "feminism" in the next unit). She believes that the interests of women are ill-served by attacking the institutions that protect both them and their children. She provides several additional arguments in favor of the (more or less) traditional family. It is, she argues, important to protect the private realm against encroachment by the state, since the traditional family shelters the weak and vulnerable in our society, teaches its members altruism, and provides a place where people are valued just because they are one's children, sisters, grandparents, and so on, and not for the functions they can perform. It therefore resists the relentless pressure of capitalism to turn everything into a commodity, and helps preserve democracy by providing a buffer between the isolated individual and the massive power of the state.

Sylvia Hewlett addresses the problem of the double burden carried by working mothers, but in a way that brings to center stage the needs of children. Failure to consider the interests of children is particularly disastrous at this time, Hewlett argues, since all the indications show that our children are significantly worse off than their parents were at their age (and worse off than children in other leading industrial nations)—financially, emotionally, physically, and educationally. Our private choices to pursue self-fulfillment at all costs and our public decisions about resource allocation have taken a very heavy toll on the weakest and most vulnerable members of our society—namely, children.

Like Okin, Hewlett is concerned about the conflict between women's roles as mothers and their participation in the workforce, but she does not share Okin's commitment to promoting the minimization of gender. She argues that we should follow the lead of European feminists and press for structural changes in the workplace and for governmental policies that make life easier for working parents of small children (leaving it up to the parents to decide how to allocate child-care responsibilities between them). Mandating lengthy paid maternity leaves without loss of seniority, requiring employers to allow parents of small children to work part-time, encouraging job-sharing and flexible work hours for parents, on-site child care provided by employers, and even outright grants of money to help those raising small children are all measures currently in place in many European countries, and Americans, Hewlett argues, must adopt some such policies if our children's need for stable families and the loving attention of both their parents is to be met. Such policies are also beneficial to women, she argues, because they would lighten the double burden and enable women to be mothers without getting completely off track in their careers.

Questions for Reflection

1. What sort of family life would you like to have and why?
2. What sort of family life is best for children, and for the larger society (making for a productive workforce, for example)?
3. If there are conflicts between your answers to questions 1 and 2, how might they be resolved?

4. Do you think that the government should step in to help parents of small children by giving them tax breaks (or other financial assistance), by directly providing or at least subsidizing day-care centers, or by mandating changes in workplace policies in order to accommodate the needs of parents? Would such policies be unfair to those adults who do not have small children?

5. When companies provide special assistance to parents—in the form of parental leaves or "mommy track" jobs—women elect to take advantage of that assistance far more often than men, even when men are equally eligible for such programs. Thus it has been argued that such policies should not be instituted because they tend to reinforce traditional sex roles. What do you think about this?

6. Do you think it is important that children be brought up with two parents of opposite sexes, or do you think that same-sex couples could function equally well as parents?

7. In light of your own experience and that of your family and friends, what sort of effect does divorce have on children? If you think it is harmful, what, if anything, do you think ought to be done about this?

8. Do you think it is better for children if at least one of their parents does not work full-time? If so, is this attainable under modern economic conditions?

9. During the 1950s, the supposed heyday of the nuclear or traditional family, there was a great deal of child abuse, including father-daughter incest. How does this consideration affect your answer to the question of what sort of family structure is good for children?

10. What was arguably the *real* traditional family was transgenerational and involved aunts and uncles, and grandmothers and grandfathers, as well as mothers and fathers, in the care of children (see Juli Loesch Wiley's article in Unit V). How does this affect your answer to the last question?

11. Should all associations that have claimed the title count as "families"? How about group "marriages"? How about stable homosexual relationships?

Glossary

absentee absent when required (for example, parents who are not home when their young children return from school).

animus dominandi a deeply entrenched need to dominate.

attendant on an airline, stewardess or steward.

basic structure of society (Rawls) those institutions evaluated from the standpoint of a theory of social justice such as that of Rawls.

career sequencing ability to shape one's career to one's familial responsibilities. For example, the "mommy track" option, which enables men and women having primary responsibility for the care of small children to postpone tenure and partnership decisions.

caregiver one person entrusted with attending to the needs of another.

circumstances of justice (Rawls) the conditions that engage the virtue of justice. *Objective* circumstances include moderate scarcity; *subjective* circumstances include lack of interest in one another's interests.

commodity good produced for sale.

communitarianism a social philosophy emphasizing bonds among human beings, usually contrasted with liberalism.

consciousness-raising groups a practice, common among feminists, especially in the late 1970s. They were designed to get participants to see that what they thought were their own personal problems were part of broader patterns of oppression affecting women as a group.

cross-cultural involving the comparison of the practices of different societies (for example, China and the United States).

custodial parent parent having primary responsibility for the care of children after a separation or divorce.

cybernetic pervaded by computer technology.

deontological asserting that obligation is prior to, or independent of, value.

erotic see *Eros* in the Glossary for Unit II.

existentialism philosophy emphasizing the human capacity for free choice.

fraternity brotherhood, one of the ideas of the French Revolution. More often called *community* so as to include women.

Gemeinshschaft opposed to *Gesselschaft*, community characterized by shared values and interest in one another's interests.

gender-structured organized according to roles defined by gender (for example, those of husband and wife).

head of household one member of a family, usually the husband and father, taken as representing the family in the public realm.

humanist taking into account the interests of all human beings (in this context, men, women, and children).

immanence confinement or presence within existing structures.

incommensurability incapable of being measured on a common scale.

individualism emphasizing the rights and needs of the isolated individual. Opposed to *corporate*.

innate present in an infant at birth, at least as a potentiality.

latchkey kids children whose parents are not present when they return from school.

legitimation crisis loss of authority by all of the institutions of our society, including the family.

liberalism political tradition that conceptualizes social life in terms of a contract among independent individuals.

love crisis crisis in intimate relationships including marriage.

maternal instinct real or supposed innate disposition of women to care for children and other small and helpless creatures.

metaphysical cannibalism a need to consume the other, grounded in the human nature (according to radical feminists, in the nature of men).

National Organization for Women (NOW) the leading feminist association, founded to combat sex discrimination during the Civil Rights era.

nurturance what is provided by a caregiver.

original position the imagined situation in which we decide upon principles of justice.

other the other human being in his or her differences. Also used of death, madness, and the unconscious by some European thinkers.

politics of displacement a form of politics that transfers discontents arising in the private sphere into the public sphere, and vice versa.

Positive Woman woman who affirms her identity as a woman, both biological and social.

primary goods things all members of a society are presumed to want, such as wealth.

principles of justice (Rawls) (1) each person is entitled to the greatest possible liberty, consistent with like liberty for all; (2) inequalities are legitimate only insofar as they benefit the worst-off.

private sector business.

recognition acknowledging the other as a having a perspective and values as legitimate as one's own.

reflective equilibrium (Rawls) reaching moral conclusions after a process of testing abstract theories against concrete moral convictions, and concrete moral convictions against abstract theories.

reflexive referring back to itself.

resource deficit failure to invest public money (in our children, for example).

self-regarding affecting only oneself.

solidaristic an association in which each party has an interest in the interests of the others.

sovereignty absolute political rule.

status accord voluntary compliance with the needs, wishes, or interests of the other, thereby according him or her extremely high status.

subjectivity pertaining to the individual person and his or her particular perspective, feelings, beliefs, and desires. Usually contrasted with *objectivity.*

suttee a Hindu religious practice in which a widow flings herself on her late husband's funeral pyre.

time deficit decline in the amount of time spent (on child care, for example).

titular in name only.

traditional family values slogan for the defense of the traditional family against various real or supposed threats.

transcendence capacity to step outside existing structures. Traditionally ascribed to God.

vassal subordinate within a feudal system.

veil of ignorance (Rawls) a situation in which we pretend not to know either our race, sex, talents, and so on—or our metaphysical and religious beliefs—in order to deliberate about the principles of justice.

visitation right of a noncustodial parent to have access to his or her children on selected occasions.

women's liberation early (1970s) feminism, characterized by extreme, vaguely Marxist rhetoric. Women's liberationists also saw a close analogy between racial and sexual oppression.

Existential Ethics and Why It's Immoral to Be a Housewife

DONALD L. HATCHER

Summarizing arguments made by Simone de Beauvoir, Donald Hatcher argues that it is immoral for women to choose to be housewives and mothers. De Beauvoir believed that women, as humans, desire freedom, meaningful labor, and sexual pleasure—which marriage, housework, and motherhood ensure that they seldom obtain. Since human freedom is the foundation of all values, this means that marriage as traditionally understood is an immoral institution. Moreover (as Sartre said in "Existentialism Is a Humanism"), man in his choices is responsible for all men. Hence it is immoral to choose to participate in an immoral institution like traditional marriage.

FOR MOST FEMINISTS, it is acceptable to criticize the institution of marriage, but it is quite another to go on and claim that it is immoral for women to choose to be housewives and mothers. Nonetheless, this position is implied in Simone de Beauvoir's early work, *The Second Sex,* and is repeated in her 1975 interview with Betty Friedan. She says, "No woman should be authorized to stay at home and raise children. . . . Women should not have that choice. . . ."

More than any other, this position sets Beauvoir apart from liberal feminists who believe that women's liberation means simply giving women a choice as to what sort of life they want to lead. Naturally, Beauvoir's position is unappealing to housewives who, at the same time, claim to be "feminists." For reasonable persons, however, whether the position is a popular one, or not, should not be the question. Rather, the concern should be whether Beauvoir's reasoning in support

From Journal of Value Inquiry, 23 *(1989): 59–68. Reprinted with kind permission of Kluwer Academic Publishers.*

of her conclusion is sound or not. If it is, those who call themselves "feminists" should no longer endorse those immoral women who choose to be housewives and mothers.

Unfortunately while Beauvoir's position is clear, it is not without apparent philosophical difficulties. First, it might appear that as a thinker who draws heavily on Sartrean existentialism with its emphasis on the value of human freedom, her position to limit women's choices is contradictory. I believe, however, that if one accepts her analysis of marriage, housework, and motherhood as given in *The Second Sex,* her conclusion that on moral grounds women should be criticized for choosing to be housewives/mothers is quite defensible. In other words, it is indeed immoral for women to choose to be housewives. Let us examine her arguments.

In *The Second Sex,* her line of reasoning is first to establish that it is for the most part imprudent for women to choose to be housewives and mothers. This is not enough, however, to show the choice is immoral, unless of course one is a strict Kantian. This is because prudentiality deals only with one's self-interest. To be criticized on moral grounds, the choice must be shown to harm other women. However, prudentiality and morality are related because as the choice harms individual women, so it ultimately harms women as a class.

Beauvoir's arguments against the prudentiality of choosing to be a housewife grow out of her view of human nature. She begins *The Second Sex* by pointing out that women, like all humans, have certain natural desires. Given these desires, prudential choices are those which lead to their satisfaction. Typically, women find themselves in social situations where marriage and motherhood at least appear to be their most prudent choices. Unfortunately, in most instances, once this choice has been made, women find that their desires are far from being satisfied. Hence, the prudentiality of the choice is questionable.

Central to her view of human nature is the innate desire for humans to dominate both the environment and other persons. This desire for sovereignty disposes all persons to try to subjugate others or turn them into what she calls the *other.* This innate disposition is "a fundamental category of human thought"; and she calls it "the imperialism of human consciousness."

The desire takes on many forms. If the subject is in a state of nature, the desire to subjugate the other might manifest itself in an open battle between persons, a kind of Hobbesian "war of all against all." The struggle may either remain a fight to the death or, if one of the parties gives up, it may result in a master-slave relationship, where one party, out of fear of death, is forced to recognize the sovereignty of the other.

In civil society the struggle is usually more subtle or "civilized." For men, it is often couched in economic terms where the members of the upper class try to command the respect of the poor by virtue of their wealth and economic power. Social status or economic power replace brute force.

Women, typically being denied access to the world of work, must use other means to gain recognition and control. According to Beauvoir, they often emphasize their beauty or seductiveness as a way of controlling others (especially men). Once women recognize their beauty (and hence power) is relatively short-lived, they see marriage and motherhood as ways of gaining both economic power and social recognition. This is because in most societies, motherhood has been seen as an especially hallowed role for women. Marriage appears to be a way to gain recognition because the wives of prominent males are able vicariously to share in the prominence.

Secondly, humans desire self-realization or fulfillment, and like Marx, Beauvoir believes this can be accomplished only through meaningful and creative labor. Apart from such labor, she says, a human is nothing. Meaningful labor, however, should not be confused with mere repetition. "Man's design," she says, "is not to repeat himself in time; it is to take control of the instant and mold the future." It is to engage in freely chosen projects which lead to a life of *transcendence* as opposed to immanence. Women, however, having been denied access to the working world and the creativity that is possible there, see choosing to be housewives/mothers as a means to creative and meaningful labor.

Finally, while critical of the Freudian tradition in psychology, Beauvoir believes that humans desire to be desired sexually and to attain sexual fulfillment. To be desired sexually, as we have seen, is a way of attaining sovereignty over the person who desires. And, to desire sexual pleasure is simply natural to the species.

Traditionally, while men were allowed to sow their wild oats, sexual relations for women were only condoned within the institution of marriage. Given the problems of pregnancy, venereal disease, and social condemnation for promiscuity, to seek sexual satisfaction outside of marriage was very risky for women. Hence, again women see marriage as the most prudential means of satisfying their sexual desires.

Hence, Beauvoir believes women, as humans, desire freedom (including the sovereignty, social recognition, and the economic wealth necessary for freedom), meaningful labor, and sexual pleasure. Traditionally, they saw marriage and motherhood as the most acceptable means to fulfilling these desires. What much of *The Second Sex* attempts to show is how marriage, housework, and motherhood ensure that these expectations are in fact seldom met. If this is the case, it is clearly not prudent for women to choose such roles. Let us examine her analyses.

According to Beauvoir, marriage tends to destroy the possibility of women becoming free sovereign subjects. Sovereignty, according to her, requires one person to become an object in relation to another who is a subject, and conversely, that the sovereign one can resist being made into an object by the other. The ability to maintain one's self as a subject requires one has some kind of power over the other person. The typical example is the relationship between a master and a slave. Masters manifest their sovereignty by the physical power they have over slaves. The slave, as other, is forced to recognize the master as a subject. How is it that males acquire sovereignty over females through marriage?

According to Beauvoir, young girls naturally desire sovereignty over their male counterparts, but lacking the necessary physical strength, they gain recognition by emphasizing their sexuality. In their struggle for dominance, young girls become experts in coquettish and flirtatious behavior. Girls emphasize their sexuality not because of nature but because other means of control, such as physical power and rationality, have been systematically thwarted in their development and education. After all, young girls may think, what do future housewives and mothers need to know of math, science, or logical self-defense?

While it may be true that at a young age sexuality is an effective means for females to control males, the question is how does marriage alter this situation? How is it that the husband becomes the subject, while the wife "becomes his vassal"?

The answer is evident when one looks at the *traditional* institution of marriage. Marriage gives the male certain rights concerning sex and establishes certain duties for the woman. As a social institution, marriage changes what began as an erotic relationship into a legal one. Rather than being seduced by the female subject who freely makes herself an object, the institution of marriage gives man the legal *right* to "take his pleasure." Conversely, the wife has an obligation to perform her "marital duties," much like the slave is obliged to submit to the will of the master. In fact the marriage ceremony itself symbolizes such a master-slave relation: the woman is "given" to the man by her father, much like a piece of property being passed from one owner to the next. As Beauvoir says, the woman has been "solemnly handed over to her husband as if to a master." The woman's control over her sexual behavior has been eliminated. Her power has been dissipated.

Secondly, according to Beauvoir, marriage destroys a woman's *sexual* power because it turns sex into an experience of *average everydayness*. The excitement and adventure of the erotic soon die after many encounters. Familiarity breeds both boredom and contempt. As the desirability of sexual relations decreases, so the power of the woman over her husband diminishes. In Beauvoir's words, after a few years of marriage, erotic adventures become "a kind of joint masturbation" based on biological need rather than erotic desire or love.

Thirdly, Beauvoir believes that while a woman's beauty was the original source of her power, both housework and pregnancy are its enemies: Pregnancy destroys her figure; housework her skin and her mind.

However, some may point out that while a woman's sexual pleasure and power over her spouse may not quite measure up to her romantic teenage dreams, at least, once safe in the fold of marriage, she has the financial security necessary for satisfying her other human desires. While such security may appear obvious, Beauvoir points out that void of outside income a married woman who is but a housewife is totally dependent upon her husband's income, and hence, his generosity. Secondly, having chosen to be a housewife, the woman lacks the training necessary to enter any adequately paid profession. In other words, lacking marketable skills, she is totally dependent upon the good-will of her husband. And, in those cases where the husband's will is not quite so good, for a woman to contemplate divorce becomes only a theoretical possibility. Void of the necessary training, the woman knows only too well that life would be very hard without her husband's financial support. And, if she already has children, her marketability as a housewife for another man is minimized.

Hence, according to Beauvoir, the traditional marriage not only destroys the sovereignty that women seek and makes sexual pleasure unlikely, but also leads to financial dependency rather than freedom. The woman who initially sought independence through marriage is in reality dependent upon her husband; she truly has become "his vassal."

Some might say, however, that while the woman may have given up her sovereignty, sexual pleasure, and financial independence, at least she has a meaningful vocation; i.e., a housekeeper/mother. Not according to Beauvoir. Rather than a meaningful vocation, housework is the epitome of stultified labor. Rather than being engaged in creative self-fulfilling acts, the housekeeper soon discovers that she is doomed to a life of mindless and repetitive activity. Cleaning the house is an endless routine with no true goal beyond the activity of maintaining the *status quo*. It is, according to Beauvoir, an endless battle against the natural forces of life. Creative projects, on the other hand, define goals beyond the present and attempt to change the world in some lasting way. The housewife though is trapped in a present which is always the same. Her days are, to quote Beauvoir, "gilded mediocrity lacking ambition and passion, aimless days infinitely repeated; life slips away towards death without ever questioning its purpose." Such an account is surely reminiscent of Marx's description of alienated labor, when he says, a person involved in alienated labor

does not fulfill himself in his work but denies himself, has a feeling of misery rather than well-being, does not develop freely his mental and physical energies but is physically exhausted and mentally debased. . . . It is not a satisfaction of a need, but only a means for satisfying other needs . . . it is not his own work but work for someone else. . . . The activity is not his own spontaneous activity.

Being, for all practical purposes, employed by her husband, like Marx's wage-laborer, the woman is denied her true human development. Her creative and rational capacities are stultified through the repetitive acts of cooking, cleaning, and doing the laundry.

The housewife, according to Beauvoir, is likewise alienated from her fellow human beings. Typically she works in a neighborhood with other housewives. True friendship between such women is impossible. Other housewives, according to Beauvoir, are as boring as the woman. "Their correspondence deals especially with beauty counsel, recipes for cooking, and directions for knitting." Beyond the shallowness of such relationships, Beauvoir believes that there is always a kind of competitive antagonism between housewives. Each seeks to impress the other with her possessions or her beauty. These are the signs of success in the world of the housewife. And in this battle for social esteem, each new acquisition of home or furniture by another is seen as a threat to one's relative status. A new dress which beautifies a friend also turns the friend into a competitor as a sexual object. And finally, because a housewife knows that ultimately her life is dependent upon her husband, her true allegiance is always to the person who can benefit her the most. In such a situation, true friendships become impossible.

In this a state of boredom, sexual frustration, alienation, and loneliness, many housewives decide to solve their problems by having children. For Beauvoir, as it was for Nietzsche, if a woman desires to have a child in order to make up for the emptiness in her life, as opposed to out of the creative joy of self-transcendence, she is criminal. A child is not a solution to her problems. A child cannot fulfill the mother's human needs. First, children make housework even more difficult. There are even more messes to clean up. Second, the child is not a substitute for mature rational companionship. The baby, rather than providing the needed intellectual stimulation, merely smiles and babbles. Third, a child cannot really be considered as a product of the woman's creativity. Pregnancy is a natural process which the woman undergoes. She submits "passively to her biologic fate." Both pregnancy and childbirth are animal as opposed to human functions. Human creativity, on the other hand, is to bring a preconceived idea into reality through labor. The fetus, as women with unwanted pregnancies know only too well, simply grows itself much like a parasite which has attached itself to the woman.

For all of these reasons, Beauvoir believes that it is clearly not in a woman's best interest to choose to be a housewife/mother. A woman's natural desires for freedom, meaningful labor, and sexual pleasure are seldom satisfied. She ends up bored, frustrated, dependent, and lonely. If the description is accurate, to choose to be a housewife/mother is clearly an imprudent choice and should be avoided.

It is one thing, however, to show that it is not in a woman's best interest to choose to be a traditional housewife/mother. . . . In order for Beauvoir to support her claim that women should not be given such a choice, she must show how such a choice harms others and is hence immoral.

In general, the form of argument is as follows: first we need to establish what, from Beauvoir's perspective, makes any act or institution immoral. Then, given our analysis of marriage, we can see how women choosing the role of housewife/mother fulfill this criteria.

Beauvoir tells us at the beginning of *The Second Sex* that her perspective is one of "existential ethics." She says such an ethical perspective can be built on the ontology of Sartre's *Being and Nothingness*. This relationship between her ethics and Sartre's ontology is important because in an almost Aristotelean fashion she employs Sartre's ontology to argue that humans *ought* to behave or be treated in certain ways because they *are* the kind of beings that they are.

. . . To put the matter simply, for Sartre, human consciousness is *freedom*. As freedom, consciousness must choose whatever objects of thought, actions, or values are to make up its content. Being

free, nothing can determine that consciousness choose one state of affairs over another. Now (and this is the crucial step), if freedom is the fundamental being of consciousness and nothing can determine whether consciousness should value one object or action over another, then if anything is deemed to have value, it is valuable only because it has been chosen by consciousness or is a means to an end chosen by consciousness. As Sartre says, "My freedom is the unique foundation of values. . . ."

If human freedom is the foundation of all values, then, without human freedom to posit or choose values, there would be no values. Hence, if anything at all has value, human freedom must. This is the argument which underlies Beauvoir's claim in *The Ethics of Ambiguity* that, "Freedom is the source from which all significations and all values spring; . . . The man who wants to justify his life must want freedom itself absolutely and above all else." Now if one is logically committed to value freedom, one is also logically committed to value those behaviors and institutions which protect or enhance freedom. Or conversely, if one values freedom, one is logically committed to oppose those behaviors or institutions which unduly limit or destroy human freedom. As Beauvoir says in *The Second Sex,* "We shall pass judgment on institutions according to their effectiveness in giving concrete opportunities to individuals. Hence, if an institution tends to limit the freedom of individuals, it must be opposed on moral grounds.

Now, if we are willing to accept Beauvoir's position that freedom is the ultimate value, and institutions or behaviors are immoral just to the extent that they limit an individual from freely choosing to "transcend himself, or engage in freely chosen projects," how is it that the practice of women choosing to be traditional housewives/mothers can be seen as immoral? How is it that such a choice is not only imprudent, but at the same time destroys the freedom of others? We should recall how the life of a housewife stultifies the development of a woman's human capacities; how such a life thwarts her creativity, dooms her to a vocation of alienated labor, makes sexual satisfaction difficult, and ensures her economic dependence upon her husband. Hence, such a life, limits the freedom of individual women. Treated as a class, when the majority of women make this choice, the effect then is to limit the freedom (especially in terms of economic and political power) of all women. In other words, *women as a class are and remain exploited, second-class citizens because they lack economic and political power necessary to escape oppression, and this is, to a large extent, because they choose to be housewives. . . .*

Our next question is, if the institution itself is seen as immoral, how is it that women who choose to enter into the institution are also immoral? Part of the answer to this question can be found in Sartre's essay, "Existentialism is a Humanism." In a famous quote from that essay Sartre explains that from the existentialist tradition, "Man is nothing else but who he makes himself," and that man is not only responsible for

> his own individuality, but that he is responsible for all men. . . . When we say that man chooses himself we do mean that every one of us must choose himself: but by that we also mean that choosing for himself he chooses for all men. For in effect, of all the actions a man may take in order to create himself as he wills to be, there is not one which is not creative, . . . of an image of man such as he believes he ought to be. . . . Our responsibility is thus far greater than we have supposed, for it concerns mankind as a whole. . . . I am creating a certain image of man as I would have men to be. In fashioning myself I fashion man.

What Sartre is saying is that morality not only deals with what we do directly to our fellow human beings, but also with how our choices indirectly influence others. By choosing a particular role, we are saying to the rest of humanity that this sort of activity is acceptable; we are endorsing that role to the rest of the world. Hence, in the case of a woman who chooses the role of being a housewife/mother, the woman is implicitly endorsing such a role. But by endorsing the role, the woman is also endorsing an institution which, as we have seen, is the primary cause of the continued oppression of women as a class. Through her endorsement she is perpetuating the oppressing institution. Through the endorsement, the effects are continued.

The most immediate effect of such a choice is on the minds of the woman's children. Like Plato in his *Republic,* Beauvoir believes that children learn through imitation. A mother is naturally an important role-model for her children. But when she chooses to be a housewife, both male and female children grow up believing that this is the natural role for women. In this way the oppressing institution is perpetuated through the attitudes of her children. Both male and female children believe that the "natural" role for a woman is to stay home as a housewife. The sins of the mother are passed on to the child.

One could see the situation as analogous to a black who chooses to be a slave, even though it is well known that the institution of slavery is responsible for oppressing blacks as a class. Whether or not the individual is happier being a slave or a housewife is not the question. Beauvoir claims that when the issue of class oppression is paramount, for an individual to be concerned with his or her happiness is simply selfishness. It does not matter whether a woman thinks she would be happier staying home, or even be socially more useful being supported by her husband. Because her actions endorse and perpetuate the oppressing institution, her actions are immoral. As a choice which harms others, "it is an absolute evil." The woman who makes such a choice is harming all other women, and hence, is immoral.

Hence, while Beauvoir's position on the morality of choosing to be a housewife may at first seem radical, when one understands the arguments which underlie and support her conclusion, it becomes, I believe, very difficult not to agree with her, whether we are emotionally inclined to do so or not. The reluctance of feminists to endorse her position is, however, understandable. The institution of the traditional housewife/mother has become so mystified, so much a part of our cultural heritage, that openly to oppose it on moral grounds is emotionally quite unsettling. Nonetheless, if choosing to be housewives is the primary cause of women's oppression, and one sees the oppression of women as immoral, then it is immoral to endorse and hence perpetuate the oppressing institution. It is immoral to be a housewife.

Study Questions on Donald Hatcher

1. De Beauvoir, as Hatcher explains, believes that being a housewife and mother is not only an imprudent choice for a woman, but also an immoral one. Explain how these two judgments differ and what reasons de Beauvoir gives for each of them.
2. Why does de Beauvoir believe that homemaking and child rearing cannot engage a woman's creative and rational abilities, at least as much as the sorts of jobs most men do?
3. It seems paradoxical (and perhaps even contradictory) to claim that freedom is the highest value and then, at the same time, deny women the choice to stay at home and raise children if they want to. Does Hatcher succeed in persuading you that de Beauvoir's position is coherent?
4. Like many other feminists, de Beauvoir thinks of women as a natural class, who share the same interests and need to maintain solidarity with one another. If so, what interests do you think are shared by women *as* women? How would she answer those who believe that different women might find fulfillment in different sorts of ways—some as homemakers and mothers, and some as professionals?

Feeding Egos and Tending Wounds: Deference and Disaffection in Women's Emotional Labor

SANDRA BARTKY

Sandra Bartky applies basic Marxist ideas to the family. She regards women's emotional labor as like that of workers under capitalism, in other words, as a form of exploitation. She speaks of domestic maintenance, children, sexuality, and the nurturing of both men and children as "goods" produced within heterosexual marriage, of which women receive an insufficient share. Male culture, she argues, is parasitical, feeding on the emotional strength of women without reciprocity. Women need to locate their subordination in the duties they are happy to perform and in what they thought were the innocent pleasures of everyday life.

(Male) culture was (and is) parasitical, feeding on the emotional strength of women without reciprocity.

Shulamith Firestone, *The Dialectic of Sex*

SEVERAL DOZEN BEST-SELLING BOOKS in popular psychology have appeared in recent years that detail what one writer calls the "love crisis"—what is presumed by the authors of these books to be a crisis in the intimate relationships of men and

Reprinted by permission of Routledge, Inc., part of the Taylor & Francis Group.

women. These writers, mostly women, tell a depressing tale of female dependency and male misconduct, often gross misconduct. While their characterizations of the "love crisis" differ in some respects, these accounts converge in one respect: All agree that men supply their women with far less of what in popular psychology is called "positive stroking"—the provision of emotional sustenance—than women supply in return, and all agree that this imbalance is a persistent source of female frustration.

Feminist theorists too have noted the gendered imbalance in the provision of emotional support. Ann Ferguson, for example, has maintained that men's appropriation of women's emotional labor is a species of exploitation akin in important respects to the exploitation of workers under capitalism. Ferguson posits a sphere of "sex-affective production," parallel in certain respects to commodity production in the waged sector. Four goods are produced in this system: domestic maintenance, children, nurturance (of both men and children), and sexuality.

According to Ferguson, economic domination of the household by men is analogous to capitalist ownership of the means of production. The relations of sex-affective production in a male-dominated society put women in a position of unequal exchange. Just as control of the means of production by capitalists allows them to appropriate "surplus value" from workers, i.e. the difference between the total value of the workers' output and that fraction of value produced that workers get in return—so men's privileged position in the sphere of sex-affective production allows them to appropriate "surplus nurturance" from women. So, for example, the sexual division of labor whereby women are the primary child-rearers requires a "'woman as nurturer' sex gender ideal." Girls learn "to find satisfaction in the satisfaction of others, and to place their needs second in the case of a conflict." Men, on the other hand, "learn such skills are women's work, learn to demand nurturance from women yet don't know how to nurture themselves." Women, like workers, are caught within a particular division of labor which requires that they produce more of a good—here, nurturance—than they receive in return. . . .

Let us fix with more precision the character of the emotional sustenance that women are said to provide more of to men than they receive in return. What is it, in the ideal case, to give someone "emotional support"? To support someone emotionally is to keep up his spirits, to keep him from sinking under the weight of burdens that are his to bear. To sink would be to fail to cope at all, to fall prey to paralysis or despair, in less extreme cases, to cope poorly. To give such support, then, is to tend to a person's state of mind in such a way as to make his sinking less likely; it is to offer him comfort, typically by the bandaging up of his emotional wounds or to offer him sustenance, typically by the feeding of his self-esteem. The aim of this supporting and sustaining is to produce or to maintain in the one supported and sustained a conviction of the value and importance of his own chosen projects, hence of the value and importance of his own person.

It is the particular quality of a caregiver's attention that can bolster the Other's confidence. This attention can take the form of speech, of praise, perhaps for the Other's character and accomplishments, or it can manifest itself in the articulation of a variety of verbal signals (sometimes called "conversational cheerleading") that incite him to continue speaking, hence reassuring him of the importance of what he is saying. Or such attention can be expressed nonverbally, e.g., in the forward tilt of the caregiver's body, the maintaining of eye contact, the cocking of her head to the side, the fixing of a smile upon her face.

Again, the work of emotional healing can be done verbally in a myriad of ways, from simple expressions of indignation at what the boss has said about him, to the construction of elaborate rationales that aim, by reconceptualizing them, to make his failures and disappointments less terrible; or nonverbally, in the compassionate squeezing of a hand or in a hug, in the sympathetic furrowing of a brow, or in a distressful sighing. The work of emotional repair—the tending of wounds—and the bolstering of confidence—the feeding of egos—overlap in many ways. A sustained sympathetic listening, as we have seen, conveys to the speaker the importance of what he is saying, hence the suggestion that he himself is important; beyond this, a willingness to listen in comforting, for hurts, if hurts there are, sting less when we can share them. To enter feelingly and without condescension into another's distress—a balm to the spirit indeed—is to affirm that person's worth, though an affirmation of someone's worth need not require any particular effort at emotional restoration. Affection is also a factor in the provision of emotional support. While emotional support might be forthcoming from some stranger on a train in whom I decide to confide, the forms of emotional caregiving as they have been described here are among the commonest ways we show affection, especially when the caregiving is underscored, as it is among intimates, by loving endearments. . . .

Emotional caregiving can be done as an expression of love or friendship. It can also be done for pay as part of one's job. Either way, it involves the same two elements—the feeding of egos and the nursing of wounds. But commercial caregiving can differ significantly from the deeper connections between intimates. In a detailed study of the emotional work done by flight attendants, Arlie Hochschild has given a fine account of the "commercialization of human feeling." These mostly female workers are paid to generate commercial affection for passengers: to smile steadily and to lay down around themselves an atmosphere of warmth, cheerfulness, and friendly attention. A relentless cheerfulness would be difficult enough to sustain under any circumstances, but it has become even harder with the speed-up associated with airline deregulation. Not only must the attendant's emotional care be expended on many more passengers per flight, but the passengers themselves are often stressed, feeling the effects of longer lines, lost baggage, and late flights.

Attendants must manage not only their passengers' feelings, but their own as well: They must work to "induce or suppress feeling in order to sustain the outward countenance that produces the proper state of mind in others." . . . Under such conditions, the provision of emotional service can be disempowering indeed. . . . Now one can well understand how the routine emotional work of flight attendants may become disempowering, leading as it often does to self-estrangement, an inability to identify one's own emotional states, even to drug abuse or alcoholism. But how

can the provision of affectionate regard and the sympathetic tending of psychic wounds—activities that require the exercise of such virtues as loving-kindness and compassion—be disempowering too? Surely, the opportunity to attend to the Other in these ways must be morally empowering for it gives us the chance not merely to be good by doing good, but to become morally better through the cultivation and exercise of important moral qualities. And are we not privileged, too, in being allowed entree into the deepest psychological recesses of another, in being released, if only temporarily, from the burden of isolation and loneliness that each of us must bear? The claim that women in intimacy are disempowered in their provision of emotional support to men may begin to seem not merely mistaken, but perverse. But let us look more closely. . . .

Love, affection, and the affectionate dispensing of emotional sustenance may seem to be purely private transactions that have nothing to do with the macrosocial domain of status. But this is false. Sociologist Theodore Kemper maintains that "a love relationship is one in which at least one actor gives (or is prepared to give) extremely high status to another actor." "Status accord" he defines as "the voluntary compliance with the needs, wishes or interests of the other." Now insofar as women's provision of emotional sustenance is a species of compliance with the needs, wishes and interests of men, such provision can be understood as a conferral of status, a paying of homage by the female to the male. Consider once again the bodily displays that are typical of women's intimate caregiving: the sympathetic cocking of the head; the forward inclination of the body; the frequent smiling; the urging, through appropriate vocalizations, that the man continue his recital, hence, that he may continue to commandeer the woman's time and attention. I find it suggestive that these behaviors are identical to common forms of deference display in hierarchies of status. But status is not accorded mutually: Insofar as the emotional exchanges in question are contained within a gendered division of emotional labor that does not require of men what it requires of women, our caregiving, in effect, is a collective genuflection by women to men, an affirmation of male importance that is unreciprocated. The consistent giving of what we don't get in return is a performative acknowledgement of male supremacy and thus a contribution to our own social demotion. The implications of this collective bending of the knee, however, rarely enter consciousness. The very sincerity and quality of heartfelt concern that the woman brings to her man's emotional needs serves to reinforce in her own mind the importance of his little dramas of daily life. But he receives her attention as a kind of entitlement; by failing to attend to her in the same way she attends to him, he confirms for her and, just as importantly, for himself, her inferior position in the hierarchy of gender.

Women do not expect mutual recognition from the children we nurture, especially when these children are very young, but given the companionate ideal that now holds sway, we yearn for such recognition from the men with whom we are intimate. Its withholding is painful, especially so since in the larger society it is men and not women who have the power to give or to withhold social recognition generally. Wishing that he would notice; waiting for him to ask: how familiar this is to women, how like waiting for a sovereign to notice a subject, or a rich man, a beggar. Indeed, we sometimes find ourselves begging for his attention—and few things are as disempowering as having to beg.

Women have responded in a number of ways to men's refusal of recognition. A woman may merge with her man psychologically to such an extent that she just claims as her own the joys and sorrows he narrates on occasions of caretaking. She now no longer needs to resent his indifference to her doings, for his doings have just *become* her doings. . . . To attempt such merger is to practice magic or to have a try at self hypnosis. A woman who is economically dependent on a man may find it natural to identify with his interests; in addition to the kind of merging I have described, such dependency itself feeds a tendency to overidentification. But given the generally fragile character of relationships today, the frequency of divorce, and the conflicts that arise even within ongoing relationships, prudence requires that a woman regard the coincidence of her interests with those of her partner as if they were merely temporary.

In this section, I shall argue that women run a risk that our unreciprocated caregiving may become both epistemically and ethically disempowering. In the course of her caretaking, a woman may be tempted to adopt morally questionable attitudes and standards of behavior or she may fall prey to a number of false beliefs that tend to mystify her circumstances.

First of all, there is the epistemic risk, i.e., the risk that the woman will accept uncritically "the world according to him" and that she will have corresponding difficulty in the construction of the world according to herself. How does this happen? To support and succor a person is, typically, to enter feelingly into that person's world; it is to see things from his point of view, to enter imaginatively into what he takes to be real and true. Nel Noddings expresses it well: To adopt a caring attitude toward another is to become "engrossed" in that other: it is "a displacement of interest from my own reality to the reality of the other," whereby "I set aside my temptation to analyze and to plan. I do not project; I receive the other into myself, and I see and feel with the other." Hence, caring "involves stepping out of one's own personal frame of reference into the other's." Here is merger of another sort, one not motivated by a failure of recognition but by the very character of emotional caregiving itself.

Now a woman need not merge epistemically with the man she is sustaining on every occasion of caregiving; there are times when she will reject his version of things, either to his face or to herself. But if a caregiver begins *consistently* to question the values and beliefs of the one to whom she is supposed to be offering sustenance, her caregiving will suffer. She is caught in the following paradox: If she keeps her doubts to herself, she runs the risk of developing that sense of distance and falseness that, as we saw earlier, is a major mark of alienated caregiving in commercial settings. If she articulates her doubts, again consistently, likely as not she will be seen as rejecting or even disloyal. Either way, her relationship will suffer. Professional therapists are required to develop a "hermeneutic of suspicion"; our intimates are not. We have the eminently reasonable expectation that our friends and intimates will support our struggles and share our allegiances, rejoice in our victories and mourn our defeats, in a word, that they will see things—at least the big things in our lives—as we see them. And so, an "epistemic lean" in the direction of the object of her solicitude is part of the caregiver's job—of any caregiver's job—it comes, so to speak, with the territory. . . .

There is then, a risk for women's epistemic development in our unreciprocated caregiving. What are its risks for our ethical life? . . .

To affirm a man's sense of reality is at the same time to affirm his values. "Stand by your man": What else can this mean? Recall that male psychologists Cowan and Kinder (*Smart Women, Foolish Choices*) did not ask for high ethical principles in a woman, much less for ethical strenuousness, but for "female tenderness." Tenderness requires compassion and forgiveness, clearly virtues under some circumstances and certainly excellences in a caregiver. But there are situations in which virtues such as forgiveness lead to moral blindness or outright complicity:

> Behind every great man is a woman, we say, but behind every monster there is a woman too, behind each of those countless men who stood astride their narrow worlds and crushed other human beings, causing them hideous suffering and pain. There she is in the shadows, a vague female silhouette, tenderly wiping blood from their hands.

This is vividly expressed, understandingly so, since it appears in a discussion of Teresa Stangl, wife of Fritz Stangl, Kommandant of Treblinka. Teresa, anti-Nazi and a devout Catholic, was appalled by what she knew of her husband's work; nevertheless, she maintained home and hearth as a safe harbor to which he returned when he could; she "stood behind her man." Few of us would take female tenderness to these lengths, but many of us, I suspect, have been morally silenced or morally compromised in small ways because we thought it more important to provide emotional support than to keep faith with our own principles. . . .

Disempowerment, then, may be inscribed in the more prominent features of women's unreciprocated caregiving: in the accord of status and the paying of homage; in the scarcely perceptible ethical and epistemic "leaning" into the reality of one who stands higher in the hierarchy of gender. . . .

Tending to wounds: this is a large part of what it is to provide someone with emotional support. But this means that in one standard scenario of heterosexual intimacy, the man appears to his female caregiver as vulnerable and injured. Fear and insecurity: for many men, these are the offstage companions of competitive displays of masculinity, and they are aspects of men's lives that women know well. To the woman who tends him, this fellow is not only no colossus who bestrides the world, but he may bear little resemblance to the patriarchal oppressor of feminist theory. The man may indeed belong to a more powerful caste; no matter, this isn't what he *seems* to her at the moment. . . .

. . . She may be willing to grant, this average woman, that men in general have more power than women in general. This undoubted fact is merely a fact; it is *abstract,* while the man of flesh and blood who stands before her is *concrete:* His hurts are real, his fears palpable. . . .

An apparent reversal has taken place: The man, her superior in the hierarchy of gender, now appears before the woman as the weaker before the stronger, the patient before his nurse. A source within the woman has been tapped and she feels flowing outward from herself a great power of healing and making whole. She imagines herself to be a great reservoir of restorative power. This feeling of power gives her a sense of agency and of personal efficacy that she may get nowhere else. We read that one of Kafka's mistresses, Milena Jesenka, "believed she could cure Kafka of all his ills and give him a sense of well-being simply by her presence—if only he wanted it." . . .

. . . The power a woman feels in herself to heal and sustain, on the other hand—"the power of love"—is, once again, concrete and very near: It is like a field of force emanating from within herself, a great river flowing outward from her very person. . . . And while she may well be ethically and epistemically disempowered by the care she gives, this caregiving affords her the feeling that a mighty power resides within her being.

The situation of those men in the hierarchy of gender who avail themselves of female tenderness is not thereby altered: Their superordinate position is neither abandoned, nor their male privilege relinquished. The vulnerability these men exhibit is not a prelude in any way to their loss of male privilege or to an elevation in the status of women. Similarly, the feeling that one's love is a mighty force for good in the life of the beloved doesn't make it so, as Milena Jesenka found, to her sorrow.

The *feeling* of out-flowing personal power so characteristic of the caregiving woman is quite different from the *having* of any actual power in the world. There is no doubt that this sense of personal efficacy provides some compensation for the extradomestic power women are typically denied: If one cannot be a king oneself, being a confidante of kings may be the next best thing. But just as we make a bad bargain in accepting an occasional Valentine in lieu of the sustained attention we deserve, we are ill advised to settle for a mere feeling of power, however heady and intoxicating it may be, in place of the effective power we have every right to exercise in the world. . . .

. . . Such disempowerment, like the disempowerment of the wage worker, may be described as a species of alienation, i.e., as a prohibition on the development and exercise of capacities, the exercise of which is thought essential to a fully human existence. The capacity most at risk here is not, as in the traditional Marxist theory of alienation, the capacity for creative labor; rather, it is the capacity, free from the subtle manipulation of consent, to construct an ethical and epistemic standpoint of one's own. Hence, Marxist categories of analysis—categories that have to do with exploitation, alienation, and the organization of the labor process—are by no means irrelevant to women's experience nor, as some postmodernist feminists have maintained, do they invariably distort the nature of this experience. Quite the contrary: Marxist questions, if we know how to follow out their answers, can lead us into the heart of female subjectivity. . . .

Conservatives argue, in essence, that women's caregiving may be properly exchanged for men's economic support. This view is not defensible. . . .

[E]ven in the dwindling number of cases in which men are willing and able to offer economic patronage to women, it would be difficult to show how such support could compensate a woman for the epistemic decentering, ethical damage, and general mystification that put us at risk in unreciprocated caregiving.

Recently, conservatives have been joined by a number of feminist theorists in the celebration of female nurturance. The motives of these thinkers differ: Conservatives extol traditional female virtues in the context of a larger defense of the sexual *status quo;* feminist theorists, especially those who are drawn to the idea of an "ethics of care" based on women's traditional nurturant activities, want to raise women's status by properly valuing our emotional work and to see this quality of caring extended to the formal domains of commerce and politics. I applaud these aims. However, many feminist thinkers who extol women's nurturance, like most conservatives, have just ignored the possibility that women may suffer moral damage in the doing of emotional labor. . . .

. . . In order to develop an effective politics of everyday life, we need to understand better than we do now not only the processes of personality development, but the ''micropolitics'' of our most ordinary transactions, the ways in which we inscribe and reinscribe our subjection in the fabric of the ordinary. The most prominent features and many of the subjective effects of this inscription can be grasped independently of any particular theory of personality formation. We need to locate our subordination not only in the hidden recesses of the psyche but in the duties we are happy to perform and in what we thought were the innocent pleasures of everyday life.

Study Questions on Sandra Bartky

1. Bartky applies basic Marxist categories to the family, regards men's appropriation of women's emotional labor as a species of exploitation like that of workers under capitalism, and speaks of "domestic maintainence, children, nurturance, and sexuality" as "goods" produced within heterosexual marriage. Does this way of talking make sense?

2. What does Bartky mean by "disempowerment and alienation from self"? (How is that of wives and girlfriends similar to, or different from, that of flight attendants?) What does she mean by "epistemic decentering" and "ethical damage"?

3. It would seem that a man who reveals his emotional needs and vulnerability to his wife or girlfriend is, in fact, showing himself to be weak and needy rather than asserting his higher position on the gender hierarchy. Why does Bartky disagree?

4. Would Bartky condemn Mother Teresa? Why or why not? How would she react to Schlafly's (see article in this unit) "two pillars of a happy marriage"? What would she say about "The Giving Tree" (see symposium by May in For Further Reading section in this unit)?

Justice and the Family

JOHN RAWLS

John Rawls proposes to derive principles of justice for what he calls "the basic structure of society," under a "veil of ignorance" concerning both our personal characteristics and our moral and religious beliefs. The issue of importance here is whether Rawls's principle applies to the family, and if so, how it applies (whether, e.g., it requires the abolition of the family). We take our selections from the revised edition of *A Theory of Justice* (1999), which represents Rawls's most recent thoughts on these issues.

The Subject of Justice

MANY DIFFERENT KINDS OF THINGS are said to be just and unjust: not only laws, institutions, and social systems, but also particular actions of many kinds, including decisions, judgments, and imputations. We also call the attitudes and dispositions of persons, and persons themselves, just and unjust. Our topic, however, is that of social justice. For us the primary subject of justice is the basic structure of society, or more exactly, the way in which the major social institutions distribute fundamental rights and duties and determine the division of advantages from social cooperation. By major institutions I understand the political constitution and the principal economic and social arrangements. Thus the legal protection of freedom of thought and liberty of conscience, competitive markets, private property in the means of production, and the monogamous family are examples of major social institutions. Taken together as one scheme, the major institutions define men's rights and duties and influence their life prospects, what they can expect to be and how well they can hope to do. The basic structure is the primary subject of justice because its effects are so profound and present from the start. The intuitive notion here is that this structure contains various social positions and that men born into different positions have different expectations of life determined, in part, by the political system as well as by economic and social circumstances. In this way the institutions of society favor certain starting places over others. These are especially deep inequalities. Not only are they pervasive, but they affect men's initial chances in life; yet they cannot possibly be justified by an appeal to the notions of merit or desert. It is these inequalities, presumably inevitable in the basic structure of any society, to which the principles of social justice must in the first instance apply. These principles, then, regulate the choice of a political constitution and the main elements of the economic and social system. The justice of a social scheme depends essentially on how fundamental rights and duties are assigned and on the economic opportunities and social conditions in the various sectors of society. . . .

The Original Position and Justification

I have said that the original position is the appropriate initial status quo which ensures that the fundamental agreements reached in it are fair. This fact yields the name "justice as fairness." It is clear, then, that I want to say that one conception of justice is more reasonable than another, or justifiable with respect to it, if rational persons in the initial situation would choose its principles over those of the other for the role of justice. Conceptions of justice are to be ranked by their acceptability to persons so circumstanced. Understood in this way the question of justification is settled by working out a problem of deliberation: we have to ascertain which principles it would be rational to adopt given the contractual situation. This connects the theory of justice with the theory of rational choice. . . .

It seems reasonable to suppose that the parties in the original position are equal. That is, all have the same rights in the procedure for choosing principles; each can make proposals, submit reasons for their acceptance, and so on. Obviously the purpose of these conditions is to represent equality between human beings as moral persons, as creatures having a conception of their good and capable of a sense of justice. The basis of equality is taken to be similarity in these two respects. Systems of ends are not ranked in value; and each man is presumed to have the requisite ability to understand and to act upon whatever principles are adopted. Together with the veil of ignorance, these conditions define the principles of justice as those which rational persons concerned to advance their interests would consent to as equals when none are known to be advantaged or disadvantaged by social and natural contingencies. . . .

. . . [I]n searching for the most favored description of this situation we work from both ends. We begin by describing it so that it represents generally shared and preferably weak conditions. We then see if these conditions are strong enough to yield a significant set of principles. If not, we look for further premises equally reasonable. But if so, and these principles match our considered convictions of justice, then so far well and good. But presumably there will be discrepancies. In this case we have a choice. We can either modify the account of the initial situation or we can revise our existing judgments, for even the judgments we take provisionally as fixed points are liable to revision. By going back and forth, sometimes altering the conditions of the contractual circumstances, at others withdrawing our judgments and conforming them to principle, I assume that eventually we shall find a description of the initial situation that both expresses reasonable conditions and yields principles which match our considered judgments duly pruned and adjusted. This state of affairs I refer to as reflective equilibrium. It is an equilibrium because at last our principles and judgments coincide; and it is reflective since we know to what principles our judgments conform and the premises of their derivation. At the moment everything is in order. But this equilibrium is not necessarily stable. It is liable to be upset by further examination of the conditions which should be imposed on the contractual situation and by particular cases which may lead us to revise our judgments. Yet for the time being we have done what we can to render coherent and to justify our convictions of social justice. We have reached a conception of the original position. . . .

Two Principles of Justice

I shall now state in a provisional form the two principles of justice that I believe would be agreed to in the original position. The first formulation of these principles is tentative. As we go on I shall consider several formulations and approximate step by step the final statement to be given much later.

I believe that doing this allows the exposition to proceed in a natural way.

> The first statement of the two principles reads as follows.
>
> First: each person is to have an equal right to the most extensive scheme of equal basic liberties compatible with a similar scheme of liberties for others.
>
> Second: social and economic inequalities are to be arranged so that they are both (a) reasonably expected to be to everyone's advantage, and (b) attached to positions and offices open to all. . . .

These principles primarily apply, as I have said, to the basic structure of society and govern the assignment of rights and duties and regulate the distribution of social and economic advantages. Their formulation presupposes that, for the purposes of a theory of justice, the social structure may be viewed as having two more or less distinct parts, the first principle applying to the one, the second principle to the other. Thus we distinguish between the aspects of the social system that define and secure the equal basic liberties and the aspects that specify and establish social and economic inequalities. Now it is essential to observe that the basic liberties are given by a list of such liberties. Important among these are political liberty (the right to vote and to hold public office) and freedom of speech and assembly; liberty of conscience and freedom of thought; freedom of the person, which includes freedom from psychological oppression and physical assault and dismemberment (integrity of the person); the right to hold personal property and freedom from arbitrary arrest and seizure as defined by the concept of the rule of law. These liberties are to be equal by the first principle.

The second principle applies, in the first approximation, to the distribution of income and wealth and to the design of organizations that make use of differences in authority and responsibility. While the distribution of wealth and income need not be equal, it must be to everyone's advantage, and at the same time, positions of authority and responsibility must be accessible to all. One applies the second principle by holding positions open, and then, subject to this constraint, arranges social and economic inequalities so that everyone benefits.

These principles are to be arranged in a serial order with the first principle prior to the second. This ordering means that infringements of the basic equal liberties protected by the first principle cannot be justified, or compensated for, by greater social and economic advantages. These liberties have a central range of application within which they can be limited and compromised only when they conflict with other basic liberties. Since they may be limited when they clash with one another, none of these liberties is absolute; but however they are adjusted to form one system, this system is to be the same for all. It is difficult, and perhaps impossible, to$\geq$ give a complete specification of these liberties independently from the particular circumstances—social, economic, and technological—of a given society. The hypothesis is that the general form of such a list could be devised with sufficient exactness to sustain this conception of justice. Of course, liberties not on the list, for example, the right to own certain kinds of property (e.g., means of production) and freedom of contract as understood by the doctrine of laissez-faire are not basic; and so they are not protected by the priority of the first principle. Finally, in regard to the second principle, the distribution of wealth and income, and positions of authority and responsibility, are to be consistent with both the basic liberties and equality of opportunity.

The two principles are rather specific in their content, and their acceptance rests on certain assumptions that I must eventually try to explain and justify. For the present, it should be observed that these principles are a special case of a more general conception of justice that can be expressed as follows.

> All social values—liberty and opportunity, income and wealth, and the social bases of self-respect—are to be distributed equally unless an unequal distribution of any, or all, of these values is to everyone's advantage.

Injustice, then, is simply inequalities that are not to the benefit of all. Of course, this conception is extremely vague and requires interpretation.

As a first step, suppose that the basic structure of society distributes certain primary goods, that is, things that every rational man is presumed to want. These goods normally have a use whatever a person's rational plan of life. For simplicity, assume that the chief primary goods at the disposition of society are rights, liberties, and opportunities, and income and wealth. (Later on the primary good of self-respect has a central place.) These are the social primary goods. Other primary goods such as health and vigor, intelligence and imagination, are natural goods; although their possession is influenced by the basic structure, they are not so directly under its control. Imagine, then, a hypothetical initial arrangement in which all the social primary goods are equally distributed: everyone has similar rights and duties, and income and wealth are evenly shared. This state of affairs provides a benchmark for judging improvements. If certain inequalities of wealth and differences in authority would make everyone better off than in this hypothetical starting situation, then they accord with the general conception.

Now it is possible, at least theoretically, that by giving up some of their fundamental liberties men are sufficiently compensated by the resulting social and economic gains. The general conception of justice imposes no restrictions on what sort of inequalities are permissible; it only requires that everyone's position be improved. We need not suppose anything so drastic as consenting to a condition of slavery. Imagine instead that people seem willing to forego certain political rights when the economic returns are significant. It is this kind of exchange which the two principles rule out; being arranged in serial order they do not permit exchanges between basic liberties and economic and social gains except under extenuating circumstances. . . .

. . . When principles mention persons, or require that everyone gain from an inequality, the reference is to representative persons holding the various social positions, or offices established by the basic structure. Thus in applying the second principle I assume that it is possible to assign an expectation of well-being to representative individuals holding these positions. This expectation indicates their life prospects as viewed from their social station. In general, the expectations of representative persons depend upon the distribution of rights and duties throughout the basic structure. Expectations are connected: by raising the prospects of the representative man in one position we presumably increase or decrease the prospects of representative men in other positions. Since it applies to institutional forms, the second principle (or rather the first part of it) refers to the expectations of representative individuals. As I shall discuss below, neither principle applies to distributions of particular goods to particular individuals who may be identified by their proper names. The situation where someone is considering how to allocate certain commodities to needy persons who are known to him is not within the scope of the principles. They are meant to regulate basic institutional arrangements. We must not assume that there is much similarity from the standpoint of justice between an administrative allotment of goods to specific persons and the appropriate design of society. Our common sense intuitions for the former may be a poor guide to the latter.

The Circumstances of Justice

The circumstances of justice may be described as the normal conditions under which human cooperation is both possible and necessary. Thus, as I noted at the outset, although a society is a cooperative venture for mutual advantage, it is typically marked by a conflict as well as an identity of interests. There is an identity of interests since social cooperation makes possible a better life for all than any would have if each were to try to live solely by his own efforts. There is a conflict of interests since men are not indifferent as to how the greater benefits produced by their collaboration are distributed, for in order to pursue their ends they each prefer a larger to a lesser share. Thus principles are needed for choosing among the various social arrangements which determine this division of advantages and for underwriting an agreement on the proper distributive shares. These requirements define the role of justice. The background conditions that give rise to these necessities are the circumstances of justice.

These conditions may be divided into two kinds. First, there are the objective circumstances which make human cooperation both possible and necessary. Thus, many individuals coexist together at the same time on a definite geographical territory. These individuals are roughly similar in physical and mental powers; or at any rate, their capacities are comparable in that no one among them can dominate the rest. They are vulnerable to attack, and all are subject to having their plans blocked by the united force of others. Finally, there is the condition of moderate scarcity understood to cover a wide range of situations. Natural and other resources are not so abundant that schemes of cooperation become superfluous, nor are conditions so harsh that fruitful ventures must inevitably break down. While mutually advantageous arrangements are feasible, the benefits they yield fall short of the demands men put forward.

The subjective circumstances are the relevant aspects of the subjects of cooperation, that is, of the persons working together. Thus while the parties have roughly similar needs and interests, or needs and interests in various ways complementary, so that mutually advantageous cooperation among them is possible, they nevertheless have their own plans of life. These plans, or conceptions of the good, lead them to have different ends and purposes, and to make conflicting claims on the natural and social resources available. Moreover, although the interests advanced by these plans are not assumed to be interests in the self, they are the interests of a self that regards its conception of the good as worthy of recognition and that advances claims in its behalf as deserving satisfaction. I also suppose that men suffer from various shortcomings of knowledge, thought, and judgment. Their knowledge is necessarily incomplete, their powers of reasoning, memory, and attention are always limited, and their judgment is likely to be distorted by anxiety, bias, and a preoccupation with their own affairs. Some of these defects spring from moral faults, from selfishness and negligence; but to a large degree, they are simply part of men's natural situation. As a consequence individuals not only have different plans of life but there exists a diversity of philosophical and religious belief, and of political and social doctrines.

Now this constellation of conditions I shall refer to as the circumstances of justice. Hume's account of them is especially perspicuous and the preceding summary adds nothing essential to his much fuller discussion. For simplicity I often stress the condition of moderate scarcity (among the objective circumstances), and that of conflict of interests (among the subjective circumstances). Thus, one can say, in brief, that the circumstances of justice obtain whenever persons put forward conflicting claims to the division of social advantages under conditions of moderate scarcity. Unless these circumstances existed there would be no occasion for the virtue of justice, just as in the absence of threats of injury to life and limb there would be no occasion for physical courage.

Several clarifications should be noted. First of all, I shall, of course, assume that the persons in the original position know that these circumstances of justice obtain. This much they take for granted about the conditions of their society. A further assumption is that the parties try to advance their conception of the good as best they can, and that in attempting to do this they are not bound by prior moral ties to each other.

The question arises, however, whether the persons in the original position have obligations and duties to third parties, for example, to their immediate descendants. To say that they do would be one way of handling questions of justice between generations. However, the aim of justice as fairness is to try to derive all duties and obligations of justice from other reasonable conditions. So, if possible, this way out should be avoided. There are several other courses open to us. We can adopt a motivation assumption and think of the parties as representing a continuing line of claims. For example, we can assume that they are heads of families and therefore have a desire to further the well-being of at least their more immediate descendants. Or we can require the parties to agree to principles subject to the constraint that they wish all preceding generations to have followed the very same principles. By an appropriate combination of such stipulations, I believe that the whole chain of generations can be tied together and principles agreed to that suitably take into account the interests of each. If this is right, we will have succeeded in deriving duties to other generations from reasonable conditions.

Finally, I shall assume that the parties in the original position are mutually disinterested: they are not willing to have their interests sacrificed to the others. The intention is to model men's conduct and motives in cases where questions of justice arise. The spiritual ideals of saints and heroes can be as irreconcilably opposed as any other interests. Conflicts in pursuit of these ideals are the most tragic of all. Thus justice is the virtue of practices where there are competing interests and where persons feel entitled to press their rights on each other. In an association of saints agreeing on a common ideal, if such a community could exist, disputes about justice would not occur. Each would work selflessly for one end as determined by their common religion, and reference to this end (assuming it to be clearly defined) would settle every question of right. But a human society is characterized by the circumstances of justice. The account of these conditions involves no particular theory of human motivation. Rather, its aim is to reflect in the description of the original position the relations of individuals to one another which set the stage for questions of justice. . . .

The Basis of Equality

The consistent application of the principle of fair opportunity requires us to view persons independently from the influences of their social position.

But how far should this tendency be carried? It seems that even when fair opportunity (as it has been defined) is satisfied, the family will lead to unequal chances between individuals. Is the family to be abolished then? Taken by itself and given a certain primacy, the idea of equal opportunity inclines in this direction. But within the context of the theory of justice as a whole, there is much less urgency to take this course. The acknowledgment of the difference principle redefines the grounds for social inequalities as conceived in the system of liberal equality; and when the principles of fraternity and redress are allowed their appropriate weight, the natural distribution of assets and the contingencies of social circumstances can more easily be accepted. We are more ready to dwell upon our good fortune now that these differences are made to work to our advantage, rather than to be downcast by how much better off we might have been had we had an equal chance along with others if only all social barriers had been removed. The conception of justice, should it be truly effective and publicly recognized as such, seems more likely than its rivals to transform our perspective on the social world and to reconcile us to the dispositions of the natural order and the conditions of human life.

Study Questions on John Rawls

1. Explain Rawls's two principles of justice. How does he derive them? Does his derivation succeed?
2. What is the basic structure of society? Does it include the structure of the family?
3. What do you think of Rawls's suggestion that the parties to the social contract can be understood as heads of families?
4. If we apply Rawls's theory to the family, what follows? Should the family be abolished on Rawls's principles?

Liberalism and the Limits of Justice

MICHAEL SANDEL

> Michael Sandel criticizes Rawls's theory of justice, with special emphasis on questions concerning family relations. Emphasizing questions of justice can cause a general decline in the moral character of family life, so that justice turns out to be not a virtue, but a vice.

The Circumstances of Justice: Empiricist Objections

THE CIRCUMSTANCES OF JUSTICE are the conditions that engage the virtue of justice. They are the conditions that prevail in human societies and make human co-operation both possible and necessary. Society is seen as a co-operative venture for mutual advantage, which means that it is typically marked by a conflict as well as an identity of interests—an identity of interests in that all stand to gain from mutual co-operation, a conflict in that, given their divergent interests and ends, people differ over how the fruits of their co-operation are to be distributed. Principles are needed to specify arrangements by which such claims can be sorted out, and it is the role of justice to provide them. The background conditions that make such sorting-out arrangements necessary are the circumstances of justice.

Following Hume, Rawls notes that these circumstances are of two kinds—objective and subjective. The objective circumstances of justice include such facts as the moderate scarcity of resources, whereas the subjective circumstances concern the subjects of co-operation, most notably the fact that they are characterized by different interests and ends. This means that each person has a distinctive life plan, or conception of the good, which he regards as worthy of advancement. Rawls emphasizes this aspect by assuming that, as conceived in the original position at least, the parties are mutually disinterested, that they are concerned to advance their own conception of the good and no one else's, and that in advancing their ends they are not bound to each other by prior moral ties. The circumstances of justice are thus summarized:

One can say, in brief, that the circumstances of justice obtain whenever mutually disinterested persons put forward conflicting claims to the division of social advantages under conditions of moderate scarcity. Unless these circumstances existed there would be no occasion for the virtue of justice, just as in the absence of threats of injury to life and limb there would be no occasion for physical courage.

The circumstances of justice are the circumstances that give rise to the virtue of justice. In their absence, the virtue of justice would be nugatory; it would not be required nor for that matter even possible. "But a human society *is* characterized by the circumstances of justice" [emphasis added]. Therefore the virtue of justice *is* required.

The conditions that occasion the virtue of justice are empirical conditions. About this Rawls is clear and unabashed. "Moral philosophy must be free to use contingent assumptions and general facts as it pleases." It can proceed in no other way. What matters is that the premises be "true and sufficiently general."

> The fundamental principles of justice quite properly depend upon the natural facts about men in society. This dependence is made explicit by the description of the original position: the decision of the parties is taken in the light of general knowledge. Moreover, the various elements of the original position presuppose many things about the circumstances of human life. . . . If these assumptions are true and suitably general, everything is in order, for without these elements the whole scheme would be pointless and empty.

From Liberalism and the Limits of Justice, *2d ed., by Michael Sandel. Reprinted by permission of Cambridge University Press.*

But an empiricist understanding of the original position seems deeply at odds with deontological claims. For if justice depends for its virtue on certain empirical preconditions, it is unclear how its priority could unconditionally be affirmed. Rawls says that he borrows his account of the circumstances of justice from Hume. But Hume's circumstances cannot support the priority of right in the deontological sense. They are after all empirical conditions. To establish the primacy of justice in the categorical sense Rawls's claim requires, he would have to show not only that the circumstances of justice prevail in all societies, but that they prevail to such an extent that the virtue of justice is always more fully or extensively engaged than any other virtue. Otherwise, he would be entitled to conclude only that justice is the first virtue of certain kinds of societies, namely those where conditions are such that the resolution of conflicting claims among mutually disinterested parties is the most pressing social priority. . . .

The notion that the primacy of justice could be grounded empirically becomes all the more implausible when we consider how unlikely the necessary generalization must be, at least when applied across the range of social institutions. For while we can easily enough imagine that certain large-scale associations such as the modern nation-state might meet its requirements in many cases, we can readily imagine a range of more intimate or solidaristic associations in which the values and aims of the participants coincide closely enough that the circumstances of justice prevail to a relatively small degree. As Hume himself observes, we need not have recourse to utopian visions or the fiction of poets to imagine such conditions, but "may discover the same truth by common experience and observation."

> In the present disposition of the human heart, it would, perhaps, be difficult to find complete instances of such enlarged affections; but still we may observe that the case of families approaches towards it; and the stronger the mutual benevolence is among the individuals, the nearer it approaches; till all distinction of property be, in a great measure, lost and confounded among them. Between married persons, the cement of friendship is by the laws supposed so strong as to abolish all division of possessions; and has often, in reality, the force ascribed to it.

While the institution of the family may represent an extreme case in this respect, we can easily imagine a range of intermediate cases of social institutions, a continuum of human associations characterized in varying degrees by the circumstances of justice. These would include, at various points along the spectrum, tribes, neighbourhoods, cities, towns, universities, trade unions, national liberation movements and established nationalisms, and a wide variety of ethnic, religious, cultural, and linguistic communities with more or less clearly-defined common identities and shared purposes, precisely those attributes whose presence signifies the relative absence of the circumstances of justice. Although the circumstances of justice might well exist in all of these cases, they would not likely predominate, at least not to such an extent that justice was engaged in all cases in greater measure than any other virtue. On the empiricist interpretation of the original position, justice can be primary only for those societies beset by sufficient discord to make the accommodation of conflicting interests and aims the overriding moral and political consideration; justice is the first virtue of social institutions not absolutely, as truth is to theories, but only conditionally, as physical courage is to a war zone. . . .

To invoke the circumstances of justice is simultaneously to concede, implicitly at least, the circumstances of benevolence, or fraternity, or of enlarged affections, whatever the description might be; such are the circumstances that prevail in so far as the circumstances of justice do not prevail, and the virtue to which they give definition must be a virtue of at least correlative status.

One consequence of the remedial aspect of justice is that we cannot say in advance whether, in any particular instance, an increase in justice is associated with an overall moral improvement. This is because a gain in justice can come about in one of two ways; it can arise where before there was injustice, or it can occur where before there was neither justice nor injustice but a sufficient measure of benevolence or fraternity such that the virtue of justice had not been extensively engaged. Where justice replaces injustice, other things being equal, the overall moral improvement is clear. On the other hand, where an increase in justice reflects some transformation in the quality of pre-existing motivations and dispositions, the overall moral balance might well be diminished.

When fraternity fades, more justice may be done, but even more may be required to restore the moral status quo. Furthermore, there is no guarantee that justice and its rival virtues are perfectly commensurable. The breakdown of certain personal and civic attachments may represent a moral loss that even a full measure of justice cannot redeem. Does it go without saying that a rent in the fabric of implicit understandings and commitments is fully morally repaired so long as everyone "does what he ought" in the aftermath?

Consider for example a more or less ideal family situation, where relations are governed in large part by spontaneous affection and where, in consequence, the circumstances of justice prevail to a relatively small degree. Individual rights and fair decision procedures are seldom invoked, not because injustice is rampant but because their appeal is pre-empted by a spirit of generosity in which I am rarely inclined to claim my fair share. Nor does this generosity necessarily imply that I receive out of kindness a share that is equal to or greater than the share I would be entitled to under fair principles of justice. I may get less. The point is not that I get what I would otherwise get, only more spontaneously, but simply that the questions of what I get and what I am due do not loom large in the overall context of this way of life.

Now imagine that one day the harmonious family comes to be wrought with dissension. Interests grow divergent and the circumstances of justice grow more acute. The affection and spontaneity of previous days give way to demands for fairness and the observance of rights. And let us further imagine that the old generosity is replaced by a judicious temper of unexceptionable integrity and that the new moral necessities are met with a full measure of justice, such that no injustice prevails. Parents and children reflectively equilibrate, dutifully if sullenly abide by the two principles of justice, and even manage to achieve the conditions of stability and congruence so that the good of justice is realized within their household. Now what are we to make of this? Are we prepared to say that the arrival of justice, however full, restores to the situation its full moral character, and that the only difference is a psychological one? Or consider again the parallel of physical courage. Imagine a society once tranquil but with little courage (not out of cowardice but quietude), now turned violent and precarious, but where the virtue of courage is on bold, even plentiful display. Is it obvious we would prefer the second from a moral point of view?

To be sure, the incommensurabilities, if they exist, could pull in the opposite direction as well. It may be that despite the harshness of the circumstances of courage, there is a certain nobility that flourishes in the new way of life unavailable to the human spirit under more protected conditions and that this goes uncompensated by even the most blissful peace. And if the demise of familial or communal *Gemeinschaft* reflects not the onset of material meanness but the flowering of diversity, or the children outgrowing the parochial ways of their parents' home, we might be inclined to view the advent of justice in a more favorable light. The general point remains. An increase in justice can fail to be associated with an overall moral improvement in at least two different ways: either by failing fully to meet an increase in the circumstances of justice, or by an inability, however full, to compensate the loss of certain "nobler virtues, and more favourable blessings."

If an increase in justice does not necessarily imply an unqualified moral improvement, it can also be shown that in some cases, justice is not a virtue but a vice. This can be seen by considering what we might call the reflexive dimension of the circumstances of justice. The reflexive dimension refers to the fact that what the parties know about their condition is an ingredient of their condition. Rawls acknowledges this feature when he writes, "I shall, of course, assume that the persons in the original position know that these circumstances of justice obtain."

The circumstances of justice, and more specifically the subjective aspect of these circumstances, consist partly in the motivations of the participants and in the way they perceive their motivations. If the parties one day came to regard their circumstances differently, if they came to believe that the circumstances of justice (or of benevolence) obtained to a greater or lesser extent than before, this very shift would amount to a change in those circumstances. As Rawls points out in his discussion of the good of justice, acting out of a sense of justice can be contagious; it reinforces the assumptions it presupposes and enhances its own stability by encouraging and affirming like motivations in others.

But what is the effect of this "contagion" when it is applied to a situation where, or in so far as, the circumstances of justice do not obtain? When I act out of a sense of justice in inappropriate circumstances, say in circumstances where the virtues of benevolence and fraternity rather than justice are relevantly engaged, my act may not merely be superfluous, but might contribute to a reorientation of prevailing understandings and motivations, thereby transforming the circumstances of justice in some degree. And this can be true even where the "act" I perform out of justice is "the same act" as the one I would have performed out of benevolence or fraternity, except in a different spirit. As in Rawls's account of stability, my act and the sense of justice that informs it have the self-fulfilling effect of bringing about the conditions under which they *would* have been appropriate. But in the case of the inappropriate act of justice, the result is to render the circumstances of justice more pressing without necessarily evoking an increase in the incidence of justice to a similar degree.

Gratuitous displays of physical courage in the midst of tranquil conditions can prove disruptive of the very tranquility they fail to appreciate and quite possibly can fail to replace. It is similar with justice. If, out of a misplaced sense of justice, a close friend of long-standing repeatedly insists on calculating and paying his precise share of every common expenditure, or refuses to accept any favor or hospitality except at the greatest protest and embarrassment, not only will I feel compelled to be reciprocally scrupulous but at some point may begin to wonder whether I have not misunderstood our relationship. The circumstances of benevolence will to this extent have diminished, and the circumstances of justice grown. This follows as a consequence of the reflexive dimension of the (subjective aspect of the) circumstances of justice. But as we have already seen, there is no guarantee that the new sense of justice can fully replace the old spontaneity, even in those cases where no injustice results. Since the exercise of justice in inappropriate conditions will have brought about an overall decline in the moral character of the association, justice in this case will have been not a virtue but a vice. . . .

Study Questions on Michael Sandel

1. What are the "circumstances of justice" and in what sorts of situations might they fail to obtain? Why does Sandel think that the family is an institution in which they do not obtain, or at least not as they do within the larger society? Do you agree?

2. Why does Sandel think that justice is not the primary social virtue? Why does he think that an increase in justice need not mean overall social improvement?

3. Okin (see next article) argues that the traditional family is unjust. Defenders of the traditional family regard some family arrangements as unjust—for example, ones in which parents are denied effective authority over children, or have the power to kill or sell them. How would such people respond to Sandel, and what might he say in reply?

4. Sandel is criticizing Rawls's *deontology,* that is, his insistence on the requirements of justice regardless of consequences, at least as applied to the family. In your view, what is the relationship between Sandel's argument and the fact that the human infant is helpless for a long time, and therefore needs a non-Rawlsian family? Are communitarian virtues important only because their practice has good consequences and their neglect bad ones?

Justice, Gender, and the Family

SUSAN MOLLER OKIN

> Susan Moller Okin maintains that the division of labor within marriage makes wives far more likely to be exploited both within the marital relationship and in the world of work outside the home. Women's greater vulnerability begins in anticipation of marriage, and continues within marriage itself and after separation and divorce. She concludes with an argument, derived from the political philosophy of John Rawls, for reconstructing the institutions of marriage and family to correct this situation.

IT IS NOT EASY TO THINK ABOUT marriage and the family in terms of justice. For one thing, we do not readily associate justice with intimacy, which is one reason some theorists idealize the family. For another, some of the issues that theories of justice are most concerned with, such as differences in standards of living, do not obviously apply among members of a family. . . . As we shall see, however, the question of who earns the family's income, or how the earning of this income is shared, has a great deal to do with the distribution of power and influence within the family, including decisions on how to spend this income. It also affects the distribution of other benefits, including basic security. Here, I present and analyze the facts of contemporary gender-structured marriage in the light of theories about power and vulnerability and the issues of justice they inevitably raise. I argue that marriage and the family, as currently practiced in our society, are unjust institutions. They constitute the pivot of a societal system of gender that renders women vulnerable to dependency, exploitation, and abuse. When we look seriously at the distribution between husbands and wives of such critical social goods as work (paid and unpaid), power, prestige, self-esteem, opportunities for self-development, and both physical and economic security, we find socially constructed inequalities between them, right down the list. . . .

Vulnerability by Anticipation of Marriage

The cycle of women's vulnerability begins early, with their anticipation of marriage. Almost all women and men marry, but marriage has earlier and far greater impact on the lives and life choices of women than on those of men. Socialization and the culture in general place more emphasis on marriage for girls than for boys and, although people have recently become less negative about remaining single, young women are more likely than young men to regard "having a good marriage and family life" as extremely important to them. This fact, together with their expectation of being the parent primarily responsible for children, clearly affects women's decisions about the extent and field of education and training they will pursue, and their degree of purposiveness about careers. It is important to note that vulnerability by anticipation of marriage affects at least as adversely the futures of many women who do *not* marry as it affects those who do. This is particularly significant among disadvantaged groups, particularly poor urban black women, whose actual chances of marrying and being economically supported by a man are small (largely because of the high unemployment rate among the available men), but who are further burdened by growing up surrounded by a culture that still identifies femininity with this expectation.

Even though the proportion of young women who plan to be housewives exclusively his declined considerably, women's choices about work are significantly affected from an early age by their expectations about the effects of family life on their work and of work on their family life. As is well known, the participation of women in the labor force, especially women with small children, has continued to rise. But, although a small minority of women are rapidly increasing the previously tiny percentages of women in the elite professions, the vast majority of women who work outside the home are still in low-paying jobs with little or no prospect of advancement. This fact is clearly related to girls' awareness of the complexity they are likely to face in combining work with family life. . . . Needless to say, such a choice does not confront boys in their formative years. . . .

When women envisage a future strongly influenced by the demands on them as wives and particularly as mothers, they are likely to embark on traditionally female fields of study and/or occupational paths. . . . Regardless of educational achievement, women are far more likely than men to work in administrative support jobs, as a secretary, typist, or bookkeeper, for example, which in most cases hold no prospects for advancement. Almost 30 percent of employed women worked in this category in 1985, compared with fewer than 6 percent of men. . . .

. . . On top of all this, recent research has shown that large discrepancies exist between male and female wages for the same job title. While female secretaries earned a median wage of $278 per week in 1985, the median for male secretaries was $365; moreover, in twenty-four other narrowly defined occupations in which females earned *less* than they would have as secretaries, males earned *more* in every case than a female secretary. Indeed, some firms designate particular jobs as male and others designate the same jobs as female, and the wage rates differ accordingly. . . .

Thus workplace discrimination *per se* is very significant. In addition, as I have suggested, some of the segregation of wage work by sex is attributable to the individual choices that women and men make in the context of their own socialization and with knowledge of the gender structure of the family in particular. . . .

VULNERABLITY WITHIN MARRIAGE

Marriage continues the cycle of inequality set in motion by the anticipation of marriage and the related sex segregation of the workplace. Partly because of society's assumptions about gender, but also because women, on entering marriage, tend already to be disadvantaged members of the workforce, married women are likely to start out with less leverage in the relationship than their husbands. As I shall show, answers to questions such as whose work life and work needs take priority, and how the unpaid work of the family will be allocated—if they are not simply assumed to be decided along the lines of sex difference, but are live issues in the marriage—are likely to be strongly influenced by the differences in earning power between husbands and wives. In many marriages, partly because of discrimination at work and the wage gap between the sexes, wives (despite initial personal ambitions and even when they are full-time wage workers) come to perceive themselves as benefiting from giving priority to their husbands' careers. Hence they have little incentive to question the traditional division of labor in the household. This in turn limits their own commitment to wage work and their incentive and leverage to challenge the gender structure of the workplace. Experiencing frustration and lack of control at work, those who thus turn toward domesticity, while often resenting the lack of respect our society gives to full-time mothers, may see the benefits of domestic life as greater than the costs.

Thus, the inequalities between the sexes in the workplace and at home reinforce and exacerbate each other. . . .

Housework and the Cycle of Vulnerability

It is no secret that in almost all families women do far more housework and child care than men do. But the distribution of paid and unpaid work within the family has rarely—outside of feminist circles—been considered a significant issue by theorists of justice. Why should it be? If two friends divide a task so that each takes primary responsibility for a different aspect of it, we would be loath to cry "injustice" unless one were obviously coercing the other. But at least three factors make the division of labor within the household a very different situation, and a clear question of justice. First, the uneven distribution of labor within the family is strongly correlated with an innate characteristic, which appears to make it the kind of issue with which theorists of justice have been most concerned. The virtually automatic allocation to one person of more of the paid labor and to the other of more of the unpaid labor would be regarded as decidedly odd in any relationship other than that of a married or cohabiting heterosexual couple. One reason for this is that, as we shall see, it has distinct effects on the distribution of power. . . .

. . . One cannot even begin to address the issue of why so many women and children live in poverty in our society, or why women are inadequately represented in the higher echelons of our political and economic institutions, without confronting the division of labor between the sexes within the family. . . .

When a woman is a full-time housewife—as are about two-fifths of married women in the United States who live with their husbands—she does less total work, on average, than her employed husband: 49.3 hours per week, compared with his 63.2. This is also true of couples in which the wife works part-time (defined as fewer than thirty hours per week, including commuting time), though the average difference per week is reduced to eight hours in this case. . . . But the *quantity* of work performed is only one of a number of important variables that must be considered in order for us to assess the justice or injustice of the division of labor in the family, particularly in relation to the issue of the cycle of women's vulnerability.

In terms of the quality of work, there are considerable disadvantages to the role of housewife. One is that much of the work is boring and/or unpleasant. Surveys indicate that most people of both sexes do not like to clean, shop for food, or do laundry, which constitute a high proportion of housework. Cooking rates higher, and child care even higher, with both sexes, than other domestic work. In reality, this separation of tasks is strictly hypothetical, at least for mothers, who are usually cleaning, shopping, doing laundry, and cooking at the same time as taking care of children. Many wage workers, too, do largely tedious and repeti-

tive work. But the housewife-mother's work has additional disadvantages. One is that her hours of work are highly unscheduled; unlike virtually any other worker except the holder of a high political office, she can be called on at any time of the day or night, seven days a week. Another is that she cannot, nearly as easily as most other workers, change jobs. . . .

Many of the disadvantages of being a housewife spring directly or indirectly from the fact that all her work is unpaid work, whereas more than four-fifths of her husband's total work is paid work. . . . This both affects the predominantly houseworking wife's power and influence within the family and means that her social status depends largely upon her husband's, a situation that she may not consider objectionable so long as the marriage lasts, but that is likely to be very painful for her if it does not.

Also, although married couples usually share material well-being, a housewife's or even a part-time working wife's lack of access to much money of her own can create difficulties that range from the mildly irritating through the humiliating to the devastating, especially if she does not enjoy a good relationship with her husband. Money is the subject of most conflict for married couples, although the issue of housework may be overtaking it. . . .

. . . Both wife abuse and child abuse are clearly exacerbated by the economic dependence of women on their husbands or cohabiting male partners. Many women, especially full-time housewives with dependent children, have no way of adequately supporting themselves, and are often in practice unable to leave a situation in which they and/or their children are being seriously abused. In addition to increasing the likelihood of the more obvious forms of abuse—physical and sexual assault—the fear of being abandoned, with its economic and other dire consequences, can lead a housewife to tolerate infidelity, to submit to sexual acts she does not enjoy, or experience psychological abuse including virtual desertion. The fact that a predominantly houseworking wife has no money of her own or a small paycheck is not necessarily significant, but it can be very significant, especially at crucial junctures in the marriage. . . .

Predominantly Wage-Working Wives and Housework. Despite the increasing labor force participation of married women, including mothers, "working wives still bear almost all the responsibility for housework." . . . [T]he resistance of most husbands to housework is well documented, as is the fact that the more housework men do, the more it becomes a cause of fighting within couples. Examining factors that caused the breakup of some of the couples in their sample, Blumstein and Schwartz say:

> Among both married and cohabiting couples, housework is a source of conflict. . . . *[A] woman cannot be perceived as doing less housework than her partner wants her to do without jeopardizing the relationship.* However, a man, who is unlikely to be doing even half the work, can be perceived as doing less than his fair share without affecting the couple's durability. *It is difficult for women to achieve an equal division of housework and still preserve the relationship* [emphasis added].

As a result, in many of the households in which men and women both work full-time—those for which much paid household help or reliance on other purchased services is not a practical option—the unequal distribution of housework between husbands and wives leads to gross inequities in the amount and type of work done by each. "Drudge wives," as Bergmann has recently termed women in such households, do more total work than their husbands, averaging 71.1 hours a week to the husband's 64.9. But of greater overall significance is the fact that a vastly higher proportion of the wife's than of the husband's work is unpaid. She averages 28.1 hours of unpaid "family" work to 43 hours of paid work, whereas he averages only 9.2 hours of family work to 55.8 hours of paid work. One important effect of unequal sharing of housework and other family work within dual working couples is that the amount of time and energy the wife has left to commit to her wage work is considerably more limited than her husband's. . . .

. . . [Women's] chances of success are significantly affected by the fact that, although they are likely to expend significant amounts of time on their homes and children, they must compete at work, not only with men from families like their own, who do significantly less family work than they do, but also with men whose wives are full-time housewives or work only part-time. . . . Because of their lower level of labor force attachment, their tendency to work part-time and at jobs that in other respects bend to meet the needs of the family, and their propensity to accommodate their own employment to their husbands', women's wages become lower in relation to men's as they get older. . . . Since the partner whose wage work is given priority and who does far less unpaid family work is likely to increase the disparity between his and his spouse's earnings, seniority, and work status, his power in the family will tend to grow accordingly. . . .

VULNERABILITY BY SEPARATION OR DIVORCE

The impact of the unequal distribution of benefits and burdens between husbands and wives is hardest and most directly felt by the increasing number of women and children whose families are no longer intact. . . . Not only has the rate of divorce increased rapidly but the differential in the economic impact of divorce on men and women has also grown. Divorce and its economic effects contribute significantly to the fact that nearly one-quarter of all children now live in single-parent households, more than half of them, even after transfer payments, below the poverty level. Moreover, partly because of the increased labor force participation of married women, there has been a growing divergence between female-maintained families and two-parent families. These dramatic shifts, with their vast impact on the lives of women and children, must be addressed by any theory of justice that can claim to be about all of us, rather than simply about the male "heads of households" on which theories of justice in the past have focused.

There is now little doubt that, while no-fault divorce does not appear to have caused the increasing rate of divorce, it has considerably affected the economic outcome of divorce for both parties. Many studies have shown that whereas the average economic status of men improves after divorce, that of women and children deteriorates seriously. . . .

The basic reason for this is that the courts are now treating divorcing men and women more or less as equals. Divorcing men and women are not, of course, equal, both because the two sexes are not treated equally in society and, as we have seen, because typical, gender-structured marriage makes women socially and economically vulnerable. The treatment of unequals as if they were equals has long been recognized as an obvious instance of injustice. In this case, the injustice is particularly egregious because the inequality is to such a large extent the result of the marital relationship itself. . . .

By attempting to treat men and women as equals at the end of marriage, current divorce law neglects not only the obvious fact that women are *not* the socioeconomic equals of men in our society, but also the highly relevant fact that the experience of gendered marriage and primary parenting greatly exacerbates the inequality that women already bring with them into marriage. To divide the property equally and leave each partner to support himself or herself and to share support of the children might be fair in the case of a marriage in which the paid and unpaid labor had been shared equally, and in which neither spouse's work life had taken priority over that of the other. However, as we have seen, such marriages are exceedingly rare. Traditional or quasi-traditional marriages are far more common, even in the case of the many wives who currently work full-time outside the home. A wife who has contributed at least her fair share in a gender-structured marriage, by undertaking virtually all of the unpaid family work while her husband pursues his work life, meanwhile greatly enhancing his actual and prospective earnings, is by no means treated equally if, at the time of divorce, she is almost entirely cut off from the benefits of his enhanced economic position. But in the typical divorce today, this is exactly what happens. . . .

If we are to aim at making the family, our most fundamental social grouping, more just, we must work toward eradicating the socially created vulnerabilities of women that stem from the division of labor and the resultant division of power within it. . . .

Conclusion: Toward a Humanist Justice

Let us first try to imagine ourselves, as far as possible, in the original position, knowing neither what our sex nor any other of our personal characteristics will be once the veil of ignorance is lifted. Neither do we know our place in society or our particular conception of the good life. Particularly relevant in this context, of course, is our lack of knowledge of our beliefs about the characteristics of men and women and our related convictions about the appropriate division of labor between the sexes. Thus the positions we represent must include a wide variety of beliefs on these matters. We may, once the veil of ignorance is lifted, find ourselves feminist men or feminist women whose conception of the good life includes the minimization of social differentiation between the sexes. Or we may find ourselves traditionalist men or women, whose conception of the good life, for religious or other reasons, is bound up in an adherence to the conventional division of labor between the sexes. The challenge is to arrive at and apply principles of justice having to do with the family and the division of labor between the sexes that can satisfy these vastly disparate points of view and the many that fall between. . . . I think we would arrive at a basic model that would absolutely minimize gender. . . .

. . . Few people outside of feminist circles seem willing to acknowledge that society does not have to choose between a system of female parenting that renders women and children seriously vulnerable and a system of total reliance on day care provided outside the home. While high-quality day care, subsidized so as to be equally available to all children, certainly constitutes an important part of the response that society should make in order to provide justice for women and children, it is only one part. If we start out with the reasonable assumption that women and men are equally parents of their children, and have equal responsibility for both the unpaid effort that goes into caring for them and their economic support, then we must rethink the demands of work life throughout the period in which a worker of either sex is a parent of a small child. We can no longer cling to the by now largely mythical assumption that every worker has "someone else" at home to raise "his" children. . . .

An equally important role of our schools must be to ensure in the course of children's education that they become fully aware of the politics of gender. This does not only mean ensuring that women's experience and women's writing are included in the curriculum, although this in itself is undoubtedly important. Its political significance has become obvious from the amount of protest that it has provoked. Children need also to be taught about the present inequalities, ambiguities, and uncertainties of marriage, the facts of workplace discrimination and segregation, and the likely consequences of making life choices based on assumptions about gender. They should be discouraged from thinking about their futures as *determined* by the sex to which they happen to belong. . . . Finally, schools should be required to provide high-quality after-school programs, where children can play safely, do their homework, or participate in creative activities. . . .

It is impossible to predict all the effects of moving toward a society without gender. Major current injustices to women and children would end. Men would experience both the joys and the responsibilities of far closer and more sustained contact with their children than many have today. Many immensely influential spheres of life—notably politics and the professional occupations—would for the first time be populated more or less equally by men and women, most of whom were also actively participating parents. . . .

PROTECTING THE VULNERABLE

The pluralism of beliefs and modes of life is fundamental to our society, and the genderless society I have just outlined would certainly not be agreed upon by all as desirable. Thus when we think about constructing relations between the sexes that could be agreed upon in the original position, and are therefore just from all points of view, we must also design institutions and practices acceptable to those with more traditional beliefs about the characteristics of men and women, and the appropriate division of labor between them. It is essential, if men and women are to be allowed to so divide their labor, as they must be if we are to respect the current pluralism of beliefs, that society protect the vulnerable. Without such protection, the marriage contract seriously exacerbates the initial inequalities of those who entered into it, and too many women and children live perilously close to economic disaster and serious social dislocation; too many also live with violence or the continual threat of it. . . .

Gender-structured marriage, then, needs to be regarded as a currently necessary institution (because still chosen by some) but one that is socially problematic. It should be subjected to a number of legal requirements, at least when there are children. Most important, there is no need for the division of labor between the sexes to involve the economic dependence, either complete or partial, of one partner on the other. Such dependence can be avoided if both partners have *equal legal entitlement* to all earnings coming into the household. The clearest and simplest way of doing this would be to have employers make out wage checks equally divided between the earner and the partner who provides all or most of his or her unpaid domestic services. In many cases, of course, this would not change the way couples actually manage their finances; it would simply codify what they already agree on—that the household income is rightly shared, because in a real sense jointly earned. . . .

In the case of some couples, however, altering the entitlement of spouses to the earned income of the household as I have suggested *would* make a significant difference. It would make a difference in cases where the earning or higher-earning partner now directly exploits this power, by refusing to make significant spending decisions jointly, by failing to share the income, or by psychologically or physically abusing the nonearning or low-earning partner, reinforced by the notion that she (almost always the wife) has little option but to put up with such abuse or to take herself and her children into a state of destitution. It would make a difference, too, in cases where the higher-earning partner indirectly exploits this earning power in order to perpetuate the existing division of labor in the family. . . .

It is also important to point out that this proposal does not constitute unwarranted invasion of privacy or any more state intervention into the life of families than currently exists. It would involve only the same kind of invasion of privacy as is now required by such things as registration of marriages and births, and the filing of tax returns declaring numbers and names of dependents. And it *seems* like intervention in families only because it would alter the existing relations of power within them. If a person's capacity to fulfill the terms of his or her work is dependent on having a spouse at home who raises the children and in other ways sustains that worker's day-to-day life, then it is no more interventionist to pay both equally for their contributions than only to pay one.

The same fundamental principle should apply to separation and divorce, to the extent that the division of labor has been practiced within a marriage. Under current divorce laws, as we have seen, the terms of exit from marriage are disadvantageous for almost all women in traditional or quasi-traditional marriages. Regardless of the consensus that existed about the division of the family labor, these women lose most of the income that has supported them *and* the social status that attached to them because of their husband's income and employment, often at the same time as suddenly becoming single parents, and prospective wage workers for the first time in many years. This combination of prospects would seem to be enough to put most traditional wives off the idea of divorcing even if they had good cause to do so. In addition, since divorce in the great majority of states no longer requires the consent of both spouses, it seems likely that wives for whom divorce would spell economic and social catastrophe would be inhibited in voicing their dissatisfactions or needs within marriage. The terms of exit are very likely to affect the use and the power of voice in the ongoing relationship. At worst, these women may be rendered virtually defenseless in the face of physical or psychological abuse. This is not a system of marriage and divorce that could possibly be agreed to by persons in an original position in which they did not know whether they were to be male or female, traditionalist or not. It is a fraudulent contract, presented as beneficial to all but in fact to the benefit only of the more powerful.

For all these reasons, it seems essential that the terms of divorce be redrawn so as to reflect the gendered or nongendered character of the marriage that is ending, to a far greater extent than they do now. The legal system of a society that allows couples to divide the labor of families in a traditional or quasi-traditional manner *must* take responsibility for the vulnerable position in which marital breakdown places the partner who has completely or partially lost the capacity to be economically self-supporting. When such a marriage ends, it seems wholly reasonable to expect a person whose career has been largely unencumbered by domestic responsibilities to support financially the partner who undertook these responsibilities. This support, in the form of combined alimony and child support, should be far more substantial than the token levels often ordered by the courts now. *Both postdivorce households should enjoy the same standard of living.* Alimony should not end after a few years, as the (patronizingly named) "rehabilitative alimony" of today does; it should continue for at least as long as the traditional division of labor in the marriage did and, in the case of short-term marriages that produced children, until the youngest child enters first grade and the custodial parent has a real chance of making his or her own living. After that point, child support should continue at a level that enables the children to enjoy a standard of living equal to that of the noncustodial parent. . . .

. . . I claim that the genderless family is more just. [I]t is more just to women; it is more conducive to equal opportunity both for women and for children of both sexes; and it creates a more favorable environment for the rearing of citizens of a just society. Thus, while protecting those whom gender now makes vulnerable, we must also put our best efforts into promoting the elimination of gender.

The increased justice to women that would result from moving away from gender is readily apparent. Standards for just social institutions could no longer take for granted and exclude from considerations of justice much of what women now do, since men would share in it equally. Such central components of justice as what counts as productive labor, and what count as needs and deserts, would be greatly affected by this change. Standards of justice would become *humanist,* as they have never been before. One of the most important effects of this would be to change radically the situation of women as citizens. With egalitarian families, and with institutions such as workplaces and schools designed to accommodate the needs of parents and children, rather than being based as they now are on the traditional assumption that "someone else" is at home, mothers would not be virtually excluded from positions of influence in politics and the workplace. They would be represented at every level in approximately equal numbers with men.

In a genderless society, children too would benefit. They would not suffer in the ways that they do now because of the injustices done to women. . . . First, the growing gap between the economic well-being of children in single-parent and those in two-parent families would be reduced. . . .

Second, children of both sexes in gender-free families would have (as some already have) much more opportunity for self-development free from sex-role expectations and sex-typed personalities than most do now. . . .

Finally, it seems undeniable that the enhancement of justice that accompanies the disappearance of gender will make the family a much better place for children to develop a sense of justice. We can no longer deny the importance of the fact that families are where we first learn, by example and by how we are treated, not only how people do relate to each other but also how they *should*. How would families not built on gender be better

schools of moral development? First, the example of co-equal parents with shared roles, combining love with justice, would provide a far better example of human relations for children than the domination and dependence that often occur in traditional marriage. The fairness of the distribution of labor, the equal respect, and the *inter*dependence of his or her parents would surely be a powerful first example to a child in a family with equally shared roles. Second, as I have argued, having a sense of justice requires that we be able to empathize, to abstract from our own situation and to think about moral and political issues from the points of view of others. . . .

To the extent that gender is de-emphasized in our nurturing practices, this capacity would seem to be enhanced, for two reasons. First, if female primary parenting leads, as it seems to, to less distinct ego boundaries and greater capacity for empathy in female children, and to a greater tendency to self-definition and abstraction in males, then might we not expect to find the two capacities better combined in children of both sexes who are reared by parents of both sexes? Second, the experience of *being* nurturers, throughout a significant portion of our lives, also seems likely to result in an increase in empathy, and in the combination of personal moral capacities, fusing feelings with reason, that just citizens need. . . .

Study Questions on Susan Moller Okin

1. Do you find Okin's argument that the traditional family is unjust convincing?
2. Okin thinks of marriage with divorce in mind. Is she just being realistic, or does thinking of marriage in this way lead to destabilization of the family and more divorces?
3. Okin claims that her proposals would be chosen under a veil of ignorance about whether one was a man or a woman, a traditionalist or a feminist. Do you agree?
4. Does Okin take the interests of traditional women sufficiently into account? Those of children? Those of males?

The Power of the Positive Woman

PHYLLIS SCHLAFLY

Phyllis Schlafly defends what she calls "the Positive Woman," who rejects the lure of women's liberation and finds fulfillment in the opportunities offered by conventional American marriage. An important part of her argument is an unappetizing picture of the opportunities presented by the world outside the home.

. . . THE POSITIVE WOMAN starts with the assumption that the world is her oyster. She rejoices in the creative capability within her body and the power potential of her mind and spirit. She understands that men and women are different, and that those very differences provide the key to her success as a person and fulfillment as a woman.

The women's liberationist, on the other hand, is imprisoned by her own negative view of herself and of her place in the world around her. This view of women was most succinctly expressed in an advertisement designed by the principal women's liberationist organization, the National Organization for Women (NOW), and run in many magazines and newspapers and as spot announcements on many television stations. The advertisement showed a darling curlyheaded girl with the caption: "This healthy, normal baby has a handicap. She was born female." . . .

The second dogma of the women's liberationists is that, of all the injustices perpetrated upon women through the centuries, the most oppressive is the cruel fact that women have babies and men do not. Within the confines of the women's liberationist ideology, therefore, the abolition of this overriding inequality of women becomes the primary goal. This goal must be achieved at any and all costs—to the woman herself, to the baby, to the family, and to society. Women must be made equal to men in their ability *not* to become pregnant and *not* to be expected to care for babies they may bring into the world.

This is why women's liberationists are compulsively involved in the drive to make abortion and child-care centers for all women, regardless of religion or income, both socially acceptable and government-financed. . . .

If man is targeted as the enemy, and the ultimate goal of women's liberation is independence from men and the avoidance of pregnancy and its consequences, then lesbianism is logically the highest form in the ritual of women's liberation.

The Positive Woman will never travel that dead-end road. It is self-evident to the Positive Woman that the female body with its baby-producing organs was not designed by a conspiracy of men but by the Divine Architect of the human race. Those who think it is unfair that women have babies, whereas men cannot, will have to take up their complaint with God because no other power is capable of changing that fundamental fact. . . .

The differences between men and women are also emotional and psychological. Without woman's innate maternal instinct, the human race would have died out centuries ago. There is nothing so helpless in all earthly life as the newborn infant. It will die within hours if not cared for. Even in the most primitive, uneducated societies, women have always cared for their newborn babies. . . .

Why? Because caring for a baby serves the natural maternal need of a woman. Although not nearly so total as the baby's need, the woman's need is nonetheless real.

The overriding psychological need of a woman is to love something alive. A baby fulfills this need in the lives of most women. If a baby is not available to fill that need, women search for a baby-substitute. This is the reason why women have traditionally gone into teaching and nursing careers. They are doing what comes naturally to the female psyche. The schoolchild or the patient of any age provides an outlet for a woman to express her natural maternal need. . . .

This is not to say that every woman must have a baby in order to be fulfilled. But it is to say that fulfillment for most women involves expressing their natural maternal urge by loving and caring for someone.

The women's liberation movement complains that traditional stereotyped roles assume that women are "passive" and that men are "aggressive." The anomaly is that a woman's most fundamental emotional need is not passive at all, but active. A woman naturally seeks to love affirmatively and to show that love in an active way by caring for the object of her affections. . . .

American women are also especially fortunate to be the beneficiaries of the Judeo-Christian tradition, which accords a status to women unknown in the rest of the world. Our Judeo-Christian civilization has developed laws and customs that, since women must bear the physical consequences of the sex act, require men to assume other consequences. These laws and customs decree that a man must carry his share by physical protection and financial support of his children and of the woman who bears his children, and also by a code of behavior that benefits and protects both the woman and the children.

This is accomplished by the institution of the family. Our respect for the family as the basic unit of society, which is firmly ingrained in the laws and customs of our Judeo-Christian civilization, is the greatest single achievement in the entire history of women's rights. It assures a woman the precious right to keep and care for her own baby and to be supported and protected in the enjoyment of watching her baby grow and develop . . . .

In some African and Indian societies, the men strut around wearing feathers and beads and hunting and fishing, while the women do all the tiresome, manual drudgery, including tilling the soil, hewing wood, making fires, hauling water, and building dwellings—not to mention cooking, sewing, and caring for babies.

This is not the American way. In America, one of the first significant purchases a man makes is a ring for his bride, and the largest financial investment of his life is a home for her to live in. American husbands work hours of overtime to pay premiums on life insurance policies to provide for their wives' comfort when they are widows (benefits in which the husbands will never share). In India, by contrast, the problem of supporting the widow was taken care of for centuries by inducing her to commit *suttee* (flinging herself on her husband's funeral pyre). . . .

The women's liberation movement makes much of the fact that, despite laws requiring equal pay for equal work, statistics show that women hold only a small minority of the high-paying executive and professional positions. The statistics are accurate, but the reason is not discrimination. No person, man or woman, rises to those high-income ranks on a forty-hour week. Ask any successful doctor, lawyer, or business executive. They have invariably spent years working nights and weekends, bringing home briefcases bulging with work, and serving clients or customers in a steady stream outside of office hours. . . .

For any man or woman who chooses that life, there is plenty of room at the top. The stakes are high, and it is a personal decision as to whether the rewards of money, power, and prestige are worth the sacrifices and the risks. Many men think they are. The plain fact is that most women don't. Why? It certainly is not because they lack a willingness to do hard and sustained work, and it probably is not even because they lack a capacity for competition. It is because, for most women, something else comes first in their lives—namely, marriage and motherhood—and business or professional success does not rate high enough in their scale of values to permit it to steal so much time from the home. Many talented women may want to have some of both careers, but home remains primary in their scale of values, while a business or professional career is secondary. . . .

Another element to cope with in the matter of women rising to top executive and professional positions is the preferences of women themselves. The Gallup Poll reconfirmed in April, 1976, what every personnel manager has always known: by a ratio of six to one, women would rather have a man than a woman as their boss. Most women would rather deal with male than female doctors, lawyers, and bankers. Should a company be compelled to make one woman happy by promoting her to "foreperson," but make twenty women unhappy who do not want to accept her as their boss? . . .

The small number of women in Congress proves only that most women do not want to do the things that must be done to win election—

drive all those thousands of miles, shake all those strangers' hands, eat all those third-rate chicken suppers, attend political meetings every night and weekend, subject themselves to press and political attacks that impugn their integrity and their motives, and face probes into personal life and finances. Most women say it isn't worth it. . . . To allocate half the seats in governmental bodies to that small minority of women who choose a political career over home and family—in the mistaken notion that they represent *all* women—would be the world's most grievous abdication of authority by a supine majority to a militant minority. . . .

The Positive Woman recognizes that there is a valid and enduring purpose behind this recognition of different roles for men and women which is just as relevant in the twentieth century as it was in the time of Saint Paul.

Any successful vehicle must have one person at the wheel with ultimate responsibility. . . .

Every successful country and company has one "chief executive officer." None successfully functions with responsibility equally divided between cochairmen or copresidents. . . .

If marriage is to be a successful institution, it must likewise have an ultimate decision maker, and that is the husband. Seen in this light, the laws that give the husband the right to establish the domicile of the marriage and to give his surname to his children are good laws designed to keep the family together. They are not anachronisms from a bygone era from which wives should be liberated in the name of equality. If a woman does not want to live in her husband's home, she is not entitled to the legal rights of a wife. Those women who preach that a wife should have the right to establish her own separate domicile do not stay married very long. That "equal right" is simply incompatible with a happy lifetime marriage.

The women's liberationists look upon marriage as an institution of dirty dishes and dirty diapers. They spend a lot of energy writing marriage contracts that divide up what they consider the menial, degrading chores. The much quoted "Shulmans' marriage agreement," for example, includes such provisions as "Husband does dishes on Tuesday, Thursday and Sunday. Wife does Monday, Wednesday and Saturday, Friday is split. . . ," and "wife strips beds, husband remakes them." If the baby cries in the night, the chore of "handling" the

baby is assigned as follows: "Husband does Tuesday, Thursday and Sunday. Wife does Monday, Wednesday and Saturday, Friday is split. . . ." Presumably, if the baby cries for his mother on Tuesday night, he would be informed that the marriage contract prohibits her from responding.

It is possible, in such a loveless home, that the baby would never call for his mother at all. . . .

If you think diapers and dishes are a never-ending, repetitive routine, just remember that most of the jobs outside the home are just as repetitious, tiresome, and boring. Consider the assembly-line worker who pulls the same lever, pushes the same button, or inspects thousands of identical bits of metal or glass or paper, hour after weary hour; the stenographer who turns out page after page of typing; the telephone operator; the retail clerk who must repeatedly bite her lip because "the customer is always right." . . .

The Price of a Happy Marriage

In their attack on marriage and the home, the women's liberationists tell young women that *Cinderella* and all fairy tales in which the girl meets her Prince Charming and they "live happily ever after" are a myth and a delusion. One thing is sure. If you make up your mind that you will never find your "Prince Charming," you won't. If you decide in advance that it is impossible to "live happily ever after," you won't. It all *can* happen to you, however, if you make up your mind that it *will* happen. I *know*—because it happened to me.

A happy marriage is truly a pearl of great price, but it isn't something to be discovered by searching in faraway places. Nor is it like a lucky strike for oil or gold. It is like a garden that yields a good crop when the seed is planted and the ground is cultivated regularly. . . .

The Positive Woman knows that there are two main pillars of a happy marriage and that she has the capability to build both. The first is that a wife must appreciate and admire her husband. Whereas a woman's chief emotional need is active (i.e., to love), a man's prime emotional need is passive (i.e., to be appreciated or admired). . . .

Is this degrading to the wife? Humiliating? Subservient? Or any of the other extravagant liberationist adjectives? How ridiculous! It is just the application of the Golden Rule with a simple male/female variation. Most women think that the prize is worth the price.

A satisfying and rewarding relationship between a man and a woman can last through the years only if she is willing to give him the appreciation and the admiration his manhood craves. . . .

Among the dozens of fallacies of the women's liberation movement is the cluster of mistaken notions that traditional marriage is based on the wife's submerging her identity in her husband's, catering to his every whim, binding herself to seven days and nights a week inside the four walls of the home, stultifying her intellectual or professional or community interests, and otherwise reducing herself to the caricature of the dumb, helpless blonde, or a domestic servant.

What nonsense. It is true (and properly so) that the husband is naturally possessive about his wife's sexual favors, but he is seldom possessive of his wife's mind, time, or talents. A Positive Man is delighted to have his wife pursue her talents and spend her time however she pleases. The more she achieves, the prouder he is—*so long as* he knows that he is Number One in her life, and that she needs him. . . .

One way of handling decision making in a marriage is to divide jurisdictions between husband and wife. The story is told about the husband who proudly told his friends: "When my wife and I were married, we agreed that I would make all the major decisions, and she would make the minor ones. I decide what legislation Congress should pass, what treaties the president should sign, and whether the United States should stay in the United Nations. My wife makes the minor decisions—such as how we spend our money, whether I should change my job, where we should live, and where we go on our vacations."

The Positive Woman is skillful enough to draw the jurisdictional line at the most advantageous point in *her* marriage. . . .

The second pillar of a happy marriage is cheerfulness. No other quality can do so much to ensure a happy marriage as a happy disposition.

Life is full of problems and everyone has his or her share. A great part of most people's time and energy is occupied with trying to cope with financial problems, health problems, social problems, and emotional problems—their own and those of their families. You may think that you are the first person in the world who ever faced tragic or intransigent circumstances, but you are not. Everyone's own problems always seem the most momentous, the most insoluble, and the most unjust. . . .

A cheerful disposition can guide you over countless obstacles. A wife's cheerful disposition will draw her husband like a magnet. Why would a husband want to stop off at the local bar instead of coming straight home? Unless he has already become addicted to alcohol, the subconscious reason is probably because everyone there is cheerful and no one is nagging him. If home is to have a greater lure than the tavern, the wife must be at least as cheerful as the waitress. . . .

The biggest problem for wives in their middle years is boredom and idleness. It can even be a fatal disease. . . .

The solution for both problems of the middle years is to keep busy. Work is the great cure for most of the ills of the world. Every community is crying for the kind of volunteer work that women can best give: welfare, hospital, educational, cultural, civic, and political. All these avenues provide opportunities for women to perform useful services to the community—and in so doing to become happier, more interesting, and more fulfilled. . . .

A woman needs to love and to show that love by serving the object of her affections. A good cause can provide an outlet for her continuing maternal urge in the years between the time when her children go off to school and when she is discovered by her grandchildren.

The women's liberationists show outspoken contempt for volunteer service. They try to dissuade women from volunteering their time and energies to any cause (unless it serves a liberationist goal). In their inverted scale of values, they judge every service by money, never by love. Yet, the social and cultural services of most communities would collapse if all their volunteers were to walk out.

But the women who quit their volunteer "jobs" would suffer even more. The woman who cheerfully volunteers her time and talents to serve others gains more than her needy beneficiaries. . . .

Only a woman who has, or somehow allows herself to be given, a negative view of herself could follow the Pied Pipers of women's liberation. The Positive Woman is too busy doing constructive work to brood over her own misfortunes, real though they may be.

Study Questions on Phyllis Schlafly

1. Do you agree with Schlafly that feminists have adopted a negative view of women? That women naturally gravitate toward occupations that provide an outlet for their need to love and care for the object of their love?
2. Some feminists hold that marriage is morally akin to prostitution, in that women provide a man with sex, emotional care, and children in exchange for protection, comfort, and security. Is Schlafly's ideal of marriage open to this criticism?
3. Is it an objection to her argument that only relatively well-to-do men can afford to have a wife who stays at home? That most people, whether men or women, do not have a real chance to rise to the top?
4. Is she a defender of female subordination?

Feminists Against the Family

JEAN BETHKE ELSHTAIN

Jean Bethke Elshtain examines the harsh attacks on the biological family, on permanent commitments of adults to children, and on childbearing itself that have occurred just when women and men have been in the best position to reduce the oppressive features of human biology. She concludes that they are an example of *the politics of displacement,* which erodes personal life even as it inhibits the emergence of a genuine public life. She criticizes the claim that "the personal is the political" and the reduction of politics to power relations, which together imply that a sex war replaces serious social and political struggle. She sees the feminist movement as a direct outgrowth of the intensification of contradictory burdens on family members produced by the Industrial Revolution. She defends the family as an institution that, whatever its flaws and stresses, can resist total domination by the values of the marketplace. In the family, a child is taught to see himself or herself as unique and unconditionally loved—as having a "dignity," and not just a "price."

WHATEVER ITS SINS AGAINST GENERATIONS of mothers and daughters, the family has served the women's movement well: located by feminists as the key to female oppression, it has been offered up as *the* institution to reform, revolutionize or destroy if feminist aims are to be realized. As a catalyst for rethinking the terms of public and private reality, the family has also provided feminist thinkers with inexhaustible material for dissecting the human condition from the vantage point of this, its central bête noire.

Much that is exciting and fruitful emerged from this ferment. Connections between sexuality, authority and power were opened up for debate in a provocative way. Women were encouraged to create conceptual and linguistic tools to help them pierce the patterns of social reality. Through consciousness-raising, hundreds of women began to view themselves less as passive recipients of revocable privileges and more as active, responsible human beings. But from the start something was terribly wrong with much of the feminist treatment

From The Nation *(November 17, 1979). Reprinted with permission.*

of the family. By "wrong" I don't mean so much careless or unscholarly by traditional canons of historic and social science methodology, though one saw evidence of both. I refer instead to an imperative more deeply rooted and bitter, which erupted from time to time in mean-spirited denunciations of all relations between men and women and in expressions of contempt for the female body, for pregnancy, childbirth and child-rearing.

In my view, the feminist movement has contributed to the discrediting of what Dorothy Dinnerstein, a psychoanalytic feminist thinker, calls the "essential humanizing functions of stable, long-standing, generation-spanning primary groups" and the "virulent, reckless, reactive quality of much feminist rhetoric against the biological family, against permanent personal commitments of adults to childhood . . . against childbearing itself [has occurred] ironically, when women and men have been in the best position to minimize the oppressive features of human biology." The result has been the creation of what I shall call a *politics of displacement,* which erodes personal life even as it vitiates the emergence of a genuine public life. This feminist politics of displacement, in turn, helps to provoke a troubling mirror-image. How has this come about?

The key to feminist politics lies in a phrase that has served simultaneously as an explanatory principle, a motto and an article of faith: "The Personal Is Political." Note that the claim is not that the personal and the political are interrelated in important and fascinating ways not yet fully explored and previously hidden to us by patriarchal ideology and practice; nor that the personal and the political may be fruitfully examined as analogous to one another along certain touchstones of power and privilege, but that the personal *is* political. What is asserted is an identity: a collapse of the one into the other. Nothing "personal" is exempt, then, from political definition, direction and manipulation—neither sexual intimacy, love, nor parenting.

By reducing politics to what are seen as "power relations," important thinkers in all wings of the women's movement, but centered in the radical feminist perspective, have preferred as an alternative to the malaise of the present a rather bleak Hobbesianism rejuvenated in feminist guise. For if politics is power and power is everywhere, politics is in fact nowhere and a vision of public life as the touchstone of a revitalized ideal of citizenship is lost. These are serious charges and I shall docu-

ment them by turning to the manner in which radical feminist images of the "sex war," centered in the family, are served up as a substitute for social and political struggle.

To have a war one needs enemies, and radical feminism (as distinguished from liberal, Marxist or socialist, and psychoanalytic feminism) has no difficulty finding him. The portrait of man which emerges from radical feminist texts is that of an implacable enemy, an incorrigible and dangerous beast who has as his chief aim in life the oppression and domination of women. Ti-Grace Atkinson attributes this male compulsion to man's a priori need to oppress others, an imperative termed "metaphysical cannibalism" from which women are exempt. Susan Brownmiller's male is tainted with an *animus dominandi* which makes him a "natural predator." Mary Daly's male is less bestial, more ghoulish, a vampire who feeds "on the bodies and minds of women. . . . Like Dracula, the he-male has lived on women's blood." Women, however, escape the curse of original sin, being accorded a separate and divergent ontological status. In their views on male and female nature, radical feminists sadly confuse "natural" and "social" categories (as they accuse apologists for patriarchal privilege of doing by manipulating the terms "nature" and "culture" for their own ideological ends). For if male and female roles in society flow directly from some biological given, there is little or nothing politics can do to alter the situation.

. . .

Although women escape the curse of an unblessed birth, they are treated to considerable scorn by radical feminists under the guise of "demystifying" their "biological functions." Pregnancy is characterized as "the temporary deformation of the body for the sake of the species." Shulamith Firestone rubs salt into the wound by relating a story of a group of malicious children who point their fingers at a pregnant woman and taunt mercilessly "Who's the fat lady?" The fetus is labeled variously a "tenant," a "parasite" and an "uninvited guest." Heterosexual sex is reduced to "using people, conning people, messing over people, conquering people, exploiting people." And love? A "pathological condition," a "mass neurosis" which must be destroyed. Childbirth is painful and hideous. Motherhood is portrayed as a condition of terminal psychological and social decay, total self-abnegation and physical deterioration. The new mother is "barely coherent . . . stutters . . . bumps into stationary objects." What has all this to do with politics? The answer, for radical feminists, is everything, given that the "personal is political."

The only way to stop all this, they go on, is to eliminate the patriarchal nuclear family. The argument runs something like this: because "tyranny" begins in biology or nature, nature itself must be changed. *All else* will follow, for it is biological "tyranny," the sex distinction itself, that oppresses women. Having accepted as a necessary and sufficient condition for social change the total "restructuring" of relations between the sexes, Firestone, for example, fizzles into a combination of trivial self-help ("a revolutionary in every bedroom") and a barbaric cybernetic utopia within which every aspect of life rests in the beneficent hands of a new elite of engineers, cyberneticians animated by the victorious Female Principle. Brownmiller's solution to the sex war lodged in male biology and the "rape culture" that is an automatic outgrowth of man's unfortunate anatomy is a loveless Sparta, a "stalemate" in the sex war in which women have been "fully integrated into the extant power structure—police, national guards, state troopers, local sheriffs' offices, state prosecuting attorneys' offices, armed forces"—in other words, just about any male activity that involves a uniform, a badge, a gun or a law degree.

These suggested solutions to masculine perfidy and biological "tyranny" exemplify a politics of displacement for they cannot be specified with any concreteness nor acted upon, remaining utopian and abstract; at other times they envisage a female takeover of the extant "power structure," thus vitiating consideration of the structural dimensions of our current crisis, which lie in the specific practices of production, the nature of life work, the problems of political accountability and of social stratification along lines of ethnicity, class and race as well as sex.

Except for its ludicrous caricature of the married person as a family fanatic busily engaged in putting single people down, a more recent and sophisticated treatment of radical feminist themes, Ellen Willis's *Village Voice* article, "The Family: Love It or Leave It," avoids many of the crude oversimplifications I have cited. Willis expresses much of the richness and ambivalence internal to family life and to an honest contemplation of that life. Finally, however, her essay collapses under the weight of several contradictions. She insists, for example, that familial matters include public issues that should be the grounds for political decision making. Yet she provides no basis for genuine political action because her strategy remains steadfastly individualistic. ("If people stopped . . . If enough parents . . . If enough women . . .")

Indeed, it is difficult to determine how and why "people, enough parents, women" could mount an effective assault on the public issues Willis finds embedded in our private lives if one of her other claims, that capitalists "have an obvious stake in encouraging dependence on the family," is as overriding as she says it is. She fails to realize that one could make precisely the opposite case—with strong support from historic case studies, something Willis never sees fit to provide—that capitalists have historically had an interest in breaking up family units and eroding family ties. The capitalist ideal is a society of social atoms, beings not essentially connected to one another, to a time, or to a place, who could be shunted about according to market imperatives alone.

Liberal feminism's indictments of family life and men are less bloodcurdling, although Betty Friedan couldn't resist the alliterative "comfortable concentration camp" as a description of suburban housewifery. Friedan's women vegetated as menfolk went off to the city and "kept on growing." Friedan's presumption that the world of work within capitalist society is infinitely preferable to the world of the home is a linchpin of liberal feminism and serves to highlight the class-bound nature of their reflections. Friedan certainly didn't have eight hours a day on an assembly line in mind when she denigrated familial life and celebrated work life. Elizabeth Janeway, another liberal thinker, insists that a man has it over a woman in contemporary society because he knows where he stands; he receives rewards according to pre-existing standards of judgment in the marketplace. Women, however, out of the running for the prizes, are confused as to their "true value" (i.e., market worth). Women can take care of this unfortunate state of affairs as individuals, acting alone and being political simply by being "role breakers," a move that simultaneously puts them into the market arena and "threaten(s) the order of the universe."

Marxist feminists put forth conflicting views of family life, but those operating within an orthodox Marxist-Leninist framework are locked into a narrow econometric model that sees both the family and politics as epiphenomenal, having no autonomous nor semiautonomous existence of their own. Within this perspective, politics is displaced onto economic concerns exclusively and, paradoxically, depoliticized as a result. Mothering becomes "the reproduction of the labor force" or "the future commodity labor power." Should a mother take umbrage at this characterization of her alternately joyous and vexing activity, it is taken as evidence of her "false consciousness." (There are, however, feminists working within the Marxist tradition who have a more complex image of familial life, and I discuss their views briefly below.)

Taken all in all, the image that emerges from contemporary feminism's treatment of the family is that of a distortion so systematic that it has become another symptom of the disease it seeks to diagnose. One of the key symptoms of this disease— this "legitimation crisis"—is a widespread draining of society's social institutions, public and private, of their value and significance. In stripping away the old ideological guises that celebrated motherhood and denigrated women, extolled the dignity of private life yet disallowed parents the means with which to live in decency and with dignity, feminists performed a necessary and important service. But unmasking an ideology and constructing a sound theory are not the same activity. Ironically, a new feminist ideology has emerged to replace the old patriarchal one. It, like the old, exerts a silencing effect over free and open debate on a whole range of issues having to do with female sexuality, the conflicting demands of contemporary heterosexuality, pregnancy, childbirth and child-rearing, and family life, even as it provides no alternative vision of a revitalized concept of "citizenship."

My concern is with that anti-familial feminist ideology that has become linked up in the popular mind with efforts to erode or destroy the meaning and relations of family life *in the absence of any workable alternative*. I have described the complex process at work as a politics of displacement, a form of pseudopolitics in which the symptoms of social breakdown are construed as the disease itself, allowing the deeper dimensions of the crisis to go unchallenged.

Feminist thinkers, in their quest to identify the breeding ground of patriarchal privilege, found a sitting duck in the family. But this is as much attributable to our confusion and malaise over the family's proper social role as it is to feminist prescience. Since the advent of the Industrial Revolution, Western society has faced a "crisis in the family" with each successive generation. The chain of events set in motion by industrialism eventually stripped the family of most of its previous functions as a productive, vocational, religious, educative and welfare unit. As these functions were absorbed by other social institutions and practices, the family remained the locus of intimate, long-term reproductive relations and child-rearing activities. The strains of these shifts are reflected historically in the works of great novelists, political and social theorists and the theory and practice of psychoanalysis.

The feminist movement is, then—at least in part—a direct outgrowth of the intensification of contradictory burdens and demands on family members. The family is a product of uneven development, existing as a purposeful and vital unit within *every* extant society, yet resisting, within capitalist society, total domination by relations of exchange and the values of the marketplace. Diverse aspects of social practices collide within the family: little girls, for example, may be inculcated with the American ideology of equality of opportunity, receive an education identical to that of their brothers yet, simultaneously, learn an ideology of womanhood and domesticity incompatible with the other ideological imperatives they also hold. Nevertheless, the family, however shakily and imperfectly, helps to keep alive an alternative to the values which dominate in the marketplace. It serves, in the words of Eli Zaretsky, as a reminder of the hope that "human beings can pass beyond a life dominated by relations of production." This vital role played by the family in modern life is recognized by a minority of feminist thinkers who hold the socialist and psychoanalytic perspectives. Indeed, one of the most lyrical evocations of the importance of holding on to that which is valuable in family life, if social relations are not to become thoroughly brutal, may be found in the words of Sheila Rowbotham, a British Marxist feminist, who writes of the family as a "place of sanctuary for all the haunted, jaded, exhausted sentiments out of place in commodity production. . . . The family is thus in one sense the dummy ideal, the repository of ghostly substitutes, emotional fictions. . . . But this distortion of human relations is the only place where human beings find whatever continuing love, security, and comfort they know."

Each child taught to see himself or herself as unique and unconditionally loved, a being (to draw upon Kant) having "dignity," not merely a "price," represents a challenge to the terms of the market system, just as noninstrumental human intimacy is a similar affront to increasingly sophisticated attempts to merchandise every area of human sexual life. Yet these family ties and relations are fragile, subject to strains and breakdowns and to a coarsening that reflects in miniature the abuses of the world outside. Reported incidents of child abuse, for example, rise dramatically during periods of widespread unemployment and economic despair as outward frustrations, in another variant on the politics of displacement, are displaced privately onto the family's most vulnerable members.

The politics of displacement is nothing new under the political sun. Past examples that spring to mind include the policies of the Romanov czars who, over the years, implicated Russia in some external imbroglio whenever they wished to shift public attention away from their domestic politics. A more sinister instance is the use of German Jews as scapegoats for the widespread social dislocation and hardship that followed the end of World War I, a politics of displacement perfected by fascism. In the history of American capitalist expansion and labor strife, one finds the frequent pitting of poor white and black unemployed against each other in such a way that each group saw the other as the source of its misery and corporate oligarchs escaped serious political challenge. Feminism's politics of displacement reveals its true colors when a feminist thinker assaults a social unit, already vulnerable and weakened by external and internal strains, as both *cause* and *symptom* of female subordination. In so doing, those feminists direct attention away from structural imperatives and constraints and promote a highly personalized sexual politics that is simultaneously depoliticizing, individualistic and potentially pernicious in its implications.

The implication of a feminist politics of displacement for politics itself is simply this: a displaced pseudopolitics vitiates attempts to articulate an ideal of public life as the deliberate efforts by citizens to "order, direct, and control their collective affairs and activities, to establish ends for their society, and to implement and evaluate these ends." Feminism's politics of displacement renders politics hollow, first, by finding politics everywhere; second, by reducing politics to crude relations of force or domination, and third, by stripping politics of its centrality to a shared social identity. It erodes private life by construing it as a power-riddled battleground, thus encouraging a crudely politicized approach toward coitus, marriage, child-rearing, even one's relationship to one's own body. It shares with all spinoffs of classical liberalism the failure to develop a vision of a political community and of citizenship that might serve as the touchstone of a collective identity for males and females alike. As Michael Walzer put it recently: "What made liberalism endurable for all these years was the fact that the individualism it generated was imperfect, tempered by older restraints and loyalties, by stable patterns of local, ethnic, religious or class relationships. An untempered liberalism would be unendurable." Feminist thinkers have yet to confront this sobering realization.

Study Questions on Jean Bethke Elshtain

1. Elshtain finds something "terribly wrong with much of the feminist treatment of the family." What is it?
2. Explain what Elshtain means by the politics of displacement. What is displaced onto what?
3. What unique values does Elshtain find in family life? Might they be found elsewhere?
4. "An untempered liberalism would be unendurable." What does this statement mean? Do you agree?

When the Bough Breaks

SYLVIA ANN HEWLETT

Sylvia Ann Hewlett begins by observing that children are now failing to flourish throughout contemporary America, both absolutely and in comparison with other rich democracies. Children suffer from two deficits: the *resource deficit,* or failure to invest public money in our children; and the *time deficit,* or sharp decline in the amount of time parents spend caring for their children. She proposes: *workplace policies,* such as flexible time for parents; *career sequencing,* or the ability to take extended parenting leave without losing one's job; and *divorce reform,* designed to bring down the rate of divorce and ensure that children of divorcing parents are not abandoned or impoverished. More broadly, she calls for *family support policies,* designed to reduce the price we ask women to pay for their children; these policies would both restore traditional family patterns and contribute significantly to achieving equality of economic opportunity between men and women.

ACROSS THE FACE OF AMERICA, children are failing to flourish. Rich kids, middle-class kids, poor kids—all deal with risk and neglect on a scale unimagined in previous generations. Problems of poverty, divorce, out-of-wedlock births, absentee parents, latchkey kids, violence, and drugs are no longer confined to the ghetto. They reach deep into the mainstream; they belong to "us" as well as to "them." Child neglect has become endemic to our society, and childhood is now "far more precarious and less safe for millions of America's children." In the words of a 1990 National Commission, "never before has one generation of American children been less healthy, less cared for, or less prepared for life than their parents were at the same age." According to an index that measures the social health of children and youth, the well-being of children has declined dramatically over the last twenty years. In 1970 the index stood at 68; by 1987 it had plummeted to 37.

The Facts of Child Neglect

Most of us know that it's rough out there. Children are not doing well in late-twentieth-century America. But few of us realize how bad things have become. Consider the following:

- 20 percent of all children are growing up in poverty, a 21 percent increase since 1970.
- 330,000 children are homeless.
- the rate of suicide among adolescents has tripled since 1960.
- 42 percent of fathers fail to see their children in the wake of divorce.
- 27 percent of teenagers drop out of high school.

Children in America are at much greater risk than children elsewhere in the advanced industrial world. Compared with other rich countries, children in the United States are much more likely to die before their first birthday; to live in poverty; to be abandoned by their fathers; and to be killed before they reach the age of twenty-five. Although the United States ranks No. 2 worldwide in per capita income, this country does not even make it into the top ten on any significant indicator of child welfare.

The problems of our youth range from elemental issues of health and safety to more complicated issues of motivation and performance. We cannot ensure the safety of children on the streets or in our homes. . . .

Nor can we keep our children healthy. Infant mortality in the United States places it twentieth in the world, behind such countries as Spain and Singapore. . . .

On the education front the news is even more grim, since underachievement and failure are now widespread. An October 1988 ABC News Special entitled "Burning Questions: America's Kids: Why They Flunk" opened with the following dialogue:

INTERVIWER: Do you know who's running for president?

FIRST STUDENT: Who, run? Ooh. I don't watch the news.

INTERVIWER: Do you know when the Vietnam War was?

SECOND STUDENT: Don't even ask me that. I don't know.

INTERVIWER: What side won the Civil War?

THIRD STUDENT: I have no idea.

INTERVIWER: Do you know when the American Civil War was?

FOURTH STUDENT: 1970.

These are not students from some inner-city ghetto. The children featured in this program attended middle-class high schools in Bridgeville, Pennsylvania, and Pine Bluff, Arkansas. But despite the mainstream contexts, these youngsters are not learning a whole lot in school. Across the nation, combined average Scholastic Aptitude Test (SAT) scores have fallen 70 points since 1963. Experts say that only half of high school students are performing even moderately well, and many of their problems seem to be rooted in the family. . . .

American kids are at or near the bottom in most international surveys measuring educational achievement: seventh out of ten countries in physics; ninth out of ten countries in chemistry; and tenth—dead last—in average mathematics proficiency. . . . The United States does do well in one area, though: it ranks No. 1 in the percentage of thirteen-year-olds who watch five or more hours of TV every day. The typical eighth-grader now spends four times as many hours watching TV per week as on homework. . . .

A Comparative Perspective

We think of America as a child-centered nation. We like to boast that our children are cherished, pro-

tected, nurtured, and offered a field of opportunity unmatched elsewhere in the world. We see ourselves as valuing children to a fault—indeed, we brag about "spoiling" them.

Close inspection reveals a much less comforting reality. Over the past twenty-five years, slowly but relentlessly, American society has been tilting in an ominous new direction—toward the devaluation of children. "There has been an alarming weakening of a fundamental assumption, long at the center of our culture, that children are to be loved and valued at the highest level of priority." In the public sphere, our policies display a weak and eroding commitment to children. We slash school budgets, build "adults only" housing, and deny working parents the right to spend a few weeks with their newborn babies. In 1987 less than 5 percent of the federal budget was devoted to programs that benefit children—one-fifth the amount we spent that year on persons over sixty-five. . . .

The other rich democracies continue to give children much higher priority. Great Britain, France, Sweden, and Canada spend two or three times as much as the United States on families with children—which helps explain why so many more American than European or Canadian children live below the poverty line.

The Twin Deficits

This *resource deficit,* this failure to invest public money in our children, is aggravated by a growing *time deficit.* Over the last decades there has been a sharp decline in the amount of time parents spend caring for their children. According to economist Victor Fuchs, children have lost ten to twelve hours of parental time per week since 1960. Parental time has been squeezed by the rapid shift of mothers into the labor force; by escalating divorce rates and the abandonment of children by their fathers; and by an increase in the number of hours required on the job. Today the average worker puts in six hours more per week than in 1973. This reduction in parental time has had an extremely negative impact on children. . . . [T]he research shows that unsupervised "latchkey" kids are at increased risk of substance abuse, and that children with little or no contact with their fathers are unlikely to perform well at school.

One thing is sure: our failure to invest either public resources or private time in the raising of children has left many families fragile and overburdened, unable to do a decent job in raising the next generation. True, some children continue to be raised in supportive communities by thoughtful, attentive parents, but the larger fact is that the whole drift of our society, our government policies, and our private adult choices is toward blighting our youngsters and stunting their potential. An anti-child spirit is loose in the land. . . .

Workplace Policy

. . . [C]orporate America is developing elaborate family support policies, which will soon reach a significant proportion of all working parents in America. The role of government in this area is to *shape and complement private sector efforts.*

- Government should encourage corporations to address the *family time famine.* This is a critical task because of the divergence of interest between what is good for employers and what is good for children—both want more of a parent's time! Government should therefore weigh in and persuade firms to provide "time" as well as "resources" in their family-friendly benefits package. . . .

In some states companies that offer on-site child care already qualify for tax concessions. Why not extend this concept? If carefully tailored tax incentives prompted companies to extend flextime to a majority of employees, many more parents would be able to work 7:00 A.M. to 3:00 P.M. and be home in time to catch up with the kids in those important after-school hours.

Time-enhancing workplace policies have impressive win-win properties. Take the issue of *career sequencing.* The ability to take extended parenting leave without losing one's job; the ability to share a job for two or ten years; the ability to construct a challenging and remunerative part-time career—these are tremendously attractive options for professional parents who are often faced with the choice of working a fifty-hour week or getting off a career ladder designed for men with at-home wives. In the contemporary economy, conventional career structures can be unfair and ineffi-

cient. Not only do rigid career trajectories discriminate heavily against women (who tend to take time out to have children) but they are wasteful of human capital. With mothers comprising more than half of all labor market entrants over the next decade, it is in the self-interest of companies to use their woman-power well, to make sure that some of their best educated and most valuable workers are not cast aside or thrown away because of a career interruption. In other words, given the demographic pressures of the 1990s, government should find it relatively easy to prod corporations into being responsive to the needs of working parents and their children, rather than attempt to make parents and children fit into the rigid structures of established business practice.

Divorce Reform

Government should *seek to bring down the rate of divorce* by constructing a set of rewards and penalties that encourage parents to stay together. In the event of marital breakdown, the role of government is to create a legal framework that ensures children are not abandoned or impoverished in the wake of divorce. Prompted by the federal Child Support Enforcement Amendment of 1984, many states have tightened their collection procedures and some have attempted to increase the value of child-support awards. . . .

[I]f you care about the welfare of children, you cannot be agnostic on the issue of divorce. When marriages break down children often become separated from their fathers—in almost half of all cases there is no contact at all in the wake of divorce—and this can be extremely harmful to children. [T]he research evidence is overwhelming: children derive a great deal of intellectual stimulation and emotional sustenance from day-to-day contact with Dad. It seems that fathers are not readily expendable.

Deciding that a father's presence as well as his paycheck is important to the well-being of children complicates policy making. We can no longer "fix" the divorce problem with bigger and more reliable child-support payments but must attempt to bring divorce rates down, and, in the event of marital breakdown, create a legal framework that maximizes contact between the noncustodial parent and the child.

In 1991 it's extremely hard to get back into the business of enforcing the value of marriage as a long-term commitment. It seems old-fashioned, even quaint, to reintroduce morality, but we must *for the sake of the children*. The thing is, government cannot be neutral. Like it or not, the state has enormous moral suasion. In moving toward no-fault divorce, we thought that we were relinquishing the responsibility of arbitrating private morality. In fact, our new policies, by giving a green light to much easier methods of ending marriage, produced a major shift in private values. . . .

. . . [T]he new legislation changed public attitudes toward divorce, and, in the end, both weakened the institution of marriage and undermined the life prospects of children. We need to undo this damage and once more bend the vast moral authority of the state to the task of strengthening families and protecting children. . . . I recommend . . . the following items:

- When a noncustodial parent evades the withholding system and fails to pay child support (and this will continue to happen in a minority of cases), *the state, rather than the custodial parent, should absorb the risk*. In practical terms this means that if a father is delinquent, a government agency rather than the mother tries to collect, in the meantime advancing the amount of child support owed, up to a limit set by law.

- *The economic obligations of the noncustodial parent should not stop when a child turns eighteen* but continue until the child has completed his or her education.

- Couples with dependent children should be *encouraged to stay married* and to live together as a family. The process of divorce has become too easy and too automatic. Couples experiencing difficulties very quickly find themselves in a one-way street leading to divorce. In the spirit of a 1990 British Law Commission report that advocated "throwing sand in the machinery of divorce," parents seeking divorce should face an eighteen-month waiting period, during which time they would be obliged to seek marriage counseling. In addition, they should be legally obliged to safeguard their children's future before winning a final divorce decree. . . .

- Finally, we should institute *guidelines for visitation,* backed up by an appropriate set of sanctions. If a noncustodial parent (normally the father) has not seen his child in, say, three months, that parent should be fined or otherwise put on notice that such conduct is unacceptable. Even if it were impossible to enforce this kind of provision fully, its very existence would communicate the message that society acknowledges the importance of fathering, and is prepared to go to considerable lengths to encourage contact between fathers and children. . . .

Toward a Better Balance

Once upon a time we didn't have to worry about constraining freedom or limiting choice. No matter how self-centered or predatory the behavior of men, women could be relied upon to stay quietly in their separate sphere, looking after children, family, and community, providing the needed balance to the aggressive individualism that dominated the outside world.

In the 1830s, Alexis de Tocqueville wrote, "No free communities ever existed without morals and . . . morals are the work of women." In his view, women provided a counterpoint to the relentless competitive pressures of capitalist societies. Men "rushing boldly onward in pursuit of wealth" led "tumultuous and constantly harassed lives," and were apt to relinquish ideals for profit.

Women, on the other hand, not being governed by the marketplace, presided over a domestic universe where an entirely different set of values held sway. In Tocqueville's upper-middle-class nineteenth-century world, wives and mothers were engaged in the creation of a comfortable home; the care and nurturing of husband and children; the handing on of a cultural tradition; the teaching of values; and the maintenance of a complex web of social and familial relationships. These tasks clearly required a great deal of selfless labor, but they also encompassed a moral dimension. In woman's domestic sphere, life was about tenderness, beauty, compassion, and responsibility to others, as well as scrambling for a buck.

In a much more modern context, psychologist Carol Gilligan talks about the difference between the "voices" of men and women. In her 1982 book *In a Different Voice,* she describes how men gravitate toward the instrumental and the impersonal and emphasize abstract principles, while women lean toward intimacy and caring and give priority to human relationships. Gilligan points out that the female "care" voice is not inferior to the male "instrumental" voice, as it is often treated in psychological theory; it is simply different. In her opinion, the voice of care plays a critical role in producing a needed equilibrium between individual and community in American society. Because it balances "self" with "other," and tempers material aspirations with those things spiritual, it goes some distance toward redeeming the ugly, urgent greed that is the spirit of capitalism.

Back in the days when families were organized along traditional lines, women provided the energy and vision that knitted together family and community. At least in the prosperous classes, a clear division of labor between the sexes allowed women to devote considerable time to nurturing and homemaking tasks. Under these conditions the voice of care rang out loud and clear through the land and children flourished. But in America (and to a lesser extent in Europe) these traditional patterns were broken by a liberation movement that urged women to get out into the world and seek money and power on the same terms as men, and by a set of economic pressures that increasingly required both parents at work to sustain any semblance of middle-class life.

According to Gilligan the main change wrought by feminism was that it "enabled women to consider it moral to care not only for others but also for themselves." She quotes Elizabeth Cady Stanton telling a reporter in 1948 "to put it down in capital letters: SELF-DEVELOPMENT IS A HIGHER DUTY THAN SELF-SACRIFICE." Modern women have struggled with this lesson. In recent years some elite women have achieved considerable status and earning power in the marketplace, the most successful being those who have traded the care voice for the instrumental voice and cloned the male competitive model. Many less privileged women have gotten bogged down in debilitating divorces, single parenthood, second shifts, and plain, old-fashioned poverty. One thing is clear: with women preoccupied with the search for self and/or the fight for economic survival, there is often no one at home to look

after the children or worry about the moral tone of society.

But before we get nostalgic about traditional roles and start dumping the blame on that easy scapegoat, liberated women, we must remind ourselves of some contemporary realities.

It's become a risky, thankless task, this business of raising children and building families. Risky in that divorce can quickly destroy a lifetime of investment in family, leaving a displaced homemaker teetering on the edge of poverty, struggling to earn a living in a labor market that exacts large penalties for career interruptions. Thankless in that we no longer seem to value these activities. The story told by our public policies is that almost any endeavor is more worthy of support than child raising. We discriminate heavily against pregnant workers and fail to provide parenting leave or prenatal care; under our tax code a couple would be better off breeding race horses than raising children; and most states do a better job regulating kennels than day-care centers. To use the words of Germaine Greer, "if the management of childbearing in our society had actually been intended to maximize stress, it could hardly have succeeded better. The childbearers embark on their struggle alone; the rest of us wash our hands of them."

No wonder individual women find it increasingly difficult to place children at the center of their lives. In the titanic struggle to get ahead, to earn money and accumulate power—the only yardsticks that count in contemporary society—children are increasingly relegated to the margins of life.

As we move through the 1990s, we have to learn how to increase the rewards and spread around the sacrifices of parenting. There is no sensible alternative. It would be foolish to expect wives and mothers to assume a more traditional role and somehow find the resources to take up, once again, the entire family burden. Modern women are intent upon a fair measure of self-realization; besides which, the economic facts of life preclude a return to a 1950s division of labor. With plummeting wages and sky-high divorce rates, it's hard to spin out a scenario where large numbers of mothers have the option of staying home with their children on a full-time basis. Tighter divorce laws, job sharing, and mortgage subsidies might well be part of the solution, but whatever the precise mechanisms, we simply have to bend the rules of the game so as to free up many more resources and much more time for children. The critical task of building strong families can no longer be defined as a private endeavor, least of all a private female endeavor. It is time to demonstrate in our laws and policies that we, as a nation, honor parents, value families, and treasure our children.

Redrawing our public policies so that children may thrive has one enormously important additional characteristic—it will greatly improve the economic status of women. Enhancing and enforcing child-support awards eases the lives of the children of divorce but also bolsters the standard of living of ex-wives; mandating parenting leave improves the life circumstances of infants but also protects the earning power of women and reduces the wage gap; job sharing and career sequencing provide time and flexibility for children but also allow a mother to work part-time and then get back on the career ladder with her promotional prospects intact. In other words, family support policies, because they *reduce the price mothers are asked to pay for their children,* contribute significantly to achieving equality of economic opportunity between men and women. Not because they necessarily produce a 50-50 split in nurturing or breadwinning tasks in any given day or week, but because they compensate mothers for childbearing and child raising and promote a greater measure of equity over the life span. When we place a high value on children, modern women, benefit enormously. . . .

Study Questions on Sylvia Ann Hewlett

1. It used to be argued that married couples who were unhappy should stay together for the sake of the children. In the light of your experience and that of your friends, do you think this was a good idea?
2. What do you think of Hewlett's proposals for divorce reform? Are they restrictive enough? Too restrictive?
3. Discuss the pros and cons of requiring business to provide: (a) maternity leaves, (b) the option of part-time work for the parents of small children, (c) flexible work hours or job-sharing for the parents of small children, (d) on-site child-care facilities. Would you advocate that the government provide assistance to firms too small to be able to afford such policies?
4. Imagine that you are an unhappily married man or woman contemplating divorce. You agree with Hewlett that divorce is a bad thing for society. Does this mean that you must remain in your unhappy marriage?

For Further Reading

Al-Hibri, Azizah. *Women in Islam.* New York: Pergamon Press, 1982.
Bane, Mary Jo. *Here to Stay.* New York: Basic, 1976.
Berger, Brigette and Peter. *The War over the Family: Capturing the Middle Ground.* New York: Doubleday, 1983.
Bernard, Jessie. *The Future of Motherhood.* New York: Penguin, 1975.
Blankenthorn, David, Stephen Bayme, and Jean Bethke Elshtain. *Rebuilding the Nest.* Milwaukee, Wisc.: Family Services America, 1990.

Blum, Larry et al. "Altruism and Women's Oppression." In Carol Gould and Mark Wartofsky, eds., *Women and Philosophy: Toward a Theory of Liberation.* New York: G. P. Putnam's, 1976.

Blustein, Jeffrey. *Parents and Children: The Ethics of the Family.* Oxford: Oxford University Press, 1982. Especially Chap. 4, Equal Opportunity and the Family.

Boswell, John. *Same-Sex Unions in Premodern Europe.* New York: Villard Books, 1994.

Bradley, Gerard. "Marriage Hawaiian Style?" In Christopher Wolfe, ed., *Homosexuality and American Public Life.* Dallas, Tex.: Spence, 1999. Chap. 10.

Chodorow, Nancy. *The Reproduction of Mothering: Psychoanalysis and Sociology of Gender.* Los Angeles: University of California Press, 1978.

Clark, Stephen. *Man and Woman in Christ.* Ann Arbor, Mich.: Servant, 1980. Available in full through The Council on Biblical Manhood and Womanhood, http://www.cbmw.org/resources/books.

Cooey, Paula, William Eakin, and Jay McDaniel. *After Patriarchy: Feminist Transformations of the World's Religions.* Maryknoll, N.Y.: Orbis, 1991.

Cooke, Miriam. *Opening the Gates: A Century of Arab Feminist Writing.* London: Virago, 1989.

Coolidge, David Orgon. "The Question of Marriage." In Christopher Wolfe, ed. *Homosexuality and American Public Life.* Dallas, Tex.: Spence, 1999. Chap. 11.

Crittinden, Danielle. *What Our Mothers Didn't Tell Us: Why Happiness Eludes the Modern Woman.* New York: Simon & Schuster, 1999.

Daniels, Norman. *Am I My Parent's Keeper? An Essay on Justice Between the Young and the Old.* Oxford: Oxford University Press, 1987.

Dinnerstein, Dorothy. *The Mermaid and the Minotaur: Sexual Arrangements and Human Malaise.* New York: HarperCollins, 1977.

English, Jane. "What Do Grown Children Owe Their Parents?" In Onora O'Neill and William Ruddick, eds., *Having Children: Philosophical and Legal Reflections on Parenthood.* New York: Oxford University Press, 1979.

Eskridge, William N., Jr. *The Case for Same-Sex Marriage.* New York: Free Press, 1996.

Firestone, Shulamith. *The Dialectic of Sex.* New York: Bantam Books, 1971.

Fraiberg, Selma. *Every Child's Birthright: In Defense of Mothering.* New York: Basic, 1977.

Haddad, Yvonne, and Ellison Findly. *Women, Religion and Social Change.* Albany: State University of New York Press, 1985.

Haddad, Yvonne, and Adair Lummis. *Islamic Values in the United States: A Comparative Study.* London: Oxford University Press, 1988.

Hassan, Riffat. "Muslim Women in Post-Patriarchal Islam." In Cooey et al., *After Patriarchy: Feminist Tranformations of the World's Religions.* Maryknoll, N.Y.: Orbis, 1991.

Lamm, Norman, ed. *The Good Society: Jewish Ethics in Action.* New York: Viking Press, 1974.

———. *A Hedge of Roses: Jewish Insights into Marriage and Married Life.* New York: P. Feldheim, 1966.

May, William F. et al. "*The Giving Tree:* A Symposium." *First Things,* no. 49 (January 1995), 22–45.

Meilander, Gilbert. "The Venture of Marriage." In Carl E. Braaten and Robert W. Jenson, eds., *The Two Cities of God.* Grand Rapids, Mich.: Eerdmans, 1997. Pp. 117–132.

Mernissi, Fatima. *Beyond the Veil.* London: Al Saqi, 1985.

Moffat, Robert L., Joseph Grcic, and Michael D. Bayles, eds. *Perspectives on the Family.* Lewiston, N.Y.: Edwin Mellen Press, 1990.

Mohr, Richard. "The Case for Gay Marriage." In Richard Mohr, *A More Perfect Union.* Boston: Beacon Press, 1994.

Nicholson, Linda. *Gender and History: The Limits of Social Theory in the Age of the Family.* New York: Columbia University Press, 1988.

Okin, Susan Moller. "Feminism and Multiculturalism: Some Tensions." *Ethics,* 108, no. 4 (July 1998), 661ff.

———. et al. *Is Multiculturalism Bad for Women? Susan Moller Okin with Respondents.* Joshua Cohen, Matthew Howard, and Martha C. Nussbaum, eds. Princeton: Princeton University Press, 1999. An extreme liberal perspective on family issues, with responses from representatives of a variety of views. (Okin's essay has the same title as the book.)

O'Neill, Onora, and William Ruddick, eds. *Having Children: Philosophical and Legal Reflections on Parenthood.* New York: Oxford University Press, 1979.

Popenoe, David. *Disturbing the Nest: Family Change and Decline in Modern Societies.* New York: Aldine de Gruyter, 1988.

Rich, Adrienne. *Of Woman Born: Motherhood as Experience and Institution.* London: Virago, 1977.

Ross, Joshua Jacob. *The Virtues of the Family.* New York: Free Press, 1994. A traditional Jewish view.

Russell, Bertrand. *Marriage and Morals.* New York: Liverwright, 1929.

Sandel, Michael. *Liberalism and the Limits of Justice.* 2nd ed. Cambridge: Cambridge University Press, 1998.

Shils, Edward. *Tradition.* Chicago: University of Chicago Press, 1981.

Sommers, Christina. "Filial Morality." *Journal of Philosophy,* 83, no. 8 (1985), 539–556.

———, and Fred Sommers, eds. *Vice and Virtue in Everyday Life.* 4th ed. Fort Worth, Tex.: Harcourt Brace, 1985. Chap. 9.

Sullivan, Andrew. "The Marriage Moment." *The Advocate* (January 20, 1998), 59–67.

———, ed. *Same-Sex Marriage, Pro and Con, a Reader.* New York: Vintage, 1997. Note especially the essays by Paula Ettelbrick and Frank Browning, arguing, "from the Left," that marriage is not an appropriate framework for homosexual couples.

Thorne, Barrie, and Marilyn Young, eds. *Rethinking the Family: Some Feminist Questions.* Boston: Northeastern University Press, 1992.

Treblicot, Joyce, ed. *Mothering: Essays in Feminist Theory.* Totowa, N.J.: Rowman and Allenheld, 1984.

Wolf-Devine, Celia. "Rawlsian and Feminist Critiques of the Traditional Family," in Wolf, ed., *The Family, Civil Society, and the State.* Lantham, Md.: Rowman and Littlefield, 1998.

Wolfe, Christopher, ed. *The Family, Civil Society, and the State.* Lanham, Md.: Rowman and Littlefield, 1998.

Yutang, Lin. "On Growing Old Gracefully." In Lin Yutang, *The Importance of Living.* London and Melbourne: William Heinemann, 1960.

INFOTRAC COLLEGE EDITION To learn more about the topics from this chapter, you can use the following words to conduct an electronic search on InfoTrac College Edition, an online library of journals. Here you will find a multitude of articles from various sources and perspectives: *www.infotrac-college.com/wadsworth/access.html*

Civil Society

Divorce

Family

Fatherhood

Marriage

Matriarchy

Motherhood

Multiculturalism and Feminism

New Family Forms

Parents and Children

Patriarchy

Seniors

Tradition

Web Sites

Child Support (Legal Encyclopedia)
http://www.nolo.com/encyclopedia/child_support_ency.html

CivNet (Civitas International)
http://www.civnet.org

DivorceNet.com
http://www.divorcenet.com

FirstGov for Seniors
http://www.seniors/gov/

Focus on the Family (Dr. James Dobson)
http://www.family.org/

Marriage Builders
http://www.marriagebuilders.com/

Matrirarchy (Columbia Encyclopedia, 6th ed., 2001)
http://www. bartleby.com/65/ma/matriarc.htm

Moms (Mothers Talking about Motherhood)
http://www.familyplay.com/moms/

Patriarchy Website
http://www.patriarchy.website.com/

Toward Tradition (Traditional Jewish perspective on family issues)
http://www.towardtradition.org/

Politics: Gender in the Public Arena

HOWEVER WE UNDERSTAND THE FAMILY, it exists in a larger society whose structure and politics affect its workings. Sometimes the family is thought of as a constraint on political and socioeconomic policy. People may reject policies on the ground that they intrude too much into the private domain of the family. For example, many people would oppose laws forbidding home schooling. But sometimes encouraging or discouraging certain types of family structure may be something people aim at directly, as, for example, Okin (in Unit IV) recommends policies designed to discourage the gender-structured family.

Many political movements and ideologies have implications for the kinds of sex and gender issues we have been discussing in this volume. These include the various movements commonly grouped under the label "multiculturalism," communitarianism, the New Right, and (especially outside North America and Western Europe) religious nationalism. Marxism in its heyday also addressed the "woman question" in ways that have continuing implications. The ideology of the free market also affects the way people think about sex and gender issues. In its most extreme form it holds that the value of everything (including people) is its price, and that if there is a demand for something and people are willing to supply it, they should be allowed to do so. This would license child selling, prostitution, live sex shows, and the sale of eggs, sperm, and embryos. In any case, the market profoundly shapes the world in which we think about these issues, for example, by generating a demand for family life as a "haven in a heartless world," as Christopher Lasch has put it.

Although many political movements have implications for the issues discussed so far in the selections, two major movements that arose during the second half of the twentieth century have made gender issues their central focus. The first is feminism, and the second is the movement for gay and lesbian rights. Feminism has focused on male-female relationships and sought to correct for the various ways in which existing institutions and sex role patterns disadvantage women, while the movement for gay and lesbian rights has focused on the way in which homosexuals have been marginalized and discriminated against in a society in which heterosexuality has been taken to be normative. Both movements have included a number of different groups with agendas ranging from concrete and practical issues such as employment discrimination or the elimination of laws against sodomy to attempts to change how people think about gender in broad and sweeping ways. And both have exhibited a sort of complex interweaving between political activism on the one hand and academic research of a more theoretical nature on the other. Since the focus in this unit is on politics, we are more interested in the way in which gender issues have been played out in the public arena than in theoretical developments comprehensible mainly to specialists. But these cannot be completely separated, since a certain amount of cross-fertilization has occurred between theory and practice.

Two Extreme Positions: Sex War and the Assimilationist Ideal

Before discussing feminism in detail, it will be useful to step back for a moment and look at the two extreme positions on male-female relationships that frame the debate. Neither extreme alternative is likely to be found acceptable by most people; therefore, neither can function directly to inform policies. But they nonetheless function as imaginative visions lying in the background of the debate, and as such they exert a powerful influence on the various political players.

One approach to the politics of gender is the sex war ("not the fun kind," as one of our selections puts it). Men and women are so different that peace and cooperation are impossible across the sex divide; each can only wish that the other were "transported / Far beyond the Northern Sea," as the old song puts it (or at least that they could avoid serious engagement with the other). In the current debate, this way of thinking is represented by what Alison Jaggar calls *lesbian separatism,* which holds that women must abstain from intimate relations with men, at least for the time being, and thus advocates lesbianism on political grounds. Men may also fear becoming entangled in intimate relationships with women, but for whatever reason they do not tend to choose a homosexual way of life on that basis. They are more likely to avoid serious engagement with the opposite sex by turning to pornography, prostitution, and sexual encounters with women who make themselves sexually available without making any serious demands on them. In any event, women and men must still cooperate as citizens if in no other way, and the sex war is for that reason political fantasy rather than a serious policy option.

Another way to go is to focus on the sameness between men and women and take it all the way. This leads to the assimilationist ideal espoused by Richard Wasserstrom and criticized by Roger Scruton under the label of "Kantian feminism" (Unit I). Male-female differences, according to the assimilationist ideal, should be regarded as no more important, even in intimate relationships, than the color of one's eyes or the length of one's toes. We ought, then, to aim for a society in which gender as such is eliminated completely. Biological differences will persist, of course, but they will be accorded no important psychological or social meaning. This ideal also is a central tenet of *radical feminism* as defined by Jaggar, and underlies Susan Moller Okin's thought about family structure and her recommendations for public family policies (in Unit IV). The assimilationist vision, then, functions for many cultural radicals as an ideal to be aimed at, but few people believe that it could ever be fully attained.

Feminism

Feminism, as a political movement, has been in part a response to conditions outside women's control (such as the economic pressures that have made it necessary for most women to work outside the home in order to maintain a middle-class standard of living), but the way feminists have responded to these changes has had a profound effect on our social institutions, which in turn has generated a wide range of responses by other social groups. For example, the New Right has fought to defend the traditional family against those feminists who want to radically alter it, and the movement for gay and lesbian rights has pressed the deconstruction of traditional mores governing marriage and family further than most feminists.

Attempts to give any sort of neat definition of "feminism" are bound to fail, and it is generally acknowledged at the present time that there are a number of different types of feminism. We have included a selection by a leading feminist, Alison Jaggar, who describes what she takes to be the leading types of feminism. She provides, however, no definition of feminism unifying these. This raises some interesting questions. Is there, or should there be, some sort of unifying definition of feminism? Or is it acceptable to admit, and perhaps even celebrate, the diversity among feminists? The only thing that appears to be shared by the types of feminism defined by Jaggar is that they all seek to promote the interests of women. But communitarian feminists like Jean Bethke Elshtain and Elizabeth Fox-Genovese (see the For Further Reading section in this unit), as well as Juli Loesch Wiley, who argue that women (and children) have a special interest in "reweaving" social bonds, also take themselves to be working in the interests of women. The same is true even of conservative women like Phyllis Schlafly. The political challenge, then, for feminism is finding a way to accommodate the genuine diversity among women without allowing feminism to become so fragmented that it can no longer function as a coherent movement.

Liberal Feminism

From the political point of view, by far the most successful and widely influential sort of feminism was what has been called "first-wave" or "liberal" feminism. A central expression of this sort of feminism was the unsuccessful Equal Rights Amendment (ERA), submitted for ratification in 1971. The proposed constitutional amendment read as follows: "Equality of rights under the law shall not be abridged or denied by the United States or any state on account of sex." The reasons for its failure were complicated, but among them were: suspicions that it might require unisex washrooms or be used to enforce abortion rights; the opposition of Mormons and traditional women like Phyllis Schlafly (who in fact was one of the most important leaders of the "Stop ERA" campaign); the tactics employed by ERA advocates (which included, for example, boycotts of hotels in states that had not ratified the ERA); and the perception by many legal scholars that the complexity of the issues concerning when sex is relevant and when it is not is too great to be captured in one sentence.

Equal opportunity in education and in the workplace was of primary importance to early feminists. Following the lead of the black civil rights movement, they sought to combat discrimination against women in the public realm of business and politics, and they coined the term *sexism* to emphasize the similarity between racial and sexual discrimination (an analogy that had a profound effect on the feminist movement in the United States and made it different from European feminism). But the demand that abortion should be readily available to all women who believe they require one was also very central to their program. Some lesser manifestations of the feminist impulse included introducing the title "Ms." (abolishing the social distinction between married and unmarried women); insisting that the generic pronoun "he" be replaced by "he or she," "s/he," or sometimes just "she"; coinages such as "chairperson"; and the rewriting of classical texts such as the Bible in inclusive language. Underlying the movement toward inclusive language was the belief that the common-gender "he" leads people to unthinkingly take males to be the norm or standard, and to thereby render women and their perspectives invisible. This could happen on a number of levels. If seat belts or airbags were crash-tested using dummies six feet tall, weighing 180 pounds, they might cause unforeseen injuries to small, slight women. Or if a psychologist were to do research on the moral development of children using only male subjects, this would bias the results obtained. It was hoped that the suggested linguistic changes would help to counteract such biases—that if people use pronouns in a way that explicitly includes women, this will impress upon them the fact that women are human beings in every bit as full a sense as men are.

Most of the less controversial feminist objectives have either been attained or at least agreed upon in principle by people all across the political spectrum. For example, even conservatives like Pat Robertson or Rush Limbaugh now favor equal pay for equal work. Women have flocked into higher education and the professions, the pay gap between men and women has narrowed dramatically in the last twenty years, middle-class parents are becoming as ambitious for their daughters' careers as for those of their sons, and so on. This is not of course to say that complete fairness has been achieved. There has been controversy over the "glass ceiling" in businesses, for example, and women are, for whatever reason, still relatively scarce in positions that carry with them significant political power. Nonetheless, if one takes the central goal of feminism to be attaining fair treatment of women in the workplace and in the political arena, then considerable progress has been made. But *is* this the central goal of feminism? Is feminism a movement to demand justice for women, or should its goal be simply to advance the interests of women? (Janet Radcliffe Richards, included in the Prologue, for example, distinguishes these particularly clearly.)

After Liberal Feminism

The leadership of the feminist movement has concluded that formal equality is not enough, and moved away from liberal feminism. Just as the demand for fairness and equal opportunity for black people gradually evolved into a demand for affirmative action, so many feminists began to call for affirmative action for women so that they could obtain a fair proportion of high-paying and prestigious jobs. Since it is often difficult to determine when bias is at work, and since the standards themselves may include a subtle bias in favor of men, they argued that to ensure fairness we need to insist that a certain percentage of those hired or promoted be women—for example, that there should be the same proportion of women among managers as there is among employees as a whole. Their support of affirmative action, then, was an exception to their general opposition to legal and social distinctions between men and women (including ones that had previously been thought to be to the advantage of women, such as women's protective legislation that had been put in place by blue-collar women's unions before liberal feminists gained ascendancy in the women's movement).

The very success of liberal feminism, however, has generated a new set of problems for subsequent feminists. For liberal feminism relied heavily on a sharp dividing line between the private and the public realm. In the public realm, women were to be treated no differently from men, but in the private realm of courtship, marriage, and domestic life, sexual differences remained very important. This set up a sort of tension between the two, since private and public cannot really be kept hermetically sealed apart from each other. If women receive affirmative action preferences for jobs, this will affect a couple's choice about who is to be the primary breadwinner; or if women do most of the homemaking and child care, this will have an impact on their ability to advance in their careers. Likewise, romantic patterns of male-female relationships can carry over into the workplace, resulting in real or perceived sexual harassment.

A number of types of feminism have emerged since the heyday of liberal feminism, but none of them has been able to attract as wide a base of political support. Although some women did not support liberal feminism, most of them did, and many men were moved to support liberal feminists' demands by simple considerations of fairness. The need for skilled labor in a highly competitive global economy made it advantageous and profitable for businesses to efficiently use women's talents as well as men's. Partly as a result of their political activism on behalf of women, and partly because of the influence of multiculturalists and post-modernists who strongly emphasized differences among people, feminists became worried that liberal feminism had been a white, heterosexual, middle-class, elitist movement, and sought to take into account the experiences of women of color, lesbian and bisexual women, and working-class women. If feminism is a movement to promote the interests of women (instead of merely a quest for fair treatment in the public arena), it is necessary to face the question of what their interests are and whether they all have the same interests. Communitarian feminists, in particular, have emphasized women's distinctive interests in child-bearing and child rearing, and some of these have taken a pro-life position in the abortion debate. In short, deep disagreements among women have come to the surface.

The political situation among women in the early twenty-first century appears to be entering a new phase. Surveys have found that the proportion of young women who identify themselves as "feminists" has declined over the last ten or twenty years. This may be simply because they believe that the important battles have been won and they can sit back and enjoy the greater freedom and opportunities won for them by earlier generations of feminists. Also, the media tend to focus on the most extreme and colorful "feminists," usually ones who express deep hostility to men, and this does not appeal to most young women. On the political level, the authority of groups like the National Organization for Women (NOW) to speak for women has been challenged by a number of other women's organizations with quite different agendas. Concerned Women for America (a conservative organization committed to strengthening the family and defending Judeo-Christian values) has twice as many members as NOW. There are also some active pro-life women's organizations (e.g., Feminists for Life and Women Exploited by Abortion) and, oddly enough, several organizations founded by independently minded women irritated by other women's claims to speak for them, whose express purpose is to stand up for women's right to think for themselves. What will emerge is anybody's guess, but it is clear that differences among women (for better or for worse) are here to stay.

Preview of Readings

Following a literary portrayal of the sex wars by Sandra Gilbert and Susan Gubar, the readings on feminism begin with Alison Jaggar's classic account of the most influential types of feminism—liberal feminism, classical Marxist feminism, radical feminism, lesbian separatism, and socialist feminism. To this list, in the next selection, Juli Loesch Wiley adds another alternative—a kind of communitarian feminism that she calls "social feminism."

Two practical issues illustrating the way feminist social thought has found expression in politics are affirmative action and sexual harassment. Sex-based affirmative action is criticized by Louis Katzner, who challenges the common feminist tendency to assimilate the problems faced by women to those faced by black people, and argues that the justifications offered for affirmative action for black people are not defensible for women. Laura Purdy argues that past prejudice against women has introduced a bias into the hiring process, and that affirmative action is needed to correct this situation. (See, also, the book by Celia Wolf-Devine on affirmative action listed in the For Further Reading section in this unit.)

Sexual harassment is addressed by Catharine MacKinnon and Katie Roiphe. MacKinnon argues that the fact that sexual harassment involves "only words" should not protect men who engage in it, and that refusal to believe a woman's complaints of sexual harassment, or even pointed cross-questioning by those defending the alleged harasser, is itself a form of sexual harassment. Roiphe raises two objections to MacKinnon: first, that the vague way in which sexual harassment regulations are written opens the door to injustice against men; and second, that such regulations teach women to regard themselves as helpless victims, unable to rebuff unwanted sexual advances with a timely slap in the face.

The Movement for Gay and Lesbian Rights

The movement for gay and lesbian rights has followed the pattern set by feminism, but goes further in the direction of rejection of traditional sexual mores than most feminists. If women have been oppressed and made to feel excluded and marginalized in various ways, then surely, they argued, the same is true in a deeper and more pervasive way of gays and lesbians. The tacit assumption that heterosexuality is the normal or standard form of sexuality and that homosexual orientation requires some special explanation—in other words, that something has gone wrong if a person is homosexual—was one that they encountered at every turn (they coined the term *heterosexism* to describe this attitude). And hostility and even violence toward known homosexuals was common. Liberal feminists generally took heterosexuality for granted and did not give much thought to the special difficulties faced by lesbians. They tended to consign people's sexual behavior (heterosexual or homosexual) firmly to the private sphere and leave it there. Many early gay rights activists, like the liberal feminists, believed that their private sexual behavior was nobody's business but their own and sought only to be accorded respect and fair treatment (and, of course, repeal of legal prohibitions and protection from verbal and physical assaults).

There are still, no doubt, sexually active gays and lesbians who believe their sexual lives are their own private business and want only to be left alone and treated fairly. How many gays and lesbians there are in America is hotly contested, and those who deliberately choose to keep their sex lives private and stay out of politics are especially hard to count. In any case, the leadership of the gay and lesbian movement has moved increasingly in the direction of demanding that they be able to be open about their sexuality and not be stigmatized for it. The core of their position, then, is that homosex is morally equivalent, or at least no worse, than heterosex. Attempts have been made to change people's ways of thinking about homosexuality, especially through education and the media. Although a fair amount of success has been achieved in this regard, especially among the younger generation, some strong opposition has been aroused. The most important opponents of the gay and lesbian movement have been conservative Christians and Jews deeply convinced that homosexual practices are sinful and that the social influence of openly gay and lesbian persons (in education, for example) is pernicious. Many, though by no means all, of these have been fundamentalists given to crude expressions of their attitudes.

The gay and lesbian movement is made up of a number of groups with differing ideas about what policies should be adopted and what sort of tactics should be employed. Some favor working within established political channels (sometimes called "mainstreaming"), while others engage in expressive politics and confrontive "in your face" tactics (such as the disruption of a mass at St. Patrick's Church in New York in 1989). Lying behind the differences in tactics are deeper questions about what direction the movement ought to take.

The most important question from the point of view of the issues covered in this anthology is to what extent gay men and lesbians should try to assimilate themselves to the patterns prevalent in straight society, and to what extent they ought to emphasize their differences from heterosexuals. This is ultimately a question that can only be answered from within the gay and lesbian movement itself. But it is worth noting the way in which gay and lesbian politics parallels at this point the way in which women and black people have wrestled with the problems of sameness and difference. Women have often been torn between trying to assimilate to male patterns and asserting their difference. And among black people there have been persistent disagreements over whether to pursue the integrationist politics of Martin Luther King, to adhere to the separatist position of Malcolm X (who had a very negative view of white people, viewing them as "blue-eyed devils" until his conversion to Islam), or to focus more on the positive aspects of their own difference, as Stokely Carmichael did in saying that "black is beautiful" and insisting on "black pride."

Preview of Readings

The first two readings focus on a broad question of social policy, namely, the extent to which heterosexuality should be regarded as normative. Michael Novak argues that the tension between male and female is essential to the good life, both for the individual and for society. He thus argues that heterosexuality should be recognized as normative by law and social custom. Though he wants to maintain the distinction between public and private, the heterosexual norm has a political as well as a psychological importance for him. According to Novak, heterosexuality and heterosexual marriage are valuable (and therefore deserving of public support) because they both require and enable us to live with the conflicts that arise out of the natural differences between men and women and ultimately to benefit from them.

Timothy Murphy responds that there are no significant differences between homosex and heterosex, to use his terms. Thus homosexuality ought to be accorded the same social and legal status as heterosexuality. Murphy's view approximates the view that Scruton, in Unit I, describes as "Kantian feminism." We are essentially only persons; sexual difference is a matter of our physical equipment only—one among many differences that exist between people—and not a matter of who we are in any deeper sense. There is, thus, a convergence between his view and that of the radical feminists who want to totally eliminate gender as such.

As a concrete issue illustrating how the theoretical differences between Novak and Murphy play themselves out in practice, we have chosen the issue of same-sex marriage. Whether or not same-sex unions should qualify as "marriages" is a different question from the question of whether or not homosexual sexual acts are immoral. One attitude, common among the ancient Greeks, was that homosexual relationships between men might be morally acceptable (and even admirable) but that such relationships just were not marriages. The focus of the selections in this unit will be on the issue of same-sex marriage, and not on the morality of homosexual behavior. Whether to legally recognize such unions is a question that public policy must decide one way or the other.

The issue of whether or not the legitimation of same-sex marriage is a goal at which the gay and lesbian movement should aim lies close to the heart of some major disputes within the movement itself. Some want to minimize their difference from heterosexuals, and assimilate themselves to behavioral patterns (such as monogamy) prevalent in the broader heterosexual culture. We are really pretty much like everyone else, except for the fact that we prefer sexual partners of our own sex. (Andrew Sullivan uses the term *virtually normal* to describe this position.) Others advocate a root-and-branch rejection of the patterns of relationships and the social institutions prevalent in straight society, and call for the affirmation of a distinctively gay or lesbian alternative vision. (Whether or not gay men and lesbians share the same vision is in some dispute. The articles by Marilyn Frye and John Preston, for example, listed in the For Further Reading section of this unit, discuss some of the main areas of tension between gay men and lesbians.) Finally, there are those who believe that homosexuals can win acceptance, as distinct from tolerance, only by a transformation of the broader society, and who therefore advocate political and cultural activism aimed at radically changing the surrounding society—particularly the way people think and feel about sex and gender. (For a more theoretical expression of this more militant side of the gay and lesbian movement, see Cathy Cohen's article "Straight Gay Politics," listed in the For Further Reading section.)

We begin with an argument for same-sex marriage by Andrew Sullivan, which he presents as conservative. Sullivan, representing the assimilationist wing of the gay movement, challenges the traditional understanding of a family, and shifts the emphasis in our understanding of marriage from children to the personal relationship between the partners ("Love Makes a Family," as the bumper sticker puts it). He argues that not recognizing same-sex unions as marriages deprives such couples of a civil right accorded to others, and that doing so will help to stabilize gay and lesbian relationships and integrate them more into the social fabric.

The traditionalist case against same-sex marriage is articulated here by Robert George. He understands marriage as a one-flesh union of the two sexes, consummated by acts that are reproductive in type (although they do not invariably issue in a new generation). George's understanding of marriage, and the reasons why he believes that marriage deserves the support of (and requires regulation by) the larger society, then, imply that it is heterosexual by definition. David Orgon Coolidge responds to the suggestion that even if same-sex unions are not marriages in some normative sense, recognizing them will do no harm. Recognizing such unions, he argues, will change the institution of marriage in deep and undesirable ways, and lead to a number of bad social consequences. He thus fills a gap in George's argument.

Paula Ettelbrick argues, in contrast, that allowing same-sex couples to enter into marriages will not change the institution in deep ways, and therefore entering into such relationships would be a betrayal of the primary goals of the gay and lesbian movement. Although she thinks same-sex couples should have the civil right to marry, she believes that marriage as an institution has been tainted by its association with property relationships and dominance of men over women, and that gays and lesbians ought to proudly affirm their identity and fight for the validation of many different sorts of relationships. She does not want to give the state the power to regulate her primary relationship, and thinks of marriage as antithetical to the sort of personal liberation to which she is committed, both for herself and for the broader society. With state validation of some homosexual relationships, but not others, would come increasing marginalization of those who do not fit the approved model, and true liberation requires that society be accepting of a variety of different sorts of intimate relationships and accord them legal protection.

Finally, E .J. Graff disagrees with Ettelbrick and reverses Coolidge's argument. Same-sex marriage is, she says, a "breathtakingly subversive idea" that will change the message of one of the most important institutions of our society. Contrary to Ettelbrick, she believes that gays and lesbians ought to insist on the right to marry and enter into marriages, because by doing so they will bring about major changes in the institution itself. But, unlike Coolidge, she believes these changes will be good.

In the final unit, we will move beyond the political realm and examine the way in which sex and gender issues are entwined with questions about the nature of Ultimate Reality. We anticipate that you will differ widely in your religious beliefs, and that some of you will have strong religious convictions, and some will be hostile or indifferent to religion. Yet the religious dimension cannot be omitted if we are to understand why sex and gender issues provoke such fierce controversy, for many people who do not practice any religion are deeply shaped by the religions they or their parents were brought up with. In addition, religious views of nature and our place in it are deeply ingrained in our culture, from casual references to "Mother Nature" to the more explicit religious appeals made by opponents of homosexuality or by environmentalists who want us to reverence the Earth as our Mother or who appeal to God's command to Adam to care for the garden and to tend it as an example of the proper attitude of "stewardship" toward nature.

Many feminists have argued that traditional Western religions have provided support for patriarchal institutions and, therefore, try to radically reform or eliminate them, or at least to limit their influence. Traditional Jews, Christians, and Moslems have opposed some actual and proposed changes in our laws and institutions on the grounds that such changes are in conflict with what their religion teaches about sexuality, reproduction, and male-female relationships. We, therefore, will turn to the cosmic dimension of sex and gender issues.

Questions for Reflection

1. As you read the selections, ask yourself how closely the problems faced—first by women, and then by gays, lesbians, bisexuals, and transgendered people— resemble those faced by black people, and how they differ from them.
2. Should heterosexuality be regarded as normative? Should laws and policies be designed on the assumption that the heterosexual family is something that is good for the individuals participating in it and for the society as a whole, and that therefore policies favoring or supporting the traditional family are a good thing?
3. Some feminists are concerned about what they perceive as a "backlash" against feminism. Do you think there is currently a backlash against feminism, and if so what do you think are the causes of this phenomenon?
4. Some women are adamantly opposed to feminism, even in its most moderate, liberal forms. Why might some women take this position?
5. What, if any, interests do you think are shared by all or almost all women?
6. Suppose that you were in a position to influence the future direction of the feminist movement (you may answer this question if you are a man). What issues do you believe feminists should focus on in the twenty-first century? What positions should they take on these issues and why?
7. Do you think the direction you would like to see the feminist movement take in the future is one that would receive widespread popular support? Does this matter?
8. If you favor a program that you believe would not receive widespread popular support, explain why you believe feminists should pursue it anyway. If you favor a program that you believe would receive widespread popular support, explain why it would have such mass appeal.
9. Many practicing gays and lesbians are uncomfortable with some of the political aims pursued by gay and lesbian activists. Why might they feel this way? Do all homosexuals have the same interests? Do they share the same interests less than, more than, or to the same degree as women do?
10. Do you think the feminist movement and the gay and lesbian movement are equally likely to achieve success by democratic methods? Explain.
11. Should controversial gender-related issues in public policy be resolved by democratic methods? Or do such methods tend to favor the status quo too much? If you find democratic methods inadequate, what would you recommend instead? What are the advantages and disadvantatages of private militant action? Of reliance on the courts? Of educational policies designed to favor (or disfavor) feminism or the gay and lesbian movement? Of dictatorship?

Glossary

affirmative action active attempt to improve the employment and educational opportunities of women and people of color, often by explicit preferences (and sometimes by quotas).

basic structures of society those practices and institutions to which a theory of social justice, such as that of Rawls, apply.

conservatism defense of existing institutions; in the present context, the view that the differential treatment of women is not, as such, unjust.

discrimination making public decisions, for example, about education and employment, in a way that unfairly disfavors certain groups (such as people of color and women).

expressive politics political activity designed to display feeling rather than change policies or institutions.

free-market ideology ideology that holds, in sharp contrast with Leftist views of all sorts, that the unregulated market is the best measure of value, and the best method of allocating resources.

glass ceiling invisible obstacle to the promotion of women.

heterosex sexual activity involving members of the opposite sex.

homosex sexual activity involving members of the same sex.

Kantian feminism the view that human beings should be regarded as persons, whose sex or gender is no more important than their eye or skin color.

liberationists roughly, cultural radicals.

loose-bolt sexuality sexual promiscuity.

multiculturalism political movement emphasizing the diversity of cultures, often opposed to the idea of a shared human nature.

narcissism erotic focus on the self.

New Right in America, a movement of religiously motivated conservatives, which arose in the 1970s in response to liberal policies on such issues as abortion.

parody a mocking imitation.

preferential affirmative action policies involving explicit preferences for women and people of color in education and employment.

religious nationalism fusion of religion and nationalism, including the militant Islam important in such countries as Afghanistan and Iran. In America, this movement uses such slogans as "Christian America" and "the values that made this country great."

reproductive-type acts sexual acts of a sort that lead to procreation, even if on a particular occasion they cannot do so.

reverse discrimination another word for preferential affirmative action, emphasizing the fact that such policies disfavor white males.

sex role stereotypes public expectations concerning the differences between male and female personality and behavior; also called *gender roles* (social expectations associated with gender).

sexual harassment words and behavior that make the workplace inhospitable to women, ranging from rough jokes to direct demands for sexual favors.

sodomy from the Biblical story of Sodom and Gomorrah (Genesis 19), a word for various sorts of sexual behavior traditionally viewed as nonstandard; in the narrowest sense anal intercourse between men.

transgendered transvestite (person who prefers to dress as a person of the opposite sex, sometimes as a means of sexual gratification) or transsexual (person who believes that his or her gender differs from his or her sex).

unitive good the intimate joining of a man and a woman in marriage. In some views, this good is also attainable in nonmarital or homosexual relationships.

Sex Wars: Not the Fun Kind

SANDRA GILBERT AND SUSAN GUBAR

> Sandra Gilbert and Susan Gubar here ask whether men and women are two different species, doomed to perpetual battle. A survey of recent fiction and nonfiction, by both women and men, suggests that the sex war is getting worse. The authors notice, especially, the replacement of "the sensitive guy . . . by the Wild Man in search of the primitive roots of his maleness."

ARE MEN AND WOMEN two different species, doomed to a perpetual battle? Are words weapons with which the sexes must fight for territory and authority? What has triggered the mass appeal of books like Shere Hite's "Women and Love," with its message that women are sick of men, and movies like "Fatal Attraction," featuring one of the goriest male-female encounters since "Psycho"? Has the battle of the sexes entered a new, violent phase?

Even a cursory survey of recent fiction and nonfiction suggests as much, for increasingly, male and female writers have been as fascinated by sex wars as by Star Wars. Indeed, at the most intense moments of conflict, men evidently seem to women like marauding Darth Vaders while women appear to men like emissaries from a sinister Death Planet.

And if sex wars are escalating, which side is winning? Predictably, there is little agreement. Men say women are triumphing. Women claim the opposite. As in real wars, body counts are unreliable.

Speaking for the female side, Susan Forward, the author, with Joan Torres, of "Men Who Hate Women & the Women Who Love Them," reports that when she went on a television talk show to describe abusive husbands who suffer from what she sees as the prevalent psychological disorder of misogyny, the network reported "one of the most overwhelming phone-call responses that they'd ever had." Even more dramatically, Andrea Dworkin claims in her most recent book of feminist theory, "Intercourse," that most men who make love to women make war on women, because "intercourse remains a means or the

means of physiologically making a woman inferior; communicating to her cell by cell her own inferior status . . . shoving it into her, over and over . . . until she gives up and gives in—which is called *surrender* in the male lexicon. . . .

. . .

As for men who feel about women the way Ms. Dworkin feels about men, they are numerous, judging by the enthusiasm with which masculine audiences have received Robert Bly's proselytizing. According to a 1986 article in the *San Francisco Chronicle*, this poet thinks "the men's movement is going through a sea change these days. The sensitive-guy model is being replaced by the Wild Man in search of the primitive roots of his maleness." At rallies that feature "30 conga drummers hammering out a tribal beat" and "men capering about in fearsome masks," Mr. Bly sermonizes to hundreds of enthralled listeners that "there is something about being a man over the last 20 years that is connected with the feeling of inadequacy." Bly notes grimly in the same article that "that 20-year period coincides with the rise of feminism" and adds glumly that right now "the force field of the mother is very strong." "In our culture," he says, "it is usually the woman who is willing to be fierce and not the man. The man now has to learn how to be fierce."

The plot of sexual battle is, of course, as old as literature itself. But it was not really until the mid-19th century, when female resistance became feminist rebellion, that the battle of the sexes emerged as a symbol of struggle over political as well as personal power. Since then, it seems that whenever sexual politics seize the public imagination writers have turned to the plot of battling sexes. It should come as no surprise, then, that the subject has resurfaced lately. Literary sex wars have escalated in the past decades specifically because of the cultural revolution set in motion by the women's movement in the late 1960s.

Parallels to what's happening now existed in the 19th century and again in the early 1920s. . . .

"Fight for your life, men," urged Lawrence in a 1923 polemic whose masculinist theory could be said to permeate many of his novels. "Fight your wife out of her own self-conscious preoccupation with herself. Batter her out of it till she's stunned." "Any man might do a girl in," confided the protagonist of Eliot's "Sweeney Agonistes" (1926–27), a fragmentary verse drama that hints at dark connections between sex and sacrifice. "Any man has to, needs to, wants to, / Once in a lifetime, do a girl in."

But if modernist men studied "sex antagonism" with intense seriousness, some of their descendants were more amused than threatened by the antics of the armies on both sides, perhaps because the "feminine mystique" that gained ground at mid-century made it easier to scoff at feminist rebellion. As early as 1945, James Thurber's hilarious cartoon sequence "The War Between Men and Women" portrayed male and female adversaries fighting in the grocery, taking each other hostage and struggling at a climactic "Gettysburg." In 40s films like "Adam's Rib" and "The Maltese Falcon," too, gender strife turned out to be good box office.

Like a number of more recent film makers, however, many male novelists are depicting an escalation in the battle of the sexes that is no laughing matter, for even some of the wittiest works on the subject picture a world on the verge of total war. Specifically, in the years that saw the founding of the National Organization for Women (1966), the publication of Kate Millett's "Sexual Politics" (1970), and the appearance of *Ms.* magazine (1972), men of letters, not surprisingly, became preoccupied with feminists who were "not the fun kind" and "wild men" in search of "the primitive roots of their maleness." Norman Mailer examined the "brutal, bloody war" between the sexes in "The Prisoner of Sex" (1971), a defensive retort to *Ms.* Millett's criticisms of him and Henry Miller in "Sexual Politics." Going on the offensive, Amiri Baraka (LeRoi Jones) entered the combat zone with "Babylon Revisited" (1969), a curse-poem directed at a 20th-century femme fatale:

*May this bitch and her sisters, all of them,
receive my words
in all their orifices like lye mixed with
cocola and alaga syrup.*

More parodically, Thomas Berger, in "Regiment of Women" (1973), imagined a world where men (who seem to have been vanquished by bullying women) are encased in uncomfortable dresses and incarcerated in sperm banks where they are "milked" by female top sergeants. Perhaps most melodramatically, John Irving's popular "The World According to Garp" (1978) offered scenes in which Garp's wife bites off her lover's penis in an auto accident that kills one of her sons and partially blinds the other, Garp's famous mother is shot by a reactionary man, and Garp himself is mowed down by a deranged women's-liberation fanatic who has had her own tongue surgically removed.

Though Mr. Irving's portrayal of feminists as self-mutilating hysterics is savage, his novel's denouement implies that, as the battle of the sexes grows increasingly violent, a triumph for either side is a Pyrrhic victory. . . .

· · ·

In other words, no matter how hard these male characters try to learn (as Robert Bly recommends) "to be fierce," they seem to feel they've failed, seem, indeed, to feel that feminists somehow have more fun. But do their female contemporaries agree? When we look at writings by women from Charlotte Brontë to Margaret Atwood, it doesn't appear that they do. While many men of letters react with rage to what they perceive as unprecedented female power, literary women analyze female powerlessness at least as often as they exult in new-found strength. For as is frequently the case in the history of sex relations, some men view the smallest female steps toward autonomy as threatening strides that will strip them of authority, while many women respond to such masculine fears with a paradoxical sense of guilt and vulnerability.

Even if we turn to women's utopian or quasi-utopian works, we don't find all that much optimism, nor do we generally find the same kind of bellicosity. Where male descriptions of sexual conflict often present women as daunting opponents, women's works often depict feminine vulnerability and masculine violence. In fact, until quite recently women writers have rarely been able to envision clear-cut female victories in the sex war, and, even more to the point, most have been unable to imagine that a female character in her right mind would try to win a battle with a man in any but the most devious ways. . . .

With the modern period women writers either became more explicitly militant or began to create more openly combative female characters. "Men ought to be horsewhipped," broods the feminist protagonist of Dorothy Richardson's "Honeycomb" (1917), while Virginia Woolf brilliantly outlines the ideology of the sexual battle in "A Room of One's Own" (1929). This great modernist draws a portrait of a representative misogynist, "Professor von X.," who sits in the British Museum "writing his monumental work entitled *The Mental, Moral, and Physical Inferiority of the Female Sex*" and jabbing "his pen on the paper as if he were killing some noxious insect." In retaliation, the feminist narrator herself, "flushed with anger," begins "drawing cartwheels and circles over the angry professor's face" until it becomes "an apparition without human semblance or significance."

Such obliterations of the enemy became increasingly difficult to imagine, however, in those decades when the pervasive feminine mystique let men poke fun at angry women and left feminist rebels feeling like freaks. By 1951, for instance, Carson McCullers's "Ballad of the Sad Cafe" depicted a woman who was a kind of monster precisely because she was a great fighter, and who was therefore defeated in a wrestling match with her estranged husband.

Even visions of victory in this period were vexed and hexed. One of Sylvia Plath's most famous poems does imagine annihilating "Daddy." But when this poet notoriously declares, "So Daddy, I'm finally through," her conclusion suggests that even if she is done with the patriarch, she herself may also be finished off.

Problematic as Plath's visions of victory may have been, though, coming when they did in the early 60s they were quickly fetishized by a generation of women suddenly swept up in the hope that, as Kate Millett put it, "a second wave of sexual revolution might at last accomplish its aim of freeing half the race from its immemorial subordination." From the moderates who began working for passage of the E.R.A. in the early 70s to the radicals who signed the manifesto produced by S.C.U.M. (Society for Cutting Up Men), which proclaimed that "the male is an incomplete female, a walking abortion," participants in the revitalized women's movement enlisted with new fervor in the battle of the sexes.

. . .

Particularly in the genres of science fiction, fantasy and poetry, a number of writers produced anti-utopias that are the very opposite of Gilman's "Herland": visions of worlds in which men have got so deeply in touch with what Mr. Bly considers the "primitive roots of [their] maleness" that they enslave and even exterminate women. The misogyny at the heart of such brutality is analyzed by a battered wife in Nancy Price's recent novel "Sleeping with the Enemy" (1987) when she explains about the psychology of men who hate women: "If you sleep with them," you're called one set of obscene names; if you won't you're still cursed, but with another set of names. But Marilyn French had already anticipated both this analysis and Ms. Dworkin's definition of intercourse when she presented the idea that "all men are rapists and that's all they are. They rape us with their eyes, their laws and their. . . ."

Strong as these accusations are, Margaret Atwood's "Handmaid's Tale" (1986) is probably the best-known anti-utopian feminist work to appear in recent years. Denied all freedoms, healthy women of childbearing age in Ms. Atwood's horrifying Republic of Gilead are forced to submit to ritual attempts at impregnation meant to transform them into baby-making machines. Ironically, this society's fundamentalist ideology proclaims the need to save women from sexual violence, but the grotesquely impersonal mating to which the "handmaid" is subjected—an experience for which no proper word can be found ("Copulating . . . would be inaccurate . . . nor does rape cover it")—reveals that the cure is at least as bad as the disease. . . .

Equally extreme is Adrienne Rich's feminist version of Amiri Baraka's masculinist "Babylon Revisited," a poem in which "white acetylene / ripples" from the speaker as she attacks a male antagonist:

raking his body down to the thread
of existence
burning away his lie
leaving him a new
world; a changed
man . . .

Still, one wonders when peaceful coexistence between the sexes—a coexistence not predicated on a separatist peace—might become possible. Surely by now some of the old wounds of the feminist struggle have healed. A key poem in Ruth Stone's new collection "Second-Hand Coat" begins as an elaborate curse of an old lover but ends with a conciliatory incantation addressed to the "Poor innocent lecher": "may you be exonerated. May you be forgiven. / May you be a wax taper in paradise." What are the circumstances that foster such impulses toward the cessation of hostilities? Ms. Stone's poem suggests that they have to do with historical nightmares (in this case World War II) that virtually annihilate gender distinctions, and the latest work by one of our most important contemporary women novelists supports the point.

Toni Morrison's tender and elegiac "Beloved" dramatizes the ways in which black men and women, enslaved by history, resisted bondage to whites by bonding with each other even when they had lost the family ties incarnated in the dead baby Beloved and in the rest of the dearly beloved dead. Brilliantly examining just the premise of infanticide on which Elizabeth Barrett Browning had drawn in the 19th century, Ms. Morrison's book ultimately honors a woman who preaches, "Don't study war no more. Lay all that mess down. Sword and shield," and concludes with its hero describing the love of a dead man for a woman who "is a friend of my mind."

Is it only under great duress and after horrifying losses that men and women can win through to a détente where they become friends of each others' minds? Given the commitment of feminists to what Kate Millett, almost two decades ago, defined as a hope "of freeing half the race from its immemorial subordination," must male and female antagonists continue substituting stalemated violence for love and friendship? Can the sexes lay down sword and shield sometime soon, or will the year 2001 witness a war of the words between feminists who are "not the fun kind" and "wild men" in search of "the primitive root" of their maleness?

Study Questions on Sandra Gilbert and Susan Gubar

1. Why might someone think that men and women are two different species, doomed to a perpetual battle? Do you agree?
2. Why is the "sensitive guy" model being replaced by the "Wild Man in search of the primitive roots of his maleness" model? How does this development in the men's movement strike you?
3. Is the sex war a recent thing?
4. How much hope do the authors extend for peace and friendship between the sexes? Do you think they are being overly pessimistic? What evidence do they cite for their conclusions? What contrary evidence might be offered?

Political Philosophies of Women's Liberation

ALISON JAGGAR

Alison Jaggar begins by observing that feminists are united in holding that the inferior social position of women is unjust and needs to be changed. She then examines four different political philosophies affecting women's liberation. *Conservatives* hold that the differential treatment of women, as a group, is not unjust. *Liberal feminists* hold that an individual woman should be able to decide her social role with as much freedom as a man. *Classical Marxist feminists* hold that the oppression of women is a direct result of the institution of private property, and can be ended only by the abolition of that institution. *Radical feminists* deny the liberal claim that the basis of women's oppression consists in their lack of political and civil rights; rather, they hold that the roots of women's oppression are biological, and that its abolition requires a biological revolution. Finally, Jaggar briefly reviews two recent developments: *lesbian separatism* and *socialist feminism*.

FEMINISTS ARE UNITED BY A BELIEF that the unequal and inferior social status of women is unjust and needs to be changed. But they are deeply divided about what changes are required. The deepest divisions are not differences about strategy or the kinds of tactics that will best serve women's interests; instead, they are differences about what *are* women's interests, what constitutes women's liberation.

Within the women's liberation movement, several distinct ideologies can be discerned. All believe that justice requires freedom and equality for women, but they differ on such basic philosophical questions as the proper account of freedom and equality, the functions of the state, and the notion of what constitutes human, and especially female, nature. In what follows, I shall outline the feminist ideologies which are currently most influential and show how these give rise to differences on some particular issues. Doing this will indicate why specific debates over feminist questions cannot be settled in isolation but can only be resolved in the context of a theoretical framework derived from reflection on the fundamental issues of social and political philosophy.

The Conservative View

This is the position against which all feminists are in reaction. In brief, it is the view that the differential treatment of women, as a group, is not unjust. Conservatives admit, of course, that some individual women do suffer hardships, but they do not see this suffering as part of the systematic social oppression of women. Instead, the clear differences between women's and men's social roles are rationalized in one of two ways. Conservatives either claim that the female role is not inferior to that of the male, or they argue that women are inherently better adapted than men to the traditional female sex role. The former claim advocates a kind of sexual apartheid, typically described by such phrases as "complementary but equal"; the latter postulates an inherent inequality between the sexes.

All feminists reject the first claim, and most feminists, historically, have rejected the second. However, it is interesting to note that, as we shall see later, some modem feminists have revived the latter claim.

Conservative views come in different varieties, but they all have certain fundamentals in common. All claim that men and women should fulfill

Reprinted by permission of the author. "This article reflects the thinking of the mid-1970s. If I were to rewrite it today, it would look very different."—Alison Jaggar.

different social functions, that these differences should be enforced by law where opinion and custom are insufficient, and that such action may be justified by reference to innate differences between men and women. Thus all sexual conservatives presuppose that men and women are inherently unequal in abilities, that the alleged difference in ability implies a difference in social function and that one of the main tasks of the state is to ensure that the individual perform his or her proper social function. Thus, they argue, social differentiation between the sexes is not unjust, since justice not only allows but requires us to treat unequals unequally.

Liberal Feminism

In speaking of liberal feminism, I am referring to that tradition which received its classic expression in J. S. Mill's *The Subjection of Women* and which is alive today in various "moderate" groups, such as the National Organization for Women, which agitate for legal reform to improve the status of women.

The main thrust of the liberal feminist's argument is that an individual woman should be able to determine her social role with as great freedom as does a man. Though women now have the vote, the liberal sees that we are still subject to many constraints, legal as well as customary, which hinder us from success in the public worlds of politics, business and the professions. Consequently the liberal views women's liberation as the elimination of those constraints and the achievement of equal civil rights.

Underlying the liberal argument is the belief that justice requires that the criteria for allocating individuals to perform a particular social function should be grounded in the individual's ability to perform the tasks in question. The use of criteria such as "race, sex, religion, national origin or ancestry" will normally not be directly relevant to most tasks. Moreover, in conformity with the traditional liberal stress on individual rights, the liberal feminist insists that each person should be considered separately in order that an outstanding individual should not be penalized for deficiencies that her sex as a whole might possess.

This argument is buttressed by the classic liberal belief that there should be a minimum of state intervention in the affairs of the individual. Such a belief entails rejection of the paternalistic view that women's weakness requires that we be specially protected. Even if relevant differences between women and men in general could be demonstrated, the existence of those differences still would not constitute a sufficient reason for allowing legal restrictions on women as a group. Even apart from the possibility of penalizing an outstanding individual, the liberal holds that women's own good sense or, in the last resort, our incapacity to do the job will render legal prohibitions unnecessary.

From this sketch it is clear that the liberal feminist interprets equality to mean that each individual, regardless of sex, should have an equal opportunity to seek whatever social position she or he wishes. Freedom is primarily the absence of legal constraints to hinder women in this enterprise. However, the modern liberal feminist recognizes that equality and freedom, construed in the liberal way, may not always be compatible. Hence, the modern liberal feminist differs from the traditional one in believing not only that laws should not discriminate against women, but that they should be used to make discrimination illegal. Thus she would outlaw unequal pay scales, prejudice in the admission of women to job-training programs and professional schools, and discrimination by employers in hiring practices. She would also outlaw such things as discrimination by finance companies in the granting of loans, mortgages, and insurance to women.

In certain areas, the modem liberal even appears to advocate laws which discriminate in favor of women. For instance, she may support the preferential hiring of women over men, or alimony for women unqualified to work outside the home. She is likely to justify her apparent inconsistency by claiming that such differential treatment is necessary to remedy past inequalities—but that it is only a temporary measure. With regard to (possibly paid) maternity leaves and the employer's obligation to reemploy a woman after such a leave, the liberal argues that the bearing of children has at least as good a claim to be regarded as a social service as does a man's military or jury obligation, and that childbearing should therefore carry corresponding rights to protection. The liberal also usually advocates the repeal of laws restricting contraception and abortion, and may demand measures to encourage the establishment of private day-care centers. However, she points out that none of these demands, nor the father's payment of child support, should really be regarded as discrimination in favor of women. It is only the customary assignment of responsibility for children to their mothers which makes it possible to overlook the fact that fathers have an equal obligation to provide and care for their children. Women's traditional responsibility for child care is culturally determined, not biologically inevitable—except for breast-feeding, which is now optional. Thus the liberal argues that if women are to participate in the world outside the home on equal terms with men, not only must our reproductive capacity come under our own control but, if we have children, we must be able to share the responsibility for raising them. In return, as an extension of the same principle of equal responsibility, the modern liberal supports compulsory military service for women so long as it is obligatory for men.

Rather than assuming that every apparent difference in interests and abilities between the sexes is innate, the liberal recognizes that such differences, if they do not result entirely from our education, are at least greatly exaggerated by it. By giving both sexes the same education, whether it be cooking or carpentry, the liberal claims that she is providing the only environment in which individual potentialities (and, indeed, genuine sexual differences) can emerge. She gives little weight to the possible charge that in doing this she is not liberating women but only imposing a different kind of conditioning. At the root of the liberal tradition is a deep faith in the autonomy of the individual which is incapable of being challenged within that framework.

In summary, then, the liberal views liberation for women as the freedom to determine our own social role and to compete with men on terms that are as equal as possible. She sees every individual as being engaged in constant competition with every other in order to maximize her or his own self-interest, and she claims that the function of the state is to see that such competition is fair by enforcing "equality of opportunity." The liberal does not believe that it is necessary to change the whole existing social structure in order to achieve women's liberation. Nor does she see it as being achieved simultaneously for all women; she believes that individual women may liberate themselves long before their condition is attained by all. Finally, the liberal claims that her concept of women's liberation also involves liberation for men, since men are not only removed from a privileged position but they are also freed from having to accept the entire responsibility for such things as the support of their families and the defense of their country.

Classical Marxist Feminism

On the classical Marxist view, the oppression of women is, historically and currently, a direct result of the institution of private property; therefore, it can only be ended by the abolition of that institution. Consequently, feminism must be seen as part of a broader struggle to achieve a communist society. Feminism is one reason for communism. The long-term interests of women are those of the working class.

For Marxists, everyone is oppressed by living in a society where a small class of individuals owns the means of production and hence is enabled to dominate the lives of the majority who are forced to sell their labor power in order to survive. Women have an equal interest with men in eliminating such a class society. However, Marxists also recognize that women suffer special forms of oppression to which men are *not* subject, and hence, insofar as this oppression is rooted in capitalism, women have additional reasons for the overthrow of that economic system.

Classical Marxists believe that the special oppression of women results primarily from our traditional position in the family. This excludes women from participation in "public" production and relegates us to domestic work in the "private" world of the home. From its inception right up to the present day, monogamous marriage was designed to perpetuate the consolidation of wealth in the hands of a few. Those few are men. Thus, for Marxists, an analysis of the family brings out the inseparability of class society from male supremacy. From the very beginning of surplus production, "the sole exclusive aims of monogamous marriage were to make the man supreme in the family, and to propagate, as the future heirs to his wealth, children indisputably his own." Such marriage is "founded on the open or concealed domestic slavery of the wife," and is characterized by the familiar double standard which requires sexual fidelity from the woman but not from the man.

Marxists do not claim, of course, that women's oppression is a creation of capitalism. But they do argue that the advent of capitalism intensified the degradation of women and that the continuation of capitalism requires the perpetuation of this degradation. Capitalism and male supremacy each reinforce the other. Among the ways in which sexism benefits the capitalist system are: by providing a supply of cheap labor for industry and hence exerting a downward pressure on all wages; by increasing the demand for the consumption goods on which women are conditioned to depend; and by allocating to women, for no direct pay, the performance of such socially necessary but unprofitable tasks as food preparation, domestic maintenance and the care of the children, the sick and the old.

This analysis indicates the directions in which classical Marxists believe that women must move. "The first condition for the liberation of the wife is to bring the whole female sex back into public industry." Only then will a wife cease to be economically dependent on her husband. But for woman's entry into public industry to be possible, fundamental social changes are necessary: all the work which women presently do—food preparation, child care, nursing, etc.—must come within the sphere of public production. Thus, whereas the liberal feminist advocates an egalitarian marriage, with each spouse shouldering equal responsibility for domestic work and economic support, the classical Marxist feminist believes that the liberation of women requires a more radical change in the family. Primarily, women's liberation requires that the economic functions performed by the family should be undertaken by the state. Thus the state should provide child care centers, public eating places, hospital facilities, etc. But all this, of course, could happen only under socialism. Hence it is only under socialism that married women will be able to participate fully in public life and end the situation where "within the fam-

ily [the husband] is the bourgeois and the wife represents the proletariat."

It should be noted that "the abolition of the monogamous family as the economic unit of society" does not necessitate its disappearance as a social unit. Since "sexual love is by its nature exclusive," marriage will continue, but now it will no longer resemble an economic contract, as it has done hitherto in the property-owning classes. Instead, it will be based solely on "mutual inclination" between a woman and a man who are now in reality, and not just formally, free and equal. . . .

Since she sees women's oppression as a function of the larger socioeconomic system, the classical Marxist feminist denies the possibility, envisaged by the liberal, of liberation for a few women on an individual level. However, she does agree with the liberal that women's liberation would bring liberation for men, too. Men's liberation would now be enlarged to include freedom from class oppression and from the man's traditional responsibility to "provide" for his family, a burden that under liberalism the man merely lightens by sharing it with his wife.

Radical Feminism

Radical feminism is a recent attempt to create a new conceptual model for understanding the many different forms of the social phenomenon of oppression in terms of the basic concept of sexual oppression. It is formulated by such writers as Ti-Grace Atkinson and Shulamith Firestone.

Radical feminism denies the liberal claim that the basis of women's oppression consists in our lack of political or civil rights; similarly, it rejects the classical Marxist belief that basically women are oppressed because they live in a class society. Instead, in what seems to be a startling regression to conservatism, the radical feminist claims that the roots of women's oppression are biological. She believes that the origin of women's subjection lies in the fact that, as a result of the weakness caused by childbearing, we became dependent on men for physical survival. Thus she speaks of the origin of the family in apparently conservative terms as being primarily a biological rather than a social or economic organization. The radical feminist believes that the physical subjection of women by men was historically the most basic form of oppression, prior rather than secondary to the institution of private property and its corollary, class oppression. Moreover, she believes that the power relationships which develop within the biological family provide a model for understanding all other types of oppression such as racism and class society. Thus she reverses the emphasis of the classical Marxist feminist by explaining the development of class society in terms of the biological family rather than explaining the development of the family in terms of class society. She believes that the battles against capitalism and against racism are both subsidiary to the more fundamental struggle against sexism.

Since she believes that the oppression of women is basically biological, the radical feminist concludes that our liberation requires a biological revolution. She believes that only now, for the first time in history, is technology making it possible for women to be liberated from the "fundamental inequality of the bearing and raising of children." It is achieving this through the development of techniques of artificial reproduction and the consequent possibility of diffusing the childbearing and child-raising role throughout society as a whole. Such a biological revolution is basic to the achievement of those important but secondary changes in our political, social and economic systems which will make possible the other prerequisites for women's liberation. As the radical feminist sees them, those other prerequisites are: the full self-determination, including economic independence, of women (and children); the total integration of women (and children) into all aspects of the larger society; and the freedom of all women (and children) to do whatever they wish to do sexually. . . .

The end of the biological family will also eliminate the need for sexual repression. Male homosexuality, lesbianism, and extramarital sexual intercourse will no longer be viewed in the liberal way as alternative options, outside the range of state regulation, in which the individual may or may not choose to participate. Nor will they be viewed, in the classical Marxist way, as unnatural vices, perversions resulting from the degrading influence of capitalist society. Instead, even the categories of homosexuality and heterosexuality will be abandoned; the very "institution of sexual intercourse," where male and female each play a well-defined role, will disappear. "Humanity could finally revert to its natural 'polymorphously perverse' sexuality.". . .

Like the other theories we have considered, radical feminism believes that women's liberation will bring benefits for men. According to his concept of women's liberation, not only will men be freed from the role of provider, but they will also participate on a completely equal basis in childbearing as well as child-rearing. Radical feminism, however, is the only theory which argues explicitly that women's liberation also necessitates children's liberation. Firestone explains that this is because "The heart of woman's oppression is her childbearing and child-rearing roles. And in turn children are defined in relation to this role and are psychologically formed by it; what they become as adults and the sorts of relationships they are able to form determine the society they will ultimately build."

New Directions

Although the wave of excitement about women's liberation which arose in the late '60s has now subsided, the theoretical activity of feminists has continued. Since about 1970, it has advanced in two main directions: lesbian separatism and socialist feminism.

Lesbian separatism is less a coherent and developed ideology then an emerging movement, like the broader feminist movement, within which different ideological strains can be detected. All lesbian separatists believe that the present situation of male supremacy requires that women should refrain from heterosexual relationships. But for some lesbian separatists, this is just a temporary necessity, whereas for others, lesbianism will always be required.

Needless to say, all lesbian separatists reject the liberal and the classical Marxist beliefs about sexual preferences; but some accept the radical feminist contention that ultimately it is unimportant whether one's sexual partner be male or female. However, in the immediate context of a male-supremacist society, the lesbian separatist believes that one's sexual choice attains tremendous political significance. Lesbianism becomes a way of combating the overwhelming heterosexual ideology that perpetuates male supremacy. . . .

Socialist feminists believe that classical Marxism and radical feminism each have both insights and deficiencies. The task of socialist feminism is to construct a theory that avoids the weaknesses of each but incorporates its (and other) insights. There is space here for only a brief account of some of the main points of this developing theory.

Socialist feminists reject the basic radical feminist contention that liberation for women requires the abolition of childbirth. Firestone's view is criticized as ahistorical, anti-dialectical, and utopian. Instead, socialist feminists accept the classical Marxist contention that socialism is the main precondition for women's liberation. But though socialism is necessary, socialist feminists do not believe that it is sufficient. Sexism can continue to exist despite public ownership of the means of production. The conclusion that socialist feminists draw is that it is necessary to resort to direct cultural action in order to develop a specifically feminist consciousness in addition to transforming the economic base. Thus their vision is totalistic, requiring "transformation of the entire fabric of social relationships."

In rejecting the radical feminist view that the family is based on biological conditions, socialist feminists turn toward the classical Marxist account of monogamy as being based "not on natural but on economic conditions." But they view the classical Marxist account as inadequate, overly simple. Juliet Mitchell argues that the family should be analyzed in a more detailed, sophisticated, and historically specific way in terms of the separate, though interrelated, functions that women perform within it: production, reproduction, sexuality, and the socialization of the young.

Socialist feminists agree with classical Marxists that women's liberation requires the entry of women into public production. But this in itself is not sufficient. It is also necessary that women have access to the more prestigious and less deadening jobs and to supervisory and administrative positions. There should be no "women's work" within public industry.

In classical Marxist theory, "productive labor" is viewed as the production of goods and services within the market economy. Some socialist feminists believe that this account of productiveness obscures the socially vital character of the labor that women perform in the home. They argue that, since it is clearly impossible under capitalism to bring all women into public production, individuals (at least as an interim measure) should be paid a wage for domestic work. This reform would dignify the position of housewives, reduce their dependence on their husbands and make plain their objective position, minimized by classical Marxists, as an integral part of the working class. Not all socialist feminists accept this position, however, and the issue is extremely controversial at the time of this writing.

One of the main insights of the feminist movement has been that "the personal is political." Socialist feminists are sensitive to the power relations involved in male/female interaction and believe that it is both possible and necessary to begin changing these, even before the occurrence of a revolution in the ownership of the means of production. Thus, socialist feminists recognize the importance of a "subjective factor" in revolutionary change and reject the rigid economic determinism that has characterized many classical Marxists. They are sympathetic to attempts by individuals to change their life styles and to share responsibility for each other's lives, even though they recognize that such attempts can never be entirely successful within a capitalist context. They also reject the sexual puritanism inherent in classical Marxism, moving closer to the radical feminist position in this regard. . . .

This sketch of some new directions in feminism completes my outline of the main contemporary positions on women's liberation. I hope that I have made clearer the ideological presuppositions at the root of many feminist claims and also shed some light on the philosophical problems that one needs to resolve in order to formulate one's own position and decide on a basis for action. Many of these philosophical questions, such as the nature of the just society, the proper account of freedom and equality, the functions of the state and the relation between the individual and society, are traditional problems which now arise in a new context; others, such as the role of technology in human liberation, are of more recent origin. In either case, feminism adds a fresh dimension to our discussion of the issues and points to the need for the so-called philosophy of man to be transformed into a comprehensive philosophy of women and men and their social relations.

Study Questions on Alison Jaggar

1. Which form of feminism do you think Jaggar favors? Which (if any) do most American women favor? Which do you favor?
2. What do feminists mean when they say that the liberation of women will also mean the liberation of men?
3. Radical feminists, according to Jaggar, find the source of women's oppression in their role in reproduction, and place great hope in the new reproductive technologies that will free women from the tyranny of biology. What sense can be made of the notion of being tyrannized by one's biological structure, and are women more tyrannized by their biological structure than men are?
4. To what extent do you think feminism is simply a movement to push for the interests of women, and to what extent can it appeal, as the civil rights movement did, to shared ideals such as justice? If it is a movement to advance women's interests, what interests are shared by all women, and how can a movement to advance them be sold to men?

Reweaving Society

JULI LOESCH WILEY

Juli Loesch Wiley begins by observing that contemporary feminism lacks a coherent, shared identity. She then proposes "social feminism," founded on the belief that stable social bonds are in the interests of women and children. She rejects "loose-bolt" sexuality and proposes a number of measures intended to bring about a "new civilization of love."

THE WOMEN'S MOVEMENT is composed of a number of strikingly different teams all wearing the same jersey. Some of these teams huddle together as allies; others clash as opponents; still others aren't even playing the same game.

Eleanor Smeal, president of the National Organization for Women, calls the Equal Rights Amendment and legal abortion the central demands of mainstream feminism. But Eleanor Roosevelt, who inspired much of the modern women's movement, saw abortion as irrelevant to female advancement, and opposed the ERA vigor-

ously for 40 years on the grounds that it would hurt working women.

Hugh Hefner's daughter Christy, president of Playboy Enterprises, claims that sexual entertainment is "liberating"; but Andrea Dworkin, feminist and founder of Women Against Pornography, insists that it is degrading—the equivalent of a sexual assault.

In her 1970 book *The Female Eunuch*, Germaine Greer glorified contraception and sexual promiscuity. But by 1984, Greer was denouncing international contraceptive promoters as "corporate

From Social Justice Review *(July–August, 1987): 122–124. Reprinted by permission.*

criminals" and urging Third World women to "defend themselves" against the Western nations' "misuses of sexuality."

Even religious feminists take strikingly different approaches. In Christian churches today, "women's spirituality" can involve anything from Teresa of Avila to witchcraft.

In short, it's almost impossible to say just what it is that the adherents of "feminism" adhere to. The unifying trait of this movement is its discontent with the lot of women in society, its sense of grievance; but as a social philosophy, it shows signs of incoherence, if not disintegration.

Some might conclude that the grievances which engendered the movement must be insubstantial. I don't believe this is the case. Rather, I believe that the modern re-organization of social life has administered a series of shocks to women's sense of well-being; and that these shocks have prompted both individual and collective attempts to re-establish a "way to live," a way to *be women*—attempts which have been variously brilliant, tragic, prodigious, and disoriented.

The entire class of modern women—whether feminists or traditionalists, agents of continued social change along the lines of the '60s and '70s, or promoters of personal and social restoration—are about the work of critiquing the society in which they live. To attend to the thoughts and observe the work of women today is to witness the making and remaking of the world.

In this paper I will sketch the social forces which have injured women's sense of well-being, and contrast the ways in which two *different* strains of feminism have dealt with areas of justified complaint. I will conclude with a view which I hope could unite the now fractured focus of women's social vision.

The Divested Homestead

The Book of Proverbs ends with a famous poem (Chapter 31) in praise of the "valiant woman." We learn that she is an accomplished textile worker in her own right (v. 13), and the manager of a number of household employees (v. 15). She purchases property with her own earnings and, displaying physical strength and skill, establishes a successful farming enterprise (v. 16–18).

This "perfect wife" provides food and clothing both for a populous and productive homestead and for the needy in her community (v. 20–23). She does fine needlework and embroidery which she sells for a profit (v. 24). Her "dignity" and the "wisdom of her instruction" are lauded. The anthem ends by proclaiming that she should receive "her share," the fruit of the work of her hands, as well as "praises at the city gates."

The Biblical woman was the center of the household; and the household was the center of the world.

For millenia before the industrial age, the home was not just a private residence where families slept and ate their meals. It was far more: it was the nexus of economic and social life.

Books like *Kristin Lavranstatter* by Sigrid Undset, which picture daily life in medieval Europe, describe bustling homesteads composed of the conjugal couple and their children, adult unmarried relatives, servants and their families, tutors, craftsmen, and travelers who might enjoy the hospitality of the estate for days or weeks.

While this description applies to a country estate, urban dwellings too were centers of industry. Dyers, metalsmiths, butchers, and toolmakers worked in shops attached to their own homes; men, women, and children old enough to be apprentices contributed to productive work.

This close integration of work and domesticity persisted in some form almost to the modern age. . . .

The real challenge to women's role as "the heart of the home" came as domestic life was denuded of almost every shred of economic and cultural significance. The industrial revolution separated the workplace from the home. In America, the completion of the Interstate Highway system, plus Federal home financing for GIs, led to the burgeoning of suburbs and "bedroom communities" which were empty from 7:30 AM to 5:30 PM every day while the commuter-husbands were at work and the children at school.

They were empty, that is, except for the housewives. Women of the 1950s were the first generation ever to be separated from the world of "real" adult challenges other than toilet-training their toddlers and devising exciting things to do with frozen dinners.

It may be that the majority of American women did not in fact live a life of suburban ennui; but it was the cultural ideal. . . .

. . . Women of the educated economic elite, their childbearing dramatically reduced by contraception and their child-rearing responsibilities largely replaced by school-based organizations and television, launched out into the professional workforce.

Their less economically favored sisters, whose domestic lives had likewise dwindled in significance, found the labor market less congenial. The occupations in which they were concentrated (food service, secretarial, and light industrial work) had low wages and few avenues for advancement. Nevertheless, the changing economy forced them to work, not for "self-fulfillment," but to pay the rent and put food on the table.

Sexuality dwindled, too, as it was cut loose from its procreative powers. What some see as a "blooming" of sexuality with the introduction of oral contraceptives and the prevalence of sexual-adventurist themes in mass culture, is like the "bloom" of algae in a dying lake. It seems to be everywhere, growing with furious vitality—for a time; then it chokes off the sources of life and begins to rot and stink.

Like a loose bolt in a machine, loose sex does considerable damage and clatters all the more noisily because it's not connected to anything.

All these changes were accompanied by a crisis of spirituality. The traditional source of woman's strength is the unquestioned centrality of her life-giving powers. But every image of women's dignity—the fire in the hearth, the babe in the womb, the candle in the window—was emptied out and extinguished; and the corresponding virtues—domestic competency, nurturance, fidelity—faced extinction.

To be "queen of the home" was to be regent of a ludicrously reduced domain, a joke. But to plunge into the labor market in a "serious" way—to make your major commitment there—was to risk losing even the shreds of family life that were still available in our culture.

Where to from here?

The Issue Is Joined: Two Paths

Despite many permutations and combinations, it might be said that feminists choose one of two fundamentally different approaches to this dilemma.

"Assimilationist feminism" insists that men and women be treated identically in law, in the marketplace and in social relations. Assimilationists oppose special benefits for women as much as they oppose adverse discrimination. Once the differences between men and women have been eliminated by equal rights legislation plus reproductive freedom (i.e., the freedom not to reproduce), women will achieve power, money, and satisfaction on the same terms as men.

"Social feminism," on the other hand, holds that it is not legal distinction or normal fertility which traps women in second-class citizenship, but rather the dual burden women carry to maintain a home and family *and* function in the workforce. Social feminists argue that because women are wives and mothers as well as workers, their mother-status needs *extra* compensation and support if they are to have equal opportunities in the world beyond the home.

In her brilliant book on women in the workplace, *A Lesser Life,* Sylvia Ann Hewlett finds that U.S. feminists' single-minded pursuit of identical treatment—formal equality—has trapped millions of women in a very unfavorable situation if they have children—as most women do.

Pregnant workers are routinely fired. Others are defined as "new hires" when they come back to work after childbirth, losing accumulated benefits, merit raises, and seniority rights. Large numbers of new mothers, unable to find affordable child care, are forced to take a third-rate or part-time job close to home, or quit the workforce altogether.

Yet most U.S. wage-earning women have to work: 75% are either single (with or without dependents), or are married to men who earn less than $10,000 a year. At some point in their lives, 90% of women have at least one child—and the percentage would be even higher if we counted women who want to have children. The market economy severely penalizes such women *precisely because it treats them like men.*

In every other industrial nation in the world, social feminists have pushed successfully for guaranteed job-protection and full or partial income-replacement when a woman takes time off to have a baby. Throughout Europe, the average maternity leave is five months at full pay.

In Sweden, both parents can opt for a 6-hour workday until their child is 8 years old. In Italy, working women get 2 years' accelerated seniority every time they give birth to a child.

The practical effect of social feminism, then, is not to redesign women to fit the labor market, but to redesign the labor market to fit women.

In the U.S., however, where assimilationists have largely set the feminist agenda, 60% of the working women have no right to any job-protected maternity leave whatsoever. Overall, women suffer a 20% drop in their earning power each time they give birth.

The practical effect of assimilationist feminism is to redesign women to fit into a male-oriented system. Don't get pregnant; or, if you do, don't stay pregnant. Don't make any demands on the system for child care or flex-time or maternity benefits ("preferential treatment") and you'll have the privilege of being treated just like a man.

The assimilationist approach is to *structurally alter the women* through gynecological surgery and chemical modification (sterilization, abortion, and contraception) to fit them more easily into the male mold.

In contrast, the social feminists would see no point in habituating people to sexual patterns which are inherently destructive. They would work instead for behavioral changes for a more socially constructive, sustainable, and wholesome sexuality. . . .

A Vision for the Future

An alliance between traditional pro-family and social feminist forces could help build a social environment which is more humane for men and women, and safer for children. This requires action on the economic, cultural, and spiritual levels.

For the rest of this century, it looks as if most women in America will spend most of their adult lives in the labor market. Action to eliminate overt discrimination and wage inequity is still needed: "give her," as the Proverb says, "her share, the fruit of the work of her hands."

In addition, there is a need for other economic supports—particularly, affordable family medical coverage and maternity benefits—to enable women to stay home with their infants and young children without causing intolerable financial hardship to their families.

Prenatal care, job-protected parental leave, family allowances, and more realistic tax-deductions for dependents are reasonable and attainable goals. They could make it possible for women to move more freely in and out of the market economy while still enjoying a richly family-oriented existence.

In the long run, strategies must be devised which would bring productive employment back into the home, or at least overcome the radical disjunction between our family lives and our working lives. Home computers now make it possible for journalism and publishing, management, marketing, research, and other work to be done largely or entirely at home. Women—and men, too—may be able to re-invest the home itself with some of the economic and social centrality which it lost over the past 50 years.

"Loose bolt" sexuality should be rejected. Cultures which dissipate bonding energy, and which override and disrupt female sexual cycles through contraception and abortion, destroy women's well-being and are not sustainable over time. For the sake of our own integrity, sexuality must be re-connected to marriage and the formation of stable families.

The trivialization of sex, which followed inevitably upon the contraceptive revolution, must be reversed. The social feminist/pro-family alliance against pornography is already underway; the potentially much more powerful alliance against destructive contraceptive and reproductive engineering practices must still be forged.

An authentic renewal of women's spirituality is likewise essential. Women must be encouraged to reflect theologically upon their lives, drawing deeply from the feminine tradition which includes such giants as Hildegard of Bingen and Julian of Norwich, Katherine Drexel and Elizabeth Seton, Maisie Ward, Catherine de Hueck Doherty, and the woman who should be the patron saint of the American Catholic laity, Dorothy Day.

The women who want to unravel the present patterns of oppression in our society are wise women indeed; but the reweaving of our common life must be done with careful hands.

It is my hope that the justified complaints of women will bring social feminists and pro-family activists together both for the unraveling and the reweaving. Together we can create, in the words of Pope John Paul II, a "new civilization of love."

Study Questions on Juli Loesch Wiley

1. Do you agree with Wiley that feminists lack a coherent, shared identity? Might not a shared awareness of the oppression of women unite them?
2. Explain the difference between assimilationist and social feminists. What, if anything, makes them both feminists? Would Jaggar regard Wiley as a feminist? What do you think?
3. What is loose-bolt sexuality, and why does Wiley reject it? Do you agree that women especially ought to reject it? Is it more harmful to women than men, equally bad for both, or do you think both men and women should be free to pursue sexual pleasure without necessarily becoming involved in committed relationships?
4. Do Wiley's suggestions for the future seem attractive to you, or is she just trying to put women back into unfulfilling traditional roles? What parts of her program would you accept and what parts would you reject, and why? How central is religion to her ideal society?
5. How much coercion or social pressure is required to control loose-bolt sexuality? Would laws forbidding adultery, divorce, or fornication be in order? What about the social pressures, largely imposed by women, portrayed in a novel such as Edith Wharton's *Age of Innocence?*

Is the Favoring of Women and Blacks in Employment and Educational Opportunities Justified?

LOUIS KATZNER

Louis Katzner examines the justice of preferential affirmative action. He argues that while the favoring of black people in employment and educational opportunities may be justified, this result is not true for women because the debilitating effects of discrimination against women are not passed on from generation to generation.

THERE IS PRESENTLY A CALL to favor blacks and women in employment and educational opportunities because in the past many of them have been discriminated against in these areas. The basic concern of this paper is whether or not reverse discrimination in this sense is justified. Given that, as

will be shown, all acts of reverse discrimination involve prejudgment, it is appropriate to scrutinize first the notion of discrimination itself. Next, the idea of reverse discrimination will be explicated by distinguishing among several different forms that it may take; and from this explication the set of

Reprinted by permission of the author.

conditions under which a bias of redress is justified will emerge. Finally, the situation of blacks and women in the United States will be examined to see what conclusions can be drawn concerning the justification of reverse discrimination for these two classes.

I. Discrimination

There are certain things that are relevant to the way people should be treated and certain things that are not. The size of one's chest is relevant to the size shirt he should have, but it has nothing to do with the size his shoes should be. The rate of one's metabolism is pertinent to the amount of food she should be served, but not to the color of the napkin she is given. People should be treated on the basis of their attributes and merits that are relevant to the circumstances. When they are, those who are similar are treated similarly and those who are dissimilar are treated differently. Although these distinctions do involve treating people differently (those with larger chests get larger shirts than those with smaller chests), it does not involve discrimination. For discrimination means treating people differently when they are similar in the relevant respects or treating them similarly when they are different in the relevant respects.

It follows that to determine what constitutes discrimination in vocational and educational opportunities, we must first determine what qualities are relevant to a career and the capacity to learn. People today generally seem to accept the principle of meritocracy—that is, that an individual's potential for success, which is a combination of his native and/or developed ability and the amount of effort he can be expected to put forth, is the sole criterion that should be used in hiring and college admissions practices. It may be that until recently many people did not accept this view, and it may be that there are some even today who do not accept it. Nevertheless, this is one of the basic principles of the "American Dream"; it is the foundation of the civil service system; it is a principle to which even the most ardent racists and sexists at least give lipservice; and it is the principle that most people seem to have in mind when they speak of the problem of discrimination in hiring

and college admissions practices. And because it is generally agreed that people with the same potential should be treated similarly in employment and college admissions, and that those with more potential should receive preference over those with less, the discussion begins with this assumption.

II. Reverse Discrimination

With the notion of discrimination clarified, it is now possible to see what is involved in the idea of reverse discrimination. Reverse discrimination is much more than a call to eliminate bias; it is a call to offset the effects of past acts of bias by skewing opportunity in the opposite direction. This paper will consider only the claims that blacks, women, et cetera, have been discriminated against in the past (that is, they have been treated as if they have less potential than they actually do); and that the only way to offset their subsequent disadvantages is to discriminate now in their favor (that is, to treat them as if they have more potential than they actually do).

It follows that those who are currently calling for the revision of admission standards at our colleges because they do not accurately reflect a student's chances of success there are not calling for reverse discrimination. They are merely saying that we should find a way of determining precisely who is qualified (that is, who has the potential) to go to college, and then admit the most qualified. On the other hand, those who are calling for us to admit students whom they allow are less qualified than others who are denied admission, and to provide these less qualified students with special tutorial help, are calling for reverse discrimination.

This example clearly illustrates the basic problem that any justification of reverse discrimination must come to grips with—viz., that every act of reverse discrimination is itself discriminatory. For every less qualified person who is admitted to a college, or hired for a job, there is a more qualified person who is being discriminated against, and who has a right to complain. Hence the justification of reverse discrimination must involve not only a justification of *discriminating for* those who are benefiting from it, it must also involve a justification of discriminating *against* those at whose expense the reverse discrimination is being practiced.

III. Justification of Reverse Discrimination: Direct

There are at least two significantly different kinds of situations in which reverse discrimination can be called for. On the one hand, a person might argue that he should be favored because he was arbitrarily passed over at some time in the past. Thus, for example, a Chicano might maintain that since he was denied a job for which he was the most qualified candidate simply because of his race, he should now be given one for which he is not the most qualified candidate, simply because he was discriminated against in the past. On the other hand, one might argue that he should be given preference because his ancestors (parents, grandparents, great-grandparents, et cetera) were discriminated against. In this case, the Chicano would claim that he should be given a job for which he is not the most qualified applicant because his ancestors were denied jobs for which they were the most qualified.

In the former case, that of rectifying bias against an individual by unduly favoring him, there are several interesting points that can be made. First of all, the case for reverse discrimination of this type is strongest when the person to be passed over in the reverse discrimination is the same one who benefited from the initial discriminatory act. Suppose, for example, that when it comes time to appoint the vice-president of a company, the best qualified applicant (that is, the one who has the most potential) is passed over because of his race, and a less qualified applicant is given the job. Suppose that the following year the job of president in the same firm becomes open. At this point, the vice-president, because of the training he had as second in command, is the most qualified applicant for the job. It could be argued, however, that the presidency should go to the person who was passed over for the vice-presidency. For he should have been the vice-president, and if he had been he would probably now be the best-equipped applicant for the top post; it is only because he was passed over that the current vice-president is now the most qualified candidate. In other words, since the current vice-president got ahead at his expense, it is warranted for him to move up at the vice-president's expense. In this way the wrong that was done him will be righted.

There are two main problems with this argument. First of all, certainly to be considered is how well the individual who benefited from the initial act of discrimination exploited his break. If he used this opportunity to work up to his capacity, this would seem to be a good reason for not passing him over for the presidency. If, on the other hand, although performing very adequately as vice-president, he was not working up to the limits of his capacity, then perhaps the job of president should be given to the man who was passed over in the first place—even though the vice-president's experience in his job leads one to think that he is the one most qualified to handle the difficult tasks of the presidency. In other words, how much a person has made of the benefit he has received from an act of discrimination seems to be relevant to the question of whether or not he should be discriminated against so that the victim of that discrimination may now be benefited.

Secondly, there are so few cases of this kind that even if reverse discrimination is justified in such cases, this would not show very much. In most instances of reverse discrimination, the redress is at the expense of someone who did not benefit from the initial act of discrimination rather than someone who did.

One species of this form of reverse discrimination is that in which the victim of the proposed act of reverse discrimination has not benefited from *any* acts of discrimination. In such a case, what is in effect happening is that the burden of discrimination is being transferred from one individual who does not deserve it to another individual who does not deserve it. There is no sense in which "the score is being evened," as in the case above. Because there is no reason for saying that one of the individuals deserves to be penalized by prejudice while the other one does not, it is difficult to see how this kind of reverse discrimination can be justified.

The only argument that comes to mind as a justification for this species of reverse discrimination is the following: The burdens of discrimination should be shared rather than placed on a few. It is better that the liabilities of discrimination be passed from person to person than that they remain the handicap only of those who have been disfavored. It follows that if we find someone who has been discriminated against, we are warranted in rectifying that injustice by an act of reverse discrimination, as long as the victim of the reverse discrimination has not himself been discriminated against in the past.

But this is not a very persuasive argument. For one thing, the claim that discrimination should be shared does not seem a very compelling reason for discriminating against a totally innocent bystander. Secondly, even if this is viewed as a forceful reason, the image of society that emerges is a horrifying one. The moment someone is discriminated against, he seeks out someone who has not been unfairly barred, and asks for reverse discrimination against this person to rectify the wrong he has suffered. Such a procedure would seem to entrench rather than eliminate discrimination, and would produce an incredibly unstable society.

Another species of this form of reverse discrimination is that in which the victim of the proposed reverse bias has benefited from a previous unfair decision, although it is not the particular act that is being rectified. In other words, he did not get ahead at the expense of the individual to whom we are trying to "make things up" by reverse discrimination, but he has benefited from bias against other individuals. In such a case, there is a sense, admittedly extended, in which a score is being evened.

Now it appears that such cases are more like those in which the victim of the proposed act of reverse discrimination benefited from the initial instance of discrimination than those in which he is a completely innocent bystander, and hence in such cases reverse discrimination can be justified. Of course it would be preferable if we could find the beneficiary of the original act of discrimination— but very often this just is not possible. And we must make sure that the reverse discrimination is proportionate to both the liability suffered by the proposed beneficiary and the advantage previously gained by the proposed victim—a very difficult task indeed. But there does not seem to be any reason for saying that reverse discrimination can only be visited upon those who benefited from the particular discriminatory act that is being rectified. It seems more reasonable to say that reverse discrimination can be visited upon those who benefited from either the particular instance of discrimination being rectified or from roughly similar acts.

Although the conclusions drawn from this discussion of the various species of one form of reverse discrimination do not seem conclusive, this discussion has brought to light three conditions which are necessary for the justification of reverse discrimination: First, there must have been an act of discrimination that is being rectified. Second, the initial act of discrimination must have in some way handicapped its victim, for if he has not been handicapped or set back in some way, then there is nothing to "make up to him" through reverse discrimination. And third, the victim of the proposed reverse discrimination must have benefited from an act of discrimination (either the one that is being rectified or a similar one); otherwise it is unacceptable to say that he should now be disfavored.

IV. Justification of Reverse Discrimination: Indirect

Not all of the claims that are made for reverse discrimination, however, assume that the individual involved has himself been the victim of bias. In many cases what is being claimed is that an individual is entitled to benefit from a rectifying bias because his ancestors (parents, grandparents, great-grandparents, et cetera) were unfairly denied opportunity. Keeping in mind the three conditions necessary for reverse discrimination that we have just developed, this form of reverse discrimination will be examined.

In a society in which wealth could not be accumulated or, even if it could, it did not give one access to a better education and/or job, and a good education did not give one access to a better job and/or greater wealth, it would be hard to see how educational and/or economic discrimination against one's ancestors could be a handicap. That is, if education was not a key to economic success, then the educational discrimination one's ancestors suffered could not handicap one in the search for a job. If wealth did not buy better teachers and better schools, then the fact that one's ancestors have been handicapped economically could not be a reason for his being educationally disadvantaged. If wealth could not start a business, buy into a business, or give one direct access to a good job, then the economic shackling one's ancestors endured could in no way handicap her in the economic realm. But if wealth and education do these things, as in our society they clearly do, and if because of discrimination some people were not allowed to accumulate the wealth that their talents normally would bring, then it is quite clear that their offspring are handicapped by the discrimination they have suffered.

It is important to note that this point in no way turns on the controversy that is currently raging over the relationship between IQ and race. For it is not being claimed that unless there is complete equality there is discrimination. The members of a suppressed group may be above, below, or equal to the other members of society with regard to potential. All that is being claimed is that to the extent that the members of a group have been denied a fair chance to do work commensurate with their capacities, and to the extent that this has handicapped subsequent members of that group, reverse discrimination may be justified to offset this handicap.

But, as we have already seen, for reverse discrimination to be justified, not only must the victims of discrimination be handicapped by the discrimination, those who will suffer from its reversal must have benefited from the original injustice. In this particular case, it may be that they are the children of the beneficiaries of discrimination who have passed these advantages on to them. Or it may be that they benefit in facing reduced competition for schooling and jobs, and hence they are able to get into a better school and land a better job than they would if those suffering the effects of discrimination were not handicapped. Or they may have benefited from discrimination in some other way. But the proposed victims of reverse discrimination must be the beneficiaries of previous discrimination.

In addition to all of this, however, it seems that there is one more condition that must be met for reverse discrimination to be justified. Assuming that if we eliminated all discrimination immediately, the people who have suffered from it could compete on an equal basis with all other members of society, then reverse discrimination would not be justified. This of course is trivially true if it is only being claimed that if the elimination of all discrimination entails the eradication of all the handicaps it creates, then only the elimination of discrimination (and not reverse discrimination) is justified. But the claim involves much more than this. What is being argued is that even if the immediate elimination of

all discrimination does not allow all suppressed people to compete equally with other members of society, as long as it allows equal opportunity to all children born subsequent to the end of discrimination, then reverse discrimination is not justified— *not even for those who have been handicapped by discrimination*. In other words, reverse discrimination will not prevent its debilitating effects from being passed on to generations yet unborn.

Thus there is a fourth condition that must be added to the list of conditions that are necessary for the justification of reverse discrimination. Moreover, the addition of this condition renders the list jointly sufficient for the justification of reverse discrimination. Thus, reverse discrimination is justified if, and only if, the following conditions are met:

1. There must have been an initial act of discrimination that the reverse discrimination is going to rectify.
2. The beneficiary of the proposed act of reverse discrimination must have been handicapped by the initial act—either directly, if he was the victim of the initial discrimination, or indirectly, if he is the offspring of a victim (and inherited the handicap).
3. The victim of the proposed act of reverse discrimination must have benefited from an act of discrimination—the one that is being rectified or a similar one—and either directly, if he was the beneficiary of an initial act of discrimination or indirectly, if he is the offspring of a beneficiary (and inherited the benefit).
4. It must be the case that even if all discrimination were ended immediately, the debilitating effects of discrimination would be passed on to generations yet unborn.

V. Reverse Discrimination Favoring Women and Blacks

A partial answer, at least, to the question of whether or not reverse discrimination is justified in the case of women and blacks is now possible. Let us begin with blacks.

It seems clear that the situation of many blacks in this country meets the four conditions shown to be individually necessary and jointly sufficient for the justification of reverse discrimination. First, there can be no doubt that many blacks have been the victims of educational and vocational discrimination. Second, given the relationships existing between wealth, education, and vocation, there can be no doubt that the discrimination that blacks have met with has handicapped both themselves and their offspring. Third, it also seems clear that within our economic framework, if blacks had not been discriminated against, there are many whites (those who got an education or a job at the expense of a more qualified black or in competition with the handicapped offspring of disadvantaged blacks) who would be in far less advantageous educational and vocational situations than they currently are—that is, there are people who have benefited from discrimination. And finally, again given the relationships existing among wealth, education, and vocation, even if all discrimination against blacks were to cease immediately, many black children born subsequent to this time would not be able to compete for educational and vocational opportunities on the same basis that they would had there been no bias against their ancestors.

Of course this in no way shows that reverse discrimination for all blacks is justified. After all, there are some blacks who have not let themselves be handicapped by discrimination. There are also undoubtedly some whites who have not benefited from the discrimination against blacks. And finally, there are many whites who have endured discrimination in the same way blacks have. In other words, so far it has only been shown that all those who have been discriminated against in a way that meets the conditions established are entitled to reverse discrimination and that some blacks have been discriminated against in this way.

To move from this claim to the conclusion that blacks as a class are entitled to reverse discrimination, several additional things must be shown. First, it must be demonstrated that it is unfeasible to handle reverse discrimination on a case by case basis (for example, it might be argued that such a procedure would be far too costly). Second, it must be proven that the overwhelming percentage of blacks have been victimized by discrimination—that is, the number of blacks who would benefit from reverse discrimination, but who do not deserve to, must be very small. And finally, it must be shown that the overwhelming majority of the

potential victims of bias of redress have benefited from the acts of discrimination (or similar acts) that are being rectified—that is, it must be that the number of whites who will suffer the effects of reverse discrimination, without deserving to, must also be very small. If these conditions are met, then although there will be some unwarranted discrimination resulting from the reverse discrimination in favor of blacks (that is, some blacks benefiting who were not victimized and some whites suffering who were not benefited), such cases will be kept to a bare minimum, and hence the basic result will be the offsetting of the handicaps with which blacks have unwarrantedly been saddled.

When it comes to the case of (white) women, however, the situation is quite different. There is little doubt that many women have been denied opportunity, and thus handicapped while many men have benefited from this discrimination (although I believe that discrimination has been far less pervasive in the case of women than it has been for blacks). But women generally do not constitute the kind of class in which the handicaps of discrimination are passed on to one's offspring. This is because, unlike blacks, they are not an isolated social group. Most women are reared in families in which the gains a father makes, even if the mother is limited by society's prejudice, work to the advantage of *all* offspring. (White) women have attended white schools and colleges and, even if they have been discriminated against, their children have attended these same schools and colleges. If all discrimination were ended tomorrow, there would be no external problem at all for most women in competing, commensurate with their potential, with the male population.

Two important things follow from this. First, it is illegitimate for most women to claim that they should be favored because their mothers were disfavored. Second, and most importantly, if all discrimination against women were ended immediately, in most cases none of its debilitating effects would be transmitted to the generations of women yet unborn; hence, for most women, the fourth condition necessary for the justification of reverse discrimination is not satisfied. Thus, reverse discrimination for women as a class cannot be justified, although there are undoubtedly some cases in which, for a particular woman, it can.

Study Questions on Louis Katzner

1. Explain what Katzner means by discrimination and by reverse discrimination.
2. Why is reverse discrimination justified for black people, according to Katzner? How does his argument apply to other racial minorities, such as Native Americans (American Indians), Asian Americans, and Hispanic Americans?
3. Why is reverse discrimination *not* justified for white women, according to Katzner?
4. Is Katzner's position fair to poor whites? To ethnic groups, such as Italian Americans, whose ancestors came here after slavery was abolished, and were themselves subjected to much discrimination?

In Defense of Hiring Apparently Less Qualified Women

LAURA PURDY

Laura Purdy defends hiring apparently less qualified women, especially in the academy. She argues that past prejudice against women has introduced a bias into the hiring process, and that affirmative action is needed to correct this situation.

A Man's mind—what there is of it—has always the advantage of being masculine—as the smallest birchtree is of higher kind than the most soaring palm—and even his ignorance is of a sounder quality.

George Elliot, *Middlemarch*. ch. 2

THERE ARE RELATIVELY FEW WOMEN in academe, and it is reasonable to believe that discrimination—conscious and unconscious, subtle and overt, individual and institutional—is responsible for this state of affairs. Affirmative action programs have been promoted to try to neutralize this discrimination. One form requires academic departments to search actively for female candidates; if a woman with qualifications at least as good as those of the leading male contender is found, she is to be hired.

Does this policy create new and serious injustice, as some contend? If a woman and a man were equally qualified, and one could be sure that prejudice against women played no part in the decision to hire, such a policy would certainly be an imposition on the department's freedom to hire the most compatible-seeming colleague. (This is not to say that such an imposition could never be justified: we might, for example, believe that the importance of creating role models for female students justifies some loss of freedom on the part of departments.) However, it is widely conceded that there is prejudice against women among academics, with the result that women are not getting the appointments they deserve. My intent here is to consider how this happens. I will argue that women are often not perceived to be as highly qualified as they really are. Thus when the qualifications of candidates are compared, a woman may not be thought equally (or more highly) qualified, even when she is. Affirmative

Reprinted by permission of The Journal of Social Philosophy.

action programs which require hiring of equally qualified women will therefore be ineffective: the hiring of women perceived to be less qualified is needed if discrimination against women is to cease.

Some people think that the latter course is both unnecessary and unfair. Alan Goldman, for instance, maintains that it is unnecessary because the procedural requirements of good affirmative action programs are sufficient to guarantee equal opportunity. He also believes it to be unfair because it deprives the most successful new Ph.D.s of their just reward—a good job. I will argue that neither of these claims is true and that there is a good case for hiring women perceived to be less well qualified than their male competitors.

The general difficulty of forming accurate assessments of candidates' merit is well-known, and it is probable that the better candidate has sometimes been taken for the worse. It is reasonable to believe, however, that the subjective elements in evaluations lead to systematic lowering of women's perceived qualifications. I have two arguments for this claim. The first is that past prejudice biases the evidence and the second is that present prejudice biases perception of the evidence. Let us examine each in turn.

Why then may women be better qualified than their records suggest? One principal reason is that many men simply do not take women seriously:

> You might think that the evaluation of a specific performance would be an objective process, judged on characteristics of performance itself rather than on assumptions about the personality or ability of the performer. Yet performance is rarely a totally objective process. Two people may view the same event and interpret it differently. In the same way, it is possible for someone to view two people acting in exactly the same way and yet come to different conclusions about that behavior.

Studies by Rosenthal and Jacobson provide experimental support for this claim. They found that students reported one group of rats to run mazes faster than another identical group, when they had previously been told that the first group was brighter. Ann Sutherland Harris quite plausibly concludes that such studies have important implications for women:

> If male scholars believe that women are intellectually inferior to men—less likely to have original contributions to make, less likely to be logical, and so on—will they not also find the evidence to support their beliefs in the women students in their classes, evidence of a far more sophisticated nature than the speed at which one rat finds its way through a maze? Their motives will be subconscious. Indeed, they will firmly believe that their judgment is rational and objective.

What grounds are there for maintaining that this does not occur whenever women are evaluated? Other studies suggest additional hurdles for women that bias the evidence upon which they are judged. For instance, male students (though not female ones) rate identical course syllabi higher when the professor is said to be a man.

Sociologist Jessie Bernard suggests that bias occurs whether women present accepted ideas or novel ones. In one study, a man and a woman taught classes using the same material. The man engaged the students' interest: he was thought both more biased and more authoritative than the equally competent woman. According to Bernard, she was taken less seriously because she did not "look the part." To support her position that novel ideas are less well received from women than men, Bernard mentions the case of Agnes Pockels, whose discoveries in physics were ignored for years. She cites this as an example of the general inability to see women in "the idea-man or instrumental role. We are simply not used to looking for innovation and originality from women." The consequences of failing to take new ideas seriously may be even more detrimental to women than the failure to be taken seriously as a teacher. Bernard argues: "The importance of priority . . . highlights the importance of followers, or, in the case of science, of the public qualified to judge innovations. If an innovation is not recognized—even if recognition takes the form of rejection and a fight—it is dead."

I have been arguing that women are likely to be more highly qualified than they seem. This fact alone would support a policy of hiring women perceived to be less qualified. However, I think there is another sound argument for such a policy. Women may sometimes be less qualified than their male competitors because as students they faced stumbling-blocks the men did not. Hence some women probably deserve their weak recommendations and dearth of publications because their work is less fully developed and their claims less well supported than a man's might be. This can occur because women's social role often precludes opportunities for informal constructive criticism; it may also be the result of the lack of a mentor to push her to her limits. Finally, a woman is likely to have had to work in a debilitating environment of lowered expectations.

Goldman argues that it would be wrong to hire such a woman if there were a more qualified candidate: ". . . the white male who has successfully met the requirements necessary to attaining maximal competence attains some right to that position. It seems unjust for society to set standards of achievement and then to thwart the expectations of those who have met those standards."

But surely hiring is ultimately intended to produce the best scholar and teacher, not to reward the most successful graduate student. Consequently, if there are grounds for believing that women turn into the former, despite not having been the latter according to the traditional criteria, it is reasonable to hold that they should sometimes be hired anyway. And there are such grounds.

The obstacles encountered by women in academe are well-documented and there is no need to elaborate at length upon them here. What matters is the nature of the person they create. Until very recently, at every stage of schooling, fewer girls than boys continued. There is considerable evidence that women graduate students have higher academic qualifications than their male counterparts. This appears to be because only the very highly qualified get into graduate school. Harris argues that it ". . . is worth remembering that women candidates for graduate school are the survivors of a long sifting process—only the very best of the good students go on to graduate school." A report issued by women at the University of Chicago supports this claim—the grade averages of women students entering graduate school were significantly higher than those of men.

Once there, women have somewhat higher attrition rates than men. But Harris thinks that this is "largely explained by the lack of encouragement and the actual discouragement experienced by women graduate students for their career plans. . . . It is not surprising that some women decide that they are not cut out to be scholars and teachers." She argues that if women were not highly committed, the attrition rate would be much higher: ". . . only the hardiest survive."

In light of all these facts, a temporary policy of hiring women perceived to be less well qualified would be reasonable, to see if the hypothesis that they will bloom is borne out. Such a policy is less risky than it might seem since junior faculty members are on probation and can be fired if they do not start to fulfill their promise.

In conclusion, there are good grounds for at least a trial of the policy I am proposing with regard to hiring in academe, since existing affirmative action programs have not been and cannot be effective. I have tried to show why women may often seem less qualified than they really are, and why they may be more promising than they seem. Unless faculty members take these factors into account, no improvements in the position of women can be expected, for women are likely to seem less worthy of being hired than their male competitors when they are judged in the usual manner. Requiring departments to hire women perceived to be less well qualified may well turn out to be the most efficacious way to force departments to recognize and remedy the situation. It might also have a more generally beneficial side-effect of promoting faculty-members' awareness of their own biases as they struggle to distinguish between truly mediocre women and those merely perceived to be so!

Study Questions on Laura Purdy

1. Purdy's article was written in 1984, and statistically women have made enormous gains in postsecondary and graduate education since then, both in terms

of degrees obtained and job placement. Do you think, on the basis of your own experience, that women still face the sorts of obstacles in their education that Purdy describes? Be concrete and specific. Do you think that the situation requires affirmative action in order to correct the problems (if any) that exist? What advantages and disadvantages might result for women if the policies Purdy recommends were put into practice?

2. Is Purdy's argument undermined by statistics showing that girls do better than boys in primary and secondary education, with the result that more women than men go to college?

3   Many prejudices influence perceptions of academic ability. What are some of them other than those based on gender? Are gender prejudices somehow special?

4. How, on Purdy's view, are we to distinguish between "apparently less qualified women" and those who are really less qualified? How would we know that we had overcome gender prejudice and hired the best person?

5. Case Study: A man and an older woman have both been teaching, on a temporary basis, at a small state college, the woman for one year longer than the man. Both of them have published books, unlike the majority of their department. The man is generally regarded in the department as the more effective teacher. When a permanent position arises, both are passed over, the man because he is a man, the woman because (despite her book) she is insufficiently "high powered." Instead a younger woman with less good paper credentials than either of them is hired from outside, and the two temporary teachers are obliged to leave. Is this decision just? Discuss the decision with reference to our readings, and defend your own opinion about what should have been done.

Sexual Harassment: Its First Decade in Court (1986)

CATHARINE MacKINNON

In this 1987 essay, Catharine MacKinnon reviews developments in the law of sexual harassment, which she argues to be a form of gender discrimination against women. She was the first to propose analyzing sexual harassment as a form of sex discrimination, a position that the courts have subsequently adopted. She addresses subsequent developments in the law, and in particular the connection between racial and sexual harassment, in chapter II of her 1993 book *Only Words*.

SEXUAL HARASSMENT, THE EVENT, is not new to women. It is the law of injuries that it is new to. Sexual pressure imposed on someone who is not in an economic position to refuse it became sex discrimination in the midseventies, and in education soon afterward. It became possible to do something legal about sexual harassment because some women took women's experience of violation seriously enough to design a law around it, as if what happens to women matters. This was apparently such a startling way of proceeding that sexual harassment was protested as a feminist invention.

Reprinted by permission from Feminism Unmodified: Discourse on Life and Law *by Catharine MacKinnon, Cambridge, MA: Harvard University Press, © 1987 by the President and Fellows of Harvard College.*

Sexual harassment, the event, was not invented by feminists; the perpetrators did that with no help from us. Sexual harassment, the legal claim—the idea that the law should see it the way its victims see it—is definitely a feminist invention. Feminists first took women's experience seriously enough to uncover this problem and conceptualize it and pursue it legally. That legal claim is just beginning to produce more than a handful of reported cases. Ten years later, "[i]t may well be that sex harassment is the hottest present day Title VII issue." It is time for a down-the-road assessment of this departure.

The law against sexual harassment is a practical attempt to stop a form of exploitation. It is also one test of sexual politics as feminist jurisprudence, of possibilities for social change for women through law. The existence of a law against sexual harassment has affected both the context of meaning within which social life is lived and the concrete delivery of rights through the legal system. The sexually harassed have been given a name for their suffering and an analysis that connects it with gender. They have been given a forum, legitimacy to speak, authority to make claims, and an avenue for possible relief. Before, what happened to them was all right. Now it is not.

This matters. Sexual abuse mutes victims socially through the violation itself. Often the abuser enforces secrecy and silence; secrecy and silence may be part of what is so sexy about sexual abuse. When the state also forecloses a validated space for denouncing and rectifying the victimization, it seals this secrecy and reenforces this silence. The harm of this process, a process that utterly precludes speech, then becomes all of a piece. If there is no right place to go to say, this hurt me, then a woman is simply the one who can be treated this way, and no harm, as they say, is done.

In point of fact, I would prefer not to have to spend all this energy getting the law to recognize wrongs to women as wrong. But it seems to be necessary to legitimize our injuries as injuries in order to delegitimize our victimization by them, without which it is difficult to move in more positive ways. The legal claim for sexual harassment made the events of sexual harassment illegitimate socially as well as legally for the first time. Let me know if you figure out a better way to do that.

At this interface between law and society, we need to remember that the legitimacy courts give they can also take. Compared with a possibility of relief where no possibility of relief existed, since women started out with nothing in this area, this worry seems a bit fancy. Whether the possibility of relief alters the terms of power that gives rise to sexual harassment itself, which makes getting away with it possible, is a different problem. Sexual harassment, the legal claim, is a demand that state authority stand behind women's refusal of sexual access in certain situations that previously were a masculine prerogative. With sexism, there is always a risk that our demand for self-determination will be taken as a demand for paternal protection and will therefore strengthen male power rather than undermine it. This seems a particularly valid concern because the law of sexual harassment began as case law, without legislative guidance or definition.

Institutional support for sexual self-determination is a victory; institutional paternalism reinforces our lack of self-determination. The problem is, the state has never in fact protected women's dignity or bodily integrity. It just says it does. Its protections have been both condescending *and* unreal, in effect strengthening the protector's choice to violate the protected at will, whether the protector is the individual perpetrator or the state. This does not seem to me a reason not to have a law against sexual harassment. It is a reason to demand that the promise of "equal protection of the laws" be *delivered upon* for us, as it is when real people are violated. It is also part of a larger political struggle to value women more than the male pleasure of using us is valued. Ultimately though, the question of whether the use of the state for women helps or hurts can be answered only in practice, because so little real protection of the laws has ever been delivered.

The legal claim for sexual harassment marks the first time in history, to my knowledge, that women have defined women's injuries in a law. Consider what has happened with rape. We have never defined the injury of rape; men define it. The men who define it, define what they take to be this violation of women according to, among other things, what they think they don't do. In this way rape becomes an act of a stranger (they mean Black) committed upon a woman (white) whom he has never seen before. Most rapes are intraracial and are committed by men the women know. Ask a woman if she has ever been raped, and often she says, "Well . . . not really." In that silence between the well and the not really, she just measured what happened to her against every rape case she ever heard about and decided she would lose in court. Especially when you are part of a subordinated group, your own definition of your injuries is powerfully shaped by your assessment of whether you could get anyone to do anything about it, including anything official. You are realistic by necessity, and the voice of law is the voice in power. When the design of a legal wrong does not fit the wrong as it happens to you, as is the case with rape, that law can undermine your social and political as well as legal legitimacy in saying that what happened was an injury at all—even to yourself.

It is never too soon to worry about this, but it may be too soon to know whether the law against sexual harassment will be taken away from us or turn into nothing or turn ugly in our hands. The fact is, this law is working surprisingly well for women by any standards, particularly when compared with the rest of sex discrimination law. If the question is whether a law designed from women's standpoint and administered through this legal system can do anything for women—which always seems to me to be a good question—this experience so far gives a qualified and limited yes.

It is hard to unthink what you know, but there was a time when the facts that amount to sexual harassment did not amount to sexual harassment. It is a bit like the injuries of pornography until recently. The facts amounting to the harm did not socially "exist," had no shape, no cognitive coherence; far less did they state a legal claim. It just happened to you. To the women to whom it happened, it wasn't part of anything, much less something big or shared like gender. It fit no known pattern. It was neither a regularity nor an irregularity. Even social scientists didn't study it, and they study anything that moves. When law recognized sexual harassment as a practice of sex discrimination, it moved it from the realm of "and then he . . . and then he . . .," the primitive language in which sexual abuse lives inside a woman, into an experience with a form, an etiology, a cumulativeness—as well as a club.

The shape, the positioning, and the club—each is equally crucial politically. Once it became possible to do something about sexual harassment, it became possible to know more about it, because it became possible for its victims to speak about it. Now we know, as we did not when it first became illegal, that this problem is commonplace. We know this not just because it has to be true, but as documented fact. Between a quarter and a third of women in the federal workforce report having been sexually harassed, many physically, at least once in the last two years. Projected, that becomes 85 percent of all women at some point in their working lives. This figure is based on asking women "Have you ever been sexually harassed?"— the conclusion—not "has this fact happened? has that fact happened?" which usually produces more. The figures for sexual harassment of students are comparable.

When faced with individual incidents of sexual harassment, the legal system's first question was, is it a personal episode? Legally, this was a way the courts inquired into whether the incidents were based on sex, as they had to be to be sex discrimination. Politically, it was a move to isolate victims by stigmatizing them as deviant. It also seemed odd to me that a relationship was either personal or gendered, meaning that one is not a woman personally. Statistical frequency alone does not make an event not personal, of course, but the presumption that sexual pressure in contexts of unequal power is an isolated idiosyncrasy to unique individual victims has been undermined both by the numbers and by their division by gender. Overwhelmingly, it is men who sexually harass women, a lot of them. Actually, it is even more accurate to say that men do this than to say that women have this done to them. This is a description of the perpetrators' behavior, not of the statisticians' feminism.

Sexual harassment has also emerged as a creature of hierarchy. It inhabits what I call hierarchies among men: arrangements in which some men are below other men, as in employer/employee and teacher/student. In workplaces, sexual harassment by supervisors of subordinates is common; in education, by administrators of lower-level administrators, by faculty of students. But it also happens among coworkers, from third parties, even by subordinates in the workplace, men who are women's hierarchical inferiors or peers. Basically, it is done by men to women regardless of relative position on the formal hierarchy. I believe that the reason sexual harassment was first established as an injury of the systematic abuse of power in hierarchies among men is that this is power men recognize. They comprehend from personal experience that something is held over your head if you do not comply. The lateral or reverse hierarchical examples suggest something beyond this, something men don't understand from personal experience because they take its advantages for granted: gender is also a hierarchy The courts do not use this analysis, but some act as though they understand it.

Sex discrimination law had to adjust a bit to accommodate the realities of sexual harassment. Like many other injuries of gender, it wasn't written for this. For something to be based on gender in the legal sense means it happens to a woman as a woman, not as an individual. Membership in a gender is understood as the opposite of, rather than part of, individuality. Clearly sexual harassment is one of the last situations in which a woman is treated without regard to her sex; it is because of her sex that it happens. But the social meaning attributed to women as a class, in which women are defined as gender female by sexual accessibility to men, is not what courts have considered before when they have determined whether a given incident occurred because of sex.

Sex discrimination law typically conceives that something happens because of sex when it happens to one sex but not the other. The initial procedure is arithmetic: draw a gender line and count how many of each are on each side in the context at issue, or, alternatively, take the line drawn by the practice or policy and see if it also divides the sexes. One by-product of this head-counting method is what I call the bisexual defense. Say a man is accused of sexually harassing a woman. He can argue that the harassment is not sex-based because he harasses both sexes equally, indiscriminately as it were. Originally it was argued that sexual harassment was not a proper gender claim because someone could harass both sexes. We argued that this was an issue of fact to be pleaded and proven, an issue of did he do this, rather than an issue of law,

of whether he could have. The courts accepted that, creating this kamikaze defense. To my knowledge, no one has used the bisexual defense since. As this example suggests, head counting can provide a quick topography of the terrain, but it has proved too blunt to distinguish treatment whose meaning is based on gender from treatment that has other social hermeneutics, especially when only two individuals are involved.

Once sexual harassment was established as bigger than personal, the courts' next legal question was whether it was smaller than biological. To say that sexual harassment was biological seemed to me a very negative thing to say about men, but defendants seemed to think it precluded liability. Plaintiffs argued that sexual harassment is not biological in that men who don't do it have nothing wrong with their testosterone levels. Besides, if murder were found to have biological correlates, it would still be a crime. Thus, although the question purported to be whether the acts were based on sex, the implicit issue seemed to be whether the source of the impetus for doing the acts was relevant to their harmfulness.

Similarly structured was the charge that women who resented sexual harassment were oversensitive. Not that the acts did not occur, but rather that it was unreasonable to experience them as harmful. Such a harm would be based not on sex but on individual hysteria. Again shifting the inquiry away from whether the acts are based on sex in the guise of pursuing it, away from whether they occurred to whether it should matter if they did, the question became whether the acts were properly harmful. Only this time it was not the perpetrator's drives that made him not liable but the target's sensitivity that made the acts not a harm at all. It was pointed out that too many people are victimized by sexual harassment to consider them all hysterics. Besides, in other individual injury law, victims are not blamed; perpetrators are required to take victims as they find them, so long as they are not supposed to be doing what they are doing.

Once these excuses were rejected, then it was said that sexual harassment was not really an employment-related problem. That became hard to maintain when it was her job the woman lost. If it was, in fact, a personal relationship, it apparently did not start and stop there, although this is also a question of proof, leaving the true meaning of the events to trial. The perpetrator may have thought it was all affectionate or friendly or fun, but the victim experienced it as hateful, dangerous, and damaging. Results in such cases have been mixed. Some judges have accepted the perpetrator's view; for instance, one judge held queries by the defendant such as "What am I going to get for this?" and repeated importunings to "go out" to be "susceptible of innocent interpretation." Other judges, on virtually identical facts, for example, "When are you going to do something nice for me?" have held for the plaintiff. For what it's worth, the judge in the first case was a man, in the second a woman.

That sexual harassment is sex-based discrimination seems to be legally established, at least for now. In one of the few recent cases that reported litigating the issue of sex basis, defendants argued that a sex-based claim was not stated when a woman worker complained of terms of abuse directed at her at work such as "slut," "bitch," and "fucking cunt" and "many sexually oriented drawings posted on pillars and at other conspicuous places around the warehouse" with plaintiffs' initials on them, presenting her having sex with an animal. The court said: "[T]he sexually offensive conduct and language used would have been almost irrelevant and would have failed entirely in its crude purpose had the plaintiff been a man. I do not hesitate to find that but for her sex, the plaintiff would not have been subjected to the harassment she suffered." "Obvious" or "patently obvious" they often call it. I guess this is what it looks like to have proven a point.

Sexual harassment was first recognized as an injury of gender in what I called incidents of quid pro quo. Sometimes people think that harassment has to be constant. It doesn't; it's a term of art in which once can be enough. Typically an advance is made, rejected, and a loss follows. For a while it looked as if this three-step occurrence was in danger of going from one form in which sexual harassment can occur into a series of required hurdles. In many situations the woman is forced to submit instead of being able to reject the advance. The problem has become whether, say being forced into intercourse at work will be seen as a failed quid pro quo or as an instance of sexual harassment in which the forced sex constitutes the injury.

I know of one reported case in employment and one in education in which women who were forced to submit to the sex brought a sexual harassment claim against the perpetrator; so far only the education case has won on the facts. The employment case that lost on the facts was reversed on appeal. The pressures for sex were seen to state a claim without respect to the fact that the woman was not able to avoid complying. It is unclear if the unwanted advances constitute a claim, separate and apart from whether or not they are able to be resisted, which they should; or if the acts of forced sex would also constitute an environmental claim separate from any quid pro quo, as it seems to me they also should. In the education case, the case of Paul Mann, the students were allowed to recover punitive damages for the forced sex. If sexual harassment is not to be defined only as sexual attention imposed upon someone who is not in a position to refuse it, who refuses it, women who are forced to submit to sex must be understood as harmed not less, but as much or more, than those who are able to make their refusals effective.

Getting recoveries for women who have actually been sexually violated by the defendant will probably be a major battle. Women being compensated in money for sex they *had* violates male metaphysics because in that system sex is what a woman is for. As one judge concluded, "[T]here does not seem to be any issue that the plaintiff did not desire to have relations with [the defendant], but it is also altogether apparent that she willingly had sex with him." Now what do you make of that? The woman was not physically forced at the moment of penetration, and since it is sex she must have willed it, is about all you can make of it. The sexual politics of the situation is that men do not see a woman who has had sex as victimized, whatever the conditions. One dimension of this problem involves whether a woman who has been violated through sex has any credibility. Credibility is difficult to separate from the definition of the injury, since an injury in which the victim is not believed to have been injured *because she has been injured* is not a real injury, legally speaking.

The question seems to be whether a woman is valuable enough to hurt, so that what is done to her is a harm. Once a woman has had sex, voluntarily or by force—it doesn't matter—she is regarded as too damaged to be further damage-able, or something. Many women who have been raped in the course of sexual harassment have been advised by their lawyers not to mention the rape because it would destroy their credibility! The fact that abuse is long term has suggested to some find-ers of fact that it must have been tolerated or even wanted, although sexual harassment that becomes a condition of work has also been established as a legal claim in its own right. I once was talking with a judge about a case he was sitting on in which Black teenage girls alleged that some procedures at their school violated their privacy. He told me that with their sexual habits they had no privacy to lose. It seemed he knew what their sexual habits were from evidence in the case, examples of the privacy violations.

The more aggravated an injury becomes, the more it ceases to exist. Why is incomprehensible to me, but how it functions is not. Our most power-ful moment is on paper, in complaints we frame, and our worst is in the flesh in court. Although it isn't much, we have the most credibility when we are only the idea of us and our violation in their minds. In our allegations we construct reality to some extent; face to face, their angle of vision frames us irrevocably. In court we have breasts, we are Black, we are (in a word) women. Not that we are ever free of that, but the moment we physically embody our complaint, and they can see us, the pornography of the process starts in earnest.

I have begun to think that a major reason that many women do not bring sexual harassment com-plaints is that they know this. They cannot bear to have their personal account of sexual abuse reduced to a fantasy they invented, used to define them and to pleasure the finders of fact and the public. I think they have a very real sense that their accounts are enjoyed, that others are getting plea-sure from the first-person recounting of their pain, and that is the content of their humiliation at these rituals. When rape victims say they feel raped again on the stand, and victims of sexual harassment say they feel sexually harassed in the adjudication, it is not exactly metaphor. I hear that they—in being publicly sexually humiliated by the legal system, as by the perpetrator—are pornography. The first time it happens, it is called freedom; the second time, it is called justice.

If a woman is sexually defined—meaning all women fundamentally, intensified by previous sex-ual abuse or identification as lesbian, indelible if a prostitute—her chances of recovery for sexual abuse are correspondingly reduced. I'm still wait-ing for a woman to win at trial against a man who forced her to comply with the sex. Suppose the male plaintiff in one sexual harassment case who rented the motel room in which the single sexual encounter took place had been a woman, and the perpetrator had been a man. When the relationship later went bad, it was apparently not a credibility problem for *him* at trial that he had rented the motel room. Nor was *his* sexual history apparently an issue. Nor, apparently was it said when he com-plained he was fired because the relationship went bad, that he had "asked for" the relationship. That case was reversed on appeal on legal grounds, but he did win at trial. The best one can say about women in such cases is that women who have had sex but not with the accused may have some chance. In one case the judge did not believe the plaintiff's denial of an affair with another coworker, but did believe that she had been sexu-ally harassed by the defendant. In another, the woman plaintiff actually had "linguistic intimacy" with another man at work, yet when she said that what happened to her with the defendant was sex-ual harassment, she was believed. These are mirac-ulous. A woman's word on these matters is usually indivisible. In another case a woman accused two men of sexual harassment. She had resisted and refused one man to whom she had previously sub-mitted under pressure for a long time. He was in the process of eliminating her from her job when the second man raped her. The first man's defense was that it went on so long, she must have liked it. The second man's defense was that he had heard that she had had sexual relations with the first man, so he felt this was something she was open to. This piggyback defense is premised on the class defini-tion of woman as whore, by which I mean what men mean: one who exists to be sexually done to, to be sexually available on men's terms, that is, a woman. If this definition of women is accepted, it means that if a woman has ever had sex, forced or voluntary she can't be sexually violated.

A woman can be seen in these terms by being a former rape victim or by the way she uses language. One case holds that the evidence shows "the allegedly harassing conduct was substantially welcomed and encouraged by plaintiff. She actively contributed to the distasteful working environment by her own profane and sexually suggestive conduct." She swore, apparently and participated in conversations about sex. This effectively made her harassment-proof. Many women joke about sex to try to defuse men's sexual aggression, to try to be one of the boys in hopes they will be treated like one. This is to discourage sexual advances, not to encourage them. In other cases, judges have understood that "the plaintiffs did not appreciate the remarks and . . . many of the other women did not either."

The extent to which a woman's job is sexualized is also a factor. If a woman's work is not to sell sex, and her employer requires her to wear a sexually suggestive uniform, if she is repeatedly sexually harassed by the clientele, she may have a claim against her employer. Similarly although "there may well be a limited category of jobs (such as adult entertainment) in which sexual harassment may be a rational consequence of such employment," one court was "simply not prepared to say that a female who goes to work in what is apparently a predominantly male workplace should reasonably expect sexual harassment as part of her job." There may be trouble at some point over what jobs are selling sex, given the sexualization of anything a woman does.

Sexual credibility, that strange amalgam of whether your word counts with whether or how much you were hurt, also comes packaged in a variety of technical rules in the sexual harassment cases: evidence, discovery, and burden of proof. In 1982 the EEOC held that if a victim was sexually harassed without a corroborating witness, proof was inadequate as a matter of law. (Those of you who wonder about the relevance of pornography, get this: if nobody watched, it didn't happen.) A woman's word, even if believed, was legally insufficient, even if the man had nothing to put against it other than his word and the plaintiff's burden of proof. Much like women who have been raped, women who have experienced sexual harassment say "But I couldn't prove it." They mean they have nothing but their word. Proof is when what you say counts against what someone else says—for

which it must first be believed. To say as a matter of law that the woman's word is per se legally insufficient is to assume that, with sexual violations uniquely, the defendant's denial is dispositive, is proof. To say a woman's word is no proof amounts to saying a woman's word is worthless. Usually all the man has is his denial. In 1983 the EEOC found sexual harassment on a woman's word alone. It said it was enough, without distinguishing or overruling the prior case. Perhaps they recognized that women don't choose to be sexually harassed in the presence of witnesses.

The question of prior sexual history is one area in which the issue of sexual credibility is directly posed. Evidence of the defendant's sexual harassment of other women in the same institutional relation or setting is increasingly being considered admissible, and it should be. The other side of the question is whether evidence of a victim's prior sexual history should be discoverable or admissible, and it seems to me it should not be. Perpetrators often seek out victims with common qualities or circumstances or situations—we are fungible to them so long as we are similarly accessible—but victims do not seek out victimization at all, and their nonvictimized sexual behavior is no more relevant to an allegation of sexual force than is the perpetrator's consensual sex life, such as it may be.

So far the leading case, consistent with the direction of rape law, has found that the victim's sexual history with other individuals is not relevant, although consensual history with the individual perpetrator may be. With sexual harassment law, we are having to deinstitutionalize sexual misogyny step by step. Some defendants' counsel have even demanded that plaintiffs submit to an unlimited psychiatric examination, which could have a major practical impact on victims' effective access to relief. How much sexual denigration will victims have to face to secure their right to be free from sexual denigration? A major part of the harm of sexual harassment is the public and private sexualization of a woman against her will. Forcing her to speak about her sexuality is a common part of this process subjection to which leads women to seek relief through the courts. Victims who choose to complain know they will have to endure repeated verbalizations of the specific sexual abuse they complain about. They undertake this even though most experience it as an exacerbation, however unavoidable, of the original abuse. For others, the necessity to repeat over and over the verbal insults, innuendos, and propositions to which they have been subjected leads them to decide that justice is not worth such indignity

Most victims of sexual harassment, if the incidence data are correct, never file complaints. Many who are viciously violated are so ashamed to make that violation public that they submit in silence, although it devastates their self-respect and often their health, or they leave the job without complaint, although it threatens their survival and that of their families. If, on top of the cost of making the violation known, which is painful enough, they know that the entire range of their sexual experiences, attitudes, preferences, and practices are to be discoverable, few such actions will be brought, no matter how badly the victims are hurt. Faced with a choice between forced sex in their jobs or schools on the one hand and forced sexual disclosure for the public record on the other, few will choose the latter. This cruel paradox would effectively eliminate much progress in this area.

Put another way, part of the power held by perpetrators of sexual harassment is the threat of making the sexual abuse public knowledge. This functions like blackmail in silencing the victim and allowing the abuse to continue. It is a fact that public knowledge of sexual abuse is often worse for the abused than the abuser, and victims who choose to complain have the courage to take that on. To add to their burden the potential of making public their entire personal life, information that has no relation to the fact or severity of the incidents complained of, is to make the law of this area implicitly complicit in the blackmail that keeps victims from exercising their rights and to enhance the impunity of perpetrators. In effect, it means open season on anyone who does not want her entire intimate life available to public scrutiny. In other contexts such private information has been found intrusive, irrelevant, and more prejudicial than probative. To allow it to be discovered in the sexual harassment area amounts to a requirement that women be further violated in order to be permitted to seek relief for having been violated. I also will never understand why a violation's severity or

even its likelihood of occurrence, is measured according to the character of the violated, rather than by what was done to them.

In most reported sexual harassment cases, especially rulings on law more than on facts, the trend is almost uniformly favorable to the development of this claim. At least, so far. This almost certainly does not represent social reality It may not even reflect most cases in litigation. And there may be conflicts building, for example, between those who value speech in the abstract more than they value people in the concrete. Much of sexual harassment is words. Women are called "cunt," "pussy," "tits"; they are invited to a company party with "bring your own bathing suits (women, either half)," they confront their tormenter in front of their manager with, "You have called me a fucking bitch," only to be answered, "No, I didn't. I called you a fucking cunt." One court issued an injunction against inquiries such as "Did you get any over the weekend?" One case holds that where "a person in a position to grant or withhold employment opportunities uses that authority to attempt to induce workers and job seekers to submit to sexual advances, prostitution, and pornographic entertainment, and boasts of an ability to intimidate those who displease him," sexual harassment (and intentional infliction of emotional distress) are pleaded. Sexual harassment can also include pictures; visual as well as verbal pornography is commonly used as part of the abuse. Yet one judge found, apparently as a matter of law, that the pervasive presence of pornography in the workplace did not constitute an unreasonable work environment because, "For better or worse, modern America features open displays of written and pictorial erotica. Shopping centers, candy stores and prime time television regularly display naked bodies and erotic real or simulated sex acts. Living in this milieu, the average American should not be legally offended by sexually explicit posters." She did not say she was offended, she said she was discriminated against based on her sex. If the pervasiveness of an abuse makes it nonactionable, no inequality sufficiently institutionalized to merit a law against it would be actionable.

Further examples of this internecine conflict have arisen in education. At the Massachusetts Institute of Technology pornography used to be shown every year during registration. Is this *not* sexual harassment in education, as a group of women complained it was, because attendance is voluntary, both sexes go, it is screened in groups rather than individually, nobody is directly propositioned, and it is pictures and words? Or is it sexual harassment because the status and treatment of women, supposedly secured from sex-differential harm, are damaged, including that of those who do not attend, which harms individuals and undermines sex equality; therefore pictures and words are the media through which the sex discrimination is accomplished?

For feminist jurisprudence, the sexual harassment attempt suggests that if a legal initiative is set up right from the beginning, meaning if it is designed from women's real experience of violation, it can make some difference. To a degree women's experience can be written into law, even in some tension with the current doctrinal framework. Women who want to resist their victimization with legal terms that imagine it is not inevitable can be given some chance, which is more than they had before. Law is not everything in this respect, but it is not nothing either. Perhaps the most important lesson is that the mountain can be moved. When we started, there was absolutely no judicial precedent for allowing a sex discrimination suit for sexual harassment. Sometimes even the law does something for the first time.

Study Questions on Catharine MacKinnon

1. To what extent do you believe that sexual harassment is a problem only in situations where the harasser has some sort of power over the victim (e.g., a boss over a worker or a teacher over a student)? Do you think it can also occur between peers? What reasons does MacKinnon provide for recognizing that women can be sexually harassed by men who are their hierarchical equals or inferiors? Do you think this analysis is right? Why or why not?

2. In *Feminism Unmodified,* MacKinnon writes, "the relation between the sexes is organized so that men may dominate and women must submit and this relationship is sexual—in fact, is sex" (p. 3). Do you think it is possible for a man to be sexually harassed by a woman? And what about same-sex sexual harassment? Consider, for example, a lesbian doctor who pressures the female nurses in her unit for sexual favors, a gay professor who makes an unwelcome advance to a male student, or for that matter a bisexual who harasses both sexes equally? In fact, MacKinnon has argued that such cases should be covered; can you imagine how her analysis could be adapted to cover them?

3. MacKinnon observes that when a sexual harassment complaint is brought to court, the woman finds it painful to repeat the words of abuse in a public forum—"rape victims say they feel raped again on the stand, and victims of sexual harassment say they feel sexually harassed in the adjudication." She speaks of what Anita Hill was put through during the Senate confirmation hearing for Clarence Thomas as a kind of "re-violation" (which she attributes in part to the saturation of the public arena with pornography). "The offensiveness, the dirt, the uncleanness stick to the woman, particularly the woman of color" (*Only Words,* p. 66). If testifying at some sort of judicial proceeding is itself a "re-violation" of the victim, how might we go about trying to establish fair substantive and procedural protections for the accused—given that false, malicious, and politically motivated charges of sexual harassment or abuse do occur? (Cardinal Bernardin, for example, was accused of sexual abuse by a seminarian who later withdrew the

charges.) Are sexual harassment charges more open to abuse than any other charges? Why or why not?

4. Free-speech law has traditionally distinguished between speech and conduct (although it does in certain cases treat speech as conduct and conduct as speech), and protects forms of speech that many people find offensive or even deeply wounding, at least if it is not otherwise injurious. Does MacKinnon's argument undermine this distinction, and if so is this a good or a bad thing? How would *you* strike the balance between free expression and sexual equality in the area of sexual harassment at school or at work (or in any other context, for that matter)?

5. Suppose you are a young man. You want to treat women respectfully, but you also want to be able to ask some of your female fellow students or co-workers out on dates or try to find out if they are interested in a sexual relationship. What should you do or not do in order to avoid engaging in sexual harassment? Suppose you are a young woman. How should you communicate your preferences and how do you want the man to respond? Students of both sexes should try to put themselves in the positions of both the man and the woman in discussing this question.

Reckless Eyeballing

KATIE ROIPHE

Katie Roiphe discusses the conflicts that heterosexual desire raises for the passionate feminist. She criticizes rules and laws based on the premise that all women need protection from all men, because they are so much weaker. She is particularly troubled by highly subjective legal definitions of sexual harassment, and by regulations that intrude into unconscious motivations or subtle patterns of human relationship. Though she recognizes the injustice of abusing power, she defends the right to leer.

HETEROSEXUAL DESIRE INEVITABLY RAISES conflicts for the passionate feminist, and it's not an issue easily evaded. Sooner or later feminism has to address "the man question." But this is more than just a practical question of procreation, more than the well-worn translation of personal into political. It's also a question for the abstract, the ideological, the furthest reaches of the feminist imagination.

Charlotte Perkins Gilman, a prominent feminist writing at the turn of the century, found a fictional solution to the conflict between sex and feminism in her utopian novel, *Herland*. Her solution is simple: there is no sexual desire. Even after the male anthropologists arrive with their worldly lusts, the women of Herland remain unruffled. Everything runs smoothly and rationally in Herland, and through the entire course of the book none of the women harbors any sexual feelings, toward men or toward each other. They magically reproduce by parthenogenesis, and motherhood is their driving passion.

Gilman erases whatever problems arise from sexual involvements with men in her happy, if sterile, vision of clean streets, clean hearts, clean minds. In her sociological work, *Women and Economics,* Gilman applies the same device—obliterating the source of conflict—to another site of struggle. She conceives of houses without kitchens as the solution to women's household drudgery. The problem is that most people want kitchens, and most people want sex.

Many of today's feminists, in their focus on sexual harassment, share Gilman's sexual politics. In their videos, literature, and workshops, these feminists are creating their own utopian visions of human sexuality. They imagine a world where all expressions of sexual appreciation are appreciated. They imagine a totally symmetrical universe, where people aren't silly, rude, awkward, excessive, or confused. And if they are, they are violating the rules and are subject to disciplinary proceedings.

A Princeton pamphlet declares that "sexual harassment is unwanted sexual attention that makes a person feel uncomfortable or causes problems in school or at work, or in social settings." The word "uncomfortable" echoes through all the literature on sexual harassment. The feminists concerned with this issue, then, propose the right to be comfortable as a feminist principle.

The difficulty with these rules is that, although it may infringe on the right to comfort, unwanted sexual attention is part of nature. To find wanted sexual attention, you have to give and receive a certain amount of unwanted sexual attention. Clearly, the truth is that if no one was ever allowed to risk offering unsolicited sexual attention, we would all be solitary creatures.

The category of sexual harassment, according to current campus definitions, is not confined to relationships involving power inequity. Echoing many other common definitions of sexual harassment, Princeton's pamphlet warns that "sexual harassment can occur between two people regardless of whether or not one has power over the other." The weight of this definition of sexual harassment, then, falls on gender instead of status.

In current definitions of sexual harassment, there is an implication that gender is so important that it eclipses all other forms of power. The driving idea behind these rules is that gender itself is a sufficient source of power to constitute sexual harassment. Catharine MacKinnon, an early theorist of sexual harassment, writes that "situations of co-equal power—among co-workers or students or teachers—are difficult to see as examples of sexual harassment unless you have a notion of male power. I think we lie to women when we call it not power when a woman is come on to by a man who is not her employer, not her teacher." With this description, MacKinnon extends the province of male power beyond that of tangible social power. She proposes using the words "sexual harassment" as a way to name what she sees as a fundamental social and political inequity between men and women. Following in this line of thought, Elizabeth Grauerholz, a sociology professor, conducted a study about instances of male students harassing their female professors, a phenomenon she calls "contrapower harassment." . . .

The idea that a male student can sexually harass a female professor, overturning social and institutional hierarchy, solely on the basis of some primal or socially conditioned male power over women is insulting. The mere fact of being a man doesn't give the male student so much power that he can plow through social hierarchies, grabbing what he wants, intimidating all the cowering female faculty in his path. The assumption that female students or faculty must be protected from the sexual harassment of male peers or inferiors promotes the regrettable idea that men are natively more powerful than women.

Even if you argue, as many do, that *in this society* men are simply much more powerful than women, this is still a dangerous train of thought. It carries us someplace we don't want to be. Rules and laws based on the premise that all women need protection from all men, because they are so much weaker, serve only to reinforce the image of women as powerless. . . .

. . . If you feel sexually harassed then chances are you were. At the university's Terrace Club, the refuge of fashionable, left-leaning, black-clad undergraduates, there is a sign supporting this view. It is downstairs, on a post next to the counter where the beer is served, often partially obscured by students talking, cigarettes in hand: "What constitutes sexual harassment or intimidating, hostile or offensive environment is to be defined by the person harassed and his/her own feelings of being threatened or compromised." This relatively common definition of sexual harassment crosses the line between being supportive and obliterating the idea of external reality.

The categories become especially complicated and slippery when sexual harassment enters the realm of the subconscious. The Princeton guide explains that "sexual harassment may result from a conscious or unconscious action, and can be subtle or blatant." Once we move into the area of the subtle and unconscious, we are no longer talking about a professor systematically exploiting power for sex. We are no longer talking about Hey, baby, sleep with me or I'll fail you. To hold people responsible for their subtle, unconscious actions is to legislate thought, an ominous, not to mention difficult, prospect.

The idea of sexual harassment—and clearly when you are talking about the subtle and unconscious, you are talking about an idea—provides a blank canvas on which students can express all of the insecurities, fears, and confusions about the relative sexual freedom of the college experience. Sexual harassment is everywhere: it crops up in dinner conversations and advertisements on television, all over women's magazines and editorial pages. No one can claim that Anita Hill is an unsung heroine. It makes sense that teenagers get caught up in the Anita Hill fury; they are particularly susceptible to feeling uncomfortable about sexuality, and sexual harassment offers an ideology that explains "uncomfortable" in political terms. The idea of sexual harassment displaces adolescent uneasiness onto the environment, onto professors, onto older men. . . .

In an early survey of sexual harassment, a law student at Berkeley wrote that in response to fears of sexual harassment charges, "the male law school teachers ignore female students . . . this means that we are afforded [fewer] academic opportunities than male students." Many male professors have confirmed that they feel more uncomfortable with female students than with male students, because of all the attention given to sexual harassment. They may not "ignore" their female students, but they keep them at arm's length. They feel freer to forge friendships with male students.

The overstringent attention given to sexual harassment on campuses breeds suspicion; it creates an environment where imaginations run wild, charges can seem to materialize out of thin air, and both faculty and students worry about a friendly lunch. The repercussions for the academic community, let alone the confused freshman, can be many and serious.

In an excessive effort to purge the university of sexual corruption, many institutions have violated the rights of the professors involved by neglecting to follow standard procedures. Since sexual harassment is a relatively recent priority, "standard procedures" are themselves new, shrouded, and shaky. Charges of sexual harassment are uncharted territory, and fairness is not necessarily the compass.

In a recent case a tenured professor at a prominent university was dismissed in a unilateral administrative action, without a faculty hearing, legal counsel, or the calling of witnesses in his defense. Some professors have been suspended indefinitely without a sense of when or what would end the suspension. As an official of the American Association of University Professors framed the problem, "There tends to be publicizing of names at too early a stage, and trigger-quick action to suspend without suggestion of immediate harm." . . .

The university has become so saturated with the idea of sexual harassment that it has begun to affect minute levels of communication. Like "date rape," the phrase "sexual harassment" is frequently used, and it does not apply only to extremes of human behavior. Suddenly everyday experience is filtered through the strict lens of a new sexual politics. Under fierce political scrutiny, behavior that once seemed neutral or natural enough now takes on ominous meanings. You may not even realize that you are a survivor of sexual harassment. . . .

. . . Many feminists in other countries look on our preoccupation with sexual harassment as another sign of the self-indulgence and repression in American society. Veronique Neiertz, France's secretary of state for women's rights, has said that in the United States "the slightest wink can be misinterpreted." Her ministry's commonsense advice to women who feel harassed by co-workers is to respond with "a good slap in the face." . . .

Instead of learning that men have no right to do these terrible things to us, we should be learning to deal with individuals with strength and confidence. If someone bothers us, we should be able to put him in his place without crying into our pillow or screaming for help or counseling. If someone stares at us, or talks dirty, or charges neutral conversation with sexual innuendo, we should not be pushed to the verge of a nervous breakdown. . . .

. . . Feminists drafting sexual harassment guidelines seem to have forgotten childhood's words of wisdom: sticks and stones may break my bones, but names will never harm me. . . .

I would even go so far as to say that people have the right to leer at whomever they want to leer at. By offering protection to the woman against the leer, the movement against sexual harassment is curtailing her personal power. This protection implies the need to be protected. It paints her as defenseless against even the most trivial of male attentions. This protection assumes that she never ogles, leers, or makes sexual innuendos herself.

History offers an example of another time when looks could be crimes, but today feminists don't talk much about what happened to black men accused of "reckless eyeballing," that is, directing sexual glances at white women. Black men were lynched for a previous incarnation of "sexual harassment." As late as 1955, a black man was lynched for whistling at a white woman. Beneath the Jim Crow law about reckless eyeballing was the assumption that white women were the property of white men, and a look too hard or too long in their direction was a flouting of white power. Reckless eyeballing was a symbolic violation of white women's virtue. That virtue, that division between white women and black men, was important to the southern hierarchy. While of course lynchings and Jim Crow are not the current danger, it's important to remember that protecting women against the stray male gaze has not always served a social good. We should learn the lessons: looks can't kill, and we are nobody's property. . . .

All of this is not to suggest that abuses of power are not wrong. They are. Any professor who trades grades for sex and uses this power as a forceful tool of seduction deserves to face charges. The same would be true if he traded grades for a thousand dollars. I'm not opposed to stamping out corruption; I only think it's important to look before you stamp. Rules about harassment should be less vague, and inclusive. They should sharply target serious offenses and abuses of power rather than environments that are "uncomfortable," rather than a stray professor looking down a shirt. The university's rules should not be based on the idea of female students who are pure and naive, who don't harbor sexualities of their own, who don't seduce, or who can't defend themselves against the nonconditional sexual interests of male faculty and students. . . .

As feminists interested in the issue themselves argue, "Many have difficulty recognizing their experience as victimization. It is helpful to use the words that fit the experience, validating the depths of the survivor's feelings and allowing her to feel her experience was serious." In other words, these feminists recognize that if you don't tell the victim that she's a victim, she may sail through the experience without fully grasping the gravity of her humiliation. She may get through without all that trauma and counseling. Buried within this description of helping students overcome the problem of "recognizing their experience as victimization" is the nagging concern that the problem may pass unnoticed, may dissolve without political scrutiny. To create awareness is sometimes to create a problem. . . .

. . . If there is any transforming to be done, it is to transform everyday experience back into everyday experience.

Study Questions on Katie Roiphe

1. Roiphe complains of the vagueness of sexual harassment regulations. How would you write them to avoid this problem?

2. In your judgment, is "sticks and stones may break my bones, but words can never hurt me" an adequate response to the problem of sexual harassment?
3. In Roiphe's view, college-aged women are quite capable of rejecting unwanted sexual advances without bringing in the police. Do you agree? If not, should we train men to be less aggressive, women to be more assertive, or what?
4. Many societies have held that women require protection from aggressive male sexuality. Roiphe disagrees. What do you think? What would the other writers represented in this anthology think?
5. What larger issues concerning the nature of male and female sexuality are at stake in these questions?

Men Without Women

MICHAEL NOVAK

> Michael Novak defends the view that heterosexuality is normative. He argues that society has a special stake in nurturing that special wisdom and powerful realism learned in heterosexual marriage and the battle between the sexes. On the way to this conclusion he casts a critical glance at feminism and the rage of homosexuals.

A PECULIAR PARADOX EMERGES from recent debates about homosexuality. On the one hand, proponents of homosexuality speak of "sexual preference" and "alternative choices." On the other hand, they speak of being "trapped," of "having been given a different nature." So there are really two different possibilities involved. First, if homosexuality is a matter of choice or preference, it lies in the realm of freedom. The argument then concerns whether such choices ought to be encouraged or discouraged; whether, in a word, homosexuality is a good choice. Second, if homosexuality is a matter of nature, it lies in the realm of necessity. The argument then does not reach so high a moral level. Those involved are not really free to choose an alternative. They suffer from a diminished range of freedom.

The moral argument about this second alternative is sometimes simply expressed as "Do what really comes naturally," or "To yourself be true." In other moral traditions, however, the limitation of freedom involved in this alternative constitutes a moral defect, like kleptomania, pyromania, or other "natural" psychic flaws. Few human bodies fulfill classical possibilities of form; so also few human psyches. Each of us carries serious flaws. In some traditions, homosexuality is such a flaw. It makes people suffer, but does not make happiness or moral courage impossible.

It is probably important to distinguish between male and female homosexuality. Male infants have a hurdle to jump—I speak as a nonscientist—which females do not have to jump: *viz.*, a transference of their sexual identity away from their mother, with her sensual closeness, to their father. A distance must be established between the male and the mother, and an identification made with the father. One must appreciate the fact that, in a percentage of cases, this transition will be handled very rudely. In addition, one anticipates the probability that the natural endowment—hormonal, neural, emotional, whatever—of a certain percentage of children will not follow the norm. Aristotle pointed out long ago that nature does not work flawlessly,

Reprinted by permission of Human Life Review.

but only "for the most part," i.e., with considerable looseness and randomness, producing a spectrum of individuals from the nearly flawless to the seriously aberrant. None of us ever chose our nature. Yet we each do become responsible for what we make of it.

When the male infant does not make a successful transfer in sexual identity to the father, the male is attracted to other males. Females may even seem to him repulsive, surrounded by an aura of conflict or disinterest. In past ages, such homosexuality was sometimes construed as a danger to the human race because it meant a) a decline in population, or b) a decline in those masculine qualities essential for survival. What happened in the socialization of the young male was perceived to be of greater significance, and of greater risk, to the race than what happened to the female. Unless I am mistaken, even today society is in a more troubled state about male homosexuality than about female homosexuality. Lesbianism may suggest infantile pleasure and regression, but it does not threaten the public, at least not to the same extent that male homosexuality does. Female handholding, public exchanges of tenderness, and the like indicate that females are permitted a more relaxed attitude than males with members of their own sex. Female homosexuality seems somehow more natural, perhaps harmless. Male homosexuality seems to represent a breakdown of an important form of socialization.

The point may need elaboration. Recent publicity about women has served to shield us from an event of far greater significance: the decline of value, status, and the need of "masculine" qualities. In modern corporate life, "mother bureaucracy" swallows the strong ego. Rewards do not come from taking risks, being aggressive, speaking out. In the rationalized, smooth world of government and corporate life, "going along to get along" wins more certain rewards.

The rules of corporate bureaucracy may be more decisive in altering sex roles than the pill. These rules weaken masculine qualities in obvious ways. Yet the male spirit leads one to put one's own body at risk; a degree of occasional physical danger is as necessary for male living as air. The modern era suffocates the male principle. (I say "male" rather than "masculine" to emphasize the high animal spirits involved, the instinctual base on which culture works.) The deep and wide-ranging changes in our experience of maleness have been too little explored. They have certainly induced vast sexual confusion.

They may also—in an odd way—help to cast light on at least part of the inexplicable rage among contemporary women. Suppose that some women, unconsciously, seek the male principle and cannot find it realized in the corporate men around them. What a vast disappointment there seems to be among women today about the men of their acquaintance. They *tell* us that we are "male chauvinist pigs." But what if they *mean* that we are not even males, that they can have no respect for us? The fact that so many men cave in before the rhetoric of militant feminists must only increase the rage, by proving its unconscious point.

Is it true that the number of homosexuals is multiplying in our day? Who could marvel if it were? Men find it perplexing to be male. Seeking the male principle, some women are trying to supply it themselves. It is not just that "sex-role stereotypes" are breaking down. Rather, basic systems of identity have been profoundly altered by the technology and organization of modern life. Personal confusion abounds. The problem is deeper than that of homosexuality alone.

Society has a special stake in the development of married family life. Without strong, enlightened, spiritually nourishing families, the future of society looks bleak indeed. The family is the original, and still the most effective, department of health, education, and welfare. If it fails to teach honesty, courage, a desire for excellence, and a whole host of basic skills, it is exceedingly difficult for any other agency to make up for its failures. Who would trust politicians to do the job?

More than that, society has an important stake in nourishing that special wisdom and powerful realism learned in marriage in the battle between the sexes. For thousands of years, masculine culture and feminine culture have been quite different. It is not easy for men and women to understand each other, or to learn to be honest with each other. "Honesty" may mean something different to males and females.

In addition, the raising of children is morally demanding in a special way. Most of what one learns is failure. A raw realism develops. The brute demands of running a house, of keeping order, of teaching all that one must teach, and of encountering the daily struggles of self-will and self-assertion on the part of each parent and each child are of great moral significance. Sometimes the moral life of families is taken to be conventional and easy. It is not. Moral health must be won against great odds by each couple and each family, starting from scratch, and battled for over and over. We are learning in our generation how many social supports are necessary to make family life successful. We are learning the hard way. In the *hubris* of pursuing "progress" through affluence, mobility, and the promotion of individual hedonism on a vast scale, we have destroyed most of these supports.

I must add here that I am a Catholic—not to say that other traditions do not have analogous concerns, but only to give my own comments moral concreteness. Morals do not come down to us in some universalist language of the lowest common denominator, but in the concrete rituals, voices, affects, and symbols of long historical traditions, internalized by individuals who carry them. To my mind, the human body is a dwelling place of God, and the joining of a man's and a woman's body in matrimony is a privileged form of union with God. The relationship is not merely that of a mechanical linking, putting genitals here or there. It is a metaphor for (and an enactment of) God's union with mankind. Marital intercourse thus reenacts the basic act of creation. It celebrates the future. It acts out in the flesh a communion of two separate persons who are not, at the beginning of their marriage, or at their fifteenth or any other anniversary, nearly as united in fact as this symbol pledges them to become.

There is no doubt that women can truly love women, and that men can have profound love for other men. (Aristotle, indeed, argued that men could only be true friends with men, not with women, because friendship depends on equality, and men and women did not have equality.) In some ways, friendships are indeed easier between persons of the same sex. Sexual relations between men and women are enormously complex, so that one short lifetime is normally insufficient to plumb even one such relationship. Heterosexual relations are full of terror. They are not as rosy and cheerful as *Playboy* and *Penthouse* would puff for our infantile fantasies.

Men have done most of the world's writing, so we are well informed about how little, and how poorly, men understand women. It would be foolish to believe—all experience tells against it—that women understand men any better. (In a secret area of bias, I confess to believing that men, at least sexually, are simpler to understand. The truth is so simple, I think whimsically, that many women cannot bring themselves to believe it. They keep looking for deeper, more complicated explanations.)

Society has a great—an overwhelming—interest in the battle between the sexes, and in its successful negotiation by its millions of couples. Even given the full social supporters of an economic and cultural and spiritual system, such as we do not now have, not all couples can be expected to be successful. In a system as fantastically successful, rich, and centrifugal as ours, the casualties must be many. Democratic capitalism necessarily develops powerful contradictions, as Daniel Bell has spelled out. It is the freest system ever devised by mankind. But it sends individuals off every which way, in general moral incoherence. The effort to nourish strong families in such a system places huge burdens upon each solitary couple.

Great strides have been made in recent years—strides which I welcome—in winning tolerance for homosexuals. Tolerance for individuals does not entail moral approval, however. In a democracy, one must live and let live. But one is free to argue against. From my point of view, homosexuals absent themselves from the most central struggle of the individual, the struggle to enter into communion with a person of the opposite sex. That is the battle most at the heart of life. Excluded from this struggle, whether by choice or by psychic endowment, the homosexual is deprived of its fruits. Those fruits are a distinctive honesty, realism and wisdom taught by each sex to the other: that complementarity in which our humanity is rejoined and fulfilled. Apart from this civilizing struggle there is a lack, an emptiness, a loss of realism. On the other hand, God knows, there are compensating riches of the spirit. Often those deprived in one way are the most sensitive and creative in others. Fulfillment does not depend on being heterosexual, or married, or familial. But the marital ideal nourishes every other ideal we have.

Psychiatrists have ceased calling homosexuality a sickness, or a lack, but one is not sure that they—or others—have ceased thinking that way about it (or that they should). There are three features in the very structure of homosexual life that tell against it. The first is a preoccupation with one's own sex. Half the human mystery is evaded. The second is the instability of homosexual relationships, an instability that arises from the lack of the full dimension of raising a family. Apart from having and raising children, a couple can hardly help a degree of self-preoccupation. The structure of family life—the same onerous structure that feels like a "trap"—places the married couple in a context larger than themselves, shields them from one another, so to speak, and opens up new avenues of realism and honesty. It is an especially important experience to exercise the authority of a parent, having rebelled against mother, or father, or both, for so many years. Only thus does one see things from the other side.

Thirdly, the homosexual faces a particular sort of solipsism, which is difficult to escape simply through companionship. Homosexual love is somehow apart from the fundamental mystery of bringing life into the world, and sharing in the birth and death of the generations. It is self-centered in a way that is structural, independent of the goodwill of the individual. Marital love has a structural role in continuing the human race that is independent of the failures of the individuals who share it.

There are also particular dangers in homosexuality. If it is true that the homosexual is lacking something that nature usually intends, then that lack is bound to be felt, at least unconsciously. A certain rage against nature is likely to be felt, and perhaps internalized and directed at the self. Of course, it is often argued that nature has made no mistake, that the homosexual is fully endowed, and that it is *society* that is the cheat. The rage will then be directed against society. Yet even in this case, one will expect to see the rage turned inward, and one will not really expect it to be assuaged by public approval. Indeed, the more the public might seem to approve of homosexuality, the more one would expect homosexuals to begin punishing themselves. For the source of this rage is not merely an anger at being different; it is deeper than that. One knows one has been left out of something. One wishes to be accepted for what one is.

But one does not wish to be told lies in the process. One can make something heroic out of a flaw in oneself, but not by lying.

In fact, the climate of the last ten years—just the years in which tolerance and "understanding" have been growing in unprecedented ways—has encouraged the growth of rage against society. Negativism and hostility are in the air. For homosexuals, however, rage against society will not alleviate rage against the self. That rage must be dealt with by the self. Self-fulfillment is at stake. (This does not mean mere self-expression, or doing what one feels like doing.) Self-fulfillment is doubly difficult for the homosexual; it is hard enough for everybody. But the married person with family has so many demands made by others upon the self that many painful blows are struck from outside-in, so to speak, and this is an inestimable advantage. (Edward Albee's hideous play about marriage, *Who's Afraid of Virginia Woolf?*, only appeared to be about a man and wife; the dialogue was unmistakably that of the soul in rage against itself. The play is an almost perfect metaphor for the rage of the homosexual against himself.)

Second, a peculiar sickness fell upon the rhetoric of blacks during the past decade. It was duly reported by the media as authentic. Incredible poses were struck, rage was faked, pantomime was acted out. Instead of seeing this charade for what it was, many good liberals employed a double standard: Blacks act "funny," so this play-acting must be true. Then everyone who wished to gain the benefits accruing to the "oppressed" through the media began aping militant blacks of that period (now already out of style). "The student as nigger" was the first act. "Women's liberation" was the second. "Gay Power" came third upon the stage. Howsoever poignant the stories to be told, they now come out as canned, bowdlerized, third-rate imitations. Can anyone doubt the inevitable result if this charade continues, long after the public has seen through the symbolic form? Demonstrations of fist-waving homosexuals carrying placards fulfill stereotypes in the public mind surrealistically. . . .

. . . Not only is politics a blunt and destructive instrument, supplanting precise reason with slogans, stereotypes, namecalling, and other campaign necessities. It is, in addition, an awakener of fierce counteraction. If one is seeking tolerance and solid shifts in underlying values, politics defeats one's efforts by stimulating and crystallizing opposition. Politics awakens irrational forces. It is not a wholly rational sphere.

That there are, and always will be, homosexuals among us (among our friends, in our families, among those we work with, throughout society) is certain. That they are often among our most talented, creative, and successful citizens is obvious. Yet the homosexual condition offers rather more inner suffering and sorrow, even with its normal quotient of human happiness, than I would wish for my children or for others. Heterosexuality is the full and complete human ideal. Homosexuality is not a preference of equal moral weight. Still, it would be good for laws specifically aimed against homosexuality to be stricken from the books, so that the coercions of the state do not enter into private life. Similarly, no one should be coerced by the state into giving approval for a way of life of which he does not approve. The state should be kept as much as possible outside such questions.

Study Questions on Michael Novak

1. Novak identifies himself as a Roman Catholic. Could his argument be nonetheless accepted by an atheist, or by an adherent of some other religion?
2. Are you persuaded by Novak's analysis of feminism? Of the rage of homosexuals?
3. Novak rejects the "politicization of almost everything." Yet his article is intended to support some political views and to oppose others. Is this an insuperable problem for him?
4. Is there reason to believe that what we can gain by trying to negotiate and learn from the differences between the sexes is more valuable than what we can learn from other sorts of differences—say, of age, race, interests, or temperament? (Consider the differences between introverts and extroverts, and between people inclined to be cerebral and analytic and those inclined to be guided by their feelings.)
5. How would Murphy (see next article) respond to Novak's argument? Which do you agree with more and why?

Homosex/Ethics

TIMOTHY F. MURPHY

Timothy F. Murphy defends "homosex" as a rich and fertile language for discovering and articulating the meanings of human life. The differences between homosex and heterosex are unimportant, except as far as they offer the opportunity to raise more significant moral questions about the relations between power and

From Journal of Homosexuality, 27, 3–4 (1994), *The Hayworth Press, Inc.*
Reprinted by permission of the publisher.

sexuality, and about the meaning of difference. He rejects arguments that homosex is cowardly recoiling from difference, and maintains that it brings opportunities for strength and heroism that are unparalleled in heterosex.

WHILE IT DOES SEEM TO ME that the moral arguments on behalf of homosex do carry the day against their competition, I do not want to rehearse here the usual arguments about pathology, normalcy, nature, or religion in order to defend the morality of homosex. Instead, I will argue that homosex stands on its own as sex because, like heterosex, it is a rich and fertile language for discovering and articulating the meanings of human life. Homosex, to say the least, permits capacities for strength, erotic possibilities, and moral meanings that are not otherwise available. Because homosex is not especially opposed to heterosex, both sexualities share many physical and conceptual continuities, and as I will try to show, moral continuities as well. In many regards, therefore, questions about the genitalia of bedroom partners are ultimately beside the moral point. Homosex and heterosex are divided only in the way that English and French are divided, and the differences are not in themselves morally significant except as they offer the opportunity to raise ultimately more significant moral questions about the relations between power and sexuality and about the meaning of difference.

In an essay called "Heterosex," Robert Solomon rightly argues that sexual desire is not a discrete, independently subsiding trait in persons, one that could be excised at will, leaving an otherwise intact person behind. On the contrary, and he is right about this as well, a complex of human desires and activities becomes "sexual" mostly through the workings of custom and ritual. One may underline his thesis by noting that orgasm in infants does not, for example, carry the "sexual" meanings adults find in it. What counts as "sexual" expression differs widely among cultures and even among generations within the same culture. One need only think of differences in dressing habits on beaches around the world to understand the variable meanings of sexuality. Sex is indeed more than the sum of anatomical parts and physiological processes. An adequate understanding of sexuality is possible and complete only through an appreciation of the functional meanings of sexuality in our

personal and social lives. Just as human *nature* ultimately signifies not what is biologically, socially, or metaphysically given in human life but what can be *summoned* from human beings, the "nature" of our sexuality depends not only on what "parts" are involved but also on what others and our society call forth from us and on how we respond.

Thus does Solomon rightly believe that a recovery of the joys of heterosex (the ostensible goal of his essay) depends on an improved understanding of the poetry of sex and not on an increasingly exact analysis of bodily function: "Heterosex is first of all a kind of poetry, and there is no clear limit to richness of interpersonal feelings that it can express, given an adequate vocabulary and what we might call, tongue in cheek, sexual literacy." . . .

Sexuality thus construed, it is hard to see why homosex should not be interpreted in the same way as heterosex. If there is no independently abiding desire in humans that is a priori (hetero)sexual, if sexuality is primarily a matter of definitions and meanings, then not only is there no reason to think of homoeroticism as anything but sex, there is also no reason to give heterosex any kind of priority in having greater claim to being the "essence" or "nature" of sex any more than there would be reason to assert that Latin or German were the "nature" of language itself and all other tongues merely a falling off from those culturolinguistic paradigms. On the contrary, homosex would seem to be conceptually continuous with heterosex insofar as it represents a similar range of intentions, desires, and definitions in the [same] manner, if not in the same configurations. No less than heterosex, homosex represents fields of attraction, culturally defined, with expressive purposes, some of them more acrobatic than others, but bearers of meanings very often little or no different from those of heterosex.

Both homosex and heterosex would share, for example, common forms in pursuit of interpersonal and social goals and means of expression. And this would remain true whether the origins of homosex belong in—as the speculations about its origins go—fetal hormone deprivation, in unhappy family dynamics, genetic heritage, prideful revolt against the order of God, or merely in the lottery of unaccountable and serendipitous human difference. Homosex is as much about the contact between bodies as heterosex. As much as heterosex, the expressions of homosex may after all be an adventure in discovery, an act of vengeance, a cold manipulation, an experiment in pleasure, a flirtation, an act of cowardice, an expression of sympathy, an act of theater, a passing fancy, an act of trust, a thoughtless relief, a defiance, a bored obligation, a willful expression of difference, a cozy evening at home, a fiery crash in the night, a rescue, and a way of belonging. By grounding the intelligibility of sexuality in its meanings rather than acts it is possible to see how the meanings of homosex are as rich, varied, and as open to invention as those of heterosex. . . .

Homosex is a "sexual" language that may appear, to be sure, foreign and unintelligible to those unfamiliar with it, but it is a language nonetheless that makes certain relations and meanings possible. Homosex is its own *lingua franca,* spoken by adherents across the world who each contribute to it, change it, define it, make themselves understood through it. It is in many regards, however, no more impervious to understanding than another spoken language. Much of its "vocabulary" and meanings can be "translated" into heterosex especially as homosex relations echo heterosex relations. But certainly all forms of translation eventually run up against structures, meanings, and concepts that find no exact equivalent in moving from one language to another. And so too will homosex have meanings that cannot be duplicated in heterosex. But it is not clear that the lack of complete conceptual or sexual equivalency between homosex and heterosex damages either sexuality any more than differences between spoken languages invite moral judgment on their comparative worth.

An understanding of sexuality that focuses on its meanings rather than its acts, moreover, makes it difficult to posit any moral superiority of heterosex per se to homosex per se. Both sexualities may be "spoken" in better or worse variants. Both forms of expression are also open to the venalities of human weakness and willful machination. No less than homosex, heterosex may involve serious moral impropriety. Heterosex may, for example, involve rape when its partners do not equally consent to intercourse. Heterosex is not beyond moral suspicion when tied to motives of manipulation and degradation, when it presupposes and perpetuates immoral social practices. Heterosex may recapitulate (and perpetuate) social phylogeny insofar as it bears the marks of objectionable inequality between sexes or other social injustices. To say that sex is merely heteroerotic is in the end to say very little about its morality. Homosex, moreover, bears the capacities for vice (and virtue) to be found in heterosex. But it is not clear that these vices are amplified in kind by being a matter of same-sex relations. The ostensible differences of gender involved in heterosex would not significantly alter this conclusion for reasons that will be discussed below.

Sexual morality, therefore, whether involving homosex or heterosex, belongs more ultimately to matters of meaning rather than to matters of genitalia or acts. It is worth saying too that the bodily expressions of homosex (and heterosex) are in an important way epiphenomenal to erotic attraction; they are a function of what biology makes possible. If men and women had body structures different from those they have now, it is likely that they would still find ways to love one another. It is Eros that invents the pleasures of bodies, not body parts that determine the predilections of Eros. . . .

. . . I do, however, want to discuss one argument that is used in various ways against homosex: that homosex is inferior sexuality because it fails to unite, as heterosex does, opposite genders.

It is this "unifying" feature of heterosex that led Solomon to pronounce heterosex as sex itself. "The central paradigm," he says, "which provides us with the 'natural' continuity with most of the animal kingdom and even a small minority of plants, is heterosexual intercourse." It is "the prototype for every alternative form of sexuality, from bestial to masturbatory. Heterosex is—sex" (206). On such a view, homosex would not appear to be sex at all, any more than talking to oneself could be called conversation. In his account of the erotic, Scruton suggests that the superior nature of heterosex might be put this way: "In the heterosexual act, it might be said, I move out *from* my body *towards* the other, whose flesh is unknown to me; while in the homosexual act I remain locked within my body, narcissistically contemplating in the other an excitement that is the mirror of my own." In its union of genders, heterosex is believed to offer the opportunities for reaching across differences to construct a relationship with another unlike one's self, to reach a complementarity that is not otherwise possible and whose benefits are set at the center of human rewards. Heterosex is therefore the occasion of courage, of adventure, of conquest, of exploration, and, finally, blessed union.

Compared to heterosex, homosex might appear to be a cowardly thing, an atavistic recoiling from difference. Indeed, some psychological accounts insist on the phobic nature of all homosex. Same-sex love has been characterized as an immurement in the idolatry of self, and its same-sex character invites the judgment that it is also narcissism. Thus are to be understood views that homosex is counterfeit sex, that male homosexuals are simply, unconsciously frightened fugitives from women, fleeing in their panic to one another, locked in love with their own images in the way Narcissus was punished—as Ovid told the tale—for spurning the love of Echo.

Against a facile understanding that heterosex represents a union of differences unparalleled in homosex, it is worth observing the many ways in which heterosex does and does not unite "opposite" sexes. After all, its unions may be as transient as those in homosex. Moreover, heterosex does not merge bodily, psychological, or chromosomal identities. Heterosex does not by definition unite disparate social roles of men and women; indeed many heterosex relations seem to be structured by profound divisions and differences between both the sexual identities and the gender roles of men and women; these divisions and differences may say more about the nature of power in these relations than they do about the differences of "male" and "female." Complementarity in sexual relations may have less to do with differences between male and female than with differences between the controller and the controlled.

Eve Kosofsky Sedgwick has observed how few ways we actually have to express all the differences that exist between persons, how a few rough-edged distinctions are forced to bear the brunt of individuation. But the same might also be said of the few ways we have for expressing *similarity*

between persons. Men and women are alike in ways that defy expression, ways that bind them biologically, emotionally, morally, culturally, even geographically. What "differences" there are between men and women in heterosex may not loom especially large against the plethora of background traits they often share. In practice and in general, individual heterosexual partners typically share significant similarities in age, social standing, health, intelligence, emotions, political views, cultural views, standards of tolerance, hobbies, food and entertainment preferences, and so on. Sexual partners, therefore, are sometimes more united by their similarities than they are divided by their anatomical differences. Hence it is not surprising that heterosex personal ads lay out often stringent criteria of similarity as the *sine qua non* of acquaintance and what comes after. It may not be the conquest of difference that stokes sexual engines in heterosex so much as the lure of the familiar. Insofar as men and women share the same language, cultural background, religion, social class, and so on, differences of anatomy in heterosex may appear vanishingly small and their conquest a minor, maybe an inevitable achievement in a culture whose sexual orthodoxy presupposes heterosex as the virtual destiny of human nature. Given the magnitude of the social, familial, and conceptual forces that impel men and women toward one another, heterosex hardly seems a venture into the unknown; on the contrary, heterosex may appear as inevitable as the working of gravity. Given all the ways in which heterosex presupposes shared traits, anatomical differences seem almost beside the point, mere ripples in the fleshy minors in which we contemplate ourselves. Men and women are, after all, *exactly the same* as regards kingdom, phylum, class, order, family, genus, and species, this regardless of their gender or sexual habits.

It is also not clear that heterosex by definition represents strength in ways that homosex cannot, represents venturesomeness that homosex evades. Indeed, homosex can represent opportunities for growth and adaptation that are otherwise unavailable. . . .

. . . [Homosexuals] do not ordinarily have the benefits of parental and social expectation to guide them. They find themselves at the mercy of public discourse and symbolism in education, media, and religion that presuppose heterosex as the order of human nature. When they go to the libraries for information, they find discussions of pathology, they find their books stacked alongside tomes about pornography and prostitution, and the newspaper indexes will refer parties interested in homosex to the subject-heading of AIDS.

Given these significant familial and culturally pervasive barriers to self-esteem and growth, gay and lesbian young people face challenges that offer them plenty of opportunity for the development of personal skills and capacities. It also requires of them risks and undertakings without analogue in heterosex. Far from being a matter of sheer cowardice, homosex brings opportunities for strength and heroism that are unparalleled in heterosex. . . .

It is the sameness of genders in homosex that perhaps drives the view—commonalities in heterosex notwithstanding—that homosex is nothing more than masturbation writ large, that its "sterility" is emotional and psychological as well as reproductive, that its "sterility" is both the cause and effect of homosex, that its uncomplementary nature is inalterably narcissistic. There are, though, many ways in which homo-eroticism does not deserve its etymology, ways in which it is indeed not homo-erotic but allo-erotic. In his essay "Homo-Narcissism; or, Heterosexuality," Michael Warner has, for example, criticized the narcissistic view of homosex, arguing, first of all, that Freud's own analysis does not show homosex to be any kind of developmental regression because homosex is, after all, not merely pursuit of one's *own* image. Beyond this specific analysis,

Warner also holds that the view of homosex as narcissism is itself a form of narcissism peculiar to modern heterosex. It is a narcissism insofar as heterosex requires all sex to reflect its own configuration in which there is an antagonistic Self-and-Other relationship, a relationship that permits and even requires forms of domination. This kind of analysis makes it clear that what is found "objectionable" in homosex is not the presence of certain behaviors so much as the absence of the traits around which identity, authority, and community have been traditionally defined. It is hard to see, therefore, in what ways the label of narcissism generates a significant objection to homosex if, in fact, the concept functions to advance its own ideology about the structure of interpersonal relations. *Even if* narcissism were the pursuit of one's own image, given the extent to which heterosex relations themselves presuppose and seek similarity, they too would be implicated in narcissism. It is not clear, that is, why similarity of body parts between partners should be seen as more indicative of narcissism than similarity of, say, deeply-held religious or political views.

Like the moral worth of heterosex, then, the moral worth of homosex ultimately depends not on questions of narcissism but on the people involved and the context of their lives. And it is here in looking at the social context of homosex that one finds moral questions worth raising, but these questions are not about the use of body parts and their "fit" or the intentions of nature.

Study Questions on Timothy F. Murphy

1. Explain how Murphy (following Solomon) thinks of sexual behavior as like a language. Are you persuaded that what counts as sexual behavior is mostly a matter of the meanings society assigns to it?
2. Do you believe that all or most human beings have a genetic propensity to heterosexuality? How can we determine whether this is so?
3. Murphy argues that homosexuality "brings opportunities for strength and heroism that are unparalleled in heterosex." Is this claim consistent with his claim that there are no significant differences between homosexuality and heterosexuality? Is violating social expectations valuable in itself, or does Murphy have something deeper in mind?

4. In your opinion, does heterosexual intercourse unify the two people in a way homosexual intercourse does not? Explain your answer.

The Conservative Case for Same-Sex Marriage

ANDREW SULLIVAN

Andrew Sullivan tries to show how every conservative argument against same-sex marriage collapses upon close examination. He concentrates on the notion that legalizing same-sex marriage would undermine traditional heterosexual marriage.

THE MOST COMMON CONSERVATIVE ARGUMENT against same-sex marriage is that the public acceptance of homosexuality subverts the stability and self-understanding of the heterosexual family. But here the conservative position undermines itself somewhat. Since most conservatives concede the presence of a number of involuntarily homosexual persons, they must also concede that these persons are already part of "heterosexual" families. They are sons and daughters, brothers and sisters, even mothers and fathers, of heterosexuals. The distinction between "families" and "homosexuals" is, to begin with, empirically false; and the stability of existing families is closely linked to how homosexuals are treated within them. Presumably, it is against the interest of heterosexual families to force homosexuals into roles they are not equipped to play and may disastrously perform. This is not an abstract matter. It is quite common that homosexual fathers and mothers who are encouraged into heterosexual marriages subsequently find the charade and dishonesty too great to bear: spouses are betrayed, children are abandoned, families are broken, and lives are ruined. It is also common that homosexual sons and daughters who are denied the love and support of their families are liable to turn against the institution of the family, to wound and destroy it, out of hurt and rejection. And that parents, inculcated in the kind of disdain of homosexuality conservatives claim in necessary to protect the family, react to the existence of gay children with unconscionable anger and pain, and actually help destroy loving families.

Still, conservatives may concede this and still say that it's worth it. The threat to the stability of the family posed by public disapproval of homosexuality is not as great as the threat posed by public approval. How does this argument work? Largely by saying that the lives saved by preventing wavering straights from becoming gay are more numerous than the lives saved by keeping gay people out of heterosexual relationships and allowing greater tolerance of gay members of families themselves; that the stability of the society is better served by the former than by the latter. Now, recall that conservatives are not attempting to assert absolute moral truths here. They are making an argument about social goods, in this case, social and familial stability. They are saying that a homosexual life is, on the face of it, worse than a heterosexual life, as far as society is concerned. In Harvard psychologist E. L. Pattullo's words,

> Though we acknowledge some influences— social and biological—beyond their control, we do not accept the idea that people of bad character had no choice. Further, we are concerned to maintain a social climate that will steer them in the direction of the good.

The issue here is bad character and the implied association of bad character with the life of homosexuals. Although many conservatives feel loath to articulate what they mean by this life, it's clear what lies behind it. So if they won't articulate it, allow me. They mean by "a homosexual life" one in which emotional commitments are fleeting, promiscuous sex is common, disease is rampant, social ostracism is common, and standards of public decency, propriety, and self-restraint are flaunted. They mean a way of life that deliberately subverts gender norms in order to unsettle the virtues that make family life possible, ridicules heterosexual life, and commits itself to an ethic of hedonism, loneliness, and deceit. They mean by all this "the other," against which any norm has to be defended and any cohesive society protected. So it is that whatever good might be served by preventing gay people from becoming parents or healing internal wounds within existing families, it is greatly outweighed by the dangers of unleashing this kind of ethic upon the society as a whole.

But the argument, of course, begs a question. Is this kind of life, according to conservatives, what a homosexual life *necessarily* is? Surely not. If homosexuality is often indeed involuntary, as conservatives believe, then homosexuals are not automatically the "other"; they are sprinkled randomly throughout society, into families that are very much like anybody else's, with characters and bodies and minds as varied as the rest of humanity. If all human beings are, as conservatives believe, subject to social inducements to lead better or worse lives, then there is nothing inevitable at all about a homosexual leading a deprived life. In some cases, he might even be a paragon of virtue. Why then is the choice of a waverer to live a homosexual rather than a heterosexual life necessarily a bad one, from the point of view of society? Why does it lead to any necessary social harm at all?

Of course, if you simply define "homosexual" as "depraved," you have an answer; but it's essentially a tautologous one. And if you argue that in our society at this time, homosexual lives simply *are* more depraved, you are also begging a question. There are very few social incentives of the kind conservatives like for homosexuals *not* to be depraved: there's little social or familial support, no institution to encourage fidelity or monogamy,

precious little religious or moral outreach to guide homosexuals into more virtuous living. This is not to say that homosexuals are not responsible for their actions, merely that in a large part of homosexual subculture there is much a conservative would predict, when human beings are abandoned with extremely few social incentives for good or socially responsible behavior. But the proper conservative response to this is surely not to infer that this behavior is inevitable, or to use it as a reason to deter others from engaging in a responsible homosexual existence, if that is what they want; but rather to construct social institutions and guidelines to modify and change that behavior for the better. But that is what conservatives resolutely refuse to do.

Why? Maybe for conservatives, there is something inherent even in the most virtuous homosexual life that renders it less desirable than the virtuous heterosexual life, and therefore merits social discouragement to deter the waverers. Let's assume, from a conservative perspective, the best-case scenario for such a waverer: he can choose between a loving, stable, and responsible same-sex relationship and a loving, stable, and responsible opposite-sex relationship. Why should society preference the latter?

The most common response is along the lines of Hadley Arkes, the conservative commentator, who has written on this subject on occasion. It is that the heterosexual relationship is good for men not simply because it forces them to cooperate and share with other human beings on a daily basis but because it forces them into daily contact and partnership with *women:*

> It is not marriage that domesticates men; it is women. Left to themselves, these forked creatures follow a way of life that George Gilder once recounted in its precise, chilling measures: bachelors were twenty-two times more likely than married men to be committed to hospital for mental disease (and ten times more likely to suffer chronic diseases of all kinds). Single men had nearly double the mortality rate of married men and three times the mortality rate of single women. Divorced men were three times more likely than divorced women to commit suicide or die by murder, and they were six times more likely to die of heart disease.

I will leave aside the statistical difficulties here: it's perfectly possible that many of the problems Arkes recounts were reasons why the men didn't get married, rather than consequences of their failing to do so. Let's assume, for the sake of argument, that Arkes is right: that marriage to a woman is clearly preferable to being single for an adult man; that such a man is more likely to be emotionally stable, physically healthy, psychologically in balance; and that this is good for the society as a whole. There is in this argument a belief that women are naturally more prone to be stable, nurturing, supportive of stability, fiscally prudent, and family-oriented than men, and that their connection to as many men as possible is therefore clearly a social good. Let's assume also, for the sake of argument, that Arkes is right about that too. It's obvious, according to conservatives, that society should encourage a stable opposite-sex relationship over a stable same-sex relationship.

But the waverer has another option: *he can remain single*. Should society actually encourage him to do this rather than involve himself in a stable, loving same-sex relationship? Surely, even conservatives who think women are essential to the successful socialization of men would not deny that the discipline of domesticity, of shared duties and lives, of the inevitable give-and-take of cohabitation and love with anyone, even of the same sex, tends to benefit men more than the option of constant, freewheeling, etiolating bachelorhood. But this would mean creating a public moral and social climate which preferred stable gay relationships to gay or straight bachelorhood. And it would require generating a notion of homosexual responsibility that would destroy the delicately balanced conservative politics of private discretion and undiscriminating public disapproval. So conservatives are stuck again: their refusal to embrace responsible public support for virtuous homosexuals runs counter to their entire social agenda.

Arkes's argument also leads to another (however ironic) possibility destabilizing to conservatism's delicate contemporary compromise on the homosexual question: that for a wavering woman, a lesbian relationship might actually be socially *preferable* to a heterosexual relationship. If the issue is not mere domesticity but the presence of women, why would two women not be better than one, for the sake of children's development and social stability? Since lesbianism seems to be more amenable to choice than male homosexuality in most studies and surveys, conservatism's emphasis on social encouragement of certain behaviors over others might be seen as even more relevant here. If conservatism is about the social benefits of feminizing society, there is no reason why it should not be an integral part of the movement for women to liberate themselves completely from men. Of course, I'm being facetious; conservatives would be terrified by all the single males such a society would leave rampaging around. But it's not inconceivable at all from conservative premises that, solely from the point of view of the wavering woman, the ascending priorities would be: remaining single, having a stable, loving opposite-sex relationship, and having a stable, loving same-sex relationship. And there is something deliciously ironic about the sensibility of Hadley Arkes and E. L. Pattullo finding its full fruition in a lesbian collective.

Still, the conservative has another option. He might argue that removing the taboo on homosexuality would unravel an entire fabric of self-understanding in the society at large that could potentially destabilize the whole system of incentives for stable family relationships. He might argue that now, of all times, when families are in an unprecedented state of collapse, is not the occasion for further tinkering with this system; that the pride of heterosexual men and women is at stake; that their self-esteem and self-understanding would be undermined if society saw them as equivalent to homosexuals. In this view, the stigmatization of homosexuals is the necessary corollary to the celebration of traditional family life.

Does this ring true? To begin with, it's not at all clear why, if public disapproval of homosexuals is indeed necessary to keep families together, homosexuals of all people should bear the primary brunt of the task. But it's also not clear why the corollary really works to start with. Those homosexuals who have no choice at all to be homosexual, whom conservatives do not want to be in a heterosexual family in the first place, are clearly no threat to the heterosexual family. Why would accepting that such people exist, encouraging them to live virtuous lives, incorporating their difference into society as a whole, necessarily devalue the traditional family? It is not a zero-sum game. Because they have no choice but to be homosexual, they are not choosing that option over heterosexual marriage; and so they are not sending any social signals that heterosexual family life should be denigrated.

The more difficult case, of course, pertains to Arkes's "waverers." Would allowing them the option of a stable same-sex relationship as a preferable social option to being single really undermine the institution of the family? Is it inconceivable that a society can be subtle in its public indications of what is and what is not socially preferable? Surely, society can offer a hierarchy of choices, which, while preferencing one, does not necessarily denigrate the others, but accords them some degree of calibrated respect. It does this in many other areas. Why not in sexual arrangements?

You see this already in many families with homosexual members. While some parents are disappointed that their son or daughter will not marry someone of the opposite sex, provide grandchildren and sustain the family line for another generation, they still prefer to see that child find someone to love and live with and share his or her life with. That child's siblings, who may be heterosexual, need feel no disapproval attached to their own marriage by the simple fact of their sibling's difference. Why should society as a whole find it an impossible task to share in the same maturity? Even in the most homosexualized culture, conservatives would still expect over eighty percent of couples to be heterosexual: why is their self-esteem likely to be threatened by a paltry twenty percent—especially when, according to conservatives, the homosexual life is so self-evidently inferior?

In fact, it's perfectly possible to combine a celebration of the traditional family with the celebration of a stable homosexual relationship. The one, after all, is modeled on the other. If constructed carefully as a conservative social ideology, the notion of stable gay relationships might even serve to buttress the ethic of heterosexual marriage, by showing how even those excluded from it can wish to model themselves on its shape and structure. This very truth, of course, is why liberationists are so hostile to the entire notion. Rather than liberating society from asphyxiating conventions it actually harnesses one minority group—homosexuals—and enlists them in the conservative structures that liberationists find so inimical. One can indeed see the liberationists' reasons for opposing such a move. But why should conservatives oppose it?

Study Questions on Andrew Sullivan

1. Sullivan presents a "conservative" case for same-sex marriage. Why do you suppose he calls it a conservative case? What does conservative mean here?

2. "Liberationists" hold that marriage is inherently an oppressive institution, and that homosexuals of all people should be happy to avoid it (see, e.g., Ettelbrick's essay and Browning's essay in the Sullivan reader listed in the For Further Reading section). Why might people take this position, and how might Sullivan answer them?

3. Sullivan argues that stable relationships are better for homosexuals (and for society) than promiscuity. How much do you think legal recognition would contribute to the stability of homosexual relationships?

4. Would same-sex marriages imply same-sex wedding ceremonies? (Could they be provided with the necessary legitimacy without them?) What sort of ceremony (secular or religious) would be appropriate? (See the essay by Henry Alford in the Sullivan reader.) How do you feel about same-sex marriage ceremonies?

5. One reason why the same-sex marriage issue has been so controversial is because people have deeply differing gut intuitions about the topic. Many people,

including some who would be happy to extend tax breaks or health insurance benefits to same-sex couples, balk at the idea of a same-sex marriage ceremony, regarding it as a farcical parody, especially of a religious wedding. In light of these differences, is there any hope of arriving at a resolution of this issue?

"Same-Sex Marriage" and "Moral Neutrality"

ROBERT P. GEORGE

Robert P. George responds both to defenders of same-sex marriage and to those who believe that the law should be neutral on the question of the nature of marriage. Marriage, he argues, is a one-flesh communion of persons that can be realized only in heterosexuality. In defense of this, he cites Germain Grisez, who says, "Though a male and a female are complete individuals with respect to other functions . . . with respect to reproduction they are only potential parts of a mated pair, which is the complete organism capable of reproducing sexually." He tries to answer those who point out that sterile heterosexuals are allowed to marry by appealing to the fact that they, unlike homosexuals, can engage in acts which are reproductive *in type*.

IT IS CERTAINLY THE CASE that implicit in our matrimonial law is a (now controversial) moral judgment, namely, the judgment that marriage is inherently heterosexual—a union of one man and one woman. . . . Of course, this is not the only possible moral judgment. In some cultures, polygyny or (far less frequently) polyandry is legally sanctioned. . . .

There are two ways to argue for the proposition that it is unjust for government to refuse to authorize same-sex (and, for that matter, polygamous) "marriages." The first is to deny the reasonableness, soundness, or truth of the moral judgment implicit in the proposition that marriage is a union of one man and one woman. The second is to argue that this moral judgment cannot justly serve as the basis for the public law of matrimony, notwithstanding its reasonableness, soundness, or even its truth.

I maintain that the moral neutrality to which this way of arguing appeals is, and cannot but be, illusory. To that end, it will be necessary for me to explain the philosophical grounds of the moral judgment that marriage is a union of one man and one woman and to discuss the arguments advanced by certain critics of traditional matrimonial law in their efforts to undermine this judgment.

Two in One Flesh

Here is the core of the traditional understanding: Marriage is a two-in-one-flesh communion of persons that is consummated and actualized by acts which are reproductive *in type*, whether or not they are reproductive *in effect* (or are motivated, even in part, by a desire to reproduce). Reproductive-type acts have unique meaning, value, and significance because they belong to the class of acts by which children come into being. More precisely, these acts have their unique meaning, value, and significance because they belong to the *only* class of acts by which children can come into being, not as

326 UNIT V Politics: Gender in the Public Arena

"products" which their parents choose to "make," but, rather, as perfective participants in the organic community (that is, the family) that is established by their parents' marriage. The bodily union of spouses in marital acts is the biological matrix of their marriage as a multi-level relationship that unites them at the bodily, emotional, dispositional, and spiritual levels of their being.

Marriage, precisely as such a relationship, is naturally ordered to the good of procreation (and to the nurturing and education of children), as well as to the good of spousal unity, and these goods are tightly bound together. The distinctive unity of spouses is possible *because* men and women, in reproductive-type acts, become a single reproductive principle. Although reproduction is a single act, in humans the reproductive act is performed not by individual members of the species, but by a mated pair as an organic unit. The point has been explained by Germain Grisez: "Though a male and a female are complete individuals with respect to other functions—for example, nutrition, sensation, and locomotion—with respect to reproduction they are only potential parts of a mated pair, which is the complete organism capable of reproducing sexually. Even if the mated pair is sterile, intercourse, provided it is the reproductive behavior characteristic of the species, makes the copulating male and female one organism."

Although not all reproductive-type acts are marital,[1] there can be no marital act that is not reproductive in type. Masturbatory, sodomitical, or other sexual acts which are not reproductive in type cannot unite persons organically, that is, as a single reproductive principle. Therefore, such acts cannot be intelligibly engaged in for the sake of marital unity as such: They cannot be marital acts. Rather, persons who perform such acts must be doing so for the sake of ends or goals which are *extrinsic* to themselves as bodily persons: Sexual satisfaction, or (perhaps) mutual sexual satisfaction, is sought as a means of releasing tension, or obtaining or sharing pleasure, either as an end in itself, or as a means to some other end, such as expressing affection. In any case, where one-flesh union cannot (or cannot rightly) be sought as an end in itself, sexual activity necessarily involves the

instrumentalization of the bodies of those participating in such activity to extrinsic ends.

In marital acts, by contrast, the bodies of persons who unite biologically are not reduced to the status of mere instruments. Rather, the end, goal, and intelligible point of sexual union is the good of marriage itself. On this understanding, such union is not merely an instrumental good, that is, a reason for action whose intelligibility as a reason depends on other ends to which it is a means, but is, rather, an intrinsic good, that is, a reason for action whose intelligibility as a reason depends on no such other end. The central and justifying point of sex is not pleasure, or even the sharing of pleasure, *per se,* however much sexual pleasure is rightly sought as an aspect of the perfection of marital union. The point of sex, rather, is *marriage itself,* considered as a bodily union of persons consummated and actualized by acts which are reproductive in type. Because in marital acts sex is not instrumentalized, such acts are free of the self-alienating and dis-integrating qualities of masturbatory and sodomitical sex. Unlike these and other nonmarital sex acts, marital acts establish no practical dualism which volitionally and, thus, existentially (though, of course, not metaphysically) separates the body from the conscious and desiring aspect of the self, understood as the "true" self that uses the body as its instrument. As John Finnis has observed, marital acts are truly unitive, and in no way self-alienating, because the bodily or biological aspect of human beings is "part of, and not merely an instrument of, their *personal* reality."

But, one may ask, what about procreation? On the traditional view, isn't the sexual union of spouses instrumentalized to the goal of having children? It is true that St. Augustine was an influential proponent of such a view. The strict Augustinian position was rejected, however, by the mainstream of philosophy and theology from the late Middle Ages forward, and the understanding of sex and marriage that came to be embodied in both the canon law of the Church and the civil law of matrimony does not treat marriage as a merely instrumental good. Matrimonial law has traditionally understood marriage to be consummated by, and only by, the reproductive-type acts of spouses. The sterility of spouses—so long as they are capable of consummating their marriage by a reproductive-type act (and, thus, of

---

[1]Adulterous acts, for example, may be reproductive in type (and even in effect) but are intrinsically nonmarital.

achieving bodily, organic unity)—has never been treated as an impediment to marriage, even where sterility is certain, and even certain to be permanent (as in the case of the marriage of a woman who has been through menopause or has undergone a hysterectomy).

According to the traditional understanding of marriage, then, it is the nature of marital acts as reproductive in type that makes it possible for such acts to be unitive in the distinctively marital way. And this type of unity has intrinsic, and not merely instrumental value. Thus, the unitive good of marriage provides a noninstrumental (and sufficient) reason for spouses to perform sexual acts of a type which consummates and actualizes their marriage. In performing marital acts, the spouses do not reduce themselves as bodily persons (or their marriage) to the status of means or instruments.

At the same time, where marriage is understood as a one-flesh union of persons, children who may be conceived in marital acts are understood, not as ends which are extrinsic to marriage (either in the Augustinian sense, or the modern liberal one), but rather as gifts which supervene on acts whose central justifying point is precisely the marital unity of the spouses. It is thus that children are properly understood and treated—even in their conception—not as means to their parents' ends, but as ends-in-themselves; not as *objects* of the desire[2] or will of their parents, but as *subjects* of justice (and inviolable human rights); not as *property,* but as *persons.* It goes without saying that not all cultures have fully grasped these truths about the moral status of children. What is less frequently noticed is that our culture's grasp of these truths is connected to a basic understanding of sex and marriage that is not only fast eroding, but is now under severe assault from people who have no conscious desire to reduce children to the status of mere means, or objects, or property.

---

[2]I am not here suggesting that traditional ethics denies that it is legitimate for people to "desire" or "want" children. I am merely explicating the sense in which children may be desired or wanted by prospective parents under a description which, consistently with the norms of traditional ethics, does not reduce them to the status of "products" to be brought into existence at their parents' will and for their ends, but rather treats them as "persons" who are to be welcomed by them as perfective participants in the organic community established by their marriage. . . .

Liberal Dualism

It is sometimes thought that defenders of traditional marriage law deny the possibility of something whose possibility critics of the law affirm. "Love," these critics say, "makes a family." And it is committed love that justifies homosexual sex as much as it justifies heterosexual sex. If marriage is the proper, or best, context for sexual love, the argument goes, then marriage should be made available as well to loving, committed same-sex partners on terms of strict equality. To think otherwise is to suppose that same-sex partners cannot really love each other, or love each other in a committed way, or that the orgasmic "sexual expression" of their love is somehow inferior to the orgasmic "sexual expression" of couples who "arrange the plumbing differently."

In fact, however, at the bottom of the debate is a possibility that defenders of traditional marriage law affirm and its critics deny, namely, the possibility of marriage as a one-flesh communion of persons. The denial of this possibility is central to any argument designed to show that the moral judgment at the heart of the traditional understanding of marriage as inherently heterosexual is unreasonable, unsound, or untrue. If reproductive-type acts in fact unite spouses interpersonally, as traditional sexual morality and marriage law suppose, then such acts differ fundamentally in meaning, value, and significance from the only types of sexual acts which can be performed by same-sex partners.

Liberal sexual morality that denies that marriage is inherently heterosexual necessarily supposes that the value of sex must be instrumental *either* to procreation *or* to pleasure. Proponents of the liberal view suppose that homosexual sex acts are indistinguishable from heterosexual acts whenever the motivation for such acts is something other than procreation. The sexual acts of homosexual partners, that is to say, are indistinguishable in motivation, meaning, value, and significance from the marital acts of spouses who know that at least one spouse is temporarily or permanently infertile. Therefore, the argument goes, traditional matrimonial law is guilty of unfairness in treating sterile heterosexuals as capable of marrying while treating homosexual partners as ineligible to marry.

. . . On the contrary, it is a central tenet of the traditional view that the value (and point) of sex is the *intrinsic* good of marriage itself which is actualized in sexual acts which unite spouses biologically and, thus, interpersonally. The traditional view rejects the instrumentalization of sex (and, thus, of the bodies of sexual partners) to any extrinsic end. This does not mean that procreation and pleasure are not rightly sought in marital acts; it means merely that they are rightly sought when they are integrated with the basic good and justifying point of marital sex, namely, the one-flesh union of marriage itself.

It is necessary, therefore, for critics of traditional matrimonial law to argue that the apparent one-flesh unity that distinguishes marital acts from sodomitical acts is illusory, and, thus, that the apparent bodily communion of spouses in reproductive-type acts is not really possible. And so Macedo claims that "the 'one-flesh communion' of sterile couples would appear . . . to be more a matter of appearance than reality." Because of their sterility such couples cannot really unite biologically: "[T]heir bodies, like those of homosexuals, can form no 'single reproductive principle,' no real unity." Indeed, Macedo goes so far as to argue that even fertile couples who conceive children in acts of sexual intercourse do not truly unite biologically, because, he asserts, "penises and vaginas do not unite biologically, sperm and eggs do."

John Finnis has aptly replied that "in this reductivist, word-legislating mood, one might declare that sperm and egg unite only physically and only their pronuclei are biologically united. But it would be more realistic to acknowledge that the whole process of copulation, involving as it does the brains of the man and woman, their nerves, blood, vaginal and other secretions, and coordinated activity is biological through and through."

Moreover, as Finnis points out, the organic unity which is instantiated in an act of the reproductive kind is not, as Macedo "reductively imagine[s], the unity of penis and vagina. It is the unity of the persons in the intentional, consensual *act* of seminal emission/reception in the woman's reproductive tract."

The unity to which Finnis refers—unity of body, sense, emotion, reason, and will—is, in my view, central to our understanding of humanness itself. Yet it is a unity of which Macedo and others who deny the possibility of true marital communion can

give no account. For their denial presupposes a dualism of "person" (as conscious and desiring self), on the one hand, and "body" (as instrument of the conscious and desiring self), on the other, which is flatly incompatible with this unity. Dualism is implicit in the idea, central to Macedo's denial of the possibility of one-flesh marital union, that sodomitical acts differ from what I have described as acts of the reproductive type only as a matter of the arrangement of the "plumbing." According to this idea, the genital organs of an infertile woman (and, of course, all women are infertile most of the time) or of an infertile man are not really "reproductive organs"—any more than, say, mouths, rectums, tongues, or fingers are reproductive organs. Therefore, the intercourse of a man and a woman where at least one partner is temporarily or permanently sterile cannot really be an act of the reproductive type.

But the plain fact is that the genitals of men and woman are reproductive organs all of the time—even during periods of sterility. And acts which fulfill the behavioral conditions of reproduction are acts of the reproductive type even where the nonbehavioral conditions of reproduction do not happen to obtain. Insofar as the object of sexual intercourse is marital union, the partners achieve the desired unity (become "two-in-one-flesh") precisely insofar as they mate, that is, fulfill the behavioral conditions of reproduction, or, if you will, perform the type of act—the only type of act—upon which the gift of a child may supervene. . . .

The Law as Teacher

. . . The true meaning, value, and significance of marriage are fairly easily grasped, even if people sometimes have difficulty living up to its moral demands, when a culture—including, critically, a legal culture—promotes and supports a sound understanding of marriage, both formally and informally. Ideologies and practices which are hostile to a sound understanding and practice of marriage in a culture tend to undermine the institution of marriage, making it difficult for people to grasp the true meaning, value, and significance of marriage. It is, therefore, extremely important that government eschew attempts to be "neutral" with regard to competing conceptions of marriage and try hard to embody in its law and policy the soundest, most nearly correct conception. Moreover, any effort to achieve neutrality will inevitably prove to be self-defeating. For the law is a teacher: It will teach *either* that marriage is a reality that people can choose to participate in, but whose contours people cannot make and remake at will *or* the law will teach that marriage is a mere convention which is malleable in such a way that individuals, couples, or, indeed, groups, can choose to make of it whatever suits them. The result, given the biases of human sexual psychology, will be the development of practices and ideologies which truly do tend to undermine the sound understanding and practice of marriage, together with the pathologies that tend to reinforce the very practices and ideologies that cause them.

Joseph Raz, though himself a liberal who does not share my views on homosexuality or sexual morality generally, is rightly critical of forms of liberalism, including Rawlsianism, which suppose that law and government can and should be neutral with respect to competing conceptions of morality. In this regard, he has noted that "monogamy, assuming that it is the only valuable form of marriage, cannot be practised by an individual. It requires a culture which recognizes and supports it through the force of public opinion and its own formal institutions." . . .

. . . Does a due regard for equality require moral neutrality? I think that the appeal to neutrality actually does no work here. If the moral judgment that marriage is between a man and a woman is false, then the reason for recognizing same-sex marriages is that such unions are as a matter of moral fact indistinguishable from marriages of the traditional type. If, however, the moral judgment that marriage is between a man and a woman is true, then Macedo's claim that the recognition of this truth by government "denies fundamental aspects of equality" simply cannot be sustained. . . .

It is certainly unjust arbitrarily to deny legal marriage to persons who are capable of performing marital acts and entering into the marital relationship. So, for example, laws forbidding interracial marriages truly were violations of equality. Contrary to the claims of Andrew Koppelman, Andrew Sullivan, and others, however, laws which embody the judgment that marriage is intrinsically heterosexual are in no way analogous to laws against miscegenation. Laws forbidding whites to marry blacks were unjust, not because they embodied a *particular* moral view and thus violated the alleged requirement of moral neutrality; rather, they were unjust because they embodied an *unsound* (indeed a grotesquely false) moral view—one that was racist and, as such, immoral.

Study Questions on Robert P. George

1. Explain George's conception of "one-flesh communion." Why does he think that sterile heterosexual marriages qualify? Are you persuaded? Why or why not? Do you think it makes any difference whether their childlessness is intentional or unintentional?

2. What about celibate marriages (i.e., ones in which the spouses refrain from sexual intercourse)?

3. Can the law (or the law of marriage) be neutral about the relative merits of homosexuality and heterosexuality? What if the state got out of the marriage business, and left the whole question to churches and other social institutions?

4. Suppose you believe that homosexual practices are legitimate, at least for some people under some circumstances. Could you nonetheless oppose proposals to institutionalize same-sex marriages?

The Question of Marriage: Two Arguments

DAVID ORGON COOLIDGE

David Orgon Coolidge addresses a question that many of you are likely to raise: How important would the recognition of same-sex marriages be really? He maintains that such recognition would have important harmful social effects.

Same-Sex Marriage Won't Make Any Real Difference to Society Anyway

PROPONENTS OF SAME-SEX MARRIAGE argue that its legalization will make no real difference. They paraphrase the now-famous words of Congressman Barney Frank, "What difference does it make to you if my partner and I can get married? How does it change you're your life in any real way?" At the same time, these advocates claim that legalizing same-sex marriage will be a tremendous achievement. In Andrew Sullivan's equally memorable words, "If nothing else were done at all, and gay marriage were legalized, ninety percent of the political work necessary to achieve gay and lesbian equality would have been achieved. It is ultimately the only reform that truly matters." Which is it? "No difference" or "Ninety percent"?

Of course the legalization of same-sex marriage will have dramatic effects; it is supposed to. The real debate is about whether these effects will be good.

For instance, legalizing same-sex marriage will send a new *moral message* to Americans about marriage: Marriage is based solely upon emotional and economic attachment, and those who disagree with this view are bigots who should not be allowed to "discriminate" against others.

It will also have a *legal impact*. This includes federal benefits, but the main effects will be at the state level, in the areas of marriage-related benefits, anti-discrimination laws based on marital status, adoption and child custody laws, public and private school curricula, nonprofit contracts with State and local government, private groups using public facilities, and professional licensing standards for lawyers, doctors, social workers and teachers, among others.

Finally, this moral message and legal impact cannot help but have profound *societal effects* over the long run. Those parents and associations who disagree with legalized same-sex marriage will be further alienated from mainstream America and its central institutions. There will be less support for marriage benefits in the workplace; benefits will be reduced, and more and more employers will give benefits only to individuals, leaving families to fend for themselves. Meanwhile, young people will grow up imbibing the official view that there is nothing special about the male-female family unit; it is only one item on the sexual smorgasboard of life. They will feel that they must experiment sexually in order to discover "who they really are." But since there will be no real answer to that question, the result will be deep confusion and many broken lives.

To some, these travails will be a sign of a transition to a more inclusive society; to others, they will be evidence of a society without standards, descending into chaos, prepared to suppress its own tradition of civic participation in the name of "equality."

Same-Sex Marriage Will Not Open a Pandora's Box, for Instance, to Polygamy

This is another argument about societal effects. Most proponents of same-sex marriage laugh off the question, or label it a diversion from the "real" issue. But the question of polygamy is not a diversion, because it highlights a perfectly legitimate substantive question: Once one drops the definition of marriage as the union of one man and one woman, why limit marriage to two people? Professor Chambers made precisely this point. Some gays and lesbians are personally interested in multiple partners, and some are not. There is no "pro-polygamy" movement on a grand scale. But that is not the issue: there is a logical implication here, and logical implications are especially powerful in legal settings. A change in the law based on the introduction of a new principle can begin "small" and quickly become "large," while its proponents deny responsibility for the results. In the case of America today, simple sexual anarchy is probably more likely than "polygamy," but anything could happen, and once the floodgates are opened, anything probably will happen. If and when it does, then the question will be whether there is any principled basis for opposing it. Supporters of the existing law have a valid basis for worrying that same-sex marriage will open a "Pandora's Box" and be unable to close it.

Study Questions on David Orgon Coolidge

1. What effects does Coolidge expect the legal recognition of same-sex marriages to have? Do you agree with his expectations?
2. Do you agree that these effects would be socially damaging? Which of the writers reprinted here would welcome them, and which regret them?
3. If same-sex marriage is legally recognized, is there any *principled* ground for refusing similar recognition to polygamous unions?
4. Would legal recognition of homosexual domestic partnerships or civil unions have the same effects as recognition of homosexual marriages? What about the repeal or judicial invalidation of laws making homosexual practices criminal?

Since When Is Marriage a Path to Liberation?

PAULA ETTELBRICK

A lesbian writer, Paula Ettelbrick argues that same-sex marriage would not further the radical program: "we will be liberated only when we are respected and accepted for our differences and the diversity we provide to this society."

A traditional leftist worries about what same-sex marriage would do to the radical agenda.

"MARRIAGE IS A GREAT INSTITUTION . . . if you like living in institutions," according to a bit of T-shirt philosophy I saw recently. Certainly, marriage is an institution. It is one of the most venerable, impenetrable institutions in modern society. Marriage provides the ultimate form of acceptance for personal, intimate relationships in our society, and gives those who marry an insider status of the most powerful kind.

Steeped in a patriarchal system that looks to ownership, property, and dominance of men over

Reprinted by permission of the author. Paula Ettelbrick is the Family Policy Director for the Policy Institute of the National Gay & Lesbian Task Force.

women as its basis, the institution of marriage has long been the focus of radical-feminist revulsion. Marriage defines certain relationships as more valid than all others. Lesbian and gay relationships, being neither legally sanctioned nor commingled by blood, are always at the bottom of the heap of social acceptance and importance.

Given the imprimatur of social and personal approval that marriage provides, it is not surprising that some lesbians and gay men among us would look to legal marriage for self-affirmation. After all, those who marry can be instantaneously transformed from "outsiders" to "insiders," and we have a desperate need to become insiders.

It could make us feel okay about ourselves, perhaps even relieve some of the internalized homophobia that we all know so well. Society will then celebrate the birth of our children and mourn the death of our spouses. It would be easier to get health insurance for our spouses, family memberships to the local museum, and a right to inherit our spouse's cherished collection of lesbian mystery novels even if she failed to draft a will. Never again would we have to go to a family reunion and debate about the correct term for introducing our lover/partner/significant other to Aunt Flora. Everything would be quite easy and very nice.

So why does this unlikely event so deeply disturb me? For two major reasons. First, marriage will not liberate us as lesbians and gay men. In fact, it will constrain us, make us more invisible, force our assimilation into the mainstream, and undermine the goals of gay liberation. Second, attaining the right to marry will not transform our society from one that makes narrow, but dramatic, distinctions between those who are married and those who are not married to one that respects and encourages choice of relationships and family diversity. Marriage runs contrary to two of the primary goals of the lesbian and gay movement: the affirmation of gay identity and culture and the validation of many forms of relationships.

When analyzed from the standpoint of civil rights, certainly lesbians and gay men should have a right to marry. But obtaining a right does not always result in justice. White male firefighters in Birmingham, Alabama, have been fighting for their "rights" to retain their jobs by overturning the city's affirmative-action guidelines. If their "rights"

prevail, the courts will have failed in rendering justice. The "right" fought for by the white male firefighters, as well as those who advocate strongly for the "rights" to legal marriage for gay people, will result, at best, in limited or narrowed "justice" for those closest to power at the expense of those who have been historically marginalized. . . .

Justice for gay men and lesbians will be achieved only when we are accepted and supported in this society despite our differences from the dominant culture and the choices we make regarding our relationships. Being queer is more than setting up house, sleeping with a person of the same gender, and seeking state approval for doing so. It is an identity, a culture with many variations. It is a way of dealing with the world by diminishing the constraints of gender roles that have for so long kept women and gay people oppressed and invisible. Being queer means pushing the parameters of sex, sexuality, and family, and in the process transforming the very fabric of society. Gay liberation is inexorably linked to women's liberation. Each is essential to the other.

The moment we argue, as some among us insist on doing, that we should be treated as equals because we are really just like married couples and hold the same values to be true, we undermine the very purpose of our movement and begin the dangerous process of silencing our different voices. As a lesbian, I am fundamentally different from non-lesbian women. That's the point. Marriage, as it exists today, is antithetical to my liberation as a lesbian and as a woman because it mainstreams my life and voice. I do not want to be known as "Mrs. Attached-To-Somebody-Else." Nor do I want to give the state the power to regulate my primary relationship. . . .

By looking to our sameness and de-emphasizing our differences, we do not even place ourselves in a position of power that would allow us to transform marriage from an institution that emphasizes property and state regulation of relationships to an institution that recognizes one of many types of valid and respected relationships. Until the Constitution is interpreted to respect and encourage differences, pursuing the legalization of same-sex marriage would be leading our movement into a trap; we would be demanding access to the very institution that, in its current form, would undermine our movement to recognize many different kinds of relationships. We would be perpetuating the elevation of married relationships and of "couples" in general, and further eclipsing other relationships of choice.

Ironically, gay marriage, instead of liberating gay sex and sexuality, would further outlaw all gay and lesbian sex that is not performed in a marital context. Just as sexually active nonmarried women face stigma and double standards around sex and sexual activity, so too would nonmarried gay people. The only legitimate gay sex would be that which is cloaked in and regulated by marriage. Its legitimacy would stem not from an acceptance of gay sexuality, but because the Supreme Court and society in general fiercely protect the privacy of marital relationships. Lesbians and gay men who do not seek the state's stamp of approval would clearly face increased sexual oppression. . . .

Marriage creates a two-tier system that allows the state to regulate relationships. It has become a facile mechanism for employers to dole out benefits, for businesses to provide special deals and incentives, and for the law to make distinctions in distributing meager public funds. None of these entities bothers to consider the relationship among people; the love, respect, and need to protect that exists among all kinds of family members. Rather, a simple certificate of the state, regardless of whether the spouses love, respect, or even see each other on a regular basis, dominates and is supported. None of this dynamic will change if gay men and lesbians are given the option of marriage. . . .

It is crucial . . . that we avoid the pitfall of framing the push for legal recognition of domestic partners (those who share a primary residence and financial responsibilities for each other) as a stepping-stone to marriage. We must keep our eyes on the goals of providing true alternatives to marriage and of radically reordering society's view of family. . . . We must not fool ourselves into believing that marriage will make it acceptable to be gay or lesbian. We will be liberated only when we are respected and accepted for our differences and the diversity we provide to this society. Marriage is not a path to that liberation.

Study Questions on Paula Ettelbrick

1. Why does Ettelbrick find the appeal of same-sex marriage fraudulent? Is there something about same-sex relationships that makes marriage inappropriate, or is marriage a bad thing for everybody?
2. What would be the implications of same-sex marriage for those lesbians and gay men who did not seek state approval for their relationships?
3. What does liberation mean for Ettelbrick? What does it require of the larger society? Do you find this ideal attractive?
4. What would Ettelbrick say about Sullivan? What would Sullivan say about Ettelbrick?

Retying the Knot

E. J. GRAFF

> E. J. Graff argues that same-sex marriage is, in fact, a radical step. She argues that it transforms one of the most powerful institutions of society.

THE RIGHT WING GETS IT: Same-sex marriage is a breathtakingly subversive idea. So it's weirdly dissonant when gay neocons and feminist lesbians publicly insist—the former with enthusiasm, the latter with distaste—that same-sex marriage would be a conservative move, confining sexual free radicals inside some legal cellblock. It's almost as odd (although more understandable) when pro-marriage liberals ply the rhetoric of fairness and love, as if no one will notice that for thousands of years marriage has meant Boy + Girl = Babies. But same-sex marriage seems fair only if you accept a philosophy of marriage that, although it's gained ground in the past several centuries, still strikes many as radical: the idea that marriage (and therefore sex) is justified not by reproduction but by love.

Sound like old news? Not if you're the Christian Coalition, the Pope or the Orthodox rabbinate, or if you simply live in one of many pre-industrial countries. Same-sex marriage will be a direct hit against the religious right's goal of re-enshrining biology as destiny. Marriage is an institution that towers on our social horizon, defining how we think about one another, formalizing contact with our families, neighborhoods, employers, insurers, hospitals, governments. Allowing two people of the same sex to marry shifts that institution's message.

From The Nation *(June 14, 1996). © 1996 by E. J. Graff. Reprinted by permission of the author.*

Study Questions on E. J. Graff

1. Explain the two different philosophies of sex and marriage that Graff believes are at work in the debate over same-sex unions. Are they the only philosophies of marriage possible?
2. Do you agree with Graff that "allowing two people of the same sex to marry shifts that institution's message"? If so, is this proposed shift of message a good one?
3. How would George respond to Graff? How would Sullivan? How would Coolidge?
4. What weight, if any, do *you* give to the fact that "for thousands of years marriage has meant Boy + Girl = Babies"?

For Further Reading

Alger, Jonathan. "Love, Lust, and the Law." *Academe,* 84, no. 5 (September 1, 1998), 34ff.

Altman, Andrew. "Making Sense of Sexual Harassment Law." *Philosophy and Public Affairs,* 25, no. 1 (Winter 1996), 36ff.

Anthony, Louise B., and Charlotte Witt, eds. *A Mind of One's Own: Feminist Essays on Reason and Objectivity.* Boulder, Colo.: Westview, 1992.

Bane, Mary Jo, and Kenneth Winston. *Gender and Public Policy: Cases and Comments.* Boulder, Colo.: Westview, 1992.

Becker, Mary, Cynthia Grant Bowman, and Morrison Torrey, eds. *Feminist Jurisprudence: Taking Women Seriously: Cases and Materials.* American Casebook Series. St. Paul, Minn.: West, 1994.

Blasius, Mike, and Shane Phelan, eds. *We Are Everywhere: A Historical Sourcebook of Gay and Lesbian Politics.* New York: Routledge, 1997.

Califia, Pat. *Sex Changes: The Politics of Transgenderism.* San Francisco: Cleis, 1997.

Cohen, Cathy J. "Straight Gay Politics." *Nomos,* 39 (1997), 572–616.

Crosthwiate, Jan, and Graham Priest. "The Definition of Sexual Harassment." *Australasian Journal of Philosophy,* 84, no. 1 (March 1996), 66-82.

Davidson, Nicholas. *The Failure of Feminism.* Buffalo, N.Y.: Prometheus, 1988.

Devine, Philip E. *Human Diversity and the Culture Wars.* Westport, Conn.: Praeger, 1996.

Elshtain, Jean Bethke. *Public Man, Private Woman.* Princeton, N.J.: Princeton University Press, 1981.

_____, ed. *The Family in Political Thought.* Amherst: University of Massachusetts Press, 1982.

English, Jane, ed. *Sex Equality.* Englewood Cliffs, N.J.: Prentice-Hall, 1977.

Epstein, Cynthia Fuchs. *Women's Place.* Berkeley: University of California Press, 1971.

Farrell, Warren. *The Myth of Male Power.* New York: Simon & Schuster, 1993.

Firestone, Shulamith. *The Dialectics of Sex.* New York: Bantam, 1971.

Fox-Genovese, Elizabeth. *Feminism Is NOT the Story of My Life.* New York: Nan A. Talese (Doubleday), 1996.

_____. "Severing the Ties That Bind." *Intercollegiate Review,* 34, no. 1 (Fall 1998), 26–30. A good short statement of her argument.

Friedan, Betty. *Beyond Gender.* Brigid O'Farrell, ed. Washington, D.C.: Woodrow Wilson Center Press, 1997. Second thoughts by a founder of the contemporary women's movement.

Frye, Marilyn. "Lesbian Feminism and the Gay Rights Movement." In *The Crossing* (1983). Reprinted in Mike Blasius and Shane Phelan, eds., *We are Everywhere: A Historical Sourcebook of Gay and Lesbian Politics.* New York: Routledge, 1997. Pp. 498–510.

Furchtgott-Roth, Diana, and Christine Stolba. *Women's Figures: The Economic Progress of Women in America.* Arlington, Va.: Independent Women's Forum; Washington, D.C.: American Enterprise Institute, ca. 1996.

Gallagher, Maggie, and Barbara Defoe Whitehead. "End No-Fault Divorce?" *First Things,* no. 75 (August/September, 1997), 24–30.

Gearhart, Sally Miller. "The Future—If There Is One—Is Female." In Pam McAllister, ed., *Reweaving the Web of Life*. Philadelphia: New Society Publishers, 1982.

George, Robert P. "Public Reason and Political Conflict: Abortion and Homosexuality." *Yale Law Journal,* 106, no. 8 (June 1997), 2475–2504.

Glendon, Mary Ann. *Abortion and Divorce in Western Law*. Cambridge, Mass.: Harvard University Press, 1987.

Greer, Germain. *The Female Eunuch*. New York: Random House, 1979.

Held, Virginia. *Feminist Morality: Transforming Culture, Society, and Politics*. Chicago: University of Chicago Press, 1993.

Hewlett, Sylvia Ann. *A Lesser Life*. New York: Morrow, 1986. Criticizes conventional feminism as not in the interests of women and children.

Humm, Maggie, ed. *Modern Feminisms*. New York: Columbia University Press, 1992. Note the plural.

Illich, Ivan. *Gender*. New York: Pantheon, 1962. An elusive discussion by a severe critic of industrial society.

Jaggar, Alison, and Paula S. Rothenberg, eds. *Feminist Frameworks*. New York: McGraw-Hill, 1993. Note the plural.

Kaminer, Wendy. *A Fearful Freedom*. Reading, Mass.: Addison-Wesley, 1990. Attempts to rally support for the assimilationist cause.

Kennedy, Eugene. *Bernardin: Life to the Full*. Chicago: Bonus Books, 1997.

Macedo, Stephen. "Homosexuality and the Conservative Mind," and articles following. *Georgetown Law Review,* 84 (1995), 261ff.

MacKinnon, Catharine. *Only Words*. Cambridge, Mass.: Harvard University Press, 1993.

Mansfield, Harvey. "Why a Good Man Is Hard to Find." *The Women's Quarterly,* no. 17 (August 1998), 4–6. Feminism liberated men, too.

Matthews-Green, Frederica. *Real Choices*. Ben Lomand, Calif.: Concilliar Press, 1997.

McKenna, George. "On Abortion: A Lincolnian Position." *Atlantic Monthly* (September, 1995), 51–68.

Mill, John Stuart. *On the Subjection of Women*. Greenwich, Conn.: Fawcett, 1979.

Millett, Kate. *Sexual Politics*. New York: Doubleday, 1970.

Morgan, Marabel. *The Total Woman*. Old Tappan, N.J.: Fleming H. Revell Co., 1973.

Nussbaum, Martha C., and Jonathan Glover, eds. *Women, Culture, and Development*. Oxford: Clarendon, 1995.

Okin, Susan Miller. *Women in Western Political Thought*. Princeton: Princeton University Press, 1979.

Patai, Daphne. *Heterophobia*. Lanham, Md.: Rowman & Littlefield, 1998.

_____, and Norette Kortege. *Professing Feminism*. New York: Basic Books, 1994.

Preston, John. "Goodbye to Sally Gerhardt." In Mike Blasius and Shane Phelan, eds., *We Are Everywhere: A Historical Sourcebook of Gay and Lesbian Politics*. New York: Routledge, 1997. Pp. 511–521.

Rawls, John. "The Idea of Public Reason Revisited." *University of Chicago Law Review* 64, no. 3 (Summer 1997), 765–802. Contains his response to Okin.

Rhaods, Heather. "Cruel Crusade: The Holy War Against Lesbians and Gays." *Progressive* (March 1993), 18ff.

Rich, Adrienne. *Arts of the Possible: Essays and Conversations*. New York: W. W. Norton, 2001.

Rutherglen, George. "Sexual Harassment: Ideology or Law?" *Harvard Journal of Law & Public Policy,* 18, no. 2 (Spring 1995), 487–499.

Sandel, Michael J. *Liberalism and the Limits of Justice.* 2nd ed. Cambridge: Cambridge University Press, 1998. Includes an up-to-date discussion of liberal ideas of "public reason," especially as applied to issues concerning abortion and gay rights.

Sen, Amartya. "More than 100 Million Women Are Missing." *New York Review of Books* (Christmas 1990), 61–66.

Sommers, Christina Hoff. *The War Against Boys.* New York: Simon & Schuster, 2000.

_____. *Who Stole Feminism?* New York: Simon & Schuster, 1994. Both books are highly polemical.

Steinem, Gloria. "Erotica and Pornography." *Ms.* (November 1978), 53ff.

Sterba, James P. "Reconciling Public Reason and Religious Values." *Social Theory and Practice,* 25, no. 1 (Spring 1999), 1ff.

Sullivan, Andrew, ed. *Same-Sex Marriage: Pro and Con: A Reader.* New York: Vintage (Random House), 1997. In addition to the selections reprinted here, see Frank Browning, "Why Marry?" for a rejection of same-sex marriage by a gay man.

Szikla, Christine. "Lesbianism: Dispelling the Myths." Published by Women's Issues and Social Empowerment (Melbourne, Australia), http://www.infoexchange.net.au/wise/HEALTH/Les0.htm.

Vaid, Urvashi. *Virtual Equality: The Mainstreaming of Gay and Lesbian Liberation.* New York: Doubleday Anchor, 1995.

Wiley, Juli Loesch. "Why Feminists and Prolifers Need Each Other." *New Oxford Review,* 60 (November 1993), 9–14.

Wolf-Devine, Celia. *Diversity and Community in the Academy: Affirmative Action in Faculty Appointments.* Lanham, Md.: Rowman & Littlefield, 1997.

Wolfe, Christopher, ed. *Homosexuality and American Public Life.* Dallas, Tex.: Spence, 1999. Includes extensive discussion of same-sex marriage.

Wolstonecraft, Mary. *A Vindication of the Rights of Women.* Charles W. Hegelman, ed. New York: W. W. Norton, 1967.

Young, Iris. *Justice and the Politics of Difference.* Princeton, N.J.: Princeton University Press, 1990.

INFOTRAC COLLEGE EDITION To learn more about the topics from this chapter, you can use the following words to conduct an electronic search on InfoTrac College Edition, an online library of journals. Here you will find a multitude of articles from various sources and perspectives: *www.infotrac-college.com/wadsworth/access.html*

Community Values	Rights
Feminism	Same-Sex Marriage
Gays and Lesbians	Sex-Based Affirmative Action
Liberalism	Sexual Equality
Private Behavior	Sexual Harassment
Public Reason	Sexual Justice

Web Sites

Biatch, Rabbi Jonathan. *"Private, Public Behavior Must Be in Harmony"* (Torah Study)
http://www.jewishorg.com/jewishnews.00512/torah.shtml

Citizens for Community Values
http://www.ccv.org

Facts About Sexual Harassment (EEOC)
http://www.eeoc.gov/facts/fs-sex

Gays and Lesbian Alliance Against Defamation
http://www.glaad.org/org/index.html

Human Rights Web
http://www.hr.web.org/

Independent Women's Forum
http://www.iwf.org

Liberalism (Stanford Encylopedia of Philosophy)
http://www.plato.stanford.edu/entries/liberalism/

Origins of Affirmative Action for Women (Feminist Majority Foundation)
http://www.feminist.org.other/ccri/aafact.html

Religion Project Web Page: Religious Declaration on Sexual Morality, Justice and Healing (Sexual Information and Education Council of the United States)
http://www.religionproject.org/declaration.html

Same Sex Marriage Laws Across the United States (CNN.com)
http://www.cnn.com/2000/LAW/05/25/same.sex.marriages

Sunstein, Cass R., *"Sexual Equality v. Religion"*
http://www.bostonreview.mit.edu/BR 23.5/Sunstein.html

Unit VI

Religion: Naming the Supreme Being

SEXUALITY HAS COSMIC SIGNIFICANCE for a number of reasons. On an individual level, there is a deep similarity between the sexual impulse and the religious impulse; both are connected with a sense of one's own incompleteness and a longing for wholeness. Thus mystics in many traditions have recourse to sexual metaphors to describe the soul's union with God, and lovers often employ religious imagery in their poems. Aristophanes in Plato's *Symposium* explains all sexual desire by the hypothesis that there were once globular creatures with four arms, four legs, and two faces who were sliced in half by Zeus, leaving each half "with a desperate yearning for the other," so that when we are "longing after and following after that primeval wholeness, we say we are in love." And Augustine, addressing God, exclaims "Thou has made us for Thyself, and our hearts are restless until they find rest in Thee."

The struggle over sex and gender issues, then, is not limited to the relationships individuals have to each other, nor even to questions about what sorts of social structures we should set up; it also extends to questions about the nature of Ultimate Reality. There has been a recurrent tendency in the religious history of humankind to think of Ultimate Reality in ways structured by the concepts of male and female, masculine and feminine, father and mother. This is the case even for religions that do not believe in a personal god. Taoists, for example, regard the *Yang* and *Yin* principles as fundamental to the deep structure of reality, and see them as complementary. *Yang* is hot, dry, active, light, and masculine, while *yin* is cold, moist, passive, dark, and feminine. *Yang* is movement; *yin* is rest.

As Eliade points out, "For religious man, nature is never only 'natural'; it is always fraught with a religious value." Being viewed as the handiwork of the gods, the world is taken to reveal various modalities of the sacred. Contemplation of the sky reveals transcendence, infinity, eternity, and a kind of absolute existence. The gods of many primitive people are called by names designating height—the "sky dweller," the "most high." Such gods are thought of in masculine terms such as

"Lord," "Chief," or "Father." The sacredness of the Earth, by contrast, sponta-neously reveals itself as *Terra Mater* (Mother Earth), universal genetrix who gives birth to all things. The sacrality of women (their magico-religious prestige), then, depends on the holiness of the earth, and feminine fecundity has a cosmic model in Mother Earth. Some religions regard the Cosmic Mother as capable of conceiv-ing alone, while others believe that creation results from a sacred marriage between the Sky God and Mother Earth. Human marriage would, in this latter view, be viewed as a kind of imitation of the cosmic marriage. "I am Heaven . . . thou art Earth!" the husband proclaims in a Hindu wedding ritual. And ritual orgies in the fields, as practiced in some ancient Near Eastern religions, might be expected by a kind of sympathetic magic to increase the fertility of the soil.

The use of parental imagery to refer to God is a recurrent pattern in human religious history also because so many of the world's religions see the world as the creation of God (or the gods), and it is through our parents that we receive life. God has no body, of course, and thus any application of sexual imagery to God is not strictly literal—among American religious groups, only Mormons might con-test this point. But it does seem that the language we use in talking about God is important. The readings in this unit focus on the problem of naming the Supreme Being in monotheistic religions; polytheistic or nontheistic religions raise a differ-ent set of problems. In choosing what language should be used to refer to God, it is helpful to look at the differing connotations of the terms *father* and *mother* first in a purely naturalistic context.

Differing Natural Connotations of the Terms Father and Mother

DIFFERING ROLES IN REPRODUCTION

Since the roles of the father and mother in reproduction are so different, calling God "Father" conveys very different things from calling God "Mother." The father is necessarily active; his act initiates the process of reproduction. Hence, as Loesch Wiley points out, paternal imagery emphasizes God's activity in creation. The child develops within the mother's body, tied to her by the umbilical cord, and literally takes his or her physical substance from the mother. To think of the source of our being as "Mother," thus, conjures up images of immanence; we are some-how within the mother or continuous with her. To think of the source of our being as "father," by contrast, emphasizes the mysteriousness, remoteness, and tran-scendence of God; He initiates the process, but remains outside it. Who some-one's mother is is never in doubt, whereas paternity can be unknown (and some nineteenth century anthropologists supposed that entire cultures were ignorant of the biological facts of paternity). These sorts of associations with the word *father,* then, reinforce the connection between thinking of God as "Father" and the notion of transcendence, which Eliade discovered in so many cosmic religions.

DIFFERENCES IN THE INFANT'S RELATIONSHIP WITH FATHER AND MOTHER

Finally, still reflecting about the notion of "God the Father" independently of par-ticular religious traditions and their revealed scriptures, Freudians have claimed that children experience maternal power and paternal power very differently, and this means that thinking of God as Father will have very different emotional and cognitive resonances from thinking of God as Mother. The infant perceives Mother as an enormously powerful person, feels helplessly dependent on her for nourishment and care, and experiences a pull toward a dissolution of the self back into the mother (hence the association of the mother with dissolution and death as well as with nurturing and life manifested, for example, in the Hindu cult of Kali, the dark goddess who wears a necklace of skulls and drinks blood). Paternal power is experienced as more remote; Father sets limits and lays down rules for us to follow. While Mother may always be ready to forgive and shelter us, Father holds us accountable for our actions. He thus calls us out of a regressive over-identification with mother and into objectivity and responsibility. This association of the father with authority and judgment is connected with Freud's suggestion that the father is associated with what he calls the "reality principle." As a result of Freud's association between the father and the reality principle, those in the Freudian tradition are likely to see in "God the Father" the principle that limits our pursuit of gratification—the objective reality that stands over and against us and our desires.

God the Father in Revelation

Those Americans who are religious are mainly Jewish, Christian, or Moslem. Revelation as understood in these traditions is connected with nature in complex ways. It takes up already existing natural imagery and symbolism, but it also builds on it and adds new levels of meaning. The very notion of revelation presupposes a God who breaks into history "from a place beyond the natural order of things" (to use Tamar Frankiel's phrase). Much of the debate in America has focused on how we should think of the one Supreme Being—for example, on whether or not Christians should call God "Father," and on the implications this has for the role of women (both within religious institutions and in society at large).

If we look at the scriptures of the three major monotheistic religions, we find that God is referred to using primarily (although not exclusively) masculine imagery. In the Hebrew scriptures, terms are used that imply majesty, dominion, and kingship. He is described as a mighty warrior, or as "Lord of Hosts," for example. Jesus teaches his disciples to call God "Father" in the "Lord's Prayer" recited by Christians everywhere. In Genesis 1-3, where pronouns are used to refer to God, they are masculine. The centrality of the male-female distinction to the created order is also clearly conveyed by Genesis 1:27 which says "male and female he created them." Allah, likewise, is thought of in strongly masculine terms. Differing and complementary sex roles for men and women in Jewish, Christian, and Moslem cultures have roots in their sacred scriptures. There are already hints of differing roles for men and women in the passage from Genesis, reprinted here, both in the meaning of the names given to Adam and Eve (as Edith Black points out), and in the different forms of punishment to which Adam and Eve are subject after the Fall. For Moslems, different roles for men and women are clearly set out in the divine law which is based on the *Koran* and the *Hadith,* and Jewish religious law assigns certain important duties specifically to women and others to men.

Philosophical and Cultural Background to the Current Debate

ATHEISTIC PROJECTION THEORIES

Theologians and philosophers have, for centuries, puzzled over how human language can possibly describe the mysterious and transcendent God of faith; but in the twentieth century, discussion about religious language took on a new character. It is not just that human language is thought inadequate to describe God; rather "God" has come to be viewed by many people as *only* a human creation—a kind of projection of human ideals or hopes onto the void (or onto chaos).

The most important sources of this type of projection theory were Marx, Nietzsche, and Freud. All three were atheists, and attempted to account for the origins of people's belief in a "God" in naturalistic terms. They understood the nature of the projection mechanism involved somewhat differently, but for all of them, God is understood as a kind of human creation. Freud, for example, thought that we project into the Heavens our infantile image of the all-powerful father who loves and protects us because the harshness of reality is too hard to bear (the "religion as crutch" view). Marx, following Feuerbach, thought that "God" was a kind of projection of the ideal human essence which we project onto God because oppressive social institutions make it impossible to realize the fullness of our human essence here below. For Nietzsche, all systems of thought, including religion, were projections onto the Abyss undertaken by people whose will to power is very strong. Ideally, these would be superior people called *Übermenschen,* who create "new values" in full consciousness of their arbitrary character. But in the case of Judaism and Christianity, they have been members of a priestly class whose will to power is expressed in a way filled with resentment. But the projection of God and an eternal realm of forms established by our spiritual forbearers has failed, and we (or rather the most perceptive and spiritually potent among us) are now faced with the task of creating "new values." (This is the meaning of his notorious claim that God is dead.)

THE POLITICIZATION OF LANGUAGE

Another important development in the twentieth century was the intense politicization of language. Philosophers became increasingly aware of the role of language in shaping our thought (in the analytic tradition, for example, through the influence of Wittgenstein, and in the continental tradition, for example, in the work of Derrida). On a more popular level, advertisers, politicians, and the media generally became very delicately attuned to the ways in which the language we use to describe something affects the way people will respond to it. Many people, therefore, sought to modify people's behavior and ways of thinking by trying to get them to use certain words and not others. Calling people "senior citizens" instead of "old" or "elderly," for example, would, they hoped, engender in us a more respectful attitude toward them, and gender-neutral or inclusive language was advocated as a way of combating sexist ways of thinking. So those who accepted the view that "God" is a human creation, if they did not simply reject religion as Freud, Marx, and Nietzsche did, often viewed the question of what language we should use to talk about God as a political choice to be made on the basis of which one would most effectively advance social movements of which they approved, such as feminism or the ecological movement.

Disputes about what language we should use to refer to God, therefore, are often highly politicized. It would, however, be a serious oversimplification to suppose that the only players on the field are traditional believers who insist on calling God "Father" and atheists who are trying to use religion as a political tool. Many people who regard the Bible as an authoritative text revealed by God also object to the exclusive use of male pronouns and images to refer to God. And in between the traditional believers and those whose approach to religion is a purely instrumental one, there is a large number of half-believers, proponents of new religions, people who advocate return to pagan religions, and a lot of people who are just generally bewildered about what to think. People are often in internal conflict about their religious beliefs, and determining when a person has abandoned enough of the traditional teachings of a religion to be classified as no longer adhering to it can be difficult. The purpose of this unit is simply to get the important arguments for and against calling God "Father" out in the open. The essays in this unit, then, include both critics of traditional religious language and responses by more traditional believers.

Reasons Given Against Calling God "Father"

Why have people objected to the use of paternal imagery to refer to God? In discussing this, we need to distinguish between reasons why a given individual might be uncomfortable with such imagery, and reasons that should persuade other people to either reject the religion entirely or insist that the religious community in question cease using masculine imagery to refer to God in its worship services. Painful experiences with one's father, for example, might make the use of the term *Father* to refer to God a stumbling block for some would-be believers. Most critics of traditional language about God, however, offer reasons for preferring other language that are not simply based on their own experiences or feelings, since others may have had quite different experiences that lead them to prefer traditional language. Bad relationships with one's father, although common, are not universal, and many people have had equally bad relationships with their mothers.

There are broadly three different types of criticism that have been offered of the use of paternal imagery to talk about God. One objection, offered from within the religious traditions themselves, is that exclusive use of paternal imagery leaves out important aspects of God's self-revelation in Scripture. (Richard Davis and Susanne Heine emphasize this point.) A second objection is that calling God "Father" reinforces a patriarchal social structure (a hierarchical one in which women are consistently kept in a subordinate position) and is therefore damaging to women (Carol Christ, Elizabeth Johnson, and Rosemary Radford Ruether all make this type of argument). And the third objection, made by ecologists, is that the emphasis on the transcendence of God conveyed by paternal imagery has led to an overemphasis on human superiority over the rest of nature (since human beings are said to be created "in the image of God"), and that this has encouraged human beings to adopt a manipulative and exploitative approach toward nature. Ecofeminists (represented here by Rosemary Radford Ruether) combine the second and third objections, arguing that oppression of women and exploitation of nature are interconnected phenomena. Some serious believers concede that their religious tradition has, in fact, interpreted some passages of scripture in ways that license oppression of women or exploitation of nature, but insist that such interpretations are one-sided and distorted and that, taken as a whole and rightly understood, the revealed scriptures do not license these sorts of sinful behavior. Tamar Frankiel and Edith Black take this approach, and Leila Ahmad (listed in the For Further Reading section of this unit) makes the same sort of argument for the *Koran*.

Preview of Readings

The first reading by Mircea Eliade documents the pervasive use of parental imagery in human religious history, particularly the pattern in which the sky god associated with the vast celestial vault is called "lord," "chief," "father," or "most high," while the Earth is regarded as sacred and conceived as the Cosmic Mother who gives birth to all things. The second reading is from the creation story in the book of Genesis and provides the biblical background for the subsequent articles. There are two slightly different accounts of creation. Scholars generally take the second one (in Genesis 2) to have an earlier historical origin, since it is less abstract and theologically sophisticated and describes God as forming Adam from the dust of the ground and breathing into his nostrils the breath of life. Genesis 3 describes the fall of Adam and Eve and their expulsion from paradise.

God the Father and the Legitimation of Patriarchy

Carol Christ, in the selection here, rejects Judaism and Christianity because she believes that religions that think of the Supreme Being as male produce an association in people's minds between masculinity and the exercise of power, so that the exercise of power by women is regarded as anomalous or suspect in some way. God symbolism in Christianity undergirds the interests of men in patriarchy by creating certain sorts of moods and motivations. Worship of the Great Goddess is, she believes, necessary for the empowerment of women—to help them affirm the legitimacy and beneficence of female power. Worship of the Great Goddess will, she argues, help women to trust in their own power, celebrate their bodies, and believe that they can achieve their own wills in the world.

Elizabeth Johnson's position is more nuanced. She does not begin with a root-and-branch rejection of the Judeo-Christian tradition as Carol Christ does. Starting instead from the theological point that God is, after all, wholly ineffable, and no human language can truly describe God's being, she argues that to fix on masculine imagery is a kind of idolatry—putting the image of a created thing in place of God. Since no language is adequate to God, she therefore concludes that it is legitimate to bring in nontheological reasons for using feminine pronouns to refer to God—for example, its effect on the social and political position of women. She considers and rejects other ways of balancing exclusive use of male imagery by emphasizing the feminine aspects of God while still thinking of God predominantly as "Father," or by feminizing the Holy Spirit. Ultimately she hopes that people will be able to use male and female images equally to talk about God, but in order to correct for the long-standing androcentric bias in God language and reorient our imaginations and recover the dignity of women created in the image of God, it is necessary now to deliberately employ feminine images to describe and name the divine.

Juli Loesch Wiley takes issue with those feminists who claim that thinking of God as "Father" supports patriarchy, arguing that in fact the authority of God the Father provides a check on the power of human fathers, since God stands in judgment of them and holds them accountable if they violate the God-given rights of women and children. She also notes that Christians call God "Father" because Jesus did (since God *was* his father) and that Christians, being "baptized into Christ" take on the same relationship to God that Jesus had. Finally, she argues that feminist psychoanalytic theory itself suggests that thinking of God as "Mother" could be disastrous.

Richard Davis, like Wiley, emphasizes the prophetic dimension of religion, and sees God as a being with power, authority, and majesty who stands in judgment of us and our ways. Since he does not regard God as merely a projection of the human psyche, he evaluates religious language in terms of the way it facilitates or impedes the worshipper's relationship with God. While noting that the Bible contains many passages in which feminine imagery is used to describe God, he opposes those who wish to feminize God by excluding male symbols, male images, and male pronouns from the common worship of the Christian community. The feminization of God is of more than merely theoretical interest to him, because as a gay man, he personally tends to think of God as a masculine lover.

Susan Heine emphasizes the transcendence of God as a check on the uses of both masculine and feminine imagery. She argues that if those who are abused by their fathers can find consolation in the figure of a heavenly Mother, those with abusive mothers can find consolation in the figure of a heavenly Father. For that matter, those with abusive fathers could find in God the good Father they need and be healed of their emotional wounds in this way.

Gary Culpepper responds directly to Elizabeth Johnson. As a theologian, he is concerned about the way in which suggested linguistic changes may affect central Christian doctrines. Specifically, he argues that the Christian understanding of the Trinity (the belief that God is three persons in one—Father, Son and Holy Spirit) makes it appropriate to call God "Father," for God is father in a more than merely metaphorical way (as, for example, He might be called "rock"), since He is the eternal father of the eternal son—Jesus. And we cannot call the same person both "mother" and "father" without falling into equivocation.

THE ECOFEMINIST CRITIQUE

Ecofeminists (represented here by Rosemary Radford Ruether) argue that by employing masculine imagery in thinking of God, we set up an ontological hierarchy in which males are above females; males more nearly reflect God's image as spiritual, rational, and transcendent, while females are identified with the body, emotion, and nature. Thus, not only do human beings generally see themselves as entitled to dominate and use nature in any way they want, since they have a mental or spiritual dimension the rest of creation lacks, but within the human species male human beings are higher than females on this same scale, and are thus entitled to dominate and use them.

The positive vision of the ecofeminists emphasizes our immanence in nature and the interconnectedness of human beings with each other and with nature.

Hierarchical dualism in which spirit is separated from nature and regarded as superior to it should be abandoned in favor of a more holistic and organic vision of human beings as part of nature. Nonviolence and egalitarianism are also important in a way they are not for people like Carol Christ. The ecofeminist critique of the status quo is thus a deeper one, since ecofeminists are not just trying to move women up the ladder into more powerful positions in society, but are also envisioning radical social changes that would make society more egalitarian. (See, also, Wolf-Devine's account of ecofeminism in her article on abortion in Unit III.)

Edith Black responds to the ecofeminists by analyzing the first three chapters of Genesis, pointing out that Adam and Eve are equally in the image of God, and that there is nothing in the text to indicate that women are less rational or more carnal than men. Since the sin of both Adam and Eve was one of disobeying God by wanting to become like God oneself—living forever and having knowledge of good and evil—it would seem that Eve was more in the grip of inordinate spiritual ambition than carnal desire (she did not, after all, eat the fruit for its taste). The fact that Eve is held responsible for her action and punished clearly indicates that she is regarded by God as a rational being with free will just as much as Adam is. And, Black argues, the text of Genesis 3 indicates that patriarchy is a result of the Fall, and not part of God's original intention. Finally, she argues, feminists have tended to focus too much on the sin of Eve, neglecting the essential role played by Mary, the mother of Jesus, in the salvation of humankind (she has been accorded the title "Mother of God" by the Church). Also called the "second Eve," Mary, by cooperating with God's plan, reversed the sin of disobedience committed by Adam and Eve, and made reconciliation with God possible by giving birth to the Redeemer. As the greatest of the saints, she stands as a model of perfected humanity.

Tamar Frankiel responds to the ecofeminist argument from within the Jewish tradition, arguing that the sort of mind/body or spirit/matter dualism the ecofeminists criticize is Greek and not Hebraic in origin, and that God's transcendence should not be understood in terms of His being made of different (spiritual) stuff, but that His transcendence is exemplified most in His mercy because it comes from a place beyond the natural order of things. God breaks into history; His thoughts and ways are not our thoughts and ways. Therefore, human beings who are in the image of God should not be understood in dualistic terms in which the mind is distinct from and higher than the body; both men and women are embodied, and both possess equally what is distinctively human—namely, will, creativity, reason, and language.

Questions for Reflection

1. Is it possible to think of God as personal without employing gender concepts?
2. To what extent do you think that religious belief of any kind is something you can simply *choose?*
3. Suppose that you are persuaded by Carol Christ that goddess worship is necessary to liberate women and restore to them the dignity taken from them by

patriarchy. A quick glance at history indicates that there have been a large number of different types of goddesses, embodying different images of female power. For example, there is Hera, the goddess of hearth and home, who got what she wanted out of Zeus by devious methods, and Aphrodite, goddess of unregulated sex (though not of a sort that seriously challenges male dominance). Demeter is the goddess of the Earth and of fertility. Kali represents the terrifying and destructive side to the mother goddess—the devouring mother, bringer of dissolution and death. How should you decide which one of them to worship?

4. Could a twenty-first century woman just decide to become a worshipper of Artemis or Demeter?

5. Could a new religion founded by people who openly regarded it as a psychologically and politically useful fantasy make any converts (or is putting us in touch with a reality outside ourselves part of what it is to be a religion)? How might those who regard their religion as a deliberate projection of their group's ideals respond if they encountered another group—say conservative Moslems—who had different ideals and made strong truth claims for their religion?

6. Have actual goddess-worshipping societies in history had better track records when it comes to treating women with respect? Have they lived more in harmony with nature or been more peaceful than other societies? If it turns out that they haven't, would this count against those who favor goddess worship as a way of improving women's social standing and self-esteem?

7. Although Roman Catholics and Eastern Orthodox Christians do not regard Mary as a goddess, she plays many of the same roles in their religious life that goddesses do: she offers believers an image of female perfection; she is regarded as holy and able through her prayers to help us in the troubles and sorrows of life; and she is a sympathetic mother, often constrasted with the harsh justice associated with God the Father and sometimes even with Jesus. Nonetheless, feminist theologians, and even more so feminist critics of Christianity, tend to be hostile or indifferent to Mary. Why do you think this is so?

8. Lenin regarded religion as functioning to reflect and ratify existing power relationships, and many feminists have applied this to male-female relationships, claiming that religion is simply a prop for the patriarchal status quo. But, if one accepts this sort of view of religion, does it make sense to try to use it for radical (or even moderate) social critique?

9. Some people have argued that if religion is to perform a prophetic role as it did for the Reverend Martin Luther King—in other words, if it is to place existing practices and institutions under judgment, it must respect God's transcendence (that is, His existing mysteriously outside both nature and society). Do you agree?

Glossary

Aeneas hero of Virgil's *Aeneid;* founder of Rome.

aggadah stories used to teach the Jewish religion.

Ahura Mazda the good God in Zoroastrian theology.

Ainu a "primitive" people living in Japan.

Allah God (in Islam).

analogy using a word in different, but related, senses; for example, *healthy* for a person, a diet, and a complexion.

Anat wife of Baal in ancient Near Eastern mythology.

Aphrodite the Greek goddess of sex.

Baal vegetation deity worshipped by the neighbors of the ancient Hebrews (and sometimes by the ancient Hebrews themselves).

conjugal having to do with marriage; sexual intercourse in marriage.

cosmologico-ritual reenactment of Creation.

cosmos natural order.

deep ecology the attempt to overcome the human propensity for destroying the environment in the most fundamental way.

Demeter the goddess of agriculture.

Demiourgos the Creator in Plato's philosophy, who fashions the world out of prime matter.

demonic destructive spiritual power.

deus ex machina (literal or figurative) god from a machine, used to untangle complicated situations in some plays.

Dido Queen of Carthage in Virgil's *Aeneid;* she has a tragic relationship with Aeneas.

dualism view of the human person that draws a sharp distinction between body and soul.

epiphany manifestation (usually of a god or goddess).

equivocation (in theology) using the same word in two different senses; for example, scales for both a butchers's scales and the skin of fish.

eschatology religious beliefs concerning the end of the world.

Fall (of Man, or Humanity) the expulsion of our first ancestors from Paradise for disobeying God and eating the fruit of the Tree of Knowledge of Good and Evil. Its effects are called *original sin.*

fecundity fertility.

Gaia the Earth goddess in Greek mythology.

genetic frenzy orgy of reproductive sexuality.

Genetrix mother; that which gives life.

halacha Jewish religious law.

Hera the wife (and sister) of Zeus in Greek mythology.

hierogamy sacred marriage.

hierophany manifestation of the sacred.

Hinduism the chief religion of India. It ranges from belief in an Unnameable Ultimate Reality among intellectuals to the worship of the phallus (or erect male organ) in some popular forms of Hinduism.

iconoclastic destroying art used in worship. Used broadly of hostility to religious symbolism.

idol false god. The worship of such a god is called *idolatry.*

imago dei the image of God. Both men and women are said to be created in the image of God in Genesis.

immanence confinement or presence within existing structures.

inclusive language language designed to include both men and women, for example, *chairperson* rather than *chairman.*

interiority inwardness.

Kali a manifestation of God in the Hindu tradition, representing death and decay.

Koran the Holy Book of Islam, believed to have been received by the prophet Mohammed (A.D. 570?–632).

Koryak a native Russian people, also called *Nymlani.*

liturgical used in church services.

Maori the original inhabitants of New Zealand.

Marduk the chief god of ancient Babylon.

metaphor figurative language, in which a thing is described as being something it resembles. For example, "He is a fox" for "He is clever."

midrash in Jewish tradition, the finding of hidden meanings in Scripture.

Moses (dates unknown), the man who led the Hebrews out of Egypt and founded the Jewish religion.

naturism identification of nature with God.

Oceania the islands of the central, western, and southern Pacific.

ontophany manifestation of Being.

orgy sex in a group.

Oroans a group centered in Bihar, Orrissa, and Magda Pradesh states, India.

Ouranos sky god in Greek mythology, ancestor of Zeus.

parenthogenisis reproduction without a biological father.

paterfamilias father of an ancient family, with power of life and death over his wife and children.

prime matter the most fundamental stuff of which the world is made, without form of any sort. See *form and matter* in the Glossary for Unit I.

projection ascribing something in oneself to the world outside oneself.

Prometheus hero-God in Greek mythology, who stole fire for human beings and was horribly punished for doing so.

reality principle in Freudian psychology, opposed to the pleasure principle. It requires us to face difficult situations and avoid regression.

Reformation movement, led by Martin Luther (1483–1546) and John Calvin (1509–1564), that resulted in the present division between Protestants and Roman Catholics.

regressive returning to infancy or the womb.

resurrection of the body in traditional Jewish and Christian belief, the re-creation of the human body at the end of time.

sacrality sacredness.

sacramental pertaining to religious rituals, such as the Eucharist (Communion), such objects are believed to achieve what they signify. Used broadly for a view of life in which symbolism is believed to disclose important realities.

Samoyed a people inhabiting northeastern European Russia and northwestern Siberia.

Scientific Revolution the founding of modern science by Francis Bacon (1561–1626) and Galileo Galilei (1561–1642).

Shekinah in the Jewish religion, God's presence in the world.

Slave Coast part of Africa where slaves were acquired by European traders (for example, Dahomey).

spirituality the experiential side of religion, often accompanied by indifference and sometimes even hostility or indifference to doctrine.

Supreme Being the most general name for God, roughly equivalent to Ultimate Reality.

Talmud the chief Jewish book of law outside the Bible.

Taoism one of the religions of China. *Tao* refers both to Ultimate Reality (which is

unnameable), and to the Taoist way of life.

telluric of the Earth.

Tetragammaton *YHWH*, the unpronounceable name for God used by the ancient Hebrews (rendered "Yahweh," "the LORD," or in older texts, "Jehovah").

theocratic identifying social and political power with divine authority.

Tiamat Babylonian mother goddess.

Torah the first five books of the Bible, traditionally ascribed to Moses; more broadly, the whole content of the Jewish religion.

transcendence capacity to step outside existing structures. Traditionally ascribed to God.

transcendentalists a group of American writers, including Ralph Waldo Emerson (1803–1882) and Henry David Thoreau (1817–1862), who protested the "corpse-cold" character of New England theology, opposed slavery, and began to absorb Hindu religious ideas.

Trinity the belief, traditional among Christians, that God is three persons in one substance Father, Son, and Holy Spirit.

Übermensch best translated *Overman*. In Nietzsche's philosophy, a superior person who creates new values. Opposed to the *last man*. An *Übermensch* can be a man or a woman, though Nietzsche thought a female *Übermensch* unlikely.

univocal using a word in the same sense in two different contexts.

Upanishad Hindu scripture.

Uranian of the sky.

Veda Hindu scripture.

Wanapum an American Indian (Native-American) people, who lived near the Columbia River in Washington state.

Yahweh see *Tetragammaton* in this Glossary.

Yang the feminine principle in Taoist cosmology.

Yin the masculine principle in Taoist cosmology.

Zeus the chief Greek god, associated with the sky.

The Sacredness of Nature and Cosmic Religion: Sky Gods and Mother Earth

MIRCEA ELIADE

> Mircea Eliade points out that for the religious person, nature is never only "natural"—it is always fraught with a religious value. The gods manifested the different modalities of the sacred in the very structure of the cosmos. In this context, he discusses both the remote Sky God, and the Earth imagined as Mother.

FOR RELIGIOUS MAN, nature is never only "natural"; it is always fraught with a religious value. This is easy to understand, for the cosmos is a divine creation; coming from the hands of the gods, the world is impregnated with sacredness. It is not simply a sacrality *communicated* by the gods, as is the case, for example, with a place or an object consecrated by the divine presence. The gods did more; *they manifested the different modalities of the sacred in the very structure of the world and of cosmic phenomena.*

The world stands displayed in such a manner that, in contemplating it, religious man discovers the many modalities of the sacred, and hence of being. Above all, the world exists, it is there, and it has a structure; it is not a chaos but a cosmos, hence it presents itself as creation, as work of the gods. This divine work always preserves its quality of transparency, that is, it spontaneously reveals the many aspects of the sacred. The sky directly, "naturally," reveals the infinite distance, the transcendence of the deity. The earth too is transparent; it presents itself as universal mother and nurse. The cosmic rhythms manifest order, harmony, permanence, fecundity. The cosmos as a whole is an organism at once *real, living,* and *sacred;* it simultaneously reveals the modalities of being and of sacrality. Ontophany and hierophany meet.

In this chapter we shall try to understand how the world presents itself to the eyes of religious man—or, more precisely, how sacrality is revealed through the very structures of the world. We must not forget that for religious man the supernatural is indissolubly connected with the natural, that nature always expresses something that transcends it. As we said earlier: a sacred stone is venerated because it is *sacred,* not because it is a *stone;* it is the sacrality *manifested through the mode of being of the stone* that reveals its true essence. This is why we cannot speak of naturism or of natural religion in the sense that the nineteenth century gave to those terms; for it is "supernature" that the religious man apprehends through the natural aspects of the world.

The Celestial Sacred and the Uranian Gods

Simple contemplation of the celestial vault already provokes a religious experience. The sky shows itself to be infinite, transcendent. It is pre-eminently the "wholly other" than the little represented by man and his, environment. Transcendence is revealed by simple awareness of infinite height. "Most high" spontaneously becomes an attribute of divinity. The higher regions inaccessible to man, the sidereal zones, acquire the momentousness of the transcendent, of absolute reality, of eternity. There dwell the gods; there a few privileged mortals make their way by rites of ascent; there, in the conception of certain religions, mount the souls of the dead. The "most high" is a dimension inaccessible to man as man; it belongs to superhuman forces and beings. He who ascends by mounting the steps of a sanctuary or the ritual ladder that leads to the sky ceases to be a man; in one way or another, he shares in the divine condition.

Excerpt from The Sacred and the Profane: The Nature of Religion *by Mircea Eliade.*
© 1957 by Rowohtt Taschenbuch Verlag Gmbtt, English translation © 1959 and renewed 1987 by Harcourt, Inc.

All this is not arrived at by a logical, rational operation. The transcendental category of height, of the super-terrestrial, of the infinite, is revealed to the whole man, to his intelligence and his soul. It is a total awareness on man's part; beholding the sky, he simultaneously discovers the divine incommensurability and his own situation in the cosmos. For the sky, *by its own mode of being,* reveals transcendence, force, eternity. It *exists absolutely* because it is *high, infinite, eternal, powerful.*

This is the true significance of the statement made above—that the gods manifested the different modalities of the sacred in the very structure of the world. In other words, the cosmos—paradigmatic work of the gods—is so constructed that a religious sense of the divine transcendence is aroused by the very existence of the sky. And since the sky *exists* absolutely, many of the supreme gods of primitive peoples are called by names designating height, the celestial vault, meteorological phenomena, or simply Owner of the Sky or Sky Dweller.

The supreme divinity of the Maori is named Iho; *iho* means elevated, high up. Uwoluwu, the supreme god of the Akposo Negroes, signifies what is on high, the upper regions Among the Selk'nam of Tierra del Fuego God is called Dweller in the Sky or He Who is in the Sky. Puluga, the supreme being of the Andaman Islanders, dwells in the sky; the thunder is his voice, wind his breath, the storm is the sign of his anger, for with his lightning he punishes those who break his commandments. The Sky God of the Yoruba of the Slave Coast is named Olorun, literally Owner of the Sky. The Samoyed worship Num, a god who dwells in the highest sky and whose name means sky. Among the Koryak, the supreme divinity is called the One on High, the Master of the High, He Who Exists. The Ainu know him as the Divine Chief of the Sky, the Sky God, the Divine Creator of the Worlds, but also as *Kamui,* that is, Sky. The list could easily be extended.

We may add that the same situation is found in the religions of more civilized peoples, that is, of peoples who have played an important role in history. . . .

There is no question of naturism here. The celestial god is not identified with the sky, for he is the same god who, creating the entire cosmos, created the sky too. This is why he is called Creator,

All-powerful, Lord, Chief, Father, and the like. The celestial god is a person, not a uranian epiphany. But he lives in the sky and is manifested in meteorological phenomena—thunder, lightning, storm, meteors, and so on. This means that certain privileged structures of the cosmos—the sky, the atmosphere—constitute favorite epiphanies of the supreme being; he reveals his presence by what is specifically and peculiarly his—the majesty (*majestas*) of the celestial immensity, the terror (*tremendum*) of the storm.

The Remote God

The history of supreme beings whose structure is celestial is of the utmost importance for an understanding of the religious history of humanity as a whole. We cannot even consider writing that history here, in a few pages. But we must at least refer to a fact that to us seems primary. Celestially structured supreme beings tend to disappear from the practice of religion, from cult; they depart from among men, withdraw to the sky, and become remote, inactive gods (*dei otiose*). In short, it may be said of these gods that, after creating the cosmos, life, and man, they feel a sort of fatigue, as if the immense enterprise of the Creation had exhausted their resources. So they withdraw to the sky, leaving a son or a demiurge on earth to finish or perfect the Creation. Gradually their place is taken by other divine figures—the mythical ancestors, the mother-goddesses, the fecundating gods, and the like. The god of the storm still preserves a celestial structure, but he is no longer a creating supreme being; he is only the fecundator of the earth, sometimes he is only a helper to his companion (*paredros*), the earth-mother. The celestially structured supreme being preserves his preponderant place only among pastoral peoples, and he attains a unique situation in religions that tend to monotheism (Ahura-Mazda) or that are fully monotheistic (Yahweh, Allah). . . .

The Dweller in the Sky or He Who Is in the Sky of the Selk'nam is eternal, omniscient, all-powerful, the creator; but the Creation was finished by the mythical ancestors, who had also been made by the supreme god before he withdrew to a place above the stars. For now this god has isolated himself from men, is indifferent to the affairs of the world. He has neither images nor priests. Prayers are addressed to him only in case of sickness. "Thou who art above, take not my child; he is still too young!" Offerings are rarely made to him except during storms.

It is the same among many African peoples; the great celestial god, the supreme being, all-powerful creator, plays only a minor role in the religious life of most tribes. He is too far away or too good to need an actual cult, and he is invoked only in extreme cases. . . .

It is useless to multiply examples. Everywhere in these primitive religions the celestial supreme being appears to have lost *religious currency;* he has no place in the cult, and in the myths he draws farther and farther away from man until he becomes a *deus otiosus.* Yet he is remembered and entreated as the last resort, *when all ways of appealing to other gods and goddesses, the ancestors, and the demons, have failed.* As the Oraons express it: "Now we have tried everything, but we still have you to help us." And they sacrifice a white cock to him, crying, "God, thou art our creator, have mercy on us."

The Religious Experience of Life

The divine remoteness actually expresses man's increasing interest in his own religious, cultural, and economic discoveries. Through his concern with hierophanies of life, through discovering the sacral fertility. . . .

It could be said that the very structure of the cosmos keeps memory of the celestial supreme being alive. It is as if the gods had created the world in such a way that it could not but reflect their existence; for no world is possible without verticality, and that dimension alone is enough to evoke transcendence.

Driven from religious life in the strict sense, the *celestial sacred* remains active through symbolism. A religious symbol conveys its message even if it is no longer *consciously* understood in every part. For a symbol speaks to the whole human being and not only to the intelligence. . . .

Terra Mater

An Indian prophet, Smohalla, chief of the Wanapum tribe, refused to till the ground. He held that it was a sin to mutilate and tear up the earth,

mother of all. He said: "You ask me to plow the ground! Shall I take a knife and tear my mother's bosom? Then when I die she will not take me to her bosom to rest. You ask me to dig for stone! Shall I dig under her skin for her bones? Then when I die, I cannot enter her body to be born again. You ask me to cut grass and make hay and sell it, and be rich like white men! But how dare I cut off my mother's hair?"

These words were spoken scarcely fifty years ago. But they come to us from very far. The emotion that we feel on hearing them arises primarily from their revealing to us, with incomparable freshness and spontaneity, the primordial image of Mother Earth. The image is found throughout the world in countless forms and variants. It is the *Terra Mater* or *Tellus Mater* so familiar to Mediterranean religions, who gives birth to all beings. "Concerning Earth, the mother of all, shall I sing," we read in the Homeric *Hymn to Earth,* "firm earth, eldest of gods, that nourishes all things in the world. . . . Thine it is to give or to take life from mortal men."

. . . And in the *Choephori* Aeschylus celebrates the earth "who bringeth all things to birth, reareth them, and receiveth again into her womb."

The prophet Smohalla does not tell us in what way men are born of the telluric mother. But North American myths reveal how things happened in the beginning, *in illo tempore.* The first men lived for a certain time in the breast of their mother, that is, in the depths of the earth. There in the telluric abyss they led a half-human life; in some sort they were still imperfectly formed embryos. At least so said the Lenni-Lenape or Delaware Indians, who once inhabited Pennsylvania. According to their myths, although the Creator had already prepared on the surface of the earth all the things that men now enjoy there, he had decided that these first men should remain yet a while hidden in the bosom of the telluric mother, so that they might better develop, might ripen. Other American Indian myths speak of an ancient time when Mother Earth brought forth human beings in the same way that she now produces bushes and reeds. . . .

The dying man desires to return to Mother Earth, to be buried in his native soil. "Crawl to the Earth, thy mother," says the *Rig Veda* (X, 18, 10). "Thou who art earth, I put thee in the Earth!" . . .

Humi Positio: Laying the Infant on the Ground

. . . This fundamental experience—that the human mother is only the representative of the telluric Great Mother—has given rise to countless customs. We will mention, as an example, giving birth on the ground (*humi positio*), a ritual that is found almost all over the world, from Australia to China, from Africa to South America. . . .

The religious meaning of the custom is easy to see: generation and childbirth are microcosmic versions of a paradigmatic act performed by the earth; every human mother only imitates and repeats this primordial act of the appearance of life in the womb of the earth. Hence every mother must put herself in contact with the Great Genetrix, that she may be guided by her in accomplishing the mystery that is the birth of a life, may receive her beneficent energies and secure her maternal protection.

Still more widely disseminated is the laying of the infant on the ground. In some parts of Europe it is still the custom today to lay the infant on the ground as soon as it has been bathed and swaddled. The father then takes the child up from the ground (*de terra tollere*) to show his gratitude. In ancient China "the dying man, like the newborn infant, is laid on the ground. . . . To be born or to die, to enter the living family or the ancestral family (and to leave the one or the other), there is a common threshold, one's native Earth. . . . When the newborn infant or the dying man is laid on the Earth, it is for her to say if the birth or the death are valid, if they are to be taken as accomplished and normal facts. . . .

Initiation includes a ritual death and resurrection. This is why, among numerous primitive peoples, the novice is symbolically "killed," laid in a trench, and covered with leaves. When he rises from the grave he is looked upon as a *new man,* for he has been brought to birth once more, this time *directly by the cosmic Mother.*

Woman, then, is mystically held to be one with the earth, childbearing is seen as a variant on the human scale, of the telluric fertility. All religious experiences connected with fecundity and birth *have a cosmic structure.* The sacrality of woman depends on the holiness of the earth. Feminine fecundity has a cosmic model—that of Terra Mater, the universal Genetrix.

In some religions Mother Earth is imagined as capable of conceiving alone, without the assistance of a coadjutor. Traces of such archaic ideas are still found in the myths of the parthenogenesis of Mediterranean goddesses. According to Hesiod, Gaia (= Earth) gave birth to Ouranos "a being equal to herself, able to cover her completely" (*Theogony,* 126 ff). Other Greek goddesses likewise gave birth without the help of gods. This is a mythical expression of the self-sufficiency and fecundity of Mother Earth. Such mythical conceptions have their counterparts in beliefs concerning the spontaneous fecundity of woman and in her occult magico-religious powers, which exert a determining influence on plant life. The social and cultural phenomenon known as matriarchy is connected with the discovery of agriculture by woman. It was woman who first cultivated food plants. Hence it is she who becomes owner of the soil and crops. The magico-religious prestige and consequent social predominance of woman have a cosmic model—the figure of Mother Earth.

In other religions the cosmic creation, or at least its completion, is the result of a hierogamy between the Sky-God and Mother Earth. This cosmogonic myth is quite widely disseminated. It is found especially in Oceania—from Indonesia to Micronesia—but it also occurs in Asia, Africa, and the two Americas. Now, as we have seen, the cosmogonic myth is pre-eminently the paradigmatic myth; it serves as model for human behavior. This is why human marriage is regarded as an imitation of the cosmic hierogamy. "I am Heaven," the husband proclaims in the *Brihadārnyaka Upanishad* (VI, 4, 20), "thou art Earth!" Even so early as the *Atharva Veda* (XIV, 2, 71) groom and bride are assimilated to heaven and earth. Dido celebrates her marriage to Aeneas in the midst of a violent storm (*Aeneid*, IV, 165 ff); their union coincides with that of the elements; the Sky embraces his wife, dispensing the fertilizing rain. In Greece marriage rites imitated the example of Zeus's secret union with Hera (Pausanias, II, 36, 2). As we should expect, the divine myth is the paradigmatic model for the human union. But there is another aspect which requires emphasis—*the cosmic structure of the conjugal ritual,* and hence of human sexual behavior. For nonreligious man of the modern societies, this simultaneously *cosmic* and *sacred* dimension of conjugal union is difficult to grasp.

But as we have had occasion to say more than once, it must not be forgotten that religious man of the archaic societies sees the world as fraught with messages. Sometimes the messages are in cipher, but the myths are there to help man decipher them. As we shall see later, the whole of human experience can be homologized to cosmic life, hence can be sanctified, for the cosmos is the supreme creation of the gods.

Ritual orgies for the benefit of crops likewise have a divine model—the hierogamy of the Fecundating God and Mother Earth. The fertility of the fields is stimulated by an unlimited genetic frenzy. From one point of view the orgy corresponds to the pre-Creation state of nondifferentia-tion. This is why certain New Year ceremonies include orgiastic rites: social confusion, sexual license, and saturnalia symbolize regression to the amorphous condition that preceded the Creation of the World. In the case of a creation on the level of vegetable life, this cosmologico-ritual scenario is repeated, for the new crop is equivalent to a new creation. The idea of *renewal*—which we encountered in New Year rituals whose purpose was at once the renewal of time and the regeneration of the world—recurs in orgiastic agricultural scenarios. Here too the orgy is a return to the cosmic night, the preformal, the waters, in order to ensure complete regeneration of life and hence the fertility of the earth and an abundance of crops.

Study Questions on Mircea Eliade

1. Explain what Eliade means in saying "For religious man, nature is never only 'natural.'"
2. How do Sky Gods differ from divinities connected with fertility and the Earth? Sky Gods are almost universally thought of as male and Earth Goddesses as female. Why? Does this make sense to you? Try to think of the earth as father and the sky as mother. Does it work just as well? Why or why not?
3. Supposing we think of the earth as mother and the sky as father, does the fact that the sky is spatially above the earth imply that the Sky God is more powerful, or are there reasons why Mother Earth might be thought of as more powerful?
4. The sacredness of the Earth in cosmic religion is a function of her power to give birth to all living things (sometimes alone and sometimes as a result of her sacred union with the Sky God). In either case, motherhood and fertility are viewed very positively. It would seem, therefore, that those who seek to return to the tradition of worshipping the Earth as a Goddess ought to hold motherhood in particularly high esteem and value fertility. But this does not seem to be true of most of the ecologists, feminists, and ecofeminists who advocate return to such religions. Are they being inconsistent?

Genesis: Chapters 1–3

The Book of Genesis describes the creation of the world and humanity, followed by the Fall, as traditionally understood within the Jewish and Christian traditions. In order to avoided biasing issues, we have used the *Revised Standard Version of the Bible,* which was prepared and won widespread acceptance among Christians of all theological persuasions before the current round of controversy about sex and gender issues within the churches.

IN THE BEGINNING GOD CREATED the heavens and the earth. 2The earth was without form and void, and darkness was upon the face of the deep; and the Spirit of God was moving over the face of the waters.

3And God said, "Let there be light"; and there was light. 4And God saw that the light was good; and God separated the light from the darkness. 5God called the light Day, and the darkness he called Night. And there was evening and there was morning, one day.

6And God said, "Let there be a firmament in the midst of the waters, and let it separate the waters from the waters." 7And God made the firmament and separated the waters which were under the firmament from the waters which were above the firmament. And it was so. 8And God called the firmament Heaven. And there was evening and there was morning, a second day.

9And God said, "Let the waters under the heavens be gathered together into one place, and let the dry land appear." And it was so. 10God called the dry land Earth, and the waters that were gathered together he called Seas. And God saw that it was good. 11And God said, "Let the earth put forth vegetation, plants yielding seed, and fruit trees bearing fruit in which is their seed, each according to its kind, upon the earth." And it was so. 12The earth brought forth vegetation, plants yielding seed according to their own kinds, and trees bearing fruit in which is their seed, each according to its kind. And God saw that it was good. 13And there was evening and there was morning, a third day.

14And God said, "Let there be lights in the firmament of the heavens to separate the day from the night and let them be for signs and for seasons and for days and years, 15and let them be lights in the firmament of the heavens to give light upon the earth." And it was so. 16And God made the two great lights, the greater light to rule the day and the lesser light to rule the night; he made the stars also. 17And God set them in the firmament of the heavens to give light upon the earth, 18to rule over the day and over the night, and to separate the light from the darkness. And God saw that it was good. 19And there was evening and there was morning, a fourth day.

20And God said, "Let the waters bring forth swarms of living creatures, and let birds fly above the earth across the firmament of the heavens." 21So God created the great sea monsters and every living creature that moves, with which the waters swarm, according to their kinds, and every winged bird according to its kind. And God saw that it was good. 22And God blessed them, saying, "Be fruitful and multiply and fill the waters in the seas, and let birds multiply on the earth." 23And there was evening and there was morning, a fifth day.

24And God said, "Let the earth bring forth living creatures according to their kinds: cattle and creeping things and beasts of the earth according to their kinds." And it was so. 25And God made the beasts of the earth according to their kinds and the cattle according to their kinds, and everything that creeps upon the ground according to its kind. And God saw that it was good.

26Then God said, "Let us make man in our image, after our likeness; and let them have dominion over the fish of the sea, and over the birds of the air, and over the cattle, and over all the earth, and over every creeping thing that creeps upon the earth." [27]So God created man in his own image, in the image of God he created him; male and female he created them. [28]And God blessed them, and God said to them, "Be fruitful and multiply, and fill the earth and subdue it; and have dominion over the fish of the sea and over the birds of the air and over every living thing that moves upon the earth." [29]And God said, "Behold, I have given you every plant yielding seed which is upon the face of all the earth, and every tree with seed in its fruit you shall have them for food. [30]And to every beast of the earth, and to every bird of the air, and to everything that creeps on the earth, everything that has the breath of life, I have given every green plant for food." And it was so. [31]And God saw everything that he had made, and behold, it was very good. And there was evening and there was morning, a sixth day.

2 Thus the heavens and the earth were finished, and all the host of them. [2]And on the seventh day God finished his work which he had done, and he rested on the seventh day from all his work which he had done. [3]So God blessed the seventh day and hallowed it, because on it God rested from all his work which he had done in creation.

[4]These are the generations of the heavens and the earth when they were created.

In the day that the Lord God made the earth and the heavens, [5]when no plant of the field was yet in the earth and no herb of the field had yet sprung up—for the Lord God had not caused it to rain upon the earth, and there was no man to till the ground; [6]but a mist went up from the earth and watered the whole face of the ground—[7]then the Lord God formed man of dust from the ground, and breathed into his nostrils the breath of life; and man became a living being. [8]And the Lord God planted a garden in Eden, in the east; and there he put the man whom he had formed.

[9]And out of the ground the Lord God made to grow every tree that is pleasant to the sight and good for food, the tree of life also in the midst of the garden, and the tree of the knowledge of good and evil.

[10]A river flowed out of Eden to water the garden, and there it divided and became four rivers. [11]The name of the first is Pishon; it is the one which flows around the whole land of Hav'ilah, where there is gold; [12]and the gold of that land is good; bdellium and onyx stone are there. [13]The name of the second river is Gihon; it is the one

which flows around the whole land of Cush. [14]And the name of the third river is Hid'dekel, which flows east of Assyria. And the fourth river is the Euphra'tes.

[15]The Lord God took the man and put him in the garden of Eden to till it and keep it. [16]And the Lord God commanded the man, saying, "You may freely eat of every tree of the garden; [17]but of the tree of the knowledge of good and evil you shall not eat, for in the day that you eat of it you shall die."

[18]Then the Lord God said, "It is not good that the man should be alone; I will make him a helper fit for him." [19]So out of the ground the Lord God formed every beast of the field and every bird of the air, and brought them to the man to see what he would call them; and whatever the man called every living creature, that was its name. [20]The man gave names to all cattle, and to the birds of the air, and to every beast of the field; but for the man there was not found a helper fit for him. [21]So the Lord God caused a deep sleep to fall upon the man, and while he slept took one of his ribs and closed up its place with flesh; [22]and the rib which the Lord God had taken from the man he made into a woman and brought her to the man. [23]Then the man said,

> "This at last is bone of my bones
> and flesh of my flesh;
> she shall be called Woman,
> because she was taken out of Man."

[24]Therefore a man leaves his father and his mother and cleaves to his wife, and they become one flesh. [25]And the man and his wife were both naked, and were not ashamed.

3 Now the serpent was more subtle than any other wild creature that the Lord God had made. He said to the woman, "Did God say, 'You shall not eat of any tree of the garden'?" [2]And the woman said to the serpent, "We may eat of the fruit of the trees of the garden; [3]but God said, 'You shall not eat of the fruit of the tree which is in the midst of the garden, neither shall you touch it, lest you die.'"

[4]But the serpent said to the woman, "You will not die. [5]For God knows that when you eat of it your eyes will be opened, and you will be like God, knowing good and evil." [6]So when the woman saw that the tree was good for food, and that it was a

delight to the eyes, and that the tree was to be desired to make one wise, she took of its fruit and ate; and she also gave some to her husband, and he ate. 7Then the eyes of both were opened, and they knew that they were naked; and they sewed fig leaved together and made themselves aprons.

8And they heard the sound of the LORD God walking in the garden in the cool of the day, and the man and his wife hid themselves from the presence of the LORD God among the trees of the garden. 9But the LORD God called to the man, and said to him, "Where are you?" 10And he said, "I heard the sound of thee in the garden, and I was afraid, because I was naked; and I hid myself." 11He said, "Who told you that you were naked? Have you eaten of the tree of which I commanded you not to eat?" 12The man said, "The woman whom thou gavest to be with me, she gave me fruit of the tree, and I ate." 13Then the LORD God said to the woman, "What is this that you have done?" The woman said, "The serpent beguiled me, and I ate."

14The LORD God said to the serpent,
"Because you have done this,
cursed are you above all cattle,
and above all wild animals;
upon your belly you shall go,
and dust you shall eat
all the days of your life.
15I will put enmity between you and the woman,
and between your seed and her seed;
he shall bruise your head,
and you shall bruise his heel."
16To the woman he said,
"I will greatly multiply your pain in childbearing;
in pain you shall bring forth children,
yet your desire shall be for your husband,
and he shall rule over you."
17And to Adam he said,
"Because you have listened to the voice of your wife,
and have eaten of the tree
of which I commanded you,
'You shall not eat of it,'
cursed is the ground because of you;
in toil you shall eat of it all the days of your life;
18thorns and thistles it shall bring forth to you;
and you shall eat the plants of the field.
19In the sweat of your face
you shall eat bread
till you return to the ground,
for out of it you were taken;
you are dust,
and to dust you shall return."

20The man called his wife's name Eve, because she was the mother of all living. 21And the LORD God made for Adam and for his wife garments of skins, and clothed them.

22Then the LORD God said, "Behold, the man has become like one of us, knowing good and evil; and now, lest he put forth his hand and take also of the tree of life, and eat, and live for ever"—23therefore the LORD God sent him forth from the garden of Eden, so till the ground from which he was taken. 24He drove out the man; and at the east of the garden of Eden he placed the cherubim, and a flaming sword which turned every way, to guard the way to the tree of life.

Study Questions on Genesis, Chapters 1-3

1. What is meant by saying human beings are in the image of God? What sort of things is God shown doing? Are these things people can also do? Are men and women both in the image of God? If so, does this mean that there is both male and female in God?

2. Do you think that Eve is portrayed as more to blame than Adam for taking the forbidden fruit? Does her taking the fruit first have any significance? Does God appear to hold them equally responsible?

3. Look closely at the differences between the way God creates human beings and the way he creates the world and the animals. What do these imply about how humans differ from animals? Also, how is Adam's relationship to Eve different from his relationship to the animals?

4. In what ways does the text sanction patriarchy (male domination of females)?

Why Women Need the Goddess: Phenomenological, Psychological, and Political Reflections

CAROL P. CHRIST

Carol P. Christ discusses the phenomenological, psychological, and political ramifications of the emergence of the symbol of the Goddess among women. She maintains that this symbol has much to offer women who are struggling to get rid of powerful and pervasive devaluations of female power, and to create a new culture that celebrates women's power, bodies, and will.

AT THE CLOSE OF NTOSAKE SHANGE'S STUPEN-DOUSLY successful Broadway play "For Colored Girls Who Have Considered Suicide When the Rainbow Is Enuf," a tall beautiful black woman rises from despair to cry out, "I found God in myself and I loved her fiercely." Her discovery is echoed by women around the country who meet spontaneously in small groups on full moons, solstices, and equinoxes to celebrate the Goddess as symbol of life and death powers and waxing and waning energies in the universe and in themselves.

> It is the night of the full moon. Nine woman stand in a circle, on a rocky hill above the city. The western sky is rosy with the setting sun; in the east the moon's face begins to peer above the horizon. . . . The woman pours out a cup of wine onto the earth, refills it and raises it high. "Hail, Tana, Mother of mothers!" she cries. "Awaken from your long sleep, and return to your children again!"

What art the political and psychological effects of this fierce new love of the divine in themselves for women whose spiritual experience has been focused by the male God of Judaism and Christianity? Is the spiritual dimension of feminism a passing diversion, an escape from difficult but necessary political work? Or does the emergence of the symbol of Goddess among women have significant political and psychological ramifications for the feminist movement?

Religious symbol systems focused around exclusively male images of divinity create the impression that female power can never be fully legitimate or wholly beneficent. This message need never be explicitly stated (as, for example, it is in the story of Eve) for its effect to be felt. A woman completely ignorant of the myths of female evil in biblical religion nonetheless acknowledges the anomaly of female power when she prays exclusively to a male God. She may see herself as like

Reprinted by permission of the author.

God (created in the image of God) only by deny-ing her own sexual identity and affirming God's transcendence of sexual identity. But she can never have the experience that is freely available to every man and boy in her culture, of having her full sexual identity affirmed as being in the image and likeness of God. In Geertz' terms, her "mood" is one of trust in male power as salvific and distrust of female power in herself and other women as inferior or dangerous. Such a powerful, pervasive, and longlasting "mood" cannot fail to become a "motivation" that translates into social and political reality.

In *Beyond God the Father,* feminist theologian Mary Daly detailed the psychological and political ramifications of father religion for women. "If God in 'his' heaven is a father ruling his people," she wrote, "then it is the 'nature' of things and according to divine plan and the order of the universe that society be male dominated. Within this context, a *mystification of roles* takes place: The husband dominating his wife represents God 'himself.' The images and values of a given society have been projected into the realm of dogmas and 'Articles of Faith,' and these in turn justify the social structures which have given rise to them and which sustain their plausibility."

Philosopher Simone de Beauvoir was well aware of the function of patriarchal religion as legitimater of male power. As she wrote, "Man enjoys the great advantage of having a god endorse the code he writes; and since man exercises a sovereign authority over women it is especially fortunate that this authority has been vested in him by the Supreme Being. For the Jew, Mohammedans, and Christians, among others, man is Master by divine right; the fear of God will therefore repress any impulse to revolt in the downtrodden female."

This brief discussion of the psychological and political effects of God religion puts us in an excellent position to begin to understand the significance of the symbol of Goddess for women. In discussing the meaning of the Goddess, my method will first be phenomenological. I will isolate a meaning of the symbol of the Goddess as it has emerged in the lives of contemporary women. I will then discuss its psychological and political significance by contrasting the "moods" and "motivations" engendered by Goddess symbols

with those engendered by Christian symbolism. I will also correlate Goddess symbolism with themes that have emerged in the women's movement, in order to show how Goddess symbolism undergirds and legitimates the concerns of the women's movement, much as God symbolism in Christianity undergirded the interests of men in patriarchy. I will discuss four aspects of Goddess symbolism here: the Goddess as affirmation of female power, the female body, the female will, and women's bonds and heritage. There are, of course, many other meanings of the Goddess that I will not discuss here.

The sources for the symbol of the Goddess in contemporary spirituality are traditions of Goddess worship and modern women's experience. The ancient Mediterranean, pre-Christian European, native American, Mesoamerican, Hindu, African, and other traditions are rich sources for Goddess symbolism. But these traditions are filtered through modern women's experiences. Traditions of Goddesses, subordinate to Gods, for example, are ignored. Ancient traditions are tapped selectively and eclecticly, but they are not considered authoritative for modern consciousness. The Goddess symbol has emerged spontaneously in the dreams, fantasies, and thoughts of many women around the country in the past several years. . . .

The simplest and most basic meaning of the symbol of Goddess is the acknowledgement of the legitimacy of female power as a beneficient and independent power. A woman who echoes Ntosake Shange's dramatic statement, "I found God in myself and I loved her fiercely," is saying "Female power is strong and creative." She is saying that the divine principle, the saving and sustaining power, is in herself, that she will no longer look to men or male figures as saviors. The strength and independence of female power can be intuited by contemplating ancient and modern images of the Goddess. This meaning of the symbol of Goddess is simple and obvious, and yet it is difficult for many to comprehend. It stands in sharp contrast to the paradigms of female dependence on males that have been predominant in Western religion and culture. . . .

. . . The affirmation of female power contained in the Goddess symbol has both psychological and political consequences. Psychologically, it means the defeat of the view engendered by patriarchy that women's power is inferior and dangerous. This new "mood" of affirmation of female power also leads to new "motivations"; it supports and undergirds women's trust in their own power and the power of other women in family and society.

If the simplest meaning of the Goddess symbol is an affirmation of the legitimacy and beneficience of female power, then a question immediately arises, "Is the Goddess simply female power writ large, and if so, why bother with the symbol of Goddess at all? Or does the symbol refer to a Goddess 'out there' who is not reducible to a human potential?" The many women who have rediscovered the power of Goddess would give three answers to this question: (1) The Goddess is divine female, a personification who can be invoked in prayer and ritual; (2) the Goddess is symbol of the life, death, and rebirth energy in nature and culture, in personal and communal life and (3) the Goddess is symbol of the affirmation of the legitimacy and beauty of female power (made possible by the new becoming of women in the women's liberation movement. . . . Some would assert that the Goddess definitely is *not* "out there," that the symbol of a divinity "out there" is part of the legacy of patriarchal oppression, which brings with it the authoritarianism, hierarchicalism, and dogmatic rigidity associated with biblical monotheistic religions. . . . Others seem quite comfortable with the notion of Goddess as a divine female protector and creator and would find their experience of Goddess limited by the assertion that she is not *also* out there as well as within themselves and in all natural processes. When asked what the symbol of Goddess means, feminist priestess Starhawk replied, "It all depends on how I feel. When I feel weak, she is someone who can help and protect me. When I feel strong, she is the symbol of my own power. At other times I feel her as the natural energy in my body and the world." How are we to evaluate such a statement? Theologians might call these the words of a sloppy thinker. But my deepest intuition tells me they contain a wisdom that Western theological thought has lost. . . .

A second important implication of the Goddess symbol for women is the affirmation of the female body and the life cycle expressed in it. Because of women's unique position as menstruants, birth-givers, and those who have traditionally cared for the young and the dying, women's connection to the body, nature, and this world has been obvious. Women were denigrated because they seemed more carnal, fleshy, and earthy than the culture-creating males. The misogynist anti*body* tradition in Western thought is symbolized in the myth of Eve who is traditionally viewed as a sexual temptress, the epitome of women's carnal nature. This tradition reaches its nadir in the *Malleus Maleficarum (The Hammer of Evil-Doing Women)*, which states, "All witchcraft stems from carnal lust, which in women is insatiable." The Virgin Mary, the positive female image in Christianity, does not contradict Christian denigration of the female body and its powers The Virgin Mary is revered because she, in her perpetual virginity, transcends the carnal sexuality attributed to most women.

The denigration of the female body is expressed in cultural and religious taboos surrounding menstruation, childbirth, and menopause in women. While menstruation taboos may have originated in a perception of the awesome powers of the female body, they degenerated into a simple perception that there is something "wrong" with female bodily functions. Menstruating women were forbidden to enter the sanctuary in ancient Hebrew and premodern Christian communities. Although only Orthodox Jews still enforce religious taboos against menstruant women, few women in our culture grow up affirming their menstruation as a connection to sacred power. Most women learn that menstruation is a curse and grow up believing that the bloody facts of menstruation are best hidden away. Feminists challenge this attitude to the female body. . . .

The symbol of Goddess aids the process of naming and reclaiming the female body and its cycles and processes. In the ancient world and among modern women, the Goddess symbol represents the birth, death, and rebirth processes of the natural and human worlds. The female body is viewed as the direct incarnation of waxing and waning, life and death, cycles in the universe. This is sometimes expressed through the symbolic connection between the twenty-eight-day cycles of menstruation and the twenty-eight-day cycles of the moon. Moreover, the Goddess is celebrated in the triple aspect of youth, maturity, and age, or maiden, mother, and crone. The potentiality of the young girl is celebrated in the nymph or maiden aspect of the Goddess. The Goddess as mother is sometimes depicted giving birth, and giving birth is viewed as a symbol for all the creative, life-giving powers of the universe. The life-giving powers of the Goddess in her creative aspect are not limited to physical birth, for the Goddess is also seen as the creator of all the arts of civilization, including healing, writing, and the giving of just law. Women in the middle of life who are not physical mothers may give birth to poems, songs, and books, or nurture other women, men, and children. . . .

At the end of life, women incarnate the crone aspect of the Goddess. The wise old woman, the woman who knows from experience what life is about, the woman whose closeness to her own death gives her a distance and perspective on the problems of life, is celebrated as the third aspect of the Goddess. . . .

The possibilities of reclaiming the female body and its cycles have been expressed in a number of Goddess-centered rituals. Hallie Mountainwing and Barby My Own created a summer solstice ritual to celebrate menstruation and birth. The women simulated a birth canal and birthed each other into their circle. They raised power by placing their hands on each other's bellies and chanting together. Finally they marked each other's faces with rich, dark menstrual blood saying, "This is the blood that promises renewal. This is the blood that promises sustenance. This is the blood that promises life." From hidden dirty secret to symbol of the life power of the Goddess, women's blood has come full circle. . . .

The "mood" created by the symbol of the Goddess in triple aspect is one of positive, joyful affirmation of the female body and its cycles and acceptance of aging and death as well as life. The "motivations" are to overcome menstrual taboos, to return the birth process to the hands of women, and to change cultural attitudes about age and death. Changing cultural attitudes toward the female body could go a long way toward overcoming the spirit-flesh, mind-body dualisms of western culture, since, as Ruether has pointed out, the denigration of the female body is at the heart of these dualisms. The Goddess as symbol of the revalua-

tion of the body and nature thus also undergirds the human potential and ecology movements. The "mood" is one of affirmation, awe, and respect for the body and nature, and the "motivation" is to respect the teachings of the body and the rights of all living beings.

A third important implication of the Goddess symbol for women is the positive valuation of will in a Goddess-centered ritual, especially in Goddess-centered ritual magic and spellcasting in womanspirit and feminist witchcraft circles. The basic notion behind ritual magic and spellcasting is energy as power. Here the Goddess is a center or focus of power and energy; she is the personification of the energy that flows between beings in the natural and human worlds. In Goddess circles, energy is raised by chanting or dancing. According to Starhawk, "Witches conceive of psychic energy as having form and substance that can be perceived and directed by those with a trained awareness. The power generated within the circle is built into a cone form, and at its peak is released—to the Goddess, to reenergize the members of the coven, or to do a specific work such as healing." In ritual magic, the energy raised is directed by willpower. Women who celebrate in Goddess circles believe they can achieve their wills in the world.

The emphasis on the will is important for women, because women traditionally have been taught to devalue their wills, to believe that they cannot achieve their will through their own power, and even to suspect that the assertion of will is evil. . . .

. . . Patriarchal religion has enforced the view that female initiative and will are evil through the juxtaposition of Eve and Mary. Eve caused the fall by asserting her will against the command of God, while Mary began the new age with her response to God's initiative, "Let it be done to me according to thy word" (Luke 1:38). Even for men, patriarchal religion values the passive will subordinate to divine initiative. The classical doctrines of sin and grace view sin as the prideful assertion of will and grace as the obedient subordination of the human will to the divine initiative or order. . . .

In a Goddess-centered context, in contrast, the will is valued. *A woman is encouraged to know her will, to believe that her will is valid, and to believe that her will can be achieved in the world,* three powers traditionally denied to her in patriarchy. In a Goddess-centered framework, a woman's will is not subordinated to the Lord God as king and ruler, nor to men as his representatives. Thus a woman is not reduced to waiting and acquiescing in the wills of others as she is in patriarchy. But neither does she adopt the egocentric form of will that pursues self-interest without regard for the interests of others.

The Goddess-centered context provides a different understanding of the will than that available in the traditional patriarchal religious framework. In the Goddess framework, will can be achieved only when it is exercised in harmony with the energies and wills of other beings. Wise women, for example, raise a cone of healing energy at the full moon or solstice when the lunar or solar energies are at their high points with respect to the earth. This discipline encourages them to recognize that not all times are propitious for the achieving of every will. Similarly, they know that spring is a time for new beginnings in work and love, summer a time for producing external manifestations of inner potentialities, and fall or winter times for stripping down to the inner core and extending roots. Such awareness of waxing and waning processes in the universe discourages arbitrary ego-centered assertion of will, while at the same time encouraging the assertion of individual will in cooperation with natural energies and the energies created by the wills of others. Wise women also have a tradition that whatever is sent out will be returned and this reminds them to assert their wills in cooperative and healing rather than egocentric and destructive ways. This view of will allows women to begin to recognize, claim, and assert their wills without adopting the worst characteristics of the patriarchal understanding and use of will. In the Goddess-centered framework, the "mood" is one of positive affirmation of personal will in the context of the energies of other wills or beings. The "motivation" is for women to know and assert their wills in cooperation with other wills and energies. This of course does not mean that women always assert their wills in positive and life-affirming ways. Women's capacity for evil is, of course, as great as men's. My purpose is simply to contrast the differing attitudes toward the exercise of will *per se,* and the female will in particular, in Goddess-centered religion and in the Christian God-centered religion.

The fourth and final aspect of Goddess symbolism that I will discuss here is the significance of the Goddess for a revaluation of woman's bonds and heritage. . . . I will focus on the mother-daughter bond, in part because I believe it may be the key to the others.

Adrienne Rich has pointed out that the mother-daughter bond, perhaps the most important of woman's bonds, "resonant with charges. . . the flow of energy between two biologically alike bodies, one of which has lain in amniotic bliss inside the other, one of which has labored to give birth to the other," is rarely celebrated in patriarchal religion and culture. Christianity celebrates the father's relation to the son and the mother's relation to the son, but the story of mother and daughter is missing. So, too, in patriarchal literature and psychology the mothers and the daughters rarely exist. Volumes have been written about the Oedipal complex, but little has been written about the girl's relation to her mother. Moreover, as de Beauvoir has noted, the mother-daughter relation is distorted in patriarchy because the mother must give her daughter over to men in a male-defined culture in which women are viewed as inferior. The mother must socialize her daughter to become subordinate to men, and if her daughter challenges patriarchal norms, the mother is likely to defend the patriarchal structures against her own daughter. . . .

Almost the only story of mothers and daughters that has been transmitted in Western culture is the myth of Demeter and Persephone that was the basis of religious rites celebrated by women only, the Thesmophoria, and later formed the basis of the Eleusian mysteries, which were open to all who spoke Greek. In this story, the daughter, Persephone, is raped away from her mother, Demeter, by the God of the underworld. Unwilling to accept this state of affairs, Demeter rages and withholds fertility from the earth until her daughter is returned to her. What is important for women in this story is that a mother fights for her daughter and for her relation to her daughter. This is completely different from the mother's relation to her daughter in patriarchy. The "mood" created by the story of Demeter and Persephone is one of celebration of the mother-daughter bond, and the "motivation" is for mothers and daughters to affirm the heritage passed on from mother to daughter and to reject the patriarchal pattern where the primary loyalties of mother and daughter must be to men.

The symbol of Goddess has much to offer women who are struggling to be rid of the "powerful, pervasive, and long-lasting moods and motivations" of devaluation of female power, denigration of the female body, distrust of female will, and denial of the women's bonds and heritage that have been engendered by patriarchal religion. As women struggle to create a new culture in which women's power, bodies, will, and bonds are celebrated, it seems natural that the Goddess would reemerge as symbol of the newfound beauty, strength, and power of women.

Study Questions on Carol P. Christ

1. What "moods" and "motivations" does Christ think are created by religions that center on worship of a male God? How does she think such religions support patriarchy? How might she answer Wiley on this point?
2. Christ sees Goddess symbolism as undergirding and legitimating the concerns of the women's movement (affirming female power, the female body, female will, and women's bonds and heritage) just as God symbolism in Christianity undergirded the interests of men in patriarchy. In order to arrive at an image of the Goddess, modern women have had to tap ancient religions selectively, omitting, for example, goddesses subordinate to gods. Is this just a case of subordinating religion to political goals (of the sort criticized by Davis)?
3. Can a person believe something because he or she believes it would be useful psychologically or politically to do so? Do you think Christ believes in the Goddess?
4. Would Christ encourage women to worship Kali, the Hindu Goddess of death? (See the section on Kali in the book by Harman listed in the For Further Reading section of this unit for more information.)

Basic Linguistic Options: God, Women, Equivalence . . .

ELIZABETH JOHNSON

The holy mystery of God, Elizabeth Johnson maintains, is beyond all imagining. In the context of this avowal, she draws on women's interpreted experience, and critical retrieval of tradition, in order to develop a liberated way of naming God. This means speaking in female symbols for the divine mystery, testing their capacity to bear divine presence and power. Hopefully in the future we will be able to use both male and female images and symbols equally, but employing the female ones now is necessary to counterbalance the long-standing tradition of using male ones.

From She Who Is, *pp. 42–60, by Elizabeth Johnson. Reprinted by permission of Crossroad Publishing.*

Why the Word God?

A certain liability attends the very word God, given the history of its use in androcentric theology. Insofar as it almost invariably refers to a deity imaged and conceptualized in male form, this word is judged by some feminist thinkers to be a generically masculine form of naming divine reality, and thus not capable of expressing the fullness of feminist insight. . . .

The dilemma of the word God itself, however, is a real one and not easily resolved. . . .

Why Female Symbols of God?

Normative speech about God in metaphors that are exclusively, literally, and patriarchally male is the real life context for this study. As a remedy some scholars and liturgists today take the option of always addressing God simply as "God." This has the positive result of relieving the hard androcentrism of ruling male images and pronouns for the divine. Nevertheless, this practice, if it is the only corrective engaged in, is not ultimately satisfactory. Besides employing uncritically a term long associated with the patriarchal ordering of the world, its consistent use causes the personal or transpersonal character of holy mystery to recede. It prevents the insight into holy mystery that might occur were female symbols set free to give rise to thought. Most serious of all, it papers over the problem of the implied inadequacy of women's reality to represent God.

The holy mystery of God is beyond all imagining. In his own epistemological categories Aquinas's words still sound with the ring of truth in this regard:

> Since our mind is not proportionate to the divine substance, that which is the substance of God remains beyond our intellect and so is unknown to us. Hence the supreme knowledge which we have of God is to know that we do not know God, insofar as we know that what God is surpasses all that we can understand of him [the "him," so easily assumed, being the problem that this book is addressing].

The incomprehensibility of God makes it entirely appropriate, at times even preferable, to speak about God in nonpersonal or suprapersonal terms. Symbols such as the ground of being (Paul Tillich), matrix surrounding and sustaining all life (Rosemary Ruether), power of the future (Wolfhart Pannenberg), holy mystery (Karl Rahner), all point to divine reality that cannot be captured in concepts or images. At the same time God is not less than personal, and many of the most prized characteristics of God's relationship to the world, such as fidelity compassion, and liberating love, belong to the human rather than the nonhuman world. Thus it is also appropriate, at times even preferable, to speak about God in personal symbols.

Here is where the question of gender arises. Given the powerful ways the ruling male metaphor has expanded to become an entire metaphysical world view, and the way it perdures in imagination even when gender neutral God-language is used, correction of androcentric speech on the level of the concept alone is not sufficient. Since, as Marcia Falk notes, Dead metaphors make strong idols," other images must be introduced which shatter the exclusivity of the male metaphor, subvert its dominance, and set free a greater sense of the mystery of God.

One effective way to stretch language and expand our repertoire of images is by uttering female symbols into speech about divine mystery. It is a complex exercise, not necessarily leading to emancipatory speech. An old danger that accompanies this change is that such language may be taken literally; a new danger lies in the potential for stereotyping women's reality by characterizing God simply as nurturing, caring, and so forth. The benefits, however, in my judgment, outweigh the dangers. Reorienting the imagination at a basic level, this usage challenges the idolatry of maleness in classic language about God, thereby making possible the rediscovery of divine mystery, and points to recovery of the dignity of women created in the image of God.

The importance of the image can hardly be overstated. Far from being peripheral to human knowing, imaginative constructs mediate the world to us. As is clear from contemporary science, literature, and philosophy this is not to be equated with things being imaginary but with the structure of human knowing, which essentially depends upon paradigms to assemble data and interpret the way things are. We think via the path of images; even the most abstract concepts at root bear traces of the original images which gave them birth. Just as we know the world only through the mediation of imaginative constructs, the same holds true for human knowledge of God. Without necessarily adopting Aquinas's epistemology we can hear the truth in his observation:

> We can acquire the knowledge of divine things by natural reason only through the imagination; and the same applies to the knowledge given by grace. As Dionysius says, "it is impossible for the divine ray to shine upon us except as screened round about by the many colored sacred veils."

Images of God are not peripheral or dispensable to theological speech, nor as we have seen, to ecclesial and social praxis. They are crucially important among the many colored veils through which divine mystery is mediated and by means of which we express relationship in return.

The nature of symbols for divine mystery is rather plastic, a characteristic that will serve this study well. According to Tillich's well-known analysis, symbols point beyond themselves to something else, something moreover in which they participate. They open up levels of reality which otherwise are closed, for us, and concomitantly open up depths of our own being, which otherwise would remain untouched. They cannot be produced intentionally but grow from a deep level that Tillich identifies as the collective unconscious. Finally, they grow and die like living beings in relation to their power to bear the presence of the divine in changing cultural situations. In the struggle against sexism for the genuine humanity of women we are today at a crossroads of the dying and rising of religious symbols. The symbol of the patriarchal idol is cracking, while a plethora of others emerge. Among these are female symbols for divine mystery that bear the six characteristics delineated above. Women realize that they participate in the image of the divine and so their own concrete reality can point toward this mystery. Use of these symbols discloses new depths of holy mystery as well as of the community that uses them. Women's religious experience is a generating force

for these symbols, a clear instance of how great symbols of the divine always come into being not simply as a projection of the imagination, but as an awakening from the deep abyss of human existence in real encounter with divine being.

The symbol gives rise to thought. With this axiom Paul Ricoeur points to the dynamism inherent in a true symbol that participates in the reality it signifies. The symbol gives, and what it gives is an occasion for thinking. This thought has the character of interpretation, for the possibilities abiding in a symbol are multivalent. At the same time, through its own inner structure a symbol guides thought in certain directions and closes off others. It gives its gift of fullest meaning when a thinker risks critical interpretation in sympathy with the reality to which it points. So it is when the concrete, historical reality of women, affirmed as blessed by God, functions as symbol in speech about the mystery of God. Language is informed by the particularity of women's experience carried in the symbol. Women thereby become a new specific channel for speaking about God, and thought recovers certain fundamental aspects of the doctrine of God otherwise overlooked. To advance the truth of God's mystery and to redress imbalance so that the community of disciples may move toward a more liberating life, this study engages imagination to speak in female symbols for divine mystery testing their capacity to bear divine presence and power.

Why Not Feminine Traits or Dimensions of God?

Having opted to use the word God, and to do so in connection with female symbols, there is yet another decision to be made. At least three distinct approaches to the renewal of speech about God in the direction of greater inclusivity can be identified in current theology. One seeks to give "feminine" qualities to God who is still nevertheless imagined predominantly as a male person. Another purports to uncover a "feminine" dimension in God, often finding this realized in the third person of the Trinity, the Holy Spirit. A third seeks speech about God in which the fullness of female humanity as well as of male humanity and cosmic reality may serve as divine symbol, in equivalent ways.

Searching the implications of each can show why the first two options lead into a blind alley and why only equivalent imaging of God [as] male and female can in the end do greater justice to the dignity of women and the truth of holy mystery.

FEMININE TRAITS

A minimal step toward the revision of patriarchal God language is the introduction of gentle, nurturing traits traditionally associated with the mothering role of women. The symbol of God the Father in particular benefits from this move. Too often this predominant symbol has been interpreted in association with unlovely traits associated with ruling men in a male-oriented society: aggressiveness, competitiveness, desire for absolute power and control, and demand for obedience. This certainly is not the Abba to whom Jesus prayed, and widespread rejection of such a symbol from Marx, Nietzsche, and Freud onward has created a crisis for Christian consciousness. But it is also possible to see God the Father displaying feminine, so-called maternal features that temper "his" overwhelmingness. William Visser't Hooft, for example, argues that while the fatherhood of God is and must remain the predominant Christian symbol, it is not a closed or exclusive symbol but is open to its own correction, enrichment, and completion from other symbols such as mother. Thus gentleness and compassion, unconditional love, reverence and care for the weak, sensitivity, and desire not to dominate but to be an intimate companion and friend are predicated of the Father God and make "him" more attractive. A clue to the use of this approach in an author is almost invariably the word *traits.* . . .

. . . God is not exclusively masculine but the "feminine-maternal element must also be recognized in Him." God persists as "him," but is now spoken about as a more wholistic male person who has integrated his feminine side. The patriarchy in this symbol of God is now benevolent, but it is nonetheless still patriarchy. And while the image of God as ruling male as well as real male persons made in "his" image may benefit and grow from the development of nurturing and compassionate qualities in themselves, there is no equivalent attribution to a female symbol or to actual women of

corresponding presumably masculine qualities of rationality, power, the authority of leadership, and so forth. Men gain their feminine side, but women do not gain their masculine side (if such categories are even valid). The feminine is there for the enhancement of the male, but not vice-versa: there is no mutual gain. Actual women are then seen as capable of representing only feminine traits of what Is still the male-centered symbol of God, the fullness of which can therefore be represented only by a male person. The female can never appear as icon of God in all divine fullness equivalent to the male. Inequality is not redressed but subtly furthered as the androcentric image of God remains in place, made more appealing through the subordinate inclusion of feminine traits.

A critical issue underlying this approach is the legitimacy of the rigid binary system into which it forces thought about human beings and reality itself. Enormous diversity is reduced to two relatively opposed absolutes of masculine and feminine, and this is imposed on the infinite mystery of God. The move also involves dubious stereotyping of certain human characteristics as predominantly masculine or feminine. Even as debate waxes over the distinction between sex and gender, and about whether and to what extent typical characteristics of men and women exist by nature or cultural conditioning, simple critical observation reveals that the spectrum of traits is at least as broad among concrete, historical women as between women and men. In the light of the gospel, by what right are compassionate love, reverence, and nurturing predicated as primordially feminine characteristics, rather than human ones? Why are strength, sovereignty, and rationality exclusively masculine properties? As Rosemary Ruether astutely formulates the fundamental question: Is it not the case that the very concept of the "feminine" is a patriarchal invention, an ideal projected onto women by men and vigorously defended because it functions so well to keep men in positions of power and women in positions of service to them? Masculine and feminine are among the most culturally stereotyped terms in the language. This is not to say that there are no differences between women and men, but it is to question the justification of the present distribution of virtues and attributes and to find it less than compelling as a description of reality. Such stereotyping serves the genuine humanity of neither women nor men, and feeds an anthropological dualism almost impossible to overcome. Adding "feminine" traits to the male-imaged God furthers the subordination of women by making the patriarchal symbol less threatening, more attractive. This approach does not, then, serve well for speech about God in a more inclusive and liberating direction.

A FEMININE DIMENSION: HOLY SPIRIT

Rather than merely attribute stereotypical feminine qualities to a male-imaged God, a second approach seeks a more ontological footing for the existence of the feminine in God. Most frequently that inroad is found in the doctrine of the Holy Spirit, who in classical trinitarian theology is coequal in nature with the Father and the Son. In the Hebrew Scriptures the Spirit is allied with female reality as can be seen not only by the grammatical feminine gender of the term *ruah,* which in itself proves nothing, but also by the use of the female imagery of the mother bird hovering or brooding to bring forth life, imagery associated with the Spirit of God in creation (Gn 1:2) and at the conception and baptism of Jesus (Lk 1:35 and 3:22). Semitic and Syrian early Christians did construe the divine Spirit in female terms, attributing to the Spirit the motherly character which certain parts of the Scriptures had already found in Israel's God. The Spirit is the creative, maternal God who brings about the incarnation of Christ, new members of the body of Christ in the waters of baptism, and the body of Christ through the epiclesis of the eucharist. In time the custom of speaking about the Spirit in female terms waned in the West along with the habit of speaking very extensively about the Spirit at all.

There have been various attempts in recent years to retrieve the full trinitarian tradition while overcoming its inherent patriarchy by speaking about the Spirit as the feminine person of the godhead. When the Spirit is considered *the* feminine aspect of the divine, however, a host of difficulties ensues. The endemic difficulty of Spirit theology in the West insures that this "person" remains rather unclear and invisible. A deeper theology of the Holy Spirit, notes Walter Kasper in another connection, stands before the difficulty that unlike the Father and Son, the Holy Spirit is "faceless." While the Son has appeared in human form and while we can at least make a mental image of the Father, the Spirit is not graphic and remains theologically the most mysterious of the three divine persons. For all practical purposes, we end up with two clear masculine images and an amorphous feminine third. Furthermore, the overarching framework of this approach again remains androcentric, with the male principle still dominant and sovereign. The Spirit even as God remains the "third" person, easily subordinated to the other two since she proceeds from them and is sent by them to mediate their presence and bring to completion what they have initiated. The direction in which this leads may be seen in Franz Mayr's attempt to understand the Holy Spirit as mother on the analogy of family relationships: if we liberate motherhood from a naturalistic concept and see it in its existential-social reality, then we can indeed see how the mother comes from the father and the son, that is, how she receives her existential stamp and identity from them both within the family. As even a passing feminist analysis makes clear, while intending to rehabilitate the feminine, Mayr has again accomplished its subordination in unequal relationships.

The problem of stereotyping also plagues this approach. More often than not those who use it associate the feminine with unconscious dreams and fantasies (Bachiega), or with nature, instinct, and bodiliness (Schrey), or with prime matter (Mayr), all of which is then predicated of God through the doctrine of the Holy Spirit. The equation is thus set up: male is to female as transcendence is to immanence, with the feminine Spirit restricted to the role of bearing the presence of God to our interiority. . . .

. . . There is real danger that simply identifying the Spirit with "feminine" reality leaves the overall symbol of God fundamentally unreformed and boxes actual women into a stereotypical ideal. . . .

Unexamined presuppositions about the doctrine of God itself raise a further theological question about this approach. In what sense can it be claimed that God has "dimensions," let alone the dualistically conceived dimensions of masculine and feminine? Such an idea extends human divisions to the godhead itself. It actually ontologizes sex in God, making sexuality a dimension of divine being, rather than respecting the symbolic nature of religious language.

We must be very clear about this. Speech about God in female metaphors does not mean that God has a feminine dimension, revealed by Mary or other women. Nor does the use of male metaphors mean that God has a masculine dimension, revealed by Jesus or other men; or an animal dimension, revealed by lions or great mother birds; or a mineral dimension, which corresponds with naming God a rock. Images and names of God do not aim to identify merely "part" of the divine mystery, were that even possible. Rather, they intend to evoke the whole. Female imagery by itself points to God as such and has the capacity to represent God not only as nurturing, although certainly that, but as powerful, initiating, creating-redeeming-saving, and victorious over the powers of this world. If women are created in the image of God, then God can be spoken of in female metaphors in as full and as limited a way as God is imaged in male ones, without talk of feminine dimensions reducing the impact of this imagery. Understanding the Holy Spirit as the feminine dimension of the divine within a patriarchal framework is no solution. Even at its best, it does not liberate.

Equivalent Images of God Male and Female

While both the "traits" and the "dimensions" approach are inadequate for language about God inasmuch as in both an androcentric focus remains dominant, a third strategy speaks about the divine in images taken equivalently from the experience of women, men, and the world of nature. This approach shares with the other two the fundamental assumption that language about God as personal has a special appropriateness. Behaviorism notwithstanding, human persons are the most mysterious and attractive reality that we experience and the only creatures who bear self-reflective consciousness. God is not personal like anyone else we know, but the language of person points in a unique way to the mysterious depths

and freedom of action long associated with the divine.

Predicating personality of God, however, immediately involves us in questions of sex and gender, for all the persons we know are either male or female. The mystery of God is properly understood as neither male nor female but transcends both in an unimaginable way. But insofar as God creates both male and female in the divine image and is the source of the perfections of both, either can equally well be used as metaphor to point to divine mystery. Both in fact are needed for less inadequate speech about God, in whose image the human race is created. . . .

Although drawing their predominant speech about God from the pool of male images, the biblical, early theological, and medieval mystical traditions also use female images of the divine without embarrassment or explanation. The images and personifications are not considered feminine aspects or features of the divine, to be interpreted in dualistic tension with masculine dimensions or traits, but rather they are representations of the fullness of God in creating, redeeming, and calling the world to eschatological shalom.

Ancient religions that spoke of deity in both male and female symbols may also be helpful in clarifying the thrust of this third approach. As evidenced in psalms and prayers, male and female deities were not stereotyped according to later ideas of what was properly masculine and feminine, but each represented a diversity of divine activities and attributes. In them "gender division is not yet the primary metaphor for imaging the dialectics of human existence," nor is the idea of gender complementarity present in the ancient myths. Rather, male and female enjoy broad and equivalent powers. . . . Both male and female are powerful in the private and public spheres. . . .

The mystery of God transcends all images but can be spoken about equally well and poorly in concepts taken from male or female reality. The approach advocated here proceeds with the insight that only if God is so named, only if the full reality of women as well as men enters into the symbolization of God along with symbols from the natural world, can the idolatrous fixation on one image be broken and the truth of the mystery of God, in tandem with the liberation of all human beings and the whole earth, emerge for our time.

Options

The linguistic options which guide this study made with the judgment that they are appropriate and necessary, converge into speech about God using female metaphors that intend to designate the whole of divine mystery. Theoretically I endorse the ideal of language for God in male and female terms used equivalently, as well as the use of cosmic and metaphysical symbols. In actual fact, however, male and female images simply have not been nor are they even now equivalent. Female religious symbols of the divine are underdeveloped, peripheral, considered secondarily if at all in Christian language and the practice it continues to shape, much like women through whose image they point to God. In my judgment, extended theological speaking about God in female images, or long draughts of this new wine, are a condition for the very possibility of equivalent imaging of God in religious speech. . . .

Study Questions on Elizabeth Johnson

1. Why is the word *God* problematic for Johnson?
2. If the holy mystery of God is above *all* imagining, on what grounds can we prefer one set of images to another? How does Johnson's position differ from that form of atheism which denies that we can talk sense about God? From an instrumentalism that uses religion as a political or psychological tool?
3. What benefits does Johnson see as following from the use of feminine symbols for God? Why is it not sufficient to speak of feminine dimensions of God?
4. Is Johnson's argument at bottom a political one? What would Johnson say to someone who finds the employment of masculine images helpful in deepening his or her relationship with God, who does not share Johnson's longing for an egalitarian and liberated society, or who finds masculine images psychologically satisfying? How would she reply to Richard Davis (see article later in this unit)?

On the Fatherhood of God

JULI LOESCH WILEY

Juli Loesch Wiley defends speaking of God as Father and criticizes speaking of God as Mother. The Fatherhood of God, she argues, imposes obligations on both men and society to serve, support, and acknowledge the God-given rights of women and (both born and unborn) children. Moreover, it frees us from the overwhelming weight of being under the Mother, and relieves all women of the burden of having to play God.

Reprinted with permission of the author.

A KEY CHARACTERISTIC of the Holy One of Israel, is that Yahweh cares for the husbandless woman and the fatherless child. "The desire of the afflicted You hear, O Lord! You pay heed to the defense of the orphan (*yatom*) and the oppressed."

Yatom is often translated "orphan," but etymologically it is more precisely "without a man," or "the fatherless." The "widow" in Hebrew society was not necessarily a woman whose husband was dead, but a woman bereft, abandoned, or alone; and the *yatom* child was not necessarily a child whose father was dead, but could also be a child rejected—unwanted, unsupported, or unprotected by a father. (It is not hard to see a woman impregnated and then abandoned as a "widow" in the Biblical sense, and her child, born or unborn, as an "orphan.")

Israel often had a hard time distinguishing the Holy One from the ever-popular Baals of patriarchal Canaanite society. But Hosea (4:14) puts the difference between Yahweh and Baal succinctly: "What we have made with our hands we will never again call 'gods'; for You are *the one in whom the fatherless find compassion.*"

According to the Psalms, the *resa'im,* the unjust, who are the enemies of God, are defined as those who do not defend the cause of the fatherless child and the woman-alone (Ps. 10:14–15; 94:3, 6; 146:9). This theme is taken up from the very first chapter of Isaiah, where the unjust are typified as those who "are merciless to the fatherless: the plight of the woman-alone is never heeded" (v. 23), and where God's people are told, "Search for justice, help the oppressed, do right by the fatherless, be an advocate for the woman-alone" (v. 17), with the significant warning, "If you refuse and rebel, you shall be devoured by the sword" (v. 20).

The *paterfamilias* in the patriarchal Greco-Roman world had life-or-death power over his entire household. His physical or symbolic paternity implied ownership. The absolute identification of *siring* and ownership was radically undercut by the Hebrew realization that God Himself is in some sense the true Father and protector of every child.

It is the Holy One of Israel who opens and closes the womb. Even the very first child, Cain, caused his mother Eve to acknowledge. the procreative power, not of Adam, but of God: "I have produced a child with the help of the Lord" (Gen. 4:1). So the Fatherhood of God did not serve to absolutize the power of earthly fathers. Precisely the opposite: it served to relativize earthly paternity. Fathers had obligations toward their offspring because children were conceived "with the help of the Lord."

When Sarah, Hannah, or (in Luke's Gospel) Elizabeth conceived, it is a triumph of the woman and Yahweh: one is almost given the impression that the earthly father is an instrument and bemused observer of it all.

This theme of God's liberating paternity reaches its apex with Jesus, Who was literally "the Son of God."

(I am reminded of a curious story about a 19th century opponent of women's rights who tried to tell the Christian abolitionist/feminist, Sojourner Truth, that men were superior to women "because Christ was a man." He received the black woman's arch retort: "And where did your Christ come from? God and a woman—man didn't have nothin' to do with it!")

One could almost say that it takes, not *two* to have a baby, but *three:* a man, a woman, and the Holy Spirit. The woman, too, knows that she is not the maker or owner of her child. In the gripping testimony of a woman witnessing the torture and death of her seven sons (2 Macc. 22–23):

> I do not know how you came into existence in my womb. It was not I who gave you the breath of life, nor was it I who set in order the elements of which each of you is composed. Therefore, since it is the Creator of the Universe who shapes each person's beginnings, and brings about the origin of everything, God, in His mercy, will give you back both life and breath.

God makes a relationship with the child He is forming in the womb from the very beginning. In Psalm 139, the singer envisions himself, an embryo, as a person in the hands of a personal God. "Truly You have formed my inmost being: You knit me in my mother's womb" (v. 13). God sees this young Hebrew's actions (v. 16) and accepts the child's praises even before birth.

Jeremiah was recognized, not only as person, but as prophet before birth. "Before I formed you in the womb," says Yahweh, "I knew you; before you were born I dedicated you; a prophet to the nations I appointed you" (Jer. 1:5).

What does this mean for us?

First, *the Fatherhood of God in no way supports patriarchy* in the sense of a male right to autonomous power in the household. A man has the obligation to serve, support, and acknowledge the God-given rights of his wife and children, or God Himself will be his enemy and judge.

Second, *the Fatherhood of God imposes collective obligations.* Society as a whole must uphold the interests of single women and provide protection and sustenance to children without fathers, whether those children are born or unborn. A nation which fails to enforce the rights of women and children will perish "by the sword."

Third, *the Fatherhood of God guarantees the rights and dignity of each person* because God wills the particular creation of each and every individual, fashions each one for a purpose, and entrusts to each a vocation. God has a right to see each of these vocations come to fruition. Thus, situations where humans fail to develop their personal gifts (as victims of war and abortion, sexual and racial discrimination, hunger, poverty, illiteracy and ignorance, widespread underdevelopment and the squandering of human potential) are an affront, not just to human rights, but to the rights of God.

"That is why I kneel before the Father, from whom every family in heaven and on earth takes its true name." The human rights of all flow from the Father-rights of God.

Is "God the Mother" Just as Good?

JULI LOESCH WILEY

FEMINIST THEOLOGIANS have said they've looked within themselves and seen a Spirit feminine. If their writings tell the story of their search for the Godhead, then the Hebrew and Christian Testaments are the story of the Godhead's search for them, and for all of us. God's choice image is that He is the Bridegroom: and Israel, and the Church, and all of us, *men and women,* are the Bride.

For all their sensitivity to sex, many of the post-traditional feminist theologians are not sexual enough. Many identify the "female imagination" as being "meditative" and "fertile," and then shy away, almost prudishly, from even imagining natural sex. Some even say their meditations become "fertile" *parthenogenetically*—that is, "not dependent on an external catalyst," as Meinrad Craighead insists.

Craighead therefore abandons the sexual metaphor altogether—as it applies to human beings—and prefers the image of procreating from an unfertilized egg, as do certain insects, crustaceans, and worms—all because she will not bring a male generative act into her inward meditations.

Many feminist theologians believe that women have been withheld from full participation in the Christian mysteries. It would be truer to say, however, that it is only women who are admitted to the Christian mysteries, and that any men who would participate must first become "women." This is because in traditional Christian mystical language *all* souls are feminine. (C.S. Lewis says something to the effect that the whole of creation is feminine in relation to the Creator.)

So it is men, *as men,* who are left out of Christian sexual mysticism. The Prophets of Israel, the Doctors of the Church—drawing upon Paul's writings—and the late medieval mystics, male and female, say we must all be Brides. In this respect, Mary is the model, not only for all women, but for all Christians. Men or women who want to unite with God must become other Marys.

It is males who must change most in the spiritual life. Thus it is *not* that women must identify with God (as Mary Daly would say) but that men must *stop* identifying with Him. We women can rejoice directly in our femaleness; men, on the other hand, must empty out their maleness.

"Ah, but you are confining yourself to the limits of patriarchal imagery" retort the feminists. They make much of the fact that all ancient peoples had pictures of gods and goddesses, and then go on as if, for all practical purposes, one is as good as another. Just scan the Jungian menu (Babylonian and Eleusian, too) and order *a la carte*. Hence, we get from feminists the image of God as "Immanent Mother."

But this is no biblical view. The Hebrew Scriptures, clear through, are a thousand-year polemic against their neighbors' myth systems. Hebrew writers drew on familiar Middle Eastern materials, of course, but only to "spike" them with Yahwism, co-opting them quite cleverly at times. But adherence to the rival images of the other nations is plainly forbidden as idolatry.

Idolatry is the sin most frequently denounced by the Hebrew prophets; and they linked it closely with their second-most-denounced sin, the oppression of the poor and helpless. The prevalence of novel and popular myths is seen as being so dangerous to the community as to bring about its ethical, and then physical, destruction.

Every created thing is, in some way, a revelation of God; and so any image the artist or poet brings up can have, in the very broadest sense of the word, a "sacramental" significance (in the sense that it is an outward sign through which the Creator acts and communicates). So there can be considerable freedom in symbolic language. But this freedom must be disciplined by core considerations.

For instance: let's say we like the Promethean myth rather than the theme of Jesus' sacrificial death on the Cross. So we redesign the Mass in certain ways so that the obedient Jesus becomes the rebel Prometheus; the loving Father God becomes the irate, cruel Zeus; and the object of human life becomes not worship but tyrannicide. This would be relevant to many an individual struggle; it would be useful to many a political and social agenda; but it would not be the Mass of the Christian *kerygma*.

The Mass is the same sacrifice as the Sacrifice of the Cross. It happened "primordially," in a sense, in that the Word is for all eternity offering Himself to the Father; but it also happened within *historical* time: on Golgotha Hill outside the city of Jerusalem, when Pontius Pilate was governor of Judea. And it has an *ethical* meaning which is not ambiguous at all, but painfully explicit. Jesus was obedient to the Father's will, and rescued us from sin through His death, to show His love. And this—both the obeying and the loving—is just what we must do. Jesus said: take up your cross.

Some feminist rite-makers defend their own liturgical revisionism by saying that we must bravely face the anxiety of "uncertain and ambiguous reality"—which is far easier to take than the offensive clarity of Mass and Cross.

Meinrad Craighead says that her Mothergod has but one law: "Create; make as I do make." Craighead explicitly puts this outside of ethical judgment, asserting that "*anyone* involved in creating *anything* new" expresses the "cosmic female force." She draws us to the clear conclusion that this is beyond the old religious concern with "rectitude"—it is beyond Good and Evil.

Some have called this doctrine of the Sovereign Will "Nietzsche for Girls." Perhaps that's too extreme; it must be admitted that the idea of human perfection through self-expression unhampered by "rectitude" can be very attractive. I think an intelligent group like feminist theologians could manufacture six or seven attractive religious ideas in any given morning, and then invent a sacrament or two over lunch.

But if we grant that this post-traditional mysticism can be attractive—even plausible and useful—we still have not asked the really important question: *Is it true?* Many true things are not necessarily attractive; some true things hardly seem plausible, and, far from being useful, seem potentially troublesome. (Take, for instance, a black hole in space. In fact, take all of them.) And this is my main argument with the feminists' Immanent

Mothergod: she has not revealed herself (outside of the devotees' subjectivity) to be true.

Hunger, emotion, duress, hormones, chemicals smoked or ingested, or any number of other factors can produce persuasive subjective intuitions. Some people fantasize hell; others, hamburgers. The fact that they are subjective does not make them false; but that they are attractive does not make them true.

Veronica Leuken of Bayside, New York, says the Virgin Mary appeared to her and said women should not wear pants. I don't say Veronica Leuken is a liar. I say she is mistaken. Any of us could make the same mistake.

Jesus' consistency in calling God His Father is one of the most striking features of His teaching. If Jesus did not have a "Theology of the Father," it's safe to say He had no theology at all. And if the content of His teaching is open to radical change, this would mean one of two things: We're saying that we have more inward freedom than Jesus did (Jesus was limited by His times but we are not). Or, while admitting that we are limited by our culture, we assert that ours is a much *better* culture: that is, 20th-century American society is more deeply and truly religious than that of Jesus' day.

Either way, we're saying we know more about God than Jesus did.

But rather than assume that Jesus' Theology of the Father, His God-language, is archaic and essentially misleading, perhaps we should ask whether calling God our Mother (while metaphorically interesting) is not actually confusing—sexually confusing.

There's one obvious reason why Jesus called God His Father. It was because God *was* His Father. God was not His Mother: *Mary* was. And this is not metaphorical or allegorical at all: it's just the way it is.

If we are baptized "into" Christ, then we take on the same relationships that Jesus has. God is our Father, others in the family of faith are our sisters and brothers, and Mary is our Mother. This has been the belief of Christians since ancient times.

Going back even further we find that exactly one-third of one verse of Genesis describes God's image as both male and female. Despite its brevity, this is said to be a crucial text: one which flashes a kind of beacon light across 72 books of

Scripture. For instance, God is portrayed as being intimately connected with feminine things: God opens and closes the womb, and delights in pregnancies; God longs to provide milk and comfort for His people (Isaiah 66). God is full of *rachmones*, the Hebrew word for "loving-kindness" which is derived from the root-word *rechem*: a mother's womb. God loves us with womb-love. It is profound.

Yet never in all 72 books of the Bible is God called, personally and directly, "Our Mother." Why? A Father with a Womb hardly seems plausible. Hardly attractive. Hardly, with the present feminist agenda, usable. Yet there it is.

The Hebrew and Christian Scriptures abound with various titles and images for God. The titles include Lord, Wonderful Counselor, Prince of Peace. The images include even animals and inanimate objects, both natural and of human making: a Rock, a Shield, a Fortress, a mother eagle urging on her young. And metaphorically, God is seen as farmer-like, shepherd-like, soldier-like—and mother-like.

But all metaphors, evidently, are not equal. Lambs, calves, and snakes may be equal; yet, while Christ can be the "Lamb" of God, we never call Him the Golden Calf or the Sacred Serpent. Why? Because serious confusion would arise, due to the other associations we have with these animals. So these terms are ruled out.

It seems that, given the prominence of both priestesses and goddesses in the religions of all of Israel's thoroughly patriarchal neighbors (Canaanite, Hellenic, Mesopotamian, and Egyptian), the Judeo-Christian avoidance of "God the Mother" and insistence upon "God the Father" was not a matter of "cultural conditioning" at all. It went against the conditioning. It was *countercultural*. It is as if "God the Mother" imagery were specifically considered, and rejected.

Again, why?

I don't know. And I know of no authoritative voice in Scripture or church tradition that tells me *why*. But without claiming any authority on my own, and drawing from my own grab bag of symbolic and psychological notions, I would make a few speculations (other than a bias in favor of Scripture and Tradition) why we theists should want to keep our old God the *Father* anyway.

There's a datum of biology I'd like to lead off with in a tentative way. Procreation requires action that is conscious or deliberate on the part of the male, but not on the part of the female. Hence, a man can have intercourse with a woman who is entirely nonactive—even unconscious or in a coma—and beget a child.

This is, admittedly, an extreme example, but it illustrates a fact that is not social or cultural, but anatomical: the act that begets life is *always* active for the male, but not necessarily for the female. In this sense (if in no other) the male initiates generation.

I simply offer this as a datum, not as the basis for a general and socially pervasive theory of female passivity (which God forbid!). But in terms of choosing natural images—sheer metaphor—this may be relevant to the idea of God's coming, God's active giving, our openness, our "letting God," our patient bearing of what God has implanted: an idea common in Christian mysticism.

With the same tentativeness—merely offering this for investigation—I suggest another reason which involves psychological theory.

Psychologist Dorothy Dinnerstein interprets our prolonged human infancy as a time of strong emotions, physical helplessness, and preverbal frustration directed—almost always—at our mother or female caretaker. Dinnerstein shows that we all have deeply ambivalent relationships with mother figures. We have depended upon them absolutely, and raged against them with infant tears because they were so controlling of every sensate need: milk, touch, comfort. She exhaustively details how we go through stages of feeling "smothered" by our mothers, and by women generally. She emphasizes that the father, the male, is *not* the object of all our fervent need and howling resentment—not in the crucial preverbal months of our infancy—

because the man's role in the day-to-day routine care of tiny infants has been marginal.

One of Dinnerstein's main conclusions—a theme found in popular feminist psychology—is that the main project for human maturity is to distribute our strong emotions more equally among men and women. Dinnerstein's prescription is to shift the earliest infant care substantially to men, so that our infant bliss and rage will be directed at men and women equally. Yet she doubts that this can actually be carried out on a wide scale. For 99 percent of the human race it's still mothers and other women who tend the babies, and it's likely to remain so. That's how *we* were raised. Can we be born once again?

Then—still following this theory—we might still compensate for the power of *all* our original "Mothergods" by transferring those emotions to a male figure in some other way.

I'm suggesting—and, ironically, feminist psychoanalytic theory itself suggests—that at this point, the resurgence of God as *Mother* could be disastrous. All our impelling hopes and wild fears, our tearful petitions, and our upwelling resentments would still be heaped upon—who? *the Mother!* It's Mother's fault. It always was. How "liberating"!

Maybe one of the sane aspects of our old "improbable" biblical God is that He gives us, at last, a chance to climb into the womb and be born again, from the Father this time.

The Theology of the Father gives us a masculine figure to love impossibly and struggle with like Jacob; a terrible Papa (not Mama) to reproach and beat with Jeremiah fists.

It frees all of us from the awful weight of being under the Mother, *again*. It relieves our mothers—and all women—of the burden of being God Almighty, so to speak, *again*.

Study Questions on Juli Loesch Wiley

1. How does Wiley believe that the Hebrew understanding of the Fatherhood of God had the effect of limiting the power of earthly fathers? How does Wiley see the Fatherhood of God as guaranteeing the rights and dignity of each person?
2. Wiley argues that in relationship with God, "women can rejoice directly in our femaleness; men, on the other hand, must empty out their maleness." Carol

Christ says that women can see themselves as like God only by denying their own sexual identity. Are they disagreeing? Or are they talking about different phenomena?

3. Why, according to Wiley, does feminist psychoanalytic theory suggest that the resurgence of God as Mother could be disastrous? How would Christ, Reuther, and Johnson reply?

4. Has Wiley persuaded you that thinking of God as "Father" does not support patriarchy? Why or why not?

Making Inclusive Language Inclusive: A Christian Gay Man's View

RICHARD DAVIS

Richard Davis points out that "inclusive language" excludes male symbols, male images, and male pronouns from the common worship of the Christian community. Many male homosexuals, in particular, feel hurt and betrayed by a language that has often neuterized or feminized God, forbidding Him ever to be Father, Lord, or King.

SOME CHRISTIANS are dead set against any change whatsoever in the language of worship. But few contemporary Christians are so hidebound. Most of us welcome language that more satisfactorily expresses the fullness of our experience of God. Scripture and Christian tradition contain a rich variety of images and symbols that have been employed to speak about God—and not only anthropomorphic ones like Father or Mother, but also images like Rock, Water, Light, Word, Wind, Silence, Mountain, Lamb, Bread, and Wine. Introducing a wider range of images into the common worship of the Christian community would give us a richer and fuller experience of the Being of God, and provide worshippers the freedom to enter more deeply into an intimate, personal relationship with God. Unfortunately, however, much of what goes by the name of "inclusive language" involves *ex*cluding all masculine images and symbols for God and not just including others. The masculine pronoun is eliminated when referring to God and replaced either with feminine pronouns or by the monotonous repetition of the sexless word *God*. Yet we see no rush to replace the numerous feminine pronouns for God in the Book of Wisdom with a monotonous repetition of the sexless word *God*. Have our notions of God advanced only so far as to eliminate our male anthropomorphic images and not our female ones?

Many men feel hurt and betrayed by a language that was supposedly created to include us all in a fuller and richer experience of worship, but which, instead, has neuterized or feminized God, forbidding Him ever to be Father, Lord, King, or any other masculine image. Many men have profoundly experienced the feminine in God and wish to express that experience in worship. However, other men wish to affirm their positive image of God as Father, Brother, Coach, Masculine Lover. How can a language that deliberately excludes the masculine be called "inclusive"?

First of all, in the name of truthful scholarship, we ought not to tamper with Scripture. Where the original languages have a particular sexual pronoun,

An earlier version of this article appeared in the newsletter of the Parsonage, *a lesbian and gay ministry of the Episcopal Diocese of California; it has been rewritten for this volume. Used by permission of the author.*

to change that pronoun in English to the opposite sex or to a neuter, or to systematically refuse to translate the pronoun, is censorship. The lesbian and gay community has always been especially sensitive to the issue of censorship because the literature and history of our foremothers and forefathers has frequently been systematically censored to conform to a heterocentric concept of society. Masculine and feminine pronouns in poetry and other works have been played with by heterosexual scholars to create heterosexual expressions of love out of works by lesbian and gay authors. We rightfully condemn such heterocentric bowdlerizations of our heritage. So also should we condemn any attempt to censor Scripture or the language of worship to make it conform to preconceived ideological notions about the nature of God. If Scripture is understood as God's self-revelation, we ought to preserve the rich variety of images and symbols found in it; we cannot do justice to the full Being of God if we refuse to ever acknowledge him in masculine-gendered terms. Despite the enforced gender neutrality of American society, perhaps male and female are two very different, but complementary expressions of what it means to be human. God created us in his image both male and female (Genesis 1:27), and when God wishes to express his Being in a way that is analogous to a peculiarly masculine form, such as Father, then that form must be masculine to be true to who God is. Mother and Father are not mutually interchangeable images, equal to each other in meaning or significance. And the fact that Jesus taught his disciples to call God "Father" provides an additional reason for retaining this way of speaking and thinking about God.

Where central doctrines such as the Trinity are involved, again we should be careful about ill-thought-out experiments in inclusive language. Unfortunately, the level of doctrinal knowledge and understanding is frequently so limited among contemporary Christians that the profound theological significance of an innovative language formula may pass lightly by. It seems to work okay and nobody worries that it may imply a change in credal affirmations! For example, the substitution of the formula "God the Creator, God the Redeemer, and God the Sanctifier" for "God the Father, God the Son, and God the Holy Spirit" on first sight seems to be theologically sound, and it has a nice ring. Yet, it reduces God to His functions and moves our attention away from His Being, His *personalness*. Moreover, does this formula imply that God exists in modalities of function or as successive immanences in human history—both heresies? Perhaps, perhaps not, but I've never heard anyone worry themselves with examining what this inclusive language formula implies about the Being of God.

Often the introduction of inclusive language formulas is motivated not by a desire to experience the God of our fathers and mothers in faith in a richer and fuller way, but by a feminist political agenda. Some materialist feminists see religion and its language as mere tools of the patriarchal social structure. Their primary goal is the restructuring of society at large, and changing the language of worship and the images religious people have of God is just a small aspect of a larger social agenda. They are not interested in God per se but in God as the projected symbol of power structures in society. Change the language used in reference to God; change the power structures. But when ideology becomes the motivation for liturgical change, the freedom and personalism of the individual's living experience of God will get squashed. How many men have been pressured into praying to "our Mother" or "our parent" when their lived experience of God is as a Dad or a Father? (And although my emphasis in this article is on the experience of men, I am sure that those nuns or other women who think of Christ as their spouse, or the many women who think of God as a brother or as a loving Father, would also find that liturgical language eliminating all masculine images or pronouns would interfere with their freedom to experience God in their own way.)

Sometimes advocates of inclusive language are not merely manipulating religion to serve political goals, but rather seeking to explore non-Christian perceptions of God. It is not uncommon for such people to introduce the worship of the goddess qua Goddess, and not only as the feminine aspect of the God of Christian faith. Various pagan and atavistic rituals and prayer formulas are also frequently adopted in order to explore new forms of faith and concepts of divinity. Some do not look back to archaic gods but wish to introduce a more up-to-date conception of God. The personal, transcendent God of Christian faith seems to them outmoded. They embrace instead a New Age vision of a pantheistic god, immanent in all things, an impersonal force. The Christian community can warmly support such spiritual searches and pray earnestly that those searching will find a deeper communion with God. We also hope to learn more about God through dialogue with people who are earnestly on the path of search. But it is misleading to introduce into Christian worship conceptions, prayers, rituals, and formulas that are not Christian; new and strange gods must not be foisted upon the Christian community under the auspices of inclusive language.

Another thing that is sometimes going on under the cloak of inclusive language is an attempt to sneak in by the back door beliefs about God that are incompatible with our Christian tradition. Many American Christians have a strong emotional reaction against the Old Man in the Sky of former piety. Authority figures are rather passé, and Yahweh Sabaoth is decidedly authoritative. We would love nothing more than to rid ourselves of that cranky old warrior-king and replace him with a cozier, more nurturing—need I say affirming?—Big Earth Mama with a soft lap and ample bosom. Thus "Lord" and "King" are eliminated because they are masculine, but they are not replaced by more neutral images of authority. Authority is identified as masculine and therefore given short shrift by those inclusive language writers motivated to convey a more affirming image of God. Male authority figures are either demonized or laughed at. A feminine image of God is thought to convey something caring and nurturing, while a masculine one carries with it negative associations with domination and aggression. Yet to enshrine this reaction against the masculine in our common liturgical language is to enforce the very gender stereotypes from which inclusive language is supposed to free us.

Which brings me to what is perhaps the most troubling thing about inclusive language—namely that it all too often springs from and reflects an antimasculine ideology. If all male pronouns and images must be excised from our common liturgical language, the clear message would seem to be that to use a masculine image or pronoun is to say

something bad about God, whereas to use feminine ones is to say something good. Or at least this is how many men will perceive it. Men in our culture are all too often seen as the perpetuators of the worst in human society—war, rape, eco-pillage, and dominance, while women are portrayed as always caring and sensitive—never aggressive or dominating. Boys, it seems, are always in trouble in school, while little girls are always good. Little boys are made of "snakes and snails and puppy dog tails," while girls are made of "sugar and spice and everything nice."

Ironically, Scripture paints a much less stereotyped image of the feminine. Yes, Naomi is an example of God's loving-kindness toward those who embrace him in faith, even if they be strangers or foreigners. Esther is the archetype of God's providence. In the sacrifice of the daughter of Jephthah we see one of the great archetypes of the sacrifice of Christ for our redemption (Judges 11:29–40). But in the Bible we also find Jael hammering her spike through the head of General Sisera—after feeding him milk and cookies (Judges 5:24–27), terrorist Ma Maccabee inciting her sons to undergo martyrdom in Jihad (2 Maccabees 7), and even the Blessed Virgin Mary is pictured marshalling the Church Militant into battle (Revelation 12).

Because of the profound neglect of much in our scriptural and liturgical tradition, many Christians approach inclusive language simply as a process of cutting out offending male pronouns and images. Well, put away those red pencils! That's not the solution. Instead we need to fully own what already belongs to us as Christians in our Scripture and our tradition. For example, the Warrior-God Yahweh already is Mother Eagle, "watching her nest, hovering over her young" (Deuteronomy 32:10, 11). The King of Israel is already Israel's mother. When Zion says that the Lord has abandoned them, Yahweh replies, "Does a woman forget her baby at the breast, or fail to cherish the son of her womb?" (Isaiah 49:14, 51). In the New Testament, Jesus frequently uses feminine imagery in reference to himself and the Father. In the parable of the lost coin (Luke 15:8–10), God the Father is already imaged as a woman sweeping her house. Jesus, lamenting his rejection by his people, cries, "how often I would have gathered your children together as a hen gathers her brood under her wings" (Matthew 23:37). Just as Scripture is already rich in feminine images of God, so also is the living tradition of our Christian faith. For example, the Council of Seville prayed to God the Father, "who bore us in His womb." One ancient icon of Christ's crucifixion shows him pregnant, heavy with child upon the Cross. In Most Holy Redeemer Church in the gay Castro neighborhood of San Francisco, there is a stained glass window picturing Jesus surrounded by children and above is the symbol of a mother pelican plucking her breast to feed her young. Our sexual stereotypes, like the idols of Egypt, lie broken forever when we embrace the true icons of God already found in Scripture and tradition. The problem with the typical heavy-handed ideological approach to inclusive language is that it destroys the delicate ambiguity of these transgendered images of God.

The untruthfulness of either exclusively male images of God or exclusively female images of God is that God is both and neither. Either masculine or feminine images can be used of God as analogies of His Being precisely because they are analogies. They give us true information about his nature but, ultimately, we see through a glass darkly. When some experiments in inclusive language neuterize God that is perhaps the worst of all, for then we are denied the vivid, concrete image of God as Father, as Mother. When speaking of God using anthropomorphic sexual analogies, the tension of opposites must be maintained.

In one sense, though, inclusive language calls us even deeper into our faith. While we cling to our anthropomorphic images of God, Father and Mother, he refers to himself as Rock, Water, Light, Word, Wind, Silence, Mountain, Lamb, Bread, and Wine. Our religion is human-centered. Might not inclusive language be calling us to open our hearts to all of God's creation, whom also he suffered and died to save? Ultimately, we may have to abandon words altogether. St. Theresa of Avila, a Doctor of the Church, is best known perhaps for her great works on prayer. Yet when she returned to her sisters after her direct apprehension of the glory of God, she could not speak, there were no images possible. She could only bring out her castanets and dance her vision of pure Being.

Whenever I have used a pronoun in place of the word *God* in this article, I have used a masculine pronoun. My primary experience of God is as a Masculine Lover. To quote the Song of Songs:

As an apple tree among the trees of the wood, so is my beloved among young men. With great delight I sat in his shadow, and his fruit was sweet to my taste. He brought me to the banqueting house, and his banner over me was love. Sustain me with raisins, refresh me with apples; for I am sick with love. (Song of Solomon, 2:3–5)

Or I think of John, the disciple whom Jesus loved who was lying close to his breast at the last supper (John 13:23). I do have some strong feminine experiences of God and when I am expressing those I may use a feminine pronoun, but that is not my primary experience and so it would be false for me to use "she" instead of "he." I am faithful to Scripture when I imagine God as my Masculine Lover and it is true to my experience as a gay Christian man that he is so, and I am free in Christ to worship him as such. Genuinely inclusive language allows me that freedom and includes my experience in the common worship of the Christian community. Anything else is not inclusive.

Study Questions on Richard Davis

1. Davis argues that "inclusive language" as is currently practiced is not in fact inclusive at all. Explain his argument for this conclusion.
2. What does he think truly inclusive language would be? What positive role does he accord to feminine language about God?

3. Davis is worried about ideologically motivated changes in liturgical worship. Why? What is the purpose of liturgy for him, and how might politically motivated changes interfere with that purpose?
4. Do you agree with Davis about the crucial importance of accuracy in Scripture translation? How would you handle other linguistic problems, for example, pronouns?

God the Father, God the Mother, and Goddesses

SUSANNE HEINE

> Susanne Heine agrees that those with impaired images of their fathers *may* find that thinking of God as "father" harms their relationship with God, although even they may be able to find in God the good father they lacked, and so find healing. But mothers also behave abusively, so that thinking of God as "mother" is not the solution. The tradition has provided us with many names and images of God, and we should welcome this richness and avoid one-sided identifications. Above all we must beware of the "theocratic shortcut" that appeals to the authority of God to authorize the absolute power of human authorities. Heine also corrects some popular misconceptions about God the Father, God the Mother, and the goddesses in light of the biblical record and the surrounding goddess-worshipping cultures of the Ancient Near East.

The Strict Name of God

Blessed art thou
O Lord our God and God of our fathers,
the great, mighty and revered God,
the most high God,
who bestowest lovingkindness,
creator of the universe . . .
O King, Helper, Saviour and Shield . . .
Thou, O Lord, art mighty for ever . . .
Thou art holy
and thy name is holy . . .
Cause us to return, O our Father, to thy Law.
Draw us near, O our King, unto thy service,
and bring us back in perfect repentance unto thy presence . . .
Bless us, O our Father,
with the light of thy countenance.

"Lord," "revered God," "King," "Shield," "Father"—that is the way in which pious Jews still address their God in the Eighteen Benedictions: in the morning, in the evening and on the Sabbath. All these names appear in the Old Testament, and more besides: as warrior hero and leader of heavenly and earthly hosts God annihilates the enemies of Israel (Song of Miriam, Ex.15.1ff.; Song of Deborah, Judg.5.1ff.). He is Lord over all other gods and men, strong and terrible, king, supreme lawgiver and judge, a divine patriarch, who—as a feminist verdict has it—justifies all the evil deeds of the male patriarchs.

God is indeed also Father, although he does not have this name in the Old Testament anywhere so often as might be supposed from a knowledge of the New Testament. But God is a strict father: "Know then in your heart that, as a man disciplines

From Christianity and the Goddess. *SCM Press, 1988. Reprinted by permission of the publisher.*

his son, the Lord your God disciplines you. So you shall keep the commandments of the Lord your God, by walking in his ways and by fearing him" (Deut.8.6). "For the Lord reproves him whom he loves, as a father the son in whom he delights" (Prov.3.12). As father God gives his people Israel, or even the individual, ethical instruction, The Torah, the "Law of God."

Nevertheless, the strict God of the Old Testament is not a cruel God to his own people: "The Lord is merciful and gracious, slow to anger and abiding in steadfast love. . . . As a father pities his children, so the Lord pities those who fear him" (Ps.103.8,13). Indeed, love virtually overwhelms the divine Father: "For as often as I speak against him (= the people), I do remember him still. Therefore my heart yearns for him; I will surely have mercy on him . . ." (Jer.31.20). God the Father has taught his people to walk, taken them in his arms and drawn them to him with "bands of love" (Hos.11.3–4). This is no blind love without criteria; just as God is a father to orphans without rights who gives them justice (Ps.68.6), so God knows that people will always remain children and in need of forgiveness. For is there anyone who with the best will in the world does not sometimes fail others? Who among the mortals can say that he is perfect? No one escapes guilt. Anyone who does not recognize that is regarded as a stubborn sinner; judgment comes upon him. But anyone who has insight and turns in confidence to the Father may be certain of the love and mercy of his heavenly Father.

Thus this God has all the traits of the caring father who is strict but just to his children, especially his sons, in the family of the patriarchate. He brings his children up to obey his law, punishes them and rewards them, loves his children and feels offended if the children do not follow him, if they forsake him or even deny him. He can be furious with them, but he wants to win them back by having mercy on them and looking after them. He does not abandon his children, and they do not get away from him. All the authoritarian features of the paterfamilias, but also the humanly understandable and lovable ones, can also be found in God the Father.

The New Testament is striking first of all for the way in which the name Father is used for God much more frequently than in the Old Testament. Here it should be stressed that the address "Abba" (Mark 1.36; Gal.4.6; Rom.8.15), the word that the small child burbles and which is best translated "Papa," is the basis of a new, intimate relationship of trust in God which is free from anxiety: the Father God, who as Son is equal to human beings in everything (sin apart), who lays aside his exaltation and authority so as not to leave men and women alone even in their dying, creates a new relationship with God. Without doubt these features of the New Testament Father God are striking, and so the favourite parable of the Prodigal Son (Luke 15.11ff.) appears in every children's service or school curriculum. Nevertheless, we should not fail to notice that the names of God which attest his power, superiority and strength are still there: he is the Lord of heaven and earth, the Lord of all men and women, the king who establishes his rule, the judge of good and evil, and the Father who surrenders his utterly obedient Son Jesus to the minions of the law. The Old and New Testaments cannot be played off against one another. Almighty as he is, God can show his people his shining countenance and lovingly lead them on the way of life; but he can also hide himself, and can be experienced as the absent God: where was God when the tower of Siloam crashed down, burying people under it (Luke 13.4)? The dark, incomprehensible, indeed apparently destructive God, who does not lay aside his strangeness, does not disappear in the New Testament. . . .

Such omnipotence removes God from human understanding; it transcends the power of the patriarchal kings, fathers and other rulers of the world. This has not prevented these rulers from continually deriving their power from the power of God, from transferring the distance between the utterly other God and humankind to the distance between them and their subjects. The parents are "partners in procreation," we read in a rabbinic text from the sixth century of the Christian era. This participation in the divine power of creation then gives the parents, and above all the father, almost divine authority over the children. . . .

This "theocratic shortcut," which has given its blessing to so much abuse, inhumanity and violence in history, has been criticized by spiritual and political revolutionary movements since the Enlightenment and has also continually been rejected, because of its association with a vehement attack on Christianity and an explicit atheism. Nevertheless, final success is still to come. Anyone nowadays who takes part in the life of the Christian community and its liturgical acts will encounter the biblical texts which I have quoted being used in an unreflective way, in prayers and hymns to the God of the "theocratic shortcut." . . .

Abused Children

Thoughtful theological literature continually stresses that the Father God and Lord God is not to be understood literally and naively: God is not male and has no sex; names and properties have "only" symbolic significance. But what does "only" mean here? Symbols are very closely connected with reality. Women who go to church must immediately get the impression that male properties are at least more appropriate to God than female ones. In addition, there is the hiatus between theological reflection, which has good intentions, and the means of communication through pulpits and cathedras, which hardly stimulate such sophisticated thinking, but naively hand on what the language of the tradition offers. But naive communication cannot lead to reflective reception.

However, what makes the "theocratic shortcut" of this language of the male God so terrifyingly "credible," false though it is, is the quite direct and personal experience which many women have of the other sex. This begins at the tenderest age. My first encounter with a case of sexual abuse of children by close relatives is now well back in the past. In a confidential conversation at that time, an unmarried middle-aged woman told me that from the age of eight she had regularly been subjected to all kinds of sexual abuse by an uncle for almost twenty years. As a result she had not established any relationship with a man and had been undergoing psychotherapy for some time. She came from a good Christian home and for a long time had been involved in various positions and activities in the church and in the community. At the time I did not believe what she said and took it to be the expression of a suspect state of mind; her psychotherapy seemed to me to be more than justified. I am writing this because I am afraid that such experiences might seem just as incredible to others if they come up against them: the literature

on this theme, which is the "best-kept secret," but which is slowly but surely coming to light, shocked me over my reaction at the time. Meanwhile I have come to pay more careful attention to my surroundings and know that such experiences on the part of women are not extreme aberrations, nor are they limited to some "lower level" of society. . . .

In view of such experiences, talk about the Father God and God the Father as the representative of law and order, as the one who loves, who has mercy on his children, becomes sheer arrogance. What else can give rise to the cynical image of a father who refers to the fact that he is a father while raping his daughter: "Don't be afraid . . . I'm your father"?

The Motherhood of God

Many women leave the church in order to have done with Christianity and the church once and for all. Others leave the church in order—grotesque though it may sound—to be able to grapple with Christian belief again. . . .

The strongest statements about the motherhood of God appear in Deutero-Isaiah, the later prophet of salvation in the exilic period (sixth century BC): "Can a woman forget her sucking child, that she should have no compassion on the son of her womb?" And the prophet goes on to greater heights: even if a mother forgot her child: "Even these may forget, but I will not forget you" Isa.49.15–16). God calls his people together: "Hearken to me O house of Jacob, all the remnant of the house of Israel, who have been borne by me from your birth, carried from the womb; even to your old age I am he, and to grey hairs I will carry you" (Isa.46.3–4). God says to the anonymous prophet whom we call Trito-Isaiah, from the period after the exile, who appears in Jerusalem in the Persian period (c.520 BC): "As one whom his mother comforts, so I will comfort you" (Isa.66.13). In the book of Job God describes his creative activity with terms from the experiential world of the mother: "Who shut in the sea with doors, when it burst forth from the womb; when I made clouds its garment, and thick darkness its swaddling band?" (Job 38.3–9). The action of mother and father can be limited to the idea of comprehensive parental functions: "Has the rain a father, or who his begotten the drops of dew? From whose womb did the ice come forth, and who has given birth to the hoarfrost of heaven?" (Job 38.28–29).

The pious person snuggles confidently up to his God-Mother: "But I have calmed and quieted my soul, like a child quieted at its mother's breast" (Ps.131.2). When the people murmur on their exodus from Egypt and long for the fleshpots of Egypt, Moses too gets weary of his sole responsibility: "Did I conceive all this people? Did I bring them forth that thou shouldst say to me, 'Carry them in your bosom, as a nurse carries the sucking child, to the land which thou didst swear to give their fathers'" (Num.11.12)? Thus Moses reminds God of his maternal duties. But before his death Moses also admonishes the people: "You were unmindful of the Rock that begot you, and you forgot the God who gave you birth" (Deut.32.18). Once again paternal and maternal features of God are combined in the "parenthood" of God.

God is like a mother bird which teaches her young to fly and takes them on its wings (Deut.32.11; Ex.19.4), like a hen who gathers her chickens under her wings (Matt.23.37; Ps.17.8; 91.4; 37.2 etc.). But the motherhood of God can also be directed aggressively against her own children if these turn away from the mother: "I will fall upon them like a she-bear robbed of her cubs" (Hos.13.8). The mention of rebirth from the Spirit (especially in the Gospel of John, e.g.3.4–7) evokes maternal associations; the parables of Jesus among other things make use of the realities of a woman's life: the kingdom of God can be compared with yeast which a woman mixes with the flour until it is completely leavened; like a woman and her friends who search the house for a lost coin until she has found it, so God seeks out sinners for them to be converted (Luke 13.20–21; 15.8–10). Some feminist theologians also see in the female gender of words a reference to the feminine aspects of the biblical God. The Hebrew word for the Spirit of God is feminine, *ruach*, and the divine mercy which is constantly mentioned in the texts is also feminine, *racham;* moreover it can be translated in its original meaning "mother's womb." . . .

So we can certainly bring together some feminine features and formulate them as a counterbal-

ance to a long tradition of one-sided stress on the masculinity of God. Nevertheless the question remains whether that is honest and meaningful. There is no doubt that male designations for the divine qualities and modes of action predominate in the biblical text. Accordingly the feminist concerns for a feminine image of God seem a little forced, especially where they use the feminine gender of a word for their arguments. The word "Spirit," for example, has a variety of genders depending on the language. In German it is male, in Greek neuter, in Hebrew feminine; in English, of course, nouns have no gender at all. What does one achieve with this argument when one reflects that in German, for example, power, violence or greatness are all feminine although in feminine judgment they are very closely related to the character of the male? Nor is that the case only in German: in Hebrew not only is the sword feminine, but also *geburah*, male power.

Moreover it is dangerous and contrary to basic feminist interests when a division of the male and female properties of God gives a boost to the usual stereotyping of roles. In addition to childbearing, we find that loving care, oversight, clothing, feeding, the household are seen as "typically" feminine; justice, law, anger, punishment, power are seen as "typically" masculine.

The maternal features of God to which some feminists refer belong to that part of the tradition which is opposed to goddess myths and cults: Hosea, Jeremiah, Deutero-Isaiah, Trito-Isaiah, Deuteronomy, the Priestly Writing. It is obvious what they want to say. Why do you need a mother goddess? Yahweh, the father, judge and warrior hero, can also give birth, breast-feed, care for and have mercy. Even if a mother left her child, God would never leave his people.

Anyone in search of the Old Testament God as mother will find indissolubly connected with this perspective the one God of heaven and earth and the strict father. That can also be seen in a positive light: male and female, separated here on earth, alien to one another or in conflict with one another, belong together in a totality. It is not God's fault that people have not always understood things like this, but instead use the power and masculinity of God as legitimation for the rule of men over men. . . .

Impaired Experiences of the Mother

Let us try another experiment in thinking. Suppose that the biblical tradition had given us a goddess instead of a god, a mother in heaven instead of a father in heaven. Let us once again take up the remarks of many women who say that their unhappy experiences with their physical father got in the way of their access to a heavenly father, but that they could have trust in a heavenly mother. We would evidently not be human were all this impossible. In the course of the feminist revolution women have discovered their problems with their physical mothers, which are worked out less in open violence than through subterranean psychological pressure, yet prove just as great a burden in adult life. Mothers no longer punish so much with their fists as with an indirect threat of withholding love or indicating that they have been insulted in a way which threatens their existence. Such mothers do send out not verbal but emotional signals: If you do that, you'll kill me. "She hardly ever punished us," wrote a woman about her mother. "She had a worse method. If we had to do something and didn't want to do it, then she would say, 'Then I'll do it myself.'" Daughters complain about being tied to mother's apron strings, about being treated like children, about being put down, about too few good words, about too few words at all. "I never understood her (= the mother); for me she was an authority of whom I was afraid"; "I could never touch her; that humiliated me a great deal"; "She recognized me intellectually but she despised me as a person and a woman in the same way that she despised herself." Daughters suffer from the fact that they feel responsible for their mothers, and already did as children; they feel as it were mothers of their mothers. They get on better with their fathers and feel accepted by them. The reverse is also true. Anything, in fact, may be the case. Mothers also exercise emotional power over their sons, just as sons have to suffer violence in various forms from their fathers. The literature is full of examples. . . .

. . . Women with bad experiences of their fathers may be helped by the mother in heaven; women with bad experiences of their mothers may be helped by the father in heaven. Again it was in a conversation with women after a lecture that I heard one of them say. "If God is a mother, I'm scared of the resurrection."

Neither the phenomenological selection of feminine features of the biblical God nor the historical-critical quest for the place where these features arose, nor recourse to human experiences of parents, seem to me to take us further. If one reflects on the terrifying variety of possibilities of violence between parents and children, then the "disembodied" and transcendent conception of God as the "wholly other" which is so reviled by feminists takes on power to release us: "Thank God" that God is different from us human beings!

You Shall Not Make for Yourself Any Image

Therefore as a fourth and last stage which can in fact help us out of many contradictions, systematic considerations about the question of God are necessary. I shall start from the statement that God *is* Father. What does this "is" mean? The Jewish-Christian tradition has always excluded physical ideas of procreation. The biblical God is not like Zeus, who occupied himself pre-eminently with begetting physical descendants and thus populated heaven and earth with demigods. The Christian confession of the virgin birth is simply meant to say that the conception of a physical procreation of Jesus by God is as out of the question as is his origin simply from a human being. The main reason why the phrase "conceived by the Spirit (of God)" keeps appearing in the biblical texts is to rule out biological associations: the word "conceived" is never to be understood literally. Nor is the phrase "God is father" to be reversed to become "our (physical) father is God." The effect of Judaism and Christianity is to portray God the creator as the "wholly Other," as the one who is defined as not being a creature.

Feminists have labelled this sexless, transcendent, spiritualized, abstract God who is critical of myth a product of a male consciousness and made him responsible for any drop of blood which human beings have shed in their struggle against other human beings: males, theologians "project" a "divided spiritual principle, the product of the development of patriarchal consciousness, on to the cradle of human culture." . . . The human course towards worshipping God without images is not spiritual progress but development towards a schizophrenic—i.e. divided—mode of human existence. The psychologically healthy person remains fruitfully bound up with his or her world of images. . . .

With the prohibition against images the biblical tradition also rejects all attempts to gain control of God as an "object" that can be manipulated and to claim him for all possible interests. The intention behind stating all that God is *not* is to keep God free from the conditions of finitude, from "contamination with the certainty of the senses," but also to prevent him from being imagined as the otherworldly being who "crouches outside the world" (Hegel), from where he stirs up world history at whim, when he feels like it (*deus ex machina*). Even if only in theory, such a world would be conceived of in as objective terms as this one and could not withstand the critical argument that it was a mere projection. But God is not a "thing" either to see or to touch or to imagine. All that would be "bad metaphysics" (Hegel). Were God an object, then objects would be interchangeable: what you set your heart on is your God, says Luther aptly in an explanation of the first commandment in the Greater Catechism. In that case what would be the difference between God and a good, fast automobile? The loss of either equally drives the "owner" to despair. Only the confession of several gods would offer the chance of complaining about the loss to a heavenly rival. By contrast, the transcendent God of the Bible is the critical principle which is implemented in the same tradition in an ethical claim: You shall not dominate, kill, exploit. . . . On the one hand feminists like Gerda Weiler, whom I have already mentioned, find quite vehement words for protesting against all possible forms of a claim to power, and on the other hand they accuse the biblical God of rigorist moralism which despises humanity. . . .

In the Fullness of Images

Let us return once again to the personal experiences of individuals with their parents. Against the background of our theoretical considerations neither positive nor negative experiences of a father must establish or damage relationships with a father God. It is clear that positive experiences form the basis of the analogy. The one who is loved by a father can say, "If my father . . . how much more my heavenly father." Let me recall the prophet Deutero-Isaiah (Isa.49.15–16), who talks about a mother like this. Many biblical texts talk about God in this way, independently of the analogies of which they make use. The one who is dominated by a father can say: "Though my father does not . . . at least my father in heaven does!" Is the repudiation of an earthly father to have so much power that it destroys any connection with the father God? Negative experiences can also lead to a longing and a hope for protection by the power of God which is superior to all human authorities. Conversation with women has shown me that that is possible, and that many women gain strength from offering resistance.

Father and mother are not the only analogies in talking of and to God. Not very often, but at decisive points in the Bible, God is the friend: God speaks with Moses face to face as with his friend (Ex.33.11); God can be called "friend of my youth" (Jer.3.4); and in the New Testament it is said pointedly that Christians are not servants but friends of the Lord (John 15.15). Abraham is called a "friend of God" (James 2.23) and Luke, the great story-teller, produces analogies in extended parables: God is like someone who does not reject his friend when he asks for a loaf at midnight (Luke 11.5ff.).

Eroticism also contributes to the formation of analogies. God is beloved, bridegroom, marriage partner. The Song of Songs, a collection of cultic love poetry, was accepted into the canon (after many difficulties, but it got there in the end) as an analogy for the relationship between God and people. Each side can complain about the faithlessness of the other (Isa.49.14; Jer.2.2). The analogy of the bride brings us to the New Testament, where the kingdom of God is compared to a wedding feast (Mark 2.19f.; Matt.22.1; 25.1). At the end of days this wedding will be celebrated in great splendour (Rev.19.9; 21.9,17). But all these analogies are in the dialectic of negation, "God is not . . .," and the claim which transcends everything, "God is always more than . . ." That can be done by anyone who has made the effort at analogy without being afraid of the many names and images of God which the tradition has brought together. It is precisely its wealth which makes it appropriate for protecting us from one-sided identifications. . . .

Idols and Whores

"They also built for themselves high places, and pillars, and Asherim on every high hill and under every green tree; and there were also 'initiates' in the land" (I Kings 14.23–24). This charge is made against Rehoboam, the son and successor of King Solomon in Judah. He was not the only one; hardly any king, whether in Judah or Israel, was regarded as being beyond reproach in this respect. Anyone like King Asa of Judah who destroyed these "alien" cults was praised. He had expelled the "initiates" from the land, removed all the idols and deprived his mother of the status of "queen mother" because she had had a statue erected to the goddess Asherah—in the Canaanite pantheon the wife of the supreme God El: "And Asa cut down her image and burned it at the brook Kidron" (I Kings 15.11–13). Jehoshaphat son of Asa completed his father's work by exterminating the "rest of the initiates." And the great cultic reform of King Josiah which—according to the text—he implemented with reference to Deuteronomy consisted in orders to "bring out of the temple of the Lord all the vessels made for Baal, for Asherah and for all the host of heaven" (II Kings 23.4ff.); he "did away with" the idolatrous priests, pulled down the dwellings of the "initiates" "where the women wove hangings for the Asherah" (v.7) and also destroyed all the places of idols in the land: "And he broke in pieces the pillars, and cut down the Asherim, and filled their places with the bones of men" (II Kings 23.14).

Monotheism was far from being something that could be taken for granted in pre-exilic Israel; we have already noted this in the previous chapter. Even the few passages I have cited show two things: first, how dominant the Canaanite cults must have been among the people of Israel and Judah, and secondly, that this domination is matched by the vehemence of the repudiation of these cults by the tradition of a later time. Those who handed it on were of the same stamp as prophets like Amos, Hosea or Jeremiah before them. Among the idols which fell victim to their verdict were in fact a series of significant goddesses. However, whether a return to them is in the interest of feminists remains to be seen. . . .

The goddess Anat is without doubt the most impressive figure. She fights, wades in the blood of her opponents, is not "sated with her killing; the heads she has cut off reach up to her waist." "She is filled with joy as she plunges her knees in the blood of heroes." . . . Anat acts just like Yahweh, at least when it comes to annihilating her enemies. Why is Yahweh then accused of violence by feminists and not Anat? At any rate it is a sign of progress that Yahweh does not wade with joy in the blood of his enemies. . . .

Since Anat and Baal, like Asherat and El, are gods of fertility, and war is identified with drought, and love and peace with growth and flourishing, Anat's battle may also be connected with this. Anat is always angry when she has to save Baal; then she couples with him, for only together do they create fertility. So Anat longs for Baal "like the heart of the mother sheep for its lamb"; they celebrate their love feast in a meadow, taking the form of cattle, so that Anat bears a calf (cf. the cult of the golden bull or calf). This form of religion is therefore aptly called a fertility cult or vegetation cult: human children, young animals, corn and fruit are to grow. What happens in "heaven," the expulsion of the gods, their defeats and victories, determines life and death. All eroticism is in the service of fertility. And again a conflict with feminist interests is clear; anyone who is on guard against reducing women to fertility and motherhood can hardly lay claim to the goddess myths. Anat certainly fights, but she fights in order to make all living things fertile. A lack of fertility at that time was probably the worst thing that could happen to a woman. We can see that from the Old Testament. As Sarah does not get any children, she sends her husband Abraham to the maid (Gen.16.1ff.); when Rachel sees that her womb remains closed her husband Jacob has to get children for her through the maid Bilhah (Gen.30.1ff.). The husbands do what their wives tell them, for descendants are of more value than the personal relationship between man and woman. . . .

All this shows how remote is the interest of women of four thousand years ago from what moves women today. Feminists again revive the myths and rites from this period therefore overlook what was decisive at that time. They do not pray to the goddesses for fertility, yet this is the cornerstone of the submerged world of the feminine deities, and the myth, thus robbed of its intention, becomes barren in both the literal and the metaphorical sense. What has it to offer us in a period and civilization for which fertility has become a burden, if not a curse? If the women of those days rose up again, from a time when fertility was overshadowed by the early deaths of mothers and children, and heard our debates over contraception and abortion, our world would seem as strange to them as on close inspection theirs must appear to us. The selection of themes by feminists, when they depict e.g. Anat as mistress of life and death, when they depict the one set over her mortal hero, the gracious, warlike one who takes the initiative in love, exclusively "proves" their interest. This is what women want to be today; they want to break the tradition of male destructive domination of their body and their soul. They are right. It is high time for that. But the arguments must be different; the arguments derived from the goddess myths can all too easily be turned against those who use them.

Study Questions on Susanne Heine

1. To what extent does the Bible refer to God as Father? To what extent as Mother? What is the attitude of the Old Testament prophets to goddess worship? What implications does Heine draw from these features of the Bible?
2. Why have feminists preferred God the Mother or goddesses to God the Father, and what about their reasons does Heine find unconvincing? (Consider, in particular, her observations concerning Canaanite goddess worship.)
3. What lessons does Heine draw from "impaired experiences of the mother"?
4. What is the theocratic shortcut, and what is wrong with it? How does Heine attempt to avoid it?

Why Christians Name God "Father"

GARY CULPEPPER

Setting aside political questions, Gary Culpepper focuses on the theological issue of how Christians should name the One God in worship and doctrine. For Christians, he argues, Jesus' use of the name Father is not metaphorical. The name *Father* refers literally to someone whose existence would otherwise be unknown and unknowable apart from the witness of Jesus the Son. Faithful appropriation of our religious traditions will, Culpepper argues, exclude the distorted readings that have supported the oppression of women.

THE DOCTRINE OF GOD is a principal area of concern in Christian feminist theology today. This follows most obviously, perhaps, for the reason that Christian understanding and worship of God is formulated primarily in terms of nouns (e.g., Father, Son, Lord, King) and corresponding pronouns

From Why Christians Name God "Father." *Reprinted by permission of the author.*

(He, His) which in ordinary English usage refer exclusively to males. To some, this exclusivity stands in the way of women's liberation. To insist upon a tradition which excludes the practice of naming God "Mother" as well, the argument runs, further confirms the complicity of the Christian religion in the history of sexist oppression.

Typically, feminist theologians link a political and sociological criticism of Christian religion with strictly theological arguments to contend that the traditional Christian grammar of speech about God embodies a distorted, "patriarchal" understanding of the nature of divinity. Speech about "God the Father," these theologians contend, supports the belief that God's "otherness" and power are best pictured by an emotionally-detached male ruler of the world, a belief which both legitimates male rule over women in Church and society *and* fails to communicate the truth about the intimate, "maternal" love that the Christian God bears for the world.

This essay will focus primarily upon the theological issue of how the One God is to be named truly in Christian worship and doctrine. The question of how Christian naming of God is related to the promotion of the equal dignity of women in Church and society will be considered as a distinct issue. In other words, in this essay, theological analysis is understood to be distinct from political or sociological analysis of how a given religion functions in a society for or against the emancipation of women. The latter area of research is rendered complex due to the lack of a discernable correlation in the history of religion between the presence of Goddesses in a given culture and the achievement of a higher social status for women. Just as the presence or absence of Goddesses or feminine language for God in ancient cultures fails to provide insight into the level of dignity accorded women in that society, so, too, it is not evident that any particular revision of religious language in the present will bring forth the results anticipated by feminist theologians.

The issue of how Christians are to address God remains complex even when restricted to the domain of theology. First, there are names for God—such as Almighty, Goodness Itself, or Being—which identify the divine nature in a general way that is open to philosophical discussion. Secondly, there are names which are more "personal" in their connotation, insofar as they communicate the identity of a "living God" who performs particular saving deeds in history. This "living God" is not discovered merely through philosophical analysis of names such as "the Almighty." For example, the name "God of our fathers Abraham, Isaac, and Jacob" identifies the personal identity of God in a way that the name "Infinite" cannot. In Christian theology, yet another dimension enters into the practice of naming God: names for God can refer to the three divine persons—Father, Son, and Holy Spirit—who are distinct from one another, though exist as One God.

This new dimension in naming God—the belief that God is a Trinity of persons each with a distinct name—has its roots in the saving revelation of this "three-person God" in the life, death, and resurrection of Jesus Christ. For our purposes, the issue can be focused most instructively upon Jesus' practice of addressing the God of Jewish faith as "Abba" or "Father," and teaching his disciples to do the same. Theologians who support the use of the name "Father" in Christian prayer believe that Jesus' own practice is *more than* merely a product of Jewish cultural conditioning; according to these theologians, the name "Father" is an integral element in the revelation of the three-person God, Father, Son, and Holy Spirit.

Feminist theologians critical of the privileged status accorded the name "Father" in Christian prayer and doctrine today typically do not deny that the practice of naming God "Father" is a distinctive feature of Jesus' life and ministry. This raises what at first seems to be a problem: the historical source of a tradition which is taken to be oppressive of women seems, at first glance, to be Jesus himself, the eternal God Incarnate. Yet, certain arguments are advanced by Christian feminist theologians at this point concerning the metaphorical nature of names for God, including Jesus' use of "Father," in order to avoid the conclusion that the God of Christian faith is the primordial sexist. While the complexity of feminist theology today precludes easy generalizations, these arguments share two basic features in common: (1) an affirmation of the incomprehensibility of God, which (2) supports the axiom that all speech about God is strictly metaphorical in character.

The theologian Elizabeth Johnson (whose work appears in this collection) has advanced such a theory of the metaphorical nature of religious language, and appeals frequently for support of her position to the theology of St. Thomas Aquinas, a 13th century theologian whose contributions are especially esteemed among Roman Catholics. Aquinas taught that the divine nature is truly said to be incomprehensible for human understanding, and acknowledged that metaphors are often employed in Scripture to communicate a real though imperfect understanding of God. Unlike Johnson, however, Aquinas argues that there exists a class of non-metaphorical names which are predicated of God, among which belongs the name "Father."

Johnson, on the other hand, employs the doctrine of God's incomprehensibility to support the position that there are no non-metaphorical names for God. In a departure from Aquinas, Johnson will argue that God is ultimately "nameless." How, then, are we to justify using any names for God at all? Johnson looks to the practice of Jesus, and points out that, while he addressed God as his Father, we should not overlook the fact that he also proposed female images of God to his audience as well (e.g., the woman in search of the lost coin in Luke 15:4–10).

Since all names for God are metaphorical, according to Johnson, there can be no substantial difference between Jesus' use of the name "Father" for God and the other images, masculine or feminine, he may have employed to communicate the Gospel. Accordingly, Johnson can maintain that the practice of Jesus himself legitimates the use of metaphors drawn from male and female experience alike in our prayerful desire to address the God revealed in and through Jesus. Johnson's proposal to integrate male and female images of God into Christian prayer is theologically sound, and merits more attention than it receives at present. Johnson, however, advocates not merely the vigorous development and use of female metaphors in our speech about God; she claims that metaphors such as "Mother" can function as *equivalents* to the name "Father" as the latter has come to be used in Christian prayer and doctrine. But it is far from clear that this is the case when the issue is considered from the perspective of how God comes to be addressed in the history of Jewish and Christian prayer and theology.

Jewish theology affirms that God is One, a Oneness which implies the holiness and transcendence of God beyond the human power to imagine or conceive. The sacred name of the God of Israel is revealed to Moses *neither* as "Father" nor "Mother," but in the words "I am Yahweh" (Exodus 3:14), a name which is variously translated "I am who I am," "I am who I will be," or "I am who causes to be." Jewish consciousness of the holiness of God led further to this name being rendered YHWH (the "Tetragrammaton") in its sacred texts, rendering it unpronounceable in liturgical prayer. From at least the time of the Babylonian exile (6th c. BC), the pronounceable name "Father" came into use in Jewish prayer as a *vocative,* a part of speech employed to address a *particular* someone in order to be heard (as in ordinary usage, "Father, will you help me with my homework?").

The Jewish use of the name "Father" for Yahweh suffers from certain limitations, limitations which suggest that it is properly classified as a metaphorical vocative. This is the case for the Jew since there is nothing that belongs to the definition of the term "Father" that can strictly speaking be said of the God of Israel. First, Yahweh is not male (nor female, nor androgynous), and secondly, "Father" implies a relation to a son or daughter, and it was the hallmark of Jewish monotheism, in its criticism of pagan polytheism, to deny that anyone or anything enjoyed this kind of relation to Yahweh. Hence, "Father" is metaphorical; the proper, non-metaphorical name of the God of Israel is "Yahweh."

To conclude that Jewish speech about God the "Father" is metaphorical is not to say that this name (as a liturgical vocative) is without theological meaning. Naming Yahweh "Father" in Judaism is not simply arbitrary. It would be a mistake, however, to think that its meaning for the Jew was derived from a general human experience of fatherhood, such that, when said of Yahweh, "Father" should be taken to mean "a being like the male head of the household." This interpretation would overlook the particularity of Jewish history which is the context in which the name gained its concrete meaning in distinction from the significance of the name "Father" in other ancient Near Eastern religions.

Among the historical associations which give Jewish use of the name "Father" its distinctive meaning, the figures of Abraham and David enjoy primacy. Abraham is remembered as the father of Jewish faith, an honor attributed to him both because he was the first to enter into the covenant of faith established by Yahweh, and because he accepted responsibility for the transmission of this faith signified in the practice of male circumcision Metaphorical extension of the name "Father" to Yahweh points out that the authority of Abraham, and the whole of Jewish patriarchal culture, derives from and has its basis in the authority of Yahweh and the covenental law. So, too, political authority is based not in man but in God. Significant here, especially for Christian theology, is the Jewish understanding of God as the "Father" of the king who presides over the people of Israel as the adopted son of Yahweh, with particular reference to that future king whom the prophet Nathan prophesied would come from the house of David to reign justly and eternally over the nations (2 Samuel 7:14).

Feminist theologians are correct to point out that the use of the name "Father" in Jewish religion is related to a patriarchal form of life. This fact, however, ought not lead one immediately to the conclusion that the exclusive use of the name "Father" for God represents an attempt to construct the image of a male God who legitimates adult Jewish male desire for unrestrained dominance over women and children. In fact, recalling the polytheistic context in which the Jewish prophets rejected the practice of naming Yahweh equivalently as "Mother" reinforced the Jewish belief that God is neither male nor female.

It was Israel's neighbors—whose religious cults were steeped in ritual prostitution and child sacrifice—who named God equivalently "Father" and "Mother" in accord with their polytheistic belief in male and female gods (see Jeremiah 2:20–28). Jewish religion distinguished sharply between created sexual life-forces and the life-force of Yahweh, and employed speech about God the "Father" to communicate that Yahweh is beyond the forms of sexual distinction which occupied the attention of those in non-Jewish religious cults. This does not mean that the use of female imagery and metaphors for God is strictly inadmissible in Jewish religion (e.g., Hosea 11:1–4), but points to the prophetic concern to distinguish polytheistic and monotheistic religious belief and practice.

The Christian theologian, however, notes a difference between Jesus' use of the name "Father" and the monotheistic purposes of naming God "Father" in the Jewish prophets. This is because the name "Father" on the lips of Jesus is understood to mean that there is a distinctive sense in which God is Jesus' eternal Father, and, reflexively, that Jesus is God's eternal Son. The Christian theologian might see things like this: *our* speaking about God as "Father" is merely metaphorical (in the sense that we are not really the eternal sons or daughters of God), but *Jesus'* speaking about God as "Father" is more-than-metaphorical. But if *all* language about God is merely metaphorical, as Johnson insists, then this difference in Jesus' use of "Father" does not really show itself to us. This then is the most important theological point in Christian understanding of God the "Father": The Christian distinction between Jesus, who is the eternal Son of God the Father, and ourselves, who are creatures of the One God, remains confused or obscured in the doctrine, which Johnson proposes, that all language about God the "Father" be considered metaphorical.

This emphasis on the importance of the Christian distinction between metaphorical and "more-than-metaphorical" speech about God demands explanation, especially in light of the concern that naming God "Father" implies that God is a male. According to St. Thomas Aquinas (to whom Johnson appeals for her own doctrine of God's incomprehensibility), metaphorical speech involves the use of a word or image to communicate some truth about the reality of God which, when pressed, will ultimately fail, because the definition of the word is inescapably bound up with the conditions of finitude and lack of perfection. In contrast, Aquinas holds that the theologian will also discover more-than-metaphorical, or "proper" (sometimes, not so helpfully it seems, translated "literal" in theological literature) names which are said of God and do not break down or fail, precisely because there exists some aspect of the definition of the term which does not communicate finitude or lack of perfection (see Aquinas, *Summa Theologiae* I, q.13,a.3).

Take two propositions which Aquinas himself offers for consideration: "God is our Rock" and "God is the Father of our Lord Jesus." In the case of naming God our "Rock," Aquinas insists that such speech is metaphorical, for bodiliness belongs to the definition of "rock" and hence is improperly said of God (though the metaphor communicates the truth that God is faithful or unchanging in His love for us). The situation is different with the name "Father" according to Aquinas, for the definition of "Father" is to be the "personal origin" of another and this relational aspect of the definition of the name "Father" implies neither finitude nor imperfection: God is the eternal Father, or "personal origin," of the Son Jesus.

Two problems might be raised against this view. First, is it not the case that both the terms "Rock" and "Father," derived as they are from our experience of the bodily, material world, communicate equally the aspect of limitation? Secondly, if "Father" is said non-metaphorically of God, does this not violate the doctrine of divine incomprehensibility?

In response to the first problem, Aquinas answers—and this is very important—that the name "Father" is *not* derived from our natural knowledge or experience of the world; rather, it is derived from our hearing the speech of Jesus the eternal Son in faith. On these grounds, Aquinas argues that the name "Father," like all proper names for divinity, is said most truly of God, and refers to our natural experience of fathers and fatherhood only secondarily and by analogy. This sheds light on the meaning of Jesus' command "call no man your father on earth, for you have one Father, who is in heaven" (Matthew 23:9): the name "Father" can be said *truly* of the human male only insofar as the sexual and interpersonal dimension of his existence embodies the perfection of the divine love manifest in Christ (see Ephesians 3:14).

In order to answer the second question about God's incomprehensibility, Aquinas developed a theological theory of language which attempts to clarify how it is that the meaning of a term said non-metaphorically of God is neither identical to (univocal speech) nor radically dissimilar from (equivocal speech) the meaning of the term when used in our ordinary discourse. Aquinas referred to this mean between univocal and equivocal speech which allowed terms to be predicated non-metaphorically of God as a language of analogy.

Theologians who, like Johnson, do not admit a distinction between metaphorical and non-metaphorical naming of God follow a trajectory closer to that of the Jewish theologian Rabbi Moses Maimonides, a contemporary of Aquinas who insisted upon the radical dissimilarity of the meaning of our words when said of God. Aquinas, whose aim was to explain the name "Father" in the new context of Christian revelation and belief in Jesus as the Son of God, rejected the adequacy of Maimonides' view (see Aquinas, *Summa Theologiae* 1,q.13,a.2). "Divine incomprehensibility" means something very different for Aquinas, who held that we can know by Christian faith *that* God is a Father (of Jesus, his eternal Son), but insisted equally that *how* God exists as Father will remain eternally incomprehensible. Aquinas' doctrine of analogy affirms the incomprehensibility of a God who is knowable to some degree, not that God is completely unknowable.

Of what consequence is this issue for Christian belief and life, especially in connection to the concerns of feminism and feminist theology? An answer to this question might be found in Aquinas' argument that the name "Father," when spoken by Jesus, reveals that God is the trinity of persons whose existence would otherwise be unknown and unknowable apart from the living witness of Jesus the Son. The Trinity is the central mystery of salvation for Christians, for it discloses that divine life is the existence of distinct persons dwelling in love without subordination of one to another. Christians understand salvation to be an entrance into personal communion with the Trinity of divine persons, not as slaves subordinated to an all-powerful male divinity, but in a relation of friendship with the One God, neither male nor female. As there exists no subordination of one to another in the divine life, so there can be no subordination of one Christian to another on the basis of sex, age, race, or class. Theologians who affirm only the possibility of metaphorical speech about God undermine this central mystery of Christian religion, for metaphorical language is always bound up with limitation and hence cannot be said to capture the truth about God. But the Christian believes that "Father" *is* said truly of

God, precisely in the sense that this name refers to that person who sent his eternal Son to offer humanity the fullness of divine life.

At the end of this essay, which has attempted to argue that the use of the name "Father" for God in Christian religion ought to point our attention, not to yet another ideological construct of a patriarchal culture, but to the liberation offered by the Son to men and women alike, the question might still remain: why is it that the name "Mother" cannot be said non-metaphorically of God as well? While there has been much discussion of whether, considered from a sexual/biological point of view, the name "Father" more perfectly captures the sense of "personal origin" than "Mother," that debate need not occupy our attention here. This is so because the names which the Christian uses for God are not derived from philosophical reflection, political or social experience, or biology, but from the personal relations manifest in the life of Jesus, the Son of God. The revelation of God in the life of Jesus and his personal relations leads one to understand that "Mother" is said non-metaphorically, not of God, but of Mary, the Mother of Jesus, whose receptivity to divine grace establishes her as the true Mother of God and the spiritual Mother of all Christians.

This differentiation in the use of the names "Father" and "Mother" inscribed in the very pattern of Jesus' own life relations, and anticipated by the use of "Father" in Jewish religion will, sadly, continue to offer the occasion for the development of distorted patriarchal interpretations of the relations of the sexes. This essay has attempted to argue that (1) such distortions are not the result of a faithful appropriation of these religious traditions, and (2) there does not exist any evidence, in the history of religions or otherwise, that a modification of this Christian pattern of naming God in prayer and theology will bring about the sort of liberation of women described in Christian feminist theology. Something more must be said, however: the practice of naming God "Father," in the spirit of Christian faith, directs our lives toward greater conformity to Jesus the Son, who offered himself in life and death for our redemption from the history of sexism, and whose Spirit makes it possible to love the good of the other, male or female, even as we are loved by Jesus and the God whom he addressed as "Father."

Study Questions on Gary Culpepper

1. Explain the difference between a political and theological approach to questions about religion. Can the distinction be kept as sharp as Culpepper wants it to be?
2. Explain the difference between metaphorical and proper uses of language. How can calling God *Father* be nonmetaphorical if we do not believe that God has a male body?
3. According to Culpepper, what difference does it make that Jesus frequently called God *Father?* What is the role of the doctrine of the Trinity in his argument?
4. Why can't both *Mother* and *Father* be used of God, since God is by common consent above all concepts?

Ecofeminism: Symbolic and Social Connections of the Oppression of Women and the Domination of Nature

ROSEMARY RADFORD RUETHER

Ecofeminism, Rosemary Radford Ruether explains, represents the union of the radical ecology movement and feminism. She argues that thinking of God as single, male, and transcendent has been used to justify human exploitation of nature and patriarchal denigration and oppression of women. She calls for a new ecofeminist culture and ethic, in which all racist, classist, cultural, and anthropocentric assumptions of superiority and inferiority will be discarded. Among other things, this means allowing women more access to public culture, and converting males to an equal share in the tasks of child nurture and domestic maintenance.

. . . ECOFEMINISM REPRESENTS THE UNION of the radical ecology movement, or what has been called "deep ecology," and feminism. The word "ecology" emerges from the biological science of natural environmental systems. It examines how these natural communities function to sustain a healthy web of life and how they become disrupted, causing death to the plant and animal life. Human intervention is obviously one of the main causes of such disruption. Thus ecology emerged as a combined socioeconomic and biological study in the late sixties to examine how human use of nature is causing pollution of soil, air, and water, and destruction of the natural systems of plants and animals, threatening the base of life on which the human community itself depends.

Deep ecology takes this study of social ecology another step. It examines the symbolic, psychological, and ethical patterns of destructive relations of humans with nature and how to replace this with a life-affirming culture.

Feminism also is a complex movement with many layers. It can be defined as only a movement within the liberal democratic societies for the full inclusion of women in political rights and economic access to employment. It can be defined more radically in a socialist and liberation tradition as a transformation of the patriarchal socioeconomic system, in which male domination of women is the foundation of all socioeconomic hierarchies.

Feminism can be also studied in terms of culture and consciousness, charting the symbolic, psychological, and ethical connections of domination of women and male monopolization of resources and controlling power. This third level of feminist analysis connects closely with deep ecology. Some would say that feminism is the primary expression of deep ecology. . . .

. . . What I plan to do in this essay is to trace some symbolic connections of domination of women and domination of nature in Mediterranean and Western European culture. I will then explore briefly the alternative ethic and culture that might be envisioned, if we are to overcome these patterns of domination and destructive violence to women and to the natural world.

Pre-Hebraic Roots

Anthropological studies have suggested that the identification of women with nature and males with culture is both ancient and widespread. This cultural pattern itself expresses a monopolizing of the definition of culture by males. The very word "nature" in this formula is part of the problem, because it defines nature as a reality below and separated from "man," rather than one nexus in which humanity itself is inseparably embedded. It is, in fact, human beings who cannot live apart from the rest of nature as our life-sustaining context, while the community of plants and animals both can and, for billions of years, did exist without humans. The concept of humans outside of nature is a cultural reversal of natural reality.

How did this reversal take place in our cultural consciousness? One key element of this identification of women with nonhuman nature lies in the early human social patterns in which women's reproductive role as childbearer was tied to making women the primary productive and maintenance workers. Women did most of the work associated with child care, food production and preparation, production of clothing, baskets, and other artifacts of daily life, cleanup, and waste-disposal.

Although there is considerable variation of these patterns cross-culturally, generally males situated themselves in work that was both more prestigious and more occasional, demanding bursts of energy, such as hunting larger animals, war, and clearing fields, but allowing them more space for leisure. This is the primary social base for the male monopolization of culture, by which men reinforced their privileges of leisure, the superior prestige of their activities, and the inferiority of the activities associated with women.

Perhaps for much of human history, women ignored or discounted these male claims to superiority, being entirely too busy with the tasks of daily life and expressing among themselves their assumptions about the obvious importance of their own work as the primary producers and reproducers. But, by stages, this female consciousness and culture was sunk underneath the growing male power to define the culture for the whole society, socializing both males and females into this male-defined point of view.

It is from the perspective of this male monopoly of culture that the work of women in maintaining the material basis of daily life is defined as an inferior realm. The material world itself is then seen as something separated from males and symbolically linked with women. The earth, as the place from which plant and animal life arises, became linked with the bodies of women, from which babies emerge. . . .

The conquest and enslavement of other tribal groups created another category of humans, beneath the familiar community owned by it, whose labor is coerced. Enslavement of other people through military conquest typically took the form of killing the men and enslaving the women and their children for labor and sexual service. Women's work becomes identified with slave work. The women of the family are defined as a higher type of slave over a lower category of slaves drawn from conquered people. In patriarchal law, possession of women, slaves, animals, and land all are symbolically and socially linked together. All are species of property and instruments of labor, owned and controlled by male heads of family as a ruling class.

As we look at the mythologies of the Ancient Near Eastern, Hebrew, Greek, and early Christian cultures, one can see a shifting symbolization of women and nature as spheres to be conquered, ruled over, and finally, repudiated altogether.

In the Babylonian Creation story, which goes back to the third millennium B.C.E., Marduk, the warrior champion of the gods of the city states, is seen as creating the cosmos by conquering the Mother Goddess Tiamat, pictured as a monstrous female animal. Marduk kills her, treads her body underfoot, and then splits it in half, using one half to fashion the starry firmament of the skies, and the other half the earth below. The elemental mother is literally turned into the matter out of which the cosmos is fashioned (not accidentally, the words *mother* and *matter* have the same etymological root). She can be used as matter only by being killed; that is, by destroying her as "wild," autonomous life, making her life-giving body into "stuff" possessed and controlled by the architect of a male-defined cosmos.

The Hebraic World

The view of nature found in Hebrew Scripture has several cultural layers. But the overall tendency is to see the natural world, together with human society, as something created, shaped, and controlled by God, a God imaged after the patriarchal ruling class. The patriarchal male is entrusted with being the steward and caretaker of nature, but under God, who remains its ultimate creator and Lord. This also means that nature remains partly an uncontrollable realm that can confront human society in destructive droughts and storms. These experiences of nature that transcend human control, bringing destruction to human work, are seen as divine judgment against human sin and unfaithfulness to God (see Isaiah 24).

God acts in the droughts and the storms to bring human work to naught, to punish humans for sin, but also to call humans (that is, Israel) back to faithfulness to God. When Israel learns obedience to God, nature in turn will become benign and fruitful, a source of reliable blessings, rather than unreliable destruction. Nature remains ultimately in God's hands, and only secondarily, and through becoming servants of God, in male hands. Yet the symbolization of God as a patriarchal male and Israel as wife, son, and servant of God, creates a basic analogy of woman and nature. God is the ultimate patriarchal Lord, under whom the human patriarchal lord rules over women, children, slaves, and land.

The image of God as single, male, and transcendent, prior to nature, also shifts the symbolic relation of male consciousness to material life. Marduk was a young male god who was produced out of a process of theogony and cosmogony. He conquers and shapes the cosmos out of the body of an older Goddess that existed prior to himself, within which he himself stands. The Hebrew God exists above and prior to the cosmos, shaping it out of a chaos that is under his control. Genesis 2 gives us a parallel view of the male, not as the child of woman, but as the source of woman. She arises out of him, with the help of the male God, and is handed over to him as her Master.

The Greek World

When we turn to Greek philosophical myth, the link between mother and matter is made explicit. Plato, in his creation myth, the *Timaeus,* speaks of primal, unformed matter as the receptacle and "nurse". He imagines a disembodied male mind as divine architect, or Demiurgos, shaping this matter into the cosmos by fashioning it after the intellectual blueprint of the Eternal Ideas. These Eternal Ideas exist in an immaterial, transcendent world of Mind, separate from and above the material stuff that he is fashioning into the visible cosmos.

The World Soul is also created by the Demiurgos, by mixing together dynamics of antithetical relations (the Same and the Other). This world soul is infused into the body of the cosmos in order to make it move in harmonic motion. The remnants of this world soul are divided into bits, to create the souls of humans. These souls are first placed in the stars, so that human souls will gain knowledge of the Eternal Ideas. Then the souls are sown in the bodies of humans on earth. The task of the soul is to govern the unruly passions that arise from the body.

If the soul succeeds in this task, it will return at death to its native star and there live a life of leisured contemplation. If not, the soul will be reincarnated into the body of a woman or an animal it will then have to work its way back into the form of an (elite) male and finally escape from bodily reincarnation altogether, to return to its original disincarnate form in the starry realm above. Plato takes for granted an ontological hierarchy of being, the immaterial intellectual world over material cosmos, and, within this ontological hierarchy, the descending hierarchy of male, female, and animal.

In the Greco-Roman era, a sense of pessimism about the possibility of blessing and well-being within the bodily, historical world deepened in Eastern Mediterranean culture, expressing itself in apocalypticism and gnosticism. In apocalypticism, God is seen as intervening in history to destroy the present sinful and finite world of human society and nature and to create a new heaven and earth freed from both sin and death. In gnosticism, mystical philosophies chart the path to salvation by way of withdrawal of the soul from the body and its passions and its return to an immaterial realm outside of and above the visible cosmos.

Christianity

Early Christianity was shaped by both the Hebraic and Greek traditions, including their alienated forms in apocalypticism and gnosticism. Second-century Christianity struggled against gnosticism, reaffirming the Hebraic view of nature and body as God's good creation. The second-century

Christian theologian Irenaeus sought to combat gnostic anticosmism and to synthesize apocalypticism and Hebraic creationalism. He imaged the whole cosmos as a bodying forth of the Word and Spirit of God, as the sacramental embodiment of the invisible God.

Sin arises through a human denial of this relation to God. But salvific grace, dispensed progressively through the Hebrew and Christian revelations, allows humanity to heal its relation to God. The cosmos, in turn, grows into being a blessed and immortalized manifestation of the divine Word and Spirit, which is its ground of being.

However, Greek and Latin Christianity, increasingly influenced by Neoplatonism, found this materialism distasteful. They deeply imbibed the platonic eschatology of the escape of the soul from the body and its return to a transcendent world outside the earth. The earth and the body must be left behind in order to ascend to another, heavenly world of disembodied life. Even though the Hebrew idea of resurrection of the body was retained, increasingly this notion was envisioned as a vehicle of immortal light for the soul, not the material body, in all its distasteful physical processes, which they saw as the very essence of sin as mortal corruptibility.

The view of women in this ascetic Christian system was profoundly ambivalent A part of ascetic Christianity imagined women becoming freed from subordination, freed both for equality in salvation and to act as agents of Christian preaching and teaching. But this freedom was based on woman rejecting her sexuality and reproductive role and becoming symbolically male. The classic Christian "good news" to woman as equal to man in Christ was rooted in a misogynist view of female sexuality and reproduction as the essence of the sinful, mortal, corruptible life.

For most male ascetic Christians, even ascetic woman, who had rejected her sexuality and reproductive role, was too dangerously sexual. Ascetic women were increasingly deprived of their minor roles in public ministry, such as deaconess, and locked away in convents, where obedience to God was to be expressed in total obedience to male ecclesiastical authority. Sexual woman, drawing male seminal power into herself, her womb swelling with new life, became the very essence of sin, corruptibility, and death, from which the male ascetic fled. Eternal life was disembodied male soul, freed from all material underpinnings in the mortal bodily life, represented by woman and nature.

Medieval Latin Christianity was also deeply ambivalent about its view of nature. One side of medieval thought retained something of Irenaeus's sacramental cosmos, which becomes the icon of God through feeding on the redemptive power of Christ in the sacraments of bread and wine. The redeemed cosmos as resurrected body, united with God, is possible only by freeing the body of its sexuality and mortality. Mary, the virgin Mother of Christ, assumed into heaven to reign by the side of her son, was the representative of this redeemed body of the cosmos, the resurrected body of the Church.

But the dark side of Medieval thought saw nature as possessed by demonic powers that draw us down to sin and death through sexual temptation. Women, particularly old crones with sagging breasts and bellies, still perversely retaining their sexual appetites, are the vehicles of the demonic power of nature. They are the witches who sell their souls to the Devil in a satanic parody of the Christian sacraments.

The Reformation and the Scientific Revolution

The Calvinist Reformation and the Scientific Revolution in England in the late sixteenth and seventeenth centuries represent key turning points in the Western concept of nature. In these two movements, the Medieval struggle between the sacramental and the demonic views of nature was recast. Calvinism dismembered the Medieval sacramental sense of nature. For Calvinism, nature was totally depraved. There was no residue of divine presence in it that could sustain a natural knowledge or relation to God. Saving knowledge of God descends from on high, beyond nature, in the revealed World available only in Scripture, as preached by the Reformers.

The Calvinist reformers were notable in their iconoclastic hostility toward visual art. Stained glass, statues, and carvings were smashed, and the churches stripped of all visible imagery. Only the disembodied Word, descending from the preacher to the ear of the listener, together with music, could be bearers of divine presence. Nothing one could see, touch, taste, or smell was trustworthy as bearer of the divine. Even the bread and wine were no longer the physical embodiment of Christ, but intellectual reminders of the message about Christ's salvific act enacted in the past.

Calvinism dismantled the sacramental world of Medieval Christianity, but it maintained and reinforced its demonic universe. The fallen world, especially physical nature and other human groups outside of the control of the Calvinist church, lay in the grip of the Devil. All who were labeled pagan, whether Catholics or Indians and Africans, were the playground of demonic powers. But, even within the Calvinist church, women were the gateway of the Devil. If women were completely obedient to their fathers, husbands, ministers, and magistrates, they might be redeemed as goodwives. But in any independence of women lurked heresy and witchcraft. Among Protestants, Calvinists were the primary witch-hunters.

The Scientific Revolution at first moved in a different direction, exorcizing the demonic powers from nature in order to reclaim it as an icon of divine reason manifest in natural law. But, in the seventeenth and eighteenth centuries, the more animist natural science, which unified material and spiritual, lost out to a strict dualism of transcendent intellect and dead matter. Nature was secularized. It was no longer the scene of a struggle between Christ and the Devil. Both divine and demonic spirits were driven out of it. In Cartesian dualism and Newtonian physics, it becomes matter in motion, dead stuff moving obediently, according to mathematical laws knowable to a new male elite of scientists. With no life or soul of its own, nature could be safely expropriated by this male elite and infinitely reconstructed to augment its wealth and power.

In Western society, the application of science to technological control over nature marched side by side with colonialism. From the sixteenth to the twentieth centuries, Western Europeans would appropriate the lands of the Americas, Asia, and Africa, and reduce their human populations to servitude. The wealth accrued by this vast expropriation of land and labor would fuel new levels of technological revolution, transforming material resources into new forms of energy and mechanical work, control of disease, increasing speed of communication and travel. Western elites grew increasingly optimistic, imagining that this technological way of life would gradually conquer all problems of material scarcity and even push back the limits of human mortality. The Christian dream of immortal blessedness, freed from finite limits, was translated into scientific technological terms.

Ecological Crisis

. . . This Western scientific Industrial Revolution has been built on injustice. It has been based on the takeover of the land, its agricultural, metallic, and mineral wealth appropriated through the exploitation of the labor of the indigenous people. This wealth has flowed back to enrich the West, with some for local elites, while the laboring people of these lands grew poorer. This system of global affluence, based on exploitation of the land and labor of the many for the benefit of the few, with its high consumption of energy and waste, cannot be expanded to include the poor without destroying the basis of life of the planet itself. We are literally destroying the air, water, and soil upon which human and planetary life depend.

In order to preserve the unjust monopoly on material resources from the growing protests of the poor, the world became more and more militarized. Most nations have been using the lion's share of their state budgets for weapons, both to guard against one another and to control their own poor. Weapons also become one of the major exports of wealthy nations to poor nations. Poor nations grow increasingly indebted to wealthy nations while buying weapons to repress their own impoverished masses. Population explosion, exhaustion of natural resources, pollution, and state violence are the four horsemen of the new global apocalypse.

The critical question of both justice and survival is how to pull back this disastrous course and remake our relations with one another and with the earth.

Toward an Ecofeminist Ethic and Culture

There are many elements that need to go into an ecofeminist ethic and culture for a just and sustainable planet. One element is to reshape our dualistic concept of reality as split between soulless matter and transcendent male consciousness. We need to discover our actual reality as latecomers to the planet. The world of nature, plants, and animals existed billions of years before we came on the scene. Nature does not need us to rule over it, but runs itself very well, even better, without humans. We are the parasites on the food chain of life, consuming more and more, and putting too little back to restore and maintain the life system that supports us.

We need to recognize our utter dependence on the great life-producing matrix of the planet in order to learn to reintegrate our human systems of production, consumption, and waste into the ecological patterns by which nature sustains life. This might begin by revisualizing the relation of mind, or human intelligence, to nature. Mind or consciousness is not something that originates in some transcendent world outside of nature, but is the place where nature itself becomes conscious. We need to think of human consciousness not as separating us as a higher species from the rest of nature, but rather as a gift to enable us to learn how to harmonize our needs with the natural system around us, of which we are a dependent part.

Such a reintegration of human consciousness and nature must reshape the concept of God, instead of modeling God after alienated male consciousness, outside of and ruling over nature. God, in ecofeminist spirituality, is the immanent source of life that sustains the whole planetary community. God is neither male nor anthropomorphic. God is the font from which the variety of plants and animals well up in each new generation, the matrix that sustains their life-giving interdependency with one another.

In ecofeminist culture and ethic, mutual interdependency replaces the hierarchies of domination as the model of relationship between men and women, between human groups and between humans and other beings. All racist, sexist, classist, cultural, and anthropocentric assumptions of the superiority of whites over blacks, males over females, managers over workers, humans over animals and plants, must be discarded. In a real sense, the so-called superior pole in each relation is actually the more dependent side of the relationship.

But it is not enough simply to humbly acknowledge dependency. The pattern of male-female, racial, and class interdependency itself has to be reconstructed socially, creating more equitable sharing in the work and the fruits of work, rather than making one side of the relation the subjugated and impoverished base for the power and wealth of the other.

In terms of male-female relations, this means not simply allowing women more access to public culture, but converting males to an equal share in the tasks of child nurture and household maintenance. A revolution in female roles into the male work world, without a corresponding revolution in male roles, leaves the basic pattern of patriarchal exploitation of women untouched. Women are simply overworked in a new way, expected to do both a male workday, at low pay, and also the unpaid work of women that sustains family life.

There must be a conversion of men to the work of women, along with the conversion of male consciousness to the earth. Such conversions will reshape the symbolic vision of salvation. Instead of salvation sought either in the disembodied soul or the immortalized body, in a flight to heaven or to the end of history, salvation should be seen as continual conversion to the center, to the concrete basis by which we sustain our relation to nature and to one another. In every day and every new generation, we need to remake our relation with one another, finding anew the true nexus of relationality that sustains, rather than exploits and destroys, life.

Finally, ecofeminist culture must reshape our basic sense of self in relation to the life cycle. The sustaining of an organic community of plant and animal life is a continual cycle of growth and disintegration. The western flight from mortality is a flight from the disintegration side of the life cycle, from accepting ourselves as part of that process. By pretending that we can immortalize ourselves, souls and bodies, we are immortalizing our garbage and polluting the earth. In order to learn to recycle our garbage as fertilizer for new life, as matter for new artifacts, we need to accept our selfhood as participating in the same process. Humans also are finite organisms, centers of experience in a life cycle that must disintegrate back into the nexus of life and arise again in new forms.

These conversions, from alienated, hierarchical dualism to life-sustaining mutuality, will radically change the patterns of patriarchal culture. Basic concepts, such as God, soul-body, and salvation will be reconceived in ways that may bring us much closer to the ethical values of love, justice, and care for the earth. These values have been proclaimed by patriarchal religion, yet contradicted by patriarchal symbolic and social patterns of relationship.

These tentative explorations of symbolic changes must be matched by a new social practice that can incarnate these conversions in new social and technological ways of organizing human life in relation to one another and to nature. This will require a new sense of urgency about the untenability of present patterns of life and compassionate solidarity with those who are its victims.

Study Questions on Rosemary Radford Ruether

1. Ruether appears to assume that if one believes in human immortality (either as disembodied souls or in "immortalized" bodies), then one will adopt an exploitative attitude toward nature. Is there a necessary connection between these? Might a person believe in human immortality and also have respect, even reverence, for God's creation? Or might one reject the idea that humans have a dimension that transcends nature and nonetheless adopt a greedy and exploitative attitude toward nature?

2. Do you think Ruether is right that culturally women have been associated with the body and nature? Is there not also a tradition of thinking that associates women with our higher and more spiritual aspirations? Consider, for example, Dante's Beatrice, or the view of femininity held by Morris (in Unit I) expressed so powerfully in the sentence Morris cites from Faust: "Eternal womanhood leads us above." Would Ruether disapprove of those female saints and mystics who have passionately desired eternal life with God above all else? Should she?

3. Is it possible to create a society in which all hierarchies are abolished? What about the authority of adults over children?

4. Is Ruether's own vision an egalitarian one? Would it be possible to institute the sort of radical social changes she advocates by consensus, or would some sort of political hierarchy be necessary in order to mandate and enforce the necessary policies? Consider, also, whether her ideal society would require more behavioral changes of men than of women. Will women go on doing what they are doing, or be free to choose? If they are free to choose but men are not, how would Ruether respond to the charge that this is unfair?

5. What implications would Ruether's "ecofeminist ethic and culture" have for the question of abortion and why (see Wolf-Devine in Unit III)?

Women in Genesis 1–3

EDITH BLACK*

Edith Black provides a commentary on the first three chapters of Genesis. Patriarchy, she maintains, was not part of God's original plan, but this does not mean that God's creation contains no gender-specific roles. The representative role of Adam provides the most adequate explanation for why God limited the Hebrew priesthood to selected males. The name given to Eve stresses her role as originator and preserver of life. While females as well as males can represent God before man as prophets, the prophetic vocation cannot be transmitted through institutional channels as can the priestly office.

THE FIRST THREE CHAPTERS of Genesis constitute, in Judeo-Christian eyes, an inspired origin story, which recounts the foundational creative events that establish the ecological-social order intended by the creator and its subsequent distortion.

In Genesis the creation of man and woman represents the climax of a series of creative events that proceed from what we would call the material universe, "heaven and earth," to plants and sentient animals. The uniqueness of humans, however, is apparent from the fact that they are created in the image of God, which is understood in the rest of Scripture to mean that they have the capacity to reason on the basis of moral law. This is not to be confused with the capacity to think, which the higher sentient animals have to some degree or another. Because of their rational capacity, men and women have a vocation to cooperatively govern the rest of creation and, in so doing, both equally manifest the creators's own image in creation:

> Let us make man in our own image, after our likeness; and let them have dominion over the fish of the sea, and over the birds of the air, and over the cattle, and over all the earth, and over every creeping thing that creeps upon the earth.

*The writer will provide a full list of scriptural citations to support her arguments upon request. Please contact the editor at cwolfdevine@stonehill.edu for information on how to reach her.

The affinity of human beings with the rest of the created natural order is apparent from the first commands God gives to them in Genesis 1: to "be fruitful and multiply." This command reiterates the command already given to sentient animals—those beings that have "nephesh," translated as "soul" or "life."

The second command, "to fill the earth and subdue it; to have dominion over the fish of the sea and over the birds of the air and over every living thing that moves upon the earth," bestows on man the right to rule. But rule here means the same as it does elsewhere in the Old Testament—a just distribution of resources that considers the needs of the ruled as much as those of the rulers. In the Old Testament, rightful rule always means stewardship, not subjugation.

At the end of Genesis 1, all living beings having "nephesh" are allocated plants as their means of subsistence, so humans in their role of managing creation are not to allocate all resources for themselves so other creatures cannot survive. Furthermore, Genesis 2 makes it clear that dominion does not mean antagonistic relationships between man and the rest of creation. Adam, the first man, is put into a garden and told to "till and keep" it. The animals all come to him, unafraid, to be named. Both Genesis 1 and 2 therefore seem to suggest that predation between animals and between man and animals is not part of God's original intent for creation.

It was not until the Fall, described in Genesis 3, and developed further in the history of the flood in

This essay was written expressly for this edition of this text and has not been previously published.

Genesis 9, that the ecological and social disintegration of the original creative order occurs as the result of human misuse of their capacity to reason—their attempt to become like a god, "knowing good and evil"—in other words, to set themselves up as the arbiters of moral right and wrong, rather than rely upon God. The fruitful garden that humans tilled becomes an unyielding ground from which they must wrest a living: "cursed is the ground because of you; and in toil you shall eat of it all the days of your life." And after the flood the companionship between man and animals that God had intended breaks down into a relationship of hunter and hunted:

> The fear of you and the dread of you shall be upon every beast of the earth, and upon every bird of the air, upon everything that creeps on the ground, and all the fish of the sea; into your hand they are delivered. Every moving thing that lives shall be food for you; as I gave you the green plants, I give you everything.

Only after the Fall does the copartnership of man and woman in stewarding the earth degenerate into the patriarchal order that feminists decry: "your desire shall be for your husband and he shall rule over you."

It is clear from the ordering of creation events in both Genesis 1 and 2 that at each successive stage creatures come into being which are of greater value than those created previously. Therefore, any interpretation of the creation of Eve after the creation of Adam as implying secondary status has no validity. In fact, the Hebrew word "helpmeet" incorporates a Hebrew word "helper" that is usually used of Yahweh, therefore meaning "helper" from a position of strength.

Moreover, the fact that Eve leads Adam astray should not be taken to imply that she is less rational than he is. For her decision to take the fruit is not primarily an act of sensual desire but one of inordinate spiritual ambition to become like a god.

Thus the patriarchal order was not part of God's original order. This does not mean, however, that there is no gender-based role distinction intrinsic to God's creation. Indeed, Genesis 1:26–27 stresses the fact that God created man in the image of himself as male and female: "So God created man in his own image, in the image of God

he created him; male and female he created them." In other words, humanity always manifests itself sexually as male or female—never as neuter.

Genesis 1:26–27 thus seems to point to a fundamental role distinction rooted in the created order that every culture, patriarchal or otherwise, prior to our modern technological one, has recognized. Anthropological evidence indicates that men universally take on the higher risk roles such as defense, while women everywhere take on the more nurturing roles such as caring for small children—though, admittedly, many of the tasks assigned to each sex have been culturally imposed and are not intrinsic to the basic role distinction between male and female.

The second account of the creation of man, Genesis 2:7, 21–22, gives us a clue to what the basic distinction is in the names bestowed upon our original parents. The first human being is a male whose name "Adam" constitutes the generic name for mankind. The role unique to males thus seems to be a representative one. The male embodies in himself the unity of the group which he represents—both in the order of nature, as with Adam who embodied in himself the unity of all humanity, and in the order of grace, as with Christ who embodies in himself the unity of the new humanity.

I believe the representative role of males provides the most adequate explanation for why God limited Hebrew priesthood to selected males—those descended from Aaron—and allowed only male animals without blemish to serve as sacrificial victims, in contrast to the general practice in the Ancient Near East, which permitted priestesses. The representative role of both priests and sacrificial victims was especially apparent once a year when the high priest stood before God in the Holy of Holies in the stead of his people to make an offering for the atonement of their sins. The priest transferred their sins into one of the victims, a male goat, by laying his hands upon its head, and then drove it into the desert.[1]

Both the high priest, who offered in Israel's stead, and the unblemished male victim, who stood in Israel's stead for her sins, are types of Christ. They prefigure the ultimate high priest who serves

[1]Leviticus 15:1–34.

at the altar in heaven and the ultimate sacrificial victim on the cross whose blood was sprinkled on that altar.[2] It was because Christ's primary role on earth was to serve as the lamb of God who took our sins upon himself that he was born a male. It was because his primary role in Heaven is to serve as the high priest who mediates between us and the Father that he rose again in a glorified male body.

The name of the second human being created by God, Eve, likewise gives us a clue to the unique female role. Her name, which means both "she who causes to live" and "she who keeps alive," stresses woman's role as originator and preserver of life. Adam honors her life-creating role further by calling her "the mother of all living"—an epithet which parallels that borne by Ancient Near Eastern mother goddesses, "mother of all the gods."[3]

When Eve gives birth to her first child she names him Cain from a Hebrew verb meaning "to create" and says: "I have created a man with Yahweh." She thus emphasizes the unique partnership between a woman and God in bringing forth human life. For it is with her body that God repeats the miracle of creation by infusing a soul into the material embryo provided by herself and her husband. The Old Testament repeatedly stresses Yahweh's intimate involvement in procreation from conception to birth. He opens and closes the womb to male sperm[4] and fashions the unborn child.[5]

Many secular feminists claim that any emphasis on the unique capacity of women to create new human life constitutes a "biology is destiny" type of argument. Yet in so doing they accept the very biological reductionism they decry, for they overlook the fact that, as all religions testify, sexual intercourse among human beings is a spiritual as well as a biological act—manifesting a mystical unity as well as fulfilling a biological urge. Genesis 2:14–28 figuratively represents this unity by the formation of Eve from Adam's rib and by his recognition of her as "bone of my bone and flesh of my flesh." They become "one flesh," a living

organism in itself. In Ephesians 25:31–32 the matrimonial union of husband and wife reflects the mystical union between Christ and his church:

> For this reason a man shall leave his father and mother and be joined to his wife, and the two shall become one. This is the great mystery and I take it to mean Christ and the Church.

Therefore, human sexuality, while incorporating the bodily sexuality of animals, also transcends it.

Old Testament prophets decried the worship of human procreative powers in the form of Canaanite male and female deities. But they never desacralized human sexuality, reducing it to a merely biological phenomenon, as does our modern secular culture. The Old Testament upholds the sacredness of the procreative process without falling into the pagan error of deifying it.

Scripture further indicates that the differentiation of man (Adam) into male and female reflects a differentiation within God himself. Surely it is not accidental that, when God is portrayed as deliberating with himself in contemplation of the creation of man as male and female, he refers to himself as plural: "Let us make man in our image. . . ." Whatever human explanation scholars may offer for the author's choice of the plural in this passage—the royal we or the plural of majesty—the fact remains that God inspired that choice with some purpose in mind.[6]

I think the personalized wisdom figure of Proverbs, the Wisdom of Solomon, Sirach, and Baruch, whom early Christians identified with the pre-existent Christ—an identification which St. Paul also seems to make in I Corinthians 1:21–24—indicates that the male and female roles that God incorporates in himself are the male representational and female creative roles. For it cannot be accidental that the creative intelligence of Yahweh is hypothesized in the Old Testament as "Wisdom," a word of female gender, and not as "Word," a word of the masculine gender. The word of God never develops into a personal figure in the Old Testament as it does in the New,[7] even

---

[2]Hebrews 5:10–15.
[3]Isaac Kikawada, "Two Notes on Eve," *Journal of Biblical Literature* 91 (1972), 33–37.
[4]A good example is the story of childless Hannah in I Samuel 1:5–6, 19–20. See also Genesis *passim*.
[5]Psalms 139:13–16; Job 10:8–11; Isaiah 45:9–18, 49:2; Jeremiah 1:5.

[6]For Christians, the fuller sense of this use of the royal we or plural of majesty becomes clear in light of Christ's revelation that God exists in three persons.
[7]See especially John 1:1–3.

though its function as an agent of creation in Genesis and as an effector of historical events in the prophetic writings would have allowed such a development.

It would seem that the Old Testament writers hypothesized the creative intelligence of Yahweh as a female figure because the focus of their interest is on her role as a cocreator and preserver of the created order.[8] Wisdom is a motherly figure who bears within herself the model ideas from which each created being takes its form and the model laws to which each created being conforms its behavior. She invokes men as her "sons" to conform their ways to hers because they alone of all earthly creatures have the intelligence and freedom to choose to do otherwise.

The New Testament writers, on the other hand, use predominantly male imagery to describe the word made flesh (the second person of the Trinity) even in his pre-existent role as the agent of creation, because the focus of their interest is on his incarnational role as the representative man who embodies in himself all humanity and through all humanity the created order.[9]

It would seem also that the fact that Christ, the second person of the Trinity, is the source of truth—whether expressed in the feminine intuitive mode (Wisdom) or in the masculine logical mode (Word)—lies at the basis of the fact that females as well as males function as his prophetic spokespeople. The Old Testament provides a number of examples of women serving as prophetesses: Miriam, Moses's sister; Deborah, one of the early Hebrew judges; Huldah, in the reign of Josiah; and Isaiah's wife. Acts in the New Testament also portrays several women acting as prophetesses in the early church.

Prophets, female as well as male, played as crucial a role in the formation of the Yahweh faith as those who held cultic office. For example, Miriam led Israel out of Egypt along with Moses and Aaron; Deborah inspired her people to fight Yahweh's battles against the oppressing Canaanites; and Huldah authorized one of the most important Yahwist reform movements in Israel's history, acting as King Josiah's prophetic counselor.

Females as well as males, therefore, represent God before man as his prophets, though only males represent men before God as his priests. The prophetic vocation cannot be transmitted through institutional channels, as can be priestly office. For the prophet or prophetess delivers a direct communication from God applicable to a specific historical circumstance, while the priest in his role as teacher explicates the law of God applicable to all times.[10]

The ultimate consummation of Eve's role as "mother of all living" is implicit in Genesis 3 when God addresses the tempter Satan, represented by the serpent: "I will put enmity between you and the woman, and between your seed and her seed; he shall bruise your head and you shall bruise his heel."

For it is through Mary, seen by the early church as the "new Eve," that the effects of the Fall are overcome. In giving birth to Christ, the "new Adam," she becomes the mother of God and, as such, a "mother" to all reborn in Christ, her son. Her free assent to God's will provides for us a model of humanity created in the image of God.

[8]Job 28:12–27; Proverbs 3:19–20, 8:22–31; Wisdom of Solomon 7:22–8:1, 9:1–4; Sirach 15:2.
[9]Romans 8:19–25; Ephesians 1:9–10.

[10]Deuteronomy 3 1:9–12.

Study Questions on Edith Black

1. Are you persuaded by Black's interpretation of Genesis 1–3? How is her account different from Ruether's and which do you find more persuasive? Could they both be right?

2. If patriarchy is not part of God's original plan, does this mean that we can get rid of it? Many contemporary Christians believe strongly in the headship and

authority of fathers within their families. Might they argue that in a fallen world such authority is necessary even if it was not God's original intention?

3. How does Black's argument apply to leadership positions in the church? Are religious leaders significantly different from political leaders with respect to her argument? Are Catholic priests different from Protestant ministers?

4 Explain the meaning and symbolism of the names given to Adam and Eve. What conclusions does Black draw from these? Do they represent unfortunate sex stereotypes, or do they express a deep truth about men and women?

5 Compare and contrast Black with Frankiel (see next article) on the appropriate role of women and the feminine element in religious life.

Traditional Judaism and Feminine Spirituality

TAMAR FRANKIEL

Tamar Frankiel attempts to introduce a woman's voice into the Jewish tradition. God, she argues, need not be understood as "uniquely alone": rather, God's one-ness, the divine unity, is a marriage of male and female, the transcendent unity which is neither mind nor body, spirit nor matter, nor anything else we can understand.

WOMEN IN THE TWENTIETH CENTURY are "finding their voices." This is perhaps the great theme of modern women's lives: we who have been silent are speaking out, describing ourselves, our experiences, our points of view in our own ways rather than—as in the past—having no voice at all or having our ideas filtered through the speech and writings of men. In religious thought—and here we will be referring to modern Christian and Jewish thought unless otherwise noted—this has resulted in a dramatic awakening and the development of ideas that sometimes seem to have the potential of reconstructing our ways of thinking altogether. . . .

We cannot consider the whole range of feminist thought here. We will be able to touch on only a few areas that in my opinion are the most crucial for Jewish women's self-understanding and self-esteem. One of the things we want to know is whether—even if we love Jewish tradition and practice—we are buying into a system that under-

cuts our full humanity, our full womanhood. Many Jewish feminists believe that we (along with women in most other religious traditions) cannot participate with integrity in our tradition unless we make radical changes. Although . . . there are many elements in our tradition that are richly relevant to women and positive for our growth, they could argue that we are fooling ourselves. Perhaps these are marginal features, while the core of tradition remains misogynist and oppressive to women. This issue needs to be addressed directly.

The way I have chosen to approach the question is to examine some of the leading writings in feminist religious thought. Many feminists are finding fundamental currents in women's spirituality that seem to appear cross-culturally and that have been opposed, denigrated, or forced underground by male dominance in religion. They have also found persistent habits of thought—basic philosophical assumptions about the nature of things—that are negative toward women and our kinds of spirituality. We must examine the extent to which these negative elements are present in Judaism and whether Jewish tradition allows and encourages women's self-expression in positive, significant ways.

To begin with fundamentals: one of the most important and recurrent issues discussed in feminist literature is the dualistic framework of Western religious thought that associates the feminine with negative characteristics. Most Western philosophical and religious thinkers assume a division between spirit and matter, or mind and body, such that spirit and mind are superior to matter and body. Further, the male is associated with spirit, the female with matter. This is worked out in a series of correlated oppositions reflected in many varieties of religious thought. Here is a partial list:

spirit/matter
mind/body
transcendence/immanence
supernatural/natural
intellect/senses
God/human beings
reason/emotion
male/female

In almost every case the first of the two is presented as superior, the second as inferior.

A second major issue has to do with the standards set for development along the spiritual path. . . . The lone ascetic in his cell, the prophet on a mountaintop, and the charismatic leader of a religious organization all emphasize the singular individual and achieving a place at the top of a hierarchy. Feminists suggest that while we may value our private communion with God, women's spirituality is essentially relational, as is expressed in one of the movement's favorite images: weaving webs of relations between self and other selves, self and world. How the experience of the individual interfaces with the networks of others is one of the cutting edges of feminist thought. But it is clear that a strongly relational orientation prevails, giving feminine spirituality a definite communal and moral/ethical bent from the beginning.

A third, related issue is the role of emotion in self and mind. Feminists tend to reject pure intellectual analysis for a more engaged, involved, or personal style. This brings us back again to the oppositions that are inherent in much of Western thought: mind and reason are usually pitted against emotion and sensuality, with reason being taken as the ultimate arbiter in human affairs. Feminists argue that cutting ourselves off from emotion and feeling has created forms of spirituality that are inadequate, unsatisfying, and ultimately unethical.

These problems are, as we will see, interrelated, but let us take them one by one before we weave them together. First, the feminist struggle with the inherited dualistic categories of Western thought—the oppositions cited above—goes back at least to Simone de Beauvoir's *The Second Sex* (1949), in which she developed an existentialist critique of Western culture's oppression of women. She showed how woman and the feminine are habitually regarded as being on the side of nature, the body, the irrational, and, theologically, "immanence." She insisted that women must refuse to accept these male definitions and regard themselves instead as "transcendent subjects"—creative and not merely receptive, initiating and not treated as an object, the Other. This means that we must affirm our freedom as creative individuals, using that liberty to move "outward, forward, and upward." . . .

Recently, however, another view has emerged. Here works like Susan Griffin's *Woman and Nature* (1978) have been extremely powerful. Griffin and others affirm that the feminine is indeed deeply connected with "nature" and "immanence," as de Beauvoir held, but this is not negative: embodiment is part of our deeply feminine mode of being. Creativity emerges from our bodies, from our physical nature, and our finite limitations, not in negation of them. We must affirm these deeply natural parts of ourselves and at the same time undercut the negative force of the dualistic system. Rosemary Radford Ruether, who sees the "dualism of nature and transcendence, matter and spirit as female against male" as "basic to male theology" insists that both sides must be rejected: "mother-matter-matrix as 'static immanence'" and "spirit and transcendence as rootless, antinatural, originating in an 'other world' beyond the cosmos."

The feminist revaluation of immanence is most clearly articulated in writings concerning women's intuited connection with the world, our sense of being inseparably a part of nature and the universe. Many have found compelling Alice Walker's characterization of women's spirituality in *The Color Purple*, when her character Shug describes herself as having "that feeling of being part of everything, not separate at all. I knew that if I cut a tree, my arm would bleed." . . .

We can see here how the feminist emphasis on immanence, undercutting what women have experienced as an oppressive dualism, connects with two other aspects of women's thought: relatedness, that is, an inner sense of connection, and reliance on feeling as a ground for judgment and knowledge. If the universe is conceived of as simply the arena of fixed natural law, or as nature wild and untamed, it gives us no ground for moral judgments—one needs a transcendent lawmaker who provides laws for both nature and human beings and some mode, beyond nature, of implanting morality in the human being. But in Carol Christ's view, it is relatedness, love and caring, a felt connection with other beings that provide, within our human nature, reasons for acting morally. This felt relationship is fundamental to women's spirituality. As she and Judith Plaskow write, the feminist sense of the self "is essentially relational, inseparable from the limiting and enriching contexts of body, feeling, relationship, community, history, and the web of life. The notion of the relational self can be correlated with the immanent turn in feminist views of the sacred: in both cases connection to that which is finite, changing, and limited is affirmed." Over against the philosopher Descartes, whose famous "I think, therefore I am" described the rational, disembodied, solitary ego, the feminine self is embodied, passionate, relational, communal. From this point of view, religious thinkers who talk about God as "being itself" or the "wholly other"—or in Judaism those who translate *Adonai echad* as "God is uniquely alone"—imply that God's lack of relatedness is a source of strength. For feminists only that divinity which is deeply related in and to the world can be authentic. . . . For these writers, relationships, connection to nature, and immanence all intertwine in their understanding of feminine spirituality.

Such features are not at all alien to what our tradition has handed down about Jewish women and the feminine. . . . In our discussion of ritual, we saw that woman's connection to nature is a persistent element. Feminine heroines and themes are strongly associated with the seasonal cycles; and women are associated with the moon, with motherhood, with food and nurturing, and with nature's sexual cycles. Whether in holidays like Rash Chodesh or special mitzvot like challah and niddah, women bring a spiritual dimension to the practical, real-life, finite embodiment of human beings.

Jewish women's life also emphasizes relationships and relatedness, with a strong connection to the concrete and personal aspects of life and a sense of interdependence. Women's traditional affinity for Tehillim (Psalms) suggests an appreciation both for nature and for personal, related spirituality—King David's intimate relation with God through all his various hardships and victories had great appeal. The women of our stories too were deeply concerned with relationships—first with family, particularly with husbands and children, then with the larger destiny of their descendants and the Jewish people as a whole.

We observed also that the very idea of motherhood in this tradition carries a strong sense of responsibility for the future: the women knew their actions would shape destiny. Jewish women were not trapped in "static immanence." On the contrary, the woman "looks smilingly to the future" and exerts her power to shape it. We saw that women often took risks and did the unconventional. Indeed, the stories of Jewish women suggest the truth of the description of premodern women given by Beverly Harrison when she says, "Historically, I believe, women have always exemplified the power of activity over passivity, of experimentation over routinization, of creativity and risk-taking over conventionality."

Jewish women are portrayed as oriented toward the immanent, the practical, and the web of relations for which they have considerable responsibility. Yet we are net simply immersed in material concerns. Jewish tradition sees us as essentially inward beings, whose essence revolves around the private sphere. The saying "All the glory of the daughter of the king is on the inside" focuses on that inwardness. That woman is the ruler of Shabbat, the day of inward orientation—toward home, community, and personal spirituality—

exemplifies this also. On a personal level Channah as the model for prayer is an example: a woman deeply connected to her feelings expressing herself to God. In the prophetic consciousness of Sarah, Rivkah, and others we also see a strong inwardness: women had their own base of knowledge that came from within. Tamar, Yehudit, and Esther all acted outside the boundaries of what was usually considered proper and right on the basis of their inner moral certainty. Thus Judaism has recognized the inner strength of women and extolled it as a feminine virtue. This actually deepens what feminists have said about basing our knowledge and morality on our inner sense of things, including our feelings and intuitions. Jewish tradition suggests that, beyond feelings and emotions, feminine consciousness can operate at a level that approaches the prophetic. . . .

. . . Some feminists have claimed that while there may be feminine dimensions to Jewish religious life, they are not really valued in Judaism—synagogue, yeshiva, and law court are more important. From an experiential point of view, many women and men within traditional Judaism will affirm that this is simply not so. Torah life is a total way of life, with women's responsibilities just as serious as men's, and equally highly valued. The question perhaps is whether women have appreciated the importance of affirming this dimension of their lives and speaking publicly about it. In the past most of the life of women remained private. In modern times, as traditional communities disintegrated, Jewish women's occupations—as with other women—were denigrated and in addition were subject to the general Enlightenment criticism of obsolete ritual. It is only in recent times that women involved in traditional practice have begun to break the silence about their experience.

Even if we grant the strengths of Jewish women in the past, there is still more to the feminist argument: Is it not true that underneath the positive features we find in Judaism a negative valuation of women or of the feminine principle? Do not the spirit/matter, soul/body, transcendent/immanent polarities appear in Jewish thought in ways detrimental to the feminine side? They do; but differently than in Greek or Christian thought. In Jewish mystical thought, for example, we often find man or the masculine associated with spirit,

woman with body; then body is associated with the "animal," and this in turn with the temptations that turn a person away from God. While Judaism never castigated Chava (Eve) and all women in the way Christianity did for bringing on the first sin, still the literature is laced with associations of the feminine to our animal nature and thus to spiritual danger. At the same time, Judaism has affirmed more consistently than Christianity a positive attitude toward body, nature, and world. Male and female are always seen as interdependent, though the male—particularly male anatomy—is the mystical model of humanity. Moreover, women are regarded as more spiritual than men. But it is clear that Judaism has absorbed to some degree the dualistic presuppositions of Western—particularly Greek—thought that tend to devalue the feminine.

Another example: the two names of God most frequently used in the Bible, "Adonai" and "Elohim," are associated with the masculine and feminine, respectively. The first is connected to the aspect of God that expresses mercy, redemption, and the assertion of God's benign will acting from outside the universe as we know it. The second, feminine aspect is associated with nature, fixed law, the eternal round of things. The first is dynamic: God's action in history that makes possible new events, new revelations. The second, feminine, appears static, moving in eternal circles. In Judaism this second aspect of God expresses justice as well—the more severe side of God that, like nature, moves in terms of fixed laws of reward and punishment.

Let us look more closely at what is at stake here. First: can we have a more benign and intimate perception of God by eliminating the idea of transcendence with its masculine associations? It would seem not. From the traditional Jewish point of view, one cannot collapse the transcendence of God into the immanence of nature. The two dimensions are absolutely essential. If one had only a transcendent God, one would have an evil, or at best a neutral and mechanical, world. But if one had only an immanent God, taking the world of nature as divine, as feminists like Carol Christ wish to do, one would collapse into paganism. Nature has divinity within it, to be sure, but that is secondary, dependent on the transcendent Creator God who formed nature and gave it its fixed laws. God is immanent in the world, but that world is totally dependent for its existence on the continually acting transcendent will, the consciousness that lies beyond nature. (Translate: the feminine is entirely dependent for her creative power on the masculine.) Similarly, the, transcendent God gave the Torah as the fixed system of laws for human beings. That same transcendent divine will which guides nature is the source of all guidelines for human action: the mitzvot and morality itself. His Torah given on Sinai is our guide, not any inner intuitions from the Shekhinah. (Translate: the masculine is the source of all morality.)

Yet part of the problem is our understanding of the word *transcendence*. Its common meaning is that which is above the limits of human thought—beyond good and evil, beyond mind and emotion, beyond male and female. In various usages, however, it takes on different connotations. As we observed, in much of Western thought it has become attached to mind I spirit/reason as opposed to body/matter/emotion. But, in another context, the literary "transcendentalists" used the term to connote a kind of higher intuition, a Reason above ordinary rational logic. The term is itself subject to much confusion. We should take transcendence to mean that which precedes any levels of being or intelligence than we, in our human finitude, can know.

But we must understand this in a Jewish context. Our idea of transcendence derives from religious experiences different from those of the Greeks, who, from Plato on down, emphasized the split between spirit and matter. The primary experience that for Jewish tradition gave rise to the concept of transcendence, the name "Adonai," was the exodus from Egypt, God's redemption of the Jewish people. "Ask if any deed as mighty as this has been seen or heard!" exclaimed Moses. "Did ever a God attempt to come and take a nation for himself out of another nation, . . . as the Lord your God did for you in Egypt in the sight of all of you?" (Deut. 4.32–34) Rabbi Abraham Isaac Kook wrote that human "sovereignty over the world's lower creatures with an idealistic motivation"—that is, our moral sense of responsibility—"began to be manifested in the miracles and wonders of the exodus from Egypt, which stamped the Jewish people with its historic character." From the unfathomable work of God in redeeming a group of slaves first came the Jewish view that God transcends the world; for it was here, according to traditional thought, that God exceeded anything known in nature. God performed miracles to overturn nature and human rulership, to liberate the Israelite slaves.

Rosemary Ruether has pointed out many respects in which the Israelite God transcended "patriarchal consciousness." Calling Abraham away from his father's house, breaking the bonds between the overlord Pharaoh and his subjects signified that rules of father and son, master and slave, king and subject could be broken to establish a higher allegiance, an allegiance formed from love. Moreover, God did this in response to the "crying out" of the slaves. It was an act of mercy, not on the basis of merit. . . .

The point of view represented in Torah, prophets, and classical rabbinic interpretations holds that it is God's mercy—not his thought, mind, intellect, spirit, logos, or other Greek philosophical characteristics—that exemplifies his transcendence, because it comes from a place beyond the natural order of things. God, in Jewish thought from the Exodus down to modern times, is unimaginably loving, giving, compassionate, beneficent. As the great seventeenth-century thinker, Moshe Chaim Luzzato, taught, God's purpose in creation is to give of his goodness to his creatures.

But this is precisely what feminists demand of God: that s/he be related, compassionate, bountiful. Part of the natural feminine moral sensibility is to recognize bonds of love—between parent and child, man and woman, friend and friend, and even between strangers—which connect us all together. We see nature as interdependent and mutually supportive. We experience relations between people, as Carol Gilligan has pointed out, as matters of care, responsibility, and responsiveness, not primarily the balancing of claims according to rules of justice. These are all reflected in the way women experience God. And these same elements infuse the Jewish view of God: when we ask why God redeemed the Hebrew slaves, the Torah tells us that he heard their cries. It is an eminently feminine answer. One can argue that the Jewish people had merit—merit as Abraham's descendents, merit for maintaining their Jewish lives in the midst of

Egyptian culture. But most simply, God heard their cries—like a mother whose child is crying, he could not let it go on any longer. So it is understandable that many women students ask me why "Adonai," the name of God representing mercy, should be male.

. . . Understood from a Jewish perspective, then, divine transcendence bridges across the supposedly male and female views. The one who redeems slaves, the one who carries the people to freedom as an eagle carries its young on its wings (Exod. 19:4, Deut. 32:11), the one who inspires Moses to care for them as a nursing father(!)—this divinity is intimately related to our lives. . . .

Yet we are not done with our Greek influences. We must look afresh at the concept of God that we have inherited from Genesis: that God is the Creator who makes the world *ex nihilo,* from nothing, and is totally independent of creation. Many feminists charge that this is another dimension of transcendence which emphasizes God's unrelatedness to us. They are attracted to myths of other cultures wherein a female deity creates the world from her own body or where the things of the world spring forth from a feminine earth. In contrast, Jewish tradition insists on the independence of the creator God who creates by his word. This later became connected with Greek concepts of transcendence, spirit, mind, and reason, setting up the full range of dichotomies we have discussed above. Also related are the emphasis on God's eternal, unchanging nature and on God as "uniquely alone." It is but a step from this to putting male (spirit/thought/creator) above female (nature/body/creation) in hierarchical fashion.

I agree with feminist theologians that we must do away with the insufferable philosophical dualism that puts women at the bottom. In fact, dualism is unnecessary if we recognize that, for us as Jews, two things are at stake: our understanding of God as totally free of limitations, absolutely free to create, and the idea that we partake of this freedom in some degree even though we, unlike God, have limitations. Since we are made in God's image, in some respect we are like God. The problem is, the part that is like God is described, in most of Western tradition, as our spirit, soul, or mind. What is left over—body, flesh, animal self—then is

regarded as not like God. This is the root of the difficulty.

Having a thinking machine in our brains or an incorporeal soul residing somewhere inside does not make us like God. Rather it is in freedom of the *will,* soul freedom, that we are like God. We have the capacity to act beyond our nature, to change ourselves, to decide and act in any moment. It is often taught that the seat of the soul is in the mind or brain. This makes it sound as if the soul (and therefore the will) is primarily a thinking entity, a rationalist creation. But this is not the case. The soul is the seat of the will. The mind or brain may formulate that will into what we recognize as "thought," but it is the will that originates any decision or nonhabitual action—the will that is beyond the mind.

Feminist thinkers, frustrated with the frequent masculine insistence on the primacy of thought, suggest an alternative: that the root of our will is not rational thought but feeling—feeling understood in the broadest sense as our experienced, embodied relation to the world and in the deepest sense as our intuition. Yet most Jewish moral perspectives hold that feelings are not a good guide to morality. They may be honored as signals of happiness or distress, but they are essentially selfish and must be trained and curbed in order not to run to excess. Anger, for example, is regarded in rabbinic tradition as an expression of idolatry—idolatry of the self. Love, while it may appear altruistic, is often a mask for self-love. Even positive feelings connected with religion cannot be trusted as certain guides to spiritual development. They may only tempt one into pride and self-satisfaction. In most ethical and Chassidic texts, the theme is rehearsed that one cannot trust one's feelings very far; only the revelation of Torah from God, as it has been passed on through authentic tradition, can give proper guidance.

Some feminists do recognize, in passing, the possibility of too much reliance on feelings. Harrison, while stressing the importance of feelings in our moral perceptions, also acknowledges that feelings do not necessarily lead to "wise or humane action." Catherine Keller also recognizes that the love expressed in the "almost animistic" idea of inseparability from other beings and things "is vulnerable to criticisms of solipsism, narcissism, and stagnation." Then, we may ask, where do wisdom and humanity to guide our actions come from? Are we then forced to return to the intellectualist tradition that insists on the supremacy of thought and the rejection of feelings?

Jewish tradition answers that the matter is complex: mind, body, emotion are all involved. As the sages of rabbinic times said, "The kidneys advise, the heart understands" (Berachot 61a). We could argue long over how we as human beings actually work—how our will comes to be active in the world and how our will can best be opened to the right way of action. It is possible that men and women experience this differently in the intricate intermingling of body, mind, and emotion. In any case, what we learn—and this is verified over and over again in the experience of the observant Jew—is that this complex wisdom is most fully embodied in our inherited body of tradition, mediated through the words of our teachers.

Specifically, we must insist, through the *words* of our teachers. Let us remind ourselves of the picture we are given in Genesis of God the Creator. God's distinctive characteristic—which he passes on to those made in his image—is that of Speaker, the Speaker-Who-Creates, the one who brings things into being by speaking them. This is an aspect of God's transcendence: what is not part of nature, not part of the round of birth and rebirth, of karmic or natural law. We are not told anything about God's thoughts or feelings here. Speech is the mode in which, so far as we can know, the Divine Will comes into being; it manifests God's freedom to create.

This is so for us as well. Speech has a freedom, a "transcendence" that the rest of nature does not have. Communication goes on among the rest of the creatures, but speech in the creative sense does not—or at least not without humans to help it come to voice. Yet we need not make this Creative Speech into the Greek *logos*, with its platonic associations of detached rationality. Plato regarded poetry and drama as decidedly inferior to philosophy; as a result, much of our Western philosophical heritage separated pure thought, and speech as its vehicle, from feeling, intuition, dream, vision, physicality. As Jews we can leave Plato behind and recover our own ways of speaking—in ritual, song, poetry, story, prophecy as well as reasoned discourse.

Again, the Jewish dual tradition is important: halacha—the speech of rationality and logic—and aggadah—the speech of story, dream, vision—never were entirely separated. The Talmud, our great classic compilation of oral law, mixes the two throughout. In practice the handing down of the law always should be from person to person, teacher to student, Rav to questioner—an ongoing dialogue, not merely laws read from books. Judaism has been, to borrow Plaskow's terms, "passionate, communal, embodied." But historically, as the speech of halacha became dominant, beginning with the monarchy and exile and increasing enormously in the Greco-Roman period, less came from the feminine side. Women, once visionaries and prophetesses, spoke less in the public realm as the centuries passed.

Now women are recovering, taking back their share of the power of speech. Women's midrash, women's prayers, women's inspiration are rising once again; and as women become engaged in the creative work of public speech, it will affect all of Jewish life, including halacha. This is the way to address the issue of dualism—not by philosophical arguments on behalf of the importance of feelings, but by what we speak. It will become apparent through our speech that our bodies also speak truth, that our feelings and intuitions can interact with Torah learning to provide guides to action. Speaking out is taking part in the creative act by which God continues to bring new things into the world, to act with compassion and caring, in ways beyond what we as women have done before. And we do this from the place of immanence, from our connection to the divine hiddenness, from our knowledge of the Shekhinah, of Rachel weeping with us. And we ask men to call back to their consciousness the knowledge of immanence: that they too are created bodies, they must speak from feeling, they must make their creative work in the world compassionate, related, feminine.

The feminine has much to say in Jewish tradition, and the years ahead promise stimulating dialogue between the community of women and that of men. This brings us to the final point. Too often when we speak as feminists we set up another "we-they" dichotomy, objectifying men in our speech as they have done to us in so many ways. But if we truly live in a relational world, where each is part of the other, men are part of us too, both inwardly in our androgynous psyches and in the web of life in which we move. The universe, according to our Jewish understanding, rests on the delicate balance of male and female, one that we must work out in our families, our communities, and the public world. As I mentioned above, *Adonai echad*—God is one—does not need to mean, "God is uniquely alone." God's oneness, the divine unity, is the marriage of female and male, the transcendent union that is neither mind nor body, spirit nor matter, nor anything else we can comprehend. For us it means we seek the unity of inner knowing and soaring mind, creative speech and compassionate wisdom from within ourselves and among ourselves, in community.

Study Questions on Tamar Frankiel

1. How does Frankiel think feminists have misunderstood God's transcendence, and how does she understand it? Why is it essential to Judaism not to eliminate God's transcendence?
2. How does she understand our being in the "image of God," and how does her interpretation bypass the problem of mind-body dualism?
3. The feminists she cites emphasize the fact that women's spirituality is more relational and communal than men's. How does Frankiel find these elements in Judaism? Has Frankiel convinced you that traditional Judaism does not in fact denigrate the feminine? Why or why not? What would Carol Christ or Elizabeth Johnson say in response to her arguments?
4. The New Testament uses Greek concepts to convey its message in the way the Old Testament does not, speaking for example of "the word (logos) made flesh" (John 1:14). In view of this fact, is Frankiel's interpretative strategy available to Christians as well as to Jews?

For Further Reading

Adams, Carol J., ed. *Ecofeminism and the Sacred.* New York: Continuum, 1993.

Ahmad, Leila. *Women and Gender in Islam: Historical Roots of a Modern Debate.* New Haven: Yale University Press, 1993.

Al-Hibri, Azizah. *Women in Islam.* London: Pergamon Press, 1982.

Aquinas, Thomas. *Summa Theologiae.* New York: Benzinger Brothers, 1948. Ia. Q. 33. (on God the Father), Q. 92. esp. a. 3. (on the Creation of Woman).

Barth, Karl. *Church Dogmatics: A Selection.* Helmut Gollweizer and G. W. Bromiley, eds. G. W. Bromiley, trans. New York: Harper Torchbooks, 1962.

Carmody, Denise Lardner. *Women and World Religions.* Nashville, Tenn.: Abingdon, 1979.

Carr, Ann. *Transforming Grace: Christian Tradition and Women's Experience.* San Francisco: Harper & Row, 1988.

Catechism of the Catholic Church. Liguori, Mo.: Liguori Publications, 1994. Nos. 232–267, 2779–2785 (God as Father), Nos. 369–373 (male and female), Nos. 1601–1666, 2197–2233, 2331–2400 (sex, marriage, and family).

Cooey, Paula, William Eakin, and Jay McDaniel. *After Patriarchy: Feminist Transformations of the World's Religions.* Maryknoll, N.Y.: Orbis, 1991. Includes Riffat Hassan, "Muslim Women in Post-Patriarchal Islam."

Cooke, Miriam. *Opening the Gates: A Century of Arab Feminist Writing.* London: Virago, 1989.

Cuneo, Michael W. *The Smoke of Satan: Conservative and Traditionalist Dissent in Contemporary Catholicism.* New York: Oxford University Press, 1997. Esp. Chaps. 3 and 5. Pelvic issues, women, and the Virgin Mary in contemporary Roman Catholic theological controversy.

Daly, Mary. *Beyond God the Father.* Boston: Beacon Press, 1973.

———. *Outercourse.* New York: HarperSanFrancisco, 1992.

Falk, Nancy Auer, and Rita M. Gross, eds. *Unspoken Worlds: Women's Religious Lives in Non-Western Cultures.* San Francisco: Harper & Row, 1980.

Fiorenza, Elizabeth Schussler. *In Memory of Her: A Feminist Theological Reconstruction of Christian Origins.* New York: Crossroad, 1983.

Frymer-Kensky, Tikva. *In the Wake of the Goddesses: Women, Culture, and the Biblical Transformation of Pagan Myth.* New York: Free Press, 1992.

Gottlieb, Roger S., ed. *This Sacred Earth: Religion, Nature, and the Environment.* New York: Routledge, 1996.

Gross, Rita, ed. *Beyond Androcentrism: New Essays on Women and Religion.* Missoula, Mont.: Scholars Press, 1977.

Haddad, Yvonne, and Elison Findly. *Women, Religion, and Social Change.* Albany: State University of New York Press, 1985.

———, and Adair Lummis. *Islamic Values in the United States: A Comparative Study.* London: Oxford University Press, 1988.

Harman, William. *The Sacred Marriage of a Hindu Goddess.* Bloomington: Indiana University Press, 1989.

Heine, Susanne. *Matriarchs, Goddesses, and Images of God: A Critique of Feminist Theology.* John Bowden, trans. Minneapolis, Minn.: Augsburg, 1989.

Heschel, Susannah, ed. *On Being a Jewish Feminist: A Reader.* New York: Schocken Books, 1983.

Hitchcock, Helen Hull, ed. *The Politics of Prayer.* San Francisco: Ignatius Press, 1992.

Jantzen, Grace M. *Becoming Divine: Towards a Feminist Philosophy of Religion.* Indianapolis and Bloomington: Indiana University Press, 1999.

John Paul II. Apostolic Exhortation, *Familaris Consortio* (November 22, 1981). On the family.

———. Apostolic Letter, *Mulieris Dignitatem.* (August 15, 1988). On the dignity of woman.

King, Ursula, ed. *Women in the World's Religions, Past and Present.* New York: Paragon House, 1987.

Lovelock, J. E. *Gaia: A New Look at Life on Earth.* New York: Oxford University Press, 1979.

Macquarrie, John. *Mary for all Christians.* Grand Rapids, Mich.: Eerdmans, 1990.

Mankowski, Paul, S. J. "The Necessary Failure of Inclusive Language Translations." *Thomist,* 62 (July 1998), 445–468.

Martin, Francis. *The Feminist Question: Feminist Theology in the Light of Christian Tradition.* Grand Rapids, Mich.: Eerdmans, 1994.

McFague, Sallie. *Models of God: Theology for an Ecological Nuclear Age.* Philadelphia: Fortress Press, 1987.

Merchant, Carolyn. *The Death of Nature: Women, Ecology, and the Scientific Revolution.* San Francisco: Harper & Row, 1980.

Mernissi, Fatima. *Beyond the Veil.* London: Al Saqi, 1985.

Nolan, Michael. "What Aquinas Never Said About Women." *First Things,* no. 87 (November 1988), 11–12.

Plaskow, Judith. *Standing Again at Sinai: Judaism from a Feminist Perspective.* New York: Harper & Row, 1990.

————, and Carol Christ, eds. *Weaving the Visions: New Patterns of Feminist Spirituality.* San Francisco: Harper & Row, 1989.

Plumwood, Val. "Ecofeminism: An Overview and Discussion of Positions and Arguments." *Australasian Journal of Philosophy,* Supplement to Vol. 64 (June 1986), 120–138.

Puttick, Elizabeth, and Peter Clarke, eds., *Women as Teachers and Disciples in Traditional and New Religions.* Lampeter Dyfed, Wales, UK: Edwin Mellen Press, 1993.

Ruether, Rosemary Radford. *New Woman, New Earth: Sexist Ideologies and Human Liberation.* New York: Seabury, 1975.

————. *Sexism and God Talk.* Boston: Beacon Press, 1993.

Schindler, David L. *Heart of the World, Center of the Church.* Grand Rapids, Mich.: Eerdmans, 1996. Esp. Chap. 9.

Sharma, Arvind, ed. *Today's Woman in World Religions.* Albany, N.Y.: SUNY Press, 1994.

Skees, Suzanne. *God Among the Shakers.* New York: Hyperion, 1998. The contemporary appeal of a celibate order founded on belief in a "Father/Mother God."

Smith, Jane, ed. *Women in World Religions.* Albany: State University of New York, 1987.

Smith, Mark S. *The Early History of God.* San Francisco: Harper & Row, 1990.

Stone, Merlin. *When God Was a Woman.* New York: The Dial Press, 1976.

Toubia, Nahid, ed. *Women in the Arab World.* London: Zed, 1988.

Vlahos, Olivia. "The Goddess That Failed," *First Things* (December 1992).

Weaver, Mary Jo, and R. Scott Appleby, eds. *Being Right: Conservative Catholics in America.* Bloomington: Indiana University Press, 1995. Esp. Chaps. 7, 9, 11. Shows the importance of women, the Virgin Mary, and "pelvic" issues in one form of religious conservatism.

INFOTRAC COLLEGE EDITION To learn more about the topics from this chapter, you can use the following words to conduct an electronic search on InfoTrac College Edition, an online library of journals. Here you will find a multitude of articles from various sources and perspectives: *www.infotrac-college.com/wadsworth/access.html (ws)*

Catholicism and Sex

Celibacy

Church and Sex

Ecofeminism